talk too much

MAN MAY DIE

FATHER DIVINE
IS
GOD
HE HEALS
BODY AND
AND SET ME
THANK YOU

RIGHTEOUSNESS
JUSTICE
TRUTH

FATHER DIVINE
DING THE WINE
UNE...I THANK
RIGHTEOUSNESS
CE TRUTH

GOD

CBS NBC CBS

Days of Sadness, Years of Triumph

Days of Sadness, Years of Triumph

The American People 1939-1945

by

Geoffrey Perrett

Coward, McCann & Geoghegan Inc.

New York

Photograph Credits for Endpaper Montage
Top, left to right:
WAACS, Fort Des Moines, Iowa, 1942, The Bettmann Archive
Car sticker, Wendell Willkie Campaign, 1940, The Bettmann Archive
Wendell A. Willkie, parading in Indiana in 1940, The Bettmann Archive
World War II Liberty ship *Samuel Adams* ready to be launched, The Bettmann
    Archive
Middle:
Japanese evacuees at reception center, Manzanar, California, U.P.I.
World War II war ration book one and ration stamps, The Bettmann Archive
Actor Errol Flynn confers with attorney on morals charge, 1942, U.P.I.
OWI poster, Culver Pictures, Inc.
Harry S. Truman, at Democratic National Convention, Chicago, 1944, The Bett-
    mann Archive
Bottom:
General Patton in Boston, Massachusetts, 1945, U.P.I.
Bobby-soxers of the 1940's in local soda fountain, The Bettmann Archive
Franklin Delano Roosevelt during Fireside Chat, The Bettmann Archive
Joe Louis, 1941, U.P.I.
Parade of Father Divine followers, The Bettmann Archive

SBN: 698-10488-9
Library of Congress Catalog Card Number: 72-87594
PRINTED IN THE UNITED STATES OF AMERICA

For permission to quote from *My Country* by Russell
Davenport (New York, 1944), the author gratefully ac-
knowledges the permission of his widow, Natalie Potter
Davenport.

For Ann

she encumbered me with help
before I reached the shore

Contents

PART III: *The Remaking of a Nation*

Introduction

When an oak tree is felled the whole forest echoes with it, while
a hundred acorns are planted silently by some unknown breeze.
—THOMAS CARLYLE

IN the 1830's De Tocqueville despaired that Americans never gave
any thought to recording their accomplishments. Government officials
casually destroyed or gave away original documents. To the visiting
Frenchman it seemed that the American people could disappear, leaving,
like the Etruscans and the Incas, only a few fragments of physical evidence to mark their existence. Were De Tocqueville to return now, to be
confronted with the annual accumulation of facts about America and the
lives of Americans, he would be overwhelmed. Within the ambit of Western civilization no people make more films, take more photographs, print
more newspapers and magazines, publish more books, make more recordings, maintain more libraries or boast larger official archives. The greatest
American newspaper is itself an international byword for conscientious
accumulation. Like other genuinely American triumphs, it is a triumph of
scale.

At an accelerating tempo the facts pile up, into mountains and entire
mountain ranges. Even as they rise, they are being riven, cleft, tunneled,
quarried, mined, rearranged. For careers can be made here, with a little
luck and much diligence. Entire subindustries and many thousands of
families have come to depend for their livelihood on this ceaseless sifting
of facts. It is partly the organic life of a vibrant community that finds its
past useful or comforting. Partly it is a form of entertainment. Partly it is
harmless drudgery. But when it is done so diligently, for whatever reason,
nothing, it seems, can escape attention for very long and nothing of real
importance can be lost. Yet, strangely enough, there are important parts
of the American experience that have gone many long years before they
received their due. The life of the American people from 1939 to 1945
provides an example.

Unconsciously we all acknowledge the profound, ongoing change that
those years brought to our times when we preface a remark with "Since
the war. . . ." We hardly ever say, "Since the Depression. . . ." No one
even has to specify which war. For who imagines that it means Korea or
Vietnam? As a reference in time we employ it more often, in fact, than
that traditional and official datum, the birth of Christ. So we daily acknowledge its fundamental importance. Yet as far as the social experi-

ence of the war is concerned, so little of it has been examined that America's domestic history appears to have jerked to a halt in 1939, then revived at breakneck speed six years later.

One might think that very little of lasting interest or importance happened at home in those six years. As this book shows, nothing could be further from the truth. Why then the neglect?

I suspect that it is partly because Frederick Lewis Allen gave us an appetite for social history in ten-year slices of life. It fitted neatly with the roughly ten years from the signing of the Treaty of Versailles to the Great Crash. It was sensationally on target when the sequel ran from the peak of the Big Bull Market on September 3, 1929, to the Allied declaration of war on Germany on September 3, 1939. Here, the twenties; there, the thirties. And though history does not carve itself into ten-year slices, that is the way we now find it most digestible. There have since been books on the fifties, and no sooner were the sixties ended than they were embraced in print. But the forties are a problem. The war cuts the decade so sharply in two that no "decade" book can be made out of it. So neither half of the decade's domestic history has been examined at length.

Nor can this be laid entirely at the door of the writers of popular social histories. Social history is not a well-developed interest among American writers, popular or academic. For both of them, political history is where the biggest battalions are to be found toiling away. Great issues of state policy are endlessly thrashed out long after the principals have closed their mouths forever. And the story of how most people lived, what they thought, what they did, what things moved them to pity or rage meanwhile goes unwritten. If, as Carlyle believed, history is really the sum of all our individual lives, then indeed almost all history goes unwritten. Obviously full justice would require a biography for each person, which is physically impossible. But intelligent summaries and distillations are possible. And for those who will never command an army, or negotiate a treaty, or confer with heads of state, this kind of history writing is truer to their own experience than the kind of political history which parades as an aid to citizenship but is really a form of escapist literature.

What, then, does the study of American society in wartime reveal? That the closest thing to a real social revolution the United States has known in this century came during those years. The six years of New Deal may have changed people's attitudes; they may have affected the way people felt about things. The six years of war changed their lives and altered the way that they lived. To some it may at first seem implausible that this actually occurred, but it did. This book describes it.

One reason why this social revolution went unnoticed was that it was in the American grain—it was nonideological. No mass movement stood behind it, nurtured it, sought recruits for it, elected candidates or defeated them as they helped or hindered. To call massive, fundamental social change a revolution may, I know, seem inflated language when one thinks of those revolutions where blood stains the fabric of society. For I am referring not to violence but to change which occurs rapidly and goes deep as a revolution in a nation's life. Even if, however, it were called reform, that would not alter the fact that no other six years in this century have brought so much real change in the lives of Americans.

It is true that the United States is notoriously set acquiver with every passing breeze, a fact remarked upon by visitors to these shores for some 200 years. But the country also changes with glacial slowness. As Lord Bryce observed half a century ago, while the leaves flutter tremulously, America's roots are firmly twined about some vast, immovable rock. Yet there has been one period at least since then when even the roots were shifted.

But what about the New Deal? I think that it is best regarded as a species of hope. Certainly there was a fair amount of experimentation and much excitement among the New Deal recruits from the universities and the law firms. Much was promised, some new principles were introduced, but its concrete accomplishments were pitifully meager. These consisted for the most part of catching up with a half century of social legislation already enacted in other Western democracies. And even there the New Deal fell short. Certainly by 1939 it had not beaten the Depression, and only the most ardent New Dealers believed it was about to. It gripped the imagination of people and does so to this day, I know. But for all that, it was a triumph of appearances over reality. The triumph of reality came, as this book shows, with the war.

It is a commonplace to remark that the war solved the unemployment problem. And as a rule, discussion of the social consequences of the war ends at this point. What goes unremarked is that enormous new groups of government beneficiaries came into existence; that barriers to social and economic equality which had stood for decades were either much reduced or entirely overthrown; that the old pyramidal class structure of the United States was cast onto the rubbish heap of history and a genuine middle-class nation came into existence; that access to higher education became genuinely democratic for the first time; that the modern civil rights movement began then; that the greatest gains in longevity occurred then; that the only basic redistribution of national income in American history occurred then; and that an entirely new role in the world was taken on. This is also only a partial list. The point is that six years of war brought more social change—desirable social change—than did six years of New Deal. It did so, furthermore, in the teeth of a massive recovery by big business and its conservative allies. Yet while the New Deal had presided with great to-do over the introduction of new principles of social justice, during the war social justice triumphed. Ironically, millions were meanwhile agonizing over the death of the New Deal, mourning that social justice had perished from the earth.

It could be argued that the New Deal paved the way for the social change of the war years. I have no wish to cast the Depression years down to raise the war years up, but I do not think that is true. For not one of the agencies created during the New Deal was adequate to the demands even of the two years of defense crisis prior to Pearl Harbor. One after another they were either cast aside, overshadowed or modified almost beyond recognition.

Besides bringing a quantum leap forward in social welfare and change, the war experience did something else. It legitimized modern American values and institutions. To Americans the test of almost anything is how it works, not whether it is old, or divine, or popular. The war years provided the last great collective social experience in the country's history, and when at the end of the war the United States bestrode the entire world like a colossus, it had proved itself to its own people. It is no accident that the war generation finds itself so at odds with its children. The theoretical and historical argument that is involved here is developed in the concluding parts of this book.

What I have written is therefore not a book about the war but a book about America; not a book about the great figures of wartime but about the lives of ordinary people. Roosevelt, for example, is not at the center of things because of the emphasis of this book; it is also true that as Roosevelt became more and more absorbed in the prosecution of the war his interest in domestic matters dropped sharply. What I have tried to portray, then, is an entire people caught up in the greatest collective undertaking of their lives. War puts individuals to the test; it puts nations to the test. Win or lose, those qualities which make them truly different from others are thrown into relief or are magnified. For that reason alone a social history of wartime is worthwhile. But there is also this: All around us—in our art, our literature, our scholarship, even our daily lives—there is fragmentation; the study of history allows us to study the unity of things. For at its best, history gives us a chance to see the order of things. Therein lies much of the fascination of the war years. That is why the theme of pulling together runs through these pages. It is comparatively easy to see the pattern when a nation is fusing around a new consensus. There is no shortage of books on the fragmentation, on the lack of unities in current American life. But even they try to make some sense of it, to somehow see things whole. And that is what I have tried to do. For this is the story of how a nation that stumbled into 1939 shaken, divided, confused and unhappy was in a sense remade, so that only six years later it was strong, united, whole, happy and confident as never before or since.

PART ONE

The Time Between

September, 1939–December, 1941

I

It Is War

THE war came as a surprise that was expected. Ordinary, sensible Americans awoke on the morning of August 23, 1939, believing that there would be no war that year. For, odd as it may seem, the nearer war came, fewer and fewer people expected it to begin. Most thought the next war would be, as it proved, the worst that had ever been fought. Some, convinced that it would be truly global, already called it the Second World War. The crises heralding its onset grew more intense, and the intervals between them shortened. Even in space Mars dipped as close to Earth as their orbits allow. Every sign, rational and mystical, announced the hour was at hand—but fewer and fewer people would admit it. As one diary entry on August 21 confessed, "Although the war may be a few days or weeks off, one reaches the singular conclusion that it is inconceivable." And despite the portents, it really was inconceivable; the closer war drew, the more dreadful it was to contemplate. The prospect of modern war pressed down on the fragile structures of modern life defeated the imagination.

Daily life went on much as it had done for years, to rhythms set by a depression whose grip was still not broken. Despite some moderation of its rigors, complete recovery seemed almost as remote as ever. About 10,000,000 people had no jobs. Uncounted millions more had work so hard, so poorly paid that only desperate people would do it. Other millions spurned relief preferring to survive, even raise a family, on the income from a part-time job. And there were still others who, defeated by despair, abandoned all pretense, stopped even the show of seeking work, went jobless and uncounted. America was becoming like Disraeli's England, settling into two nations, not explicitly along class distinctions but just as clearly setting off those with decent work from those without it. In Washington was an administration that dedicated itself to relieving the hardships which the poor and jobless nation paid for with its flesh— "ill-housed, ill-clad, ill-nourished." The sight of an exuberant, humane government in the world's largest democracy grappling with the fiercest social challenge of the age was exhilarating. It fired men's hopes and gripped their imaginations, even beyond the borders of the United States. But the touchstone of its failure after six years of struggle was a national income more unfairly divided than at any other time for more than twenty years. The poor saw their already tiny share shrink to swell the portions of the comfortable and the rich. Later ages might invest these times with romance and simply call them hard; for one of the two nations they were bitter beyond calculation.

As a people they knew little of modern war, but that little they despised. Their single taste of it had been brief, exciting and not very costly. But they damned it as a blunder best repented by going unrepeated. They were not cynical about war's uses in the hands of states. What passed for cynicism was retroactive and selective—it was reserved solely for the "war for Versailles"—and was therefore spurious. There were proud declarations that in future America would only enter war on its own terms, for its own purposes and in its own time. To those ends—and as if to atone an earlier lapse or bind a weak resolve, or both—the government had enacted laws forbidding the sale of arms to belligerents. Most people wanted to go still further and require a popular referendum before American forces could ever again be sent abroad to fight. Far from being cynical they were really sentimental, convinced that "War is a crusade or it is a crime. There is no in-between."

So people talked and argued, of wars past and wars to come. And with the talk went fears. People in the West visualized their towns razed by the Japanese while people in the East pondered havens in the West safe from German air attacks. The events, places, issues that marked the road to war seemed to them grotesque, archaic, remote and arbitrary quarrels with which they generally had little sympathy. Pressed to a choice between Britain and France on the one side and Germany on the other, they over-whelmingly took the British and French side. But not very warmly; the business of unpaid war debts and the rebukes of "Uncle Shylock" still rankled. One thing, at least, almost everyone agreed upon: When the war began, whenever it was, the country should stay out of it. But beyond that was a near conviction that America would be drawn into the fight, that no matter what it did, the country would be dragged or would slip into the war. For a people not unused to considering themselves the new Romans they were oddly like the ancient Greeks: men who saw their will set strong one way but fearful that the gods, with stronger wills, would set theirs in opposition and force on them exactly the fate they had tried hardest to avoid.

Then, with almost no forewarning, came the German-Soviet Treaty of Friendship and Alliance, signed on the night of August 23. There was shock and surprise, but almost everyone now took for granted that the upcoming Labor Day weekend would prove the last peacetime vacation for years. And when the weekend ended, the war had begun.

With almost everyone wanting to stay out of the war, wanting the Allies to win it and gloomily expecting that both those wishes were vain, it was little wonder that the United States reacted like Stephen Leacock's young man who jumped on his horse and rode off in all directions. The head of the American Legion demanded "absolute neutrality"; Senator Henry Cabot Lodge, Jr., told a cheering Veterans of Foreign Wars convention in Virginia that the prime duty of every American was to keep his country out of war; the New York *Times* wanted to minimize the risk of going to war by selling arms, but only to the Allies; the President's wife was publicly scolding the Germans; native Fascists cheered German victories; Communists and ultraconservatives formed a noisy chorus singing the glories of isolation; while ultraliberals, still mourning Spain, demanded a holy war against Fascism.

Yet there was really very little that anyone could do for the moment. The State Department banned foreign travel. In New York workmen slapped camouflage paint on belligerents' liners and painted the Stars and Stripes along the flanks of American ships. The ambassador to Germany, Hugh R. Wilson, expressed his own contempt by resigning his post on the first day of the war.

To a world alternately fascinated and appalled Germany proceeded to unveil modern war by land and air. Here was the military force that Americans had thought was indifferent or demoralized. But where was "the German people's growing spirit of revolt," the subject of a best-selling book that summer?

Now all was the war. Like a sponge, it absorbed every other topic of discussion. Newspaper circulation soared. Distracted editors ran front-page pleas begging people to stop telephoning for late war news—their switchboards were awash with incoming calls. Hopelessly out-of-date maps, some predating the Treaty of Versailles, were snapped up. The shelves of Rand McNally were cleared. Poland served yet another generation of cartographers. And at its World's Fair pavilion in New York sad-eyed Polish officials continued to invite visitors to enter the essay contest: "I would like to visit Poland because. . . ."*

Street-corner orators thrived. Provided they were willing to talk about the war—and who was not?—they drew huge crowds. Congressional mail surged to record heights, surpassing half a million letters a day. When debate on amending the Neutrality Act began in October, the House and Senate galleries were jammed while overflow crowds roamed the corridors and Capitol grounds. Here was the most tumultuous foreign policy question since the League of Nations debate twenty years before.

People openly vented their partisanship. For though 90 percent wanted the country to stay out of the war, more than 80 percent wanted the Allies to win it. Roosevelt did not even try to disguise his own sentiments. Wilson had greeted the outbreak of war in 1914 by calling for neutrality in thought, word and deed. Roosevelt called for neutrality only in deed,

* First prize was a vacation in Warsaw.

for after all, Americans not only could tell good from bad but would do so whatever he said. And when they could express their feelings in deeds, they did. The war found Germany's crack transatlantic liner *Bremen* in New York Harbor. Her captain prepared to leave at once. But U.S. customs officials kept his ship tied up for another two days by inspecting the swimming pools with unprecedented care, putting the German sailors through repeated lifeboat drills and making them prove their skills by rowing up and down the East River to a chorus of Bronx cheers sent up by a large and appreciative crowd. Meantime, a British cruiser was slipping down from Bar Harbor, Maine, to shadow the *Bremen* across the Atlantic.

But while they were partisan, most people still kept their passions on a short tether. When the British liner *Athenia* was sunk in the first hours of the war with a loss of more than 100 lives, 28 of them American, there was no upsurge of outrage. Instead there was a pointedly deliberate exercise in calm, inspired by memories of the Great War and the idea that public panic over sinkings had pushed the country into a war it should have avoided. There would never be another *Lusitania*, no matter how many ships were sunk.

Perhaps one person in twenty supported Hitler and Germany; less than one in a hundred would admit to hoping for a German victory. The rest of the people, when they thought about Germany at all, no longer thought of Huns extracting the fat from the bodies of their victims; of the sack of Louvain Cathedral; of bayoneting pregnant, defenseless women for sport. They thought rather of an intelligent, hardworking people possessing a great cultural heritage. Many believed that Germany had been treated unfairly at Versailles, that the atrocity stories from the Great War were clever inventions of British propaganda. They blamed Germany for initiating this new war, but what little antagonism they felt was reserved for Hitler and his cronies, who, for all their power, seemed slightly unreal. The American Psychological Association convening in Palo Alto in the first days of the war took up the question of Hitler's sanity.

Most people soon wanted the Neutrality Act amended so that the Allies could buy American arms. But by the end of October the British had done almost nothing to confound the enemy, and France had done even less. And with Poland's capitulation a shifting fog that was neither war nor peace cloaked the belligerents. A week after the debate on the arms embargo began the Congressional galleries were almost empty. Excitement turned to confusion and impatience.

But Russia suddenly turned without warning on Finland, demanding frontier revisions that would put Leningrad beyond the range of modern artillery. There instantly flared into life a widespread, unaffected sympathy for "Little Finland." The Finns were admired for their honesty, their modernity, their literacy—"There are no slums in Helsinki." There

was a widespread myth that Finland alone had faithfully discharged its
war debts to the United States.*

American Communists, having done somersaults for the Nazi-Soviet
Pact, proceeded to stand on their heads for Moscow's benefit. The *Daily
Worker* created its most famous headline—RED ARMY HURLS BACK INVAD-
ING FINNISH TROOPS. The first major foreign relief operation of the war
got under way, chaired by Herbert Hoover. (Poland had succumbed too
fast for Polish relief to do much more than open an office.) In newsreel
theaters people cheered films of Finnish troops along the Mannerheim
Line. And through most of the winter the Finns held the Russians to a
standstill. For a while it looked as though a Finnish word, *sisu*, denoting
stubborn courage in the face of enormous odds, would enter the English
language. But Finland's *sisu* was not enough. Early in 1940 it was forced
to accept humiliating terms and a vast loss of territory.

The war at sea had meanwhile become a variety of spectator sport. A
multiplicity of charts and graphs, of ship silhouettes and registries, was
published for plotting the tonnage sunk this week, this month, this far.
The scuttling of the *Graf Spee* in Montevideo Harbor, the rescue of
British sailors from the prison ship *Altmark*, evoked cheers and admiration, while Royal Navy losses, such as the sinking of the battleship *Royal
Oak*, caused genuine sorrow. When the brand-new pride of Britain's
merchant fleet, the *Queen Elizabeth*, turned what was supposed to be her
shakedown cruise into a dash across the Atlantic to the safety of New
York Harbor, her arrival was broadcast live. But there were limits to
sympathy and admiration, especially when the British seized U.S. mail to
and from Germany and adjacent countries. "In the U.S. armed robbery
of the mails rates a twenty-five year prison sentence," grumbled *Life*.

Throughout this first winter of the war every week that passed with the
United States still at peace brought a sharp drop in the earlier fears. War
aims, who was to blame, the ultimate significance of the war—such
considerations lost their importance. Once the first shock had passed and
the United States was still essentially neutral, there was a profound
sense of relief, as if some great hurdle had been cleared or some massive
disaster avoided. But the Phony War, the Bore War, the *Sitzkrieg* must
eventually give way to . . . what? A smashing, cataclysmic offensive

* Finland had in fact managed by good luck and good judgment to remain a noncombatant. In 1919, however, it had received a large shipment of food from the
United States as part of a general program of European relief. For this it had paid
$9,000,000. Later, as part of a relief program to prop up weak European economies,
the United States had returned the money. Finland thus owed the United States
$9,000,000. Even after their economy had recovered, the Finns did not repay that
sum, so that by 1939 almost the entire $9,000,000 was still outstanding. But the
interest was paid, promptly and in full, every year. For much less than other small
countries were spending to court American goodwill the Finns were drawing a
handsome return, thanks to a widespread misunderstanding. This was the country
Russia now attacked.

seemed out of the question now that the element of surprise was forgone. Yet unless some sort of peace was patched together, the most likely prospect was for more of Hitler's "Artichoke Plan"—conquest of a leaf at a time. But one thing, at least, was certain: France was too strong for Hitler to take by storm.

The tenor of everyday life when the war began is caught in the contrast between two commonplace terms, the Roaring Twenties and the Depression. The haze spun off by the former is entrancing to the point where ordinary, everyday life is almost impossible to see. We easily forget that most people's lives went on untouched by extravagant joys. Yet the speakeasy, the hip flask, the inexpensive Ford lent to popular amusements a whiff of outlawry. A deflated economy had worked an opposite effect. A serious cast of mind possessed an entire generation so thoroughly that even their diversions could not escape it. A quality of earnestness penetrated countless films, books, plays; even radio was not immune. In films its strongest expression was the documentary movie of social concern. In literature there were scores of strike novels and sympathetic portraits of the dispossessed, such as *The Grapes of Wrath*. On the radio programs such as *Information Please* and *Town Meeting of the Air* were popular for years.

Despite the earnestness, there was still some luxury and frivolity, of course. Gambling ships prospered beyond the three-mile limit. There was a growing market in summer homes. A new 30,000-ton luxury liner, *America*, was launched the day war began. In New York and San Francisco large crowds thronged to the international fairs. And newspapers on the last weekend of peace were fat with advertisements for back-to-school clothes and the new wasp-waist fashions from Paris.

But underneath there was an unshakably serious mood. For the principal boast of American life, the ultimate proof of the country's success—the fabled American economy—not only had collapsed, but was not yet revived. And so long as it refused to respond to the ministrations of government, so long as it refused to fill a nation's unmet needs, there could be no real recovery in body or spirit.

There was demand enough to keep the factories humming, but it was ineffective demand—demand without money behind it. So it went unmet. There was some money for new investment, money that could create new jobs. But to invest is to gamble on the future. And very few would gamble now.

On the surface of things, it is true, recovery appeared at times to be within reach. The solid middle and upper middle classes were deceptively prosperous. One distinguished foreign visitor that spring, André Maurois, thought that the country had already recovered, in pocket and soul. While

New York intellectuals despaired, it seemed to him that ordinary people were packing into the inexpensive restaurants, thronging to the World's Fair; their children were pounding on the colleges' doors; old people could at last contemplate their final years with no more than mild anxieties; for the 10,000,000 unemployed, distress was moderated by relief; America's characteristic sentimental optimism was reasserting itself; almost everyone accepted the principle of governmental responsibility for individual welfare; and the businessman no longer swaggered in the marketplace but went hat in hand to government. America, he was certain, had regained its feet. Maurois' perception of the new place of the businessman in national life was accurate. But he did not see that it cast the rest of his views in doubt. For business and the interests it represented in society had been neither crushed into extinction nor cajoled into cooperation. They had taken a beating, but they still had strength enough to fight an unending series of defensive battles. Business and those who supported its values could frustrate genuine recovery; not out of deliberate malice, but effectively all the same.

Moderates—that is, people neither fervently pro nor anti New Deal—now thought that perhaps business had taken too much of a beating. Investment stayed down, and so long as it did, there would be no recovery. Business, for its part, generally despaired of investment in this new economy where government writ ran large. The administration had recently forced the great corporations to distribute their reserves. Once again the best of intentions had produced a stupid result, for it left the corporations little or nothing with which to invest. A small recovery fueled by $14 billion in relief payments, a billion-dollar Soldiers' Bonus and a brief upsurge in credit purchases had been engineered between 1934 and 1937. But the hostility to business remained, reciprocated by a conviction that all New Dealers were bunglers. Thus, when the fuel of the 1937 recovery burned out, it had cast no sparks to ignite new fires. The economy tumbled down again, producing what conservatives dubbed the Roosevelt Depression. Unemployment rose; wage rates dropped; the economy again limped painfully along, trying to inch itself up toward general recovery.

Unemployed men, the historic symbol and irrefutable shame of the Depression, were still present in too many millions. And if the problem was unemployment, then relief, though it might moderate distress, was not —could never be—the answer. The answer was jobs. But there were no new jobs. So men accepted relief to curb their hunger and the hunger of their families, while the number of jobs offered by a government which avowedly considered itself "the employer of last resort" was dropping. In the first half of 1939 the ranks of the unemployed (roughly 10,000,000) were expanding, and total relief spending was on the rise.

Massive unemployment had come, in fact, to seem a normal part of

American life. When *Business Week* suggested in August that an unemployment rate of 5 percent was necessary as a labor reserve for business expansion, there was barely a whisper of protest. With unemployment around 15 to 20 percent of the total work force this was more a goal to be striven for than a piece of reactionary callousness.

More worrisome perhaps was the tendency of government to become more and more wedded to relief as the answer to social problems. And not only government, but people generally were coming to think of cash grants as the direct path to social justice. California voters went to the polls in November, 1939, to vote on "Ham and Eggs," otherwise known as Thirty Every Thursday. Rationalized as a combination of relief for the old and pump priming for a stagnant economy, it would provide $30 in cash each Thursday to all the unemployed aged fifty and over. The money would be raised by a state tax on incomes above $3,000 a year and on securities sales. Ham and Eggs had lost at the polls in 1938, but this time its prospects were bright. It enrolled some 400,000 dues-paying members, had more than 12,000 trained volunteer workers, and even by California standards it was an impassioned movement. Up and down the state Ham and Eggers held hundreds of rallies and demonstrations, endlessly chanting "Ham and Eggs! Ham and Eggs!" utterly impervious to criticism. Stiffly they marched their aged limbs along, taking the most militant tune in the hymnal and adding lyrics of their own: "Onward, Pension Soldiers, Marching as to War. . . ."

Conventional politicians took alarm. Similar movements were already stirring in Ohio and Nebraska; there were offshoots in Texas, Colorado and Kentucky. Success in California would encourage elderly militants everywhere. California's rich grew increasingly nervous. The San Francisco Stock Exchange threatened to move to Reno, Nevada, if Ham and Eggs won. But it lost, by a margin of two to one. In Ohio a similar plan went down to equally crushing defeat shortly thereafter. And once Social Security went into operation, schemes such as Ham and Eggs lost their appeal.

But the very poor were still battered between conflicting authorities, petty political ambitions and ingrained public callousness as in Ohio. That state's governor, John Bricker, openly nursed Presidential ambitions, and his claim to national attention in 1939 was success in accumulating a budget surplus. When the resources of local government ran dry that winter, tens of thousands of people on local relief turned to Ohio's state officials with their famous multimillion-dollar surplus. But they turned in vain, for that was Bricker's ticket to the 1940 GOP convention. Federal surplus foods were eventually rushed in to feed the many thousands who were, quite literally, starving. But federal relief consisted entirely of flour and apples—no milk, no yeast, no eggs with which to make bread. So while they froze through a Midwest winter of unusual harshness, Ohio's poor dined on bowls of flour and water. Bricker's surplus remained intact.

With such reminders at hand, after six years of New Deal programs and the establishment of a more humane and reasonable system of help for the poor, the United States knew no sense of triumph. No one really liked relief—not the government, not the nation at large, certainly not the recipients. But no one held much hope for anything better.

And not only was the economy flat, not only had the reforming zest gone out of the New Deal, not only were the poor still poor, but stagnation had worked its way to the very roots of society—even into the womb. America was rapidly growing older. The birthrate had declined dramatically, and what increase in population occurred was due more to the survival of the old than to the birth of the new. Between the 1930 and 1940 censuses the number of people under sixteen dropped by 2,000,000; the number of those over sixty-five rose by 3,000,000. A declining birthrate might be desirable, but where is the future in a gerontocracy? The United States now had 131,500,000 people. The Census Bureau forecast that population would peak at 150,000,000 about 1980, and would then start to decline. That projection spoke less of the future than it did of the present.

The most sensitive barometer of national life, however, was still the economy. Not surprisingly, it had a clear-cut response to the outbreak of war. After dithering about in the first hours until the invasion of Poland was confirmed, the stock market then turned sharply upward. The New York Stock Exchange began the day at 134; it closed at 138. Senator Robert Taft, to the horror of conservative-isolationist purists accustomed to considering him one of themselves, demanded the Neutrality Act be thrown out and war materials be offered to anyone who wanted to buy—for cash, of course. Consumer prices shot up as a housewives' panic cleared the shelves. Thanks to hoarding on the one hand and gouging on the other, the prices of staples—e.g., meat, cooking fats, sugar, flour—rose by 10 to 25 percent in the first week. Memories of World War I's spectacular inflation were revived. Real estate brokers placed half-page advertisements in the New York Times reading "BUY NOW—Anything from Anybody." And on Wall Street a boom that was almost entirely psychological kept roaring along from week to week.

No large arms orders were pouring in. For the moment the most promising prospect was export orders from neutral countries no longer able to depend on Britain, France or Germany for manufactured goods. Still, the economy grew by more during the last quarter of the year than it had done during the first nine months; those final months in fact more than doubled the growth of the gross national product for the year. Detroit had expected to sell 3,000,000 automobiles in 1940; it now raised its sights by a million. In vain did the U.S. Chamber of Commerce preach caution. Here was a nation that could not get out of the thirties fast enough. And businessmen were as eager to shake off the dust of that decade as anyone.

Labor was equally interested in a war boom, and strong enough to be sure of a share in the benefits. With the aid of a sympathetic administration union membership had grown rapidly. Of 48,000,000 people currently at work, 9,000,000 were enrolled in unions.

With growth there had gone a growing respectability. Labor's former radicalism had been tamed, and the fears it had once inspired now seemed slightly absurd. The mainstream of American labor had, in fact, never sought a social revolution. Corporate welfarism required no great compromise of principles and philosophy. Organized labor was, therefore, genuinely big, moderately respectable and generally nonviolent. It had come to power and maturity. And if there were a defense or war boom, labor would be cheek by jowl with business when the orders came in.

Even before the Neutrality Act was amended to permit arms sales to the Allies, iron and steel towns were alive with anticipation. In New Castle, Pennsylvania, whose obsolete tinplate mills had stood silent for years, one man greeted the news of the beginning of war by standing in the street shouting "Glory Hallelujah!" Euphoria, urged on by ever more plausible rumors, swept through the town in ensuing weeks. Of New Castle's 50,000 people more than half were already on some type of relief. Across Pennsylvania, West Virginia, Ohio and Kentucky stood hundreds of steel and coal ghost towns. They now stirred themselves awake. War's demands might easily make obsolete ways of producing tinplate and steel profitable again. In October New Castle's tinplate mills fired up, for the first time in years, and stood by for war orders.

Away from the offices and factories new life was already stirring. Florida in the winter of 1939 had its best season since 1929, despite unusually cold weather. Part of Florida's boom was generated by rich sun lovers fearful of taking their usual winter cruise. But most of the state's visitors were families of modest means, many taking their first vacation in years.

Those who felt they were being left out of the new prosperity were quick to complain. Farmers, for example, thought that this war should, like the last one, provide a boom for farm products. But the Allies wanted metal guns, planes, aircraft. Britain was actually buying less American tobacco, cotton, wheat, fruits, meat and fats; it was conserving its dollar reserves to purchase arms. In Congress the farm bloc pressed to tie the sale of arms on to the sale of farm products. But even as they made their arguments, the boom appeared to vanish as quickly as it had come.

By February, 1940, people asked, "What happened to the boom?" And soon it was being dismissed as an inventory boom, stocking up for the future. New Castle's ancient tinplate mills shut down. The farmers lowered their sights. Economists argued that there had been no war boom at all. It was just a temporary upturn which had begun the previous summer and come to fruition in the fall and winter, they said. But whatever it was, it was over. Things were still the same. Or so they seemed.

II

To Arms!

WHEN March gave way to April, there was a strong sense that great things were about to happen. It was plain that with the advent of spring one side or the other must strike a major blow, or both must sue for peace. And a nation that went to bed one April evening wondering which it would be awoke the next morning to learn that while it slept, Norway and Denmark had been conquered.

In the next few days there was a sense of shock, not without a rueful admiration for the sheer technical brilliance of German arms. Yet underneath the current mood there was a feeling of outrage, which was made keen by apprehension. No one appeared less deserving of sudden attack and the cruelties of Nazi occupation than the hardworking, high-minded, peaceful Scandinavians. And by conquering Denmark, Hitler had acquired a claim to Greenland.

As a rule most people knew little more of Greenland than that it was in the general vicinity of the North Pole and consisted chiefly of snow and ice. Overnight it became "the world's largest unsinkable aircraft carrier" or "Greenland . . . with its unexploited riches and its strategic nearness to the United States." In vain did Hitler protest that he had no desire for Greenland (imaginary riches and all). Germany was beginning to seem to many people a menace to America itself.

Just as this conviction was beginning to take hold, Hitler launched his next bolt. The Netherlands was overrun. More than ever now the war cast everything else into the shade. Daily attendance at the New York World's Fair fell to a trickle until war bulletins were piped over the public-address system every few minutes.

In five days the Dutch were completely defeated. And what of their imperial possessions? In German hands the Dutch West Indies could threaten the Gulf Coast and the Panama Canal. In Japanese hands the Dutch East Indies would make Japan rich in rubber and tin. The United States, which had long depended on these sources, would be so much the poorer.

From the Netherlands the Luftwaffe at last had bases close enough to England to mount a sustained air offensive. England it must be, thought lay and military opinion, for France was surely too strong even for the dazzling blitzkrieg tactics which had devastated five small, weak countries.

Three million French soldiers stood ready along the Maginot Line, the most spectacular piece of military engineering of an age both military and engineering. With all hope of surprise gone, Germany would be forced to concentrate on launching sea and air attacks. That, people reasoned, must have been the purpose of the conquest of the Dutch.

It was around these points that public opinion, shaken and tremulous from the five-day war against the Dutch, hastily rallied. Indeed, the bewilderment of the Dutch at being invaded had been matched by American astonishment at invasions which were no sooner launched than they triumphed.

Just as this new equilibrium was being fashioned, Hitler launched the battle of France, with his Panzer divisions slicing through the undefended and presumably impassable forest of the Ardennes, outflanking the Maginot Line. The new equilibrium was at once overthrown, all its assumptions confounded. Hitler and his generals suddenly took on the aspect of something malignant, uncanny and inexplicable. They appeared as men who possessed a new knowledge, masters of a new technique that made rubbish of old certainties. And their military prowess had all the terror of an evil magic. With German armies closing in on Paris, the President tried to reassure a deeply frightened country by calling it to arms.

When he went before a hurriedly convened joint session of Congress in the middle of May, not a hint of lightness broke Roosevelt's gravity. Those close enough to see, or presciently equipped with opera glasses, thought he looked tired and careworn. It was a tense moment. And the hushed commingling of expectation and excitement betrayed a self-conscious sense of the historic. Outside was rain and cold spring winds; inside red "Buddy" poppies glowed in buttonholes. Every hint of fixed purpose, every call for national defense brought cheers. Not since his earliest days—the Hundred Days—had Congress cheered Roosevelt with such unaffected warmth; not even then had there been such stormy applause. No one seriously entertained fears of impending air raids, yet when he told them what every schoolchild knew—that the country was three hours' flying time from this place, and four hours away from that—graying, aging, often willful, heads bobbed in vigorous assent. And when he asked for 50,000 planes, there came the longest, loudest cheer of all from the House's floor and galleries.

He had rallied them. For one brief, exhilarating moment the old springs of confidence were refreshed. America would build the 50,000 planes and build a two-ocean navy. But France could not be saved. Paris was soon occupied by German soldiers; the Maginot Line passed into history as a byword for grand folly; and the British were fleeing for the deadly beaches of Dunkirk. Hitler had gambled on a short war; he appeared to have won. And the bilious fear bubbled up even stronger than before. A vocabulary of military terms already swollen beyond digestion was suddenly inadequate. Not quite believing it, people talked numbly now of the British fleet in German hands. And cartographers, among the few to profit so far from the war, gave up. Events moved just too fast to be captured in colored inks and sharp lines, no matter how diligently they tried.

Now "The U.S. felt defenseless. The hurricane that had swept Europe, the gathering clouds in the Three Easts, had come, with nightmare speed, close, real and threatening. The reaction was profound—broad and deep. As in few times of peace the nation spoke as a whole and the voice came clear to Congress: Arm. Arm the U.S. for what may come." Everywhere there was a burning impatience for dramatic action, for something like another Hundred Days. "Everyone wanted to help. Hundreds of gossips wrote to the FBI volunteering to spy on their neighbors." Home defense corps sprang up in nearly every state. The National Legion of the Mothers of America organized a Molly Pitcher Rifle Brigade to pick off descending parachutists. In Sioux Falls, South Dakota, a group of young men vented their feelings of helplessness in the face of Nazi savagery by beating, covering with paint and then blinding a dachshund named Hans.

Isolationist and pacifist correspondence to the press dropped off abruptly. The New York *Times* reversed itself and called for conscription. The New York *Herald Tribune* called for a declaration of war on Germany. (The editorial calling for war was written by Walter Millis, author of an isolationist best seller a few years before called *The Road to War*.) Polls had shown nearly two-thirds of the nation opposed to conscription a few months previously; they now showed the opposite. In the Senate Claude Pepper of Florida concluded an impassioned speech by calling for a resolution committing the United States to seeing Nazism destroyed, and the galleries burst into spontaneous cheers and applause. Yet the fear would not down, the fear that whatever the country did would prove too little and too late. The Army was said to be capable of nothing more than riot control. One popular rumor had it that the entire country possessed a total of four modern antiaircraft guns. A diversion that might have been called "What If Hitler Wins?" cropped up; not a few people found it too painful to play for more than a few minutes.

Trying to plumb the swirl of emotion verging on panic, Walter Lippmann thought he glimpsed beneath the guilt, the fear, the pity and the anger a moral crisis unparalleled in the nation's history, a profound sense of having failed some great existential test. Among Anglophiles and anti-Fascists there was simply despair, so deep that even Chamberlain's resignation and Churchill's appointment as Prime Minister could not dispel it. "Some day," as one of them wrote:

the survivors of this generation will tell their grandchildren what it meant to live through a critical week in the world's history. They will tell of the newspapers bought, edition after edition, each with its record of new disasters. About the perfect May weather . . . the shudder as an airplane passed overhead. . . . About turning the radio knob for news, and instead getting sales plugs and dance music—till a new voice broke in to announce that Antwerp had fallen, or St. Quentin, so that the war seemed to be fought in one's living room. . . . About the sense of absolute dehumanization rising from these stories of dive bombers and tanks . . . what the radio suggests is a world of machines for reducing human flesh to shreds and cinders. . . . But worst of all, they will say, was the feeling of helplessness.

Nearly all believed now that Britain would soon be defeated and that when it was, their own country would find itself in grave danger. Nearly all, that is, except the staunchest isolationists. The chairman of the Senate Foreign Relations Committee, Key Pittman of Nevada, unabashedly advised the British to surrender at once. "It is to be hoped," he concluded, with an eye on the Anglophiles, "that this plan will not be too long delayed by futile encouragement to fight on." The British declined to accept Senator Pittman's advice. How to keep their own country from being forced into a position as desperate as Britain's was a problem all must consider. For as long as this generation of Americans could remember, "Three thousand miles of good green water" had been security enough. But if the Royal Navy were captured or surrendered and combined with the French, Italian and German fleets, Hitler would at a stroke become absolute master of the Atlantic. If only for that reason almost no one opposed a defense buildup at flank speed. But isolationists wanted to keep every useful piece of military equipment here, while interventionists argued that some American arms would be best used in British hands. Isolationists grumbled over the *quid pro quo* which sent fifty destroyers of World War I vintage in exchange for a string of bases screening the Eastern seaboard.

The first anniversary of the war came and went with the Battle of Britain working to a furious pitch, both sides claiming great victories, both conceding moderate losses. No one believed that either was truthful. Yet the benefit of doubt went, spurred on by wish, to the British pilots. Despite its tremendous victories over the Polish and French air forces, almost no one believed or wanted to believe that the Luftwaffe had scored the hat trick. But it was impossible to think that there would be no invasion. The general opinion held up—by Thanksgiving Britain would be ruled from Berlin. The beginning of heavy and almost nightly bombings of London late in September seemed a prelude to cross-Channel attack.

Yet these bombings, ironically, signaled German defeat in the air. By switching its attacks from the RAF airfields onto civilians, the Luftwaffe had, in panic and despair, groped its way into a fatal error: It had thrown

away all chance of winning control of the air. It was possibly the decision
which cost Hitler the war, for it kept Britain alive, forcing on him the war
on two fronts that Germany could never win. Of course, this could not be
seen at the time. But as September gave way to October, the realization
grew that somehow the British had won.

When the Dutch Army surrendered, the United States moved up to
nineteenth place on the scale of world military powers. Active-duty soldiers
and reservists totaled barely half a million men in September, 1939; the
modest increases since then made no substantial difference. Most of the
planes now in service were too old for combat; even Italy was better
equipped in the air. Only at sea was America strong; but even there it had
only one great fleet, and that guarded the Pacific. The military establishment was small and professional. Much of it was out of date. And it
pared costs to the bone.

This was not, as commonly assumed, the fault of a resistant public. Most
people wanted a bigger army and navy even during the Depression; by
overwhelming margins they supported bigger defense budgets. And they
invariably expressed willingness to pay higher taxes for them. Rare was the
American who wanted less money spent on defense. But the New Deal
administrators had more pressing concerns; they effectively opposed any
but incremental increases on military spending. Even when the war began,
they maintained their opposition, sadly missing an extraordinary opportunity to promote social welfare as national preparedness. And in that folly
they also did less than they might have done to arm the nation. A Congress
which would have appropriated billions in 1939 to build ships, planes and
guns was not even asked. As one student concluded:

> The vision of Roosevelt's liberal administrators was just too narrow.
> Instead of welcoming international pressure for the irresistible pressure it
> would put on government to spend, they joined Roosevelt's conservative
> critics in counting the cost. . . . [Forrestal] told them that the practical
> way to put the New Deal programs across [in 1939] was to sell them as
> Preparedness, not as Reform—indeed, the TVA had its beginning under
> the Defense Act of 1916. In two years Forrestal's judgment was to be
> vindicated by all the shortages from dams to dentistry for which the New
> Dealers had been fighting. But the liberal mind shrank back from the
> temptation to gain the substance by denying the doctrine.

The principle preceded even the First World War. The land-grant colleges
were created by the Morrill Act of 1862, which was a piece of defense
legislation designed, among other things, to provide the Union Army with a
large supply of officers. So Forrestal had both history and public opinion
behind him. Both were persistently ignored.

People wanted a bigger army, it seemed, so long as they did not have to join it. Roosevelt had increased its active-duty strength by 100,000 when the war began, but it was difficult to find the men. Millions were unemployed, yet recruits were hard to find; healthy, literate recruits a rarity. The military was no longer esteemed. Just before the war began *Time* had offered a feature called "Background for War." The maps and text lingered over traditional European battlefields such as the strategic Baltic Plain. "But logic," it cautioned, "cannot predict where the next battles will be fought because military men are often stupid." When in public, high-ranking officers were invariably diffident; most wore their uniforms only for ceremonial occasions.

But here was a new day. The purse strings had not simply been loosened; they had been cut. Roosevelt asked for less than $2 billion for military appropriations in January, 1940. By mid-June the requests had shot up to $5 billion and were on a climbing curve. Republicans, desperately thrashing about in search of a campaign issue, grumbled that $7 billion had been spent on defense the past seven years and the country was virtually unarmed. (It should be noted that they had no idea how little defense could be bought for a billion dollars a year.) As a conservative magazine put it:

NATION BACKS UP DEFENSE PLAN
BUT DEMANDS JOB BE DONE RIGHT
What Has Happened
To Billions Poured
Out Since 1933?

The Army's authorized active duty strength was raised to 400,000, and James Montgomery Flagg's dramatic World War I poster* with the accusing finger—"I Want You"—was already beginning to reappear on billboards and handbills. But if they really wanted you, why didn't they draft you?

Most people favored conscription. But only Congress could enact a draft law, and despite the fervent pleas for national defense, Congress was extremely reluctant to enact a peacetime draft. Congress was less worried about the symbolism than it was about the fact that even though two-thirds of the people wanted conscription, there still existed a host of potential opponents, and if the war somehow disappeared and the demands for conscription died down, Congress would find itself burdened with the responsibility for having passed an act suddenly made unnecessary and

* A classic case of transatlantic borrowing. In 1917 Flagg took a popular British recruiting poster of three years before, putting Uncle Sam in Lord Kitchener's pose and using exactly the same words, to great effect.

unpopular. In that event both Houses would be decimated. That was why the White House was also lukewarm to conscription.

So, when the Burke-Wadsworth bill (formally known as the Selective Service Act of 1940) made its debut in early August, its chances of passage were rated poor to fair, despite the public clamor for it. Opposition to it touched a dozen bases; it was attacked by liberals who still smarted over their role in the First World War; by college students; by the Communist Party; by the American Youth Congress; by labor leaders, who feared conscription might be used to wreck the unions by drafting strikers into the Army; by clergymen of almost every denomination; by conservatives and isolationists; and by the Vice Presidential nominees of both major parties. The most effective argument to issue from this mixed bag of frights was that voluntary enlistments would do until the country plunged into war—conscription was therefore unnecessary and potentially dangerous. Burke, a Democratic Senator from Nebraska, and Wadsworth, a Republican Representative from New York, countered that their bill was not designed to create a standing army; its aim was to create a large reserve of trained soldiers who could be mobilized if the need arose. And they called on the President to support them. To their dismay he agreed with the principle, but not the bill.

Almost everywhere Burke and Wadsworth now turned they found opposition. They patterned their bill after the draft law of 1917 and proposed to draft men aged twenty-one to thirty-one. The Army had wanted younger men in 1917, but popular sentiment was strong against sending men to fight who were too young to vote. The compromise on a minimum age of twenty-one was adopted in the Burke-Wadsworth bill. Yet the most fiercely antiwar group in the entire country was comprised of young men in their twenties. And their mothers and clergymen, afraid for their morals, supported them. As one Methodist clergyman explained it to the Senate's Military Affairs Committee: "Conscription takes boys shortly out of high school—boys who all their lives have been trained to respect women—and places them in situations where the absence of contact with normal girls induces a mass lust which has always characterized Army units."

SENATOR SCHWARTZ: What?
CLERGYMAN: Mass lust. I will clarify that.
SENATOR SCHWARTZ: (Hastily) That's not necessary. That's clear enough.

The public hearings grew angry indeed. At one point a fistfight broke out on the House floor after one Congressman referred to another as "a son of a bitch." Senator Pepper, the staunchest of liberal interventionists and an ardent supporter of conscription, was hanged in effigy on Capitol Hill by representatives of "Mothers of the USA" and the "Congress of American Mothers." Anticonscription forces packed the House and Senate galleries, with one group of heavily veiled women melodramatically calling themselves the Death Watch, and one of them mumbling over and over, "Oh, my novena, my novena." Below them, Senator Burton K. Wheeler and other isolationists hammered hard at Burke-Wadsworth. Wheeler, once a Socialist-Progressive candidate for the Vice Presidency, argued at one moment that conscription would destroy democratic government, at another that Hitler had no designs on American territory. "If you pass this bill," he concluded, "you slit the throat of the last democracy still living— you give to Hitler his greatest and cheapest victory." And among the liberals with no stomach for Wheeler's isolationism were many who feared that he might be right about this case. When they recalled the Army of the First World War, it was with horror, not pride.

To the critical eye it had looked very much like the worst army in the world. Even the German Army was, by 1917, reasonably easygoing and fair-minded, but the American Army was full of martinets and viciousness. It was heavy with MP's, rife with class distinctions and staffed from top to bottom with petty despots. The MP's were particularly hated and feared. Their most celebrated figure was a lieutenant nicknamed Hard-Boiled Smith and notorious for his tortures, murders and wanton cruelty. Fame had its drawbacks; it brought him a short, essentially symbolic, stretch in prison. Others like him, Hard-Boiled Smith in all but fame, were never called to account. And as recently as 1932 the Army's *Training Manual 2000–25* explained:

> Democracy: A Government of the masses. Authority derived through mass meeting or any other form of "direct" expression. Results in mobocracy. Attitude toward property is Communistic—negating property rights. Attitude toward law is that the will of the majority shall regulate, whether it be based upon deliberation or governed by passion, prejudice and impulse, without restraint or regard for consequences. Results in demagogism, license, agitation, discontent, and anarchy.

Many were convinced that views such as this, imbibed by millions during their military service in the Great War, had been partly to blame for the right-wing terrors of 1919–1922. And liberals now feared that another draft of all the healthy young men into the Army might turn them into lifelong worshipers of property and strong government.

There was also the problem of conscientious objectors. With widespread antiwar, antimilitary sentiments in recent years, especially among the young, there was every reason to believe that there would be many tens of thousands of objectors instead of a few thousand as in the First World War. Existing laws and former practices stilled no apprehensions, for there was no recognition of an individual's right to conscientious objection; there was merely a concession to the handful of religious groups traditionally opposed to military service.

With so much and so varied opposition before it, Burke-Wadsworth would have been doomed at any other time. Not now, for there was one overriding theme drawing even these disparate strands together: a growing consensus that the nation must arm, no matter what. There was also a growing desire to do something, even if that included drafting young men. The potential draftees, keenly sensitive to the currents of opinion, proceeded to prophesy how Congress would vote by marrying in record numbers. Marriage-license applications shot up 24 percent in Atlanta, 25 percent in Chicago and an estimated 40 percent in Los Angeles. Lines formed before licensing offices opened each morning and were still there when they closed at night. Despite many denials that Burke-Wadsworth exempted married men, the suspicions and hopes to the contrary survived. As did rumors to the effect that future war widows would go pensionless if married after September 1 or some other such date in the immediate future.

Despite strong opposition, Selective Service would pass, and Roosevelt now declared his support for it. After three days of debate the Senate approved, 58–31. By an equally comfortable margin, so did the House. And the day after Roosevelt signed it into law Grover Cleveland Bergdoll —"notorious draft dodger of the World War"—began a seven-year jail sentence. Bergdoll had become famous by evading federal authorities for more than twenty years rather than serve in the Army. Most of the time he was assumed to be living in exile, while he had actually been living comfortably at home. At one time his mother had stood on the front lawn tearfully pleading before film cameras for Grover to come home and ask for mercy, while Grover looked on from inside the house. But Grover had been caught at last. As if writing finis to the last draft law, he went off to jail just as the new one went into effect.

Passage of Selective Service showed a heartening willingness to sink deep differences when danger required it. Seen in that light, conscription was a symbolic tie which bound the entire nation even though less than one person in a hundred would serve. Even before the draft law was passed, the country had plunged into a spontaneous outpouring of patriotic emotion.

By mid-July "Americans had dragged their patriotism out of the closet . . . and were wearing it in the streets as they had not done since 1918. Every musical show on Broadway featured the national anthem as a curtain-raiser or finale. Red, white and blue gallantly gleamed on lapels, umbrellas, hats and suspenders. Patriotic pins, pendants, clips and bracelets 'walked off the counters' of department and five-and-dime stores as fast as they could be stocked." The Society of Hay Fever Sufferers of

America was trying to replace "Gesundheit!" with "God Bless America!" And everywhere there were flags: bracelets and necklaces consisting of miniature flags in everything from brightly colored enamels to precious stones; scarves decorated with the words to the "Star-Spangled Banner"; flag bags with the Stars and Stripes appliquéd in felt. Then as now, the foremost expression of patriotism was the flag.

Just as a dearth of political theory had made "Democracy" the vague but magic touchstone of American politics, so the absence of multiple channels for patriotic sentiment had raised the flag to an eminence unknown in other democratic countries. Even now it is a thing almost sacred to the majority of Americans. Other nations may have a monarchy or a dazzling cultural heritage or many strong and ancient traditions, or all of these, to provide an abundance of symbols on which to lavish their pride. But America had to make its symbols in a hurry and make them potent enough to harness a large, polyglot, far-flung population. American patriotism thus runs deep in a few channels, while in older countries it runs broad over many. One result is that American patriotism looks more like that of a new, undemocratic state such as the Soviet Union or Nazi Germany than an older, democratic one such as Britain or France.

And by the fall of 1940 the similarity between the Nazi salute delivered to the swastika flag by German youngsters every morning and the straight-arm salute to the flag offered by American schoolchildren while reciting the pledge of allegiance was too obvious to be ignored any longer. Variations on the military hand-to-forehead salute were attempted. But this brought noisy grumbling among military men and veterans who considered that salute their own. It was also discovered that the current flag code made the straight-arm salute mandatory for children in the public schools. So the modifications were dropped and the traditional salute reinstalled.

In itself, of course, there was nothing odious to this "flag worship"; given the needs of a new country, or rather a new government, it was a necessity. Carried into another age, however, it could work real mischief and real injustice. One of the first victims of this new rush to wave the flag was a twenty-year-old girl who was sentenced to one to two years in jail in November, 1940, for the simple act of hurling an American flag to the ground.

Flagmakers were overjoyed. Theirs is an uncertain business at best. During the heady 1920's the new sophistication sent flag sales plummeting. The collapse of the stock market introduced them to rock bottom. And then, about 1931, defying the blows of hardship to their spirits, people took to buying flags again. The NRA years of 1933–1935 were boom times for flagmakers. But the 1937 collapse turned the mood sour; the tides of patriotism ebbed; a huge backlog of flags went unsold. But now flagmakers were running six weeks behind on their orders.

Business, as quick to join a boom as to promote one, leaped aboard this one with a will, and thousands of items were soon packaged patriotically. But only one campaign enjoyed any popular success, and how much it boosted product sales is questionable. Sipping noisily, a character named Gaston imbibed the products of a California winemaker named Chateau Martin, then whooped, to a sprightly tune and in a strong fake-French accent:

> I am NUTS about the good old Oo Ess Ay.
> She have everything—I hand her the bouquet.
> I go quick to government and I say
> "Please give to me citizen papers today."
> I wave the flag for good old Oo Ess Ay.

Nightclub singers offered variations on Gaston's theme. Gaston himself became something of a celebrity. Everyone knew his slogan, and schoolchildren could be heard chanting lustily, "I am NUTS about the good old Oo Ess Ay."

Across the country people were singing patriotic songs old and new. Most of them were banal, but the sentiments behind the singing were sincere enough. *Time* loved it: "The U.S. was singing, as it had not sung in years, of pride in its past, of hope in its future." Some new songs enjoyed a fleeting popularity, such as "I Am an American" ("and proud of my lib-er-tee") and "He's My Uncle." Less popular but more enduring than these was a wistfully lovely song inspired by the Nazi conquest of France, "The Last Time I Saw Paris." And most popular of all was "God Bless America." Irving Berlin had written it in 1918, but he had put it aside. Twenty years later he had offered it to Kate Smith. It quickly became a sentimental favorite. By fall, 1940, there was no escaping it. It was played at baseball games, races, bingo sessions, school meetings and films. It soon became a common and spontaneous practice for people to rise and bare their heads when it was played.

But the most extraordinary patriotic song was a cantata, thirteen minutes long, difficult to sing, not particularly tuneful, musically little more than a chant with antiphonal responses, called "Ballad for Americans." Originally composed for a WPA Theater Project by Earl Robinson and John Latouche, it was subtitled "A Pamphlet for Democracy" and addressed itself to a newly militant unity. Its national debut had come during the previous winter on *The Pursuit of Happiness*, a weekly radio program of Americana ("to balance the ugly weight of war news"). The studio audience was electrified, and as the last notes faded away, they stood on their chairs and cheered, sobbed, clapped, hugged one another. The studio switchboard was alight with incoming calls.

The President had issued a call to arms. Congress had voted money and, in a sense, men. People had literally rallied "round the flag." Government was reorganizing itself, however clumsily. But ultimately all would depend on the Army and Navy. At that time, a daunting thought.

More often than not, defense orders were placed according to purely political considerations. States in the Northeast and Midwest consequently enjoyed the lion's share of defense contracts, and the rest of the country got only crumbs; thus, tiny Delaware had more than Texas and California combined. The system of military posts and bases made some sense in terms of fighting the Indian wars and even more sense in terms of cloak-room lobbying. Most military bases were in locations of no strategic impor-tance and far from terrain hospitable to maneuvers. Key positions in the War and Navy Departments were held by special interests, such as the Assistant Secretaryship in the War Department, which for twenty years had been the property of the American Legion. At the best of times the military makes haste slowly; with problems such as these, which by no means exhaust the list, it was surprising that it could move at all.

The Navy was not as hobbled as the Army. Its biggest single problem was time, and almost an entire year had been lost. The country had long maintained a Pacific Fleet and an Atlantic Squadron. That squadron was stronger than the name implied, but the country's chief defense in the Atlantic was the British fleet. And it was threatened. With less than two hours' debate and not one dissenting vote a two-ocean navy bill passed the House late in June. Yet it would take six years according to current estimates to build the 200 new Navy ships. It was a very annoyed Chief of Naval Operations, Admiral Harold Stark, who snapped back at the Navy's critics, "Dollars can't buy yesterday."

The Army's situation was enough to inspire despair. Besides the problem of time, the Army had serious problems with its equipment, with its person-nel and in its thinking. Its newest model tanks were armed entirely with machine guns. The 12-ton tank (reported as "acknowledged in all Armies as the best in its class") had no periscope. So the tank commander's head poked up through the turret, exposed to dust and flying shell fragments, while his feet rested on the driver's shoulders. And because his voice could not be heard above the engine's roar, he delivered his instructions through his feet—a kick in the back meant forward, a kick in the right shoulder meant turn right, and so on. Even after the armament of this tank was augmented by adding a 37mm cannon, it had less firepower than the fighter planes currently engaged in the Battle of Britain. Yet this was the machine around which the Army proposed to build its armored divisions. Even the 23-ton tank introduced at the end of the year was still, ton for ton, the least powerful tank in the world.

Bad as the problems with equipment were, personnel problems were even worse. The Army might become large but almost useless if what was coyly referred to as "the Problem"—racism, that is—was not defused. Black people and white Army officers had painful memories of the Army's experience with Negro* soldiers in the First World War. One nightmarish day at Fort Sam Houston, Texas, in December, 1917, some thirteen Negro soldiers who had participated in a deadly race riot were hanged. Postwar military appraisals of the performance of black soldiers were unanimous on two points: They were unreliable in combat, and they performed better under white officers than under black. Army policy had since been that Negro soldiers should be placed in service units, and if they were to see combat, it must be under Caucasian officers. Better yet, Negroes should be discouraged from enlisting. Thus, when the war began, there were less than 4,000 black soldiers in the Army; or less than 2 percent of the total active-duty strength.

A brief, exciting hope had flared among young Negroes that perhaps those days were now over, that perhaps an unprecedented peacetime conscription might bring an unprecedented non-Jim Crow Army. But the old policy of segregated units and an all-white officer corps (or nearly so) was to be continued. Even the bare chance to get into the Army's only glamorous branch seemed closed with a War Department announcement that "Applications from colored persons for flying cadet appointments or enlistment in the Air Corps are not being accepted." This was too much; it touched off a storm of anger among Negroes and white liberals just a few weeks before the November elections. Presto! The Army's highest-ranking Negro officer, Colonel Benjamin O. Davis, was suddenly promoted to brigadier general, making him the first black general in American history. It was an obvious sop, and Colonel Davis was only eight months away from scheduled retirement. Sops would neither solve the Problem nor even keep it within tolerable limits.

Mentally this was an Army time had passed by. It still had a horse cavalry division and, thanks to a suddenly generous Congress, was adding another. Because the National Defense Act of 1920 defined a tank as "an Infantry Unit," the Army could not even discuss tanks openly unless it called them Combat Cars, as required by its own security regulations. This was an army that still talked of "AEF," "Doughboys," "Over There" and "Over the top." It did not even look like an army. In its canvas leggings from a bygone age and its forest ranger hats it looked like a hiking club.

To these burdens was added another: public impatience. There was a wealth of criticism, most of it uninformed. There was also much praise—chiefly that American planes, pilots, tanks and soldiers were the wonder and terror of the world's military forces—which was equally uninformed. The criticisms could only inflame impatience; ignorant praises could only delude opinion. After six months had gone by and there was not much

---

* I use "Negroes" and "blacks" interchangeably not because I am insensitive to the irritation of young blacks to the term "Negro," but because it seems to me a matter of common sense. I write of their parents, people who preferred to call themselves Negroes. They did so unashamedly, and so do I.

visible change, the impatience turned to anger. The essential trouble was discovered to be bottlenecks. And as tempers flared, President Roosevelt began to appear as the biggest single bottleneck in the entire defense program. All authority was centered in his hands. Yet he gave neither visible direction nor impetus to the defense effort. The National Defense Advisory Committee he had created during the summer had seemed uninspiring; now it seemed inept. There was a public chorus of demands that Roosevelt name a defense commissioner and give him the power to marry the economic resources of the nation to its military needs, bringing forth a nation in arms.

An impatient, energetic people was taking measures of its own. Some were pure hokum, with not a little boosterism, false courage and hysteria. But behind them was an important historical fact: Washington was weak, local initiative strong. The result in past years had been a luxurious undergrowth of private associations, everything from the Ku Klux Klan to the League of Women Voters. Home guard units loosely patterned after Britain's Home Guard began springing up throughout the summer of 1940. Some were small, like Carson City, Nevada's 25-man unit; others, like Miami's 400-man McCallister Volunteers, were quite large. Most were predominantly male. But Mrs. Virginia Nowell of Chapel Hill, North Carolina, had organized the Green Guards, an all-female militia dedicated to the defense of hearth and home. Her command embraced nearly 1,000 volunteers. Mrs. Nowell, whose interest in public service began with membership in the Chapel Hill PTA, now commissioned herself "the first woman general in the United States." To a song written by their leader, the Green Guards marched and drilled and sang:

> We will keep the beacons burning
> For our soldiers out there yearning
> Just to crush the warriors turning
> To our shores, America.
> Guard our homes, our land, our young ones,
> Blast to hell invading wrong ones. . . .

Many towns were trying, without success, to induce state and federal officials to instruct the local citizenry in the arcane arts of guerrilla war. The town of Hamilton, Ohio, refused to be discouraged. It devised a plan under which local businesses would subsidize those of the town's young men who joined the National Guard or participated in any other government-supervised military training. More than fifty other towns and cities copied the Hamilton plan. Many more, however, followed the lead of Lexington, Massachusetts, which armed, drilled and organized its citizens as partisans. The War Department consistently refused to encourage these local efforts. It was cool even to the revival of the Plattsburg Camp system made famous in the First World War.

These camps had begun in 1913, with the vigorous blessing of Teddy Roosevelt, to prepare the nation for war by giving military training at Plattsburg, New York, to middle-class professional and businessmen who would then be available as an officer reserve. And in 1916 Congress had taken over this essentially private initiative as a valuable contribution to preparedness. Between the invasion of Norway and the fall of France, the Plattsburg idea was reborn as the Military Training Camps Association. By mid-July there were ten camps in operation. For $43.50 trainees could savor the joys of thirty days of pork and beans, rifle drill, KP and bugle calls at 5:45 A.M. Small boys in the immediate vicinity were endlessly amused by the sight of middle-aged men, plainly flaccid and short of breath, hurling their protesting bodies into ditches, up netting, over walls and through mud. They were slyly praised for their foresight: Had not Nazi blitzkriegs demonstrated that the physical demands placed on middle-aged refugees were fully as strenuous in their own way as those placed on young soldiers?

But the nearly 15,000 officers in the Army Reserve were not amused. They resented the notion that businessmen should qualify for commissions after thirty days of training at their own expense when reservists had been attending summer camps and weekly meetings for years. The Army General Staff agreed with the reservists, and the Secretary of War, Henry Stimson, was mildly sympathetic. The Army could not stop these private training schemes, but it did nothing to aid them.

The question of reserve commissions was always sensitive. It was tacitly accepted that for the most part commissions went to class and status. Now and then it proved embarrassing, notably in the case of the President's youngest son, Elliott. With no overt qualifications for it, Elliott received a commission as a captain in the Army Reserve and was then assigned to a pleasant job in procurement. If called to active duty, he would receive a salary which, with allowances, was well above the national average. More important, reserve officers were exempt from the draft. This looked like two faults, not one: nepotism and draft dodging. "I Want to Be a Captain, Too" clubs appeared in hundreds of towns; millions of people wore "I Want to Be a Captain, Too" buttons in their lapels, while thousands of young men who, like Elliott, were college dropouts and business failures, descended on recruiting stations insisting that they were equally entitled to commissions.

The Army's success or failure would eventually depend on how well and how quickly it managed to expand. The draft had gone into effect on October 16, which was declared National Registration Day, when all males aged twenty-one to thirty-six were to register themselves. The Army had run, and bungled, the Civil War draft. The World War I draft had consequently been managed by civilians, a principle retained by the new Selective Service Act. Of the 16,500,000 registrants no more than 900,000 could be called in any one year. After a year of service draftees would then be enrolled in the reserves for ten years.

To delight and surprise National Registration Day passed with absolute calm. After so much passion everyone expected demonstrations and protests. There were none. There seemed certain to be at least hundreds, possibly several thousands, who would publicly refuse to register. There were thirty-six.

Two weeks after registration had been completed Brigadier General Lewis B. Hershey, the deputy director of Selective Service and the man who had set up the system of 5,500 local boards in civilian hands, presided over the first drawing of draft numbers. Every registrant had a number between 1 and 7,836, which was the highest number of registrants any draft board was permitted to carry. Thus no two registrants of any one draft board would have the same number, but there were thousands of other young men with the same number elsewhere in the country. Thousands of blue capsules were placed in the fishbowl used in 1917, Stimson drew the first capsule, and Roosevelt announced the number: 158. A woman in the audience shrieked, part fearful, part excited, "That's my son!" The most common greeting became "What's your number?" And overnight the most popular song was "Goodbye Dear, I'll Be Back in a Year."

The country had an anxious eye on the first peacetime draftees. Mothers and clergymen still feared for their morals, while the Army promised that vice would not be tolerated. Liberals feared for their politics; so did conservatives, who worried that the Army might have been infected by the New Deal. One journal offered up what sounded like a prayer: "Ours must be a democratic army, an army from which every man who serves will come back into the community a better democrat and citizen than when he entered it." Parents, politicians, teachers, even the draftees said similar things. Radio stations and commercial sponsors hurried to set up broadcasts from and about Army training camps. When the first contingents of draftees arrived, they were met by military bands playing "In the Good Old Summertime," "Hail, Hail, the Gang's All Here" and other favorites.

All the while Army officers wondered how they were to maintain morale without a real war to fight and would there be any more where these came from once the draft law expired next October. And General George C. Marshall, whom Roosevelt had appointed over the heads of thirty-four other generals to be Chief of Staff of the Army, was offering his candid opinion that even with all the billions in appropriations and the sense of urgency that now prevailed, the Army would not be ready for war until December, 1941.

III

Miracle at Philadelphia–Sort of

THE first question of politics these days was whether Roosevelt would run for a third term. And it is altogether possible that he himself was wondering the same thing. No one is sure just what Roosevelt, in the summer of 1939, intended to do in the summer of 1940. Like most successful politicians, he was slow to shut doors or make unbreakable commitments. Yet here was an instance where the decision could be sensibly left to the fates. If things continued much as they were until mid-1940, the decision would be made for him, for he could not then, in all likelihood, win another term. By the time of the Democratic convention he would know if that was the case; so would everyone else. And if he could not win, it was hardly worth trying. On the other hand, war might break out in Europe before then; again, the decision would be made for him. For he would then be a wartime President, and in all likelihood unbeatable. There was no need to decide anything for months to come. And even then his choice would be dictated by events beyond his control.

Since 1938 there had been a general rise in conservative fortunes; one result was an unmistakably hostile Congress. There were also some soft spots in Roosevelt's support: Farmers, probably the chief beneficiaries of the New Deal, were going back to the Republican Party; blacks were becoming restive; even labor seemed disenchanted. The country as a whole was cool to the idea of a third term; polls taken shortly after the 1936 election showed 69 percent of the population opposed. By March, 1940, less than half the nation approved a third term, and reading the polls led *Time* to conclude: "The shift toward the GOP is now so marked that nothing short of a Rooseveltian miracle . . . can save the election for the Democrats." But the real determinant was the war, as almost everyone realized. If it continued, so would Roosevelt. Yet if peace, no matter how rickety, were contrived, the Republicans would make a massive comeback, possibly strong enough to capture both Congress and the White House. With peace, concluded one noted political reporter, "The bottom would drop out of the new prosperity; there would be a quick revival of interest in domestic politics; there would be an intense dissatisfaction with the party in power and a surge of sentiment for throwing the rascals out. Restoration of peace in Europe would be an unmitigated calamity for the Roosevelt Administration." In short, with a break in the war the Republican nomina-

41

tion might well become a prize ticket to the White House. And then came the Nazi conquest of France.

Among the demands of a badly shaken nation was a plea that Roosevelt follow Britain's lead and create a coalition cabinet for the duration of the state of national emergency. And to the utter consternation of Republicans he made Henry Stimson Secretary of War and Frank Knox Secretary of the Navy only days before the Republican Convention opened. Stimson had been Taft's Secretary of War thirty years before. He had also been Hoover's Secretary of State. Enormously respected in Washington and the country at large, Stimson knew the upper reaches of both government and society better than any man alive. He was the patron saint of that part of the Eastern Establishment which, operating largely from prestigious Wall Street law firms, had made foreign policy its chief love (besides status and money) since the early 1920's. Knox was a more colorful, faintly ridiculous figure. A rich publisher and the GOP Vice Presidential candidate in 1936, the supreme moment in his life had come many years before in the comic-opera heroics of Theodore Roosevelt's Rough Riders. He had raced up San Juan Hill—they were all, alas and unglamorously, afoot rather than, as myth has it, on horseback—alongside his beloved TR. Since then, and especially after TR's death in 1920, Knox's worship had turned into an unconscious parody: the same toothy grin, the same glittering pince-nez, the same short, jerky movements, the same high-pitched, slightly nasal voice and the same tendency to reduce human speech to bristling epithet.

Just as Roosevelt expected, these appointments enraged the Republican leadership. The two heretics were instantly excommunicated. Angrily the GOP proceeded to cleave more firmly than ever to isolation, which left the Democrats as the war party. But more immediately, Roosevelt's creation of a modest coalition brought overwhelming approval from a people avid for unity or a show of unity in the presence of danger.

Long before the Republican Convention opened, there was no mystery about who the party's Presidential nominee would be. Opinion polls for months past had shown Thomas Dewey as the first choice of nearly 70 percent of the Republican rank and file. Far behind came Senator Arthur Vandenberg with approximately 15 percent, Senator Robert C. Taft with 10 percent and, leading the dark horses, Wendell Willkie with 3 percent. Among party leaders Taft and Vandenberg stood somewhat higher and Dewey correspondingly lower, but the general shape of preferences was not significantly different. Barring some serious misstep, Dewey would be nom-inated; barring a miracle, Willkie would not.

Following the capitulation of France, Dewey's standing in the polls had dropped for the first time, not fatally, but enough to inspire a joke that "Tom Dewey was the first American casualty of the Second World War."

Dewey was not only new to national politics but, at thirty-eight, perhaps too young. His reputation rested on spectacular, well-publicized convictions of major racketeers in New York City. Even then, his record was not entirely to his credit: One innocent man spent eight years in prison. Years later even journals usually well disposed toward him would criticize Dewey's "over-zealous prosecutions" and "railroading." Yet he had several considerable assets in his drive for the nomination: A smooth, trained baritone was valuable in the age of radio; he had an attractive family; the Republican Party leadership liked him; he had a national reputation. And he worked tirelessly to appeal to as many voters as possible. Before German-American groups in the Midwest Dewey was clamoring for isolationism; before Eastern interventionists he called for increased aid to Britain. He wanted both a balanced budget and a two-ocean navy. And though his standing in the polls was beginning to slip, his chief worry as he bid for the Presidential nomination was a Taft-Vandenberg coalition to knock him out of the race. Taft had already made an agreement with Bricker: Bricker would support Taft in 1940; Taft would support Bricker in 1944. Some such agreement between Taft and Vandenberg would shut Dewey out entirely.

When the convention opened, Willkie's support had grown to a still minuscule 5 percent of registered Republicans. But other polls showed that with the electorate as a whole he was more popular than Dewey or any other potential Republican nominee. Had his attempt for the nomination ended just then, it would have been remarkable. His star was rising, and the pro-Willkie press was puffing his candidacy at every opportunity. Reporters had taken to tormenting Dewey, who usually arrived at press conferences late and slightly flustered, with chants of "Bring in Willkie!" But nominations are not secured by polls, or newspapers or miracles; they are the result of hard work, organization and realistic planning with, occasionally, a little luck. Dewey and Taft could afford to concentrate on each other; Willkie, they were certain—and who was not?—was just another of those flashes in the pan which divert every convention, especially those of the party out of power. There was a sign of sorts, however, that this convention might labor to the consternation of some of them, possibly all of them. For on the day that it opened, an elephant named Lizzie died quietly on the other side of town in the Philadelphia Zoo. And if anyone should look on this and tremble, it was the party regulars. For Willkie presided over one of the most brilliant nominating campaigns in American history. The mark of its genius was that it was virtually invisible and would appear so even in years to come, creating that pleasant myth the "Miracle at Philadelphia."

Willkie's drive for the nomination had begun in the summer of 1939. While Dewey and Taft and Vandenberg were strutting and preening, Willkie was courting, and being courted by, some very powerful business and publishing interests. As president of Commonwealth and Southern Utilities Corporation he had wrestled the federal government—in the shape of the Tennessee Valley Authority—to the ground and forced it to pay far more for Commonwealth and Southern than it was worth. Businessmen, feeling long persecuted and misunderstood, warmed to Willkie. Here was the first business executive in years to beat the New Dealers publicly in a fair fight and do it with charm and graciousness. In July, his portrait appeared on the cover of *Time* over a caption ambiguously wondering, "Wouldn't he be a fool to say No?" In the accompanying text Willkie was smothered under hairy-chested praise: "To hell with formality. He talks as men do in the locker room, and spices his profanity with the Bible, Shakespeare and the law." By the spring of 1940 the same journal was hailing him as "brilliant," "the best domestic brain on politico-economics."

Willkie had voted as a Democrat in 1938, which might have appeared a handicap; in American politics, however, it rarely is, for the parties are coalitions, not disciplined bodies of true believers. Willkie need only say he was a Republican to be one. With the enthusiastic support of friends and patrons he became, in less than a year and without a single spectacular stunt, a national figure. The *Time-Life-Fortune* empire of Henry Luce adopted him; he was written up in the Cowles chain of newspapers and magazines, especially *Look*; the New York *Times* and the New York *Herald Tribune*, the two most important moderate Republican papers, smiled upon him; and business publications such as *Business Week* took a special interest in his meteoric rise.

A young editor at *Fortune*, Russell Davenport, organized Willkie's publicity campaign, while a twenty-nine-year-old enthusiast named Oren Root organized Willkie Clubs to turn the mounting national interest into organized support. By the summer of 1940 Root had established nearly 2,000 Willkie Clubs, and with a minimum of publicity. For while Willkie himself was the object of a great publicity campaign, too much attention to the clubs might easily destroy them. Apparently spontaneous organizations of impassioned amateurs smitten by Willkie worship, most of them were in fact built around a nucleus of volunteers provided by local power companies. Yet this was no insidious plot by utilities executives to take over the country and disband the TVA. In fact, they fully expected Willkie to lose his bid for the nomination and, even if he secured it, to lose to Roosevelt. But as his star flashed across the heavens, they hoped to enjoy a little reflected glory and reap some measure of goodwill for their, to them, much-maligned endeavors. Too close a scrutiny of the Willkie Clubs, however, might discredit the entire operation and turn Willkie's slender hopes to ashes.

Davenport's campaign was a great success. Following his appearance on the cover of *Time*, Willkie had secured a much-coveted guest appearance on *Information Please,* one of the most popular radio programs of the day; much of the April, 1940, issue of *Fortune* was devoted to him; and half a dozen of the most popular newspaper columnists regularly sang Willkie's praises. Willkie became well known very quickly. And Davenport's campaign cast him as a liberal nonpolitician. Willkie obliged by roundly excoriating the leadership of both major parties. Not that there was anything spurious to these attacks; he was utterly sincere. His family was of that variety of German liberals who removed themselves to the United States after the failure of the Frankfurt Parliament in 1848 had destroyed the final chance for a peaceful and liberal unification of Germany. All his life Willkie had voted as a Democrat. He favored government regulation of business; he supported the social aims of the New Deal with all his heart. But he was convinced that the New Deal had gone beyond regulation and was now trying to offset its economic failure by taking direct control of important parts of the economy. The result, he was convinced, would be to destroy the already-battered confidence of investors; the economy would fail even further, producing still greater social distress.

By the time the Republican Convention began Willkie's name was nationally known; his Indiana twang, which turned power into "pahr" and interests into "intersts," was becoming widely recognized, his voracious appetite for books and his personal library of 2,000 volumes had been dwelt on at length, his hometown of Elwood, Indiana—self-styled "Tomato Capital of America"—had been scoured for reminiscences of Wendell's earlier years; but what almost no one noticed was that Willkie controlled the machinery of the convention. A master of indirection he had everyone looking elsewhere—namely, at himself.

When he arrived in Philadelphia, he announced, "My campaign headquarters are in my hat. Be sure to put it down that I'm having a swell time." Meanwhile, Taft's forces were setting up their headquarters in 102 rooms of the Benjamin Franklin hotel; Dewey occupied 78 rooms; Vandenberg settled for a spartan 48. But Willkie, as all could see, had only 2. What they did not perceive was that he also had thousands of feet of floor space at the nearby Land Title Building and the use of an empty store less than a hundred yards from his hotel. Willkie, however, was everywhere else: being interviewed over his lunch (a cheese sandwich); in a corner drugstore; even in his bath. He trod the streets of Philadelphia for several hours each day with reporters at his heels, attracting crowds wherever he stopped. "He took street corner positions on anything and everything—a Third Term, the chances of war, economic recovery, farm policy, the party platform, his own chances of being nominated—all subjects normally covered in carefully worked out press statements," recalled one reporter. Because he was constantly on the move and because he was the most attractive, quotable candidate there, covering Willkie soon became a full-time job for political reporters, while Taft and Dewey aides could only gnash their teeth in rage and frustration. And in the convention hall the galleries were full of tireless youngsters chanting over and over again the slogan of the Willkie Clubs—"We Want Willkie."

The galleries, in fact, were stacked with the younger employees of New York and Philadelphia businesses, released for a few days, sometimes with expense money, and loaded down with Willkie banners and buttons, to cheer for Willkie. These attractive youngsters, often not old enough to vote, spilled across hotel lobbies and downtown streets, in high spirits, enjoying a paid vacation from the boring routines of Wall Street. The delight they took in what they were doing was genuine and infectious. The ever-watchful *Time* exulted that here was a "political children's crusade." Delegates were deluged with Willkie buttons and handbills. Telegrams poured into their mailboxes from people they knew back home urging them to vote for Willkie. Their clothes came back from the cleaners with the pockets stuffed with Willkie literature. It surpassed any solicitation they were accustomed to. Many were infuriated. But by the time the first ballot was taken they all knew who Willkie was: He was the most famous person there.

The party's nominal leader, Herbert Hoover, delivered a welcoming address which asserted that he had beaten the Depression, but the New Deal had revived it. Slightly embarrassed and not wanting to give the ex-President false hopes, the assembled delegates replied with carefully polite applause, and the galleries chanted, "We want Willkie!" Even when no formal business was being conducted, they chanted, "We want Willkie!" And on the floor below were men silently endeavoring to secure that end. For "Although no one outside the Willkie camp realized it at the time, the whole convention machinery was Willkie's." The GOP national chairman, John D. M. Hamilton, was a secret Willkie supporter. The keynote speaker, Harold Stassen, was Willkie's floor manager. Joe Martin, the permanent chairman of the convention, planned to swing to Willkie after the first ballot. The chairmanship of the very important Committee of Arrangements, one of whose responsibilities was gallery passes, fell into the lap of Sam Pryor, a Willkie supporter. There was, however, one key weakness: Willkie had no organization working the floor of the convention canvassing delegates, striking bargains, holding hands and performing the dozens of small chores that are often the margin of victory or defeat on a close ballot. But this possibly fatal handicap was offset by the failure of Taft and Dewey to combine in a stop-Willkie alliance. They too believed it was all a children's crusade, until it was too late. The trend of the balloting should have disabused them, for Willkie forged ahead on every ballot until on the sixth ballot Pennsylvania gave him all its votes and he was nominated.

Ballots	1	2	3	4	5
Dewey	360	338	315	250	57
Taft	189	203	212	254	377
Willkie	105	171	259	306	429

Groggy from lack of sleep and obviously surprised at what they had wrought, the delegates staggered numbly off to bed at two in the morning having chosen, though they willed it not, the best available candidate.

The following day they proceeded to give him a running mate. Looking for someone to offset their nominee's handicaps and to complement his strengths they latched onto Senator Charles McNary of Oregon, a man who only a week before had predicted that the Willkie boom would vanish when the first ballot was taken. McNary was a solid, respected party regular, unassuming and, now that he was a Senator, unambitious. Willkie was youth; he was age. Willkie was a new Republican; he was an old Republican. Willkie was from the middle of the country and the East Coast; he was from the West Coast. Six years earlier he had rhymed:

> The Presidential bee is a deadly bug;
> I've seen it work on others.
> Oh, Lord! protect me from its hug,
> And let it sting my brothers.

He did not want to be stung by the Vice Presidential bee either, assuming there is one. Only after the most solemn entreaties from the party leadership would he consent to accept his nomination. At last, he sighed, "I'll be a good soldier," and resigned himself.

Willkie accepted his nomination with far greater enthusiasm and less tact, beginning, "So, you Republicans. . . ." The old guard bristled, but the galleries were deliriously happy and broke into Willkie's theme song:

> Heigh-ho, heigh-ho, it's back to work we go;
> With Wendell Willkie leading us the jobs will grow.
> Heigh-ho, heigh-ho, we've all been feeling low,
> But Willkie's hand will save the land,
> Heigh-ho, heigh-ho, heigh-ho.

The New York *Times*, the Luce and Cowles empires, *Newsweek*, in fact, the press generally, hailed Willkie's nomination as being not only the selection of the best man, but a triumph of the people over the party bosses. The "miraculous nomination" revived interest in domestic politics. Somehow it seemed to be a sign of national regeneration and democratic vitality. It shone forth like a beacon in a dark and terrible time. And Oren Root, the young overseer of the We Want Willkie deluge, was not the man to blight fond hopes. To anyone who suggested that the outpouring of telegrams, letters and emotion was not entirely spontaneous, he turned his cheek: "There was absolutely no one directing it. There couldn't have been; it was just too colossal!" Irreverent Democrats taunted nonetheless that Willkie's nomination had been rigged by the utilities companies; they dubbed it "The Charge of the Electric Light Brigade." Alice Roosevelt Longworth, a peerless convention watcher, said laughingly that Willkie's nomination "comes right from the grass roots of every country club in America." But perhaps the last word should be allowed the eighty-one-year-old governor of Michigan, Luren Dickinson, who was ever a watch-dog of public morality. The convention, he was happy to say, had been all that a Republican convention should be—"safe, sinless, and sexless."

Moral or not, the Democratic Convention in Chicago several weeks later was sure to be a more prosaic affair. Democrats pride themselves on the turbulence and drama of their gatherings in contrast with the dullness of Republican conventions. Not so in 1940. All was in the hands of two men: Harry Hopkins, Roosevelt's every-ready, ever-faithful man of all work, and Chicago's mayor, "Boss" Kelly, who had once gurgled, "Roosevelt is my religion. I'd die for him just as I'd give up my life for my country." Other big-city bosses such as Frank Hague of Jersey City and Ed Crump of Memphis, Tennessee, were reliable, but none was so devoted as Kelly. The slogan "For Roosevelt and Humanity" was his invention. Whatever convention business was not in his hands rested with Hopkins, who, wreathed in aureoles of blue-gray smoke from an endless chain of cigarettes, brooded over the convention from Suite 308-309 in the Blackstone Hotel, the "smoke-filled rooms" in which Harding's nomination had been arranged twenty years before. Between them these two men ran the convention. There would be one surprise in these proceedings, but it too, like everything else, came from the top.

Roosevelt was not an inordinately vain man. It is a commonplace to call him patrician or aristocratic. But he was not the kind of aristocrat who is too proud to be ambitious—a sort rare in American life, especially outside the South, but not altogether unknown. For nearly eight years he had served his country by inspiring confidence or at least getting the better of fear. Nothing so erodes the foundations of any human society as a vague, free-floating fear. It becomes a useful instrument to the worst elements and destroys the final resource of good men—trust. Roosevelt, like others, sensed that. But he also had a great facility for defeating it. So that, even though he had not solved the riddle of the Depression, he had still done his country good service. Now he wanted some show of affection, some semblance of genuine gratitude and loyalty from the party he led. Also, of course, something that resembled a spontaneous, emotional draft would lend a graceful note of reluctance to his bid for an unprecedented third grant of executive powers. He would leave all in the hands of Hopkins, Kelly and the delegates; he would not lift a finger on his own behalf. But here was a blunt instrument called to a fine task. The result was a flattering myth clung to by Democrats and other liberals of how the delegates paraded and chanted for an hour in an outpouring of devotion, spurred on at times by the public address system. The actual result was a shabby parody, to no one's credit.

Having cast himself as Cincinnatus (the reluctant deliverer of the state), Roosevelt addressed himself to the convention through Senator Alben Barkley. He, Franklin Roosevelt, was tired—so ran the message Barkley read aloud—and had no particular desire to run for another term; the delegates were free to chose whomever they wished. They were absolutely stunned, bewildered; it simply did not seem credible. If it was sincere, why had he not even hinted at it before? They reacted much like people informed of some spectacular disaster. But while they buzzed and reeled at this intelligence, Kelly's men quietly went about the hall securing physical possession of the system of amplifiers and microphones without which several thousand people in a vast auditorium could not effectively transact business.

In the basement, Chicago's superintendent of sewers, Tom Garry, was now able to cut into the public address system with his stentorious voice: "We want Roosevelt!" It reverberated around the hall. The delegates stopped buzzing. Again, "We want Roosevelt!" And again. The Voice from the Sewers was in full stride now: "The party wants Roosevelt. . . . New Jersey wants Roosevelt. . . . The world needs Roosevelt. . . . Everybody wants Roosevelt." By this time Boss Kelly's men were parading through the aisles. A few minutes earlier they had forced everyone into his seat at the end of Roosevelt's message to preclude any genuinely spontaneous demonstration. After all, if they did not control it, how could they be sure it would not be for some Democratic Willkie? But now they were prying people from their seats and thrusting banners into their hands to create the illusions of a spontaneous stampede to Roosevelt. All they had created was a tasteless bore, killing off any genuine display of affection. This dreary farce dragged on for nearly an hour at the direction of Kelly's men, and then, when they too appeared to weary of it, they quickly killed it.

Roosevelt was nominated without difficulty after a forlorn bid by James Farley to keep the nomination from being unanimous had run its ignominious course. There was some problem getting the big-city bosses to accept Henry Wallace as the Vice Presidential nominee, but that too was managed. By then it was late at night, and it was not until nearly half past one in the morning that Roosevelt was able to address them from the White House and accept his nomination for a third term.

That done, the tired party faithful could then stumble off to bed. Having

abandoned "Happy Days Are Here Again" in deference to "so many people suffering the horrors of war," they put new words to "God Bless
America" and, tired but happy, sang:

> Goddamned Republicans—scum of the Earth,
> We will meet them, and beat them
> In a fight with the right on our side.
> Out of Wall Street came a Willkie,
> He's a silky S.O.B.
> Goddamned Republicans—that G.O.P.
> Goddamned Republicans—that G.O.P.

The fall brought a Presidential election that was both historic and
exciting. The third term question had evaporated as a serious issue once
the conventions were finished.

Had the election taken place just after the Democratic Convention, Willkie would have won easily, said the polls. Roosevelt would have carried
little outside the Solid South; the big industrial states of the North, such as
New York and Pennsylvania, would have gone to Willkie. But Landon
had led in the polls for more than two months following his nomination in
1936, and by mid-August Willkie had dropped into a neck-and-neck race
with Roosevelt.

Willkie had a clear advantage in the press. Nearly 700 newspapers
were openly for him. The New York *Times*, which had supported Roosevelt
in 1932 and 1936, came out for Willkie. Even the Cleveland *Plain Dealer,*
which had not endorsed a Presidential candidate for 100 years, endorsed
him.

Willkie began his campaign by addressing a Willkie Club audience as
"Fellow amateurs." Republicans, who love to see themselves as plain,
honest citizens defending the Republic from the depradations of a libertine
mob led by "politicians" and demagogues, glowed. Republican newspaper
editors slapped "Fellow Amateurs" across their front pages in large type.
And Willkie returned to Elwood, Indiana, to deliver his formal acceptance
of the nomination.

On a hot day in August, 1940, that small town of 10,000 hosted a
crowd of more than 250,000 people, drawn from every part of the country. This particular day it would be memorialized in one of the most
famous photographs in the country's political history as Elwood's most
famous son rode down Main Street, standing in the back of a convertible,
waving a straw hat, looking rumpled and exuberant. Willkie had no strong
peculiarity of feature which lent itself to caricature, so that in cartoons he
looked very much like Huey Long. But this picture made up for it. And
in and around Elwood there swirled the biggest partisan political crowd
in American history.

They had come to hear an exciting, hard-hitting speech. Willkie openly reveled in the prospect of taking on "the Champ." Yet his speech was flat, meandering, punctuated with fervent pleas to Roosevelt to join in face-to-face debate. As evening descended, the tens of thousands started to drift out of Elwood, glad they had come, but disappointed all the same. They had been ready to be thrilled, fused by a single voice, made to feel participants in a mighty movement. But Willkie was earnest and conscientious; more than that, he had no experience in electoral politics. And Roosevelt was too shrewd to help him secure a national audience by engaging in debate. Instead, the administration set its "Old Curmudgeon," Harold Ickes, Secretary of the Interior, onto the contender. Ickes had greeted Dewey's announcement of his candidacy for the Presidency with "Tom Dewey has tossed his diapers into the ring." He now laughed at "Wendell Willkie—the simple, barefoot Wall Street lawyer."

Until Roosevelt decided to come out fighting, Willkie must box with shadows. His campaign strategy, he joked, would be that "wherever and whenever two or more Americans are gathered in my honor, I will make a speech." Before very long it looked like no joke at all, for midway through September he had dropped ten points behind Roosevelt in the polls. Every professional in the GOP was ready to concede defeat, in private. Willkie had already driven them wild by agreeing with virtually every foreign policy move Roosevelt had made, including the destroyers for bases. He had supported conscription. His speeches were invariably logical and unemotional. Audiences which greeted him enthusiastically nearly always went away feeling disappointed. He had got off to a bad start by charging headlong into every issue in sight. But by October he had narrowed his scope down to a few major points, and the issue, as he defined it, was state Socialism. Efforts to implement it would destroy private initiative. And in tones oddly presaging those of another Presidential candidate twenty years later he would conclude in a voice now hoarse with wear, "Only the productive can be strong, and only the strong can be free." Willkie then set off on a whirlwind campaign, hammering away at this theme, and at the end of every speech, his voice reduced to a husky whisper, he would fling his arms wide, imploring, "Join me, join me in this great movement." To the surprise of almost everyone he began to narrow the gap in the polls just as his campaign looked most hopeless.

The contest grew hotter, much hotter. Roosevelt took off on highly visible "inspection tours" of defense plants, and the Democrats did their best to cast the election as Roosevelt versus Hitler. When Henry Wallace had made his acceptance speech for the Vice Presidential nomination, he had mentioned Roosevelt twenty-eight times, Hitler twenty-three times, Willkie none. The usually high-minded Wallace skirted very close to calling a vote for Willkie a vote for Hitler. Certainly, he insisted, the defeat of Roosevelt would cause wild rejoicing in Berlin. Willkie too began to lash out wildly. He tried, without much success, to portray a third term as a form of totalitarian rule that was one tiny step short of Fascism, hinting darkly that this might be the last free election in American history.

As election day neared, Willkie stormed about the country like an elemental force, and the campaign degenerated into one of the nastiest ever waged. Willkie faced such a steady barrage of missiles that the New York *Times* ran a daily box score of objects thrown and hits registered. The objects included an office chair aimed at Willkie's head from a high window, a steel wastebasket similarly propelled, a big-city telephone directory, several light bulbs, many rocks and eggs, and a large volume of produce. Most of it was pelted down on him in the big Democratic cities. With it went intense booing. Willkie was hit by several of the objects thrown at him; his wife was splattered with eggs; and the five-pound steel wastebasket thrown in Detroit by a government secretary split open the head of a teen-age girl.

No one could really explain the rise in viciousness. Perhaps it was a product of the country's ambiguous role in the war. Some blamed it on the New Deal, claiming that it had fanned class hatreds to the worst pitch in memory. Whatever the reason, it was a sorry business. By choosing Willkie, the Republicans had actually complimented Roosevelt: They had chosen the candidate whose appeal was most like his own. And of the four men Roosevelt defeated for the Presidency, Willkie was the only one he liked and respected.

In the stretch Willkie's furious barnstorming not only narrowed the gap, but cast a romantic haze that saw it celebrated only a few years later as "the fabulous Willkie train, the most wonderful political caravan that has travelled the U.S. in this generation." But Roosevelt was himself a great campaigner, and he too was in high gear by the end of October, chiding the isolationists in Congress and waving the banner of the New Deal. John L. Lewis vowed to resign as head of the CIO if Roosevelt was reelected; George S. Harvey, president of the Borough of Queens, vowed to move to Canada; and General Hugh S. Johnson swore that he would eat a copy of the Gallup Poll if, as Gallup now predicted, Willkie lost.* Republicans pinned their hopes on a different poll, the Dunn Survey, devised by Rogers C. Dunn. As director of Research on Public Opinion to the Republican National Committee in 1936 he had forecast an overwhelming victory for Alf Landon. Having learned from his errors in that election, Dunn had invented a new formula, taking the circulation of the newspapers endorsing each candidate as the base vote, then adding an extra four votes on the Democratic side for every worker on WPA. He forecast a Willkie victory of 334 electoral votes to 197 for Roosevelt.

---

* General Johnson later pleaded lack of appetite; Lewis kept his pledge and resigned as president of the CIO.

Willkie made a strong showing. No Republican candidate had ever done so well at the polls, and not until Eisenhower's victory twelve years later would a Republican win more votes. It was the closest Presidential election since 1916, even if it was lopsided in the electoral college. But Willkie lost all the same. He could take some comfort from the fact that those polls which were most accurate on how the voting would go also showed that he would have won but for the war. There had simply been too many, however, who felt that this was not a time for taking chances. As Fiorello La Guardia expressed it, they preferred "Roosevelt with his known faults to Willkie with his unknown virtues."

In the wake of the election Willkie called on his followers to form "a loyal opposition." There were insistent calls on both sides for "unity." "Good Losers" clubs sprang up. There was a sense of having done a brave thing in a dangerous time. No one wanted to see the fruits of that success destroyed now by a national falling out. They had, in a way, pulled themselves into a circle much as their ancestors had done under Indian attacks when crossing the broad, exposed plains of the West. Minor parties had made their worst showing since 1876, winning a combined total of less than 250,000 votes in an electorate of 50,000,000. In 1939 such a thing would have been thought impossible.

IV

Quarrel at a Crossroads

THE country went on with its political routines as though the war were peripheral; yet not only was it not peripheral, but it had forced a national debate over America's future. Because of the war, the country stood at a historic crossroads and knew it. As soon as the shock over the Nazi conquest of France had passed, the debate on isolation resumed, more vehement than ever.

Behind the argument over isolation there was really an argument that went far beyond the strict merits of the question of aiding Britain. That was the most obvious issue, but not the most important. Essentially instrumental foreign policy questions—those of necessity, security and expediency—rarely evoke impassioned popular responses. But those great foreign policy debates which virtually split the nation into two or three factions have roots deep in sharply antagonistic conceptions of American society, especially over what the nation should be. And debates of this kind are both more frequent and more bitter in the United States than they are anywhere else.

This is a political democracy for the most part. People are free to take an interest in the broad issues of government, and the press is free enough and diverse enough to promote controversy. But Americans are also unaccustomed to organizing their conceptions of society around ideologies. The two great parties are coalitions of very different groups, not convocations of the faithful; differences between the parties run far more to means than ends; sharply antagonistic views are subsumed under amorphous generalities, such as the American Dream, which mean all things to all men—provided they are American. That is why the country has added almost nothing to Western political thought since the generation which made the American Revolution passed into history. America has offered itself as an example, as proof, not argument, that it has found the way to social, economic and political success. Not that it has always and everywhere been seen as such, but whether for better or worse, the role of political ideologies has been implicit, indirect and inarticulate.

Opposed conceptions of how the nation should be shaped have existed all the same. With no outlet in ideology they have been expressed in other ways. Usually they have fixed on whatever broad decision the hour posed: Union, or Silver, or Prohibition, or Isolation, or Vietnam. On the opposing sides have stood not simply a pro and con but a congeries of related points of view on everything from the equality of women to the proper scope of governmental power. Because there are no ideologies and ideologues to impose discipline and weed out heretics, the lines are invariably fuzzy. But there is one important consequence of this vagueness: On the subsidiary questions there is always ample room for compromise.

It is in this light that the debate on isolation should be regarded. Generally it was the last stand of the generation which looked back to the time before the First World War when the country was strong and prosperous (even though many people were poor), undisputed in its sway over two continents, possessing an island empire, most of its people close-knit within small towns or on the land, threatened by no powerful enemies and aloof from the perpetual quarrels which taxed the energies of less favored lands. The great achievements of its foreign policy came swiftly and satisfyingly with a rush that crammed them into less than a decade's span and were every one of them a cause for pride—victory over the once proud and powerful Spanish Empire; building the Panama Canal after the French had given up; negotiating peace between Russia and Japan; maintaining an Open Door in China which, people believed, had saved China from extinction; becoming a great power at a trifling human and economic cost— and all without creating powerful enemies who would seek revenge on their children or grandchildren. These were the great days of McKinley and TR. And to a degree that is now almost impossible to conceive, Americans who had been alive then looked back nostalgically during the 1930's and yearned for the years before the Great War. When they talked of "the good old days," they referred invariably to the last decade of the last century and the first decade of this. Here was the world they knew as Main Street. And as Bernard De Voto concluded sadly in 1940, "Main Street no longer exists."

Since the Great War they had been obliged to suffer the modern world with its noisy, dirty cities, its vague but ubiquitous anxieties, its anonymity and its flirtation with European ideas in books, art, politics, and even everyday life. Communism, Socialism, Fascism—all came from Europe. So did Keynes, and whoever heard of "spending yourself rich"? And the paintings that didn't look like paintings, the novels where everything was broken up into tiny pieces and you had to put it back together. Before their eyes America was being remade, and into something they could barely recognize as being truly American. And while these evils were becoming more entrenched, the people who had known the real America were dying off. Under the banner of Prohibition they had made a historic stand. For a moment they had been victorious. But the hated cities now had most of the people. The victory had vanished in an orgy of lawlessness and was swept aside by superior numbers. Yet they had strength enough for one more stand. They rallied around isolation. This was rural, pre-

Great War America trying for the last time to hold the country to a vision of itself which time in its cruelly indifferent way had eclipsed. And the scorn they heaped on Europe, with its never-ending wars, its poverty, its tyrannies and its ideas, was utterly sincere. Their opponent was the twentieth century, in the shape of interventionists and internationalists. But true to the American way, none of these three (really two) sides was ideological: There was no definitive statement of the faith, no hierarchy of acknowledged teachers and no identifiable body of organized disciples.

Even had they possessed such characteristics, the isolationists would probably have still failed to impose their will on the rest of the nation. The ground they stood on was infirm, for reasons as important as the fact that theirs was the cause of a generation that was literally dying out.

America's existence rested, in fact, on those very divisions which almost all Americans in 1939 took as proof of European stupidity or wickedness. A united Europe in the nineteenth century would never have left Americans to occupy and peacefully exploit an entire continent, especially when there were, relatively, few to defend it and many millions of Europeans with whom to attempt to wrest it away. Suppose for a moment that Europe was united under one government and adopted such a policy, where then would the United States have found enough immigrants to develop and defend it? Those quarrels which were denounced with unrelieved self-righteousness had guaranteed the nation's independence since its founding. And there was an unconscious acknowledgment of that fact when, in the spring of 1940, Americans for the second time in their history faced the prospect of a united Europe, united by force . . . united by Hitler . . . united, they were certain, against themselves. The great fear that people felt was no purblind anti-Fascism. The fear which struck isolationist and interventionist alike welled up from unspoken recognition of a historic fact: Isolation depended, as it had always depended, on a disunited Europe.

Both Britain and America owed their independence, or at least their chance to grow into prosperous democracies, to the fragmentation of Europe. They shared a deep, mutual interest in it. Britain was so close to the Continent that it never lost sight of it; America was far enough away that it hardly ever thought of it. And behind Britain's fleet America had dreamed its dreams of peace and comfort, securing a rare measure of both. But it had grasped the point in the Great War: When Germany had threatened to defeat the Allies, America had been forced to intervene. Though intervention was damned two decades later as a great mistake, people rarely went on to acknowledge that the alternative was German victory. To most people a victorious Germany looked only too likely to yoke all its victims into a great military engine which could carry war across the Atlantic or, at a minimum, shut America off from the rest of the world and make it truly isolationist.

The third great stumbling block to isolation arose from the fact that the roots of genuine isolationism had been tainted at the outset of the American adventure: A people who have preempted an entire continent hardly consists of stay-at-homes. Nor, once settled, had they isolated themselves from the rest of the world. Even in colonial times New England had traded with China, Africa and the East Indies. And was it not one of America's proudest boasts that it had "opened" Japan—which, ironically, was genuinely isolationist—to the world? Before this century began, America possessed an island empire stretching across half the globe to the rim of Asia. Nor had Americans been averse to force or threats of force: How else are continents taken and empires acquired? Nor had the country even after the disappointments of Versailles kept unto itself. Several times during the 1920's the marines went ashore in Central America. There had also been the Washington Naval Conference in 1922 and the Kellogg-Briand Pact six years later. By 1939 the United States, and every other great power in the world, had treaty obligations to promote peace and support resistance to aggression. In at least three treaties the United States, Germany, Italy and Japan were joined as cosignatories. And the public declarations of Hoover's Secretary of State, Henry Stimson, and Roosevelt's, Cordell Hull, made clear a deep American involvement in international politics.

The fourth and probably most fundamental barrier to genuine isolation was the historic failure to create a genuinely new man. In an existence of more than 300 years the new American nation had not created a genuinely independent civilization, as different from Europe's as, say, the Chinese or the Mayan. Though self-consciously different, Americans differed where all peoples differ from one another—in the secondary characteristics which go to make up a folk or popular culture. America differs as France differs from Germany and as both differ from Britain and, like all of them, is a full participant in the European heritage. Despite a war for independence, despite a score of historic disagreements, America had not in more than three centuries developed an alternative civilization. What chance then in the mid-twentieth century, with its infinitely better communications across the Atlantic, to take up a truly independent stand and hold forth a genuinely different civilization: as different in its faith as Shinto is from Christianity; as different in its language as Swahili is from English; as different in its laws as the common law is from the Talmud; as different in its moral code, architecture, social structure and artistic standards as Islam differs from Europe? An America actually left to its own devices was not likely to find much satisfaction in it. Isolation was then a frail flower if it would sever the connection between America and the civilization of which it was a part and could offer nothing in its place. The noted historian Charles Beard might well insist that "America is not to be Rome or Britain, it is to be America." But what did that mean in concrete, specific terms? Even Beard was unsure.

Isolationism had never exercised predominant control over American life and policy except for short periods. The nation's foreign policy has always borne a strong resemblance to that exotic animal the Pushme-Pullyou. It has always faced in two directions: It has always shown isolationist elements; it has always shown interventionist elements. And the predominance of one over the other has always been set by the current state of the debate over American society. In 1940 isolationism was but the latest recrudescence of anti-Europeanism and antimodernism. Onto it those who had loved TR or William Jennings Bryan, once bitter foes, had cast their memories and dead dreams, united at last in the twilight of life. It was Europe from which they wanted to be isolated, not the world. But the best they could manage was a peacetime indifference. Once the war began and Hitler's victories threatened to bring forth a seamless Europe bound to a single will, indifference must turn into alarm, cut isolation at the knees and hand initiative to interventionists. Thus it was no accident that the Committee to Defend America by Aiding the Allies predated the Committee for America First by half a year. And the initiative stayed with the interventionists and internationalists for the duration of the historic national debate into which the country was plunged.

Just days after the battle of France began, the Committee to Defend America by Aiding the Allies announced its existence. Its origins as a pressure group went back to a Non-Partisan Committee for Peace through Revision of the Neutrality Act, formed under the chairmanship of a famous Kansas newspaper editor, William Allen White. White was a Midwestern Republican who was much loved by liberal Democrats, including President Roosevelt. Those provisions of the Neutrality Act which placed a complete ban on the sale of arms to warring governments had long aided countries with large arms production capacity, such as Germany, Italy and Japan, when they turned on countries less well armed, such as China, Republican Spain and Ethiopia. And Germany had the Allies outgunned. The Non-Partisan Committee worked hard, and successfully, to permit arms sales to the Allies on a cash-and-carry basis. Once that was done, the Non-Partisan Committee quietly expired, believing that it had done its best to keep the country out of war.

But when the round of Nazi conquests revived a few months later, the members of that committee came together again in a larger, more ambitious organization. White was again prevailed on to lend his prestige to the chairmanship of a nonpartisan lobby dedicated to providing the Allies with the assistance they needed. For himself, White had another hope—to keep the Republican Party from becoming the Isolationist Party. There was no future in that. A serious misstep might destroy it, already a decidedly minority party, as the pre-Civil War Whig Party had been destroyed, and on whose bones the GOP had itself arisen.

Besides the CDA, another, more militantly interventionist, splinter group came into existence almost simultaneously. Called the Century Group (after the New York club where it held its early meetings), it pressed for a declaration of war on Germany. But for the moment the interventionist tides were with the moderates.

On the CDA board were Frank Knox and Henry Stimson, soon to be appointed to Roosevelt's Cabinet; Herbert Lehman, the governor of New York; Nicholas Murray Butler, the president of Columbia University; and a galaxy of distinguished journalists and academics. Their aim was vague, "to aid the Allies." They had no one demand or set of demands, but their strategy fluctuated with the tides of war: sending planes directly from American stocks, or feeding French and Belgian refugees, or transferring American destroyers to Britain, or putting an end to oil sales to Fascist Spain, which served as a funnel to German planes and tanks.

The committee's efforts would have availed nothing had it not enjoyed a broad appeal. And about 60 percent of the nation in fact was in general agreement with the CDA—that is, they believed that an Allied victory was America's best hope of avoiding war. But the CDA was a coalition, and while White and other members honestly believed that they were promoting formal neutrality, a sizable wing of the committee was pressing for direct American intervention. What bound them all together was a common agreement on aid to Britain.

Chapters of the CDA seemed to pop up out of the ground in the first few weeks of its existence. The enthusiasm behind the local chapters was clearly spontaneous, encouraged by the autonomy they enjoyed. So long as a chapter adhered to the general policy of the national organization, it was free to employ whatever means it chose. CDA units were organized geographically, generationally, around professional interests, as church affiliates, as college or university units, on almost every conceivable basis that a common purpose allowed. By the end of October, 1940, there were 750 chapters, 10,000 active workers and a membership of nearly 1,000,000. And millions more had signed its petitions demanding aid to Britain.

Beneath the emotional outpouring now being tapped were all manner of fears and beliefs, but outside the emotional depiction of Hitler and Fascism as evils incarnate there were, in general, two arguments which prospered. One was expressed by White in a letter to his niece; the other by a noted academic and journalist, Max Lerner. White reasoned that if Hitler won, the peace which followed would, given his past record, surely be unjust, and the United States would be helpless to influence its terms or modify its consequences. But if the Allies won, a just peace was possible if only because the United States carried some weight with them, a weight which would be undeniable if it had made their victory possible. A Nazi victory would also deliver into Hitler's hands the trade and colonies of the defeated, which might easily bring him into the Caribbean and South America. Lerner saw the issue more starkly: "Anyone with even the most elementary knowledge of Nazi writings on America knows that we have always hung before Nazi eyes as a succulent prize." (One wonders what on earth Lerner was reading.)

Both Lerner and White, and the millions who believed as they did, ultimately pinned their hopes on the President, whose personal sympathies were never in doubt. When he had visited the University of Virginia, he had slowly, dramatically intoned "On this, the tenth day of June, 1940 . . . the hand . . . that held the dagger . . . has struck it . . . into the back . . . of its neighbor!" This stinging expression of contempt for Italy's entry into the war at the last moment to pick up a few crumbs held out a fleeting prospect that quickened interventionist hearts. *Time*, whose publisher, Henry Luce, was a member of the Century Group, trumpeted: "The U.S. had taken sides. Gone was the myth of neutrality." Another journal thought it signaled a change "from neutrality to partisan non-belligerency" (whatever that was). In that moment they expected all-out aid to materialize, but it did not. For though most of the nation thought much as the CDA did, there was still a sizable minority that did not. And the President had to govern them both.

The Committee to Defend America had the field to itself for the first few months of its existence not because there were no isolationists but because the isolationist one-third of the nation had not been organized. There were half a dozen isolationist Senators, and every one of them stodgy. The ex-President, Herbert Hoover, had the same problem. At first it had looked as though isolation had found its great champion in Colonel Charles A. Lindbergh. Shortly after the war began, he had made his first radio address in eight years to a national audience, which listened politely. He was, after all, much esteemed. During the great crisis sparked by the battle of France he had taken to the radio again and scolded the fearful, now numbering many millions. They were told they "must stop this hysterical chatter of calamity and invasion." Lindbergh scoffed at ideas that air or sea attacks menaced the Eastern seaboard. He may have been right, but as a champion he was a disaster, for his cold, schoolmarm tone, slightly high-pitched and frosted with derision, dug a ditch so wide that his enormous reputation could no longer bridge it. There was, it is true, a smattering of tiny, *ad hoc* isolationist groups, but they were so feeble that even if Lindbergh had been a success, they would have been unable to exploit it.

Yet even as Roosevelt spoke at Charlottesville, two students at Yale were creating a national isolationist organization. One was a law student named R. Douglas Stuart; the other, Kingman Brewster, Jr., edited the student newspaper (and would one day be president of Yale). They had circulated through the Republican Convention in June, 1940, pleading with delegates to write an isolationist platform and, beyond that, to help establish an isolationist organization.

Stuart had succeeded before the summer was over in convincing General Robert Wood, the president of Sears, Roebuck and Company, that such an organization was both necessary and possible. Late in September the America First Committee announced its existence. Its headquarters would be in Chicago. On its board were General Hugh S. Johnson, who had headed the National Recovery Administration in the early years of the New Deal; a former commander of the American Legion; a big meatpacker; Teddy Roosevelt's daughter, the redoubtable Alice Roosevelt Longworth; the heir to the Morton salt millions; Eddie Rickenbacker; a Nobel prizewinner in medicine; and a dozen others who were Midwestern, newly rich and conservative.

The AFC called for an "impregnable defense." It opposed aid to Britain, contending that it would weaken American defenses. Organized along almost identical lines to the CDA, the AFC grew almost as fast. Membership reached an estimated 850,000 spread among 450 chapters. But the vast majority of members and chapters were within 300 miles of Chicago, inspiring a long-standing belief that isolationism was overwhelmingly a Midwestern phenomenon to be explained by geography and ethnic ties. There is now much proof that this was not so. But the important thing is that the AFC was never truly national in scope. For one thing, it had virtually no success in the South, where several entire states did not even have so much as a token chapter. Nor did it have much success in New England, where large pockets of isolationist sentiment had long existed. Yet the AFC was still strong enough to make the President wary of ignoring isolationism. It was now a force to be reckoned with.

At first the AFC's activities consisted of little more than radio broadcasts and newspaper advertisements. General policy guidance, literature, speakers and slogans issued from Chicago to the various chapters. But there was no overall program. Instead, it waited for the CDA to formulate its most recent set of demands and then generated a campaign to oppose them. Isolation was always on the defensive and negative side of the debate. And theirs was just as uneasy a coalition as the CDA's, perhaps more so. America First cast a wide net, dragging in the anxious parents of healthy young men; Europaphobes; Anglophobes; German-Americans; Roosevelt haters; native Fascists; Communists; pacifists; liberals apprehensive that entry into war would end the social gains of recent years; and conservatives who feared that exactly the opposite would occur. The leadership of the AFC tried to cast the net still further and attempted to win over labor, Negroes and intellectuals, with no real success. Possibly the keenest sense of failure, however, arose from its inability to attract young people, who were generally, but erroneously, thought to be isolationist. The AFC also failed, despite its geographical base, to have more than marginal success with the leadership of major farmers' organizations. And while it was laboring to bring these elements into the fold, it tried, and failed, to keep Fascists and Communists out.

While the rank and file were plainly Anglophobic, the leadership frequently expressed hopes that Britain would somehow survive. But they insisted that Britain was not fighting for democracy or Western civilization; it fought for its own survival and the preservation of its Empire. America had no interest in such a fight. American intervention would be worse than foolish, it would be disastrous; it would prolong the war, bring curbs on democratic institutions and civil liberties and promote the growth of extremism at home and abroad. Neither Germany nor Britain was capable of conquering the other; only the prospect of American intervention kept the war going because it encouraged the British to refuse Hitler's offers of a negotiated peace. Thus, they argued, they were not promoting the destruction of Britain; rather, they were promoting an end to the war. Even so, of course, some were hoping for a German victory and the destruction of Britain.

As the interventionists pinned their hopes on the President, the isolationists pinned theirs on Congress. Prominent Republicans, including Governor Bricker of Ohio and Senators Taft and Vandenberg, had already come out explicitly for a policy of "fortress America" several months before the formation of America First. In the Republican primaries that spring Dewey had campaigned in the Midwest on "100% isolationism." But the crisis mood occasioned by the fall of France had brought second thoughts. Vandenberg damned Hitler as "the anti-Christ" and despairingly confessed that isolationism was no longer possible. Dewey backed away from isolation. Yet when Roosevelt appointed Knox and Stimson to his Cabinet on the eve of the Republican Convention, he had goaded the Republican Party into a more isolationist position than it had ever intended or wanted. As a consequence, the party hierarchy was angrily divided, and the GOP dropped more than ever out of touch with the mainstream of American life and politics. Roosevelt had made the Republican Party safe for isolationists, which was to prove a mixed blessing for both isolationists and Republicans. The original "America First" had been a movement popular in 1915–1916. It promoted the Americanization of immigrants and became, in time, a synonym for bipartisan patriotism. This America First could never become bipartisan so long as it was married to the GOP, and the GOP could never again be the majority party so long as its leadership was stuck with isolation.

Isolationism had a more fundamental weakness, or rather, connected set of weaknesses: From beginning to end it was dogged by stodginess, silliness and faintheartedness. Three examples should suffice. The AFC's slogan was "The Path to War Is a False Path to Freedom." Not much there to stir men's hearts like "Fifty-Four Forty or Fight" or "Peace, Land, Bread." The AFC's slogan invited debate, not agreement. Further, its spokesmen were trying so hard to combine compassion and hardheadedness that they sometimes found themselves treading a short path to fatuity. Congressman Bruce Barton, a noted advertising man (and author of a best-selling book portraying Christ as the first great salesman), declared that he was willing to be shot if that would help the Allies win the war. But he would never agree to an American declaration of war on Germany. For that would produce the inevitable wartime inflation, inflation would doom democracy in America, and he would rather be dead than live under a dictatorship. Finally, many conservative elements simply broke ranks and abandoned isolationism. Only a month after the AFC was formed, the American Legion held its annual convention. For years it had embraced isolation, yet now it did a *volte face* and voted for all practical aid to Britain and China. Lest anyone misunderstand, however, the Legionnaires paraded through the streets of Boston under banners which said (among other things) "America—Love It or Leave It."

Military assistance was already going to the British, and the principle upon which it was based might be said to date from 1859, when a British force in China bent on forcibly admonishing the proud, recalcitrant Chinese was brought up short by the Taku forts on the banks of the Yellow River. The United States was neutral in this particular dispute. But an American squadron in the river below steamed to the assistance of the pinned-down British and bombarded the forts. Some of the American officers protested the orders of their commander, Commodore Josiah Tattnall, arguing that this was an illegal act. "Blood," he retorted, "is thicker than water." And far from being rebuked when this news reached home, he was hailed as a hero. But another principle also seemed to be at work now, and it was expressed in the family motto of Lord Lothian, Britain's ambassador to the United States in 1940: *Sero Sed Serio*—"Late, but in earnest."

Individually and collectively Americans tried to aid the British and French as a supplement to, occasionally as a substitute for, government action. The Red Cross usually managed to raise about $7,000,000 to $8,000,000 in its annual fund drive; a refugee relief drive launched in June, 1940, raised $14,000,000 in the first week. And "in homes, clubs, churches all over the country, American women were making dresses, socks and sweaters for refugees, bandages for soldiers." More than 300 relief organizations were at work collecting money or other items for war relief, such as Allied Relief Fund, Bundles for Britain, American Friends of France and Le Paquet au Front. As in the First World War an American

Volunteer Ambulance Corps sprang to life. For the more combative there was the Royal Canadian Air Force, which was especially interested in people who could already fly, and it enrolled so many Southerners that the RAF nicknamed it the Royal Texas Air Force. The RAF itself contained an all-American unit, the Eagle Squadron, patterned after the Lafayette Escadrille of the First World War. And London boasted a mobile defense unit of the Home Guard which was composed entirely of Americans with business or property interests in England. Like their British counterparts, they were middle-aged and did not look particularly ferocious. But they roared about the countryside armed with Thompson submachine guns and called themselves the Gangsters.

In some areas, notably the South and Pacific Northwest, spontaneous movements arose to promote buying British-made goods. No one, however, took the fate of Britain—the land of Shakespeare and Shaw—more to heart than the American theater. It was virtually impossible for anyone in Hollywood or on Broadway to avoid being either in or at a benefit for Britain. In the fall of 1940 Congress added to these private efforts by making an outright gift of $50,000,000 for the relief of Britain's wounded and to help those who had been bombed from their homes. Harvard established a hospital in England and financed its operation for the duration of the war. As these and countless similar acts demonstrated, Commodore Tattnall's dictum still held true. But the efforts of private citizens could not help Britain stave off Hitler's Army and Air Force.

In early September, however, fifty World War I destroyers were exchanged for long-term leases to eight island bases along the Eastern seaboard. Thanks to the efforts of the Committee to Defend America by Aiding the Allies, Roosevelt was assured of massive public support before he even announced that the agreement had been made. When he revealed this *fait accompli,* which was done without Congressional approval, there was some surprise and annoyance over the way it had been done, but almost no opposition to the agreement itself. Most of the nation, including the conservative press, agreed:

SWAP OF DESTROYERS FOR BASES
MAKES U.S. DREAM COME TRUE
Nation's Eastern Flank
Thus Made Impregnable:
General Public Thrilled

When the first of the fifty destroyers slipped out of Boston Harbor a few days later, motorists on the Charlestown Bridge flashed their headlights and sounded their horns while pedestrians along the shore waved and cheered.

There was still two potentially formidable barriers to large loans or gifts of arms, however. There was the Johnson Act, which banned loans to debtors from the First World War; its foundations were deep in the belief that the United States had entered the First World War largely because the Allies were $4 billion in debt for American arms purchases. There was also the ingratitude of the Allies once victory was won and what looked like a refusal to pay their debts. "They borrowed it, didn't they?" asked President Coolidge rhetorically. But these objections had not survived the occupation of France and the onslaught on Britain. By early December, 1940, most people had changed their minds: The country had been right after all to go to war in 1917. "The mistake was made, not in winning the war, but in losing the peace." And a clear majority now favored all possible aid to Britain, on credit if necessary, and at the risk of war if need be.

Aid-to-Britain sympathies had become strong even among people who were quick to fault the British for their inefficiency, their "decadence," their classes and their Empire. When the administration moved to sell the RAF nearly fifty of its older model B-17's, the anti-New Deal *Newsweek* thought this was a "tame and timid step." The reactionary Texas banker Jesse Jones, who presided over the Reconstruction Finance Corporation, an instrument at least equal in economic power to the Treasury Department, announced his opinion that "Britain is a good risk for a loan." (Senator Taft's response: "Nonsense!") But for the moment all talk of U.S. aid— and even Roosevelt spoke of "our aid to England"—was misleading. For so far it was all cash and carry, at a handsome profit and no risk. "What an inspiration we are," cracked the Louisville *Courier-Journal,* "we are opening our hearts. We are opening our order books."

Despite heavy hints from Lord Lothian that loans would very soon be necessary, Roosevelt had already said that assistance to Britain had just about reached its peak. There also seemed to be a growing apathy along with the sympathy: Britain no longer appeared to be in mortal danger as it had a few months back.

But American identification with Britain's fate hardly wavered, despite the strains and tensions. No one was more roundly criticized than the British, yet no other people ever supplanted the preference that Americans felt for the British when compared with other nations. Concrete reminders of the ties were all about: The desk at which the President sat was carved from the timbers of a British warship, HMS *Resolute*, a gift from Queen Victoria to President Rutherford B. Hayes; when the English after their grittily perverse fashion waited with something not unlike enthusiasm for the invasion that never came, 1,500 American government officials had joined most of the Washington diplomatic corps at a special service in Washington's National Cathedral to pray for the people of Britain; six of the New York *Times'* foreign correspondents were British; top Eastern prep schools bore an undeniable resemblance to Britain's famous public (exclusive, private) schools, and from these had issued many of the men to whom Britain now looked, now that the gold and dollars had gone, and gone not into planes and ships, but into factories to build the planes and launch the ships—in short, into financing American rearmament. They were gambling, and it was not a bad gamble, that the United States would not let them be snuffed out because they could not pay. They pinned their hopes on Roosevelt. Christmas, 1940, was to bring them a full sack.

Britain and the United States had formerly shared new war matériel from American factories on a fifty-fifty basis; henceforth Britain would have priority on such crucial items as fighter planes. Better still, there would be no danger of going without weapons for want of money. In a homely parable to a neighbor with a house on fire, Roosevelt compared arms to a garden hose loaned for a momentary emergency on the double assumption that it would help keep the fire away from one's own house and that the hose, or one like it, would be returned once the danger had passed. Roosevelt's garden hose was a lifeline.

With greater cheer than would have seemed possible a few months before, the British settled down to Christmas, 1940, anticipating a long but victorious war. And even with the promise of lend-lease ordinary people still pitched in to help them. Workers at Lockheed sent their own Christmas present to the British people: With their own skills, and on their own time, and with their own money, they built, paid for and dispatched a brand-new Hudson bomber as a Christmas gift. At about the same time, the popular British ambassador, Lord Lothian, died in the hour of his greatest success, a victim to uremic poisoning and a Christian Scientist to the last.

V
Creating a Defense Economy

PERHAPS there was once a time when courage, daring, imagination and intelligence were the hinges on which wars turned. No longer. The total wars of modern history give the decision to the side with the biggest factories. The economically inferior may win battles; they do not win the all-out wars. Nor is it just a matter of machines. Big, strong economies rest upon disciplined, educated populations, from which large, mechanically adept armies can be drawn and quickly trained in the use of modern weapons. The nation had committed itself to a massive program of national rearmament, and its economy was coming to life again. But who would direct and control the new economy? On the answer to that question would depend not only how well or how badly the job of arms production was done but what influences would predominate in national life. Business, government or the military—all would gain something, but who would gain most?

The decision rested with the President as much as it rested with any man. There were generally two sets of experience that he could draw on as he tried to make up his mind: America's experience in the last war and Great Britain's experience so far in this one. Roosevelt was extraordinarily well placed to draw on both of these. He had been Wilson's Assistant Secretary of the Navy during the First World War. And through his close contacts with the British he had a wide knowledge of how Britain was organizing its war effort. As we shall see, these two influences shaped much of the course the country followed.

During the First World War big business had been handed the economy on a plate and commissioned, at a large profit, to turn out the arms. By the time of the Armistice in November, 1918, America had raised an army of 4,000,000 men—and their planes, tanks and artillery came chiefly from French and British factories. The postwar opinion of laymen and experts alike was that the nation's war management had rarely gone beyond stupidity and incompetence. Except for the production of ships there was certainly nothing to boast of.

The British were equally disenchanted with the strong role private enterprise had played in their own part in the First World War. "No one now believes," a British historian later observed, "that laisser faire was the best method for conducting a war, or even a possible one." Thus, the second time around, the British employed a very different approach. The government took the economy into its hands, divided the sacrifices as fairly as a middle-class bureaucracy was able to and in the end created a more Socialist country than even Socialists had thought possible just a few years before. To the best of their ability, the British were fighting "a people's war." Their wartime government was a broad-based coalition which enjoyed the warm support of almost the entire population. Only the Communists believed that it was all a cleverly wicked plot to serve the narrow interests of business and the military at the expense of the people. American liberals wanted something of the same sort here and, as time went by, pressed the President to follow Britain's lead.

He was also being pressed hard by the military services. They had not forgotten the shambles the civilians had made of production in the last war. In the twenty years of peace since then, the Army and Navy had jointly prepared the nation's Industrial Mobilization Plan, making two crucial assumptions as they did so: They assumed a total war and a complaisant Congress. As it stood in 1939, their plan called for direct military control of the economy: All useful manpower, raw materials and machinery were to be turned over to them for the duration of the war. But this simple, and to its creators logical, plan was summarily voided by the President in the summer of 1940, to the disgust of military officers. The issue did not end there, however. In the years that followed, "the Army never gave up the effort to increase its control" over labor, industry and public opinion. But the principle of civilian control was never entirely overthrown. The military's role in the nation's life was bound to increase in time of defense crisis, and if the country got into the war, it would grow even further. Yet complete control of the economy would always be just beyond its reach.

And what of business? Many people frankly doubted that it could do the job. But business had rallied at the prospect of an arms boom during the first winter of the war. The advertising journal *Printer's Ink* had solemnly intoned: "The American businessman, shrinking as he must at the thought of making money out of the European tragedy, must be strong enough to face the facts as they are." If any shrinking persisted, it was not recorded.

Beyond the welcome prospect of a defense boom's restoring their livelihood was the more important question of power. What of their lost prestige? What of their lost place as national movers and shakers? Roosevelt had appointed a War Resources Board a few days before the war began, and its chairman, Edward Stettinius, Jr., president of U.S. Steel, had tactlessly acted as if it were 1928. He had gestured to his fellow members, faced the cameras and said, "We of the business community. . . ." New Dealers groaned aloud, and a few months later the WRB was quietly abandoned.

To appreciate what was happening now and what would happen in the years ahead, we must first touch briefly on the New Deal's approach to the challenge posed by the Depression. There was not one economic problem, but two. Either was daunting; together they had proved unsolvable. One was to create confidence in a milieu of failure. The other was to create new jobs in a deflated economy.

Roosevelt's New Dealers had attacked this two-headed monster with an amateur's zest and an abundance of goodwill. At first, they had pressed hard for an alliance between government and business; working in tandem, they could advance the general welfare. It failed as business scrambled for what might be the last chance to pick up a few crumbs. This was the First New Deal, *circa* 1933–1935.

On their second attempt the New Dealers had pinned their hopes on laws and courts. Government would still refuse to take over business, but judicial control over business life would be broadened and deepened. Business would be nudged and prodded into promoting social goals whether it wished to or not, and all without government take-over.

But the legalist approach had also failed by 1938. One final palliative was thrown into the fight—deficit spending à la Lord Keynes. Government could, by running up deficits, invest in the economy. But where deficits applied on a massive scale in a climate of public trust might work, when done on a modest scale in a milieu of dwindling confidence they became little more than relief, under a different name. In practice, therefore, this policy was like the others, concerned more with fair distribution rather than creating more wealth, with social justice rather than economic revival. And even there the New Deal had failed.

In the years ahead, once confidence in present and future was restored, deficits which would have created panic during the thirties were plumbed to the alarm of no one. The factories, the skills, the manpower for full-tilt production stood all about. Missing was anything that might pass for spontaneous, genuine, obvious social imperative. The sociology of the economy —that is where the New Deal had really failed. Ironically, though, that was exactly where the New Dealers believed they had done their best and most important work.

Businessmen now had three fears: first, that they might be shut out of the higher levels of government during this crisis as they had been shut out during the Depression; second, that the crisis might be used to promote the social goals of the hated New Deal; third, that defense boom profits might be subject to confiscatory rates of taxation. Foolish though these fears might have been, they were sincerely felt. More important, they governed business's actions in the years ahead.

All through the spring of 1940 conservative elements clamored that what the country needed was a "practical go-getter." Conservative publications brayed more loudly than ever at Cabinet members who were "unacquainted with industrial processes." The National Defense Advisory

Committee was very much like the conservative, probusiness Advisory Committee that Wilson had created in 1916 and had followed up a year later by handing the economy over to the interests it represented. The chairman of Roosevelt's NDAC was a "practical go-getter" any businessman could admire, William S. Knudsen. Arriving as a poor immigrant from Denmark at the age of twenty-one, he had since become president of General Motors. New Dealers groaned, even though Sidney Hillman of the CIO was on the NDAC, and Roosevelt took pains to assure them that rearmament would not deliver the New Deal over to the tender mercies of reaction. But by now liberals were convinced of the worst. When Roosevelt appointed James Forrestal to his staff that spring, it brought an angry roar from the *New Republic*: "Mr. Forrestal's appointment is the most marked step so far taken to turn the New Dealers out [of the rearmament program]. Just how chummy can the New Deal be with Wall Street and continue to be the New Deal?"

It was against this background of a three-way struggle for control— among business, military and liberals—and Roosevelt in the middle that the defense boom of 1940 began to forge ahead. It had looked for a moment that the boom triggered by the outbreak of war had run its course. At the end of May one economic reporter shrugged: "The war has been a dud as a stimulant. And the domestic picture presents nothing better." But in fact, the mild boom of the Phony War was giving way to the greatest boom in American history. And no one knew it.

The last boom had washed across the country fifteen years before—the great Florida land boom. And its collapse had, say the economists, signaled that the Great Depression lay just ahead. By August, 1940, towns with defense plants were well on their way to being bona fide boom towns. Many already felt the effects of an acute housing shortage. And after so many pinched, unhappy years there was no shortage of towns which envied them their torments.

Midwest towns, unshakable in their isolationism, had no qualms now about demanding a share of the defense contracts which were breathing new life into towns up and down the Eastern seaboard. There were also any number of suggestions that defense expenditures be arranged in a way that would make old "ghost towns" boom once more; liberals and conservatives alike favored the idea. The premise was that much productive capacity lay idle all across the land; intelligent subcontracting, the argument ran, would harness these pockets of unused capacity and remedy the foolish concentration of vital industries in the most militarily vulnerable parts of the country. They pointed to Britain, where bicycle shops in remote villages were making small parts for aircraft.

After traveling across the country during these impassioned months, one reporter confessed to being "edified at the splendid activity among civic groups wherever I have been, to offer their communities to the government as sites for defense factories and locations for government war expenditures." Not every would-be boom town could be satisfied, but the administration was already responding to new demographic and political realities. The bulk of defense expenditures was shifted to the South, the Southwest and the Pacific coast. California, for example, secured 13 percent of all the defense monies contracted for between June 1 and Christmas, 1940. But most ghost towns, wherever they were, were left undisturbed. The best that could be done (and was done, as we shall see) was to put new life—that is, new money—into towns which had been slowly running down.

Beneath this upsurge in the economy was a nation springing to arms. But would it succeed where the New Deal had failed; would it fire the economy in such a way as to revive the well-capitalized risk taking that relief and mild deficit spending could not provide? After all, "It was the disappearance of production for the future market which wiped out so much employment between 1928 and 1940." Unless it could revive the confidence of private investors, this defense boom might turn out to be no more than a fleeting, cruel hoax. Private capital was obviously still wary. Caught between fears of a Nazi victory and hopes for a sustained defense or war boom, it had responded to the attack on France by driving the stock market to its lowest level in two years. During July, 1940, trading had slumped to the lowest level since 1918; that entire month saw only 7,300,000 shares change hands on the New York Stock Exchange. "Nobody invests money any more. Nobody wants to put out new issues of stocks . . . the people with a few dimes keep their money in cash," an economic reporter concluded. Until confidence in the future revived, private capital would not fuel the war boom; government would have to, with the people's money and credit.

Only by extraordinary measures, however, could government meet the current appropriations for defense. There was no more than marginal opposition to higher taxes. The problems were really the problems of all taxation: raising enough money for the nation's needs and doing it fairly. But there were two complications. There was the matter of heavy borrowing against the future. There was also the issue of excess defense profits.

Only days after the capitulation of France the first Revenue Act of 1940 was rushed through Congress to help pay for the new defense programs. The ceiling on the national debt (which had dropped substantially since 1929) was raised; income tax exemptions were cut by 25 percent; and a multibillion-dollar defense bond issue was authorized. This latter was the worst possible way to finance defense expenditures. By issuing interest-paying bonds, the government turned the sacrifices of the wealthy into a sound investment and passed the real cost of the war off onto the shoulders of the poor and moderately well-off. What hope then for an excess profits tax?

The British had simply declared a 100 percent tax on all excess war profits. American businessmen were appalled. What if Roosevelt took it into his head to try to do the same thing here? Nervously and at the top of their lungs, they wondered aloud how any good could ever be expected to come from such clumsy strangling of initiative. The *Wall Street Journal* had already proclaimed: "Industry will demand many concessions in the way of tax exemptions, amortization policies, relaxation of labor laws, et cetera" in return for rapid expansion of production. The U.S. Chamber of Commerce flatly opposed any excess profits tax. And in the event, the administration called for "a steeply graduated excess profits tax," rather than 100 percent. Government economists were set to devising a workable and fair tax on defense profits.

They could not adopt the British principle, and the country's experience with excess profits in the First World War had left a very bad taste. A mystifying, unworkable tax law with levies ranging from 20 to 60 percent had been passed. Any abuses which occurred were to be corrected once the war was over; they never were. As economists saw it, there were two ways in which an excess profits tax might be devised. They could take earnings over a base period—say 1936–1939—as the average and hold future profits to that level. Or they could set some arbitrary rate of return on invested capital, say, 10 percent per annum. Whatever approach was adopted, they were determined that as "defense profits were being made out of the sacrifices of the people as a whole [they] should be returned to the people in taxes." Congress took a markedly different approach and produced a bill which combined both of the two principles mentioned above—combined them in a single, thoroughly baffling, unworkable measure. Loaded with amendments, exemptions, exceptions and diversions, it was a 489-page confession that Congress had thrown in the towel. This was the second Revenue Act of 1940.

There was probably no need to capitulate so readily to big business. Most business in 1940 was small business: 97 percent of manufacturing was in small businesses employing just a few hundred people and modest capital outlays; more than 60 percent of the nation's income was generated by small business; most of the nation's workers were employed by small business. Yet Congress was becoming inordinately sensitive to big business. And the administration was almost as solicitous of its desires now that it had to cope with a crisis in national defense.

Business and its friends were calling for even greater concessions. *Newsweek* had applauded the call to arms but detected two great problems on which all might founder: "governmental cliques that mix defense with politics, and the attitude of labor. For success of the program, labor must bow to the national common effort. . . . The Walsh-Healy and the Wage-Hour laws will have to be relaxed to allow the needed speedups." General Marshall informed Congress that for every dollar spent by European armies on their soldiers the United States must spend $21—all because of labor laws. Yet the administration had made it a policy since 1937 to deny government contracts to firms which failed to comply with New Deal labor legislation or National Labor Relations Board decisions. It huffed and it puffed that this policy would remain in force. And the Attorney General, Robert Jackson, was issuing legal opinions at the beginning of October that defense contractors must obey NLRB decisions or lose their contracts. But later that same month the policy was quietly shelved.

People generally agreed that given a choice between labor's demands for higher wages or job security and their own demands for national defense, the latter must prevail. And it was never difficult to present labor problems in terms of those alternatives. The result was a widespread demand that labor, especially in defense plants, be denied the right to strike. But this was not probusiness sentiment; more than 70 percent of the people thought that any company that refused to accept defense orders should be seized by the government. And these days there was indeed an evident reluctance on the part of many companies to make guns at a small profit when they might produce butter at a larger one now that the economy was reviving.

No one overtly refused to accept the orders. They merely shrugged that the President's demands exceeded what was possible. Henry Ford had responded to Roosevelt's call for 50,000 planes a year by saying that he could himself turn out 1,000 planes a week; later he raised his sights to 1,000 per day. But when the young president of the United Automobile Workers union, Walter Reuther, called for Detroit to turn its idle capacity to aircraft production, Ford and his fellow automobile manufacturers ran for cover, one of them snorting pedantically, "Guns are not windshield wipers." Not an edifying performance. Yet the responsibility for it was not theirs alone. It was shared by people generally, who simply had neither the desire nor the intention of going without automobiles, not when the boom was putting money into their pockets.

By December, 1940, the legendary peaks of 1929 were already being encroached on throughout the economy. Unemployment remained high, but the national income and the gross national product were sharply up. And automobile manufacturers looked at 1941 as the most promising year in history.

In Washington, meanwhile, the first dollar-a-year men since Baruch's notorious legion of a generation before had started to settle for a long stay. Like their predecessors, many planned to frame their paychecks, for like their predecessors, many were still on the company payroll. Theirs was a profitable, if inglorious, heritage. Liberals and old Progressives shed bitter tears. The Secretary of the Treasury, Henry Morgenthau, joined their lamentations. But there was still one measure of hope. The Temporary National Economic Committee had held hearings for two years into business restraints on the economy. The TNEC was a joint creation of the White House and Congress. From top to bottom it was unhappy with big business and showed it. Time and again business had sent its lawyers down to Washington to put the professors of economics who dominated the TNEC in their place; time and again the despised professors—men who "had never met a payroll"—showed the corporation lawyers up to be bluffers with not the faintest notion of how, in concrete terms, economic institutions work. The TNEC's report was due to be released before the end of the year. It was hoped it would disabuse the administration of any lingering notions it might have about the indispensability of big business.

Roosevelt was already scrapping his Advisory Committee on National Defense, replacing it with an Office of Production Management for National Defense. It too would be headed by William S. Knudsen, but it was not so top-heavy with business types—and Sidney Hillman would have equal rank with Knudsen. No one was sure now who was really in charge of this strange creation, which, like the imperial Russian eagle, had two heads facing in opposite directions. A great struggle was under way between New Dealers and big business for control of the defense program. As yet there was no clear-cut winner. In fact, there might never be one. Roosevelt appeared to enjoy these protracted bureaucratic wars; perhaps they gave him more control than a tidier, more sharply defined arrangement would have afforded. Essentially, the business types would act, the New Deal elements (including labor and blacks) would pounce on them at every misstep. And both sides would then appeal to the President for his decision.

VI

Year of Meteors! Brooding Year!

NINETEEN forty-one had begun with the debut of HB 1776, "A Bill to Further Promote the Defense of the United States, and for Other Purposes." In a word, lend-lease. It was an extraordinary document. No President had ever held such a grant of power. Everything came down to "any." In a document only several pages long "any" appeared thirty-five times. Regardless of any existing legislation to the contrary, the President could at any time take anything he wished and put it to any purpose he deemed in any way important to the nation's security. Even at the height of the Civil War Lincoln had not exercised so much authority. Republicans were acidulous. Yet, with a solid Democratic majority in both houses and strong public support behind it, HB 1776 was certain to pass.

It was ironic, but the committee before which Willkie, Stimson and the other supporters of lend-lease appeared, the Senate Foreign Affairs Committee, was the most isolationist body in Congress. Yet even there isolation was in the minority and thus could neither thwart nor seriously alter the proposed legislation. The best the committee's isolationists could do was to give a warm welcome to the bill's opponents.

They greeted Lindbergh with a standing ovation and struck reverential attitudes throughout his testimony. Stimson and the others were absolutely wrong, said Lindbergh. With 20,000 modern combat planes America would be safe from invasion or serious attack for as long as any man could foresee. The Western Hemisphere could easily be shaped into a single economic unit, utterly independent of the rest of the world.

But no matter how many witnesses the isolationist bloc produced to testify against lend-lease, they could not alter HB 1776. Isolationist sentiments were overrepresented in Congress, given the vagaries of Congressional districting, but they were not vastly overrepresented. Frustrated at every turn, isolationists began to lash out wildly. Senator Burton Wheeler secured a footnote of notoriety by fuming that "the result of Lend-lease will be to plow under every fourth American boy." Roosevelt pointedly branded it the rottenest public utterance he had ever heard.

On the eve of the Congressional vote Churchill made a worldwide broadcast on Britain's needs and prospects. Americans listened to that by now familiar, sibilant voice, its volume rising and falling on the shifting tides of radio atmospherics, lisping out that Britain did not want America's young men; it needed arms and food. "Give us the tools, and we will finish the job." Several days later lend-lease passed both chambers of Congress by a wide margin. Its term was limited to two years.

When Roosevelt signed lend-lease into law, it occurred to many that fine distinctions to one side, the country was now directly involved in the war. The administration insisted that lend-lease would keep the United States from entering the war, but hardly anyone believed it.

Roosevelt had himself begun the year in an assertive, vigorous mood. His State of the Union message to the opening session of the new Congress advanced a set of aims he had been pondering for months past: "Freedom of speech and expression—everywhere in the world. . . . Freedom of every person to worship God in his own way—everywhere in the world. . . . Freedom from want—everywhere in the world. . . . Freedom from fear— anywhere in the world." This Four Freedoms speech became the most famous single address of Roosevelt's long public career. It sounded exactly the generous, forward-looking, expansive, assertive note a confused and worried people was longing to hear.

Enactment of lend-lease clearly carried forward the thrust of his "struggle to intervene." Tensions rose as April neared—April, the traditional first month of America's wars: the Revolutionary War, the Civil War, the Spanish-American War, the Great War. And by the first of April the idea had taken hold that the next hundred days would settle the great question of war or peace. Gamblers offered high odds that the German response to lend-lease would be to strike back in such a way as to provide an undeniable *casus belli*. Germany possessed a new, undamaged aircraft carrier. With this, so speculation ran, it could launch a heavy air attack on Boston, New York or Washington itself, in retaliation for U.S. aid to Britain.

During that first week of April some sort of showdown seemed likely when all the German, Italian and Danish shipping still in American ports was seized without notice, ostensibly on the ground that sabotage to these vessels was thought to be likely, and sabotage would render these ships "a menace to the safety of American harbors," a thing forbidden by law. In all, some 66 vessels totaling 300,000 tons were seized. Delivered to Britain, they offset its staggering shipping losses for the month of March. Most people approved; many, in fact, thought it was a step long overdue. But it nonetheless prompted Berlin to recall many of its officials in the United States, fanning even further the widespread mood of impending war.

Those private organizations which had provided various kinds of assistance to the British were dwarfed now by a multibillion-dollar aid program. But they continued to operate. Probably these were the people most at ease with their own consciences these days. In any event, even after the passage of lend-lease they worked as diligently as ever. Gypsy Rose Lee was stripping for Britain. In Seattle there was Bingo for Britain, the proceeds from which bought Spitfires. Every major city saw an endless round of benefit dances, sales, balls and concerts for British relief. More than forty volunteer societies toiled away at these ventures. By far the most popular with the prosperous middle classes was Bundles for Britain. With more than 1,000 chapters and 500,000 members it was also the largest relief operation of all. From it there flowed a steady stream of useful items across the Atlantic, everything from sweaters to X-ray machines. The British-American Ambulance Corps now boasted hundreds of ambulances and drivers. Adventurous young men still went to Canada to enlist in the RCAF. And even convicts were trying to help; those at the Walla Walla, Washington, state penitentiary were staging benefit concerts for Britain. The financial value of all these efforts was, by the summer of 1941, somewhere between $50,000,000 and $100,000,000. And a sizable number of Americans (apparently well into the hundreds) had been killed or maimed in Britain's war on Hitler.

Certainly almost the entire country now hoped passionately that Britain not only would survive but would triumph. Eighty percent said they favored lend-lease, and by the end of April, 1941, two-thirds of the country was convinced that aiding the British, even at the risk of war, was preferable to staying out of it. The United States was firmly committed to providing the British with lend-lease assistance. The question Americans now had to face was how that assistance was to reach its destination without American help. Would the country, in short, put it to the test and actually run the risk of war in order to aid Britain?

More than 10,000 tons of Britain's merchant shipping were currently going to the bottom of the Atlantic every day. Without American protection, much of the lend-lease assistance would never reach British ports. The administration said that it was willing to authorize American escorts until the shipments were out of the Western Hemisphere. There was a vague notion that that meant halfway out into the Atlantic. But to many the answer seemed the simplest thing in the world: Why bother with finding or setting boundary markers when these could be vaulted over by a "Bridge of Ships"? America, these people said, should convoy the goods all the way. But only the President could authorize a policy of convoys.

Roosevelt was still cautious. He moved as far as he dared, and no farther. He gave the British ten oceangoing, 2,000-ton Coast Guard cutters to help convoy lend-lease shipments. He also demanded, and received, Congressional authority to seize and pay for any and all foreign vessels found in American waters; these too he gave to the British. In order to deliver arms to British forces in the Middle East, he declared the Red Sea exempt from Neutrality Act restrictions. Crippled British warships were already being repaired in American shipyards. Thousands of British fliers were to be trained in the United States. And when Germany declared the war zone of the Battle of the Atlantic extended to within three miles of Greenland, Roosevelt responded quickly and provocatively. He established American bases in Greenland with the explicit purpose of protecting lendlease shipments on their way to Britain. American forces were thus only three miles away from the war.

Yet the essential problem—the problem of convoys—remained unsettled. By May rumor had it that 40 percent of lend-lease aid was being sunk; in fact, very little was. Still, the rumors continued to fly, while "From the Florida Everglades to the pine forests of Washington state, Americans asked themselves, asked each other, told each other, polled each other" about convoys. A thousand Princeton students petitioned for convoys; another thousand petitioned against them. The American Legion and Wendell Willkie favored convoys; the majority of registered Republicans opposed them. Congressional debate boiled down to a furious session on the Senate floor, climaxed by a demand from Senator Pepper (to a mixed chorus of boos and cheers) that the United States reach out to occupy strategically vital points around the globe—Iceland, the Azores, the Canary Islands, Cape Verde Island, Dakar. . . . More than that, fleets of American heavy bombers should be stationed in China. "Fifty of them can make a shambles of Tokyo," Pepper enthused. Even his friends thought this was pressing things too far. Interventionism was battling wildly partly because its champion, Roosevelt, was vacillating, giving neither guidance nor shape to the debate. It had become every man for himself. By June a majority of people favored convoys, and still there was no lead from the President.

The war had already taken another of its unexpected turns, with a German descent on the Balkans. There was surprise, but no great emotion; after all, the past three years had seen twelve countries brutally occupied or conquered. For a moment there was a sudden lifting of spirits, for it appeared probable that Britain would last another year—in which event, it was often assumed, it would somehow prevail. But when the British followed up with an inept and losing campaign along the Mediterranean's eastern rim, the mood dropped back into gloomy despair. "Morale" was bad. Roosevelt grumbled that the country was not up to the demands of the moment; people were "not aware." Everywhere the mood was fatalistic. The country appeared to be sliding into war, and no one was enthusiastic. Nor, however, was there any strong movement to stop it. Support for the President remained high. But why didn't he act?

Roosevelt finally broke his silence on convoys. But all that he offered was an uninspiring system of neutrality patrols. Sometimes they would extend 1,000 miles out to sea, sometimes only 100, depending on the circumstances. This deliberately fuzzy formula satisfied no one, not even the President. It prompted one exasperated private citizen to dash off an angry letter:

Sir:

The American people, according to Gallup, believe that the country should risk war, but that it should not actually wage it.

We are not at war with Germany, but Germany is our enemy.

We will use the Navy for "patrolling," but not for "convoying."

There is a terrible danger of Germany winning, but Lindbergh is a traitor for saying so.

The President murmurs "Let's do it and say we didn't."

What this country needs is a good 5¢ psychiatrist.

THOMAS H. JOYCE
Los Angeles

At this juncture, in late May, 1941, Greece fell. Here, it seemed, was an almost perfect example of the dangers and embarrassments the country's foreign policy skirted. Roosevelt had pledged the Greeks in October, 1940, that if they were attacked, they would have American military assistance. Now the country had been completely defeated, and not so much as one American bullet had been on hand to defend it. More, the performance of the British had been pathetic and that of the Germans so undeniably brilliant that people once again talked openly and fearfully of Britain's imminent conquest. The spectacular descent on Crete by thousands of German paratroopers looked like nothing so much as the prelude to an even more massive—and equally decisive—assault on Britain itself.

Thus, when Roosevelt addressed the nation on May 27, he addressed a people afraid, unhappy and bewildered; the largest radio audience up to that time, estimated at 85,000,000 people, hung on his words. What they wanted was a sense of direction and purpose, a clear line of national policy. What he gave them was a great deal of tough talk. He reviewed in detail the terrible effects a Nazi victory in Europe would have on American life. For himself, he said, he was unalterably opposed to any such outcome of the war and would do everything he could to prevent it. On no account would he tolerate Nazi encroachments on the Western Hemisphere. He concluded by declaring a state of unlimited national emergency.* And that was all. What did it mean in concrete terms? No one knew. So the sense of drift persisted.

Yet at sea the Battle of the Atlantic was raging at a furious pitch, and here was the first battle in this war in which the United States was in any real danger of becoming directly involved. Whether called convoys or patrols, American ships were almost certain to clash sooner or later with German submarines. And from the very first days of the neutrality patrols, stories circulated of American destroyers attempting to sink U-boats laying in wait for lend-lease shipping. The SS Robin Moor, carrying no military cargo at all, was sunk. But there was still no great popular outrage. Instead,

* Not until 1952 was Roosevelt's state of unlimited emergency declared at an end by President Truman.

a grim fatalism prevailed. Even German announcements that such sinkings would continue failed to shake most people from their resolve not to be panicked. Even so, when the administration responded to the sinking of the *Robin Moor* by closing down all twenty-five German consulates in the United States and freezing all assets owned by Axis and Axis-occupied countries, the popular response was strongly favorable. More than ever, but tight-lipped and somber, the country was edging into the war; at least, that is how it appeared to most people. And the most worrisome thing about it was not the slide into war but the unshakable feeling that the hand on the helm was irresolute.

It was at this juncture that Hitler delivered himself into the hands of his enemies by attacking the Soviet Union on June 22, 1941. With an active war still unresolved on one front, he thrust to the east in the most preposterous gamble of his long gambler's career.

No one doubted that this was a decisive moment. Official Washington hailed it, quietly, as perhaps the most fortuitous break in the war; fortuitous at least for the United States. One day Britain's destruction had seemed certain, war with Germany seemed imminent; the next day both were not only postponed but conceivably placed forever beyond reach. A path which followed a logical, if reluctant, course from national rearmament, to aiding Britain, to acquiring an advanced line of military bases, to aggressive patrolling far out to sea, to—finally—war had been turned sharply aside at the last moment. Churchill, who wasted no time in embracing any enemy of Hitler's, now had a fighting ally. And the United States would have time enough in which to build up its military forces to formidable strength. For even if Russia were defeated, it would take anywhere from six to twelve months for the Germans to do it.

There was also a barely concealed glee now that the two great tyrants of the age were at each other's throats. And yet, if forced to choose between them, most people preferred a victorious Stalin to a victorious Hitler. For while "Soviet ideology was hated, Soviet power was not feared." But no one wanted a quick decision regardless of the outcome; the longer the war lasted, the more Germany and Russia would bleed themselves white, while the United States would wax ever stronger.

The country was finally on its way to becoming a major military power. At times it was hard to see through the confusion, the delays, the shifting emphases and catch sight of the growing military power and the revival of the production base on which it must rest. People were also impatient, very impatient. The focal point of popular interest remained the Army, now that it was a conscript army.

Through the winter months of 1940–1941 some 20,000 generally middle-aged, middle-class volunteers had freely given their leisure time to setting up local draft boards. In some resolutely spartan offices with rough furniture and an omnipresent clutter of lists, address cards, coffee urns, pencils, paper, steel wastebaskets, they could be seen milling about to no readily apparent purpose while two or three people huddled in a corner, desperately checking off old lists or compiling new ones. And they had been enthusiastic; they at least were doing something.

But by the spring of 1941 the high spirits were gone. Even the most dedicated volunteers were beginning to wonder if the draft was worth the effort it involved. For they had learned by now that a wartime measure enacted in peacetime had all the disadvantages of emergency legislation and none of the ostensible benefits. It was neither universal military training nor mobilization. It was a shapeless hulk deposited in a bureaucratic no-man's-land, drawing fire from every side.

If they agreed on nothing else, Army officers and draftees were usually agreed on at least one point—that the draft boards were incompetent. Time and again the local boards would hurry potential draftees through the preliminaries of induction, rule that they were fit to serve, tell them to give up their jobs and say their farewells, pass them along to the Army— and the Army would send them back a few days later because they were physically and mentally unfit. This sort of bungling and the still troublesome doubts that the draft was needed at all threatened to spell the end of Selective Service. Six months after the draft went into effect, the country generally was becoming alarmed, and the crucial principle of civilian control began to lose much of its appeal.

There were also frequent objections that a year of training added little more to national defense than equipping the Boy Scouts with rifles would do. Army officers and civilians alike tended to look on a one-year draft as giving "too many men too little training." The Army also grumbled that the local boards kept sending them men over thirty: men who were simply not up to the physical demands of basic training. Time and again they pleaded that the boards send them no one over twenty-seven; to no avail. Civilians worried for the health of the draftees; half of them were being trained in the South, which was, so far as public health was concerned, the most pestilential region in the entire country. And there were still millions of people who worried, as Dorothy Dunbar Bromley did in the New York *Post*: "Now that there is no turning back, we ask ourselves, will they come out as robots trained only in the use of force, jobless, an easy prey to some home-grown Führer?"

Clearly something had to give, and at the end of March the civilian head of Selective Service, Clarence Dykstra, resigned. To a chorus of acclaim from most local boards, most Army officers and most civilians, the officer who had designed the Selective Service System, Brigadier General Lewis S. Hershey, was named the new director. Hershey had in fact been director in all but name. He was hailed nonetheless as a potential savior (quite a contrast with his resignation twenty-nine years later). Local boards soon adopted a policy of drafting men between the ages of twenty-one and twenty-five.

Conscious that they were very much on trial, Army officers kept trying to calm civilian fears over what they were doing to, for and with the draftees. Efforts to keep them at least moderately happy varied from post to post, but the policy was everywhere the same. Its spirit was captured in the concluding paragraph of an order posted by a colonel in the infantry: "The squad leader and his second in command should be father, mother and big brother to all the other members of his squad." Both Army and Selective Service authorities never passed up an opportunity to portray the draft as being the most democratic of institutions; an inducted stockbroker was certain to be photographed cheek by jowl with inducted janitors and Western Union messengers. There was also a Morale Division of several hundred officers and several thousand men, responsible for keeping spirits from ever falling too low.

Yet the Army was still fumbling with personal problems, poor equipment and dated notions of contemporary warfare. When the body of Private Felix Hall was found hanging by a rope attached to the limb of a tree at Fort Benning, Georgia, the Army insisted that it was suicide; most blacks, and many whites, thought it looked suspiciously like a lynching, carried out by white soldiers and on federal property. The new 28-ton tank, the M-3, came equipped, for no apparent reason, with a police siren. And the War Department proudly reported that the Army was more lavishly equipped with horses than it had been at any time since the Civil War. In the early weeks of 1941 the Army had purchased 20,000 horses; it was looking forward to buying thousands more. Despite the rush to arms, antimilitary feelings were still quite strong. A single year could not undo the sentiments of nearly twenty years. In large cities, especially in Washington, military officers continued to wear their uniforms only for ceremonial occasions. Anything but mufti was still considered an affront to civilian feelings. But most officers dressed so badly in civilian garb that Westbrook Pegler taunted, "They look as if they had just crossed the continent by day-coach in a slow train and hadn't undressed for a week."

Government itself was committed to haste but, like everyone else, made it slowly. There was a new passion for security and timesaving. All government employees and workers in defense plants were being fingerprinted, photographed, numbered and required to apply for identification badges. Defense industries were ordered into round-the-clock operations. And the War Department eliminated waste by ordering Army officers to stop saying "Hello" when they answered the telephone.

In June the government was authorized to establish production priorities throughout American industry. The government could, by law, prescribe what was made, how much was made, and the price to be charged the consumer. As if that was not enough, Roosevelt blandly asked Congress for authority to seize any privately owned property he might find useful for defense. Until now Congress had been relatively complaisant, but it balked at this. Here, Congressmen protested, was a "Send-Seize" bill, a "Draft Property Act," a "Brass-knuckle Law." Hiram Johnson, the old California Progressive, hauled his ancient frame erect in the Senate and, red in the face, proceeded to attack it as "the damnedest piece of legislation I have ever seen."

Congress was not without resources of its own during all this. In a fit of absentmindedness it had already established a watchdog to investigate the uses to which the new powers and vast appropriations were being put. But the watchdog was so small and so unheralded that hardly anyone took any notice of it at first. An obscure Midwestern Senator, named Harry S. Truman of Missouri, had been angered—as had many of his colleagues—by constituents' stories of massive waste and incompetence in the construction of Army bases. Truman's constituents who watched the Army slap together a huge training camp, Fort Leonard Wood, in the middle of Missouri considered it little more than a calculated insult to the sensibilities of hardworking taxpayers. Truman became convinced (and as a protégé of Boss Pendergast he was better informed on such matters than most) that the crux of the problem was the contracting—a few contractors operating under marginal supervision meant unconscionable waste and enormous profits. The distribution pattern of the new Army installations also had little or nothing to do with economy. Truman was prompted to ask for a $25,000 appropriation to investigate new military construction, and he received, essentially as a courtesy, an appropriation of $15,000. Almost no one expected anything to come of it.

Formally known as the Senate Special Committee to Investigate the National Defense Program, Truman's committee got under way in March, 1941, composed mainly of freshman Senators. There were several precedents for such a committee, all of them discouraging. In every American war but one (the war with Spain: McKinley had just beaten Congress to the punch by setting up his own committee) a Congressional investigating committee had monitored the government's performance. Without fail, the wartime investigating committees were failures. The most notorious—the Committee on the Conduct of the War—had in fact been the bane of Lincoln's Presidency. Lee had once remarked that it was worth two divisions to him—a quote Truman never tired of repeating. Truman, however, was convinced that no postwar postmortem could ever rectify the errors made in wartime, and the country's experience in World War I he took as proof of that. Despite some strong opposition, led by the New York *Times*, Truman's committee was determined to find a way of correcting abuses as they were committed and to do so without hampering defense.

Truman hoped to avoid becoming a nuisance by studiously steering clear of matters relating to how the war was to be fought—when and if the United States entered it. But his committee would not wait for scandals to develop, then lament it had not acted earlier. As each new defense program emerged, the committee would probe for incompetence, waste or mismanagement, make its results public and suggest possible remedies. The rest it would leave to public opinion, the courts and the administration. Truman was convinced that this method would work. Yet it could do so only if it was carried out as honestly and as fairly as possible. "I want no smears," he insistently told his staff, "and no whitewashes."

No one doubted any longer that the country was well into a boom, with all the attendant problems of waste and confusion; defense boom, war boom, partisan nonbelligerency boom, call it what one will, it was here, and everyone knew it. But there was no rejoicing over it. America is a land of great historic booms; it was also in 1941 a country which could see beyond a boom to a bust. Memories of the collapse which followed the Great War were still lively; more vivid yet were the memories of 1929. So businessmen loudly demanded to know what would happen to the plants that were built now; would they be of any possible use once the war ended? Labor wanted to know what assurance it would have of full employment at fair wages; if it agreed to a relaxation of current labor laws, would they be revived once the war ended? No one as yet, however, could answer such questions. And whatever the fears and doubts, the fact remained that the country had a boom on its hands, or the boom had its hands on the country. And this was the crux of the defense effort: Only on the basis of a rapidly growing economy could the country build the massive military strength it needed.

These, then, were boom times, and reminders were all about. Nowhere was the boom itself bigger than in the South. The South which Roosevelt— a constant visitor to Warm Springs, Georgia—had called "The nation's Number One economic problem"; the South which had suffered unbroken economic stagnation since the Civil War; the South, many of whose enduring social and educational failures could be traced directly to a permanent depression economy. Now, spearheaded by the construction of more than 60 of the Army's 100 new camps, the boom struck the South earlier and with more force than it struck any other region in the country. Southern textile mills were humming with orders for blankets and uniforms. Along the 1,200-mile stretch of Gulf Coast from Tampa to Galveston, shipyards were alive with activity. Three years before not a single oceangoing ship was built along that coast; but in May, 1941, four shipyards were working around the clock on oceangoing merchantmen and warships, and four new shipyards were under construction. And the greatest boom town in the nation was that most famous of Southern cities Washington, D.C. Washington had grown during the Depression when government had increased by more than a third, but here was an expansion which dwarfed that. Even so, however, the South had seen something like this before—during the Great War—and clung to bitter memories of the blasted hopes it left behind. There was no whooping it up, at least, not yet, even in the South.

Wherever Army bases or new defense plants went up, in the South or elsewhere, the local economy changed overnight, especially in rural areas. And the most unlikely, unsuspecting towns were swept up in the rush; even quiet, pleasant, old Cape Cod discovered (doubtless to the horror of longtime residents) that it had become the locale of an Army training camp. Local manpower was sucked up during the winter of 1940–1941 and put to work constructing barracks. Soon unemployed men from dozens of states flocked to this spot—usually deserted in winter by all save the sea gulls and a few thousand permanent residents—as Muslims flock to Mecca. In ten weeks a stretch of formerly open ground became Camp Edwards: 1,400 buildings, 12 miles of paved roads, a 100-bed hospital, a sewage plant, a railroad spur and most of the amenities of a sizable town. All around the camp there then sprang up all manner of businesses to cater to its various needs.

Starke, Florida—a not inapt name by all accounts—had greeted 1940 as a sleepy, depressed backwater boasting 1,500 residents, most of them poor or unemployed. Starke greeted 1941 as the home of Camp Blanding (overnight it became Florida's fourth-largest city) and principal beneficiary of a federal payroll of $3,000,000 a month—that is, a sum equal to $2,000 per month for each permanent resident. Not all this money, of course, found its way into Starke, but much of it did. Not a room or a bed was unoccupied, and still they came, the mobile army of carpenters, laborers, bricklayers and anyone else willing to suffer the rigors of boomtown life for $60 to $70 a week for unskilled labor and up to twice as much for those with skills. At one point hiring had hit the rate of 1,600 new workers a day. By March, 1941, more than 20,000 men were busily sawing, hammering, bricklaying and mixing to construct a permanent camp for 60,000 soldiers. To house this small army of civilian workers, government officials, private contractors and the local Chamber of Commerce had formed an alliance and forced the people of Starke to open their homes to the transients. But even that was not enough. Before long many thousands of people were sleeping in their cars, living in pup tents, leantos, even brush piles and packing cases along local roads and ditches. Some commuted every day to and from Jacksonville—80 miles a day over narrow, congested country roads. Starke's one paved street bulged day and night. Along it, and in the short alleys just off it, a motley brigade of fiddlers, blind balladeers, beggars, cripples and hookers plied their respective trades by daylight and moonlight. Not since the semilegendary days of the Old West had there been anything like this, but here it was again, and probably for the last time. And just as the workers began to drift away, their task at this camp done, to another waiting to be built somewhere else, thousands of soldiers came swarming into the newly finished camp and brought the boom to life again.

More numerous than the towns which hosted Army camps were those which became the sites of defense plants, such as Charlestown, Indiana. In September, 1940, this small town of 3,000, located 15 miles north of Louisville, Kentucky, was picked as the site of a powder plant. Like Starke, Charlestown was soon crammed with defense workers until it was literally groaning. Workers poured into town, and hot on their heels came the speculators. Every boom town had them. Here it was a trio consisting of a local lawyer, a local contractor and a stranger—a "promoter" who arrived like the dew in the morning "with a wife, a dog and a car with California license plates."

These three set about finding a parcel of undeveloped farmland. Once they had located it, they divided it into lots 40 feet by 100 feet and proposed to sell these to defense workers as sites for prefabricated homes, which were offered by the local contractor. The speculators invested not a cent in the land. They merely held an option on it that was contingent upon securing the zoning approval of local officials; with that they could collect enough in deposits from prospective purchasers to exercise their option. If local officials did not approve, then the scheme fell through—but it cost them nothing. If their project was approved, however, then several acres of swampy, undeveloped land would make them all thoroughly rich. In the case of Charlestown, the local officials turned their noses up and their thumbs down. Yet such ventures did not always come to naught. And the proof was to be seen in scores of communities in the summer of 1941 where tacky prefabs jutted up on overpriced, underdeveloped lots creating instant rural slums.

For all the inconvenience, the swindles, the ugly, repellent side of the boom and the fears that bust would follow it, what mattered most to most people, however, was the unalloyed fact of economic resurgence. Boom-town life may have been hellish, it may have enriched the unworthy and caused hardship to the unoffending, but most people preferred its cruelties to those of the Depression. By mid-1941 most people were better off than they had ever been at any other time in their lives, including the heady days before the Great Crash. Never having had so much money before and not at all sure that it was worth trying to save, people were spending it freely. Retail sales soared by 16 percent in a single year, and automobile sales shot up 40 percent. Detroit raised its estimate from 4,000,000 to 5,000,000 units in 1941. And a government committed to unprecedented expenditures started to tap this flow of new money to pay for national defense. On May 1 the first issue of Defense Savings Bonds went on sale. People were urged to buy them as a hedge against the inevitable postwar (whenever that was) economic collapse.

VII
Who's Hysterical?

MOST Americans in 1939 could still remember, many of them with shame, the hysterical excesses of the First World War: arbitrary arrests, mob violence, lynchings. Apprehension over entering this war was in millions of cases inspired by fears for civil liberties. And the way Canada dealt with civil liberties in the first flush of war—denial of free speech even in one's home, midnight raids, secret trials on secret charges—could only exacerbate America's own fears. Who could be sure, when one recalled the previous war, that the same things would not happen here?

Even before the war began, the climate was tense. Conservative publications, such as the *Saturday Evening Post,* never let an issue go by without an exposé of subversion in the schools, or in Hollywood, or in labor unions, or in government. On the day before the war began, the Department of Justice announced the opening of a new campaign against espionage, sabotage and subversion. A week later the Attorney General, Frank Murphy, was pleading for private citizens to assist the government's anti-espionage campaign.

Since then the tide of intolerance had risen, lapping at the feet of aliens, ethnic and religious minorities, labor unions, Communists, non-Communist radicals and the simply idiosyncratic. With every Nazi victory a new round of spy rumors took wing. By the summer of 1940 a book called *The Fifth Column Is Here,* based on the claim that there were more than a million domestic fifth columnists, was a best seller. Administration officials had drawn up a loyalty pledge for all workers in defense industries. Congress had required that the 2,000,000 people still employed by the WPA must swear that they were not members of the Nazi or Communist parties or forfeit their jobs. Ordinary people were eager to catch spies and subversives: By June, 1940, the Justice Department was receiving tips at the rate of 3,000 a day. But of all the agencies of government pandering to this growing panic none was more clamorous than the House Select Committee on Un-American Activities, more popularly known, after the name of its chairman, Martin Dies of Texas, as the Dies Committee.

When it was established in 1938, no one expected anything of it. Hamilton Fish, the perfervid isolationist Congressman who represented Roosevelt's home district of Hyde Park, New York, had set up a similar committee in 1932. It was laughed out of existence when Fish's crowning triumph, a crate of anarchists' bombs, turned out to be a crate of lettuce.

This new committee had come into existence at the urging of a Jewish Representative from New York's East Side, Samuel Dickstein. He wanted a Congressional investigating committee to expose the activities of native Fascists. Dies, with objectives of his own, supported him. Out of real events, imaginary fears and personal ambitions they managed to conjure up half a million Nazis, mostly fictitious, and one very real House investigating committee. Dies then doublecrossed his partner, and by the time assignments to the committee had been completed Dies was its chairman, and Dickstein was out in the cold.

In September, 1939, the committee had been in existence for a year. With a year's experience behind it and an increasingly receptive public opinion before it, the committee was ready to pioneer some new techniques. It began publishing the names of purported Communists and fellow travelers. Its first list labeled 563 government employees as Communists or Communist sympathizers and tried to tie them to a Communist front, the League for Peace and Democracy. The evidence against them consisted solely of having their names—whether they knew it or not—on the league's mailing list. Suggestions that there was an injustice here were usually dismissed out of hand. "The country as a whole has welcomed the controversy as a healthy one, in that it brought into the open a long-standing condition in Washington which permitted Federal employees to dabble in the ideologies of foreign governments," huffed *Newsweek*.

The administration found HUAC a noisy embarrassment. But it had rapidly managed to establish itself as the most popular Congressional committee in memory; more than 75 percent of the public wanted it to be retained.

HUAC was not, for all its popularity, alone at center stage in the spotlit hunt for subversives. The FBI had become accustomed to regarding that terrain as its own, and it was popular in its own right. Before the war was very old, Dies and Hoover were quarreling publicly over which of them was the greatest scourge of spies, subversives and fifth columnists.

In Hoover, Dies had really met his match. Liberals loathed the director of the FBI, they denounced his abuses of power, they derided him as a petty tyrant and a publicity seeker, but no one rested more snugly in the bosom of popular esteem. Mass circulation periodicals such as *Time, Saturday Evening Post* and *Newsweek* adored him, as did the large and powerful Hearst newspaper chain. As if his work did not bring him opportunity enough for confounding the foes of decency, democracy and the American way of life, Hoover wrote crime fantasies in his spare time for magazines such as *True Detective*. In nearly twenty years of playing to the galleries he had become an adept at shaping popular emotions to his own ends. At a critical juncture he could always discover a dangerous new plot, and often did. A new Attorney General was often greeted with a plot. A moment of national crisis could be helped along with a conspiracy or two. And when both these eventualities conjoined, such discoveries were no surprise.

In January, 1940, shortly after the appointment of Frank Murphy as Attorney General and while Dies was claiming the crown as the number one foe of subversives, a plot was discovered. Another was revealed later in the year when Murphy was named to the Supreme Court and was replaced by Robert Jackson. When Jackson followed Murphy's path in early 1941, his successor, Francis Biddle, would be similarly honored. And when Congress took up a wiretap bill, a huge spy ring was unearthed the day before the vote was taken.

The plot in January, 1940, revolved about seventeen young men, unemployed or very poor, who were rounded up and charged with conspiring to overthrow the federal government. That done, they would establish a Fascist dictatorship. Several of them were indeed members of the anti-Semitic, pro-Fascist Christian Front. But the details of the plot were so lurid, and the conspirators such a pathetic collection of obvious misfits and incompetents, that the conspiracy was credible as nothing more than wild vaporings. Yet, Hoover insisted, they had planned to "knock off about a dozen Congressmen," seize City Hall and "blow up the goddam Police Department." The skeptical were reminded: "It only took twenty-three men to overthrow Russia." Several months later nine of the defendants were acquitted, five were freed after mistrials were declared, two were freed without a trial, and one had sought refuge in suicide.

Hostility to outsiders usually runs strong in times of collective fear, and the current crisis was no exception. Aliens generally were in for cruel handling. Unmolested and allowed to assimilate as best they might in peaceful times, they become almost perfect objects for abuse in wartime: They are easily identified, are numerically weak, have no great political leverage, have few powerful friends, are split into scores of fragments, and are often at odds with one another. There were more than 4,000,000 aliens currently in the United States. Some states, most notably Pennsylvania and Georgia, had met the outbreak of war by forcing all aliens to register with state authorities and take up a status similar to that of prison parolees. They were required to report periodically to state officials, and every change of address or occupation had to be immediately reported. Aliens in Pennsylvania were already forbidden to take out hunting or fishing licenses. They were also forbidden to own dogs. Other states had comparable restrictions. But federal authorities had never imposed such curbs. By March, 1940, however, more than seventy bills to curb or exclude aliens were before Congress. And in June the Department of Immigration, which had traditionally been a branch of the Department of Labor, was shifted to the Department of Justice. Aliens were now a federal police problem.

At about the same time, Congress passed the Smith Act, more formally known as the Alien Registration Act of 1940. Under it, all aliens—who were by now applying for citizenship at a record rate—were required to register themselves and be fingerprinted. They must also submit to inquiries into their political beliefs and activities. Nor was this concession to hysteria enough. The Smith Act went far beyond controlling aliens. It was the first peacetime sedition law since the notorious Alien and Sedition Acts of 1798. The Smith Act comprehended everyone, alien and citizen alike. It made a federal crime of any act or utterance which would incite disaffection among military personnel or promote the forcible overthrow of "any government in the United States." At its furthest limit the Smith Act also made it a federal offense "to conspire to teach the overthrow" of lawful government. Membership in organizations deemed subversive was made a federal crime, thus raising guilt by association to a new pinnacle of respectability. The fears of those few who had foreseen that attacks on aliens might be but a prelude to attacks on the civil liberties of citizens were now come true.

The brunt of the current outbreak of intolerance would be borne by American citizens. Thanks in part to the Nazi-Soviet Pact, but chiefly to a historic hostility toward Communism, it would fall heavily on Communists, such as Earl Browder, and those believed to be Communists, such as Harry Bridges.

Bridges, the Australian-born head of the West Coast longshoremen's union, was in the thick of a deportation fight even as the war began. The Department of Labor was trying to prove that Bridges was a secret Communist. The dean of Harvard Law School, James M. Landis, presided at hearings in San Francisco. After several months Landis decided that there was no proof that Bridges had ever been a member of the Communist Party. The House of Representatives then passed a bill ordering Bridges deported. He was accused of no crime. His deportation was simply declared to be "in the best interests of the United States." Here was a modern bill of attainder.

Browder, the head of the American Communist Party, was in even more serious trouble when the war began. Before the Dies Committee he was explaining his travels, especially the passports he had used. He had, he admitted, forged names to three passports since 1921. Yet each offense was more than seven years old—they came within the statute of limitations. The government, unable to prosecute him directly, then charged him with criminal fraud: When he applied for a passport under his true name, he had declared that he had never held a passport before. A federal judge then sentenced him to four years in jail and a fine of $2,000. (Shortly afterward, another person convicted of exactly the same offense was simply rebuked and fined $500.) One prominent Washington correspondent was convinced that "This country is now on the edge of a Red hunt," and he was right.

Browder proceeded to emulate the radical Socialist Eugene Debs. During the First World War Debs had been prosecuted for opposing the country's entry into war. At the conclusion of his trial, he had delivered his own summation and plea to the jury. Browder did the same thing. And like Debs, he was convicted all the same. Debs had run for the Presidency from his prison cell in 1920. So did Browder in 1940. He was running from the safest place available.

Canvassers for the Communist Party in Illinois were jailed, charged with treason and had bail set at $80,000 each (later reduced to an equally impossible $15,000). In Oklahoma membership in the Communist Party was itself a crime. Two local Communists were sentenced to jail terms of ten years each in 1940, and more than a dozen others were awaiting trial on the same charges when the year ended. A more rigorous sentence was given a fifty-four-year-old goatherd, Oscar Wheeler, who ran for governor of West Virginia. He received six to fifteen years for "fraudulent solicitation of names." The petitions he circulated to secure the signatures necessary to place his name on the ballot had COMMUNIST PARTY emblazoned across the top, with a red hammer and sickle half an inch high. Wheeler's crime was failing to inform would-be signatories orally that he was a Communist. The usual sentence for this was one to ten years. But because this was his second conviction, an extra five years were tacked on. (Wheeler had been convicted of conscientious objection in the First World War.) His bail was originally set at $5,000, whereupon he surprised the court by offering that amount of U.S. savings bonds; it was rejected as being inadequate surety. His lawyer was beaten up in the courtroom and, on at least one occasion, was shot at on the courthouse steps.

For sheer mindless violence, however, there was one group that suffered more than aliens and Communists combined. This was the small sect of Jehovah's Witnesses. From the invasion of Poland to the Battle of Britain the Witnesses were the principal victims of mob violence. More than fifty attacks on them in those months resulted in injuries to more than 500 people, many of them women and children. There were, during that same year, only two mob attacks on Communists: one in Detroit that injured 50 people, another in San Antonio that injured 30. Unable for the most part to strike at Witnesses through the arms of government, people literally took matters into their own hands. And then, at the worst possible time (June, 1940) and by a vote of eight to one, the Supreme Court struck at them. The Court ruled that the children of Jehovah's Witnesses, whose religion explicitly forbade it, must salute the flag. And reputable conservative periodicals such as the *Saturday Evening Post* joined the Court in encouraging persecution, *e.g.*:

JEHOVAH'S WITNESSES MAKE HATE A RELIGION
The Biggest Source of Conscientious Objectors.

Refusal to salute the flag was required, the Witnesses believed, by the Second Commandment. Far from being pacifists, as was commonly assumed, they would gladly fight—but only for Jehovah, not for the man-created state. There was a general belief that their paper, *The Watchtower*, was a pro-Fascist pamphlet, financed by the Third Reich. They were said to be Nazi agents and fifth columnists. No one appeared to know or care that there were thousands of Witnesses in German prisons, that their activities were banned by the Gestapo and their literature publicly burned. In the months following the Supreme Court decision, Witnesses and their children were beaten, tortured and killed in more than forty American states. Not infrequently, local police looked the other way.

The tides of hate and violence were running strong indeed. The Ku Klux Klan had grown by 50 percent in a single year, so that by December, 1940, it boasted more than 300,000 members. Killings and floggings by the Klan rose proportionately. Some seven out of every ten people now wanted to "curb, lock-up or deport Communist and Nazi sympathizers." Yet, as we shall see, there was no particular concern over any of these things. On the contrary, the same journals which reported such manifestations of hysteria were singing the loudest hosannas of national self-praise. The worst depths of viciousness which had marred the nation's course in the First World War had indeed not yet been plumbed. On that everyone was agreed. But that did not make the violence, the sedition law, the parolee status of aliens, the flag case, the rise in harsh and unjust jail sentences and the demands for more of the same all so much ephemera.

The outbreak of war had been a torment to American liberals. For years they had excoriated Fascism and all its works; they saw themselves as being in the vanguard of opposition to Hitler; they cursed appeasement policies; they openly accepted the necessity of war as the only way to be rid of the Fascist dictatorships. But once the war began, they shrank from seeming to be warmongers. They had been embarrassed by the Nazi-Soviet Pact, for many had publicly defended the Soviet Union. Many also felt guilty about their part in the Great War hysteria. Having painted themselves into a corner, they now clung to Objectivity with the desperation of the damned.

To Roosevelt's fervent appeals for national unity they bristled suspiciously. The *Nation* snapped back, "We fear that if we are all to be taken into the great camp of National Unity some of us may be taken in in another sense. Washington is full of rumors of business appeasement." Having been duped into an alliance with the state in the former war, they were not about to succumb to defense or preparedness hysteria again, and be duped again, and see social advances go aglimmering again.

Or so they believed. But the Nazi-Soviet Pact was a tremendous blow to them—it had struck both at their standing in the nation and at their own self-confidence. And now, as they tried to rescue something from the wreckage and carve out a new place for themselves, they set up purges all along the left. Wherever there was Communist influence, it would be excised. And before very long they assumed the methods and outlook of more predictable hysterics and became indistinguishable from them.

Objectivity quickly disintegrated. By early 1940 liberals such as Walter Lippmann were giving the Dies Committee their blessing. Its methods, they agreed, were disgusting, but un-American, unjust methods were necessary because the committee was dealing with un-American, unjust activities— "it takes a crook to catch a crook." And despite the strong elements of farce that marked the "plot" by the seventeen young Christian Fronters the *Nation* was absolutely certain—without a shred of connecting evidence —that the odious, anti-Semitic radio demagogue Father Coughlin had masterminded it, intending to overthrow the government. But the most extraordinary defection from traditional postures was the American Civil Liberties Union's purge of Elizabeth Gurley Flynn.

No private organization is more indispensable, and none is more self-righteous, than the ACLU. In February, 1940, it decided to bar all Fascists, Communists and anyone else who sympathized with antidemocratic organizations from holding office or serving on any of its committees. Liberal journals applauded this as a brave, sensible decision. There was, as everyone knew, only one acknowledged Communist in the ACLU hierarchy —Elizabeth Gurley Flynn, one of its founders. She had been reelected to the board in 1939, having become, and having announced that she had become, a member of the Communist Party. No one had objected then.

How the climate had changed! The chairman of the board of directors for twenty years, Dr. Harry F. Ward, resigned in outrage and disgust at the resolution of February, 1940. And even though Mrs. Flynn's son had recently died, the board pressed ahead with its sacrificial ritual. Her expulsion was achieved principally by using an old acquaintance, guilt by association. No one claimed that Mrs. Flynn was an insincere champion of civil liberties. Four of the members of the board hearing the charges against her and voting on them were the people who had brought them. The moving spirit from first to last was the most famous civil libertarian of the age, Roger Baldwin. The chairman of the hearing, who concluded by casting the tie-breaking vote for expulsion, was the Reverend Mr. John Haynes Holmes; he had already announced that as "a symbol of difficulties" Mrs. Flynn should be booted out. And she was. The national committee ratified the act by a margin of two to one, with such vocal friends of decency, democracy and tolerance as A. J. Muste, Robert Sherwood, Harry Elmer Barnes, Oswald Garrison Villard and Van Wyck Brooks approving. From start to finish it was the kind of hearing that the ACLU had denounced elsewhere. Even the Dies Committee had mounted nothing of this kind. These techniques would appear again, in a more public forum, almost exactly a decade later, presided over by a Senator from Wisconsin. No doubt these devoted anti-Fascists, unable to directly savage either Hitler or Stalin in this perilous hour, believed they had fought the good fight. They had persecuted a helpless and probably foolish old woman.

All through 1940 the country's two leading liberal journals, the *Nation* and *New Republic*, grew increasingly bellicose. No one clamored more stridently for overwhelming military force; no conservative sang louder praises of strength over weakness. In September the *New Republic* reluctantly, and "with heavy hearts," approved the Selective Service Act. Yet one month later when the bill went into effect, it adopted a ferociously off-with-their-heads attitude toward the thirty-six young men who had openly refused to register (mostly theological students who were exempt from the draft but opposed to the principle of conscription; they received prison sentences of a year and more). "We do not see how any court can fail to convict," it thundered, "a person who violates the law by deliberately refusing to register." This was not the same as refusing to fight. No; this was an evil far surpassing cowardice: "Democracy, especially when it is endangered by authoritarian aggression, cannot countenance such an extreme challenge to its sovereignty."

During these same excited months the high priest of aggressive liberalism Lewis Mumford produced *Faith for Living,* a sequel to his earlier *Men Must Act.* Liberals generally hailed Mumford's virile, aggressive liberalism. To them this was an age of moral and spiritual sickness, and Mumford offered a number of specifics: a National Board of Censorship, which would ban all speech or literature it considered pro-Fascist; plays which "spread defilement" (*Tobacco Road*?) would be banned; the Nazi and Communist parties would be outlawed; compulsory labor service would be required for all children; there would be no labor unions; business would be minutely regulated by government; private lives would be made spartan and "frivolous occupations" would be eliminated—all of which would be capped by a massive military establishment that no enemy would ever dare provoke.

This was a time when the country's most revered man of letters, Van Wyck Brooks, was bitterly upbraiding the literary modernists (of which he had himself been one) as "rattlesnakes," and Archibald MacLeish, poet and Librarian of Congress, was blaming the moral failings of the young on the writers of post-Great War disillusionment, such as Hemingway and Fitzgerald.

Certainly there had not yet occurred anything to match the hysterical excesses of 1917–1918. There had been nowhere near the number of physical assaults. The 200,000-man army of domestic spies—"Voluntary

Coadjutors"—maintained by the Department of Justice had not been revived. But the country was not yet even in the war and was already manifesting all the symptoms of war hysteria, and on a far from negligible scale. Though it would be a great mercy if nothing more than this emerged, no one could take much comfort from the factors which had so far limited expressions of hysteria. They were made of feeble stuff indeed.

For one thing, it was the United States that was provoking Germany. In the First World War, German sabotage and intrigue against American attempts to aid the Allies had put a severe strain on the nation's temper; a strain that made the declaration of war after Germany's resumption of unrestricted submarine warfare in 1917 almost a relief. In this war however it was the United States that was taking increasingly belligerent steps and Germany which was trying hard to avoid a *casus belli*. Moreover there were very few openly pro-German sympathizers against whom anti-German sentiment could be vented. And there was no strong antiwar group on the left, except for the tattered remnants of Depression Communism, small in number and influentially negligible. Most of the antiwar opposition in 1914–1918 had come from the left, especially from the Socialists. Violence against antiwar liberals and leftists had been the focal point of earlier wartime persecution and hysteria. Now it was the liberals and leftists who were generally the most bellicose for war.

It should have also been recalled that the worst excesses of the Great War came in 1918, not in 1914. If anything, compared with 1914–1915, there was nothing here for sensible people to be proud of.

But this was the Holy War against Fascism. The ardor aroused by the Spanish Civil War was gone, yet all across the liberal and non-Communist left there was eagerness to smash Fascism once and for all. They would show no more regard for those who opposed them now than they had been shown more than twenty years before. After all, they *knew* their cause was just.

Another indication of how strong was the current sway of superstition was the growing harshness of popular attitudes and government policy toward the victims of foreign persecution. To the dangers and humiliations European refugees suffered, America made its own contribution—a firmly closed door. Overwhelmingly, people wanted to keep the refugees out. Government made policy accordingly. And though it may seem odd at first to include immigration policy in a chapter on civil liberties, I am using the refugees here much as miners use canaries—to detect poisons in the atmosphere.

Roughly two-thirds of the nation was opposed to letting European refugees in. Even Roosevelt's suggestion in the summer of 1938 that unused immigration quotas be assigned to refugees had been opposed by most people. Nor did public opinion relent when the persecution worsened. After the terrible Night of Crystal, which saw tens of thousands of Jews beaten and murdered in the streets of Germany's major cities while their homes, synagogues and businesses were looted and destroyed; when the glittering shards of broken glass so covered the streets to make *Kristallnacht* a synonym for terror; when the survivors were rendered homeless and destitute, and thousands were taken to concentration camps; when it was suggested that the United States provide a haven for 10,000 of the homeless children; even then, more than two out of three Americans said no. Britain took 9,000 of them; the United States a token 240. It was to Roosevelt's personal credit, not his countrymen's, that he then used his executive powers to permit more than 15,000 refugees already here on visitors' visas to remain permanently rather than go back to persecution and worse. Still, the generally exclusionary policy remained in force. As a consequence, in only one year (1939) of the twelve-year Reich was the combined German-Austrian immigration quota filled. For the period overall, the figure was 35.8 percent.

The plight of the refugees, who were usually Jewish, was caught up in one of those incidents which at the time, and even more in retrospect, stand as both example and symbol. In the spring of 1939 a merchantman called the *St. Louis* set out from Hamburg on a sadder odyssey than any novelist could dream of. Her cabins were crammed with 907 German Jews, sailing to Cuba. More than 700 of them held places on the U.S. immigration quota for dates ranging from three months to three years away. But every one of them held a Cuban entry visa. There they would stay until America let them in.

But in Havana it transpired that the agent who had sold them their visas was not who he said he was, or they had not paid enough, or they had dealt with the out faction in Cuban politics. It all amounted to the same thing—the visas were void. They must leave Havana immediately. The *St. Louis* weighed anchor and sailed on from port to port, frantically radioing the United States, begging that her passengers be allowed to land. After all, for most of these people it was simply a question of speeding up something already tacitly agreed to—their eventual entry into the United States. The alternative, if they were forced to return to Germany, was Dachau, or Belsen, or Sachsenhausen, or some other such place. To all the pleas federal officials, firmly supported by public opinion, were unshakably deaf and blind. Low on food and fuel, her passengers in their despair turning suicidal, the *St. Louis* sailed back across the Atlantic, her cargo apparently doomed. Then, at the last moment, as the *St. Louis* sailed into the Channel, the governments of Britain, France, Belgium and the Netherlands agreed to take most, but not all, of the refugees in. The rest (no one knows exactly how many there were) sailed into Hamburg, to torture and death.

The American policy seemed pointlessly harsh. In the decade of the 1930's the difference between emigration and immigration had added to the population a total of 19,398 persons—hardly a flood tide of foreigners. Of 1939's entire immigration quota less than 40 percent was filled. Embarrassed, *Time* confessed in March, 1940: "The American people have so far shown no inclination to do anything for the world's refugees except read about them." And once the country was worrying itself frantic with fears of fifth columnists, spies and saboteurs, there was certainly little prospect that any of the barriers to immigration would be lowered. It would be remarkable, in fact, if they were not raised even higher.

Liberals pointed to the great benefits that might accrue to a less ruthless policy. Since 1933 European scholars, artists and scientists had been flocking to the United States. Even countries not yet overrun, especially England, were contributing to what must by any standard be considered an epochal enrichment of American cultural and intellectual life. The great international literary organization (or so it was then) PEN (for Poets, Essayists, Novelists) was forced from its various European homes and came to America. Several committees were hard at work by 1941 trying to bring as much of Europe's living genius to America as was possible, but they had to do so in the face of a wrong-headed policy.

Hundreds of thousands of refugees were by now clamoring for entry, a privilege extended only to 4,000 each month. And in June, 1941, this figure was cut even further when it was decreed that no one with close relatives in Germany could henceforth enter the United States.

The State Department was asking for a refugee screening committee composed of representatives from the Departments of Justice, Army and Navy. Existing immigration laws barred all save "free white persons and persons of African descent" (to maintain the racial mix as of 1920). Such a committee was capable of weaving a net so fine almost no one would be able to wriggle through.

There was, however, one important exception to this policy built on good old-fashioned superstition, and that was the case of British children. No sooner had France fallen than Harold Ickes, himself a former social worker, was promoting an organization called Save Europe's Children. Its aim was to bring British children to the United States and Canada, far from German planes and pilots. But existing immigration laws stood in the way. People who wanted to shelter British children were required to endure all the rigors of standard immigration procedures: They had to guarantee that the child would be cared for, educated and would never become a public charge; exhaustive inquiries into religion, income, education and family background had to be dealt with; an impressive array of personal references had to be furnished; credit had to be checked; and bank statements, insurance policies and other testaments to one's worth had to be produced.

There were, nonetheless, more than 5,000,000 American families willing to take in a British child (preferably "a blonde English girl, about six years old"). On the other side of the Atlantic were hundreds of thousands of English parents willing to send their children to the United States and Canada, believing all the while that they might never see them again. Yet unless the immigration laws were modified, very few children could leave even if respectable middle-class Americans successfully cleared all the hurdles. People angrily protested these restrictions. One journal grumbled bitterly in July, 1940, "If Britain is defeated during the next few weeks, quite possibly when our grandchildren ask 'What did the United States do during the Hitler War?' the answer will be '[we] helped arrange to have as many children as possible bombed to death.' " Under mounting popular demands government yielded, and Congress passed a Mercy Ships bill which authorized unlimited entry to evacuated British children.

But this generous step could amount to little more than a gesture unless the Germans provided safe conduct for the Mercy Ships. Unfortunately the Germans had few scruples about sinking ships bearing children to safety, and a number of these, such as the *City of Benares*, sunk in September, 1940, took hundreds of children to the bottom of the Atlantic. Britain's children remained at home for the most part, in no greater peril on land than they would have been placed in at sea. The American people persevered, however, by sponsoring hostelries in the English countryside to which children might be evacuated from the cities, which were now more and more targets for German air attacks.

Those refugees who did manage to reach America's shores had, often at an advanced age, to begin life anew. In the early and middle 1930's they had tended to be relatively young, skilled, mobile and adaptable. By 1939 the refugees were older; they were usually those who had left only as a last resort, when the terror was close enough to force them to put even their tired bodies on the road into exile. Often only a single member of a family would be able to escape to the United States and would try from this side of the Atlantic to save the rest. Situation Wanted in October, 1939: "Austrian agriculturalist, 43, anxious to bring wife and children from Germany, seeks position."

As we have seen, the nation's 4,500,000 aliens had been made scapegoats to the crisis mood which gripped the country in 1940. For the first time, they were set off by law and policy from the rest of the nation and became a federal police problem. The individual states had followed suit by making it even more difficult for aliens to compete with citizens for jobs. The extreme was reached in Illinois. There the state legislature barred refugees from all but the poorest-paying, hardest, dirtiest jobs; even low-status positions such as barbering, chiropody, hairdressing and horseshoeing were forbidden them. And even when defense production began to revive the economy, both labor and management did their best to keep aliens out of the job market.

The recent aliens—the refugees, that is—were particularly resented because the idea had somehow taken hold that they resisted assimilation into American society, yet if that was true of anyone, it was true of the long-established aliens who were still not citizens. Anyway, the myth was what people believed. There was also a general conviction that New York was foundering under a tidal wave of refugees. But, in truth, they never amounted to as much as 1 percent of the city's total population. Refugee organizations worked diligently to distribute the newcomers as widely as they could. They were not without success. But it was not remarkable that people who had lived in the great cities of Europe would gravitate as if by nature to the great cities of the United States, particularly New York, Chicago, Los Angeles and San Francisco.

Yet the resentments and the rumors persisted. Part of the problem was that refugee intellectuals crammed into New York City—a place whose artistic and intellectual life was already organized around tight little intellectual universes, each with its own galaxy of stars, moons and planets. A few hundred or a few thousand newcomers pressing upon this milieu quickly made their presence felt and were, no matter how deferential, highly visible. There was much irritation. But some established figures resolved to make the best of it and suggested that the city was "acquiring the literary atmosphere of Paris in the 1920's."

There was also a blossoming of avant-garde refugee magazines. Most of them were very modest, very retrospective. But one of them was very ambitious: *Dissent*, founded by Klaus Mann (son of Thomas Mann). Its avowed aim was to become "One of the greatest literary publications the world has ever known." And to that end it offered itself as a common ground whereon émigré intellectuals and American liberals could meet and exchange ideas. Like all such ventures, it soon foundered on the seas of assimilation.

One might modify an ancient remark to say that whom the gods would make vicious they first make blind. Blindness it must have been; the liberal elements which are normally the fiercest champions of individual liberties were, by 1941, lashing out angrily, intemperately, and the only thing that kept them from the worst excesses was the fact that they did not command the governmental instruments of force. It is also true that unlike some other elements—the KKK, the American Legion—liberals tend to shrink from dirtying their own hands. But many freely used the weapon they knew best—the word—to promote intolerance, bigotry, superstition and panic.

One eminent professor of government at Harvard, Carl Joachim Friedrich, was preaching that American public opinion was the fulcrum on which the outcome of the war was balanced, that the Nazis had grasped that fact, and that they were now working twenty-four hours every day to break American morale; their main weapon was propaganda. Anything which sounded like Nazi propaganda must be suppressed. And he suggested neighborhood pro-democracy get-togethers; in other words, people should monitor the political views of their neighbors.

Another equally distinguished professor and a noted student of international politics, Edward Meade Earle of Princeton, promoted fifth column hysteria. The first wave of German troops would arrive, he said, "disguised as tourists or, typical of Nazi cynicism, even as refugees." This advance guard would foment dissension, commit sabotage and encourage the gullible to engage in treason. All of which would "soften us up" for conventional attack.

The ever-vigilant Dorothy Thompson, famous for her defense of the Supreme Court in 1937, thought that the time had come to nullify the Bill of Rights in order to save it. Miss Thompson had been a reporter in Germany during the 1920's. She now told a meeting of 1,200 women in Manhattan that freedoms of speech and assembly had doomed the Weimar Republic. Worse, "They were the very instruments by which the Nazis came to power." The lesson was plain: Such rights should be allowed only to the friends of democracy. The audience, meeting ostensibly to honor the Bill of Rights, applauded vigorously.

The *New Republic* was meantime clamoring noisily for an investigation of America First, because it was "waging war against the whole American democratic heritage." They demanded strict curbs on Congressional franking privileges; isolationist Congressmen had used the free mailing privilege to pour "a stream of anti-democratic propaganda into the homes of millions of Americans." They demanded "definite action on Lindbergh's speeches by the National Association of Broadcasters"—that is, Lindbergh should not be allowed on radio. Finally, they demanded that the Pope openly declare his personal opinion of Fascism.

Civil liberties had for years been the touchstone of leftist and liberal sentiment. Yet even the Social Democrat *New Leader* was demanding suppression of Communists and anybody else who was, in its judgment, "Fifth Column." Attacks on defenders of America First in New York City were becoming frequent and bloody. If many liberals had had their way, it would have been impossible for isolationists to speak anywhere. To them, America First was not simply an organization with a position of its own and a right to express it, but the beginning of "a powerful Fascist movement." When one of the *New Republic*'s editors, John T. Flynn, declined to abandon the isolationism that his fellow editors had long defended (and only recently renounced), Flynn was booted out. The other editors conceded their fallibility, but "when the existence of the country is at stake, it is better to be safe than sorry." Yet this is surely the formula of tyrants great and small, from the Dies Committee to the KKK and, it is not stretching the point too far, the Gestapo.

By refusing to strike sufficiently virile anti-Fascist postures, Edmund Wilson was frozen out of the leading liberal magazines and moved over to the less ideologically inclined *New Yorker*. One disgruntled longtime subscriber to the *Nation* wrote in that he had read it faithfully "because I think it part of wisdom to know what the enemies of our nation are publishing and writing, but lately your 'liberal weekly' has got so extremely conservative that I feel sure I shall cancel my subscription before long." And a noted liberal author, McCallister Coleman, simply despaired. He severed his connection with the *Nation* because it was "throwing overboard in hysterical panic the old cargo of tolerance, integrity and passion for freedom."

I mention such things, let me add, not to be censorious but because it was the liberal journals and the sadly tarnished ACLU which insisted then —and they do to this day—that there was no general crisis in civil liberties during the war. To them, whatever abuses occurred were anomalous and usually minor. As we shall see, however, the worst was yet to come and the road to it well paved.

These were boom times for the FBI. In two years its appropriation had shot up from $6,000,000 to $16,000,000. Every worker in defense industries had been fingerprinted. Hoover publicly gloated over his massive card indexes on subversives and, despite a 1934 law forbidding it, made no secret of the fact that telephones were being tapped. As recently as February, 1940, Hoover had personally opposed wiretapping as "archaic and inefficient" and "a definite handicap or barrier to the development of ethical, scientific and sound investigative techniques." But here was a crisis to be exploited. Thus, when a wiretap bill came up in Congress in the early summer of 1941, Roosevelt supported it in principle, Attorney General Robert Jackson recommended it, and Hoover insisted that he could not do his job properly without it. The night before the vote was taken Hoover helpfully announced the arrest of twenty-nine German spies.

The wiretap bill failed anyway; the House still mustered enough New Deal liberals and old Progressives to turn it back by a vote of 154 to 146. But the FBI continued to tap telephones. And when a new Attorney General, Francis Biddle, was appointed, he acknowledged that wiretap evidence was null and void in court. But he countenanced it when employed in cases of espionage, sabotage, kidnapping and extortion. He then proceeded to authorize its use in the seemingly endless effort to deport Harry Bridges. Few people paused to wonder which one of Biddle's four categories Bridges fell into. In short, Congress and the courts could be, and were, openly flouted when they refused to join in the sport of defending civil liberties by denying them to the cranky, the unpopular and the pathetic.

Biddle was himself much admired by civil libertarians. He was hailed as a true friend of civil liberties because he had refused to truckle to the Dies Committee. Liberal journalists never tired of writing mistily how much Biddle loved the Bill of Rights. But there were some items that a critical mind might have pondered. The wiretap business was one. Harry Bridges was another. Bridges had eluded earlier attempts to deport him as a secret Communist. Biddle, nothing daunted, began yet another campaign for Bridges' deportation. The Justice Department also devoted much of its energies in the latter half of 1941 to a massive "Americanization" program for aliens as part of its drive on fifth columnists. Millions of dollars were spent on having Biddle's agents teach a million aliens over the age of fourteen how they should love the United States.

Federal officials were currently pressing ahead with prosecutions of conscientious objectors. More than 200 convictions were secured during the first year of Selective Service. Hundreds more CO's were awaiting trial. Sentences commonly were for as much as five years. Something must be done with objectors, of course. But there was something vindictive about a policy which, unlike the practice in other democracies, refused to permit complete exemption for genuine objectors and pacifists.

Imprisonment for holding unpopular opinions had been made law. Those states which already had similar laws were using them. Oklahoma sent six persons to jail in the summer of 1941 under its "criminal syndicalist" statute. Their sentences were for ten years. The evidence against them—a stack of pamphlets which they admitted having read. No act or intent to act was even charged. Flushed with this success Oklahoma indicted another twelve persons on the same charges. In Minneapolis eighteen self-confessed Trotskyites were convicted of "seditious conspiracy" in the country's first peacetime sedition case since 1789. Again, no overt acts. But their opinions and the literature they read were ruled seditious. They received sentences of up to fifteen years in federal prison.

Communists, of course, were suspect even after the attack on the Soviet Union. Before June 22, 1941, anti-Communist purges were flourishing all across the left. Philip Murray, Lewis' successor as president of the CIO, responded to a strike at North American Aviation by demanding that all Communists be purged from CIO locals. In New York the state legislature ousted sixty-four professors from Brooklyn, City and Hunter colleges, because they had been denounced as Communists. Not one of them was ever shown to have breathed so much as a syllable about Communism to his students. But criminal indictments were secured, and all were expelled from their jobs by the city's famously liberal Board of Higher Education. The secondary schools had similar purges. The entire New York and

Philadelphia locals of the American Federation of Teachers were cast out for "having come under Communist influence."

To the Communists the attack on the Soviet Union changed everything; for most Americans it changed very little. Consequently, when the Communists tried now to reenter the left side of American politics, they were rebuffed just as vigorously as they had been expelled in the wake of the Nazi-Soviet Pact. Efforts to revive a new United Front failed utterly. Liberal interventionists would press for a second front and all aid to Russia, but they would never again embrace domestic Communists as true friends in a common struggle. Instead, they applauded when in the fall of 1941 the leftist Newspaper Guild purged its "clique of Stalinists and fellow travellers who hung securely on the Communist Party line."

For their own part liberals were meanwhile beginning to discover that the climate which they had so enthusiastically helped bring about was being turned on them. The Alien Registration Act barred from federal employment anyone who was or had ever been a member of the Communist Party. To make that provision effective, a background investigation had to be made of every applicant for a government job. And here was a stick for Dies to use on the liberals now flocking into Washington to take their rightful places in the front ranks of the Holy War on Fascism. New Dealers already in government were investigated, pestered and basely smeared as Communists or fellow travelers. After all, Communists in government were a rarity, but liberals were a commonplace. And Dies, Hoover and others of their kind had never been noted for an ability to discriminate between the two.

VIII

Knowledge Is Power

TOO much of the Depression's cost had been borne by America's children. The public schools had traditionally been the prerogative of local authorities. Before the Depression was very old, it became a commonplace for hard-pressed local governments to pass the burden of failing revenues onto the schools. Consequently, school expenditures per pupil were lower throughout the New Deal than they had been in 1930, as much as 30 percent lower. And the quality of public school teaching was, at best, undistinguished. On an average salary of $1,800 a year a big-city schoolteacher might be able to maintain herself in genteel poverty; a rural schoolteacher earning half that amount did without the gentility. Low salaries meant low educational requirements or none at all. Local government could not meet its obligations to the children, nor could poor families. A 1940 White House Conference on Children counted the cost: of 36,000,000 children under the age of sixteen, 22,000,000 were going without the food they needed, living in substandard housing and denied a proper education; 8,000,000 were in families on relief; and more than 1,000,000 had absolutely no schooling at all.

Besides chaotic finances and poor teachers, the schools were in the throes of pedagogical turmoil. Elementary and secondary schools were torn in two directions at once: On one hand, they were becoming less restrictive; on the other, they were becoming more restrictive. The middle ground had virtually disappeared. Conscription in 1917–1918 had introduced intelligence testing of the masses. In the years following the war most American pedagogues proceeded to fall head over heels for quantification: Credits, units, points, standard tests, standard scores swept through the nation's schools. Choice was restricted and curiosity severely circumscribed; so many units of this and so many points for that henceforth added up to graduation. It was literally education by the numbers.

Yet while education was becoming more authoritarian in most school districts, it was becoming less so in others. Under the aegis of progressive education a strong challenge had been mounted to reverse the mainstream of American education. The organizational impetus was provided by a Progressive Education Association, which explicitly held itself out as an alternative to the much larger, older, more prestigious National Education Association.

Progressive education had its roots in the Progressive political movements at the turn of the century. But since the Great War it had drifted away from the political Progressives, and it had lost its provincial roots. In the hands of New York intelligentsia, professional pedagogues and devotees of scientific fact gathering, progressive education had become a byword for testing and tabulating—little more than a crude venture into social engineering; more scientism than science. And with the onset of the Depression political radicals had made a strong bid to make progressive education their own, casting it into even further disrepute. By 1932 its future looked extremely bleak, and membership in the PEA, never very large, shrank to 5,000 members. Progressive education had offered itself as an alternative and, so far as anyone could tell, had failed.

No one doubted that existing elementary schools were abysmal; the secondary schools were even worse. Teachers and administrators generally neither knew their students nor cared what happened to them. Curricula bore only a chance relationship to the interests and needs of young people; many courses were hopelessly irrelevant to anything, including scholarship. Hundreds of thousands of youngsters were graduated each year incapable of reading or writing adequately for the ordinary needs of adult life. There was no continuity between subjects from one year to the next. All that the diploma attested to was the accumulation of a requisite number of units and points. And schools were run so autocratically that they frequently resembled nothing quite so much as penitentiaries for child prisoners. There was also an unrealistic relationship between secondary schools and colleges. Students were normally required to complete a college-oriented curriculum, whether they were going to college or not—and 85 percent were not. They must therefore either be neglected or coerced.

This was the background against which progressive education, splinter that it was, had secured the support of the very staid American Historical Association and the very rich Carnegie Corporation to prove its boast that it had a better way.

Starting in 1932, the progressives had launched an experiment scheduled to come to fruition in 1940. It was designed to conform to the cardinal tenets of their faith. The progressives believed that education should overcome the traditional gap between school and society; education, in their view, should teach youngsters how to act collectively and democratically. It should also be tailored to individual needs, interests and abilities. By 1939 they held the initiative in secondary education.

More than 100 colleges and 30 secondary schools took part in the experiment begun in 1932. The secondary schools ranged from expensive, private schools in New England to schools deep in New York's ghettos and slums. They hewed to no overall plan; each school drew up its own program. But all were innovative, and some were more innovative than others.

They agreed on one point, however; they wanted to teach children how to be active citizens of a democratic society.

Their students were confronted with traditional subjects, but core curricula were developed, around which each student's education could be tailored to fit his or her needs and interests. Teaching methods eschewed autocracy, and student interest in class work was actively solicited. Grades were minimized, and detailed reports of progress compiled. Gifted students who had been held back in traditional programs were allowed to forge ahead. The less gifted were allowed to find their own levels and were offered courses which matched their abilities without being made to feel stupid or useless.

Two thousand graduates of the thirty high schools in the experiment had gone on to college in 1936. This first class was graduated from college in 1940; five other classes were to follow them. The criterion of success—or failure—was the traditional criterion employed by non- and antiprogressives: college performance. In other words, they set out to prove that even by their critics' standards progressive education was superior.

The colleges ranged in distinction from Oklahoma A & M to the University of Chicago, the University of Michigan, Smith, Wellesley, Amherst, Harvard and MIT. Each student from a progressive school was matched with another student of similar educational, social, religious and economic background who had graduated from a nonprogressive school. They were also matched by standard test scores of intelligence. But the students from progressive schools were not required, in all but a few cases, to meet the usual academic criteria for college admission.

When the results were released for the first class, in 1940, they surpassed even the most inflated expectations. In one of the most remarkable social experiments in American history the progressives had utterly defeated the traditional schools. Progressively educated students finished college with higher grades than their traditionally educated counterparts; they accumulated more academic honors; they were rated as showing more curiosity, more initiative, more sociability and more ambition; they expressed a greater interest in, and responsibility for, the welfare of their country and the rest of mankind; they played a larger role in student organizations; and even in nonacademic achievements, such as athletics, they were more impressive. Most significant perhaps was the fact that the graduates of the most thoroughly progressive high schools had the best records of all.

The college administrators who evaluated this performance conceded that the conventional high school curricula and the traditional college entrance criteria had been utterly defeated. The New York City Board of Education, which had run its own six-year experiment in progressive education in 10 percent of the city's schools thought the time ripe to announce that the entire city school system would henceforth take up progressive methodology and philosophy. Progressive educators stood, they were certain, at the dawn of a new day.

They were still ridiculed in the press. Their greatest champion, John Dewey, had been, like Marx and Jesus, cursed with more than a few fools for disciples. As Marx had at one point been driven by his followers to argue that he was not a Marxist, Dewey could have been excused for saying that he was not a progressive educator. But progressive education had, at long last, soberly, systematically and overwhelmingly established that it did indeed offer a sound alternative to traditional education.

There was one more hurdle to cross, however, and that a formidable one. Progressive education was not merely unpopular, but widely despised. The general run of opinion rarely went much beyond the titles of two magazine articles that appeared during 1940: One was called "Lollipops vs. Learning" and the other, "Treason in the Textbooks." In short, progressive education was either rubbish or subversive, or both. It would take years to overcome such hostility. With so much now in flux who could say that progressive education would be given enough time?

Schools and colleges were generally in turmoil over how to cope with a world whose certainties were going up in flames. No Federal agency or any great convocation of pedagogues provided guidance. Each school district and each college was left to find its own way. Staggering through 1940 and 1941, most were content to cast out subversives and to hymn the praises of democracy.

The American Federation of Teachers was meanwhile expelling suspect locals. Individuals did what they could, such as the professor at City College of New York who denounced his colleagues as Communists and obligingly produced a list of fifty names. Scores of state and city school boards followed the trail which New York authorities had blazed, bringing indictments against suspected Communist teachers. The National Association of Manufacturers pitched in by underwriting a massive study of textbooks in order to excise subversive passages. Chicago's superintendent of schools in 1940 had teachers and principals combing textbooks and children's classics such as *Grimm's Fairy Tales, Robinson Crusoe,* and *The Swiss Family Robinson* for evidences of subversion by long-dead fifth columnists.

Among living authors of textbooks the principal target was Harold Ordway Rugg, of Columbia. Rugg's textbooks had been in use since 1930. By and large they had gone unremarked, but they were now discovered to be dangerous. Rugg was accused of, among other things, presenting a distorted view of the United States by observing—and in the mildest of terms—that racism made this a land of less than truly equal opportunity. In small towns American Legionnaires occasionally managed to get

Rugg's textbooks publicly burned. When the National Education Association held its annual convention in July, 1941, it girded for battle by establishing a sixty-member committee for the defense of American education against its critics. This committee would attend to the public relations of "the education industry"; it would expose subversive teachings; it would investigate all criticism of the schools, textbooks, curricula and teachers to determine if the source of the criticism was the dreaded fifth column; and it would lay bare the financial sources of all organizations which criticized the schools. A lady who ran for president of the NEA won on a two-point platform that schoolchildren should be taught "to hate tyranny" and "to love the U.S.A." But while most teachers and school districts favored both those things, how would students respond?

High school students were reported to be far from frivolous; they were, on the contrary, said to be "furiously concerned with preserving Democracy." And the question the schools ("now fluttering with programs for teaching Democracy") faced was this: "Are they convincing U.S. youth that Democracy is worth defending?"

Each school district searched its own soul for the answer. Hundreds of programs were attempted, in the hopes of hitting upon the right one. One high school developed a thoroughly democratic student government, or so it appeared. Students ran assemblies, hall traffic, the library and the cafeteria. The core of this miniature democracy was a score of student clubs, each with sharply defined responsibilities. Membership in the clubs was voluntary, of course; but even admiring visitors were impressed with the overwhelming pressure, bordering on coercion, that was brought on students to join a club, *any* club.

Another high school, this one on Long Island, celebrated Bill of Rights Week by going totalitarian for a day. The principal became dictator. He and his faculty sported distinctive armbands and had a great time Heiling one another. In every classroom two students were told to be secret police agents; they had a brief taste of the joys of spying on their fellow students, making arbitrary arrests and breaking up all groups of two or more students. The luckiest were the storm troopers; they cracked down on the recalcitrant and subversive, putting them to work at hard labor, and in slack moments occupied themselves by making sure that everyone Heiled the dictator and his cronies. Alas, at the end of the day it all came to an end; the dictator resigned, his one-man state crumbled. He gave it all up because he had come to appreciate the democratic way of power, especially as practiced in the United States of America, "the finest land in the world."

From the sound and the fury of these days one might have thought that the high schools were seething with radicalism. But when an exhaustive opinion survey was conducted in the Rochester, New York, high schools in the fall of 1940, it developed that 99.22 percent of the city's high school students believed that in the entire world America had the best form of government. At about the same time a check on the sentiments of very young children was conducted by the Child Welfare Research Station at the University of Iowa. Children were placed in three different milieux, or "social climates"—democratic, autocratic and laissez-faire. Under the first, activities were planned collectively and decisions made by majority vote. Under the second, activities were set by one child alone. Under the third, there was no planning, and the brightest children were kept aloof from the rest. Finding: Children liked democracy best.

Democracy had already taken over in the textbooks. In colonial days school readers had been pious and God-fearing; during the heady days of nineteenth-century laissez-faire industrialism they glorified industry and thrift; now Democracy Readers held sway through the first six grades, and comparable texts were available for older students who could already read. Here, in outline, is a sample story: A poor and struggling young journalist falls heir to his dead uncle's estate. This comprises a country house, $25,000 in cash and a prospering newspaper—all of which are located in an unnamed European dictatorship. At first the young man is elated. But when he starts to think about the significance of this inheritance he begins to doubt that it is worth very much after all. At story's end he decides to remain in the United States, poor and unknown, but in a country with a free press. On such fare did millions of youngsters learn to read.

These were hard times for many colleges and universities. Falling interest rates during the Depression had hit the private colleges and universities hard. And they had been unable to offset the loss of endowment income by attracting more students and raising tuition; in fact, enrollments were dropping. From elementary grades through high school, enrollments were lower in 1939 than they had been a decade before. And aggravated by a falling birthrate, the drop in enrollments would probably force the closure of scores of financially weak colleges once the full impact hit them some time in the early 1940's. The public institutions were equally hard pressed. State legislatures became niggardly as tax revenues fell. During the 1920's college enrollments—public and private—had more than doubled. In the thirties they had barely kept pace with the increase in population growth. Colleges and universities everywhere were forced to pare their budgets, lay off professors, stop promotions.

The colleges would gladly have accepted federal aid, but there was little to be had. Ironically, the strongest opposition to government assistance came from the students, not the professors. The social sciences had come into their own during the 1930's when "Undergraduates turned in unparalleled numbers to courses in social and economic subjects . . . [and] more and more the government turned to the universities for expert advice." Yet though students would take part-time jobs in the chemistry lab washing retorts and test tubes for a few dollars each week from the National Youth Authority, they feared far more than did their professors any massive government presence on campus.

If government could not or would not bail out the colleges, the only other possible source of large sums of money was big business. But the relations between the academy and the marketplace had long been strained. The Depression had not made them any easier. Yet attempts at a rapprochement were still broached from time to time. One such effort made in 1939 brought academics and business executives together at a Congress on Education and Democracy convened at Columbia University. It was not a success. One speaker denounced the direct election of Senators; another set out to prove that economic equality would destroy democratic government. The large shadow which business had cast over higher education in 1929 was much diminished ten years later.

Like the elementary and secondary schools, the colleges and universities were also torn by worries other than a shortage of money and a gloomy future. The entire purpose and methods of higher education were in serious doubt, giving rise to many angry quarrels. Behind the turbulence there was no mere psychological torment but a fundamental shift in power. Humane studies had dominated university education for centuries, ever since the Renaissance had brought the revival of higher secular learning. College courses and university research reflected this fact. The humanists monopolized the best posts in administration and teaching. But starting in the latter half of the nineteenth century, the scientists had begun to encroach upon the traditional near monopoly of the humanists. By the time the Second World War began the scientists were pressing hard for equality.

It was really an old, old fight; its roots went deep in Western civilization, and the proper place of science was a problem that all society had to wrestle with. But nowhere was the clash noisier or more hotly fought than on the campus. On its outcome rested the future thrust of higher education —plus such immediate incentives as money, power and prestige. Complicating things even more was the appearance in the middle ground between the traditional territories of humanism and the clearly delimited terrain of modern science of a plethora of exotic growths, collectively (and with disparate merits) calling themselves social science and claiming parity with the other two. In this garden of exotica the strangest hybrids were able to bloom. Some of the social sciences had managed to win a grudging measure of respectability by 1940. In later years they would prosper. But science would prosper more than any of them.

Almost unnoticed beneath the hurly-burly of the war, the draft and the boom, the country was already organizing its scientific resources for war. The government began to register everyone it could find who had advanced training or experience in science. By the spring of 1941 more than half a million scientists of greater or lesser note had been enrolled. This national roster of scientific and specialized personnel was inspired by Britain's response to its own foolish policy in World War I of sending off highly trained men to serve, and often die, in the trenches of the western front. Too late the British realized that many of these men could have served their country more usefully than by dying for it. When this war began, the British had set up a roster of scientists to preclude any repetition of that earlier, costly mistake.

The United States also had reason to be chagrined over its casual approach to science in the First World War, which was typified by the Army's staunch resistance to radio. After trying everything else—telephones, telegraphs, semaphores, carrier pigeons—one officer at an observation post under heavy bombardment in 1918 was reported to have radioed his headquarters: "Situation urgent. Am completely without communications."

Organization of science on a large-scale, systematic basis as an instrument of national defense had got under way in June, 1940, when Roosevelt had taken up a plan proposed by Dr. Vannevar Bush. Under Bush's prompting Roosevelt had created a twelve-man National Defense Research Committee. The NDRC would issue contracts to universities, independent scientific research institutes, industrial science departments; even individual scientists might hold contracts. The contracts were summaries, in effect, of the War and Navy Departments' scientific and technical needs. The contractor was someone who proposed to find a solution. Money was never a problem, but manpower always was. As a result, the U.S. roster of scientific personnel was far more extensive than the British, and involuntary. It was a polite but effective draft of the nation's scientists. And already, by mid-1941, the NDRC had one-fourth of them at work on defense projects. In subsequent months the NDRC exercised a virtual monopoly on scientific manpower.

The scientists would also work henceforth under the auspices of a larger entity, the Office of Scientific Research and Development. This too was patterned, loosely, after the emerging British organization of science for war. The OSRD would be responsible for all scientific work done in the United States whether related to defense or not. The NDRC would remain, headed by Harvard's president, James B. Conant, himself a former professor of chemistry. Its function now was to lay down policies for the much larger—indeed sprawling—OSRD.

Much of what was being done had of course to be done quietly, even though some of the current projects were beginning to dwarf any scientific effort ever before undertaken. Most awesome of all was a project to tap atomic power and harness it to military purposes. This was also thought to be the project least likely to succeed. It was a commonplace that the atom was a potentially great source of power; as it was sometimes expressed, a cup of water contained enough atomic energy to drive a liner across the Atlantic, if men but knew how to tap it. A Dane, Niels Bohr, and an Italian, Enrico Fermi, had reported to their American colleagues in February, 1939, that it was possible with current knowledge and techniques to produce a chain reaction in Uranium 235. No one had yet done it, but the race was clearly on. Not only did successful military applications of this power seem immeasurably remote, but there was little evident enthusiasm for it. Vannevar Bush, the head of the OSRD, at one time sighed, "I hope they never succeed in tapping atomic power, it will be a hell of a thing for civilization if they do."

The nasty little freshets of panic which buffeted the secondary schools also struck at colleges and universities. At first they aggravated an already-antagonistic division between students and professors.

Generally, and certainly at the more prestigious institutions, the faculty was pro-Allied, pro-intervention, and pro-national defense. Students tended to be either isolationist or pacifist. But very few were attracted to the overwhelmingly middle-aged America First. The ultraisolationist splinter group, the No Foreign Wars Committee, was more to their liking, yet it was still run by their elders. Some proceeded to create their own ultra-isolationist student organizations. During the Battle of Britain college students suggested that everyone should hope and pray for a Nazi victory—"It's the only way we'll stay out." At Ivy League colleges pickets were set up around the classes of overtly pro-Allied professors.

Graduation ceremonies in 1940 saw fervent pleas by professors and alumni for an end to the Third Reich, which were greeted by a stony silence or irreverent catcalls from the assembled undergraduates. They were convinced that their parents had made the ghastly mistake of being panicked into war in 1917 and were about to do it again. The president of Fordham University was pledging to turn his campus into an armed camp if that was necessary to save democracy, and Harvard's Conant was demanding compulsory military service. When classes resumed in September, 1940, the atmosphere was tense on almost every campus. But quiet prevailed, with one notable exception. At Berkeley more than 2,000 students noisily demonstrated against the impending Selective Service Act and were, every one of them, threatened with expulsion by President Robert Gordon Sproul if they dared repeat this performance once the act was signed into law.

An enormous gulf divided the two generations, the one pre-, the other post-Great War. They differed not simply over the war but over a broad range of judgments on life and society. On the campus, where the cleavage was deepest, it seemed absolutely irreparable. Here was cause for despair indeed. What kind of future did the nation have to look forward to if the educated young were to move into adulthood still thoroughly at odds with the rest of society?

Their professors, and adults generally, explicitly insisted on the importance of ethical considerations in the life of nations, especially on questions of war and peace. All this was derided by students as emotional and impractical. Young people struck sharp postures of toughness, avoiding moral issues or moral judgments; at least, they tried to. One observer concluded: "They distrust even words in general." Very few were overt pacifists—for that required moral convictions. Yet there went with their carefully cultivated amorality a strong moral smugness that moved several hundred students at Amherst to resolve that in case of invasion the East Coast should be immediately abandoned—it was too decadent to be worth fighting for.

Part of this was doubtless no more than the normal tension between generations. Part of it was the brittle cynicism of an unhappy time. Another part was no more than the current intellectual fashions of antistatism. And part of it was the result of the Depression, which had made material success or economic security more desirable than ever in living memory. Because it held out the possibility of security and postponed entry into a depressed job market, graduate education had become more attractive. The result was a glut of PhD's by the time the war began, leading one chastened young scholar to conclude gloomily that it had all been in vain: "I have educated myself out of a job."

The initial and chief response of the colleges and universities as they tried to come to grips with the war was to revise the curriculum. Through the summer of 1940 new, and presumably relevant, courses were created for the academic year that would begin in September. Chicago, for example, would offer a course in ballistics. Columbia established a program of courses on the effects war had on society, the family, government and the individual. Courses on the history of war, the psychology of war, the causes of war and so on *ad nauseam* were to be found in hundreds of college catalogues. The new courses, it was hoped, would add in some way to the sum total of national defense. And at Harvard much of the faculty had banded together in American Defense, Harvard Group in June, 1940, to offer their particular skills to the need of the hour. The government was lukewarm, but they pressed ahead anyway. Hundreds of other college faculties soon established similar units of their own.

Among those students who did support the program of national defense there was a demand for more ROTC units. There had been a Student Army Training Corps during the preparedness crisis of 1915–1916. But the Army's memories of that venture were so painful that it would not willingly try it again. There were already some seventy ROTC units in operation at land-grant colleges. (Under the Morrill Act of 1862 students at land-grant colleges were required to engage in military training.) From these the Army expected to secure an adequate supply of officers. It refused to expand the ROTC program. There was, however, a large and important government-financed program for teaching college students to fly, run by the Civil Aeronautics Board. Its aim was to provide the military services with a large pool of qualified pilots. The program had begun operation in the fall of 1939 and grew rapidly in scope.

Given the tense, crisis-ridden atmosphere that ran just below the surface of higher education in the 1930's, it would have been unreasonable to expect that colleges and universities would be unmoved by the uprush of hysteria. And the worst excesses tended to occur at the best universities. Columbia's president, Nicholas Murray Butler, began the 1940 academic year by calling a meeting of the entire faculty to inform it that the university would do everything it could to support national defense. "Before and above academic freedom of any sort comes university freedom, which is the right and obligation of the university itself to pursue its high ideals unhampered and unembarrassed by conduct on the part of any of its members which tends to damage its reputation. . . ." Butler had long run the university according to his own autocratic lights. Twenty-three years before, he had purged pacifists from the faculty. And this war, he said, was "a war between beasts and human beings. . . . Let there be no doubt where Columbia University stands in that war."

At the University of Michigan twelve students had already been expelled for activities the university's president, Alexander G. Ruthven, considered "detrimental to the work of other students or to the public interest." Four of them had helped organize a union among nonacademic employees. Two of them were young blacks who had sought service at an Ann Arbor restaurant under a federal civil rights law. Two white students who had accompanied them shared their fate. The other four students had either defended the Soviet attack on Finland or participated in antiwar rallies.

The noisiest purge of all occurred at Brooklyn College, long damned by the Dies Committee as a hotbed of Communist sympathies. In the wake of the uproar over Bertrand Russell's appointment to teach at CCNY the New York state legislature mounted a public investigation of Brooklyn College. Its liberal president, Harry Gideonse, welcomed the investigators with open arms. A professor of English made a dramatic public confession to being a member of the Communist Party and, more particularly, a member of a party cell composed entirely of Brooklyn College faculty members. In great detail he told of his discovery that Communist influences were rife in all the student organizations. He told too of how he had striven since to expunge subversive influences. The hearings produced dozens of firings and sudden resignations, riots in the corridors, pickets around

Gideonse's house, fake telegrams arriving at all hours of the night and hundreds of nuisance calls clogging both his home and business telephones. On Brooklyn's streets students were openly taunted as "Reds! Reds!" and pelted with overripe produce.

Most colleges actually had hardly any radicals to purge. It had not been so very many years since the British political scientist Harold Laski had been forced to leave Harvard because of his views, and he was a Fabian Socialist. Now, however, anyone of radical views was less welcome on campus than ever. Harvard, Dartmouth and Princeton all responded to the outbreak of war by refusing to let Earl Browder address their students. The Harvard Corporation banned him on the grounds that he was under indictment for using a false passport—although not only was Browder not yet convicted of that offense and presumably innocent of it, but he was never even tried for that. The University of Chicago's president, Robert M. Hutchins, who was probably the country's most outspoken champion of liberal education, also refused to let Browder speak. With a straight face, Hutchins announced: "If the university banned a red-headed man it would be an infringement of civil liberties. If it banned a murderer it would not. This case is somewhere in between."

Although it generally went unremarked at the time the federal government was rapidly becoming a major partner in secondary and higher education. During the Depression it had been obliged to render temporary assistance to some distressed school districts; without that assistance, many thousands of schools would have been forced to close; even with it, several thousand perished. And this aid was a mere stopgap; it held no promise of permanence. The National Youth Authority had provided loans and jobs for tens of thousands of high school and college students. Thousands of school buildings were put up by the WPA. But traditional principles and practices still obtained: local financing, local control. With the defense crisis, however, a silent revolution began. Its course would run for decades and smash the old system into pieces.

The change was manifested foremost in the colleges and universities, but soon penetrated to the secondary institutions. When colleges opened in the fall of 1941, more than 200 of them offered federally funded programs in engineering, science and defense industry management. These courses were usually of one semester and were offered to people already working as scientists, engineers and administrators. It was not basic education but an upgrading in vitally important skills. From such small beginnings grew a program which would send more than 1,500,000 people back to college to acquire technical training at federal expense.

University science departments by the fall of 1941 were taking up weapons research for the Office of Scientific Research and Development. Usually a department would specialize in a particular area: Princeton did ballistics, Penn State worked on hydraulic fuels, Cal Tech specialized in rockets, and so on. No one ever dreamed that this union of science, government and higher education would obtain for decades to come.

The War Department began to relent in its opposition to setting up more officer training programs in colleges and universities. The antimilitary, pro-isolationist mood of the first year of the war had almost entirely disappeared by the beginning of the new school year in September, 1941. A final note of defiance had been hurled by the Class Orator of the Harvard Class of '41, who laughed off President Conant's fears of invasion and concluded his oration, "Fellow classmates—let us avoid being sent overseas." That was in June. The mood at most Ivy League colleges in September was martial and interventionist. For the isolationism and pacifism of the campuses was rooted not in experience or reflection but in emotion and the normal tension between generations. As the menace of Nazism became immediate, pacifism and isolationism became both intellectually less justifiable and emotionally less appealing. The ardor and spirit of youth quickly responded to the challenge posed to its civilization once that challenge was clearly perceived.

But it was impossible for the War Department to provide enough ROTC units to satisfy current student demands. The colleges rushed to fill their needs by offering substitutes for the military training that had overnight become the envy of most college students. The typical curriculum was fattened with hastily contrived courses in military history, national security and geopolitics. Physical fitness programs scaled new heights of popularity, especially when they offered something like an assault course. Women's colleges were just as aflame with martial ardor. They did what they could. Wellesley, for example, offered courses in ambulance driving and automobile mechanics, while Russell Sage taught its students how to censor mail. With characteristic brashness the Graduate School of Business Administration at Harvard put itself on a war footing. It canceled the 1941 summer vacation, set up a Quartermaster ROTC program, created a course on naval supply and established a one-year program in management for defense production. Yet perhaps the most important program of all was still the one offered by the Civil Aeronautics Agency. Since its inception in September, 1939, it had quietly and effectively taught 60,000 college students how to fly by December, 1941.

While colleges that fall were worrying about military training or how to play a major role in the defense effort, they were also struggling with the combined effects of the draft and the boom. Across the country freshman enrollments were down by 10 percent; a comparable drop reduced the ranks of upperclassmen. College presidents agonized over the draft. Most of them had favored it, in principle. They merely wanted to be spared the burden that the draft represented in terms of falling enrollments and the loss of income attached thereto. Conant of Harvard and Butler of Columbia, the two most ardent academic champions of national defense and all-out aid to Britain, led a chorus of distressed university presidents demanding that college students be exempted from military service. In these times, military colleges alone were swamped with applications for admission.

There was also the problem posed by the sudden interest in well-paying jobs, thanks to the boom. The lure of high wages for marginal skills was extremely seductive, and young men responded. Then too there was the declining youth population. It had already shaken the secondary and elementary schools, and sometime about 1941–1942 it was a safe bet that it would hit the colleges and universities. And after a decade of falling interest rates many colleges were on the brink of ruin; only sudden riches could save them. The draft, however, might be the final straw.

The colleges turned to Selective Service and asked, in effect, for exemption. Yet though local boards were often sympathetic, General Hershey was not. He thought college students were privileged enough already. Still, the local boards could be induced to show considerable leniency to students in science, medicine and engineering. And the colleges began to take steps of their own to minimize the impact of the draft. Hundreds of them began to offer three-year BA's. Students who entered at seventeen or eighteen would be able to graduate before reaching the draft age of twenty-one.

The impact of the current crisis was no less forceful in the elementary and secondary schools but it was more diffuse. In most elementary and secondary schools enrollments were down, but in some classrooms congestion was worse than anyone could remember. At least, this was true in the boom areas. The population shift triggered by the boom threatened to bring thousands of school districts to grief. So now, after years in which local financing and local control had been matters of faith, school districts began begging for long-term federal aid. Where expanding defense industries and military installations swamped the schools—and the number of such areas was growing at a staggering rate—local authorities demanded federal money, immediately, in large amounts, and for as long as it was needed—*i.e.,* indefinitely. Almost unnoticed, then, in the summer of 1941 the federal government began with an initial appropriation of $150,000,000 to rescue these "impacted" school districts.

Implicit in this new program (which is still with us more than thirty years later) was the hope that much justice might be effected. School expenditures per pupil varied from New York's average $147 per year to

Mississippi's $28—a difference of more than 500 percent. The areas whose schools were "impacted" tended very much to be those rural and Southern regions where the schools were worst. Here at last was a federal school program whose end no man could see and through which a valuable measure of social justice might be achieved. And because it went almost unnoticed, it had no opposition.

IX
The Meaning of It All

ONE of the important characteristics of the modern age is our persist-
ence in trying to make some sense out of the swirl of great events. Not
for us the fatalism, the mute acceptance, the fear of tampering with things
best left unknown that marked earlier ages of man. And while it is impossible
to say what every single person thought about something, it is possible
to trace the broad streams of opinion and point out some of the more
remarkable tributaries. The broad streams of opinion of the war have
already been considered. But how was it interpreted by the country's
intellectuals?

By intellectuals I mean people who cultivate the capacity for abstract
reasoning to the point where it becomes the most important single source
of direction and value in their lives; where others, such as lawyers and
engineers, are likely to live off their mental abilities, intellectuals live for
them. Overwhelmingly they are people of the word, written and spoken.
Whether the world is willing or not to listen, they continually analyze,
prophesy, criticize and explain the natural and social orders by the lights of
reason, the most effective of which is formal logic. And because intellectuals play a disproportionately large role in helping to set the terms in
which millions of other people contemplate the meaning of the times, their
impact, though diffuse, is important.

The murderous chaos of the 1930's had pressed them hard. The rise of
Fascism had sent the Lost Generation and its heirs skittering back across
the Atlantic in a frantic sort of homecoming. It was, as Alfred Kazin said,
"a crisis-begotten nationalism."

And in this time of the breaking of nations, what sense did they make of
it all? No single view was embraced by all. Each tried after his own
fashion to reach the bottom of things and peer upward through the murk
toward the light. But there was a general notion that traditional Western
liberalism had played itself out in politics, society and economics—a point,
ironically, with which both Hitler and Stalin agreed. There was also a hazy
but widespread conviction that these were revolutionary times and the
world war some sort of revolution or "civil war of the world." Hermann
Rauschning saw it as "the revolution of Nihilism"; Archibald MacLeish
pronounced it "The Revolution Against"; Max Lerner considered it "a
bastard revolution"—that is, from the top down rather than from the bot-

119

tom up—and there were hundreds of other variations on this theme.

There was also profound pessimism and despair; as Bertram Wolfe said, an optimist was the man who thought that the future was uncertain. Yet besides the despair and the notion that a revolution was under way, there were two general convictions: One was that Fascism was evil; the other was that no intelligent person could refuse to fight it. Even Bertrand Russell abandoned the pacifism for which he had gone to jail in the Great War. "Since this war began," he sighed in the spring of 1940, "I have felt that I could not go on being a pacifist. If I were young enough to fight I would do so."

Not all American and émigré intellectuals were interventionists. Most were, but there were some notable exceptions. Charles Beard, the famous historian, was unshakably isolationist. Even as the European war began, he was sternly lecturing his countrymen that "Those Americans who refuse to plunge blindly into the maelstrom of European and Asian politics are not defeatist or neurotic. They are giving evidence of sanity, not cowardice." The University of Chicago's *wunderkind* president, Robert M. Hutchins, thought the United States was too immoral to fight Hitler successfully and joined America First.

The 1930's had brought an uprush of interest in economic theories, not the least of them economic theories of Fascism. A refugee intellectual who became famous for having predicted the Nazi-Soviet Pact, Peter Drucker, was convinced that what was really at work was the end of economic man. For two centuries, he said, Western civilization had been rooted in a conception of Economic Man—Man the Consumer, Man the Producer. Under Fascism, however, the Heroic Man was to emerge. Noneconomic aims would take precedence; socially desirable ends—such as full employment —would become more important than mere economics. Heroic Man would be brave, resourceful and, above everything else, nonmaterialistic. This champion of the *Volk* would strike terror into the hearts of pusillanimous, inferior peoples. Production of the arms to be wielded by Heroic Man would eliminate unemployment. The cost of those arms would be reduced domestic consumption, a reduction which would be cheerfully borne by people who no longer cared very much about economic goals. Economic Man was dead in Fascist countries. And, said Drucker, only a new noneconomic society, given heart and soul to freedom and equality, could successfully cope with the menace which Fascism now posed to the world.

Even better known than Drucker's analysis was James Burnham's *The Managerial Revolution*. Capitalism was doomed, said Burnham. See how it limps from crisis to crisis, unable to avoid massive unemployment, unable even to regulate exchange rates intelligently, staggering along under a load of public and private debts that it could not carry any longer. Capitalism was on its last legs—but this did not spell victory for Socialism. Just look at Russia, and think again. Soviet Russia with its despotism, its new class, slave labor, mass murder and starvation. No. What lay ahead was the Managerial Revolution.

Burnham announced that this phenomenon had burst upon the world at about the time of Sarajevo. Within fifty years—that is, *circa* 1964—it would have run its triumphant course and carried all before it. No barrier could deflect it from its path; no human deed could stay its triumph; come what may, world war not excepted, it would have its victory. And the foundations of this Managerial Revolution would rest securely on the principle of state ownership of the means of production. "There will be no direct property rights in the major instruments of production vested in individuals as individuals," concluded Professor Burnham. The state will own the means of production, and the Managers will, in effect, own the state. They will thereby become the new ruling class. Their values will predominate; society will be shaped after their image. And who are the Managers? Defined by Burnham, they are neither more nor less than those people who bring *technical* direction and coordination to the processes of production. Not social or economic or political values and methods will predominate, but technical ones.

What will it look like, this managerial state? How are we to recognize it when it arrives? Well, said Burnham, under the "unlimited managerial state" money will have marginal importance; there would be only one employer—the state; labor will no longer be free to move about but will be assigned by central planners; profits would be a thing of the past, a distant memory.

What then of the present? Of a world at war? The prospects were very grim, so far as he could see, for the United States was lagging far behind in the Managerial Revolution, and as "Modern war is not profitable for capitalism, capitalism cannot adequately fight it." Only if the country placed itself firmly, and rapidly, on the path toward the Managerial Society —along which Germany and the Soviet Union were already well advanced —could the United States hope to survive. And Europe, he concluded, would continue to dominate the Soviet Union for decades to come.

Such was the work which made Burnham famous. How many people actually read his work it is impossible to say, but not enough, it seems, to jeopardize his reputation.*

There were still others who tried to see beyond all the immediate alarums and excursions. The most eminent of these was Harvard's Pitirim Sorokin. To him, the war and its outcome were completely irrelevant.

---

* Burnham is frequently and vaguely assumed to be the man who had first analyzed and explained the growing separation of ownership and control within the great corporations which dominate the modern American economy. Once these corporations were unresponsive to the public interest; now they are unresponsive to their ostensible owners. The managers—mere technicians—run them pretty much as they choose. This was the thesis of a seminal work published in 1932, *The Modern Corporation and Private Property*, by A. A. Berle and Gardner Means.

Civilization and Western culture would be neither shattered nor saved; though nations would be broken into bleeding mounds of flesh, they would somehow endure. The crisis of our age, said Sorokin, was not Hitlerism versus democracy, or any variant thereof, but a reworking of that central value around which Western civilization had revolved for half a millennium. Civilizations, according to his interpretation, rested on appeals to the senses, or to reason, or to a combination of these two; they were sensate, ideational or idealistic. Ancient Greece, for example, had been ideational. The medieval church was idealistic. Since the Renaissance, the central value had been sensate: It appealed to the senses and celebrated the senses. And now that central value was well into a period of decline; for only the fourth time in Western history a reworking of the central value was under way. As it disintegrated, sensate appeals worked to a frantic pitch—became ever more sensational—in art, in literature, in education and in everyday life. More and more intense stimuli were applied, with less and less satisfaction, for even nervous systems follow the law of diminishing returns. This was the real crisis, a crisis of values, and it neither began with the war nor would end with the war. How that crisis would be resolved Sorokin confessed that he did not know. But of one thing he was convinced: Its outcome would make the Second World War pale in importance.

A distinguished refugee psychoanalyst, Erich Fromm, was meanwhile offering a psychohistorical analysis of Nazism, as part of a larger study of modern man. As the Middle Ages gave way to the Renaissance, Fromm argued in *Escape from Freedom,* the free individual had emerged: free from the constraining, personality-stunting bonds of a community that was also close-knit, noncompetitive, and supporting; free to develop the individual personality but burdened also with choice, responsibility, insecurity. To Fromm, Nazism was no purely psychological or economic phenomenon, but combined elements of both. More fundamentally, however, it was a mechanism of escape, offering security in submission to a total authority. And Fromm traced its history back to Luther and Calvin, not Hitler.

While the intellectual disputes raged on without resolution, there was a strong sense that no matter how violently intellectuals disagreed with one another's analyses, they owed it to themselves and others to at least join together in this critical hour. To that end, therefore, a National Conference on Science, Philosophy and Religion in Their Relation to the Democratic Way of Life was held in New York in September, 1940. Ostensibly it was a gathering to bring hundreds of academics and intellectuals, specialists in diverse fields of inquiry, to a common appreciation of the crisis. They hoped the barriers between them would be broken down or at least much reduced. What transpired instead was a stern scolding by the University of Chicago's Mortimer Adler. Other business was conducted, but Adler's outburst turned into the central event of the three-day gathering. Adler was always on the lookout for Culture Criminals; he had once excoriated John Dewey as "Public Enemy Number One."

To the assembled conferees he proceeded to offer a set of sixteen propositions, belief in which set off the true defenders of democracy from its Judas Iscariots. Adler's propositions included such worthies as: "Sacred theology is superior to philosophy, both theoretically and practically"; "Faith is more certain than knowledge"; "Religious faith is a divine gift." These, he insisted, were the test of democracy's real friends, and he argued that while democracy was threatened by many enemies, the deadliest of all was positivism. And positivism was rife among academics. Hitler was a positivist, but he was far less dangerous than the academic positivists. In fact, Adler concluded, "Until the professors and their culture are liquidated the resolution of modern problems—a resolution that History demands be made—will not even begin." After that the conference broke up in acrimonious discord.

There was one point on which more and more intellectuals were in agreement. It was also, importantly, a point which was supported by most people, whatever their politics, whatever their age, wherever they lived, regardless of class or status, and that was that America must defend democracy. But no one was very sure of how to go about it. When the *New Republic* ran an essay contest for college students in 1940 in which they could select their own topics, from almost all of the contest entries there arose one fervent plea—"Provide us with a decent social philosophy," one superior to both Fascism and Communism.

The schools were already trying to satisfy this need. Outside the schools other efforts were launched to achieve the same end. One was the work of Edward Bernays, a nephew of Sigmund Freud. Bernays set up a public relations campaign on behalf of democracy. He produced a one-dollar outsize paperback called *Speak Up for Democracy*. It provided guidance on "where, when and how to speak up for Democracy."

By the end of 1940 Mr. Bernays' book had sold hundreds of thousands of copies, and his campaign had enlisted the support of literally millions of people, through the Boy Scouts, the YMCA, veterans' organizations and various service clubs such as Elks and Rotary. And beyond that the nation's intellectuals were beating the same drums—in their own way, of course.

Archibald MacLeish established a "Democracy Alcove" in the Library of Congress; there the only offerings were the classic works of liberal democracy, such as John Stuart Mill's *On Liberty* and Locke's *Second Treatise on Government*. From Hollywood there were flowing Frank Capra's paeans to the common man and the democratic way, such as *Mr. Deeds Goes to Town, Mr. Smith Goes to Washington* and *Meet John Doe*.

Others followed suit in their own work, and journals such as the *Nation*, *New Republic* and *Saturday Review* became more and more worried about democracy and more and more militant on its behalf.

There was something disturbing about most of this. A neutral observer might have been forgiven for asking what, specifically, was this democracy which America must defend? For so far as anyone could judge from the noisy invocations the answer looked like nothing more or less than the American way in politics and society. There was, in short, a fundamental confusion of what was American with what was democratic and a confusion of what was political with what was social. De Tocqueville's *Democracy in America* provides a classic example of how to avoid both these pitfalls, but its precision had been forgotten. Perhaps even here it might be instructive to recall that democracy, properly understood, has two branches. In politics, for all its myriad nuances, when strictly defined it is nothing more or less than majority rule. In society it is similarly multifaceted, yet when used precisely, it denotes conditions of social equality. And it is possible, in fact, for a society to settle political issues by majority rule while maintaining very sharp social inequities, as Great Britain did up until the Second World War. Conversely, social democracy may prevail even though political power still rests with a numerical minority, as it did in Switzerland until 1971.

There is, it is true, a tendency for each of these—political and social democracy—to press toward the other, but neither in fact nor in theory are they the same thing. Yet they are commonly confused and simple majority rule mistaken for democracy incarnate. But if these distinctions are kept clearly in mind, it becomes easier to appreciate just how much democratic institutions in the United States are not democracy itself but simply America's own answers to the modern search for political and social democracy. From the simplistic Democracy Readers in the schools to the pronouncements of the sophisticated professors of political science, such as Friedrich and Merriam, to the liberal journals, it was impossible, however, to discover that essential fact.* In trying to fashion a fighting faith from the materials closest to hand, these erstwhile champions of democracy betrayed a clumsiness that marked them as Johnny-come-latelies in the ideological wars. More than that, they became hopelessly confused and started to confuse one another.

* Charles Merriam, the very distinguished head of the Department of Political Science at the University of Chicago, jumped onto the democracy bandwagon with a series of lectures, *What Is Democracy?* Struggling to be precise, he skated into intellectual flummery: "Democracy is a form of political association in which the general control and direction of the community are habitually determined by the bulk of the community in accordance with appropriate understandings and procedures providing for popular participation and the consent of the government" (p. 6). He ended up gushing frothily: "Democracy is a spirit, an attitude toward our fellow-men . . . it is the means to an end—the happiness of mankind" (p. 92). It was also eternal and perfect.

Convinced that democracy was about to perish from the earth if they were not nimble and vigilant, they hastily jettisoned the cumbersome apparatus of detachment and criticism. And once the best-educated had reached this point, who was going to disabuse the less well-informed? Certainly no one ever did; perhaps there was no one left to do so. And from the most blissfully ignorant barfly to the most exalted minds in the most prestigious universities there now prevailed an unchallenged assumption that democracy was the American way of life, and vice versa. The neutral observer mentioned before might therefore have also been forgiven for thinking that if this muddle were ever to collide with the realities it ignored, there would be a nasty jolt.

There was still no consensus among intellectuals about the meaning of it all, but now there was at least a conviction that the country must defend democracy. And around this conviction two themes were beginning to emerge, both of them encouraged by liberal intellectuals. The first was expressed in many ways, such as Stewart Alsop's "Wanted: A Faith to Fight For." The general notion was that the country must live up to its own democratic ideals. It occurred to Alsop, looking about him, that "The kind of democracy we fought to make the world safe for leaves a bitter taste in the mouth. A kind of democracy which leaves between nine and sixteen million unemployed for ten years in the richest nation on Earth hardly seems worth imposing on the rest of the world." The remedy he suggested was to "Give the soldiers of America a dream. Give them the dream of an America in which any man willing to do his honest share will receive his honest share of America's plenty. . . ." In short, make this a genuinely middle-class democracy; end the social injustice. Such was the plea of millions of people, not intellectuals alone.

And once social democracy had been achieved here, what then? "The most important task is still to be done," said Professor Friedrich. "To sell democracy abroad . . . [and] as in other battles, the best defense is to attack." Or, as Professor Merriam expressed it, "Free states cannot exist in modern times unless there is a free world." The most moving expression of this theme was to be found in Lillian Hellman's *Watch on the Rhine,* with its high-minded insistence that all men must be free, or those who are must bear the moral responsibility for those who are not—wherever in the world they may be. A proud and generous sentiment; only the despised isolationists caught sight of the other side of this sharp and flaming sword.

Both these ideas—that America must achieve social justice at home in response to the challenge abroad and that it had a liberating mission—moved through the ranks of the educated and concerned like a freshening wind. They took on these ideas, articulated them, embroidered them, rang the changes upon them and held them out to their countrymen—a people becoming receptive to appeals based on these ideas. Was it a conversion then? No. They had been able to link hands, these intellectuals, with the rest because rather than being novel, these ideas of justice at home and crusading abroad were deeply embedded in the nation's history. They had lain dormant for a long while, victims to Sophistication, Isolation and Depression. It is true that no one revived them with a greater will than the intellectuals and the academics, yet these notions belong in truth to the entire country. And America had thus pulled itself together a little tighter, a little more united, a little more resistant to contradiction.

X

Life Goes On

DAILY life was now in a twilight state where minds and hearts were caught up in currents of war but bodies were not; where everyone wanted to help but there was nothing for them to do; where life itself seemed to be more dangerous, more important, more lively than it had been for many years. With so much turmoil almost anything might take root.

For those with access to shortwave radio the war had never been very far away. Even those who could not listen in directly on the propaganda war felt its presence. As one writer taunted, "a specter haunts the U.S.— the specter of propaganda." For millions were convinced that British propaganda had been responsible for America's entry into the Great War in 1917.

Beside radio there were propaganda films. The Germans celebrated their spring offensive with *Blitzkrieg im Westen*. The Russians were offering *Mannerheim Line*. Both contained remarkable combat photography. Both were roundly booed by film audiences. In contrast, the more restrained, less exciting films offered by the British were warmly applauded.

This was all very well, but Americans are an active people. And at the beginning of May, 1940, there appeared an advertisement in the New York *Times* which ran:

IN ORDER TO PREVENT FURTHER BLOODSHED AND OUTRAGE
IN THIS WAR OF GERMAN AGGRESSION, I AM AUTHORIZED
BY COMPETENT AMERICANS
TO OFFER A REWARD OF
$1,000,000
TO BE PAID IN CASH
TO THE PERSON OR PERSONS WHO WILL DELIVER ADOLF HITLER
ALIVE, UNWOUNDED AND UNHARMED
INTO THE CUSTODY OF THE LEAGUE OF NATIONS FOR TRIAL
BEFORE A HIGH COURT OF JUSTICE FOR HIS CRIMES
AGAINST THE PEACE AND DIGNITY OF THE WORLD.
This offer will stand good through the month of May, 1940.

The advertisement was placed by Dr. Samuel H. Church, president of the Carnegie Institute in Pittsburgh. The response was a flurry of telegrams and letters along the general lines of one which ran "Plans complete. . . .

Need twenty-five thousand. . . . We take off on receipt of expense money. . . ."

For all the alarums and excursions, however, the war was often little more than a backdrop against which life went on much as it would probably have done anyway. The general nostalgia for Main Street, the good old days and the Gay Nineties was growing stronger rather than weaker. It brought a new interest in barbershop quartets. The previous year a Society for the Preservation and Encouragement of Barber Shop Quartet Singing in America had been founded in Tulsa, Oklahoma. At the end of the 1940 session of the New York World's Fair, a five-day national championship drew thousands of entries.

Young people revived another pre-Great War pastime—roller skating. There had been a brief flurry of interest in it in the early years of the Depression as an inexpensive form of recreation, but nothing like this. On weekends and almost every night 3,500 roller rinks were jampacked with lively adolescents and young adults. Where their parents had gone silently around and around the rink, these young people danced and sang popular songs as they skated. To those old enough to remember the first roller-skating boom it brought back memories; some even recalled a poem popular in the days of their youth:

> Our Jane has climbed the golden stair
> And passed the jasper gates;
> From now on she'll have wings to wear,
> Instead of roller skates.

The quality of earnestness in everyday leisure was still there. It had once prompted Sherwood Anderson to remark that since the Great War the whole country had seemed to be "on a culture jag"; even now an Ivy League professor was sarcastically half-joking that "instead of leading a natural life in the state to which God has called them most people want to rise to power by way of the Harvard Classics." Never had the opportunities been better. Modern production and marketing techniques were working a small revolution in the enjoyment of books and music.

Radio had almost driven the recording industry to the wall in the early 1930's. But records had managed to survive and were now beginning to prosper, not least the purveyors of classical music. People, it developed, would buy inexpensive recordings of classical pieces even if performed indifferently by obscure music groups. There was a bottomless well into which recordings of Schubert's "Serenade," Beethoven's *Moonlight Sonata*, Brahms' "Lullaby" and Tchaikovsky's *Pathétique Symphony* could be poured. Starting in September, 1940, these low-priced recordings went on sale in thousands of drugstores and five-and-dimes. Some sold for as little as twenty-nine cents. All sold very well.

But a still more impressive advance in the diffusion of general knowledge had been scored by a small businessman, Robert F. De Graff. A number of attempts had been made to copy the success of England's Penguin Books in creating a market for paperbacks. All had failed. The financial backbone of American publishing remained the $2.50 novel. Publishers were certain that a vast book-buying market existed if only some way could be found to tap it. De Graff saw what others had missed; the key to this market was distribution. In June, 1939, he created Pocket Books, with an initial list of ten reprints, standard items such as *Wuthering Heights*, Shakespeare, Agatha Christie. He sold his reprints, with eye-catching permagloss, color-illustrated covers, in drugstores, cigar stores, department stores, grocery stores, on newsstands and through mail-order houses. The average publisher had 900 to 1,200 outlets for his goods; De Graff had 10,000. By August, 1940—one year after he launched his scheme on a national scale—Pocket Books was the biggest publishing success since Simon and Schuster had mushroomed out of a book of crossword puzzles. De Graff's success made him a rich man; more than that, it had created a vast new clientele of book buyers and readers running into the millions.

Hoping to redeem their losses, the two fairs opened again in the spring of 1940. At the New York World's Fair the austere chrome and plastic tributes to the World of Tomorrow were gone. The atmosphere now was calculatedly Country Fair. The limits to the World Fair's aspirations and vision were set in its second edition by Elmer, a paunchy, fortyish, easygoing character given to folksiness and whimsy. Elmer was a Madison Avenue creation of what account executives thought the average American thought the average American—that is, himself—looked like. The part of Elmer was played by a professional character actor. He strolled about the fair glad-handing the paying customers and extolling the virtues of the common man.

The corn was heavily overlaid with patriotic spectacle. The principal entertainment spectacular was a gigantic, supercolossal extravaganza called "American Jubilee." Across a stage nearly as large as a football field a cast of 300 tirelessly paraded back and forth, usually flag in hand. From time to time they would congeal into some epic moment in the nation's history—Lincoln at Gettysburg, TR and his Rough Riders taking San Juan Hill, and the like. And "in a stand-up-and-cheer finale Mr. X is inaugurated as President in 1941." The fair finished as it had begun—a financial and cultural disaster.

In San Francisco the Golden Gate Exposition opened for its second year, with cut-rate prices, a less formal atmosphere and unstinted patriotic spectacle, epitomized by "America: Pageant of a Nation!" Sally Rand was back at the same old stand, doing the same old thing. But now she had to compete with a striptease extravaganza called (a tribute to the Allies?) "Les Folies Bergère." For art lovers there was Diego Rivera performing in "Art in Action"; only fifty cents to watch the master paint a mural.

The backers of all this fake folksiness and studied informality at both fairs did not profit by it. Millions came, but millions more who represented the difference between success and failure stayed at home.

What might have aptly been called the National Defense Christmas of 1940 was celebrated by a people still shaken by events and anxious for the future. They had come through a hotly fought election, but they felt divided. They had decided to arm to the utmost, but they were still militarily weak. This Christmas they spent more lavishly than any Christmas since 1929, but there were still 8,000,000 unemployed, and millions more were poor. They had managed to remain free from direct involvement in the war, but they found little satisfaction in ambiguity. "In a mood of bitter self-examination, of no less bitter doubt, Americans were entering another crucial period. Anxious, edgy and uncertain. . . . The whole web of U. S. life, thought and conviction was involved."

There were no more protests against toy tanks, planes, ships and guns. One journal even remarked: "Today's toys can provide a useful home education in the military arts."

When Roosevelt went on the radio in the evening of the last Sunday in the year and delivered his fifteenth fireside chat, streets were deserted, restaurants and movie theaters were almost empty. His message was short. America, he said, must be, and during the year ahead would become, "The Arsenal of Democracy."

Nineteen forty-one brought the V-for-Victory campaign. It was launched by the BBC as a device for bolstering the morale of people in the occupied countries, as a counter to defeatism. From the response it awoke here one might have thought that a Nazi garrison was stationed in every American town.

Advertisers, civic organizations, schools, even the Communist Party embraced the three dots and a dash (which was, by coincidence, both the Morse code for V and the opening phrase of Beethoven's assertive Fifth Symphony) as if life itself depended on it. V symbols appeared everywhere. A large restaurant chain adorned its windows with vegetable displays of V's; newspapers used rows of V's as copy breaks; professional dance teachers devised a V-for-Victory dance; there were V-shaped pastries, jewelry, salt-and-pepper shakers; hairdressers whipped up widow's peak hairdos and V-shaped pompadours; and at night municipal and business buildings glowed with enormous floodlit V's.

In occupied Europe the V came to symbolize resistance to oppression; here it was an emblem of frustrated passions flowing from a hotly partisan neutrality. And behind every V sign there appeared to lurk, it must be said, a dollar sign. Commercialism threatened to turn it all into a V-for-Vulgarity campaign. Yet the emotional response was undeniably genuine and spontaneous, and no one was immune.

Now that people had money in their pockets, they were generally living it up. Not wildly or extravagantly but with less and less of the seriousness of recent years when the comforts of the middle class stood in such stark contrast with the miseries of the poor. Book sales, movie attendance and radio listening—all dropped sharply, while liquor consumption, roadhouse crowds and automobile accidents rose with offsetting abruptness. Cigarette consumption rose by 12 percent in the first three months of 1941 (during World War I it had doubled). The record industry roared through 1941, stamping out as many records as there were Americans, finally surpassing the mark set in 1921. Recording companies were working three shifts a day to keep up with the demand, turning out recorded music, patriotic speeches, birdcalls, language lessons, poetry and drama.

The war itself had generated a new interest in the inexplicable, and palmists, hypnotists, astrologers and other dabblers in the occult had a boom of their own under way. Hypnotists were to be found on the radio, touring Army bases, giving public demonstrations and in the schools. No college psychology course was complete without a discussion of hypnotism. One practitioner, Andrew Salter, profited handsomely by teaching people how to hypnotize themselves. Another went about the country lecturing on the uses of hypnotism in politics; as one example he cited Lindbergh, who, he said, had been hypnotized by Hitler when Hitler pinned a medal on him; Lindbergh's recent behavior struck him as the actions of a man under the influence of posthypnotic suggestion.* In 1940 the *Oracles of Nostradamus* had been reprinted and had sold very well. There now appeared a film version, *More About Nostradamus*. During the First World War both the Germans and the French had resurrected the medieval sage to prove that they would win. And Americans were now pondering the aptness of such prophecies as this: "A humane rule of Anglican breed, the daughters of the British Isles, shall re-establish unity and justice. . . ."

The urge for simpler, older pastimes created a sudden interest in square and folk dancing. Such diversions had always been popular in rural areas, but now big-city bankers, lawyers and businessmen could be seen in ever-larger numbers cavorting to the sounds of a down-home jug band. At the same time there was a new interest among the urban middle classes in gardening. As a famous literary critic who had succumbed explained it, "To dig in the earth, to transplant seedlings or drop seeds, gives one a feeling of direction and potency that is disappearing in political life. The laws of cause and effect are still valid among vegetables."

---

* In fact, Göring pinned Lindbergh's medal.

Young people had their own ways of responding to an economic and emotional revival. Most of them simply indulged the harmless pleasures which had been long denied or sharply restricted: They bought new clothes, cars, records; went out more often; and pushed the marriage rate up by 20 percent. A sizable number began to emphasize the distance between themselves and the rest of society by donning the most outlandish clothing since their parents were young—that is, since the fabled twenties. Their parents were baffled and outraged. Aided by a hit song called "A Zoot Suit," the new look went from being a mere curiosity in 1940 to being a national phenomenon in 1941. It was adopted chiefly by the children of the poor and lower middle classes. Boys wore the legendary suit; girls wore a "juke jacket," a garment which flaunted an extravagance all its own.

The song described it as "A zoot suit—with a neat pleat—with a drape shape—with a stiff cuff." The shoulders bulged with the aid of three to six inches of padding; the trousers measured three feet at the knees and narrowed at the ankles to less than twelve inches. The trousers' waistband was up in the armpits, while the jacket reached to the knees. With such extravagant dimensions only the most dazzling colors would do, preferably ornamented with string ties, pearl buttons and a yard or two of gold watch chain. It was nothing less, in short, than a frontal assault on traditional Western conceptions of symmetry, proportion, balance, taste and moderation. Respectable people considered so much excess faintly pathological. *Newsweek* called it "a disease." But despite—perhaps because of —such attacks, the zoot suit became more, not less, popular.

So young and old were living it up in their various ways with money churned out by the defense boom. Yet the new prosperity had a less welcome side—inflation. The Office of Production Management had been explicitly charged with building up the country's defenses without ruining its money. But the OPM was fighting a losing battle. There was no real shortage of goods; there was just an enormous rise in demand for everything now that people had money to spare. The administration established an Office of Price Administration in April, 1941, with the task of holding prices steady, and from it there soon issued a flurry of directives commanding that the rises stop.

Business proclaimed that it was complying with the letter of the new directives, then quietly lowered the quality of the goods. Before long, "cotton" shirts consisted chiefly of low-grade percale; "leather" soles had a suspicious tendency to get soggy and waterlogged, just as paper might; "wool suits" were conjured up from rayon waste; by sleight of hand cheap broadcloth was transformed overnight into premium quality broadcloth; and boxes of breakfast cereal quietly shrank by an ounce or two. The real burden of all this fell, of course, on the traditional victims of inflation— the poor.

Yet unwelcome as inflation was, and uneven as were the rewards and penalties of boom times, hardly anyone thought the boom cruel or unfair. For it was a fact that the rewards of the boom were starting to trickle down into parts of the economy not directly involved in defense production. Farmhands made a living wage for the first time in memory. In industry as a whole, the average daily wage had gone up to $6 a day. And a man with any skills at all was being ardently wooed by employers.

The shortwave continued to provide a steady outpouring of rubbish, but people were gradually becoming bored with propaganda and talk about propaganda. They listened to Radio Berlin now and again out of idle curiosity or for a little inexpensive amusement, but they no longer feared it or worried about analyzing it. The earnest, self-important Institute for Propaganda Analysis closed down.

Nineteen forty-one was also a year when most of the popular songs were absent from the radio, thanks to a strike which managed to annoy almost everyone. The root cause was a strike by the American Society of Composers, Authors and Publishers for higher royalties from radio. Most of its members pursued a precarious livelihood at best. But how to collect royalties from the radio stations that played their music was a problem capable of defeating intelligence and goodwill.

Negotiations between ASCAP and the stations broke down, and the networks proceeded to establish a counterorganization to ASCAP, the Broadcast Music Institute. Popular sympathies were with ASCAP: BMI's repertoire consisted almost entirely of music in the public domain, such as "Camptown Races" and "Jeanie with the Light Brown Hair," heavily padded with Latin American rhythms. By spring, "Jeanie" had been played so often that there were rumors her hair had turned gray. A group of students at UCLA grew so fed up with hearing "Jeanie" on the radio they publicly burned her in effigy. And ASCAP's members turned their own talents to mocking the opposition, e.g.:

> Little Jack Horner sat in a corner,
> His radio turned up high;
> He listened aghast, then turned it off fast,
> And said, "What a bad B.M.I."

When the strike dragged on for months on end without a break, the government ended it by threatening ASCAP with antitrust indictments.

August, 1941, brought the first taste of sacrifice on behalf of defense, and it was a disaster. It might have worked. There was an understandable tendency after so many dreary years to whoop it up and spurn restraint, yet there was a willingness to serve the nation that might have been tapped. The newly created post of Oil Coordinator for National Defense had been given to Harold Ickes, and he proceeded to cut the distribution of gasoline and oil along the Eastern seaboard by 10 percent. Sales of gasoline were also forbidden from 7 P.M. to dawn. There were stern lectures on the wickedness of "jack-rabbit starts." And it all seemed reminiscent of the "gasolineless Sundays" of the First World War, which had limited pleasure driving but left people free to drive to work. Yet this was an unworkable approach; people simply said, "Fill 'er up," before 7 P.M. Consumption dropped not a whit, and service station owners felt themselves harassed for no good reason at all. A Senate investigation very quickly established that the oil shortage which was supposed to have made the curbs necessary simply did not exist and demanded that this exercise in silliness be stopped at once. Tempers rose, as did gasoline consumption. Ickes quickly backed down. His elaborate and clumsy attempt at making people more "war-conscious" had been a flop. But it had done something far worse than that; it had discredited the government's first attempt at rationing. What confidence there might have been in government's ability to manage wartime rationing had been shattered, and the country was not yet in the war.

The new spirit abroad these days showed up more openly in women's fashions than it did anywhere else. Bareness was back, or, at least, it was evidently coming back. More flesh was being exposed than had been on view since the heady days of the flapper and the hip flask. Skirts rose above the knee, at first in walking, golfing and riding wear, then for every day. Overnight, women became conscious of their knees; beauty parlors were soon selling treatments and exercises to create the knee beautiful.

Even milliners were, for once, dictating less rather than more. In recent years hats had grown to smothering proportions until, with the attempted return of the veil in the first winter of the war, they virtually covered everything—head, neck and face, fore and aft. But all that had vanished; women's hats assumed the "Pompadour Look." Here was little more than a skullcap pitched so far back from the forehead it could hardly be detected on a frontal view. There were variations—beret pompadour, pillbox pompadour, neck bows, nets adorned with flowers—but the barehead look had clearly swept the veil before it.

Oddly, there was also a trend to masculinity these days. But it was restricted almost entirely to a fringe group—college coeds. Slacks were already part of women's wardrobes. Shorts were popular. But this was a craze for men's shirts, jackets and trousers, to be worn with deliberate sloppiness and bagginess. Its charms were entirely lost on the primary audience for all this disheveled nonchalance.

The biggest fashion news of the year—perhaps of many years—was the introduction of nylon stockings on May 15. Stores which offered them opened that day to mobs of eager customers. Prices ranged from $1.15 to $1.35 a pair (in 1972 terms, roughly $3.75 to $4.50), and all were gone within four days. At full production Du Pont would only be able to meet 15 percent of the current market for women's stockings. Those who secured a pair or two in 1940 counted themselves lucky.

As if demonstrating that they were as sensitive as anyone else to the need for patriotism and national unity, the big fashion houses put on cooperative, not competitive, showings in 1941. The offerings were "100% American," in materials, design and production. Alas, the styles rarely rose above feminized militarism. Even the colors ran strongly to navy blue, highlighted by patriotic red and white. There were also variations on the forest green shade of the marines. With the military colors and motifs went a wide assortment of patriotic pins, flags and badges. The sailor hat popular before the First World War made a comeback. And there could be discerned within these "all-American" collections the strongest traces of the last fashions to escape from Paris the year before.

There was also more jeweled embroidery, sequins, gold braid and fur trimmings. Necklines were lower. There was much draping and sculpting about the breasts. Floppy picture hats and long gloves in the French style were popular once more. And men generally liked the new trends to elgance and exposure.

Most women, however, were far more concerned with the availability of the small necessities which soften, flatter and attract than they were with the larger currents of fashion. For the fashion industry was beginning to feel the pinch of defense priorities. By August, 1941, silk stockings were being rationed: three pairs to a customer. Burly guards patrolled the aisles of department stores in what was conceded to be a stampede which dwarfed the Christmas rush. Once the stockings had vanished, there came a descent on silk panties and slips. Well before the year ended, women were dabbling with leg paint, trying to make naked legs look sheathed. Not a few gave up in disgust and bought stockings of cotton or wool. Cosmetics manufacturers took to nervously wondering aloud about the blow to national morale that a shortage of glamor would bring.

All this was the backdrop to the great defense skirt controversy in the fall of 1941. Garment manufacturers had proposed, solely as a patriotic gesture, they said, to raise skirts and slips by two or three inches. Up to 10 percent of valuable fabrics would be thereby saved for national defense. But cynics noted that no mention was made of an offsetting 10 percent drop in prices. And designers were adamantly opposed to shorter skirts, which, they said, were inelegant; besides, "hemlines are just as short today as decency and grace will permit." Yet there were forces at work beyond man's power to add or subtract. There had been for decades an astonishing correspondence between the state of the economy and the length of women's skirts. With uncanny precision they rose and fell together. If the nation's economy continued to rise, so would the skirts of its women.

Despite the defense boom, unemployment was still a critical problem. The number of people on WPA had fallen below 2,000,000 by the spring of 1941 and offered every prospect of dropping to less than 1,000,000 by the end of the year. But no one could plan, or did plan, on an indefinite boom. People being dropped from relief did not automatically find their way into steady employment, not when there were still 6,000,000 to 7,000,000 unemployed. Beggar brigades still graced big-city streets. Some, like New York's Broadway Rose, who panhandled only from celebrities and for large denominations, were famous. But for most it was a miserable, anonymous life. And the sympathetic attitudes of the Depression were rapidly wearing thin. Subways in New York now carried a message from La Guardia about the city's estimated 6,000 full-time, professional beggars, reading:

BEGGING IS UNNECESSARY

* * * * * * * * *

The City Provides for Its
Destitute and Homeless

DO NOT GIVE TO BEGGARS!

Refer Begging Men and Women
to the Department of Welfare

* * * * * * * * *

Economic revival had of course brought some significant moderation of general misery. Food stamps had firmly established themselves as that comparative rarity in public life, a bureaucratic and popular success. By the summer of 1941 more than 5,000,000 people in 300 cities and towns participated in the program. Another 1,200 communities and 10,000,000 people had asked to participate. A cotton stamp program which was, in truth, a disguised form of clothing stamps, had been launched on an experimental scale. There was even a possibility of housing stamps in a few more years.

But perhaps the best measure of what the Depression had done to a great nation was what it had done to people's bodies. There was no more dramatic index than the health of the millions of young men now being examined for selective service. Their general level of health was so bad that it was an undeniable disgrace. General Hershey might insist that these young men were no worse in mind and body than their doughboy fathers had been, but what comfort was that to a nation that set its heart on progress from one generation to the next? Even Hershey was forced to concede that these young men should have been healthier. The standards of induction had been raised since the last draft, but the health of draftees had not.

Selective Service also ran up against another disheartening fact: One adult in five was functionally illiterate, which was only a modest reduction from the 1917 figure of one adult in four. In despair, the Army turned to the WPA, which had taught millions to read and write in the thirties, and asked it to set up literacy classes for several million potential draftees. Federal authorities moved meanwhile to protect the health and morals of the nation's soldiers by making prostitution in the vicinity of military bases a federal offense.

The country also had to cope with the massive social problems posed by the boom.

Most towns simply could not cope with it. Much of the new money completely bypassed municipal authorities, for time and again the new defense plants were built just on the other side of the town or county line. The boom thus brought them massive problems, yet denied them the means of counterattack. Utterly beaten, towns which had never turned to the federal government before, not even during the Depression, turned to it now and demanded that it provide them with transportation, housing, education and public health facilities.

Washington responded. A tiny office set up in November, 1940, in the Farm Security Administration for the purpose of gathering information on welfare problems created by defense production was rapidly transformed into an Office of Defense Health and Welfare Services. Organized on regional lines parallel to the Social Security Administration, it was, by the fall of 1941, a national program for relieving boom-town welfare problems. It was also the first agency ever created by the federal government with the avowed aim of directly providing essential services to local communities.

And underneath all the hurly-burly new life was stirring. The whole fabric of American society was pulsing with confidence once again. People grumbled and complained and ran around in circles, but they made love more often and with greater abandon. The birthrate at the end of 1941 was at its highest point in ten years and still rising spectacularly. Eminent scholars and clergymen were pleased, for many of them believed that France had been defeated by allowing Germany to outbreed it. To make democracy safe, America's women were being urged to conceive. Not all women were flattered by the arguments. But whether for democracy or not they were giving birth at a rate not seen since the end of the frontier.

Daily life was changing, indelibly, sometimes imperceptibly, in a hundred different ways. Technical novelties which had a charming simplicity and primitiveness were on the threshold of maturity. People were too busy to notice, but radio, television and aviation were coming into their own at last.

Radio had long been the clear-cut first choice as a form of entertainment. And since September, 1939, it had gone on to supplant newspapers as the preferred source of news. For radio alone was able to keep pace with the lurching changes of speed and direction of this helter-skelter kind of war where countries were conquered in days or hours, where the lightning bolt had supplanted the meat grinder.

More than news, radio provided commentaries on, and analyses of, current events. There was a variety of styles, to suit a variety of tastes: H. V. Kaltenborn, pontifical, with a rapid-fire delivery and lots of lively flourishes of color; Elmer Davis, a celebrated journalist and Rhodes scholar, but with a comfortable Indiana twang; Raymond Gram Swing, possessing a nice Olympian touch of detachment and high-mindedness; and there were many others. Devoted admirers coalesced about these radio commentators. Swing, for example, was the reputed preference of Felix Frankfurter, the British ambassador, Tallulah Bankhead and Nicholas Murray Butler. Radio also offered the ultimate in immediacy—live broadcasts from where the fighting was taking place. In August, 1940, when the Battle of Britain was at its height, CBS inaugurated *London After Dark*, with Edward R. Murrow; it was a runaway success. Murrow, in fact, quickly became a national celebrity, and thanks to him, millions of ordinary people learned what England faced, learned something too of how and why it fought and came eventually to wish it safe from harm.

Radio had plunged with a will into the crisis. It very rapidly asserted itself as a central link between ordinary people and the defense program. When Selective Service began, the networks produced dozens of programs to, from and about the basic training camps. With no war at home it did the best it could by broadcasting blow-by-blow coverage of the Army maneuvers which were becoming more and more frequent. A climax of sorts came in the fall of 1941, when the Second Army was locked in mock battle with the Third Army all up and down the state of Louisiana. Live accounts were broadcast to an audience of millions, and some correspondents had the joy of being captured and interrogated. Seizing upon the spirit of the thing, the more quick-witted gave their captors false information. One managed to lead the "enemy" into an ambush.

Television still hung suspended between experiment and commonplace reality. When the war began it was little more than an expensive toy. There was one station, in New York City, and fewer than a thousand sets in operation in 1939. The Federal Communications Commission banned the sale of air time to commercial sponsors, making problematical the question of how future expansion was to be financed. No one doubted that television would eventually succeed, and against that day RCA was marketing radios with an attachment which would mate them to television screens once these dropped in price where all could buy; television sets currently sold at prices ranging from $199.95 to $600 (in 1973 terms, about $700 to $2,000).

Among the handful of people involved in television there were many who feared that unless some major development transpired very soon, American television might never catch up with the British, who already had ten times as many sets in operation and broadcast a much wider range of programs. A potentially large audience was already at hand in baseball and football fans. One imaginative producer hoped to generate interest in television by offering live broadcasts of crap games.

RCA tried to hurry the pace along by slashing the price of its most expensive models by nearly 50 percent in the spring of 1940 and pressed the FCC very hard to permit commercial broadcasts. The first frail buds of a national audience were being nurtured on a diet of televised baseball, and the Republican National Convention in Philadelphia had been carried as far as Tulsa, Oklahoma. Grudgingly, in September, 1940, the FCC agreed to commercial television, and the sale of sets jumped from 200 a month to 25,000. Then the FCC had second thoughts: Perhaps thousands of people would buy sets only to find them obsolete by the time television was "perfected." CBS, after all, was experimenting with color; it had even made its first color broadcast. But RCA assured the commissioners that color would be little more expensive than black and white. Owners of current sets would need only a small, inexpensive attachment for color reception, they said.

By the spring of 1941 there were thirteen stations in operation; forty-four more had received permission to get under way. In July commercial broadcasting began. Sponsorship of a thirty-minute show, such as Lowell Thomas with the news, sold for $100. Television stood on the threshold of success, it seemed.

But it was really a false dawn. The trained manpower and raw materials that went into television sets were needed for radar. By the fall of 1941 the production of television sets began to drop, a victim of defense priorities.

Aviation in these years was no longer in its infancy, but it was still in its innocence. Commercially and militarily it was still hedged about by novelty. Aviation was not yet an integral and integrating part of daily life. Only a relative handful of people were, as the saying went, "air-minded." Very few people, in fact, had any direct experience of flying, despite thirty years of commercial aviation. The Great War had held out a fleeting promise of ushering in the world's air age. But when the war was over, 90 percent of the new aircraft factories built in the United States were dismantled. During the twenty years that followed, flying remained a novelty, its course highlighted by the occasional triumphs and disasters of a mere handful of pilots. Commercial aviation trod a narrow, unspectacular path and by the outbreak of the Second World War the country had a total of 300 commercial airliners. In the entire United States there were only 2,500 licensed pilots (commercial and military), and less than 1 percent of the population provided 100 percent of the passengers.

As novelties will, flying attracted the idle and curious. On weekends, tens of thousands of people would journey to La Guardia Field (which opened in December, 1939) to watch the planes take off and land. The star attraction was always the four-engine Clipper flying boat providing twice-a-week service to Europe. Flying had its villains and heroes, whose lives were followed with the kind of interest that attended film stars or prize-fighters. Trophies and prizes were offered every year, to bring forth an endless series of colorful fliers. Head and shoulders above them all was the three-time winner of the Thompson Trophy, Colonel Roscoe C. Turner— "Colonel Roscoe C. Turner is a splendiferous character. A Beau Brummel of the skies, wearer of a fastidious waxed mustache and owner of a closet-ful of resplendent uniforms he designed himself. Turner often carries an eleven year old African lion named Gilmer on his flights. . . ." Blacks had a champion of their own, Colonel Hubert Fauntleroy Julian, who loved to be called the "Black Eagle of Harlem." When both these men retired from flying, they tried, without success, to become motion-picture stars.

Commercial flying boasted a graciousness it would never know again. The ultimate in airborne elegance was to be found aboard the 40-ton Pan Am Clippers which had gone into service in the spring of 1939, New York to London by way of Newfoundland. Because of the war, the route was changed to New York to Lisbon by way of the Azores. The trip took twenty-seven hours, and flying was never more charming: a few passengers, a comfortable bed for each person, dinner tables with crisp linen, fresh flowers, meals cooked to order, a sense of adventure and privilege, and the captain mingling easily with the passengers.

Yet there hung over flying, commercial and military alike, the prospect of violent death. That might thrill in the abstract or on the screen, but it discouraged the sale of airplane tickets.

The Air Transport Association persisted in trying to counter the fears and the painful memories by arguing that flying was not really any more dangerous than other means of transportation. One advertising campaign in the winter of 1939 had businessmen's wives earnestly debating the question "Should Husbands Fly?" Another campaign had Eleanor Roosevelt, modern-minded as ever, in public-service advertisements explaining the comforts and conveniences of flying. When, therefore, in March, 1940, the airlines had gone twelve consecutive months without an accident, they could barely contain their delight. For the next five months it was repeated at every opportunity that commercial aviation had gone without a fatal accident for more than a year. But when that happy skein ended, as inevitably it had to, there was the worst aviation disaster in American history (up to that time). And among the twenty-five dead was one of the most popular politicians of the day, Senator Ernest Lundeen of Minnesota.

Ensuing months brought a steady flow of air disasters; almost one a month, in fact. Overnight, commercial aviation was struggling with what looked like an epidemic of falling planes. Clumsy efforts were made to blame it all on the administration, which had abolished the tiny Civil Aviation Agency and replaced it with a much larger Civil Aeronautics Board. What had happened was that the airlines had enjoyed an extraordinary run of good luck, and it had turned on them. More than that, however, was the spectacular rise in the number of flights. The defense crisis placed a premium on time; time had become more important than safety or comfort. More planes, more haste, more crashes. And in November, 1941, came the first multiple disaster when two planes crashed in a single day, carrying thirty-four persons to their deaths. As if finally throwing in the towel on their claims of safety, the airlines had already taken to issuing parachutes to their passengers; no one liked it, but no one questioned its wisdom.

Yet the important thing was that the days of innocence were finally over; aviation would come to maturity in this war, both as a means of transportation and as an effective instrument of destruction. The number of licensed pilots in the U.S. had risen fifty-fold in just two years. Half a million people were becoming "air-minded" through serving in the Civilian Air Warning Service. Hundreds of thousands more were now in the Army Air Corps. And the textbooks used by millions of American schoolchildren were being rewritten so that these youngsters would think explicitly about the world in terms of the new air age. Even in the elementary grades the curriculum was being reordered to keep up with the new importance of aviation.

Certainly this was a mechanically minded generation already. The country boasted millions of hobbyists, tinkerers and inventors. No sooner had the war begun than an old standby, the "death ray," was revived. One inventor, a Cleveland physician, claimed to have obliterated a pigeon on the wing at a distance of four miles. In the months since then, Washington offices had been deluged with proposals, addressed to everyone from the President to "Boss of Guns, U.S. Navy," for military inventions. Yet in the First World War more than 100,000 ideas had yielded only three devices which proved practicable, and nothing so far appeared likely to threaten that record. Among the most frequent proposals were torpedoes, bombs and rockets directed by birds, fish, seals, cats and other creatures; steel umbrellas for warships; remote-control tanks, planes, ships, guns; and, of course, all manner of death rays.

A brief flurry of excitement and popular interest had swirled up about an inventor named Lester Pierce Barlow after he described to the Senate Military Affairs Committee a new and terrible device of his own creation. Dropped far above the ground, the explosive he had invented would, "by sending out detonation waves which act on objects precisely as depth charges act on objects underwater," wreak unparalleled destruction. Barlow called this explosive, which was based on a liquid-oxygen formula, Glmite, after his employer, Glenn L. Martin. He proposed to prove his claims by tethering a herd of goats several hundred feet from a 1,000-pound charge of Glmite, detonating the explosive and recording the results. The committee, much impressed and braving the protests of the ASPCA, which hurriedly mounted a national campaign against the Glmiting of goats, encouraged Barlow to proceed. Alas, to his chagrin and the relief of the ASPCA, the Glmite was exploded, but the goats grazed contentedly on.

The spirit that moved the citizen inventors, aside from a desire for prestige or just a harmless pleasure in tinkering with things, was not to be discouraged by failure; it could never be discouraged by failure, deflated claims, laughter or scorn. It was a spirit that by now ran through the whole society. Short of putting everyone into uniform, there would be many tens of millions who felt themselves unfairly or unnecessarily denied an opportunity to play a full part in national defense. The excessive emotionalism of 1940 had passed. The melancholy, the quiet despair that followed the fall of Greece was attended by a fatalistic conviction that the country would soon be at war. Shooting gallery receipts jumped 50 percent in June, 1941. There were still the publicity seekers, of course, such as the stripper whose act featured seven doves fluttering strategically at breasts and groin; she volunteered to train pigeons for the Army. But most people simply wanted some direct and satisfying role in the nation's drive to build up its forces.

What to do with so much untapped activist sentiment? How could it be kept from turning into a nuisance? Fortunately a number of outlets were being developed. The cities began to organize large-scale civil defense programs. (New York City alone registered more than 60,000 air-raid wardens in the summer of 1941). Volunteer fire brigades—an institution long dead in most urban areas—were being formed. First-aid classes were offered and attracted hundreds of thousands of students. Classes in survival techniques during air raids drew hundreds of thousands more. And after several regional experiments, the government began to establish a nationwide net of amateur aircraft spotters who would track potentially hostile aircraft. Modeled after the British system (although not yet, like theirs, backed up by radar) and known as the Civilian Air Warning System, it would soon enroll half a million volunteers.

XI

Negroes, Blacks and "Persons of Color"

THE Negroes' struggle for equality had split into two great factions about 1900; these two coalesced in response to the imperatives of national unity during the First World War; in the twenties and thirties they splintered into half a dozen groups; then they fused into a new, more assertive, more effective and independent coalition during the Second World War. And from that coalition has flowed the civil rights movement, which brought *Brown v. Board of Education of Topeka* and all that that implies. Not until the 1960's, when new, separatist militant organizations came to the fore, did the integrationist coalition lose its momentum.

Before the First World War the majority of Negroes had followed the teachings of Booker T. Washington. He counseled them to tolerate short-term discrimination while they built up economic self-sufficiency. Once a strong economic position was achieved, Negroes could then bid for genuine political and social equality. The minority, but it was a sizable minority, followed W. E. B. Du Bois. Its demand was equality now, and in full, as a matter of right. Yet Du Bois also emphasized that Negroes should cultivate their own natural elite, the Talented Tenth. From this privileged group would come the requisite leadership in the long and painful struggle for social justice.

But when the country entered the First World War, Du Bois had put his own enormous prestige behind Wilson's call for national unity. In a famous editorial he called upon American Negroes to "Close the Ranks!" And most black people complied. Had this patriotic act been reciprocated by a grateful government Du Bois' policy would have produced a historic advance in racial equality. Alas, there was only a cold indifference. Negroes were angry and hurt. Du Bois had been discredited and Washington's moderatism appeared hopelessly out of touch with reality. The result was a rise in both general militancy and confusion during the interwar years. Yet three essential features could be discerned: There was a sharp rise in black nationalism; there was a new upsurge in the consolations of religion; and the most militant demand of all—complete integration—became the most popular.

Following the 1918 Armistice, racial turmoil devastated scores of American cities, leaving hundreds of dead and wounded. Young Negroes nurtured little but bitterness for the self-righteously Progressive government

143

which had used them so badly. They reaped the whirlwind for their rage. The 1920's brought the KKK to the most powerful and terrifying position it had occupied since the years just after the Civil War. And long after angry blacks wearied of rioting, asking now just to be left alone, they continued to pay a horrendous price for their brief fling with lawlessness.

It was onto this turbulent, unhappy, bloody scene that there appeared a West Indian Negro named Marcus Garvey. Garvey ridiculed and badgered the established black leadership. And to their middle-class sensibilities he seemed a dangerous, irresponsible clown. But Garvey was able to succeed where they had failed—he reached the mass of black people. Garvey scorned alliances with liberal whites; he derided the defensive, timorous, "be a credit to the race" attitudes of other blacks. Above the tortured flesh, the scarred souls, the nagging thought that perhaps they were inferior after all, Garvey defiantly hoisted the banner of black pride. Where it was necessary, he simply invented a glorious black heritage.

For nearly a decade Garvey stood head and shoulders above every other black leader in the struggle for equality. But he too came to grief, through a series of badly managed business ventures, particularly the Black Star Line, which was to carry American Negroes back to Africa. Hundreds of thousands of poor people lost their hard-earned dollars on Garvey's ventures. But his militant black nationalism had also touched their hearts; it had brought ordinary black people into a mass movement for the first time. That twin legacy—of militancy and black nationalism—would live on even after Garvey's followers split into a dozen different sects, each with its self-styled "Race Missionary" or "Race Apostle."

The thirties brought to prominence another kind of leader, exemplified by Father Divine, preaching peace, love and unity. Garvey was a product of the post-World War I bitterness; Father Divine was created by the Depression. Garvey had, by adoring all that was black, unintentionally prepared the way for a "Black God." And that was precisely what Father Divine claimed to be.

Like Garvey's Back-to-Africa movement, Father Divine's Peace movement was a refuge from painful realities. Where Garvey taught separation and racial antagonism, Divine taught peace and love. And many of Father Divine's followers, who greeted one another with "Peace! it's wonderful!" were former Garveyites. The messiah himself was often regarded as either a confidence man or a clown. Divine was calculatedly flamboyant, ending his letters with "This leaves me well, healthy, peaceful, lively, loving, successful, prosperous and happy in spirit, body and mind and in every fiber, atom and cell of my bodily form." Other religious sects, including a Muslim sect led by Elijah Muhammad, also began to flourish, and it appeared for a while that the struggle for equal opportunity and justice might be swamped by a flood tide of black religiosity. But the cowardly Italian descent on Ethiopia in 1935 revived the latent spirit of black nationalism.

Here was a cause which Negroes could, and did, take as their own. For the first time in memory a black country was pitted in war against a white one, and for the first time that anyone could recall American blacks took an active interest in the fate of another country. Many Negroes readily formed an anti-Fascist alliance with white liberals now. There was some chagrin when it turned out that Ethiopians did not consider themselves Negroes, a name they associated with slavery, a state of which they happily knew nothing. To themselves, they were a nation, not a race. But to American Negroes they were still black, like themselves, and Ethiopia's cause was therefore their own. Black neighborhoods and communities held mass meetings, money was raised, and solidarity groups were formed. By the simple act of dispatching a correspondent to the Ethiopian War, the Pittsburgh *Courier* doubled its circulation in three months.

The climax to this reverie of black nationalism came on the night of June 25, 1935, when Joe Louis met an Italian challenger, Primo Carnera, at Yankee Stadium in a world heavyweight championship fight. Louis was a true champion to American Negroes, and not since the great Jack Johnson had there been a black fighter who had held the heavyweight crown. When Louis knocked Carnera out, Negroes set off on a double celebration, and young Negroes took to calling themselves "Afro-Americans."

The Depression had sparked a number of mass-action movements among Negroes. The best known of these, Jobs-for-Negroes, was national in organization but local in practice. It tried to force creation of jobs for black workers and failed utterly. Even educated Negroes could not get jobs, at least, not while there were so many unemployed white workers. Of the 170 Negroes who received PhD's between 1931 and 1941 only one was able to find a teaching job in a predominantly white university. Even the urbane, polyglot City College of New York had only one black teacher, and he had been there for twenty years. Yet from Jobs-for-Negroes and other movements like it, valuable experience in pressure-group politics was being acquired.

In ways that are best known only to themselves, Negroes managed to survive the Depression years. It is neither flattery nor blame to think that they, being reared to hardship from the first, probably survived the psychological pressures of the Depression more successfully than did unemployed white people. Yet tensions there always were. And occasionally they erupted, as they did in Harlem one night in March, 1935, leaving three people dead and two dozen wounded by gunfire in a brief, bloody race riot. Much of Du Bois' Talented Tenth drifted during these years into Marxism or Socialism. But those blacks who responded to the ardent overtures of the extreme left did so as individuals; most black people stayed resolutely in the political middle.

When the war began, I think it is fair to say, American Negroes were fragmented, confused, desperately poor for the most part and hardly any closer to equality than they had been in 1914. But they were much more militant than they had been in 1914. The mass of Negroes had been stirred. They were now sufficiently conscious to be shaped into an active force in national life. No one, it is true, knew how it was to be done. But sensible people were nervously hoping that it would be done peacefully. As one reviewer drew the moral of Richard Wright's best-selling first novel, *Native Son*, in 1940, it was a book about "the murderous potentialities of the whole U.S. Negro problem."

Not even the Census Bureau knew how many Negroes there were. Selective Service provided a way of double-checking at least part of the Census Bureau's figures, and it established an undercounting of anywhere between 3 and 15 percent. Negroes were assumed however to constitute roughly one-tenth of the total population. When this one-tenth attempted to exercise the influence of its numbers on the machinery of politics, it was effectively shut out. In Southern states, where more than two-thirds of the Negro population lived, the most effective single device was the poll tax, and this same mechanism was an equally formidable barrier to poor whites, who outnumbered Negroes. The tax appeared to be a token, say, $2, as in Mississippi and Alabama. But to a sharecropper who saw only $300 in cash each year that was two days' pay. And in some states the tax was cumulative. Thus, a man of forty voting for the first time might have to pay $30 or more for all the past elections he had not voted in.

On its own, of course, the poll tax did not stop people from voting. In Vermont, which had a poll tax, Negroes voted as a matter of course; Florida and Louisiana had no poll tax, and Negroes there rarely voted. But as a symbol the poll tax stood out as an indelible sign that through a variety of means, from outright physical coercion to subtler discouragements, tens of millions of poor people, black and white, were systematically disenfranchised.

Besides political emasculation, Negroes bore on, and within, their bodies the consequences of discrimination as unmistakably as the backs of slaves had once borne the marks of an overseer's lash. It was a truism that the country's "Number One public health problem" was the wretched physical state of Negroes. The incidence of syphilis and tuberculosis was three times what it was for whites; maternal and infant mortality rates were 60 percent higher. No wonder that at birth a Negro baby looked forward to a probable life-span of forty-seven years, or twelve years less than a white baby born at the same time.

White people knew that Negroes were discriminated against. Some were disturbed and thought it wrong. But to most people it was all vague and remote. They had little personal contact with blacks. For the most part Negroes, like poor whites, were invisible to the comfortable, powerful middle and upper classes. More than that, without any explicit sanction for it something very like apartheid had developed over the years, in North and South alike.

The reminders of racial separation were so pervasive that they hardly seemed remarkable any longer. Only a few can be cited here, though there were thousands of them. Anyone who turned to the twelve-pound *Directory of the American Medical Association* in search of a physician would find 300 names followed by the notation "Colored," and make his choice accordingly. Black athletes could distinguish themselves at football or baseball, but there was no chance for them to play professionally with whites. There were 16,000 movie theaters, 400 of them were "Negro movie theaters"; there was even an incipient black film industry in Harlem and the Bronx turning out all-black films. There was also an all-black American Tennis Association, with 25,000 registered players, which held its twenty-third National Championship in 1939. Sometimes the effort to maintain a separate-but-equal front was a cruelly unconscious parody, such as the 1940 "Negro World's Fair":

> At 12:30 Thursday afternoon, President Roosevelt pushed a button at his Hyde Park home turning on the lights at the American Negro Exposition in the Chicago Coliseum, "the first real Negro World's Fair in history." Marking 75 years of freedom 20,000 cheered James W. Washington, the Fair's president, and listened to laudatory speeches by Senator James L. Slattery of Illinois and Mayor Edward J. Kelly of Chicago.

When Negroes went to court to seek redress, they found that the aim of Supreme Court decisions was to require more equality in separation, not an end to separation. When separate-but-equal was asked for, the courts would grant it. So the University of Missouri opened the 1939–1940 academic year squirming under a court order that it provide a separate-but-equal law school for the black students to whom it had denied admission to the existing all-white law school. The university took over a former hair-tonic factory and tried to whip up a new law school, complete with state accreditation, to satisfy the courts. The next year it was ordered to create a new journalism school when its prestigious School of Journalism turned down a qualified Negro applicant. When the only Negro in Congress, Arthur Mitchell of Chicago, was forced to move from his Pullman berth into the day coach as the train he was on crossed into Arkansas, Mitchell sued for redress. And the Supreme Court ruled that he should have been provided with all-black Pullman accommodations just as comfortable as those he had been forced to leave. The issue, the Court reiterated, was "not a question of segregation but of equality of treatment." For his part, Mitchell praised the Court's decision; he hailed it as "the greatest advance in civil rights in my lifetime."

It should also be recalled that this was a time when white discussions of race had an easygoing callousness to them that our self-consciously race-troubled age has forgotten. There was an overriding notion that as much had been done for blacks as any reasonable person could hope for and that things would probably continue to improve—provided no one tried to force the pace. When Langston Hughes' autobiography, *The Big Sea*, appeared in 1940, he was severely rebuked for his lack of optimism: "If one lifts his eyes above Harlem and considers the strides made by the Negro—even since 1930—still greener pastures seem to lie ahead." *Time*, whose publisher, Henry Luce, publicly denounced racism, had no qualms about referring to labor dissidents as "the noisy nigger in the woodpile." When a fire roared through a shanty called the Rhythm Night Club in Natchez, Mississippi, it turned a structure composed chiefly of sheets of corrugated iron into a natural furnace. One hundred and ninety-eight patrons were burned to death in less than five minutes. But because all the victims were black, this disaster went almost completely unnoticed by the white press. The sole exception was one small photograph in *Life*, and that was because the photograph had some graphic merit, not because it was news of interest to the magazine's readers. When *Newsweek* took up *Native Son*, it was able to turn it into a pat on the back for the status quo: "It makes uneasy reading, but it is a virtue of our system of government that an indictment of the status quo such as this can be openly printed, discussed and answered."

So there was segregation by another name, callousness, indifference and smugness. This was also a time when the most radical demand was not separate-but-equal, for that would be conceded in principle and a few tokens given up, but the demand for complete and immediate integration. White society generally considered that both impossible and dangerous. To many people such was the program of hotheads and Communists. And this was still a time when the most famous expression of racism—not merely a symbol of it—was a black body hanging from the limb of a tree by some dusty Southern road.

Every few years Congress took up an antilynching bill. It did so again in 1940. The last time it had considered an antilynching statute, three years before, a mob in Mississippi had shown its contempt by demonstrating what it could do without rope: it had carefully shot down two Negroes, doing only enough damage to disable them and make escape impossible, then slowly roasted the victims to death with blowtorches.

Each year the Tuskegee Institute in Alabama announced the annual number of lynchings. And when in May, 1940, it claimed that there had been none for the past twelve months, almost no one believed it. The National Association for the Advancement of Colored People dismissed its claim out of hand as obvious nonsense. The ACLU counted three lynchings; the leftist International Labor Defense Committee counted six. The root of this dispute was the fact that in recent years, as the 1937 incident had shown, rope could be dispensed with, or as one journal expressed it, "the horrible fact that lynchings have been streamlined to the point where it is almost impossible to prove them to have been lynchings." And as the NAACP officials pointed out, mere statistics on lynchings proved very little when considered on their own: There had been a sharp rise in Klan terror in the first nine months of the war that resulted in more than thirty floggings, and three of the victims died of their injuries. It was in the midst of this dispute that Austin Calaway, an eighteen-year-old Negro, was taken from his jail cell in La Grange, Georgia, and lynched by a mob. Even conservative journals counted this as the sixth lynching of 1940, and Georgia's fourth.

The lynchings and floggings were, unhappily, only the spectacular side of a murderous rise in racial tensions. As we have seen, the country teetered on the verge of hysteria from the moment the war began. In factories, in schools, in cities large and small, racial clashes broke out more readily than at any time in recent memory. Dallas, for example, was rocked with racial violence all through the winter of 1940–1941 with riots, bombings and burnings as blacks, crammed into one tiny corner of the city, began to encroach on formerly all-white neighborhoods. Federal judges eventually managed to work out a compromise acceptable to both sides, but not before scores of people had spilled their blood. And everywhere throughout the South the Klan was moving from strength to strength.

Yet Negroes these days had something they had lacked during the First World War: a large and vocal Negro press. There had been a handful of black newspapers in 1918; now there were more than 200, and their combined circulation ran into the millions. An Associated Negro Press service provided national and international coverage. The black press was race-conscious; understandable enough, but many whites—especially white journalists—interpreted this as being antiwhite. The black press was accused by its prosperous, respectable white counterpart of encouraging race hatred and of promoting racial strife. But they were not antiwhite; they were simply problack. And their significance was that they provided Negroes with something they had never had before—a powerful and independent national voice.

Black newspapers and magazines did much to educate and mobilize Negroes to fight racism instead of accepting it as a burden to be stoically borne. No one person spoke for Negroes, no one movement joined them together; they were fragmented and segregated. But Negroes could no longer be ignored or kept ignorant. And once the defense boom began breathing new life into the economy, they would not be kept from its benefits without putting up a fight.

Negroes were, in fact, better prepared to fight for their rights than they had ever been. For besides the Negro press and the general increase in consciousness of their collective ills and grievances, there was the Depression experience of creating effective pressure groups. Among its triumphs were the Scottsboro boys and the Buy Where You Work movement. A corps of Negro labor organizers and militant civil rights workers had emerged from these struggles. There was even an all-black union, the Brotherhood of Sleeping Car Porters, headed by A. Philip Randolph.

Like other AFL unions, Randolph's Brotherhood voted resolutions against Fascism, Nazism and Communism and purged Communists from leadership positions. It came out firmly for the defense program and, like other unions, opposed the draft. But it bumped up against the fact that organized labor was generally indifferent to the problem of getting jobs for Negroes. With only a few exceptions, such as Reuther's United Automobile Workers, Negro labor organizers had few white allies. On the contrary, organized labor had persistently tried to exclude black workers from whatever new jobs opened up during the Depression. There was also spontaneous bitterness over Ford's cynical use of black workers as strikebreakers. And during the defense boom there was still much hostility. One union organizer in Seattle expressed his anger over suggestions that Negroes should be hired now that a boom was under way: "Organized labor has been called upon to make many sacrifices for defense, and has made them gladly; but this is too much."

If the unions would not help them get into defense work, Negroes would have to turn to government, even though they had been double-crossed when they turned that way in the First World War. Then a token Division of Negro Economics was created within the Department of Labor. It was abolished as soon as the war ended. But this time there was the Negro press, the new consciousness, the new leadership corps, and a growing number of Negroes in government. The importance of this latter development was often exaggerated; two entirely mythical creations—"the Black Cabinet" and "the Black Brains Trust"—were conjured up from it. The handful of Negroes in government were able and intelligent men, but their posts were advisory and their concerns almost exclusively those of Negroes. Though highly privileged themselves, they constantly lobbied the administration to use the power of the federal government in the struggle for racial equality. They now concentrated on fighting the exclusion of Negroes from defense jobs and military service. The administration at first responded by offering a few sops and tokens, such as making Robert C. Weaver an assistant to Sidney Hillman on the OPM and giving Stimson a black aide, William Hastie (later a federal judge). But the mass of black people would no longer settle for vague promises and expressions of good-will.

Not only in Washington but at every level of government from munici-palities to state and federal agencies Negroes and white liberals insistently demanded antidiscrimination legislation. Indiana was a fairly typical exam-ple. A bill forbidding race discrimination in employment breezed through the lower house of the state legislature by a vote of 91 to 0. But the upper house defeated it easily, thanks to strong opposition from the Indiana Chamber of Commerce. Yet something had to be done; if it was not, the current spate of racial clashes was certain to get worse. Consequently, a biracial committee was established, comprising the governor, the president of the Chamber of Commerce and several prominent local black leaders. The committee also secured the grudging cooperation of the AFL and the CIO. By November, 1941, some two dozen Indiana cities had similar committees at work trying to put Negroes into defense jobs or any other jobs they could find. For once, it was not a token or an excuse for failure; the employment level of blacks was soon measurably higher in Indiana than in the nation as a whole. State and local successes could only spur on the demand for federal action.

It was true that the New Deal had brought more Negroes into govern-ment than any previous administration, yet they still amounted to a mere handful. To force Roosevelt's hand, Negroes turned to direct action. Under the leadership of A. Philip Randolph some 50,000 to 100,000 Negroes prepared to march on Washington on July 1, 1941. They would parade down the Washington Mall so that all the world could see how American incantations to democracy and social justice were hollow mockeries. So long as Negroes were frozen out of the defense boom, they intended to embarrass the federal government and the administration as deeply and as often as they could. Roosevelt realized, at the last moment, that they were serious, that kind words and promises had lost their magic. Through the intervention of Eleanor Roosevelt he managed to get the march called off just days before it was scheduled. In return, he promised to use the govern-ment's power to end job discrimination. He proceeded to issue a statement deploring racism in American society and announced the creation of the Fair Employment Practices Commission to fight it. And that was all.

Negroes were bewildered. If that was all Roosevelt would do, they asked, why had Randolph surrendered so much leverage for it? Randolph's prestige plummeted. He had not been able to provide jobs after all. Nor, it appeared, could the FEPC.

The Executive Order 8802 which established the new commission bore a fatal weakness: It was all or nothing at all. Compliance could be ordered by FEPC officials, and government contractors who disobeyed could lose their contracts. Yet the FEPC could not fine them, or reduce their profits, or send them to jail. And in this hour of crisis, just how many tanks, planes, ships, guns, shells, life jackets, parachutes, how much food, penicillin, quinine, and how much time, was the country prepared to go without in order to make the FEPC's powers effective? Both the regulators and the regulated knew that Congress and the public would never allow any major contract to be canceled. Whatever the FEPC did, therefore, it had to be by persuasion, or it could not be done at all.

There was also dissension within the FEPC. One member, Mark Ethridge, a liberal journalist from Kentucky, saw nothing wrong with segregation and publicly argued that the commission should devote its energies to assuring separate-but-equal practices. Most black people angrily disagreed. But as Ethridge and his supporters pointed out, there was nothing in the executive order which banned segregation—it simply insisted on equality.

The FEPC's members used the small appropriation granted them to travel around the country holding public hearings into discrimination. They found, and publicized, the kind of runaround Negroes had experienced for years. Employers would be brought in to explain why they hired only a few Negroes or none at all. The reasons were many and sometimes mutually contradictory: Negroes never apply; white and black cannot mix together easily on the job; we do not have the time or money to build separate toilets; trained Negroes are not available for this work; Negroes are racially unsuited for the job; the union will not allow Negroes to join; the workers dislike Negroes and do not want them around; this is a rush job, and there is no time for experiments; and so on. But Negroes knew the excuses only too well. They wanted jobs, not publicity, and the FEPC was soon considered only another broken promise.

Besides, the FEPC was concerned only with discrimination in employment. Who would put an end to discrimination in the draft? It was no secret that the military would be happy to have an all-white Army and Navy if it could. The Army had maintained a policy of proportional representation during the First World War, so that roughly 400,000 of the 4,000,000 soldiers in 1918 were black. But though the Army was bulging with draftees these days, only 3 percent of them were black. Negroes wanted to be drafted, but local boards would induct them only when they had to. So a mere 2,000 Negroes were drafted during the first year of Selective Service. It was, however, relatively easier for Negroes to enlist, so that by December, 1941, 100,000 black soldiers, mostly enlistees, were in the Army. Even this was far short of 10 percent of the Army's total strength.

The grievances did not stop there. The Army still held to its policy of segregated units. Officer candidates trained together regardless of race, but black and white enlisted men were rigidly segregated. Recreation, health and eating facilities were roughly equal and always separate. Most galling of all was the segregation of Negroes in service units; the dangerous glories of combat were for whites only. As long as that policy stood, the revival of the proportional representation policy would produce not gratitude, but anger, for the only way the 10 percent level could be accomplished was by creating more of the Jim Crow service battalions.

All through 1941 race riots erupted at Army bases, leaving dead and wounded soldiers of both races in their wake. Some of the clashes were pitched battles in miniature. One, in Fayetteville, North Carolina, in August, 1941, left two soldiers dead and five with gunshot wounds. At another post an entire company of Negroes fought an hour-long gun battle with a company of military police, leaving a dozen dead and wounded. Ironically, the first man ever killed with the basic infantry weapon of World War II, the M 1 rifle, was a Negro sergeant in the U.S. Army. And because the Army placed most of its training bases in the South, bloody racial conflicts neither began nor ended at the post gates but spilled back and forth between town and camp.

The War Department tried to moderate black rage by backing down from its earlier determination to keep the Air Corps lily-white. In 1940 there had been fewer than 100 Negroes in the entire country who could fly a plane. Nearly all of them were college students trained by the CAB. Yet not one of them held a commission in the Air Corps. When one black flier, Walter Robinson, applied, he was quickly turned away. (Robinson went to Canada and was immediately signed up by the RCAF.) But in the fall of 1941 the Army reversed itself and created an all-black fighter unit, the 99th (Negro) Pursuit Squadron at Tuskegee, Alabama. To service the squadron's twenty fighter planes, an all-black ground crew was being trained in Illinois.

In a heavy-handed attempt to assure Negroes that the War Department was neither as hostile nor as indifferent to them as current policy suggested, the Undersecretary of War, Robert Patterson, went on radio to praise the courage of black soldiers, past and present. He explained in great detail how well the policy of separation was working and carefully explained its benefits. Negroes were generally disgusted by this unasked-for tribute to the mythical glories of segregation.

Yet Patterson's address, the FEPC, the various local and state biracial committees, the growing number of Negroes in the Army and in defense jobs all indicated, whether it was acknowledged or not, that a major change in the status of Negroes was well under way. Not because of the kindheartedness of white society, nor thanks to any great rise in enlightenment, but because Negroes now had enough leverage to force concessions. A rare opportunity was at hand, if they could but realize it. White people were conscious in a remote way before the war began that Negroes were treated unfairly, and some feared that they might turn on their oppressors, forming a vast, fatal fifth column. "During the World War," one writer recalled, "German propagandists tried to undermine the loyalty of American Negroes." Yet he was confident, he went on, that "Today the patriotism of our thirteen million Negroes is as strong as ever." Other people were not quite so confident. And the rise in racial tensions and clashes, the increased capacity for bringing pressure all served to make the country more sensitive to Negro demands than it had been since the far-off days of Reconstruction.

There were frequent reminders of a growing willingness to concede things which were formerly denied. Eighty percent of the nation now favored spending as much to educate Negro children as was spent on white children. When *Birth of a Nation* was shown in Denver over the opposition of local black leaders, the exhibitor was fined and threatened with a jail sentence for endangering the peace.* *Native Son* was a Book-of-the-Month Club selection and a best seller, thereby taking into hundreds of thousands of white, middle-class homes Wright's portrayal of the deadly fruits of white racism. And when the Federal Office of Education presented a series of hurrah-for-democracy radio shows in the winter of 1940, one of them, called *Freedom's People* (!), was aimed specifically at Negroes; its purpose was "to improve the Negro's status by dwelling on his contribution to U.S. civilization." Maladroit perhaps, yet well meant.

Tensions continued to rise, of course. The rage and frustration were not to be dispelled by soft words and symbolic deeds. And to many people it appeared, as 1941 drew to a close, that racial problems were getting worse, not better. In the big cities, especially in New York, a wave of violent crimes by young blacks against whites spread terror. It also inspired a sudden rush of interest in alleviating the miseries of Harlem. That November, something occurred that should have taken place long before: Two hundred New York politicians, lawyers, businessmen, teachers, policemen and government agents convened to probe Harlem's sufferings and devise palliatives to them.

---

* A clear violation of civil liberties. I cite it here only as an example of growing white sensitivity to Negro grievances.

XII

Isolation and the Rediscovery
of Latin America

LEND-LEASE had passed, and the argument over isolation ran on as
noisily as ever. But public opinion was not split neatly into antagonistic halves; rather, it was fragmented. And foreign policy, instead of shaping opinion, reflected it. The result was a strange half-in, half-out relationship with the war, satisfying absolutely no one. Roosevelt was warily
pushing his fingers farther and farther into the trap, palpably anxious not
to outdistance public support. But given opinion like this, who could be
sure just where the limits of support were to be found? Rollin Kirby summarized the sense of frustration in a cartoon which showed Uncle Sam on
a bicycle with one square wheel and one round one. And the antagonisms
showed up in private lives, as with Dorothy Thompson and Sinclair Lewis
—that is, Mr. and Mrs. Lewis. She was interventionist and for all aid to
Britain; he was isolationist and a member of America First. The longer
the foreign policy debate went on, the more muddled it became.

While isolationists were fulminating that the Committee to Defend
America had drifted from Measures Short of War into Stop Hitler Now,
the CDA was in fact torn by the bitterest dissension. White wanted aid to
Britain that did not involve the United States in the war, did not require
the repeal of the Johnson Act, did not involve convoys of American ships.
America First could—and did—support that kind of aid, but White's
fellow members in the CDA did not. Many of them, therefore, resigned
from the CDA, convinced that it had been captured by the isolationists.
Ironically, at almost exactly the same time, a sizable number of America
First members were resigning from their organization in protest of what
they considered interventionism in the higher echelons.

Sick at heart, White resigned his post, complaining that the CDA operations in New York and Washington had fallen into the hands of warmongers, "and there is no way to oust them. . . . I just can't remain head of an
organization which is being used to ghost dance for war." Characteristi-
cally, La Guardia responded by calling White a traitor, and compared him to
Laval. And General Wood proceeded to embarrass the old man by inviting him to join America First.

The CDA survived the loss of its famous and popular chairman. It fought for lend-lease with as much energy as it might have mustered under White. Throughout 1941 it supported every forward step the President took. But the initiative had in truth passed to the ultras, now organized in the Fight for Freedom committee, the most virulently prowar organization ever to flourish in the United States in a formal time of peace.

Fight for Freedom's roots went back to June, 1940, when thirty prominent people had placed newspaper advertisements calling for a declaration of war on Germany. In the months that followed, they and others who thought as they did coalesced into an organization called the Century Group. At the outset it was very small and very distinguished. The founding members included Henry Luce, James B. Conant and the playwright Robert Sherwood; Joseph Alsop was a member, so was Dean Acheson, and so were two dozen big bankers, Wall Street lawyers, liberal journalists and divines and a former Chief of Naval Operations. Drawn predominantly from New York City and New England, they tended to be relatively young —that is, in their forties. They were the junior officers of the Great War. They numbered both Democrats and Republicans but were overwhelmingly Protestant. They were as urbane and well traveled a group as the country could boast, and when they raised their eyes from America's shores, they saw Europe; only one—Henry Luce, the son of missionary parents in China—saw Asia.

Early in 1941 the Century Group blossomed into the Fight for Freedom committee. Now that the CDA was badly split, it was only a matter of time before this new interventionist organization tried to supplant the older, larger body. Like the Century Group itself, the FFF was overwhelmingly white, Anglo-Saxon and Protestant. No one could dismiss as a foreign body something so undeniably Eastern Establishment and All-American. (That had to await a Senator from Wisconsin, some ten years later.) The FFF therefore carried far more weight than interventionist groups of comparable size which were larded with Jewish and foreign-sounding names. The members of the FFF were men of moderate to conservative political views. They were rallying to the preservation of Anglo-Saxon culture. And they were moved by no mere Anglophile sentimentality. They were sincerely convinced that if Britain were conquered by Hitler, then the United States would come under attack. To save Britain was to serve the safety of their country.

The people on the FFF committee were determined to remedy what they believed was a lack of passion and vision on the White committee; once that was done, they would carry the fight for intervention into every section of the country. A set of attractive, positive war aims was thought to be a priceless asset, and they set about providing one. The result was something of a disappointment, for it ran strongly to clichés and platitudes. "Brotherhood can be made real in this world" was one typical assertion. "Democracy is a code of conduct" was another. Yet these expressions probably filled some genuine need. The FFF also called for a declaration of war on Germany, something the CDA had never seriously considered. The declaration of war very rapidly became the sum and substance of the FFF's existence.

Hundreds of FFF chapters were formed in scores of cities. More than 600 small-town newspapers carried the FFF's message into rural America and the smaller towns. Mergers between FFF and CDA chapters became a daily occurrence. In every one of these it was the policy of the FFF which predominated. Many members of the CDA and many people who were vaguely pro-aid to Britain were annoyed by the FFF's militancy. But the important thing to realize was that the entire thrust of the debate on the interventionist side had taken a new, more clear-cut, more vigorous edge. Interventionism was no longer to be seen picking its way carefully through a smoke screen of hazy part-peace, part-war, part-aid, part-chastity formulas. With the FFF at its helm, it came out unequivocally, unabashedly, unashamedly for war.

There could no longer be any doubt that isolationists were in the thick of a losing fight and would be lucky if they could keep from being routed. Roosevelt's fireside chat at the end of 1940, followed by the assertive, popular Four Freedoms speech, had thrown them more than ever onto the defensive. Isolationists were openly, and often, branded "appeasers." They scoffed in turn at the interventionists, the logic of whose arguments, they said, reduced the British to the point where "It is as if the British were our mercenaries."

America First had campaigned vigorously against the lend-lease bill, reviling it as "the War Dictator bill." But no matter what they said, public support for lend-lease had risen with every week. Isolationists fervently pinned their hopes on Senator Wheeler. Had he not defeated the Supreme Court reorganization bill in 1937? Why should he not repeat that triumph over the hated Roosevelt? But Wheeler had pressed too hard, losing the uncommitted by his tasteless prophesy about "every fourth American boy." In his rage Wheeler followed up by attacking an old target—Hollywood, for turning out anti-Nazi films; for "carrying on a violent propaganda campaign intending to incite the American people to war." Isolationists could be found lingering over the roster of Jewish names in Hollywood and ominously drawing their own conclusions. But though it was true that the big studios had ground out a spate of anti-Nazi films in the first year of war, as soon as they discovered that there was no profit in it, they had stopped.

After lend-lease went into effect, isolationists—from Norman Thomas, who now threw in his lot with America First, to Earl Browder, who was still demanding that America stay neutral, "like Russia," to Colonel Mc-

Cormick of the Chicago *Tribune*—were convinced that it would lead to war. To them, as to almost everyone else, it was obvious that the Germans would be forced to attack any "bridge of ships" carrying lend-lease, thus giving Roosevelt the *casus belli* he plainly wanted. Progressives such as Thomas were convinced that once the United States entered the war, it would very rapidly degenerate into a capitalist-imperialist dictatorship. Reactionaries such as Colonel McCormick dreaded the very opposite, the triumph of Socialism, possibly even Communism. As events were to prove, both Thomas and McCormick were wrong. But the important thing was that vain though their fears were, they revealed just how much the quarrel over isolation was really a quarrel over American society, not over foreign policy. They (and there were many thousands like them) were in each other's arms not because they shared precisely the same vision of the country but because the vision that each held had no room for the uncertainties of war; neither trusted the country to emerge from total war as anything that resembled the America they knew and loved.

Beyond that crucial fact, there was very little binding together the disparate elements of isolationism. There was no common program. There was no set of positive aims which claimed the loyalties of all, or nearly all. Some countenanced substantial aid to Britain. Others, the ultras, simply demanded no foreign wars. And every point between these two had its adherent. But just as the absolutists were in the ascendant on the interventionists' side of the spectrum, the absolute isolationists went into a spectacular decline. Their nominal leader, an Iowa journalist named Verne Marshall, made such a laughingstock of himself with his wild ideas on how to end the war that he took to calling himself "the Wild Man from Borneo." His appearance on radio's *Town Hall of the Air* during the lend-lease debate ruined what was left of his credit. He began by delivering a long and boring recital of his antecedents. He then spent several minutes reminiscing over the Pulitzer Prize he had won some years before. Again and again he appealed for money. And all the while he kept up a running battle with the program's moderator, who was trying desperately to adhere to the program's format. As the meeting staggered to its close, Marshall had succeeded in creating a hostile audience. He concluded by inviting those present in the studio to come up and fight him, "even though I'm twenty pounds under weight." Shortly thereafter the No Foreign Wars Committee vanished quietly at dead of night. America First inherited a near monopoly on what was left of isolation.

America First survived its divisions better than had the CDA, but only just. It was plain that the more distinguished members of the committee were becoming increasingly embarrassed by many of their followers. Some journalists claimed they could actually see repugnance darken the faces of the platform luminaries at isolationist rallies. Pleas for religious or racial tolerance would be greeted by boos, scurrility and noisy invocations of purblind hatred. And the committee's leading spokesman attracted such types whether he wanted them or not, and there is good reason to believe he did not.

When Lindbergh told an America First rally that Britain's shipping losses placed it in danger of starvation, that its cities were "devastated by bombing," that its situation was desperate, his litany of Britain's agonies was interrupted by furious applause. Native Fascists, anti-Semites, petty and vindictive types of every description, plus any number of Irishmen with legitimate grievances, were by now packing the meetings of America First. Here then was no crowd of sober, responsible citizens debating the great issues of the day; it was a mob which might easily explode. The possibility of violence always hovered over the big-city meetings; less so over those in small towns. In Chicago it finally became necessary to ban "God Bless America" at America First's rallies in deference to the chorus of catcalls and boos it invariably triggered, for Irving Berlin was a Jew. Lindbergh appeared genuinely embarrassed by these outpourings of hate. He was not himself given over to hate, but a man who sincerely believed his country could and should have a separate destiny from its European parents'. He was also unable to grasp that because Germany was a part of Western civilization did not mean it was not a menace to it.

Yet Lindbergh became, against his will, the darling of the worst elements of isolationism. And for decades after, he was despised by liberals, intellectuals and interventionists generally. Roosevelt himself at one point called Lindbergh a copperhead—that is, a man whose sympathies lay with his country's enemies.* Lindbergh, his pride stung, immediately resigned his commission in the Air Corps Reserve. He was subjected to a torrent of abuse. The *New Republic* cast a few dark hints, then went on to ask, "Who Is Behind Lindbergh?" And Dorothy Thompson cast a few of her own: She suggested that his actions were just what one could expect from a man who expected to be one of Hitler's Gauleiters in an occupied America.

As 1941 wore on, it became increasingly difficult for America First even to hold its meetings. Many cities simply refused to permit them. And in the unkindest cut of all, the American Legion was now denouncing isolationists and everything they advocated. In vain did the American First leadership insist that it held no brief for Fascists or Communists; that when it came to national defense it was as martial as anyone (it had rewritten its slogan: "National Defense at Any Expense, but Keep the Boys at Home"); that it investigated the source of every contribution over $100; that any contribution accompanied by the merest hint of anti-Semitism, anti-Rooseveltism, pro-Nazism or pro-Communism was returned to the donor.

All in vain, and the embarrassments not only continued, but grew far

---

* The original copperheads were northern Democrats whose sympathies during the Civil War were with the Confederacy.

worse. With some kind of showdown looming, tempers were becoming shorter than ever. Both sides in this historic debate were abandoning reason and moderation. But the isolationists were on the losing side; they were to pay the highest price in terms of shattered reputations and lowered public esteem. Collectively, they would generally be regarded for years to come as stupid, vicious, pro-Nazi reactionaries or at least as people blind to the realities of a new day and a menace to their country's safety.

Senator Wheeler had already damaged isolation. He dealt it another blow when, in July, it developed that more than a million isolationist postcards had been sent out under his frank. Each card went to a soldier or his family, asking them to petition the President to keep the country out of war. Stimson fumed that this was "subversive . . . if not treason," and the administration hinted at legal action. This brought the aged Hiram Johnson of California to his feet. If Wheeler went to jail, then he, Johnson, would go with him. And not one Senator was willing to defend the Secretary of War. Still, the main result was that the prestige of the Congressional isolationists dropped still further.

But the gaffe of gaffes came in the fall, and it was historic, the stuff of myth, rumor and legend. Lindbergh blandly told an America First rally in Des Moines that there were three elements responsible for most of the agitation to get the United States into the war. These were "the British, the Roosevelt Administration and the Jews." Just behind these three he also discerned Anglophile capitalists and intellectuals. For himself, he had strong sympathies for the Jews and understood the enmity they must cherish for Germany. He unequivocally damned German persecution and terror. But intervention, he insisted, would only make the persecution of German Jews worse, not better. More than that, the thin crust of tolerance which protected American Jewry was likely to crack under the strain of war. And the lot of unpopular minorities such as the Jews would worsen. Consider for a moment, he said, the highly visible role Jews play in entertainment, in journalism and in government. If intervention did make this a less tolerant country, how could they then hope to escape the inevitable consequences of that fact? So, he concluded, the current pressure for intervention exerted by American Jewry was in the best interest of neither themselves nor their coreligionists in Germany.

Even if Lindbergh's analysis was wrong,* it was not that of a Fascist or a religious bigot. But it was not difficult to make it appear to be both these things by breaking off a fragment and holding it up for comment, such as "Their [American Jews'] greatest danger to this country lies in their large ownership and influence in our motion pictures, our press, our

---

* As we shall see, there was in fact a rise in anti-Semitism in the United States during the war years, though thankfully not on a massive scale. It is also noteworthy that the systematic extermination of European Jews, Hitler's "Final Solution," was not undertaken until it became obvious that Germany had lost the war.

radio, and our government." Only a reading of what preceded and followed would reveal that the reason Lindbergh thought them dangerous was that from these eminent heights American Jewry might succeed in helping the United States into a war which would destroy both all that it held dear *and* all that they themselves held dear.

Nor was his essential thesis wrong. No one could seriously claim that the elements he held out as pressing for intervention were not doing so. What he said was not wicked but impolitic. The leadership of the America First Committee was thrown into utter confusion. The rank and file cheered Lindbergh, but liberal isolationists dropped away, disgusted and disheartened. From one coast to the other Lindbergh was reviled as a patent bigot and Nazi. Interestingly, about the only liberals who appear to have kept their heads during this uproar were American Jews. The important thing about this episode, however, is that it put an end to the effectiveness of America First. Its other important consequence was that street-corner oratory took on a new viciousness. Angry crowds spilled from Columbus Circle and Union Square into Fifth Avenue. Orators and hecklers snarled "Jew" and "Nazi" at one another with a dangerous bitterness, and time and again fistfights broke out. With baited breath New York's police waited for a major riot to erupt, but the isolationists were by now so outnumbered that simple prudence cleared them from the streets, and as they vanished, the threat of riot dwindled.

Yet, undaunted, Lindbergh continued to speak out, despite a growing coolness between himself and the national committee of America First. Few chapters would host him any longer. When he was welcomed at Fort Wayne, Indiana, he intemperately suggested that the 1942 elections might well be the last free elections ever held in the United States. It was a foolish idea, yet from it the *New Republic* felt able to conclude that Lindbergh was "building a Fascist movement" and declared this address was "the groundwork for possible Fascist action." They expected that the next isolationist step would be an attempted right-wing revolution.

Far from being part of some vast Fascist effort to topple the government, Lindbergh, the Lone Eagle, was in truth little more by now than a Lone Voice. Isolation had been defeated; because it never graced a Presidential ballot with a candidate of its own, a myth would arise that it was never given a fair test, that it was cheated. But well before the end of 1941 it had lost its hold on anything more than the fringes of public opinion. From the day the war began, every major battle it fought it lost. Every important segment of opinion it appealed to deserted it. And in Congress its champions were reduced to staging pathetic charades. Their chief effort in the fall of 1941 was to hold hearings into Hollywood's "warmongering," with the heavily isolationist Senate Commerce Committee leading the attack. In charge of the defense was none other than Wendell Willkie, retained as the movie industry's lawyer. So they sat there, a little rump of querulous old men, champions of a defeated cause, and demanded to know why Hollywood had turned out such films as *Sergeant York, Convoy, Flight Command, I Married a Nazi* and *The Great Dictator*. Senator Champ Clark of Missouri had, in fact, already made up *his* mind: Hollywood, he said, was "turning 17,000 movie theaters into 17,000 nightly mass meetings for war."

Americans have always looked upon Latin America as being next door, regardless of what geography says: that Moscow is closer to Chicago than is Buenos Aires or that London is closer to San Francisco than is Santiago. No one questioned the aptness of calling Roosevelt's insistence on less bullying and arrogance in dealings with that continent a Good Neighbor Policy. But it is really history that has bound the two Americas together, not geography. History and disparity. The North has held and exercised its sway over the South almost from the first days of independent American republics. Latin Americans have found the embrace stifling, yet the embrace itself has seemed entirely natural to North Americans. Physical contiguity was always reason enough, especially when the relationship was that of superior to inferior. And it was ironic that when the two continents were physically severed at last, by the construction of the Panama Canal, they were bound more tightly than ever.

Roosevelt's policy was well meant; most people thought it desirable. They were prepared to fashion a new relationship which took Latin Americans as good neighbors rather than as people who were letting down the neighborhood. But the shift in policy had little or no impact on American life. There was no upsurge of interest, no rush to invest money south of the border, no sharp increase in Spanish language classes. Perhaps it was because the Depression blunted interest or initiative in anything but itself. For whatever reason, it had little impact.

But with the war there had come a veritable rediscovery of Latin America. It was a back-door revival of internationalism in American life. While the war was painfully, clumsily dragging the country in through the front door, a new interest in Latin America was quietly, easily ushering it in at the back.

Not surprisingly, the emphasis at first was on Latin America's bearing on national security. An inventory of America's friends in the crisis months of 1940 made this sort of reading: "Where are our friends? France is in chains; Britain battles for her life; Japan, our ally of 1917, is, if not actively hostile to us, uncooperative. The South American countries? It is perilous to our security to lose them [even though] they have little to give us by way of active support." A hundred stories told of how Berlin was looking covetously at South America. In fact, said one journal, "The conqueror is already reaching greedily for the South American pear. Already the Nazi agents crawl over it like beetles . . . searching out the soft spots . . . nibbling at morale . . . burrowing tunnels underneath the surface." Here, in short, were "90 million Americans who may go to work for Hitler." And from Brazil an American businessman wrote home: "It is current *vox populi* that with 15,000 men they [the Nazis] can overrun this nigger country at a moment. . . ."

There were strong fears for the safety of the Panama Canal. And the military could not discuss the Canal's defenses openly. So it let loose a flood tide of color photographs in which the straight lines of powerful coastal guns crossed those of tropical palms. When officials were reticent, imagination took over. In the summer of 1940 rumor had it that the locks of the Canal had been bombed by unmarked aircraft; a train full of ammunition for the big guns had mysteriously blown up; and a landslide at Culebra Cut had stranded the Pacific Fleet, leaving the Eastern seaboard open to attack. The New York *Daily News* discovered that "265 known Nazis" were working on the Canal's defenses—and could not be dismissed because of military red tape. Hard on the heels of the rumors came proposed countermeasures, the most popular of which was to place a roof over the entire Canal.

There was considerable popular anxiety over the presence of German and Italian airlines in South America, a concern which American business encouraged. The Axis controlled 20,000 miles of South American air routes; their American competitors some 30,000. Given the limited current role of commercial aviation, a little thinning out would cause no real hardship and might easily increase profits. And besides, the Axis airlines posed a military threat—they were likely to shuttle in thousands of storm troopers disguised as tourists, weren't they?

Business, in fact, was beginning to look at Latin America with fresh interest. American export trade was cut off from much of the world market; here was a possible alternative. The Mexican seizure of American-owned oilfields during the late 1930's had dampened a level of interest already dulled by the Depression. But no sooner did the war settle down for an indefinite run than the possibilities of investment in and trade with Latin America revived. As one journal cheered, "The Latin American market is more than a windfall: it is a New Frontier."

Isolationists made the strongest case they could that anything the United States lost in trade with Europe could be compensated for simply by freezing European countries out of South America. General Wood, the chairman of America First, went even further. He thought that it might be possible to satisfy Hitler by giving him half of South America. The lower half, of course; farthest from America's shores. The United States would take the northern half for itself. Hitler's share would total 70,000,000 people and 5,000,000 square miles of almost virgin territory. Was that not a far, far better haul, he asked, than a handful of war-racked colonies along the Eastern seaboard and a war with the rest of the United States that might last for many years?

The administration responded to this new set of concerns in its own way. A big businessman's son (also a Republican), Nelson Rockefeller, was made Coordinator of Cultural and Commercial Relations between the American Republics for National Defense, in July, 1940. Rockefeller was charged with forging closer economic and emotional ties between the United States and its southern neighbors. It appeared that the State Department was too accustomed to routine, and too small, to take on a special venture of this kind. Or so it was said. By the summer of 1941 Rockefeller's position had become much more important, his staff had risen enormously and his appropriation correspondingly increased by several hundred-fold. The objective of his office was clearly that of countering Axis agents in Latin America.

The interest of ordinary people kept pace. They started studying Spanish in unheard-of numbers. Language classes generally had profited from the outbreak of war, with one notable and foolish exception—German classes lost their students. The chief beneficiary of the boom in foreign languages was Spanish. Through her column, "My Day," Mrs. Roosevelt was urging that Spanish be made the second language taught in the nation's schools. Hundreds of school districts were already doing that. In May, 1941, every single one of the 10,000 commissioned officers in the Army Air Corps had signed up, with official blessing, to learn the language. And a great national shortage of qualified Spanish language teachers had made itself felt.

Reader's Digest, an organ usually conservative and isolationist, went international in 1941 by publishing a South American edition, in Spanish. Within a year it had become the largest-selling Spanish-language magazine in the world. The two biggest radio networks began in 1941 to broadcast weekly programs to and from South America. *Time* inaugurated its first air edition, for South America. John Gunther produced the third of his Insides, *Inside South America,* in 1941.

But the strongest expression of this new interest in Latin America was the unconditional surrender of the country's night life. In nightclubs, dance halls and theaters the Latin American craze threatened to sweep everything before it. The New York *Times* concluded: "There were more and better rumba bands in Manhattan than Havana." Popular numbers such as "South of the Border" and "The South American Way" were played over and over again, and no one seemed to tire of them. The conga had made its entrance on American dance floors in 1939; less than a year later well-dressed matrons could be seen flailing across the dance floor each night shouting "Vamos a la Conga!" In Harlem it inspired the congeroo, conceivably the most violently acrobatic dance of an age which was inured to the frenzy of the lindy hop. The congeroo concluded with the female partner traversing the length of the floor on her backside with her heels and hands waving in the air.

To keep up with this Latin America craze, big-city nightclubs were first compelled to install rumba bands to alternate with the "straight" musicians. By 1941 this stopgap would serve no longer. Latin nightclubs were opening now on the promise of nothing but Latin music and decor— no swing, no straight, no Hawaiian, just Latin. The most glittering of all was New York's Copacabana; close behind it came the Latin Quarter; trailing off into the distance were scores of less imposing but equally all-Latin restaurants and clubs. For Broadway, Cole Porter whipped up *Panama Hattie*, a musical in which Ethel Zimmerman of Astoria, New York, continued her rise to international fame as Ethel Merman. Genuine Latin American performers flocked into the United States, and some, such as Carmen Miranda of Brazil, became famous. There was also Carmen Amaya, billed as "the world's greatest Flamenco dancer." When Toscanini saw her, he swooned. "Never," said the maestro, "have I seen such fire and rhythm!" And Michigan's Tom Harmon, who spent the 1940 college football season running over and around Michigan's opponents, received the accolade of having "rumba hips."

In these innocent, pleasant ways isolation had suffered yet one more defeat, while the country moved ever closer to assuming the role which interventionists considered America's true destiny.

XIII

Action in the North Atlantic

IN 1940 it had been the isolationists who had insisted that the British spell out their war aims. Now it was the liberal interventionists. Such was at least one of the consequences of the rallying around democracy and the general search for the larger meaning of the war. Isolationists had argued that all the British fought for were their own necks and interests. By 1941 liberal interventionists were wondering if they were right.

Here was a potentially explosive question. When the Bolshevik government had published the secret treaties of the Allies of 1917, showing them to be not sincere champions of peace and justice, but cynical self-servers and trimmers, the entire war and its sacrifices had been discredited in the eyes of millions. And that war had been oversold; on both sides of the Atlantic its aims were grotesquely inflated: H. G. Wells hailed it from the first as "The War that will end War" and President Wilson went just as far by declaring on America's entry that the war would "make the world safe for democracy." Neither of these noble ends was attained, or ever could be, and the reaction was profound. That experience might have recommended modest war aims now that a truly world war had erupted. Yet that was impossible. The sacrifices exacted from entire peoples in total war are simply too great; only staggering war aims, to match the sacrifices, will do. And even though they were not yet in the war, Americans felt more and more that they were entitled to an opinion. Overwhelmingly they had identified themselves with Britain's cause, and after lend-lease went into effect, the whole country had a direct interest in learning what that cause was. By the summer of 1941 liberal interventionists and conservative isolationists were demanding to know the "positive democratic ideals" Britain was fighting for.

Churchill had, in fact, already defined Britain's war aims by setting the terms for negotiation with Germany during the darkest hour of the war—that is, in August, 1940. Britain required, he said, "Effective guarantees by deeds, not words . . . from Germany which would ensure the restoration of the free and independent life of Czechoslovakia, Poland, Norway, Denmark, Holland, Belgium, and above all France, as well as the effectual security of Great Britain and the British Empire in a general peace." Not a word about democracy, about an end to war forever, about a millennium of peace or a new world devoted to peace and justice. How those countries governed themselves does not appear to have concerned the British very much, if at all; the important thing was that German occupation and conquest must end.

Yet to many Americans that was not good enough. The *Nation* sternly lectured that mere survival was no cause, nor was the defeat of Hitler and an end to Fascism and its works. With the revival of the crusading spirit, there had come a rediscovery of Randolph Bourne. And Bourne spoke to this generation of liberals. Bourne, a tubercular young Greenwich Village bohemian, had adamantly opposed America's entry into the Great War, though all his friends supported it. He had died young, unknown and, to his later admirers, vindicated. Where others had considered the Great War just because its ends were noble, Bourne remained unconvinced. The war's aims were not positive enough: War "must not be used for the negative ends of making the world 'safe' for anything," he wrote, "but only for affirmative ends of forward movement in class relations and economic welfare within America and in the world at large." Liberal intellectuals such as Max Lerner seized upon this heritage. Lerner was convinced by 1941 that nothing was more important than a clear-cut statement of positive, democratic war aims: "Only a statement of [British] war aims as the extension and not simply the defense of democracy can possibly hope to energize the forces throughout Europe and throughout the world which will eventually beat Hitlerism."*

But the British still stubbornly refused to promise the millennium. Tempers were frayed. The mood that summer was already sour: The whole defense effort looked clumsy and unmanageable; inflation was spiraling upward; Congress was obviously unable to deal with the tax problem; and Selective Service was about to expire. Nothing seemed to be working. And now the country was tiptoeing sideways into the war—and for what? Little wonder that the argument about war aims turned angry at times. Yet the British, keeping their own counsel, issued no grand panoply of aims to move men's hearts and justify war's dangers.

Then, after a week of growing speculation, the President, it was announced, had met with Churchill on a warship "somewhere off Maine." To no little excitement the two leaders issued an Eight-Point Program, popularly known as the Atlantic Charter. There were some fears that Roosevelt might have secretly tied the United States a little too closely to Britain, but except for this, there was the warmest approval. Those who inspected the contents of the Charter closely were not very impressed. "It seemed an uninspired plagiarism of Wilson's Fourteen Points," said one. The Charter merely declared that Britain and the United States cherished no territorial ambitions, that they sought only a world which was

---

* This was fantastic. If it meant anything in concrete terms, it was that the French, the Russians, the Danes, etc., would resist Hitler only if the British gave India its independence.

peaceful, one wherein all people might move about freely and in which all nations would have equal access to the world's natural riches.

To most people the important thing was not the Charter, but the fact that the two leaders had met face to face at last. And they did it in a stirring fashion: aboard two powerful modern warships anchored in Placentia Bay, Newfoundland, while the Battle of the Atlantic was raging in the waters outside. And the New York *Times* concluded that for all the platitudes and clichés the Atlantic Charter represented something epochal: "The end of isolation. It is the beginning of a new era in which the United States assumes the responsibilities which fall naturally to a great power."

The United States was indeed acting more and more like a great power in world politics. But whatever isolationists and other critics might say, every step was taken hesitantly; Roosevelt obviously feared to get too far ahead of public opinion, while his supporters were grumbling that, on the contrary, he was failing to keep up with it. The Atlantic Charter was all very well, they agreed, but what of aid to Russia?

When Churchill, explicitly embracing any enemy of Hitler's as an ally of his, formed a partnership with the Russians in the first flush of Hitler's invasion, millions of Americans insisted that the President do the same thing, following the same principle. Interventionists thought two things at least were obvious: Russia was finished as an ideological force for decades to come, even if it somehow managed to survive, and to them June 22 was the final, conclusive, irrefutable proof that Hitler was the real threat to American interests, now and for years to come.

Isolationists, of course, drew a very different conclusion from the same events. Britain had a fighting ally; there was therefore less need than ever for the United States to run the risk of getting embroiled in war for Britain's sake. There was also a hope, verging on glee among conservatives, that Russia and Germany would destroy each other. An overwhelming majority wanted the Russians to win, even if by more than two to one the country expected Russia to lose. But during the first few weeks of the Nazi invasion it was only a minority which favored aid to Russia. Roosevelt's efforts to help the Russians somehow had to overcome the strong opposition from conservatives, isolationists, Roman Catholics and people who simply could not for the life of them see anything to choose between Hitler and Stalin. And having breathed hatred for godless Communism for so long, most Roman Catholics found it impossible to stop now. Isolationists assiduously cultivated the Catholic opposition. At one point Roosevelt allowed himself to be drawn into a maladroit discussion of religious liberty in the Soviet Union. But as the summer drew to a close, the President had sent some modest assistance to the Russians, holding out the hope of more to come. An old foe, Herbert Hoover, fumed to a national radio audience:

"Now we find ourselves promising aid to Stalin. . . . If we go further and join the war and we win it, then we will have won for Stalin the grip of Communism on Russia. . . . It makes the whole argument of our joining the war to bring the Four Freedoms to mankind a Gargantuan jest." Yet most people were beginning to believe that to withhold aid much longer would endanger America's own security.

Once possessed of Russia's oil, wheat and metals, Hitler might well become invincible. And simply by surviving the initial onslaught, the Russians had given the people of the United States enough time to digest that crucial fact. Once it had sunk in, there was no longer any way for isolationists, Catholics and conservatives to block aid to the Soviets. So, early in November, with almost no forewarning, Roosevelt announced that he had at last "found the defense of the Union of Soviet Socialist Republics vital to the defense of the United States." And with a stroke from his pen, Russia became entitled to lend-lease. An initial appropriation of $1 billion sailed through Congress. Bitterly, but quietly, isolationists swallowed yet another defeat.

Aid to Britain had meanwhile become a matter of routine; isolationists had long since given up even grumbling about it. In fact, sentiment favoring aid to Britain at the risk of war had gone from 35 percent in June, 1940, to 85 percent by December, 1941. There were still misunderstandings, of course. Some businessmen complained that the British were using lend-lease goods to compete with the U.S. export trade to South America. And British diplomats were supposedly living it up in Washington and New York at American expense. One fantastic rumor had them flaunting cynicism and greed by publicly singing (to the tune of "There'll Always Be an England"):

> There'll always be a dollar,
> As long as we are here. . . .

But these outcroppings of puerility to one side, expressions of pro-British sentiment ran on unabated. A Flight Ferry Command of American pilots was (for several hundred dollars per trip) ferrying aircraft to Britain, thereby freeing RAF pilots for combat. The Eagle Squadron had overcome its earlier shortcomings and turned out to be a useful addition to the RAF. Throughout 1941 the chief concern of the American Red Cross was assisting Britain's civilian wounded and homeless. And when the British government advertised in U.S. newspapers for technical personnel to be trained in Britain as radar operators, 1,500 applications piled up in the first three days.

The British still counted heavily on lend-lease to bridge the billion-dollar gap in monthly war production vis-à-vis Germany, Italy and their occupied territories. Yet even as 1941 drew to a close, lend-lease on a scale large enough to close the gap was far in the future. The total amount of lend-lease assistance delivered during the year had been $1 billion, or about 7 percent of the munitions Britain had expended during the course of 1941.

The country seemed to be on an irreversible collision course with Germany. The Germans were desperately trying to avoid war with the United States. They already had more than enough to keep them busy for a long time to come. Yet incidents between American and German ships were becoming a commonplace in the cold waters of the North Atlantic. Almost from the beginning of lend-lease shipments there had been whispers of clashes, near misses, sinkings. Even huge naval battles were rumored to have been fought. The administration was so patently eager to enter the conflict by this watery gate that one periodical cautioned, "It was a great question whether the U.S. public would not dismiss as a manufactured 'incident' the first conflict that came." "Incidents" were notorious; Hitler had given them a bad name. Still, might not the President be tempted?

There was also the heritage of the Great War: Every embarrassing memory of the period before April, 1917, was bound up with sinkings on the high seas. Even if people had been panting to get into this war, clashes at sea were just about the last way they wanted it done. Strong measures of another sort were far, far preferable. When, for example, American troops occupied Iceland in July—in direct challenge to the Germans—support had run on the order of three to one.

Yet whether the country preferred it or not, and despite the empty rumors, American ships were certain to clash with Hitler's submarines if they kept up the aggressive system of patrols that kept pushing farther and farther into the Atlantic and offering more and more assistance to the Royal Navy by broadcasting the position of whatever German ships they found. The first real incident came in September, just off Iceland, when a U-boat launched a torpedo at an American destroyer, the USS *Greer*. The torpedo missed. The *Greer* responded by trying to sink the submarine but failed. To the President's evident disappointment, most people shrugged the entire affair off as predictable and not worth worrying over. After all, the *Greer* was tailing the submarine and reporting its position to the British when the German commander desperately turned and fired a torpedo.

With the sinking of American merchant ships, however, sentiment for repealing the Neutrality Act, which still forbade arming merchantmen, rose sharply. And just as tempers began to rise, there came, in mid-October, another attack on an American destroyer, the USS *Kearny*. The *Kearny* had been aiding a British convoy under attack by German submarines and was struck by a torpedo, forcing her to limp away from the fight with eleven dead and more than a dozen grievously wounded. Here, exulted the editor of the *Nation*, it had come at last, "A good test of public and Congressional reactions—like a drop of acid on the foot of a frog." By the end of October the country counted the cost of the war at sea to date: 10 merchant ships sunk, 2 warships attacked, more than 100 dead.

On Navy Day (October 27) Roosevelt felt the time had arrived to make his first foreign policy speech since his address at the end of May declaring the state of unlimited national emergency. Unhappily, he resorted to the purest demagoguery and fraud. He possessed, he said, a German map which showed just how the Germans planned to conquer the United States and go on from there to eliminate religion throughout the entire world. Roosevelt went on to portray the attack on the *Kearny* as a deliberate attempt by Hitler "to frighten the American people off the high seas." Surely no one could be indifferent to such provocation. "America has been attacked. The U.S.S. *Kearny* is not just a Navy ship. She belongs to every man, woman and child in this nation." His response was to fling the challenge back to the German Navy and its Führer: "In the face of this newest and greatest challenge we Americans have cleared our decks and taken our battle stations." *Time*, and others, whooped with obvious glee: "The U.S. is at war with Germany." But still, Roosevelt would not ask for a declaration of war. For Congress might refuse. And what would he do then? There was growing anger to be sure, but there was no irresistible sense of outrage rolling across the country and sweeping Congressional caution before it.

Only days after the Navy Day speech came another attack, and this time the USS *Reuben James* was sunk in the North Atlantic, taking more than 100 officers and men to their deaths. There was anger, but again it was heavily muffled in fatalism and resignation; it did not flow up in a great surge of emotion. *Time* was now fretting that Roosevelt was "fighting the first great undeclared war in U.S. history." And it tried to egg him on: "People no longer wondered whether the U.S. was in it. They wondered now whether the U.S. was winning." *Life* was annoyed that to date "the incomparable U.S. Navy" had "torpedoed nothing, sunk nothing, scored zero." People were becoming more combustible, so the prospect of great popular anger was still there, but the spark to ignite it had not yet been struck. The country was like a man in a dark cellar fumbling furiously with a box of damp matches.

Even so, Congress gutted the Neutrality Act, thereby removing the last legislative barrier to a declaration of war. Merchant ships could be armed. More important, it meant that American ships could now carry arms across the seas into British and Russian ports. Reluctantly, and with evident misgivings, Congress had taken what looked like the penultimate step on the road to war. If this did not get the country into it, then nothing of Roosevelt's devising seemed likely to. The narrowness of the margin on the Neutrality Act vote was connected with labor problems, as we shall see. But even if the margin had been wider, there would still have been profound misgivings in both Congress and the nation at large. For in their hearts people feared that the country was not yet in any condition to fight and win a war against Hitler. By acting rashly, they might be pushing America into a catastrophe.

But for all that, they would not back down. Some 15,000 Americans were already in the war, from England and Libya to China, as fliers, sailors, mechanics, ambulance drivers, foot soldiers, in British and Canadian uniforms or in no uniforms at all. The rest of their countrymen were resigned to joining the fight in which they had been among the first to risk their lives and shed their blood.

XIV

"Arsenal of Democracy"

ROOSEVELT'S main problem—really the nation's main problem—was to create a war economy in a nation still formally at peace. The solution he settled for, however reluctantly, was to rely on big business. And by the fall of 1941 big business had done so badly that there was no longer any way of hiding it. The administration was bitterly disappointed, businessmen were depressed, and most people were thoroughly fed up with the incompetence and the bickering that characterized defense production.

Military production was overlaid on a civilian economy whose fundamental purpose was the satisfaction of civilian needs. As the essentially civilian economy was expanded most, or all, of that expansion could be devoted to arms production. Provided the economy had room to grow—and after ten years of Depression it had ample slack—it would not have to use the sector devoted to consumer goods to turn out guns, ships, planes, and so on. The country could, in an old phrase, have both guns and butter. The challenge confronting this new marriage of government and business was to expand the civilian economy and to turn that expansion of capacity to military production.

Despite their clumsiness, the economy did expand. When they tried to curb it (and, as we shall see, they did), events and opinion forced their hand: The growing imminence of war, an angry, rising popular demand, a Congress which appropriated billions every week forced the dollar-a-year men streaming into Washington to create a burgeoning defense economy atop a growing civilian base. The business executives were slow to act; they were haunted by the prospect of a new Depression at boom's end. And try as they might, they simply could not believe that the goals Roosevelt had set—the 50,000 planes, the two-ocean navy in five years, the tens of billions of dollars of arms production each year—could be achieved. The more they drew upon their experience, the more convinced they were that it could not.

They started with the assumption that the new arsenals should be built from scratch, alongside the consumer-goods economy rather than on top of it, and that government should pay for everything. After all, they argued, the defense plants would be useless once the defense crisis ended. They proposed, in effect, to establish two parallel economies. The revived civilian economy would profit them. And the building of the other, at a

173

handsome commission, would also profit them. Once that second had to be discarded . . . well, that was no more their problem than what people did with their old refrigerators. But this approach ran up against a problem that was entirely predictable: There was not enough raw material even in this rich country to supply two such economies at the current, and rising, levels of demand. One must be sacrificed to the other, or both must be meshed into a common system of priorities. The government, for its part, had placed $6 billion of productive capacity at the disposal of defense production by the summer of 1941; more was promised, but there was simply not enough steel, rubber, aluminum and other materials to postpone the question of priorities any longer.

Business managed to raise the price of its help another notch. The crucial defense industries such as steel and aluminum had to be expanded; that was obvious. But if government financed the expansion, might not government then come to control important parts of the peacetime economy? The dollar-a-year men had been able to block the expansion of the crucial defense industries throughout the first year of the defense crisis. They could do so no longer. Yet when large infusions of taxpayers' money began to go into the expansion of private corporations, it did so with assurances that it was the next best thing to a gift.

Most people were by now convinced that the entire program of defense production had been bungled. Washington talked of a $100 billion effort, but only half that amount had been appropriated by the fall of 1941; less than $20 billion had been contracted for and only $7 billion spent by the end of the year. It must be said that what people too often failed to perceive was that clumsily or not the arms were starting to appear. The percentage of the country's total productivity which was going into defense tripled in the twelve months following Roosevelt's "Arsenal of Democracy" speech. Each month in the fall of 1941 more than $2 billion in arms was stamped, welded, soldered and rolled out, including planes at a rate of 25,000 a year and increasing. But these things were lost sight of in the noisy arguments over failure and greed and the cutbacks in announced goals. The boom stood at the point where it would pour forth arms in quantities few men had ever dreamed of, yet everywhere there was hand wringing.

The boom itself still seemed a very mixed blessing. For every problem it solved, it appeared to create two more. Everyday life in many communities was becoming a form of torture broken only by sleep, and sometimes not even then. Look at a town like San Diego: It spent the late 1930's happily thinking that it was growing so fast it would double its population and reach 300,000 inhabitants by 1960. Before 1941 was over, San Diego had its doubling in population—and critical shortages of gas, water, electricity, housing, transportation, schools and sewers. In boom towns it was impossible to escape the congestion and the strain it placed on nerves, courtesy, goodwill and the simple decencies of life. All hope of comfort, convenience, silence, cleanliness and privacy had been abandoned. On the frontier such things might have counted for little, but frontier sensibilities were a thing of the past.

In all the country the capital of boom towns was now Detroit. Though it was only the nation's third industrial city, after New York and Chicago, it was the home of the automobile industry, and that made it the capital of defense production. No such eminence was ever forced on a more unwilling community. There was a rising public demand that Detroit stop making cars and start making tanks. Already, late in 1941, where a cornfield had once been there already stood the Chrysler Tank Arsenal, about to turn out 100 tanks a week. Just 30 miles to the west of the city the largest bomber plant in the world was going up at Willow Run.

The most important fact of all, of course, was that the economy was now soaring to heights no one had ever foreseen. An economy that was clicking along at a rate of $98 billion a year in the middle of 1940 hit a rate of $138 billion a year and a half later and was still rising dramatically. Growing by leaps of this scale, it would forgive slowness, mistakes and ineffectual opposition; without wanting to be or sound callous, one might suggest that it made individual hardship a small matter. It was, in the most basic sense, the defense of the nation. Once the economy had taken up all its slack and increased its capacity to produce, it could turn out tanks or toothpaste, or both, as the nation's needs required. This vastly expanded economic base and the changes in outlook that accompanied it would support an indebtedness that three years before would have rendered half the population semicatatonic.

All the fabled highs of 1929 were being eclipsed—in gross national product, national income, retail sales, new investment. And in national income, where men and institutions come into direct contact with economic life, the economy meets social psychology, lifting or depressing the current mood and outlook. There was cause enough for buoyancy now: National income in 1929 had reached $83 billion; in 1939, $69 billion; in 1941, $92 billion and rising. And even with a rate of inflation that raised the level of wholesale prices 20 percent during the first two years of the war, real earnings were up by 30 percent.

Not only was more money coming into more hands, but ordinary people were generally willing to pay for defense out of their sudden prosperity. New tax laws raising income taxes on an average of 50 percent and lowering exemptions so that another 5,000,000 people came onto the tax rolls passed without protest. Defense bonds sold well, and growing numbers of Americans were becoming accustomed to taking their change in defense stamps rather than cash.

The administration was trying with increased determination to keep inflation down. But by now there had developed an almost classic example

of too much money hotly wooing too few goods. The only weapon immediately available was persuasion. Occasionally it worked; usually it failed.
A price-control bill under which the administration would have been able
to enforce its anti-inflation decrees was submitted to Congress. Like every
other strong measure proposed by the Office of Price Administration, it
was gutted by farm interests, conservative Republicans and anti-New Deal
Democrats. So inflation continued to rise, eroding many of the gains of the
boom, yet never quite outdistancing the rise in real prosperity.

With their paychecks Americans were fueling the growth of the total
economy, making even more arms production possible. Having paid off old
bills, had their teeth fixed, bought new clothes and taken a vacation, they
were now creating a boom in high-priced durables such as radics, refrigerators, washing machines and furniture. This second wave of consumer
demands was beginning to bump into the defense priorities on essential
raw materials. Yet many still felt as the man who said, "It's a great war,
if we don't get into it." And in October, 1941, there appeared the James
Agee and Walker Evans classic work on the Depression years, *Let Us
Now Praise Famous Men*. The Depression was finally a thing of the past.

Most people had never known such prosperity, yet not only was there
still a high level of unemployment, but unless something unforeseen
occurred, even the current boom would not put an end to it. The imminent
demise of the WPA and CCC stemmed from Congressional hostility rather
than from any great rise in private industry's demand for unskilled labor.
By the end of this year the first of 1,000,000 draftees were expected to be
returned to civilian life. Somewhere between 5,000,000 and 7,000,000
people would still be unemployed at the end of 1941. Yet the competition
for skilled workers was becoming intense. Companies with defense contracts desperately started raiding each other's payrolls.

The result of these conditions was severe labor unrest. Defense contractors resorted to putting unskilled labor to work at carpentry, plumbing
and stringing electrical wires. Skilled craft unions responded in predictable fashion at this encroachment of their prerogatives. Yet there was no
way to stop this mushrooming of neophyte plumbers, carpenters and
electricians. The most innocent amateur carpenter could earn $60 a week,
twice the pay of high school teachers and as much as that of junior
executives.

Public and private vocational training schemes sprang up in cities and
towns everywhere. The government had launched a pioneer program in
the summer of 1940 to train 300,000 mechanics and 50,000 engineers
for national defense. Federal officials had since gone on to train another
1,500,000 defense workers and placed them in the jobs they were trained
for.

The problem of labor unrest, however, grew steadily worse all through 1941 until it seemed likely to jeopardize the entire defense effort. Government had become accustomed in the late 1930's to occupying the third leg of a triangular relationship, with labor and business at the other two. Usually it had supported labor. And there was nothing novel about cooperation between labor and government during a crisis in defense. Woodrow Wilson had courted labor's cooperation during the preparedness days of 1915–1916. He had made a rough, but fair, agreement with the founder of the AFL, old Samuel Gompers: In return for labor peace, government would help bring organized labor to wealth and power. By 1919 organized labor had scaled new heights in prestige, power and numbers. It had moved away from the working class as a whole. The skilled workers of the AFL, 5,000,000 strong in 1919, were now content to cultivate their own garden.

Roosevelt acted much as Wilson had done. In this instance he relied on Sidney Hillman of the militant, unskilled CIO (and this war would do for the CIO what the last one had done for the AFL: bring it to power—and sever it from the unorganized parts of the working class). Sternly Hillman chided labor militants; he worked faithfully alongside the big businessmen, first on the National Defense Advisory Committee, later in the Office of Production Management. Hillman was convinced that labor had more to gain as a willing partner than it could ever hope to gain as an independent, militant, antagonistic force.

To curb labor unrest, Roosevelt created a National Defense Mediation Board in March, 1941. The NDMB supplanted the New Deal's National Labor Relations Board, for between the urgency of the crisis and the frequency of strikes, the NLRB was no longer adequate. The NDMB was a faithful reflection of the triangular partnership of labor, management and government, each represented with absolute equality. As a rule the government representatives would sit back, let the other two fight it out and intervene only when tempers reached a dangerous pitch or a deadlock ensued.

If the President had any hopes that the NDMB would end the turmoil in defense plants or quell the rising public and Congressional anger at labor troubles, he was quickly disabused. Strikes, usually wildcats, broke out against defense contractors and subcontractors almost every day. Labor demanded, and Hillman agreed, that defense contracts should go only to firms which obeyed existing labor laws. Roosevelt himself at one point threatened to seize those plants which were brought to a halt by strikes arising from management's violation of the law. But public opinion was emphatically not sympathetic and would sanction nothing that hampered, or appeared to hamper, defense production. In the spring of 1941 three people out of every four were in favor of a complete ban on the right to strike, regardless of cause, heedless even of whether it involved defense or not. Newsreel films of strikers—no matter where, no matter what the grievance, no matter what the merits of their case—were noisily booed. Newspapers and magazines received, and were by no means averse to publishing, a torrent of antilabor abuse. Opposition to labor's right to organize had dropped to little more than 20 percent in 1936; by June, 1941, it stood at 33 percent and was steadily growing.

More disquieting was that strikes were becoming bloody once again. Both labor and management had one eye on the main chance and the other on the end of the boom; it added an element of desperation to the current disputes. And workers were convinced that now prosperity or something like it was at hand, they should be first in line, not last.

The crest of this tide of bitterness peaked in June at the North American Aviation plant in Inglewood, California, a community on the southern edge of Los Angeles. The average wage at NAA, including overtime, was nearly $200 a year below the "minimum health and decency budget" for workers in urban areas suggested by the Department of Labor. North American held billions of dollars' worth of lucrative defense contracts. NAA's profits in 1940 had amounted to 57 percent of the company's net worth. Its workers demanded an across-the-board increase of ten cents an hour and a slight increase in starting pay. The NDMB endorsed the increases. The company promptly turned them down. The local—one of whose executives was an admitted Communist—called its workers out on strike.

The fact that a Communist was involved overshadowed every other consideration. For years afterward the NAA strike would be cited as a classic case of Communists hamstringing national defense. Roosevelt ordered the Army to smash the strike, a feat accomplished at bayonet point, backed up by tear gas and a display of machine guns at the ready. The pickets fled, leaving one of their number behind with a deep bayonet wound, inflicted perhaps *pour encourager les autres*. This operation and a similar one conducted by the Navy in San Francisco were applauded even by the prolabor left and liberal elements which would have usually been aghast. General Hershey followed up by threatening future strikers in defense plants with the loss of their draft deferments.

It was at this juncture that Hitler attacked the Soviet Union. And the notion took hold that now Russia was in the war, there would be an end to strikes.

Business, especially big business, had much to be pleased with, despite its problems with labor. The defense boom had revived both profits and some of the old prestige of commerce. There was a new assertiveness to businessmen these days; as everyone could see, they prospered. Overall profits in 1940 had been 27 percent higher than a year before, and 1941 held out every promise of even larger gains. Nor were they about to lose those gains to a rigorous excess profits tax. Stockholders were nonetheless mourning "profitless-prosperity" while collecting their ever-fatter dividends.

Even when government was forced to smash a monopoly, as in the case of ALCOA's monopoly on aluminum, it bent over backward to avoid giving offense. ALCOA could not produce enough aluminum to meet the needs of national security. Washington officials authorized Reynolds Metals to produce aluminum—in a $250,000,000 plant paid for by the taxpayers, and all the profits would go to Reynolds' stockholders.

American business was simply not going to risk its fortunes on anything so transient as a defense boom. If it had its way, it would have concentrated on satisfying the swelling public demand for consumer goods and let the government worry about defense, at least, for a while longer.

In Detroit and elsewhere the administration forced some modest cuts in production for 1941 and cut even deeper into projections of consumer-goods production in 1942. It was all very public and very noisy, yet the prestige of business was certainly on the rise. Two-thirds of the country was convinced by the early summer of 1941 that whatever delays and failures dogged the defense program, they were the fault of labor and the administration, not business.

Yet as the year wore on, it became only too evident that turning the defense program over to businessmen had been a cardinal mistake. Nothing was going according to schedule, and instead of driving harder to meet the goals Roosevelt had set, Knudsen and the dollar-a-year men were busy dreaming up reasons why they could never be met and started to cut back on production goals. Often the problem could be traced to a shortage of raw materials. There had been ample warnings that there would not be enough steel unless production expanded, and Edward Stettinius, a former president of U.S. Steel and now in charge of raw materials for national defense, laughed them all off as stupid calumnies. Six months later fourteen shipways were lying idle for lack of steel. With the steel shortage nearly 11,000,000 tons as winter approached, the administration placed all steel production under government control.

Roosevelt also put a watchdog on the flagging Office of Production Management—the Supply Priorities and Allocation Board. By infusing New Dealers into the defense program to goad the businessmen, it might be possible to inject new life.

The contrasts could certainly not have been sharper. While the captains of industry had looked upon the American economy as the nation's pride, they also did not believe it capable of outproducing the combined factories and fields of the Axis. Ironically, it was Roosevelt and the "impractical theorists who never met a payroll" who, possibly from a combination of enthusiasm and ignorance, held to a vision of the country's potential that revolved about an economy capable of outproducing most of the rest of the

180 180 DAYS OF SADNESS, YEARS OF TRIUMPH

world. They had more faith and, as events would prove, better judgment. Knudsen and his dollar-a-year men projected a maximum schedule of arms output just touching $33 billion a year; liberal and New Deal visionaries drew up a Victory Program at the end of the year calling for $45 billion in arms a year. This could have been the difference between victory and defeat.

As the government became more disillusioned with business in defense, it finally started to take over plants where management had persistently rejected NDMB rulings. But it did so with the most obvious reluctance, releasing the plants at the first possible moment after the take-over.

And all this was going on while business was profiting beyond anything the normal avarice of commerce had ever known. The big bull market of 1929 was now serving chiefly as a yardstick for what surpassed its legendary peaks. Big business waxed profitable, and none so richly as those with defense contracts to fill. A check was run on a sample of eighty-eight of those fortunate few and found that only two had annual rates of profit below 6 percent; half earned more than 40 percent; one even surpassed its own worth, with earnings of 112 percent. Overall, business profits this year would prove to be 20 percent higher than the year before, or approximately 33 percent above the level of 1939.

Yet there was still the grudging cooperation of business in defense production and, beyond that, the ludicrously low level of investment in the stock market. The reasons are not hard to find, however fanciful they may appear now. An overwhelming majority of businessmen sincerely believed that the defense crisis was being cynically used "as a pretext for pushing still further the more radical social and economic aims of the New Deal." More than half of them believed, in fact, that no matter what else the future held, it would bring more official intervention in the economy. As for the bungling of the businessmen who had been called to Washington, that was Washington's fault for picking men of poor ability.

We should remember that business had been the whipping boy of government and popular opinion for ten years and more. Before the Temporary National Economic Committee its experts had been riddled by professorial economists. Why then, they reasoned, should they bail out a panicky government and nation simply because the flag was being waved? If the government and people wanted industrial expansion for defense, let the government and people pay for it.

The sour irritation that prevailed among businessmen and the rich and upper middle classes generally was expressed with the greatest sincerity on the stock market. Soldiers vote with their feet; the well-off vote with their money. On the stock market they offer a rough guide to their current mood and expectations. And in November, 1941, with the economy surging ahead, with their dividends fattening nicely, with no end to the boom in sight, they let the stock market drop to its lowest level since the frightened, panicky days of June, 1940. After which, in the teeth of an economic boom, it continued to drop so steadily that it stood at a level below that of August, 1939. Throughout 1941 dozens of stock brokerages folded up or merged with stronger units. And in what amounted to a willful resistance to a 60 percent rise in commodity prices over the previous two years, the commodities market was just as depressed as the stock market.

As a rule, inflation pushes the stock market along. Not now. The turn-over in shares dropped to an anemic 450,000 per day, while all across the big board profits were advancing to record heights. Along Wall Street the fear would not down that once the boom ended, the Depression would take up where it had left off. Economics had once again been put to flight by social psychology. "The market," one observer concluded, "frightened by the thought of peace is almost equally frightened by the thought of war; tired of livin' and scared of dyin' it barely manages to just keep rollin' along."

Beneath the obvious nervousness, beneath the fear of bust following boom, the vain prophecies that the defense program would saddle the country with a vast and useless munitions capacity, there ran a deeper fear. Small investors with a little extra money to back a hunch or seek a hefty profit—and their numbers were growing, thanks to the boom—were buying stocks. It was the big individual and institutional investors who were fleeing the stock market, turning to bonds. The fear that moved them was, like most unreasoning fears, historic; it was by now almost a reflex: "Eight years of the New Deal have aroused among capital owners a profound sense of apprehension concerning the stability of the so-called capitalistic structure as a whole, which has caused them to seek shelter for their money at almost any cost in places which seem to be least subject to seismic disturbances."

Not a few of them genuinely feared that today's defense boom profits would be expropriated tomorrow and used to underwrite Socialism or worse. It was with that in mind that they apprehensively awaited the report of the Temporary National Economic Commission, and that remarkable document did indeed give them cause to worry. It found that about one person in three was burdened with low income, job insecurity, poor health, inadequate housing and no opportunity for personal development—and all thanks to monopoly in basic industries. Not only that, monopolistic prac-tices had aggravated the Depression and, by stifling competition, made it almost impossible for the economy to revive. To rectify these wrongs, the TNEC called for an application of federal power on a scale that would make the New Deal appear marginal in contrast. At most, the country had caught up with half a century of social legislation enacted elsewhere in the Western world; what the TNEC proposed, from slum clearance to more hospital beds, went far beyond that. But conservatives' fears were in vain. The TNEC issued its report, was thanked for its labors, and its report was quietly shelved. The administration was no longer struggling with the Depression, for which the TNEC had been commissioned to find a remedy. And the country was now far too busy for any ventures into social reform that were not disguised as defense necessities.

Yet the sentiments of most people were clearly on the side of the TNEC recommendations. By two and three to one they wanted closer regulation of banks, utilities, oil companies, railroads, steel and automobile manufacturers; they especially favored official regulation of the supply and price of basic commodities, such as bread, milk and meat. Less than one person in three wanted to see the New Deal dismantled, even partially. Even if the war ended tomorrow, what would it bring? Wrecked economies in Europe and a massive slump here. Businessmen themselves confessed that traditional laissez-faire could not assure full employment. In this climate it was not so very remarkable then that the stock market languished.

Businessmen were not yet tired of reminding one another that "business is in the doghouse." And not until it was back in the living room, it seemed, would it cooperate wholeheartedly in national defense. Admittedly, much of the criticism leveled at business was both wrong and wrongheaded. There was incompetence and self-seeking among businessmen. But where is there not? Most of the critics, and they were legion, did not appreciate the essential fact that enormous strides had been taken. And there were many steps along the way which could not have been executed more rapidly no matter who was in charge. To build thousands of planes required the construction of hundreds of plants; the plants were now almost finished. The same was true of many parts of the defense program. Talk of "business strikes" and "business blackmail" was rife; much of it was unwarranted. Even as the weapons were pouring out, the air was thick with acrimony.

Business could not, for one thing, refuse point-blank to make the weapons. For another, arms production *was* profitable. (As one cynic said, America's wars are fought on "patriotism plus 10%.") The tide of public opinion was too overwhelming to be resisted outright. Even if with faint heart (and the workers were not driving themselves very hard), the weapons were made. Simple incompetence probably cost more than resistance. None of these things—the lack of enthusiasm, the incompetence, the strikes—was fatal; together they were not fatal. For the key to defense production was not, in the final analysis, either the vastly overrated "know-how" of businessmen or the state of labor-management relations. America would outproduce the world in arms because it already possessed the physical and psychological tools: a large, skilled, disciplined population, mechanically minded, well fed and energetic, occupying a land rich in natural resources and possessed of a capital investment, accumulated over decades, worth hundreds of billions of dollars. It was accumulation, accretion, the physical strengths of a tearing, roaring heritage.

Superficially, labor unrest looked as perverse as business's aversion to the stock market. Organized labor was thriving; unemployment had been halved in the past two years; the AFL had grown by 15 percent, the more militant CIO by 70 percent; each of them boasted more than 4,000,000 members. Yet even after the Army and Navy had been used to smash defense strikes, even after the German invasion of Russia, the incidence of strikes in defense plants rose by 50 percent. These strikes could no longer be explained as part of a Communist conspiracy; no one, in fact, was more adamantly opposed to strikes after June 22 than the *Daily Worker*.

Behind the rash of defense strikes stood neither ideology nor greed, but insecurity. Most of the disputes were over union recognition or jurisdiction. Few strikes were over wages and hours. The usual dispute was over a union shop. Business was pressing for a rollback on recent labor gains. Most of all, management wanted to reestablish the open shop—that is, entirely voluntary membership in the union. Such a development would be a mortal blow to organized labor. Whether it is the fault of human nature or of human society, many people will take something for nothing if they can. In this instance, workers would accept the benefits secured by the union without paying dues unless they were obliged to do so. And if they were not required to join the union, then the union would atrophy, would gradually lose its leverage. Eventually it would perish. The unions therefore insisted with all the determination born of a struggle for survival that there must be a closed or union shop.* And over this issue each side was trying to use the current crisis to serve its own ends.

Labor was also faced by an uncertain job market. Already, "priorities unemployment" was throwing hundreds of thousands of workers back onto the streets as the drive for defense production cut its tortuous path through the economy, shutting down this plant, cutting back operations in that one, creating a new factory over there to turn out something never produced before, and leaving the workers to find out where the emphasis had shifted. There was also a fear that once the expansion of physical plant was completed—the factories, docks, barracks, shipyards—up to 2,000,000 workers would be displaced.

The soil in which labor turmoil now flourished was one where an uncertain job market occupied ground which should have been filled by a coherent national labor policy. Yet there was no policy. Instead there was the National Defense Mediation Board. And in the nation at large there was a potentially explosive public anger.

The showdown between labor, government, business and public opinion came at the end of November. It pitted John L. Lewis and his United Mine Workers against the rest.

* Closed shop: In order to be hired one must first join the union. Union shop: Initial union membership is not required, but after a specified period of time—usually ninety days—union membership becomes mandatory.

There are a number of things that should be recalled here, not least that mining is incredibly dangerous work, and nowhere was this more true in 1941 than in the United States. (Unhappily, it is still the case.) During 1940 nearly 1,300 American miners were killed at their jobs; thousands more were irreparably maimed. So commonplace were mine disasters that only if the death toll ran to a score or more were they considered newsworthy. And there was no national mine-safety legislation. Mine operators, abetted by compliant legislators, were determined that there would be none. As a result, American mines were three times deadlier than mines in England, four times more dangerous than those in France, six times more perilous than those in Holland. Labor conflicts in the coalfields could still move men to murderous rage. Strikes which produced killings were quickly becoming a memory in other industries. In Harlan County, Kentucky, a miners' strike in 1941 left four dead and a dozen grievously wounded.

These fatal passions could be found in every coalfield. Nowhere were they stronger than in the mines owned by the steel companies. Mines usually had a union shop, but not in what Lewis with his Welsh gift for language, called "the captive mines." Lewis offered a guarantee of labor peace in exchange for a union shop. U.S. Steel, with Roosevelt's support, rejected the offer. When existing contracts expired, Lewis called for a strike, and the CIO convention, evidently fearful but convinced that it must, supported the mine workers.

When the miners struck the captive mines, they struck at steel production—the central pillar in the house of heavy industry. The NDMB voted nine to two against a union shop. Three times the President called on Lewis to end the strike; three times Lewis said no.

At this juncture even those liberal and leftist elements which had long embraced the working classes and shed tears for them were cursing Lewis and his miners. Liberals who thought in July, 1941:

> The Administration has failed to give labor equal representation with employers in the defense organization . . . failed to force expansion of productive facilities early enough . . . failed to check inflation and a rising cost of living . . . failed to put the heat on Congress to prevent war profiteering . . . [and] used troops against striking workers without ever having resorted to force against recalcitrant employers

changed their tune in November. Now, they said, labor must "refrain from exercising the right to strike"; workers must take anything the NDMB offered them. No strike which affected defense could be tolerated. The strikers were little more than fifth columnists.

Still defying almost the entire nation, comprehending everyone from the Communists to men of impeccable reactionary credentials, the 53,000 "captive" miners went out on strike. And no one outside the poor who lived in the mining towns gave a damn about the conditions under which these men lived and worked. The clash between those two titanic figures— Roosevelt and Lewis—overshadowed the genuine grievances of the miners. Then, after a week, as if showing off his muscles to a crowd of small boys, Lewis ordered his miners back to work and agreed to arbitration.

Lewis had long since tested the NDMB. Only two weeks after its creation in March, 1941, he had called the 400,000 bituminous coal miners out on strike. When they went back to work, they went back to an extra dollar a day plus paid vacations. And now he agreed to sit on a three-man panel charged with ending the captive mine dispute. The panel reversed the earlier NDMB ruling against a union shop. This reversal was the death-blow of the NDMB: Lewis had shown what a determined, intelligent and powerful opponent could do to it.

An irate Congress was meantime taking up legislation to outlaw strikes. Congressional disgust with the administration's approach to labor disputes was reflected in the close vote on abolishing the Neutrality Act. There were many in Congress who were convinced that a country which would not curb striking workers was simply unready for war. And a national railroad strike was set to begin on Sunday, December 7, 1941; a railroad strike would bring the entire defense effort to a jolting halt.

XV

And So to War

ON the day that Hitler's armies crossed the Polish frontier a Japanese goodwill flight landed at Boeing Field in Seattle on the first leg of an American tour. Local officials, accompanied by 3,000 well-wishers, turned out to greet them. Off to one side throughout the formal ceremonies of welcome and congratulation could be seen a knot of fifty anti-Japanese demonstrators grimly marching back and forth under crudely lettered signs. Though they were heavily outnumbered, time and events were on their side.

Despite this show of amity in Seattle, antipathies between the two great Pacific powers were already corrosive. Americans could not any longer ignore the brutal, unjust war the Japanese were waging in China. The Japanese were convinced that the United States was intent on thwarting their legitimate national aspirations. Each country found in the other a historic rival to its supremacy in the Pacific; tacitly they divided that mighty ocean between them. There were incidents, clashes, angry words, yet something approximating normal relations still obtained and goodwill fliers could still make their flights in peace.

People generally were beginning to take an interest in the Far East; sluggishly but unmistakably Americans were starting to look far beyond their own shores to events in distant lands. In the fall of 1939, with war raging in Europe, John Gunther's *Inside Asia* surged to the top of best-seller lists. A deep sympathy with the Chinese supported a steady flow of books and articles about them. And there was a gnawing uneasiness, close to guilt, about the sale of war matériel, especially scrap metals and oil, to the Japanese. To some it was stupid—arming a potential enemy. To others it was wicked—participating in Japanese aggression. And most people (in this instance 80 percent) wanted it stopped. The back pages of American magazines carried the photograph of a Chinese father cradling in his sticklike arms the broken, lifeless body of his child. Below it ran the question: "Did YOU Help Pay for This Bomb?" It went on to say that you did if you bought even harmless items such as Japanese-made Christmas ornaments. Several efforts were launched to boycott the sale of Japanese consumer goods, but they could not stop the direct sale of war matériel. Only the administration could do that, and it moved slowly, if not in circles. As one angry, baffled citizen wrote to the New York *Times*: "This business of sending bombs to Japan and bandages to China has puzzled a great many of us."

In fairness, it should be noted that the government moved as fast and as far as it dared, even if its judgment was open to debate. While millions nagged it to do more, the general trend was unmistakably toward a rupture of relations with Japan: Every major step was in that direction, and not one step was taken in reverse. When the 1911 Treaty of Trade and Navigation came up for renewal in 1940, Washington, over the most ardent protests from Tokyo, allowed it to expire. It produced no immediate curb on Japanese goods, nor did it embargo oil and steel sales, but its significance was lost on no one. To the Japanese, it was an ax poised above their heads and might fall without warning. In the long run it was certain to increase the tariff on Japanese goods and to limit U.S. exports. While the total of U.S.-Japanese trade was only $400,000,000 a year, and the United States had the better of it, the items imported by Japan were essential to its war machine. Some, such as Walter Lippmann, were convinced that the United States had taken a giant step along the road to war. Most were, like the editors of *Newsweek*, delighted with the expiration of the treaty, whether or not it meant war. "With it [the expiration]," they exulted, "died an 86-year old policy of attempting to solve problems between the two countries on the presumption of basic friendliness. From now on the U.S. will be able to swing a big stick." To many it appeared that the country now had an economic club with which to beat the Japanese into fundamental changes in its foreign policy, and given a choice between trade or war, if the Japanese opted for the latter, they were certain to lose.

When the Germans conquered the Netherlands in April, 1940, the Japanese Foreign Minister rashly warned Washington not to declare a "protectorate" over the Dutch East Indies. Secretary of State Cordell Hull threatened back that Japan would find it dangerous to tamper with the status quo.

With the formation of the Axis alliance in October, 1940, a watershed of sorts was reached. Germany, Italy and Japan joined in a pact which bound each to regard an attack upon one as an attack upon all. By it Hitler hoped to turn American interest away from Europe and across the Pacific. Japan acquired allies. And both had marked themselves indelibly upon American minds as enemies, for no one interpreted the Axis Pact, not even for a moment, as anything but a threat aimed directly at the United States.

The State Department immediately ordered Americans in the Far East to return home. The British announced their intention to open the Burma Road, which would materially improve Chiang Kai-shek's position to resist the Japanese. Tokyo threatened to declare war on Britain. Stories raced from town to town that National Guard units were being sent posthaste to Hawaii; that more than, 4,000 sailors had been stripped from other naval units and dispatched secretly to bolster the Pacific Fleet. The former commander of U.S. naval forces in the Far East, Admiral Harry Yarnell, helped rising tensions along by urging that this was the most propitious time of all for a war with Japan, better far than some point in the future. Washington correspondents informed their editors that war was in fact no more than ten days away. Bets were offered and taken on the day the shooting would begin. And the ten days came and went with no attack save that on nervous systems. Nonetheless, the Japanese had now clearly cast themselves as *the enemy.* It would take years of delicate rebuilding to undo the hostility which now prevailed between Washington and Tokyo. Only the most diligent efforts could postpone war between them indefinitely and secure enough time for passions to cool, attitudes to be refashioned. But in the face of the Axis Pact most Americans were interested less in conciliation than in tougher measures.

A large, loosely organized pressure group was already at work to secure that end. Within it were to be found the staunchest reactionaries and the most impassioned liberals—the suspicion of Japan ran very broad and very deep. Even in the first weeks of the war one noted commentator on military affairs had reminded his countrymen: "Japan has invariably sought the achievement of her ambitions in the Far East at times when the Western powers were otherwise occupied." (One should note how something that was in itself merely an intelligent approach became, in Japanese hands, something insidious.)

Liberal journals were so keen on smiting Japan that even when Germany was poised to smash through Europe in the spring of 1940, the *New Republic* was arguing that the United States was more likely to get into the war by way of the Pacific, thanks to a Japanese lust for conquest. And conservative journals, such as the *Saturday Evening Post,* had already reached a similar conclusion: "The fact is that our most dangerous frontier is in the Pacific. In our excitement over the highly dramatized events in Europe, we have overlooked that. We cannot afford to overlook it for very long, ever."

Not all isolationists were quite so sensitive to the Far East. And when some of them, such as Senator Vandenberg, Colonel McCormick, General Wood and Captain Patterson (publisher of the New York *Daily News*), applied their tunnel vision to Asia, as well as Europe, liberals turned on them with a vengeance. Normally there was no love lost here; these men were usually chauvinists of a stripe that made liberal flesh creep. They had been blind to the evils of Fascism and Nazism in Europe. And they were now trying to appease Japan.

Of course, they did not call it appeasement. They simply asked if Asia contained anything worth a major war? The sum of American assets in China when the Chinese-Japanese War began in 1937 was less than $250,000,000; there were dozens of American corporations worth more than that. Surely, they argued, such a small economic stake was not worth the lives of tens of thousands of Americans and billions of dollars in arms. The Philippines? With the best will in the world they could not be defended if the Japanese were determined to take them. Furthermore, they were due to become independent in a few years; they must then stand on their own two feet. Let them go now. As for the tin and rubber of Southeast Asia, why not simply divide them with Japan? Going to war, both countries would be forced to pay more than all the tin and rubber were worth. Finally, an accommodation with Japan would have the effect of doubling the strength of the U.S. Navy overnight by relieving the pressures in the Pacific. I mention all this because I think it is of some interest. Could it have worked? I do not know. But even Walter Lippmann began to think it had merit, because like many other people at the time, including the President and his advisers, he did not think that the United States could fight and win a war on two fronts.

Yet Roosevelt would not back down from the current policy of toughness. He had prohibited the export of oil and steel without a federal license, thus effectively cutting some of the trade. He followed the Axis Pact by slapping a complete embargo on the export of scrap metals to Japan. At the end of the year he stopped the sale of machine tools to that country, leaving only one strategic material—oil—still being exported.

So long as there was even one item, however, there would continue to be strong pressure to discontinue the sale. The President wanted to keep the oil sales simply to retain some leverage on the Japanese; for many people that was too much. And they were furious when they discovered, in the spring of 1941, that more American oil was going to Japan than was going to Britain, while the administration was staffed by thousands of people who believed that war with Japan was only a matter of time.

That summer brought the showdown over the question of trade with Japan. The administration did not will it; it stumbled into it when Ickes made that ill-fated attempt at fanning the spark of national sacrifice into a flame by curbing gasoline distribution along the East Coast. No sooner was that done, on the ostensible grounds of an oil shortage, than continued oil exports to the Japanese could no longer be defended. The administration had boxed itself in, and the State Department's policy of trying to keep the Japanese from doing anything rash, long denounced as "appeasement," became politically exorbitant. If there was an oil shortage, let the Japanese go without, not Americans. Ickes refused to sign any more export permits for shipments of oil to Japan. The State Department muttered darkly that it was unwise, but popular sentiments could no longer be denied.

Roosevelt himself followed up by freezing all Japanese assets in the United States and closing the Panama Canal to Japanese shipping. The possibility of war seemed very close now. Steel and machine tools went into making ships; lack of oil would render the ships useless. Experts on the Far East were positive that war was at hand. As one of them, Mark Gayn, pointed out, the United States had followed a policy of harassing the Japanese without forcing them to submit to its will—a policy which could have but one result. Once the United States had constructed its two-ocean navy by 1945–1946, Japan would not have the slightest chance of waging a war against it. It must strike now or forgo the opportunity forever.

The administration had followed a policy of trying to get into the war through the North Atlantic; it was blind, though its critics would never believe it, to what the outcome of its policy in the Pacific would be. It was tough with the Japanese because it thought that that was generally the best policy; certainly it was the only policy the nation would support. There was no desire to fight a two-front war. Yet the prospect of war with Japan itself frightened no one. When Japanese soldiers in China were described as "sex-hungry," American women were not seen to pale. For no one doubted that the United States could defeat Japan with comparative ease. War in the Pacific would be a job for the Navy, and Americans were prouder, surer of their Navy than they were of their half-trained, clumsy-looking Army.

There was also less public division over the prospect of war with Japan. Most isolationists were as virulently anti-Japanese as the liberal interventionists. Far from seeking to avoid a clash, almost the entire country was willing to countenance war with Japan in the late fall of 1941. And the huge anti-Japan bloc was now insisting that the administration "Call Japan's Bluff!" while a former Chief of Naval Intelligence was pressing for a forward strategy in the Western Pacific: "The Hawaiian Islands," he concluded, "are overprotected, the entire Japanese fleet and air force could not seriously threaten Oahu."

Intervention had scored all the major victories, and what remained of isolation had been outflanked by the growing crisis with Japan. This latter showed more than ever how much isolationism was really anti-Europeanism, and Senator Wheeler led his isolationist followers in applauding every step which the administration took to press the Japanese harder.

The isolationists were by now a vestige of what they had been. In numbers and enthusiasm they were little more than a corporal's guard. Every major strategic point had been lost: Among the Republican rank and file 75 percent supported the President's foreign policy; the National Association of Manufacturers, hospitable to isolationist speakers in 1940, was not even polite to them at the 1941 convention—instead, there was Alfred P. Sloan, chairman of GM, trumpeting to a sleek, prosperous group of fellow tycoons that "The war abroad can only be won on the American industrial front"; the editor of *The Republican* pronounced isolation dead if it counted on conservatives within the GOP; at most, one person in five was willing to admit to being an isolationist; even the *Saturday Evening*

Post had deserted. Isolation had been outflanked and was about to be routed.

More than half the country was now overtly interventionist. Manifestations of interventionist supremacy were frequent: Half the Episcopalian clergy wanted a declaration of war on Germany; so did the director of the Progressive Education Association; the New York *Post* came out for war in July; the *New Republic* followed suit in August; in the following weeks a swelling parade of big-city dailies such as the San Francisco *Chronicle* joined in; and the president of Harvard added his support. Newspaper advertisements sponsored by the Associated Leagues for a Declared War began to appear with growing regularity. And interventionists could look back on an unbroken string of successes—destroyers for bases, Selective Service, lend-lease, convoys—while the isolationists had lost every round. Why not expect to secure the declaration of war and cap these efforts with the ultimate success? Because the country was afraid to take the final plunge.

Isolationists girded themselves for the final battle. Since Lindbergh's costly blunders Herbert Hoover had become the leading spokesman for this ill-starred cause. He agreed to aid to Britain, pressed for impregnable defenses, but argued that Hitler had overreached himself. Above all, he insisted, the administration should stop the "provocative steps" which could only lead to war. He had prepared his memoirs, for posthumous publication. Hoover now threw them into the breach, for they contained a solemn cautionary tale of how at Versailles American ideals had been twisted by the Europeans and applied to their own selfish ends.

But the trump card in isolation's dwindling hand was the fact that Congress would simply not declare war. So isolationists taunted the President to ask for such a declaration, confident that Germany had not yet been drawn in so far. And even though most military officers openly talked of how near war was, Congress refused to repeal the legislation banning the dispatch of American soldiers beyond the Western Hemisphere.

No one, in short, would take the responsibility for the final step—not the people, not the President, not the Congress. And even though isolation claimed the certain loyalties of perhaps only 20 percent of the nation, it still kept the country from that near unanimity almost everyone agreed it needed to brave the risks of war. This was a people that did not want to step straight into the war but preferred to be pushed, pulled or kicked into it. An odd sight, this, of grown men jostling and nudging, daring and egging one another on; of tough talk and rearmament yet trembling on the brink; of handholding and reassurances; of isolationism going one way and bellicosity going the other; of that most unhappy sight of people, singly or together, adrift for lack of sure purpose on which to attach their will.

Nebraska's redoubtable Senator George Norris, now eighty, a former pacifist and an old Progressive, was trying to get the administration to act by interpreting the growing Japanese hostility on one side and German U-boat attacks on the other as a "squeeze play." That, to his mind, was reason enough to declare war on Japan. When Tojo was named Japan's Prime Minister, any lingering doubts that Tokyo had abandoned its military ambitions were finally destroyed.

Yet desperately the Japanese made one last bid to avert war. The merits of their offer are endlessly debatable. The important thing here is that as their special envoy, Saboru Kurusu, journeyed from San Francisco to Washington in the middle of November, everywhere he went he was greeted politely, but coldly. Over a photograph of Kurusu and the Japanese ambassador to the United States, Admiral Kichisaburo Nomura, ran the headline

JAPANESE BOW AND GRIN FOR THE CAMERA
BUT GET NOWHERE IN WASHINGTON

and that was true. The betting among reporters and officials in the capital stood at nine to ten there would be war in the next few days or weeks. In the nation at large, two out of three Americans expected war to begin soon between the two countries.

Now the *New Republic*, all moderate sentiments long since abandoned, was urging that Japan be given an ultimatum: Abandon the Axis Pact, evacuate China and pledge "in future to behave like a civilized nation." To the *Nation* Kurusu's last-ditch mission was a final vindication of the wisdom of a hard-line policy toward the Japanese—a policy it had long demanded. It too called for an ultimatum.

By the beginning of December the odds on war had risen to ten to one. Kurusu had nothing new to offer. Everyone was now braced for Japan to strike; like the United States, it was tired of talk. According to the conventional wisdom, it would probably attack Thailand, Malaya, the Dutch East Indies, possibly even the Philippines; perhaps even all of these. Yet no matter where it struck, America was ready. Congress had finally overcome the last remnants of isolation and gutted the Neutrality Act, removing the last remaining barrier to the President's power to intervene directly in the war. And that, one journal concluded, was "probably the last foreign policy test unless or until Congress is asked to declare war." Thus, in the Pacific and the Atlantic, war was now at hand.

On December 4, a Thursday, two dozen of Washington's most important men sat down to a splendid dinner. There was Henry Wallace, the Vice President; there was also the new head of defense production, Donald Nelson. With them were Knudson, Knox and Stettinius. The rest were only slightly less distinguished. In this hour the talk naturally turned to the prospect of war with Japan, which seemed much closer now than war with Germany, which did not itself seem so very far away. Knox, bristling in his best bully-pulpit, TR-at-his-damnedest fashion, bellowed that even if war was about to break out, "no matter what happens, the U.S. Navy is not going to be caught napping." As for the power of Japan, the war would last no more than six months.

So the country stood, poised, ready to plunge into war, literally waiting for it. There is no need to reach for suspense. Let us instead pause a moment for one last look at the United States on the threshold of its last national crusade.

Army officers had spent an anguished few weeks in the summer wondering, as a headline expressed it, WILL CONGRESS BREAK UP A HALF-TRAINED ARMY? Under the current draft law the Army would have to begin releasing nearly 1,000,000 draftees, national guardsmen and reservists starting in September. Army officers wondered if these men might respond to appeals to stay on voluntarily. But there was already a keen and growing resentment among men earning $30 a month of their friends who were earning six and seven times as much in defense plants. General Marshall called for an indefinite extension of the draft; Roosevelt asked Congress to extend it for another year or two.

Morale at Army bases collapsed. With the current draft law due to expire in October there began to appear on walls, vehicles and weapons a cryptic notation in chalk: OHIO—for "Over the Hill in October."

Talk of simply leaving at the end of a year's service, of mutiny, of massive nonviolent protest was rife among draftees. They regarded themselves as martyrs. This was an unhappy Army to begin with. Most of a soldier's time went on close-order drill (fine in small doses, ruinous in large ones) and kitchen police. Training for combat was either rudimentary or nonexistent and carried out with poor equipment under inexperienced officers. Racial tensions were at once deep and close to the surface. Hatred for the President was the rule, not the exception, as was also true of their hatred for striking workers. And hostility between town and camp bordered on the murderous; the days when the draftees were the nation's darlings were long past. One story had it that restaurants in Southern Army towns posted signs which read SOLDIERS AND DOGS—KEEP OUT, or COFFEE 5¢— SOLDIERS' COFFEE 10¢. Perhaps the signs were apocryphal; the point they made was real.

There was no strong popular opposition to renewal of the draft law, but Congress was still leary of conscription. There was also a sense of bungling and futility, of depression, and a vote against conscription was a rebuke to the administration for doing a poor job of national defense. Had not the isolationists come around by now to supporting the draft, it might well have been defeated. As it was, only the unflagging efforts of the American Legion saw the bill through the House, and then by only a single vote.

The most important thing however was that the Army was growing. In one year it had established more than 100 new posts and bases. Its combat strength had gone from five infantry divisions and a cavalry division (approximately 15,000 to 20,000 men per division; divisions are the cutting edges of modern armies) to twenty-seven infantry divisions, two armor divisions and two cavalry divisions. It had 260,000 men in May, 1940; it would have 1,500,000 by January, 1942. Where it had had 6,000 pilots and 5,000 planes in May, 1940, it would have 22,000 pilots and 16,000 planes by the end of 1941.

The Navy was also growing at a spectacular pace. The Annapolis Class of '42 would graduate six months early, in December, 1941. In all, the Navy planned to add 17 battleships, 12 aircraft carriers, 54 cruisers, 201 destroyers and 175 other ships from submarines to minesweepers by the end of 1945. Sixty-nine of these ships were already under construction in the spring of 1941.

Gone was any lingering notion of limiting military spending or of avoiding huge deficits. In the first year after Roosevelt's call for 50,000 planes and a two-ocean navy, some $5 billion was spent on national defense, another $13.5 billion was contracted for, and requests totaling $44 billion were sent before Congress. There were critics, of course, to whom even these sums seemed inadequate. The critics wanted even more of the nation's resources to go into defense, and to them it was obvious that business was hampering the effort, or else it was the New Deal, or Roosevelt, or the country as a whole. And the newly created two-headed Office of Defense Management inspired the confidence of no one.

Manpower was a problem still, but not a critical one once Selective Service had been extended. More worrisome to most military officers was the congeries of problems which clogged the course of arms production. Lack of steel idled shipyards; lack of aluminum was likely to cut back airplane production. The government called for an aluminum scrap drive in the summer: Ten thousand tons of aluminum pots and pans would be enough for 740 heavy bombers or 4,000 fighter planes. The response was overwhelming. Seventy thousand tons of aluminum piled up around courthouses, fire stations and city halls. But months had passed, and that hoard was still there, turning into a vast collection device for dirt, dead leaves and soggy paper. In time, it was bought up by scrap dealers. They melted it down, refined it, and it reappeared—as pots and pans: Only virgin aluminum was good enough for modern planes. Unwittingly, American housewives went out and bought back what they had given away.

To wring the full measure of assistance from the clock, Roosevelt had instituted daylight saving time, over the vigorous protests of farmers who insisted that dairy cows would not be able to adjust to it, thus endangering the flow of milk and butter for national defense.

More worrisome was the prospect that American weapons could not stand the shock of battle. Critiques made by the British Army and RAF, which were currently using American planes, tanks, and artillery, led at least one American reporter to conclude: "For want of better armament, better planes, better engines, many a U.S. youngster will die."

Yet while there were problems, there was also progress that to less harried minds would have been stunning. In January the President had called for 200 cargo ships of 10,000 tons. Four months later the order was doubled. They were so ungraceful, so unattractive to look upon that the ship-loving Roosevelt, mourning their ugliness, wanted to call them "Ugly Ducklings." Other minds prevailed; they were called Liberty ships. And as the year ended, the nation's shipyards were working twenty-four hours a day on a backlog of 1,400 vessels, totaling 10,000,000 tons. Almost half those ships were scheduled for completion in 1942, and the two-ocean navy would be realized, not in 1946, but in 1944. Even now, a new merchant ship headed out to sea each day, and every three days a warship.

A country which had turned out 2,500 planes in all 1939 was building nearly that many each month. Where there had been 2,500 pilots in 1939, there were now 100,000. In June, 1940, about 7 percent of total production went into defense; in December, 1941, 25 percent, and scheduled to rise to 49 percent by the middle of 1942. Already, in fact, British and American war production was greater than that of Germany, Italy and Japan combined. And on January 1, 1942, the United States would surpass Germany as the world's foremost manufacturer of aircraft.

Fully as important as these efforts, these triplings and quadruplings of military-industrial might (henceforth there would be mainly doublings and less) was the organization for war. Literally thousands of defense plants had been built in eighteen months. They were about to turn out the thousands of ships, the tens of thousands of planes, the millions of guns, the billions of shells that modern war required. Behind them stood a reconstruction of government; not one important new agency would be required when war began that had to start from scratch. In structure and personnel the organization for war was in place when the Army finished up six months of mock battles at the end of November—a series of large-scale maneuvers in Tennessee, Louisiana, California and Washington, involving nearly 1,000,000 men. A great country, only a short time before hopelessly unready for war, was ready now for battle.

The United States proceeded to occupy Dutch Guiana; the first U.S. ships to take lend-lease directly into British and Russian ports were loaded, armed and ready to sail; the Japanese had been stymied and were prepared to discuss a possible withdrawal from China; Roosevelt gave Congress a blank check to write antistrike legislation; isolation was no longer a force to be reckoned with. The President prepared to leave for a short rest in Warm Springs, Georgia, and he could leave now, thought *Time*, "with a higher heart than at any time in 1941."

That confidence reflected the nation's armed might. But there were still lingering doubts about the will to fight and endure. For though the country was now predominantly interventionist, ready to accept war, it was still a damp explosive. It could be roused—what modern people could not?—but no one, not even Roosevelt, had found a way to do it.

Two views were in the ascendant and, as we have seen, some of the crusading mood of earlier times was reviving; these two divided that sense of crusade between them. The one had been expressed by Walter Lippmann just before the war began. It pleaded the necessities of history. America, he said, had a duty to fulfill that nostalgia or moral reservation could not shunt aside:

> What Rome was to the ancient world, what Great Britain has been to the modern world, America is to be to the world of tomorrow. We might wish it otherwise. I do. Every man who was young in the easier America of the pre-Great War world must long for it at times. But our personal preferences count for little in the great movements of history, and when the destiny of nations is revealed to them, there is no choice but to accept that destiny and to make ready in order to be equal to it.

And by now, among liberal interventionists, the necessities of history, which included the destruction of Fascism, were abundantly clear.

The other view, more attractive to conservatives, found its most important expression in Henry Luce's vision of the "American Century"; it was more assertive, more bumptious, more xenophobic than the other. Like Lippmann, he too pleaded the iron laws of history. But it is worth considering how Luce arrived at it and why his short essay became historically important.

Look at England, said Luce, in February, 1941. Eighteen months ago it was as we are now: disorganized, unhappy, insecure and apathetic; its policies fragmentary, betraying no higher aim than surviving the month in which they were made; pettiness, moral cowardice, evasion of hard realities marked the course of government and people. What a transformation since! Its body feels the iron; its spirit soars to the skies. It makes mistakes, but now it has purpose, is proud, defiant, truly great, every one of its people part of a historic cause. And here . . . here, all is miserably adrift.

And while America stumbles blindly along as if the outcome of this war was of no consequence to itself, its future is inextricably bound up in it. How large or small the role the United States chooses to play, it cannot avoid the consequences of that fact. And it alone in all the world can determine the aims of the war. Britain cannot, for it cannot win without American help. Germany cannot, for it cannot win unless America lets her. In short, the United States holds the outcome of the war in its hands, because the twentieth century has seen it develop into the world's greatest industrial power. This was a matter of fact, not opinion. Yet by not using that power affirmatively, America had abused it. It must, Luce urged, rise to the duties of that power and use it "to exert upon the world the full impact of our influence, for such purposes as we see fit and by such means as we see fit."

In the modern world, he went on, peace is indivisible, justice is indivisible, freedom is indivisible. And as this century is, whether people like it or not, the American century, the hour is now at hand for the country to assert its preeminence by holding out to the rest of the world "our Bill of Rights, our Declaration of Independence, our magnificent industrial products, our technical skills." The United States was already an international power in all save politics; indeed, it was "already the scientific, intellectual and artistic capital of the world." And, he concluded, the rest of the world was now demanding that the United States assert its political supremacy. To that goal he called his countrymen.

Conservative isolationists were slow to respond, as were some of the old Progressives. But liberal interventionists such as Robert Sherwood, Dorothy Thompson and Quincy Howe were much impressed. Some liberals were cool because of the source, but even they thought this was indeed the American century; they simply feared that American supremacy might be turned to serve illiberal ends.

And there was much truth in Luce's assertion of the country's industrial might. Even before the war began, it was, in economic terms, the preeminent power in all the world. It need only put the slack in its economy into the production of arms and it would become invincible. By all conventional estimates of power and greatness—words men linger over when thinking of their country—it had no serious rival. But that was a fact recumbent; the war had made it a fact erect. This war would savage Europe in its heart and limbs. America alone would move from strength to strength in arms and spirit. On that, such disparate organs as the *New Republic* and the *Saturday Evening Post* were agreed; agreed too in hopes that it would not turn into an American imperium.

But the temptations of imperial sway are strong and stir the souls of even sedentary men. A philosophy professor at Columbia felt the tug, and rejoiced in the impending demise of European ascendancy in artistic and intellectual fields. "Europe as Nirvana is over," he crowed, shattered by Nazi depredations. The hold of Europe on the minds of educated Americans had been smashed by Hitler's armies. And now, "only in America is there, for the long present, a chance for the survival of culture."

The country was then growing assertive; on its feet, in a sense, and ready for war. Yet a notion that people were soft lingered on. A noted anthropologist and author, Margaret Mead, was convinced of it. The traditional independence and easygoing, democratic character of the people had been eroded by the New Deal—or so it appeared to her—and a spineless, dependent generation was taking its place. Another who detected the same phenomenon was a journalist named Philip Wylie. He leaped to instant fame by blaming it all on "Momism"—mother worship. And still a third, Roy Helton, had blamed it on "The feminization of Western culture."

These fanciful notions had their roots in a widespread fear that the country was about to be put to a severe test and perhaps it would fail—a common kind of nervousness. Often it was put down to "The Failure of Propaganda," as one article expressed it. "Morale" was said to be bad. Yet one lifelong student of the public temperament was convinced that it was all froth obscuring a substantial reality: "Our morale today is probably higher than during any other critical period the nation has faced," he concluded late in November, 1941. There was a great task at hand—the defense of democratic institutions—"a job big enough to challenge us Americans. It is a job that is lifting us out of an era of tinsel, libertinism, cynicism, bitterness and disillusionment; it is a job which forces us to plan, to cooperate, in a common task."

The country was, in fact, on the brink of the greatest collective enterprise in its history; since then, there has been no other. America was about to pass through an experience both painful and priceless, and never more so in a country as diverse as this one. It was already more bound together in heart and mind than it had been for more years than anyone wished to remember. Angry quarrels still churned the surface—between business and labor, between isolation and intervention, between government and people. But under the umbrella of national defense they had gathered, and each month there arose solid proofs of a growing unity. As the great differences were leveled, those which remained stood out more than ever and seemed less tolerable: Remove the mountains and hills look large. The more unified the country was, the more unified it wanted to be.

The economy was humming now, moving into high gear. The defense industries were built or building; massive quantities of arms were beginning to appear. Strikes involved fewer and fewer workers. Isolation had been reduced to a rump. Government seemed clumsy, but there was no alternative to it. Business shunned the stock market, but it built the weapons. Science was organized for war. Boom towns were now receiving direct federal assistance. Schools and colleges had thrown themselves into national defense. Millions of workers had been retrained for defense, and millions more were learning. Military forces were now in the millions. The far left and the far right were almost gone; nearly everyone had crowded into the middle of the road. There were hardly any pacifists, and no strong antiwar bloc had emerged.

Militarily, "Everything was ready, from Rangoon to Honolulu, every man was at his battle station. And Franklin Roosevelt had to return to his. This was the last act of the drama." Any Japanese move might trigger war. "A bare chance of peace remained—of a kind of peace very close to war but not quite war." And the war of nerves that Roosevelt was conducting was "so realistic as to scare even his own people." But if the Japanese chose war, said *Time*, "Japan is a land of paper-houses and few anti-aircraft guns."

So "the stage was set for war; a distant, dangerous, hard amphibious war. . . ."

America was ready for it, a fact forever obscured because of what happened next. It was ready for war, indeed; it was not ready for Pearl Harbor.

PART TWO

The Most Incredible Year

December, 1941–December, 1942

XVI

Pearl Harbor Christmas

The war came as a great relief, like a reverse earthquake, that in one terrible jerk shook everything disjointed, distorted, askew back into place. Japanese bombs had finally brought national unity to the U.S.
—*Time*, December 15, 1941

AT two twenty-five that Sunday afternoon news tickers clicked out a seven-word bulletin: "White House says Japs attack Pearl Harbor."

For the rest of their lives the people old enough to remember that day would do so. They could invariably recall where they were and what they were doing when they heard the news.

Once the first shock passed and the ritual exclamations had died away (usually a variation on "Those dirty yellow bastards"), rage followed. Then, as the magnitude of the Japanese stroke sunk in, the mood became solemn. In recent weeks people had talked of defeating the Japanese in a matter of months. It was obvious that that would be the bloody work of years.

Recruiting stations were jammed and in some cities went onto a round-the-clock schedule. The rush to buy defense bonds exhausted the available supply.

Inevitably, there were rumors: "My brother says a man high up in Washington told him we lost eleven battleships and forty-four cruisers" and so on. But no one doubted that Japan would eventually be defeated. The overriding theme of editorial cartoonists was to show the attack on Pearl Harbor as a form of national hara-kiri. Talk of defense stopped; the word now was "Victory." Victory rallies were quickly arranged in the big cities. One, held at Madison Square Garden, sold tickets at prices ranging from 28 cents to $1.10 and offered "3 Choruses—3 Dramatic Tableaux." But already it occurred to at least one journal that "It may be that America's greatest danger is overconfidence." For, as they foresaw, there would be more defeats before there would be victory.

On that first day that the country was in the war many people found it impossible to go on as if nothing had occurred. They were restless. Large crowds silently gathered in front of the White House, the War Department, the Navy Department and the State Department. All that night a monumental traffic jam snarled the capital's streets. Yet the great federal agen-

204 DAYS OF SADNESS, YEARS OF TRIUMPH

cies seemed as somnolent as on any other Sunday. Only Selective Service had its lights on.

Elsewhere large crowds were milling aimlessly in city streets. They wanted to be told something or to be given something to do. But no one addressed them; no one told them what to do. Bars prospered. Portable radios blared on street corners. Every few hours an extra edition would arrive onto the streets, to be snatched up. And though the mood was hard to gauge, one reporter mixing with the crowds in Norfolk, Virginia, thought that "No one seems sorry to see war come, except that they hate to see the youngsters killed."

On the other side of the continent at about the same time it was raining in Los Angeles. A wandering balladeer named Woody Guthrie tramped into town with a folk-singing friend nicknamed the Cisco Kid. As evening wore on, they trudged from bar to bar along Los Angeles' skid row, singing for nickels and dimes and free drinks. But "this December night was bad for singing from joint to joint. The rain had washed the trash along the streets, but had chased most of the cash customers on home."

Singing in the Ace High Bar, Guthrie passed the hat, but there were few customers and fewer donors. A group of sailors arrived. Guthrie began to sing a song he had been working on the past few hours, of how the Japanese were sure to lose the war they had begun. Suddenly breaking into the strains of his song there came the splinter-tinkle sound of shattered glass—a not-unfamiliar sound along skid row. But this was no bottle being smashed. It had the crashing overtones of a plate-glass window coming down. The patrons of the Ace High looking into the street saw that in front of the Imperial Bar next door—owned by a Japanese and his wife —the inhabitants of neighboring pool halls and flophouses were being exhorted to strike a blow in retaliation for Pearl Harbor.

"We came to git 'em an' dam' me we're gonna git 'em," roared one of the putative leaders of the quickly gathering mob. "Japs is Japs. We're at war with them yeller-belly Japs! An' we come down to git our share of 'em," agreed another. "Get 'em! Jail 'em! Kill 'em!" chanted the mob.

Guthrie, his partner, the sailors, the bartender and the rest of those in the Ace High moved into the street. On the far side the mob, noisily working up its courage, was plainly bent on bloodshed. On the near side, framed inside their shattered window, huddled the terrified Japanese bar owner and his wife. Taking up his guitar, Guthrie, his partner, the sailors and a woman brandishing a gallon jug of cheap red wine picked their way over the shards of broken glass and eased themselves between the intended victims and their tormentors. Those in the front ranks of the mob took several threatening steps toward the intruders. Calmly Guthrie began to strum the strings of his guitar and in his flat, Oklahoma voice softly began to sing these words:

> We will fight together;
> We shall not be moved
> We will fight together;
> We shall not be moved
> Just like a tree
> That's planted by the water,
> We
> Shall not
> Be moved.

The mob still edged forward. But the song rose, its wistful melody cutting through the drizzle, and singly or in small groups other people in the street began to take it up. Some of them quietly filed in beside the group in front of the broken window and linked arms. The singing grew louder. The mob began to lose the advantage of numbers. It faltered. And its ranks began to break up just as police cars arrived on the scene. All that the police, summoned they believed to a riot, could see was the surrealistic sight of a motley congregation gathered in the rain in front of a broken window singing an old union song while a disheveled, wet, grumbling crowd shuffled shamefacedly away.

Roosevelt appeared cheerful and confident now, a strong contrast with his mood in recent months. To a visitor he conceded that the country had taken a hard blow, but he had not the slightest doubt that the United States would prevail.

By and large people expected the war to last two or three years. But eclipsing the long, painful road ahead in their consideration was the deep satisfaction derived from a new sense of community. Something of a family feeling prevailed. They were openly thankful for the newfound feelings of national unity and purpose. Typical was the headline that read:

AMERICANS ALL
National Disunity Is Ended

Or, as a University of Oregon coed expressed it, "We're all together now; that ought to be worth a couple of battleships."

No one at first seriously expected direct attacks on the United States. But the day after Pearl Harbor air-raid alarms sounded in San Francisco, triggered by a false Army report of thirty Japanese planes flying inland. Thereafter some San Francisco buildings were sandbagged. The Pacific Northwest had its "first invasion scare since Fifty-Four Forty or Fight." There were blackouts as far inland as Boise, Idaho, encouraged by rumors that one, perhaps two, Japanese aircraft carriers were standing to off the mouth of the Columbia River. Extra guards were placed on the Bonneville Dam. Radio stations went off the air rather than unwittingly serve as navigation aids to enemy aircraft. The Rose Bowl game was moved from Pasadena to North Carolina. Mobs started to prowl the streets at night, smashing stores that showed lights and beating up uncooperative motorists. And the Japanese submarines did indeed begin to stalk the Pacific coast, sinking little but sowing fear.

The war news was unrelievedly bad as the Japanese thrust toward Manila and captured Guam. Just before Christmas the British lost the brand-new battleship *Prince of Wales* and the battle cruiser *Repulse* in the waters off Singapore. (In terms of combat effectiveness the Royal Navy had suffered a worse blow than had the U.S. Pacific Fleet at Pearl Harbor.) On a cold, drizzly Christmas Eve a heavily guarded convoy sailed into San Francisco Bay carrying a sad cargo indeed: shiploads of the maimed, burned, shrapnel-torn survivors of Pearl Harbor.

Yet while there were dead to be buried and wounded to be succored, and there would be more of both before the war was done, there was cause for good cheer even in these days of defeat. There was the unexpected arrival of Winston Churchill on Christmas Eve. When Roosevelt made his Christmas Day broadcast, the British Prime Minister sat at his side. The following day Churchill addressed a special joint session of Congress, most of its members hurriedly returning from their Christmas vacations.

It proved to be a rousing, emotional occasion. The House gallery was packed. In the grounds outside, thousands of people stood in the wet and cold just to be near. Churchill wept openly at the outpouring of welcome and good cheer he received from everyone from the President to the humblest citizen. At the end of his Congressional address he flashed the V-for-Victory sign he had made famous. The Chief Justice of the United States, Harlan Stone, seated opposite him, grinned and flashed it right back. Churchill later called it "The biggest day of my life."

In that Christmas week some twenty-two new ships were launched, nine of them merchantmen, the rest Navy ships. It more than compensated for the material losses at Pearl Harbor. Christmas Day also brought the cheering news that the Navy had sunk its first Japanese submarine, off the California coast. And the much-derided defense program proved, to no little surprise, to need nothing more than minor adjustments now that war was here. In fact, "The U.S. need only step on the gas."

So on New Year's Eve almost the entire nation went out and greeted the New Year—a year certain to bring defeats, heartaches and the deaths of many young men—as bibulously and as lightheartedly as the occasion traditionally requires. The West Coast alone clung grimly to its war fever.

XVII

What News from the Front?

WHEN Congress had convened on December 8, it seemed to one Congressman that the mood was unmistakable. "Everywhere there was a quiet relief that unity had come upon us as suddenly as the Japanese had come upon Oahu." Only one vote was cast against the declaration of war on Japan, by Montana's Jeannette Rankin. (She had also voted against the declaration of war on Germany in 1917.) Tears rolled down her cheeks; pale and shaken, she mumbled her nay.

Yet when Roosevelt called for a declaration of war on Germany a few days later, there was not a single opposing vote. There was no discussion, no opposition; no one even bothered to make a speech pointing out the dangers and hardships of the road ahead. Yet Germany was commonly acknowledged to be a more formidable opponent than Japan; it was an astonishingly nonchalant way of going to war—and ironic, considering that the attack on Pearl Harbor was as stunning to Berlin as it was to Washington. Germany had sought to avoid war with the United States, but its Japanese ally had made the decision for it.

In the following months the Japanese continued to inflict defeat after defeat on the American, British and Dutch forces in the Western Pacific. There was little to ease these humiliations save confidence in ultimate victory and an occasional light or heroic note. Wake Island fell after two weeks of stubborn resistance. Just before the end its defenders defiantly radioed, "Send us more Japs." An Army pilot, Captain Colin P. Kelly, Jr., was credited with a suicidal attack that sank the Japanese battleship *Haruna* and was posthumously decorated. Roosevelt, like Lincoln and McKinley before him, wrote a letter to his successor fifteen years hence asking that the hero's son be considered for a place at West Point.* But beyond these things, the war news was sobering. People braced themselves, as if prepared to accept that "This year [1942] may be one of the hardest of all years to face. . . ."

Guam fell. The day after the New Year began, Manila surrendered to the Japanese. To a generation which had grown up thinking of that city not as a foreign capital but as the crown jewel of America's overseas pos-

---

* The *Haruna* was, in fact, almost the last Japanese battleship to be sunk, going down in August, 1945. Colin P. Kelly III went to West Point. He later became an Episcopalian priest.

sessions the loss came as a shock. Only the fall of Honolulu could have been more bitterly mourned. It was lamented as "the worst news since the British burned Washington 128 years ago." Angrily people asked, "Where is our fleet?"

February brought even worse disasters. The 65,000-ton French liner *Normandie* was being refitted in New York Harbor for eventual conversion into an aircraft carrier. Just before three o'clock on the afternoon of the tenth Abraham Goldfeather, one of the civilian workmen, saw smoke drifting toward him across the promenade deck. "They must be trying out the boilers," he said. By three o'clock Goldfeather found himself scrambling over the side of the ship to escape the sea of fire that was roaring up from belowdecks.

All this while a slight middle-aged Russian immigrant named Vladimir I. Youkovich was watching, heartbroken, from under the West Side El. "Such a terrible sight," he sighed. Youkovich had spent five years designing the *Normandie*. Now, thanks to a workman's carelessness with his welding torch and the Navy's clumsiness in pumping water in to extinguish the flames, his creation was rolling over, settling heavily into the mud.

Two days later the German battleship *Scharnhorst* and the heavy cruiser *Gneisenau* made a daylight dash up the English Channel to the relative safety of German waters and did it so brilliantly that it was taken as another defeat for Britain's RAF and the Royal Navy. On the fifteenth Singapore, the key to Southeast Asia, surrendered to the Japanese. Meantime, American forces were being pushed into the Bataan Peninsula, with no hope of escape. German U-boats, which seamen grimly described as being "as thick as catfish," prowled the East Coast, sinking a ship a day. A vague, ill-defined, yet disquieting notion that it might be possible to lose the war began to sap the country's confidence.

An angry, bitter tone crept into discussions of the war as it became painfully clear what a problem the Japanese now posed. With the fall of Singapore, as one journal concluded, "the United Nations find themselves up against a situation they never expected to face"—to wit, a ring of steel behind which the Japanese could shelter, building up their economic strength, digging in so firmly that when Allied forces took the offensive they would be forced to pay a staggering price in human and material losses. Instead of the Allies shutting Japan into the Western and South Pacific, Japan was shutting them out. The tables of blockade had, with the capture of Singapore, been neatly turned. *Time* mourned: "This was the worst week of the war. . . . It was the worst week of the century. . . . Now, as in 1864, the fate of the nation was in the balance."

As February dragged to its dismal close, Roosevelt delivered his second fireside chat since Pearl Harbor. Patiently he defended the strategy of

Germany First. He soberly tried to quell the preposterous rumors still being whispered about Pearl Harbor—of more than 100 ships sunk, of thousands of planes destroyed, of mass graves and coffin ships. But he could not still the impatience defeat inspired. A current headline bannered: ATTACK! BECOMES WATCHWORD OF A U.S. WEARY OF RETREAT. Yet the humiliating defeats went on and on.

March brought the fall of the Dutch East Indies on the twelfth. On the night of the fifteenth a combined fleet of U.S., British and Dutch warships engaged the Imperial Japanese Navy in a running battle that concluded with the Allied force being shattered and the survivors fleeing for safety by the next day's dawn. Among the losses was the heavy cruiser *Houston*, taking more than 1,000 American sailors to their deaths.

Tempers grew short. Two themes became increasingly popular: "Wake Up, America!" and "Attack Now!" Private citizens and government officials alike turned on the country at large and berated it as being apathetic and complacent. *Life* tried to shake the imagined complacency with a lengthy portrayal of "Six Ways to Invade the U.S." Every one of the six ways involved an enormous fifth column: "As one man, a hundred thousand German, Italian and Jap Fifth Columnists rock the country with explosives, wrecks and sabotage." Accompanying illustrations portrayed the fate in store for complacent Americans: "Captured Americans, their arms bound by a cord with a special pain-producing knot [!], are led off to the rear."

Time took up the other theme: "A people that had cravenly debated neutrality now looked forward to the fight. . . . The cry was *action, attack, offense, let's quit fooling around* [original italics]." Wendell Willkie told the 1942 Academy Awards dinner, "It sickens me to think of America in terms of defense." And surging to the top of current best-seller lists was a book called *Defense Will Not Win the War.*

Throughout this noisy, nervous debate there ran appeals to open up a second front somewhere—anywhere—in Europe. Such, ironically, was one of the responses to defeat in the Pacific, but it also reflected the general acceptance of the strategy of Germany First.

The growing realization that Bataan had to fall excited fears for the safety of General Douglas MacArthur. A national demand arose simultaneously that the general must not be allowed to fall into Japanese hands. It was a happy country, therefore, which learned as March ended that MacArthur had been successfully smuggled out of the Bataan Peninsula. How he escaped (by plane, at night) was kept secret for months. Roosevelt amused himself by spinning a tall tale about how the country's most distinguished military commander had disguised himself as a humble Japanese fisherman and managed to pass through the Imperial Japanese Navy in a leaky rowboat.

The escape lifted everyone's spirits for a moment. It provided a welcome

respite from the run of defeats. HERO-HUNGRY NATION GOES FOR MAC-
ARTHUR IN BIG WAY summarized one headline. Even journals which normally disliked him hailed MacArthur's escape as "an important victory in
the field of morale."

He was lauded as the man who struck terror into Axis hearts. He was
the man who would avenge Pearl Harbor. He was the greatest military
hero since "Black Jack" Pershing. For though he had yet to confound the
enemy (save by his escape), the country was indeed hungry for a hero. So
it made one. Streets were renamed in MacArthur's honor. A new dance
was danced to celebrate him. Alabama dedicated its first statewide blackout
to him. A flood of MacArthur songs, such as "Fightin' Doug MacArthur"
and "Here's to You, MacArthur," gushed forth. Then, on April 9, Bataan
fell, and the somber, gloomy mood returned.

MacArthur's second-in-command, Lieutenant General Jonathan Wainwright, removed his decimated forces to the island of Corregidor in Manila
Harbor and awaited the inevitable. And MacArthur, now situated in
Australia, prepared to parry an expected Japanese thrust against that
island continent.

At about the same time the Navy announced the loss of three more ships
in the Java Sea. The U-boat sinkings along the East and Gulf coasts were
currently running at two per day, outstripping the pace of construction.
Angrily, Roosevelt demanded more sacrifices from his people. That Easter
Sunday of 1942 church attendance was up sharply all over the United
States.

April, however, also brought the most exciting news in months: Tokyo
had been bombed. The news came first not from Washington but from
Berlin and Tokyo. "The news was so good that some people couldn't
believe it and asked if, after all, it might not turn out to be another Japanese trick." But once the truth sank in, the whole country thrilled to it.
Newspapers and magazines dwelled rapturously on the combustibility of
Japan's cities. The concrete physical damage of the raid led by Brigadier
General James Doolittle was slight. The raid was a token, but as a token
it was heavy with menace. Roosevelt spun another tall tale, inventing an
imaginary, secret air base in the Pacific called Shangri-La. From there, he
announced, the strike had been launched.* Like MacArthur's escape, it
provided a needed, sudden lift to people's spirits.

But May brought more defeats and reverses. On the nineteenth Corregidor surrendered, and its defenders were marched off into captivity. An
inconclusive naval battle was fought in the Coral Sea. Each side claimed
a victory in what was really a draw. The loss of coastal shipping rose to
three vessels sunk each day.

---

* In truth, Doolittle's planes were ferried to a point 800 miles from Japan aboard
the carrier *Hornet*.

The sinkings had become so frequent, in fact, that it seemed inconceivable that they could be accomplished on such a scale without supplies and information from shore. Thousands of tips were carefully tracked down. Yet, said the FBI, not a single case of treachery could it find. The U-boats, however, were receiving help from people onshore, albeit unwittingly.

Sailing along the fringes of the coastal shipping lanes, they would surface at night. Then they would wait for a ship to come along, an easy target silhouetted by the lights shining from the shore. Not until April had the brightest lights been extinguished and then only over the strenuous opposition of local businessmen who argued that blackouts would lower their profits. And not until summer was the coastal blackout effectively and systematically enforced. Admiral Samuel Morison later wrote with evident passion: "Ships were sunk and seamen drowned in order that the citizenry might enjoy business as usual." So the shipping losses mounted. And a country which had long loved its Navy above the rest of the services was becoming disenchanted: first Pearl Harbor; then the Battle of the Java Sea; now this.

The country's morale might have reached rock bottom had it not been for the promise of certain victory that was forming in their midst, before their eyes, the product of their own energies and skill. The war news was bad. The Battle of the Atlantic was being lost. Hitler was poised for a new offensive in Russia. But incredible numbers of tanks, planes, guns and ships were pouring forth from the factories built during the eighteen months of defense crisis. Lovingly the country's newspapers printed the totals and ran pictures of the weapons piling up.

And June brought the turning point of the war in the Pacific, however little it was appreciated at the time. In the waters around the tiny island of Midway, some 1,200 miles northwest of Hawaii, a smashing, undeniable, incredible victory was scored in which four Japanese carriers were sunk for the loss of one American flattop. From this point forward the U.S. Navy would never look back. Henceforth the victories would be American, and the defeats Japanese, right up to the end of the war. By this much, then, was the United States unready for war in December, 1941: Six months after Pearl Harbor it had turned back the Japanese in the Pacific, while at home its factories were producing more than all the factories of the Axis nations put together.

But at the time these things were not grasped. Instead, June seemed another generally bad month. By the end of it the country counted some 300 ships sunk along the East and Gulf coasts since the first of the year. The U-boats had become so bold that they were sailing in close to shore and sinking ships in broad daylight. The night of June 13 also brought one of the war's less edifying incidents, one which inevitably promoted more rumors, more myths and more fear of fifth columnists, spies and saboteurs.

That night one of the U-boats sailed in close to the beaches of Amagansett, Long Island. A heavy fog shrouded both sea and shore. Along the beach strolled a young coast guardsman named John C. Cullen, armed only with a flashlight and a signal flare. Other people may have been expecting a Nazi descent on the East Coast. Cullen was not. He suddenly stumbled out of the fog into a group of men hastily scrabbling away at the wet sand.

One, in a tongue Cullen did not recognize, cursed angrily (so much can be told whatever the tongue). "Shut up, you damn fool," hissed another man, in English. This one took Cullen firmly by the arm and led him away. Here, he said, is $300.* Just forget you ever saw us. O.K.? Cullen, mumbling agreement, took the money and gingerly walked back into the fog. Once sure he was not being followed, he ran back to his post.

Less than an hour later, when Cullen and his chief returned to the beach, the men had gone. But they could see in the early morning light the submarine U-202 aground on a sandbar at low tide, trying desperately to free herself. Combing the beach, Cullen and his chief found a packet of German cigarettes, four German uniforms, bombs disguised as coal and several boxes of explosives, all hastily and clumsily hidden. But the saboteurs had disappeared, into Manhattan.

In vain the FBI searched for them. Yet they were pursuing not dedicated, intelligent, highly trained men—merely the desperate pathetic sweepings of German society's petty criminal fringe. Under the strain, one of them broke. As soon as he could and to save his own neck, he called the FBI, turning in not only his three companions (any one of whom was capable of doing the same) but four other saboteurs who were to be landed later on the Florida coast. Alerted, the FBI was able to follow the latter to their contacts in the United States. The only damage done by these eight Nazi agents and their friends was to the reputation of German espionage. For as a British civil servant involved in spying had noted during the First World War, the German Secret Service always seemed clever, yet always proved hapless.

As attention shifted from this diversion back to the war, the principal question was what Hitler intended to do in Russia. The war seemed suspended in ice. Stimson warned everyone to expect air raids on both coasts, but no one took him seriously. For it was clear that Hitler was not concerned with pinprick attacks on the United States but with how to conquer Russia. When stymied the Germans had already descended to a level of savagery unheard of since the Thirty Years' War. And when a group of Czech partisans assassinated Reinhard Heydrich, the Nazi ruler of Czechoslovakia, the butchery that followed was so thorough and so terrifying that it shattered Czech resistance for the rest of the war. Goebbels meantime issued a new threat: If the British terror bombings of German cities

* Cullen later discovered that he had been given $240.

were not halted, all Jews in German hands would be exterminated. Yet so far hardly anyone took that to be a serious threat.

To keep up popular spirits while the country was still saddened by half a year of defeats and was awaiting Hitler's next, possibly decisive move, municipal authorities staged a variety of morale-boosting events. There were special bond drives. Parades of war heroes were arranged. Mothers with more than one son in uniform were specially honored. A week after Midway New York held the biggest parade in its history, a 30-mile extravaganza called "New York at War." It took eleven hours for the more than 500,000 marchers to file past the reviewing stand. Their ranks were dotted with tableaux such as "Hitler—the Axis War Monster," a replica of Roosevelt's head some 25 feet high and reenactment of SS killers shooting unarmed hostages.

The answer to what Hitler would do came almost exactly with the first anniversary of his invasion of Russia. By the end of June Hitler's armies were sweeping the Red Army out of its defensive positions and smashing it at will. As the Wehrmacht pressed farther into Russia, said *Time*, "Russia was in mortal peril, and with her the whole Allied cause." The British meanwhile were driven out of Tobruk. Rommel's Afrika Korps was poised to capture Egypt, and with it the entire Middle East. The mood was now one of unalloyed gloom. The morale-boosting, bond-selling tours of war heroes fell flat. And whereas at the time of Midway, when a small Japanese force had landed at the tip of the Aleutians and shelled Dutch Harbor, almost no one had been alarmed, the entire West Coast was suddenly in panic.

The war news was undisguisedly, unrelievedly bad. This was the nadir. Civilian morale was sullen. There was no good news to offset the bad. Yet it was still true, as one reporter concluded after visiting a boom town, "If the war ended today with a victory for us the mass of folks here could truthfully say that the war was the best thing to ever happen in their lives." Because for all the bad news there was unhappiness, but no despair. There were defeats, but there was no defeatism. In their personal, daily lives this was not an intolerable or a particularly painful time. There was a sense of alarm, but that was about the war news, not about life.

Still, that sense of alarm provided flagellants with new opportunities to purge the shades of defeat by mortifying their countrymen's flesh. A noted behaviorist famous for his work with rats, Professor Norman R. F. Maier, of the University of Michigan, proposed that everyone be denied gasoline, civil liberties and tires. The resulting frustration would, he promised, produce an aggressive response that could then be directed against the enemy. This would be much more effective than appealing to people's ideals.

Frustration and anger were vented in large newspaper advertisements placed by the Citizens for Victory Committee, whose members included Stephen Vincent Benét and Walter Millis. The war was being inexcusably mismanaged, they grumbled, and called for a united war command comprising Roosevelt, Churchill, Stalin and Chiang Kai-shek; a joint Army-Navy command, to put a stop to service rivalry; better management of war production; a second front at once to relieve the Russians; attack now!

Just as the country reached the first anniversary of the signing of the Atlantic Charter, one of those demands was satisfied. American forces went on the offensive at both ends of the Pacific, in the Aleutians and the Solomons. Midway had been a great victory, but a defensive one. It had brought no fundamental change of mood. But here was an offensive at last; that was the news people wanted to hear.

Even now, of course, the mood did not become immediately euphoric. There were still disappointments to be borne that fall. It was a blow to national pride to learn, for instance, that the planes which countless advertisements hailed as the wonder of the world were no match in combat for German planes. American pilots were asking for Spitfires. The Truman Committee angrily threatened to find out why.

In October the Navy admitted to the loss of a third carrier, the *Wasp*. It also announced the loss of three more cruisers. In North Africa a great battle was just beginning between the Afrika Korps and the British Eighth Army at a place in the desert called El Alamein. Egypt hung in the balance, and few people would bet on a British victory. The Russians were grimly hanging on in the rubble of Stalingrad. No one doubted that this would be the decisive battle of the war in Russia. Like the British in North Africa, the Russians were the objects of more and more hope and charity and less and less faith.

Captain Eddie Rickenbacker, the heroic air ace of the Great War, was missing, presumed dead, somewhere in the South Pacific. His loss would be mourned as a nation's loss. And as the operations in the Solomons bogged down, people began to brace themselves subconsciously for news of fresh disasters. At first they had believed (save for the inevitable fringe of scandal- and rumormongers) what government officials and military officers told them about the war. That confidence had virtually disappeared in recent months. In its place there was a growing suspicion that the news was being manipulated, and through it the country.

There was thus a ready-made audience for Melvin J. Maas, a Minnesota Congressman who was also a colonel in the Marine Corps Reserve, when he returned enraged from a visit to the Pacific war fronts. Over the radio he attacked official information policies which passed off defeats and reverses as victories and advances; military secrecy and government censorship were being used to cover up blunders, he charged; and he bitterly attacked the policy of letting the Army and Navy fight separate wars. Maas concluded by demanding a strategy of Japan First.

All during the months of defeat the government had indeed exercised more and more control over the news. Some agencies were disbanded;

new ones were created, first to simply give the facts, then to sell the war and counter defeatism. But the defeats continued, and there was no way to entirely disguise them for long. What kept defeatism and war-weariness from setting in was not the inept, clumsy juggling of information policy, but the expectation of final victory and the sense of underlying unity. At times, as we shall see, that latter broke down, but only in regard to certain fringe groups. For, as one writer observed that summer of 1942, "We are a more united nation now than we were at any time before, during or after the First World War. There is at the moment no opposition worthy of the name."

The country was fused as it had never been before in living memory. Not all the defeats, setbacks and frustration could break down that sense of national union and purpose. It was a precious thing, a strong sense of genuine community. It sustained almost the entire country during the long, bitter months from December, 1941, to October, 1942.

XVIII

We Lose, They Pay

LOOKING at the past is much like looking down from any high point: What we see is foreshortened. And there is a tendency to think about the evacuation of the West Coast Japanese as if it occurred on the heels of Pearl Harbor. In large historical terms perhaps it did. But the view from ground level is far more complex and instructive.

With the exception of a very few incidents, such as the episode on Los Angeles' skid row, West Coast Japanese and Nisei at first had little to fear, and in many cases they were shown sympathy for their awkward position. The FBI rounded up some 3,000 enemy aliens—Japanese, German and Italian—in the first few days, but that was simply a matter of routine precaution. Yet it was a tense Christmas for Issei and Nisei. Everywhere in the Pacific the United States and its allies were being defeated by the Japanese.

The strain began to tell, and tempers grew short, as defeat followed defeat. So much might have been predicted. But it was an incalculable misfortune that one of the first people to break under the pressure of war was Lieutenant General John L. De Witt.

De Witt was a general's son who had followed his father into the Army. Where the father, however, had been a much decorated combat hero, the son spent the Great War as a supply officer. The father had been a strapping, self-possessed figure, while the son was short, bald, myopic and excitable. From his office in the Presidio at San Francisco De Witt exercised command over all U.S. Army units west of the Mississippi. On the night of December 8 De Witt's headquarters alarmed the entire city by claiming that some thirty Japanese planes were flying over San Francisco Bay. All that night searchlights probed the sky while Army planes vainly hunted for the intruders. Navy officers laughed it all off the next day as another Army blunder. But not De Witt.

He called a meeting of the city's political and business elite. His pince-nez glittering, his bald head soaked by sweat, De Witt attacked them for taking the air raid calmly. They were fools, he sneered. Japanese planes flew over this city last night; the Japanese despise the rules of war; the Japanese are criminals and should be treated as criminals. His captive, angry audience seemed unmoved. His voice rising to a scream, De Witt shrieked that he wished there had been deaths and property destruction to

216

"wake up the fools in this community who refuse to realize that this is war."

A few days later Frank Knox returned from Honolulu to deliver his preliminary report. He credited the Japanese success to a fifth column which he claimed was second only in size and effectiveness to that which had betrayed Norway. "Successful Fifth Column work," not Navy negligence, was responsible for the Pearl Harbor disaster.

But still there was no persecution of the Japanese and Nisei. Even De Witt thought at this point that it would be "damned nonsense" to try to round up and move 120,000 civilians inland. Most military officers, in fact, were opposed to major evacuations. There were scares, encouraged by suggestions that at least one Japanese aircraft carrier was poised off the coast, but there was as yet no panic. The demand for Japanese goods and services dropped sharply, and someone chopped down four of Washington's cherry trees. But when asked if the country contained aliens who were secretly loyal to a foreign government 82 percent said the Germans were, 29 percent said the Italians were, and only 24 percent said the Japanese were.

Long before the war began there had been some groups, such as the American Legion, claiming that the Issei and Nisei were disloyal. (The former were born in Japan and barred by law from becoming American citizens; the latter were their American-born children, citizens by birth.) And the loyalties of the Issei at least were often assumed to be divided between the United States and Japan. But such fears were not general, and the war would prove how groundless they were.

The Japanese had been discriminated against for many years, as had the Chinese and Filipinos. But unlike the Chinese, they were rarely the objects of physical attack. The Japanese, in fact, had won a grudging respect as the Orientals most like Caucasians, while the Chinese were openly despised. The growing tension with Japan in recent years had brought increased friction between the West Coast Japanese and local racists. The war would inevitably aggravate latent hatreds. Even so, the Nisei at least might expect to be spared official persecution. Their parents were technically enemy aliens, but they were not. They enjoyed the constitutional protections of full citizenship. On the day before Pearl Harbor there had appeared a magazine article by a noted federal judge (and close friend of the President), Jerome Frank, which observed, "If ever any Americans go to a concentration camp, American democracy will go with them."

With the publication of the report on January 24 of the President's official inquiry into the Pearl Harbor attack, Knox's claims received—or appeared to receive—confirmation. With vaguely worded references to Japanese spies and saboteurs it sounded like an indictment of the islands'

Issei and Nisei for committing treason. From this moment the pressure to arrest them mounted sharply, not only in California but throughout the nation. The mayors of several West Coast cities began to demand their evacuation. And the more venal, irresponsible West Coast newspapers stepped up their long-standing hate campaigns.

Yet these demands should be seen in relation to a larger phenomenon. For all across the country there was a rising anger and impatience. Not only on the West Coast but throughout the United States tolerance plummeted in the wake of a steady succession of defeats and setbacks. A wave of prosecutions was set under way, many of them verging on persecution, and it kept up for as long as Allied forces were losing. The virtual arrest and imprisonment without trial, or even charges, of the West Coast Japanese and Nisei was the largest and most disgraceful episode, but it did not stand alone.

Five days after the Roberts report on Pearl Harbor the Attorney General announced that *all* enemy aliens would be removed from the Pacific coast: All Germans, all Italians and all Japanese would be moved to the interior and kept under guard. For the moment his order did not include Nisei. They were, as Biddle repeatedly pointed out, American citizens, entitled to all the constitutional protections. The Army proceeded to bar *all* enemy aliens from areas it deemed sensitive, limits were placed on their freedom of movement, and they were kept to a dusk-to-dawn curfew. California's governor, Culbert Olson, moved to repeal the business and professional licenses of *all* enemy aliens in his state.

Some aliens, including more than 7,000 Germans and Italians living near sensitive facilities on the West Coast, were moved inland. In New York pro-German propagandists were being prosecuted in the federal courts. The woman flier Laura Ingalls was convicted of being an unregistered Nazi agent. If anything she was an ultraisolationist and a political innocent. Nonetheless, she was sentenced to two years in prison. At the same time George Sylvester Viereck was tried on similar charges. His activities predated the act under which he was prosecuted, making it a clear case of post facto prosecution. He received a six-year sentence. Besides Ingalls and Viereck, scores of lesser pro-German lights were being prosecuted and their publications suppressed. In most cases the acts and utterances involved dated from before Pearl Harbor. Why then had the prosecutions not occurred earlier? What had occurred was a change in the climate, and suddenly people who were formerly dismissed as nuisances and cranks were viewed as menaces.

Despite official assurances to the contrary, millions of people were convinced that saboteurs were at work all over the United States. Pearl Harbor, the sinking of the *Normandie* and every major industrial accident were put down in the popular mind to saboteurs and fifth columnists. The annual Washington Cherry Blossom Festival was suddenly canceled as a concession to the present mood. When a race riot broke out in a Detroit housing project, the Justice Department charged those involved with "seditious conspiracy." Such was the climate in which pressure was mounting for the evacuation of the West Coast Japanese.

By the beginning of February the number of people on the West Coast who believed that the Japanese were loyal to another government had risen to 40 percent (though more than 40 percent still believed they were loyal to the United States). More worrisome, however, was the fact that by two to one people on the West Coast now believed they were more dangerous than the Germans or Italians, while in the rest of the country Germans were the most feared. Regionally, the breakdown could not have been more graphic: The East Coast feared Germans most, the West Coast the Japanese. Yet there was still no thought among federal officials of evacuating the Japanese to the interior.

To the north, the Canadian government had already ordered all Japanese males aged eighteen to sixty-five to work camps away from the Pacific coast. Canada had more than 50,000 Japanese and Japanese-Canadians, but those who were citizens were exempted from the order. American policy was more restrained by comparison—so far. The Hearst newspapers were busily reviling the Japanese and Nisei. Local politicians were starting to do the same. Popular sentiments appeared to be moving toward those of a man who was quoted as saying, "Throw them all [Japanese and Nisei] into concentration camps and work it out after the war's over!" There were also various proposals for throwing Nisei off the relief rolls; it proved impracticable because there were hardly any Nisei on relief. The pressure was obviously rising. But it is still hard to say just where temporary spitefulness ended and genuine hatred began.

The most vigorously anti-Japanese views were held by a relative handful of people, most of them already known for their bigotry and self-seeking. One reporter visiting there in February found that "In general the West Coast is more conscious of the war than the rest of the country. It hears more facts and rumors about Pearl Harbor. It witnesses the country going into action. It is also more jittery." The rich were said to be moving inland and some people feared that their vegetables were being poisoned by Japanese truck farmers. Yet he was left with the indelible impression that the hate campaign was the work of a few venal journalists and politicians, and most people simply went along with it.

But at the same time there was also a surprising, unfortunate campaign in the national press to intern the Japanese and Nisei. In more than 400 daily newspapers there appeared columns by the distinguished liberal journalist Walter Lippmann on February 5, 12 and 14 not only demanding internment, but offering a rationale for it that no one else appears to have thought of before. Lippmann traveled around the West Coast, reporting back that it was a fact, not speculation, that the Japanese were about to attack the coastal states. They would do so with the assist-ance of a massive Japanese fifth column. But while the brave defenders of the West were trying to guard their country, they did so with one hand tied behind their backs—tied by ignorant, spineless bureaucrats in far-off Washington, D.C. These were the people who were preventing the evacua-tion of the Japanese and Nisei.

National security required that all the Japanese and Nisei be rounded up, he insisted. And by a line of reasoning that seemed to anticipate 1984, Lippmann showed how innocence was proof of guilt. There had been no sabotage attributable to Japanese and Nisei; that meant they were waiting for some future time when such acts would be most effective; therefore, they were preparing to rise up in conjunction with a Japanese invasion; they were a clear and present danger and must be arrested at once.

Their right to legal protection was thus null and void. They were traitors to the United States. Lippmann had provided General De Witt and Cali-fornia's Attorney General Earl Warren with an argument they would soon use to great effect. And other journalists took up Lippmann's themes. They had held back before, they explained, because it seemed that the current anti-Japanese agitation was the work of local racists. But once Lippmann opened the floodgates, they poured through.

On February 14 De Witt drew up his final recommendation on the issue of the West Coast Japanese and forwarded it to Washington. "The Japa-nese race is an enemy race," he concluded, "and while many of them [the Nisei] have become 'Americanized' the racial strains are undiluted." Or, as he expressed it elsewhere, "A Jap's a Jap. . . . It makes no difference if he is an American citizen." Like Lippmann, he found that innocence was definitive proof of guilt: "The very fact that no sabotage has taken place is a disturbing and confirming indication that such action will be taken." He then asked for authority to remove "all Japanese, all alien enemies, and all other persons" who were, or were suspected of being, actual or potential spies, saboteurs or fifth columnists.

The pressure on Biddle to countenance wholesale evacuations was now immense. His own representative on the West Coast, Tom Clark (later a Supreme Court Justice), was recommending it. The Attorney General of California, Earl Warren, was demanding it. And Biddle, a supposed rock of civil liberties scrupulosity, crumbled in the dust.

The White House thus found itself confronted with an unbroken phalanx of state and federal officials supporting the Army's request for authority to evacuate anyone and everyone it, in its wisdom, wanted to move. Roose-velt, never more than vaguely interested in civil liberties, granted the authority requested. On February 19 he issued Executive Order 9066.

Military officers in the Western Defense Command who had been argu-ing for two months that massive evacuations of enemy aliens were unneces-sary now had authority to undertake them if they wished. They had argued that there was no military necessity for such action. But with this new grant of authority they began overnight to plead that overriding military necessity required the removal of enemy aliens and potential saboteurs. Thus some sort of evacuation was going to take place. Why the sudden turnabout? The commonest view is regional public opinion. But that really begs the question of what lay behind the shifting tides of public opinion.

Certainly it was not an expectation that the United States was going to be overrun by Japan. Early in February people were asked to say whether Germany or Japan posed the greatest danger to the United States. Nationally the results were:

Germany 47.5%   Japan 10.2%   Equal danger 32.3%

On the Pacific coast the results were even more instructive:

Germany 57.4%   Japan 10.5%   Equal danger 28.8%

We might therefore expect greater hostility toward German aliens than Japanese. The difference is usually put down to racism. But that explains very little. Why not round up the Japanese in January? Why wait until April? More, the early actions and recommendations applied to *all* aliens and only later shifted to the Japanese. Racism there was. It was generally believed "that it is impossible to distinguish between loyal and disloyal Japanese and Nisei, but that it is quite possible to make such a distinction [with] . . . German and Italian aliens."* Yet the racial element was only one factor among others, and possibly not the most important. All over the country the crisis which had been building for two years was coming to a head. Like all such crises, it was one which fed on human sacrifice. This we may call the horizontal crisis, stretching in linear fashion from 1939 over the whole course of the war. Intersecting it vertically in the spring of 1942 was the run of Japanese victories, and American defeats, in the Pacific. Where they crossed was over the West Coast Japanese and Nisei. The evacuation was partly inflamed regional opinion, partly racism, partly venal local interests out to acquire the victims' property at fire-sale prices. But most of all it was that ancient phenomenon—the ritual sacrifice.

Nearly all the fighting that Americans were doing in the first six months of the war was in the Pacific. The steady succession of humiliations there called out for vengeance. Also, the West Coast felt closer to the war than any other part of the country and thus bore the greatest psychological strain. It cracked under that burden.

Up to February 19 the vocal expressions of hostility were strongest against the Japanese, but they had not been treated differently from any other group of enemy aliens. On February 2 *all* enemy aliens had been

* Indeed, before 1942 ended, in fact, only 228 enemy aliens of Italian descent were still being held. With some bitterness the Japanese asked how it was possible to check on the loyalties of 600,000 Italians and not one-tenth as many Japanese.

ordered to register with the Western Defense Command. Thousands of German and Italian aliens were forcibly evacuated from their homes. De Witt asked for, and received, authority to remove any and *all* enemy aliens if he wished. So far, then, official action had been relatively even-handed. But late February and early March brought a series of policy changes reflecting the fortunes of war and their effect on popular and official tempers.

On February 10 the *Normandie* (renamed the *Lafayette*) burned and sank in New York Harbor. Five days later came the fall of Singapore. *Time* lamented on the twenty-third that this was "the worst week of the war." That same day a Japanese submarine shelled an oil refinery near Santa Barbara, doing little damage, but making the entire coast more jittery than ever. The following night, February 24, a weather balloon strayed into the skies over Los Angeles. For the rest of that night, searchlights probed for enemy raiders and the city endured a rain of spent shell fragments as Army antiaircraft batteries blazed away into the void. (For months after, the Western Defense Command continued to insist that an attack had taken place.) The results of this noisy, nervous fiasco included two persons dead from heart attacks presumably owing to the excitement, three more killed in the attendant stampede in the city streets and dozens injured by the hail of jagged steel and brass. Not the least consequence was widespread panic and hysteria throughout Southern California. Two days later came the first large-scale evacuation when Terminal Island in Los Angeles Harbor was suddenly cleared of hundreds of Japanese and Nisei fishermen. A new stage had begun.

On March 2 De Witt issued a proclamation declaring that all enemy aliens, all Nisei and all persons suspected of sabotage or espionage would be required to move away from the coast. To ease the blow, De Witt suggested that the Japanese and Nisei make their own arrangements and move voluntarily, as soon as possible. He indicated that if they did as he suggested, they would henceforth be left to their own devices.

On March 12 the Dutch East Indies fell into Japanese hands, which was followed by the stunning destruction of a formidable Allied fleet in the Battle of the Java Sea on the night of March 15.

Meantime, thousands of Japanese families had left for interior states, while thousands more prepared to follow. But wherever they went—Arizona, Nevada, Utah, Wyoming, Idaho, Montana, New Mexico—they were turned back at the state line or forced to leave the state after entering it. In many towns they were attacked by mobs. Colorado alone had a governor who would welcome them. But how to get there if not by crossing the other states? On March 27 De Witt halted the voluntary evacuation. Two days later the Army began forcible evacuation. At about the same time the restrictions on German and Italian aliens were eased.

Once the forcible evacuation and internment were under way, there was virtually no opposition to it. The civil liberties crisis was about to reap its most important harvest. And it was not coincidental that the liberal elements which are normally the staunchest opponents of the abuse of governmental power raised barely a murmur of protest. Liberal commentators such as Walter Lippmann, the House's Tolan Committee (which actually recommended evacuation and internment), the ACLU, the liberal journals—all acquiesced in the systematic and unjustifiable persecution of 120,000 people, most of them citizens of the United States.*

The reputable press had long since gone over to the side of hysteria. *Time* insisted that the Nisei and their parents posed a threat to the country and claimed that "California is Japan's Sudetenland." Unless the government acted soon, it hinted darkly, an outraged citizenry might find itself with no choice but to take action on its own behalf. *Newsweek* resuscitated one of history's more transparent hoaxes, the *Tanaka Memorial*, which made the conquest of the world Japan's historic mission. And for good measure *Newsweek* also hailed the Dies Committee's wildest attacks on the Japanese and Nisei as conclusive proof of their treachery.

In the country as a whole the thirst for vengeance was growing demonstrably. On December 24, 1941, people were asked if the United States should wage all-out war on Japan, including attacks on its civilian population, or restrict itself to military targets. These were the results:

All-out	Military only
59%	30%

When the same question was asked on March 28, 1942, these were the results:

67%	23%

It is worth noting, however, that even now when people were asked which group of enemy aliens was the most dangerous, the Germans clearly outdistanced the Japanese. It seems even more curious that only the West Coast Japanese and Nisei were being evacuated. Those in Hawaii and east of the Mississippi were generally left alone by officials, except for a relative handful of suspect individuals. The explanation is that the Hawaiian Japanese were too many, and those in the East were too few, to make adequate scapegoats. Even so, there was some spontaneous harassment in both cases. Life became very difficult for New York's 2,000 Japanese, for instance. Those in business were soon bankrupted. Those with jobs were fired. La Guardia warned them to stay off the streets, the buses and the subways. Most were quickly reduced to dependence on religious charities and occasional odd jobs.

---

* The ACLU was unhappy over the Nisei, but considered the Issei beyond its purview.

In the West, meanwhile, some 120,000 people, young and old, were being rounded up and herded into temporary, makeshift camps. From there they were to be forced out into the desert. For most it was a heartbreaking experience. Yet one would never imagine so from the accounts at the time. Almost every photograph showed smiling, cheerful Japanese going off as if to a picnic; no photographs of the suicides who laid their heads on the Southern Pacific Railway and waited for the train. *Life* described the removal of "Coast Japs" to the barren Owens Valley as "spontaneous and cheerful." The camp itself was "a scenic spot of lonely loveliness." As *Time* described it, "All they forfeit is their freedom."

Even liberal journalists gave the camps their blessings. One thought the evacuees were "living in very decent conditions and uncomplaining." Carey McWilliams, who would later denounce the entire operation, thought at the time that most of the inmates were actually living better in the camps than they had at home. Indeed, "In the long run the Japanese will probably profit by this painful and distressing experience." In short, it was good for them. This was lost on people who were in effect prisoners without possibility of parole. They had not even had trials. They cooperated in the evacuation out of simple prudence and in the hope that cooperation might be taken as a sign of innocence. But the bitterness they felt was profound. Though they frequently refused to show it openly, what they felt was "fear, frustration and anger."

They saw themselves as victims of racism and war hysteria; they believed they had been robbed, with the connivance of government, of the economic gains painfully built up over many years; they regarded American talk about democracy and the higher aims of the war and the reputed devotion to civil liberties as a tissue of lies and half-truths; and those things involved in the evacuation to which the press and government pointed with pride—such as the façade of self-government in the camps—appeared to them as pathetically lame excuses for decent, humane treatment.

In contrast with the press portrayals, one young Nisei described his surroundings:

> [It] is actually a penitentiary—armed guards . . . barbed wire . . . confinement at nine, lights out at ten. The guards are ordered to shoot anyone who approaches within twenty feet of the fence. The apartments, as the Army calls them, are stables . . . mud is everywhere. The stalls are eighteen by twenty feet; some contain families of six or seven persons. . . . We have had absolutely no fresh meat, vegetables or butter. Mealtime queues extend for blocks; standing in a rainswept line, feet in the mud, for scant portions of canned wieners and boiled potatoes, hash . . . or beans . . . and stale bread.

Sewage mixed with the mud, there was no hot water, the dishes from which they ate were unwashed, and there was an endless regimentation extending to the pettiest and most personal details. Such was life in the camps. Federal officials insisted such descriptions were lies or half-truths. Those who knew best, however, knew better.

Most of the evacuation was carried out in April and May. By August it was virtually complete. Anyone who had at least one Japanese great-grandparent—*i.e.,* was, one-sixteenth Japanese—was interned. This decision led to cases both ludicrous and pathetic. At the camp near Pomona, for instance, there was an Irish laborer named Hayward (whom the Army insisted on calling Hayabashi). With him were twenty members of his family, all of them white of skin, red of hair and round of eyes. Hayward himself had one Japanese grandparent.

The camps had self-governing councils and their own newspapers. These were patterned after high school government and newspapers: all sham, and no one more aware of it than those involved. In the early weeks, however, there was at least no censorship of what people could read. And the inmates tried to make the best of things. But even after the internment the war continued to worsen. So as if the internees had not been victimized enough, life in the camps was made even more painful, indicating even more clearly just how much they were scapegoats for American defeats. The sad little camp papers were suddenly reduced to nothing more than bulletin boards carrying official announcements or stories praising the internment. The number of visitors allowed each inmate was sharply reduced. Outside reading matter was cut off, and nothing could be read but dictionaries, hymnbooks and Bibles. All Japanese phonograph records were confiscated. Arbitrary searches, calculated harassment and the imposition of solitary confinement became commonplace. On the outside, the Army stopped drafting Nisei. They were declared 4-F or 4-C ("aliens not acceptable to the armed forces"), and those already in uniform, approximately 5,000, were put behind desks—in the East. Such petty cruelties and humiliations continued until August, when American forces went on the offensive in the Pacific. After that, the Army lost interest in its prisoners and turned them over to a civilian agency, the War Relocation Authority.

The civil liberties crisis had been building for more than two years. The evacuation was the most spectacular part of it. Others also bore the brunt of panic and fear, for the crisis was not one which made for fine distinctions. It was a general lapse in civil liberties, not a specific one.

Just days before Pearl Harbor the eighteen Trotskyites convicted in Minneapolis went off to jail, ridiculed in the press as "mice." Their ten-year sentences were considered fitting even after it was conceded that all they were guilty of was "having wicked and revolutionary ideas." As the war went from bad to worse, so did the general mood. In February the

Nation was clamoring, "We can lose this war," while the Hearst press was blaming all the disasters on the morally rotten British Empire. The FBI was protesting that it was trying to fight the fifth column but was hobbled by not having authority to tap telephones (which did not actually keep it from doing so) and thereby evaded any share of responsibility for not catching the traitors supposedly responsible for Pearl Harbor. And Roosevelt helped things along by creating attack scares. "Enemy ships could swoop in and shell New York," he told a press conference in February. "Enemy planes could drop bombs on war plants in Detroit. Enemy troops could attack Alaska." Asked if U.S. forces were not able to repel attacks like this, he bristled: "Certainly not."

At a press conference a few weeks later, on March 24, Roosevelt too seemed to succumb to the growing sense of anger and helplessness. Worse, he tried to aggravate it. He furiously attacked "Sixth Columnists"— these were defeatists, rumormongers and people who harbored pro-Fascist sympathies. *Life* forthwith called for a crackdown on defeatists and glowered, "The fact is that subversive doctrines are widespread in the U.S. today." The magazine's editors went on to draw up a list of people to be arrested. They were mainly anti-British and anti-Semitic crackpots, and the editors acknowledged that. But "crackpots who spread enemy propaganda are a dangerous luxury." Even the New York *Times* was not immune. It turned on conscientious objectors, "The Men Who Refuse to Fight." They were divided into mindless religious zombies doing whatever their leaders told them or well-meaning but ignorant pacifists, such as the Quakers, and intellectuals who arrogantly thought that those of their fellowmen who went to fight were fools.

The Selective Service was meanwhile carrying out its own crackdown on objectors and pacifists. It made it much harder to be classified as a CO. The criteria for CO status had been a sincerity of belief in religious teachings combined with a profound moral aversion to war. In March, 1942, that was suddenly changed to a single criterion: belief in a transcendent creator-deity—preferably one with a large following in the West.

A new round of attacks was also launched against Jehovah's Witnesses. Once again the Supreme Court took the side of the persecutors instead of their victims. In one of its most astonishing decisions the Court ruled that local government could curb religious freedom. In this instance municipal authorities were permitted to require that Witnesses pay a peddler's tax before they could distribute their literature. Sometimes the tax was small; sometimes it was exorbitant. But more than that, the Court also upheld the right of the authorities who imposed and collected it then to ban the distribution of the literature for which the tax had been paid. They could do so, furthermore, without cause, notice or hearing.

This extraordinary decision ruled, in effect, that free speech, a free press and freedom of religion could be curbed by even the humblest lawmaking bodies so long as the curbs were consonant with "the preservation of peace and good order." The New York *Times*' Arthur Krock expressed his own admiration for the "beautifully-reasoned argument" of the majority opinion.

At about the same time the Court reviewed the case of a Jehovah's Witness in New Hampshire who had turned on a policeman who was badgering him and snarled "damned Fascist." New Hampshire had what was in all other instances a dead letter of a law forbidding one person to address another with "any offensive, derisive or annoying word." Instead of ruling the statute too vague to be enforced, the Court upheld the conviction and the six-month jail sentence by a vote of nine to zero.

Meanwhile, the mob attacks on Jehovah's Witnesses were becoming bigger, bloodier and more frequent. They peaked when in the course of a single day in the summer of 1942 three different cities—Klamath Falls, Oregon, Little Rock, Arkansas, and Springfield, Illinois—were the scenes of mob attacks on Jehovah's Witnesses. One mob numbered more than 1,000 people.

Attorney General Biddle, still described as "an almost fanatical believer in civil liberty," kept up his pursuit of Harry Bridges. Roosevelt had pardoned Earl Browder, signaling a new policy toward the administration's radical critics. Biddle, nevertheless, and to the evident dismay of the White House, only increased his efforts against Bridges. Even some of his fervent admirers thought this was "stupid, ill-advised and undemocratic."

Liberal journals and politicians were themselves meanwhile carrying on a noisy protest movement for the suppression of native Fascists and former isolationists. The editor of the *Nation* demanded "Curb the Fascist Press!" which consisted of "the publications of native Fascists . . . of Jew-baiters, Britain haters and foes of democracy. . . . There are a lot of these in the country. . . . All of them should be suppressed. . . . Tolerance, democratic safeguards, trust in public enlightenment—these happy peace-time techniques have demonstrated their inadequacy."

The country's premier foreign correspondent, William Shirer, agreed, because "The United States is in the midst of a grim war knowingly harboring an aggressive Fascist Fifth Column whose open and avowed purpose is to make us lose the war, accept defeat. . . ." Like Dorothy Thompson, he pointed to the Weimar Republic which had been laid low by people who were dismissed as cranks, whose publications were a "vermin press." The same fate was in store for the United States if it did not suppress them. At the same time the *New Republic* and Archibald MacLeish were carrying out a hunt for "divisionists." These were people who aggravated the divisions which ran below the country's surface unity. Once located, they were to be suppressed. "It is fatal to adopt the defensive on the home front."

The Attorney General was, in fact, already rounding up Axis sympathizers, often on what appeared to be preposterously inflated charges. Some were infamous, such as William Dudley Pelley, head of the avowedly pro-Fascist Silver Shirt Legion of America. But others were simply unlucky, like the Denver gymnast who was tried and convicted on sedition charges after telling a group of Army officers that the United States was not fighting for democracy. There was a Justice Department crackdown on the "vermin press" at the end of April. Father Coughlin's odious *Social Justice* was banned from the mails, along with dozens of lesser known publications.

Ironically, the act Biddle employed as his principal weapon in the crackdown on the "vermin press" was the Sedition Act of 1918. Years before, the Supreme Court had upheld that law over the impassioned dissents of Brandeis and Holmes. These were the two Justices Biddle said he admired the most.

With the war still going badly as spring gave way to summer, the liberal press called for even stiffer measures. And in July a federal grand jury handed down indictments (later dropped, presumably for lack of evidence) against twenty-eight persons for undermining military morale. Liberals were furious that Coughlin and Lindbergh were not included. If they could not be prosecuted under existing laws, the *New Republic* fumed, then new laws must be passed to secure their conviction. There must also be more compulsion and less voluntary cooperation in the war effort. The Axis employed compulsion; for the United States to do less would be fatal. The journal's editors wanted "compulsory buying of war bonds, compulsory contributions to the rubber and scrap metal campaigns, compulsory curtailment of automobile driving." All in the name of democracy.

American liberals were also once again reaping what they had busily helped sow. Liberals who went to work in Washington were being forced to endure persecution by background investigation. The principal device for blackening their names was guilt by association. Redress was virtually impossible. By June the liberal daily *PM* counted more than 200 liberals who had been driven out of government service. Past, or present, opinions were considered proof of Communist affiliations when they accorded with the Communist Party line. It was cowardly and inexcusable. Yet this was the very formula whereby the liberals themselves had tried to tie all manner of people, from Lindbergh to grass-roots members of America First, to Hitler and Fascism.

In early June the Navy scored its stunning defensive victory over the Japanese at Midway. Yet what the country wanted was offensive victories. Besides, the war was going badly in Russia, North Africa and the Atlantic. The full-page newspaper advertisements began to appear during July, placed by Citizens for Victory. The advertisements were full of bitterness and anger. Such emotions were widely shared at the time. Citizens for

Victory mourned the losses in Alaska, Egypt, Russia and Washington, D.C., in all of which the forces of the United Nations had suffered major defeats. At the same time, as we have seen, life in the internment camps was being made more miserable for the internees.

There are three principal theories for the internment. One is racism and anti-Orientalism. Another is the actions of local interest groups. The third is sheer political expediency. Any or all these combined, it is said, was able in the heightened atmosphere of war to bring about the arrest and imprisonment without trial of more than 100,000 people. Military necessity was a complete fiction; on that everyone is agreed.

The interest group theory is plausible. But the sequence of military and governmental decisions does not support it. As for political expediency, the demands of West Coast politicians for the internment came *after*, not before, February 14. Until that date very few local political figures were demanding the removal of the Japanese and Nisei. After February 14, they vaulted onto the evacuation bandwagon.

The case of Hawaii, where there were 90,000 Japanese and 160,000 Nisei, must also be explained. There was racism in Hawaii, but it was rarely overt, and as a political issue it was fatal to anyone who raised it. But after Pearl Harbor tensions were high, and anti-Japanese rumors grew uglier than ever. The new Army commander, Lieutenant General Delos C. Emmons, was under considerable local pressure to sanction the internment of the Japanese and Nisei. He refused. Some homes were searched; a few hundred Japanese of suspect loyalty were arrested. But to the consternation of many Caucasians, Japanese newspapers were permitted to continue publication.

Vigilante groups sprang up and harassed Japanese and Nisei into giving proofs of loyalty, such as donating a pint of blood. Nisei in the university and high school ROTC programs were dismissed. But, interestingly, these humiliations came in late February and March, not just after the attack. And they peaked in April and May. It was at this point that bloodshed seemed likely if the situation was not quickly resolved.

Long before Pearl Harbor, however, local Japanese had been actively assisting Army and FBI officials in the surveillance of those few among them who were willing to serve Japan. And with the crisis worsening rapidly, most of Hawaii's influential Japanese and Nisei petitioned the government to create an all-Nisei combat unit, through which they could offer an irrefutable proof of their community's fidelity to the United States. Emmons and his staff gave the proposal their blessing. But in the current climate it was agreed to only in principle; it could not be put into effect at the moment. And the Navy, which had primary responsibility for the security of the islands, was now pressing for the internment of the islands' Japanese and Nisei. It was interesting, this, for where the Army had primary responsibility, on the West Coast, it pressed for internment while local Navy officers scoffed at the whole idea. But where the Navy had primary responsibility, the position was reversed.

Nonetheless, Hawaii's Japanese were not interned. Japanese language schools and Shinto shrines were forced to close. About 1,000 Japanese were moved to the mainland and interned with their relatives, at their own request. But there was no wholesale internment despite mounting agitation all through the spring and early summer. The reason was not that the Army protected them, for the Navy could overrule the Army. Nor was it that there was no pressure from local interests and politicians, for that there certainly was. The real reason was that once internment was considered, it became obvious that the islands' economy would have been destroyed. The Hawaii Japanese and Nisei made up a third of Hawaii's work force. They were much too valuable to make adequate scapegoats.

A scapegoat is definitionally someone who can be dispensed with. Otherwise his sacrifice becomes our sacrifice. And all major civil liberties crises have this much in common: They involve the persecution of some fringe group in conjunction with some large disappointment that involves the entire society. Such crises do not occur in tranquil times. They come instead when all is turbulent and their victims are sacrificed to the current troubles. But there are limits to the number and kind of scapegoats. The West Coast Japanese and Nisei, conscientious objectors and pacifists, a few hundred pro-Fascist cranks, a few thousand Jehovah's Witnesses—all were expendable. Too many victims, however, would destroy the emotional satisfactions of ritual sacrifice by creating a problem of disproportionate size. After all, a troubled village offers only one or two virgins to placate its angry gods, not the entire supply.

XIX
What Can I Do?

WITH the country in the war both coasts braced for possible attacks by German and Japanese raiders. People looked to the fledgling civil defense organization established the previous May, headed by Fiorello La Guardia. And it was all, said La Guardia, "magnificently organized." No one believed it.

Most big-city air-raid sirens could not be heard from more than a few blocks away. During the bustle of daytime they could barely be heard at all, emitting a bovine "Moooo-ooooh" that was swallowed up in the traffic's roar. There were more than 1,000,000 volunteers already enrolled in some 6,000 local councils of the Office of Civilian Defense at the time of Pearl Harbor, but they were so hapless that most towns and cities soon started to organize their own civil defense. Ordinary people simply refused to cooperate with La Guardia's volunteers. By trying to do two jobs at once, the mayor was falling short on both. Under mounting public pressure he resigned from the OCD.

The confusion in civil defense could not dampen the enthusiasm most people had for doing something, anything, to help. In February, 1942, there were more than 5,000,000 volunteers in local organizations all seeking to assist their communities' war efforts. But with the enthusiasm there was also frustration, and at times it gave way to anger. Mobs prowled the streets of West Coast cities at night, enforcing the blackout by the application of sheer terror. And nervous local officials and military officers added to the panicky confusion. Blackouts were liable to occur at any time, without forewarning or justification. And when the lights came on again, no one could be found to take responsibility for ordering the blackout.

False alarms threw even the biggest cities into turmoil. There was the false alarm of an air raid over San Francisco on the night of December 8. Some thirty Japanese planes were reported by the Army to have flown over the city and headed inland. A few weeks later the air-raid alarms sounded in New York. Blasé New Yorkers poured into the streets to watch their city under attack and seemed slightly disappointed when it did not occur. Los Angeles was similarly kept up all night by an imaginary air raid that had hundreds of antiaircraft guns firing into the darkness. Scores of civilians were injured by falling shrapnel. Newspaper reporters,

Army officers and scores of policemen all swore they had seen swarms of Japanese aircraft flying overhead.

The sudden, unnecessary blackouts, the false alarms and ugly incidents were too widespread to be merely comic. People in the East were preparing to evacuate their children. Local PTA chapters were torn by angry squabbles over air-raid safety measures for schoolchildren. State legislatures and municipalities decreed astronomical fines and long jail sentences for anyone who talked back to an air-raid warden. Every day in cities all over the United States police cars cruised up and down the streets ordering people to return to their homes, with not an enemy aircraft within thousands of miles. Blackout accidents were beginning to take a heavy toll of life and limb.

But after the first few months of war had passed without enemy attacks, civil defense started to become rational and effective, and a modicum of good sense returned. The blackouts still created problems, but the mob attacks stopped.

On the East Coast Times Square was dimmed out at the end of April, presumably for the duration, and Manhattan had its first complete blackout. On the West Coast visitors noticed an almost palpable tingle of excitement. Barrage balloons hovered over important targets, radio stations went off the air without warning, steel helmets appeared on unmartial heads, and at night scores of planes could be heard circling in the sky. From the Canadian border to San Diego, "people slept with their clothes and flashlights near at hand, and a suitcase packed. Stores were quickly sold out of flashlights and long lines of people waited to buy candles."

By the summer some 11,000 Local Defense Councils were in operation, carrying nearly 10,000,000 volunteers on their rolls, in either Civilian Protection or Civilian War Services. The former was another name for civil defense; the latter involved everything that affected a community's war effort from scrap drives to child care for working mothers.

Civil defense was attempting blackouts without casualties. Some cities tried "whiteouts." Thousands of smudge pots would spew a thick white chemical smoke into the air over important facilities such as docks and airfields. But blackouts were becoming more, rather than less, popular. As one woman wrote, "It was an exciting experience for an unbombed people to rush to switch off the lights at the sound of weird sirens." Usually, an "Air Raid Warning—Yellow" signal would sound at about nine in the evening from the local military headquarters. Each community would have about fifteen minutes to get its spotters out, man its stirrup pumps, bring its ambulances and emergency shelters into complete readiness and cover up or extinguish almost every visible light. A "Blue" warning would sound, indicating the approach of enemy aircraft, giving the stragglers a few more minutes. Then came the "Red" warning: enemy aircraft within 10 miles. All traffic stopped. All advertising and public lighting was extinguished. The air-raid sirens would begin to wail; searchlights flicked on; Army planes roared overhead.

Shortly the reports would start to flow in, of churches blown up, the railway station bombed, of huge craters pitting Main Street, of hundreds of casualties. Ambulances and air-raid rescue workers would rush to the scene, to find the streets littered with Boy Scouts groaning piteously, while catsup flowed freely from sleeves and trouser legs.

Elsewhere some 40,000 civilian pilots joined the Civil Air Patrol. They flew antisubmarine patrols over coastal waters and carried high-priority materials or official documents from place to place. Thousands of small-boat owners also threw themselves, over the Navy's reluctance, into the coastal antisubmarine watch. And under the impact of the various civil defense efforts the volunteer guerrilla units which had sprung up during the past two years began, albeit reluctantly, to disband.

The OCD had preempted the field at last. It was still hamstrung by jealous, uncooperative local officials and it was plagued by a shortage of equipment for fire fighting, rescue work and decontamination. Yet these things mattered very little, for the real future of the OCD lay not in its practice blackouts, its air-raid alarms and coastal patrols. Lacking enemy attacks, these had to come to an end. Its real achievements would come when it tried to help local communities deal with the social problems attendant upon the country's efforts to get on with the prosecution of the war.

Only about 40 percent of the population was actually doing volunteer war work in the middle of 1942. But there were other ways to participate. The typical American family was one which was donating blood, buying bonds, saving its tin cans and fats, collecting old newspapers and hunting up scrap metal. The press encouraged what might be called every-man-his-own-aircraft-spotter by turning out elaborate charts of front, side and underviews of enemy planes. The supplementary information, however, was usually bewildering—*e.g.*, "The Nakajima 96 is almost indistinguishable from the Nakajima 90 and 94 fighters." High school students were meanwhile carving, sandpapering and gluing together millions of model airplanes for military and civilian use. There was a near mania for first-aid instruction. The best-selling book of 1942 sold more than 8,000,000 copies. But because it was considered a pamphlet, it never appeared on best-seller lists. It was the official Red Cross handbook on first aid. The biggest efforts though went into scrap drives and Victory gardens.

The previous fall's aluminum fiasco did nothing to crimp the national ardor for rounding up scrap. Every drive proved a decided success. When phonograph records were called for (to recover their precious shellac), they piled up by the hundreds of millions. A steel scrap drive kicked off under the slogans "Slap the Jap with the Scrap!" and "Hit Hitler with the Junk!" Bing Crosby came up with a song called "Junk Will Win the War." The WPB called for 4,000,000 tons of scrap metal to be collected in two months. The response was 5,000,000 tons in three weeks.

All sorts of junk was offered, including the autogiro used by Admiral Byrd on his trip to the Antarctic in 1936 and parts of the USS *Maine* dredged up from Havana Harbor. In McAllen, Texas, a pair of horseshoes said to be from Robert E. Lee's Civil War mount were donated. "Key Kans" seemed to be everywhere. San Francisco's courts would take a traffic violator's bumper in lieu of a cash fine. And Peetz, Colorado, claimed at the end of the drive to be the national champion. Its 207 citizens had rounded up 225 tons of scrap metal.

These drives helped make up for the shortages in strategic raw materials, the most critical of which was rubber. With synthetic rubber still in its infancy and the largest source of natural rubber in Japanese hands, a massive drive for scrap rubber was launched in June after Roosevelt went on the radio to stress the urgency of the need. The whole country thereupon threw itself into the hunt. Sally Rand gave fifty balloons, reportedly leaving her with only two for the duration. When Roosevelt declared that the rubber floor mats from the White House cars had been sacrificed, Boy Scouts staked out service stations to plead with passing motorists to surrender their floor mats. Federal agencies even donated their spittoon mats, including 500 from the Senate and 1,200 from the House.

For all these drives the slogan was "Give Till It Hurts." So people gave it, or sold it for almost nothing, to the junk dealers, who then sold it to the government at full market prices. As with the aluminum they gave in 1941, much of what people salvaged in 1942 proved to be militarily useless. The floor mats, for instance, could only be turned into more floor mats. People gave up their precious spare tires, and most were put away to gather dust or show up in later years on the black market. "Paper will win the war"—so people gave paper. And the "waste paper piled up in the greater cities until, attracting rats, it became a menace to public health and was burned." Yet the zest for the scrap drives was so high that the bungling and the swindles went almost unnoticed. People were simply glad to take part.

The Victory gardens were an echo from the First World War. They sprang up spontaneously at first, over the open disapproval of Department of Agriculture officials who shuddered at the prospect of "radishy Victory Gardens." People started digging anyway. The Farm Security Administration launched "An Acre for a Soldier" in rural areas, which became a gratifying success. The crop grown on that acre or the cash raised from the crop went into such things as canteens for servicemen. For those without an acre to spare, a pig or a couple of sheep would do.

City dwellers, lacking either acres or livestock, dug all the more furiously. By April, 1942, more than 6,000,000 self-confessed amateurs were digging away for vitamins and victory. In the face of so much determination the Agriculture Department at last admitted defeat and set out to organize what it could not prevent. In the fall Claude Wickard, the Secretary of Agriculture, was calling for a national program of 18,000,000 Victory gardens. Urbanites with tiny vegetable plots in their backyards spent the long winter evenings of 1942 poring over the new *Burpee's Seed Catalogue* torn between the Coreless Carrot ("Its coreless, rich orange-red flesh possesses a sweet, melting tenderness") and the Tender Pod Bush Bean ("Surpasses all others in quality, tenderness, succulence and flavor. . . . The pods are 4½ to 5 inches long, thick, round in cross-section, smooth, deep dark green in color, curving slightly, with long and distinctively curved tips").

With mounting draft calls, enlistments and the lure of well-paying jobs in the war industries, ordinary agriculture faced a massive manpower crisis in 1942. The Victory gardens helped offset the threatened loss of millions of tons of food. But thanks to the best growing weather in years and the efforts of hundreds of thousands of volunteers, supplied chiefly by the YWCA, the High School Victory Corps and the American Women's Voluntary Service, nearly all the harvest was saved.

Besides the scrap drives and the Victory gardens, the call on America's communities varied widely from one time to another, from one region to another. When a thousand men went to their deaths in the sinking of the cruiser *Houston* at the Battle of the Java Sea, 1,000 young Houstonians were sworn into the Navy at a mass induction ceremony held several weeks later. The people of Houston meantime raised $50,000,000 to build another cruiser with their city's name. Six months to the day after the attack on Pearl Harbor some 12,000 self-styled "avengers of Pearl Harbor" were sworn into the Navy in more than 500 simultaneous induction ceremonies all across the country.

The Office of Strategic Services sent people rummaging through their attics and old photograph albums for any pictures taken in Europe and Asia in recent years which showed terrain features or recent construction, especially when they pictured cities, ports, islands and roads.

At times the initiative was assumed by local citizens. When the Germans utterly destroyed the Czech village of Lidice in retaliation for the assassination of Reinhard Heydrich, Stern Park Gardens, Illinois, and Bohemia, Long Island, voted to change their names so that the name of Lidice would live on.*

---

* After the war the Czechs rebuilt Lidice; these two towns then returned to their former names.

As if to show just how much the spirit of the nation had changed, American cities, towns and villages in April celebrated the twenty-fifth anniversary of the entry into World War I with parades, open houses at nearby military bases and interminable speeches praising the courage and foresight of President Woodrow Wilson. It was ostensibly a celebration in honor of the nation's armed forces. But who would have guessed just two years before that either the military or Wilson would ever stand so high in public esteem?

The community war effort was well under way. Its greatest triumph was still Selective Service (after it survived its first, chaotic year). And the emphasis was beginning to shift more and more toward community services. Volunteers from the Junior League ("a serious endeavor for young ladies of leisure") and the AWVS found the change welcome. There would still be occasional blackouts and scrap drives, of course, but from now on they would be dealing more with hospitals, day care centers and schools, and less with simulated incendiary bombs and air-raid alarms.

XX

Life and Leisure in Wartime

WE all know what a social revolution the automobile has worked in modern life. For most people 1942 knocked the clock back thirty years with a jolt. Car production stopped, gasoline was rationed, tires became invaluable, and the accustomed rhythms of life and leisure were confounded. The streets of Eastern cities were hushed. Pleasure driving, which had become the commonest form of weekend family diversion, virtually ceased. Sunday drivers were sure to be stopped by an OPA investigator and asked to explain why this trip was necessary. "Wherever the pattern of life had been set by the automobile . . . the routine of living was revolutionized."

With the cuts in gasoline consumption went more worrisome cuts in the supply of fuel oil. Restaurants stayed open only during the warmest hours of the day. In the winter months schools and colleges opened for no more than two hours each day. The rich shivered along with the poor. "Prosperous families (now servantless) found themselves living in two rooms with the rest of the house shut off, and the suffering in some communities was intense."

During that summer people found themselves with more money than ever, and nowhere to go. Eastern beaches were sticky with oil from torpedoed tankers. Periodically the bodies of drowned seamen and sailors washed ashore. Bathers at Virginia Beach one day in June watched in fascinated horror while a German U-boat calmly sank two ships in broad daylight. And following the capture of the Nazi saboteurs, beaches from Newfoundland to Key West were patrolled around the clock by guards carrying loaded rifles with bayonets fixed. On the Pacific coast, meanwhile, the beaches were full of barbed wire, antiaircraft guns and spotlights. On both coasts all buildings visible from the sea were blacked out at night and coastal traffic drove blind. And there were the rumors: "that a complete blackout was to be enforced for ten miles inland from Maine to Florida; that all hotels and summer places fronting on the ocean were to be closed for the duration. . . ." The exaggeration was unnecessary. The truth was daunting enough. For hoteliers that summer was a nightmare of few guests and no help. And many of the hotels were commandeered by the Army.

The most extraordinary military camps in the whole country were in Miami Beach and Atlantic City. In each hundreds of resort hotels were taken over to house tens of thousands of new recruits. The famed Boardwalk became a drill field. Beaches were converted into firing ranges. Every light visible from the ocean was painted dark blue. In Miami Beach a city park became an obstacle course. Famous names, such as Eden Roc, were blotted out and "Military Reservation—RESTRICTED" put in their places. Young airmen learned how to march and salute on the glittering white beaches, to an appreciative audience of girls, small boys and retirees. A stockbroker's office was turned into a clinic. Classes in military subjects were held in coffee shops, bars and nightclubs. Parades were held on the golf courses. And all over the city, in front of revolving doors and french windows, there were armed guards. Yet Miami hoteliers wooed the cash customers all the same. The city's boosters called for a "blitzkrieg of joy" to sustain national morale. The Florida tourist bureau placed advertisements boasting that the lack of war industries made the state an unlikely target for German attacks. But nearly everyone, whether from choice or necessity (and probably it was both), stayed home.

They got to know their neighbors better. Social life improved noticeably. Pleasures became simpler and less frantic. Formal wear was put away for the duration, and people seemed to mingle more easily than before. Most parties broke up before 11 P.M. so that the guests could catch the last bus home. Public library circulation of books jumped 15 percent that year. There was a new interest in cooking; the *Fanny Farmer Cookbook* became something of a best seller after lying dormant for more than twenty years. Crossword puzzles enjoyed a new vogue. There was a sudden gust of interest in the ancient Japanese game of strategy called Go. Parlor games had something of a boom. Rising prices and declining quality encouraged a revival of sewing and dressmaking.

But even the simple leisure activities at home were circumscribed by OPM directives successively forbidding the production of tennis balls, golf balls, hand balls and so on. Hunting and fishing were also forbidden, so that by 1943 America's backwoods and mountains were teeming with game and wildlife and its rivers were full of plump fish.

With money to spend, but fewer goods to spend it on and fewer places to travel to, some outlet had to be found. People went without vacations. They spent more time entertaining at home. And they went out far more often at night. By the fall of 1942, in fact, the country looked as if it were out on a permanent celebration. While roadhouses were folding, urban nightclubs and bars were as packed, as frenzied, as prosperous as they had ever been during the fabled twenties. Even humble neighborhood taverns were thriving. At night, New York swarmed with people out on a spree—Harlem, midtown, the Village, the East Side—all threw themselves into a round of dusk-to-dawn gaiety. Other cities, large and small, were doing the same.

There was, however, one tragic note to all this merrymaking. On a Saturday night in November more than 800 revelers crowded into Boston's Coconut Grove. In a side room one of the patrons playfully removed a light bulb from its socket. A young busboy attempting to replace it by the light of a match inadvertently held the flame too close to the crepe paper fronds of a fake palm. Instantly the entire palm burst into flame. At that moment the band in the main room was striking up the national anthem as the prelude to the floor show. Seconds later a young girl, her hair blazing like a torch, writhed in agony into the main room shrieking "Fire." The paper and plywood flora glued to the ceilings and walls carried the blaze to every part of the club within minutes. Panic-stricken, the 800 customers rushed the revolving doors, blocking them and thereby sealing their own deaths, ignorant in their terror of other, more practical exits. Four hundred and eighty-four were burned to death. Scores more were scarred for life.

Save for this one disaster, the country hardly paused in its merrymaking. Uniforms and money were everywhere. Not only did the nightclubs prosper but the palmists, astrologers, mind readers, hypnotists and fortune-tellers who worked them had found their own El Dorado. This was their golden age.

The Latin American craze was as strong as ever. The biggest dance hit of 1942 was the newly introduced Brazilian samba.

The movie industry in recent years had been staggering along from one flop to another, always pitying itself for being on the brink of financial disaster. In 1942 it fell heir to sudden riches. Movie attendance jumped 50 percent over the 1940 level, reaching 80,000,000 paying customers a week. Boom-town movie theaters stayed open twenty-four hours a day to accommodate the swing shifts. No more free dishes, bingo, breakfasts and other gimmicks. The customers packed in regardless of what was being shown. But these were also the rowdiest audiences in memory, booing, hissing, cheering and leaving demolished seats and tattered draperies in their wake.

Along with the night life there went, predictably, a rise in the consumption of alcohol. But while there was more drinking than during the previous war, it seemed to people that there were also fewer drunks and less open drunkenness. Still, the forces of Prohibition dreamed of repeating that earlier success, whose first great victory had been the 1917 ban on selling liquor to servicemen. On Mother's Day, 1942, they launched a new campaign. Prohibitionist propaganda blamed the fall of France on French soldiers too besotted to fight. Pearl Harbor was put down to drunkenness among the base's defenders. They even claimed that Hitler's armies were as dry as a bone. Opinion polls revealed a new rash of interest in Prohibition.

But the experiment at enforced sobriety was too widely recalled with shame to be given a second chance.

Reminders that there was a war on encroached on daily life in countless small ways. First the copper was taken out of pennies, and gray steel pennies took their place. Then the nickel disappeared from nickels. Miss America for 1942, Jo-Carroll Dennison of Texas, stoutly pledged her own sacrifice—she would not marry for the duration. The demand for maps cleared the shelves once more as Americans traced the course of the war in the Pacific. Lapel buttons, most of them clamorously anti-Axis, flourished again. And tattoos, always popular in wartime, had a revival of their own.

West Coast tattooists catered to tastes for the more exotic designs, such as death's heads, a militant Mickey Mouse, an angry Donald Duck, elaborate variations on one's Social Security number. East Coast parlors catered to a more conservative trade that ran strongly to flags, eagles, anchors. Marines, however, invariably asked for *Semper Fidelis*, no matter where they were.

Boom-town living had, though it hardly seemed possible, grown more aggravating than before. There were also more boom towns than ever. There were hundreds of them, each identifiable as such by the problems it faced. But Washington still clung to its reputation as the one where living was worst.

In the earlier war Washington had filled up with amateur bureaucrats drawn from industry and the professions. That experience had been repeated. So had the confusion and waste. The mood in the capital, which was commonly viewed by the rest of the country as the place where the war was most likely to be lost, was "a queer mingling of confusion, congestion and consecration." Roosevelt angrily lashed out at the overcrowding, scolding people who occupied more space than they needed as "parasites." Washington newspapers spent the next few days asking their readers "Are *You* a Parasite?"

All the while the congestion grew worse. People came to the capital in droves to work for the government; months, sometimes only weeks, later they left in despair. To cash a check, buy a bottle of beer, go to a movie, catch a bus, buy a towel or have lunch, there was always a long line of people, even in the most expensive places and even for the most expensive goods. Restaurants that only two years before had served a quick, appetizing lunch for 50 cents now served a slow, tasteless one for $1. "Washington in wartime," said a visitor, "is a combination of Moscow (for its overcrowding), Paris (for its trees), Wichita (for its way of thinking), Nome (in the gold rush days), and Hell (for its livability)."

But with the miseries the boom also brought money. And in some areas, notably the West and South, it brought real economic growth. The West Coast, in fact, had been transformed. With 10 percent of the country's population it was now producing 20 percent of the war goods. The industrial growth of twenty-five to fifty years had been achieved in less than three. To local chambers of commerce it was "the second winning of the West." So much rapid growth was bound to spawn problems. Delinquency, illegitimacy and venereal disease rates soared. Commercialized vice had a boom of its own under way. There was a critical housing shortage. But what was formerly a pleasant backwater for the exotic and bizarre had almost overnight been transformed into the most vibrant region—socially and economically—in the entire United States.

Under the pressure of war preexisting trends toward standardization and routinization were much accelerated, nowhere more visibly than in the boom towns. In the factories work was being broken down and simplified to a degree never before attempted. And more and more of the workers returned home each day to housing which reflected the triumph of the same principles. Prefabrication, "the unwanted and long-ailing stepchild of the U.S. housing industry," was taken by the government as a principal answer to the staggering shortage of war workers' housing. For a decade the advocates of prefabrication had begged for the mass market where its merits could be given a full test. But only a few thousand prefabs were constructed each year. At the start of 1942 federal authorities let contracts for 42,000 units. Before the year ended, they followed up with orders for tens of thousands more.

Officials said that this kind of housing was merely a temporary measure dictated by war's necessities. The prefabs were so ugly, they said, that they would be dismantled at the end of the war. But the builders knew, the architects knew, and the occupants knew, that what is supposed to be temporary can easily become permanent. And in this the prefabs were symbolic of much in the wartime experience.

All through 1942 the search for *the* war song was pursued. At first Tin Pan Alley had ground out a spat of songs that must rank among the worst ever composed: "You're a Sap, Mister Jap," "The Japs Don't Have a Chinaman's Chance," "Let's Take a Rap at the Jap," "We're Gonna Find a Feller Who Is Yeller and Beat Him Red, White and Blue" and "We've Got to Do a Job on the Japs, Baby" all rapidly sank into a well-deserved oblivion. So did the Pearl Harbor marching songs, like the "Remember Pearl Harbor March," performed by Swing and Sway with Sammy Kaye.

The radio ban on militant songs which had been imposed to help keep the country out of war was lifted. But the current militancy in popular songs never provided a worthy successor to "Over There." Instead there was:

> You're a sap, Mister Jap,
> To make a Yankee cranky.
> You're a sap, Mister Jap,
> Uncle Sam is gonna spanky.

J. Parnell Thomas, a Pennsylvania Congressman (who later went to jail for mail fraud), was lamenting, "What this country needs is a good five-cent war song. The nation is literally crying out for a good, peppy marching song, something with plenty of zip, ginger and fire." The number one song hit at the moment was "White Cliffs of Dover."

By the summer a concerted effort was under way to make "Praise the Lord and Pass the Ammunition" *the* war song, but it never really caught the popular fancy. Nonetheless, it was played over and over again on radio, so much so that federal officials asked that it be played less often, fearing that people might turn against it. The most genuinely popular war song, "Der Führer's Face," was never even played on the radio. Its suggestions on what should be done in the Führer's face kept it off the air.

For the most part the war seems to have turned popular tastes toward the sentimental, making popular hits of songs like "You'd Be So Nice to Come Home To." It revived older sentimental songs like "You Made Me Love You," which dated from before the First World War. Even the most popular of the "swing" bands (as distinguished from the avowedly "sweet" bands, *e.g.*, Guy Lombardo's Royal Canadians), led by Glenn Miller, had its greatest 1942 success with:

> Don't sit under the apple tree
> With anyone else but me. . . .
> Till I come marching home.*

Nostalgia for the pre-World War I years ushered in a new dance, at a time when most of the new dances were Latin. Called the Boomps-a-Daisy, it was a runaway success. Entire dance floors were soon taken up by people participating in what was really a communal, not a personal, dance, all of them noisily singing (while they clapped their hands, slapped their knees and waved their backsides in the air).

> Hands . . . knees . . . and BOOMPS-a-Daisy
> I like a bustle that bends.
> Hands . . . knees . . . and BOOMPS-a-Daisy
> What is a BOOMP between friends?

So the times were sentimental and nostalgic. And the greatest sentimental, nostalgic song hit of 1942 is still with us. Paradoxically, it appeared in a film called *Holiday Inn* which was released that sweltering August,

* *Don't Sit Under the Apple Tree*. Words and music: Lew Brown, Charlie Tobias and Sam H. Stept. Copyright 1942; Renewed 1970. Robbins Music Corporation. Used by permission.

with Christmas still months away. Yet soon thereafter American soldiers in the steaming jungles of Guadalcanal and the hot sands of North Africa could be heard mistily singing:

> I'm dreaming of a White Christmas
> With ev'ry Christmas card I write.*

It is to this day the best-selling song in history.

Though people were listening to more music these days, they were making less of their own. The makers of musical instruments were turning out precision parts for airplanes. But "canned music" had realized its promise. Industry at last acknowledged something that housewives had known for years: Music boosts both spirits and productivity. American industry had toyed for years with the idea, but not until 1942 did it become a standard feature in the factories. Some plants went further, bringing in live music groups to perform at lunchtime.

Radio had leaped into the war, as we have seen, as soon as it began in 1939. After Pearl Harbor most radio stations began and ended each program with a plea to their listeners to buy defense bonds, join the Army, become air-raid wardens, learn first aid, donate their scrap, give blood. Every one of the cleaner war songs, no matter how banal, was played over and over again.

All four networks joined together to offer *This Is War!* For one hour each week there was nothing else on the radio. Dissidents grumbled that Archibald MacLeish was no better than Dr. Goebbels. The tenor of these shows was set from the start with: "What we say tonight has to do with blood and bone and with anger, and with a big job in the making. Laughter can wait, soft music can have the evening off. No one is invited to sit down and take it easy. . . ."

Behind all the strident let's-get-on-with-the-war themes of this and other radio shows there moved the shade of Walt Whitman. But the result was never Whitman's grab bag of greatness and pretentiousness; merely sophomoric parodies of Whitman's directness and exuberance. And though government and the press endorsed these radio efforts, popular interest in them quickly paled, seeking out more prosaic fare.

There were expectations that war would crimp the thirst for violence in popular entertainments; just the opposite occurred. Before the year ended, films and radio both found themselves striving to satisfy a growing taste for violence and horror.

Radio's biggest failing as far as most people were concerned was the failure to provide coverage from the war zones. It had done very well with coverage from Pearl Harbor. Ample warnings of an impending showdown had both radio and the press ready to cover that story as soon as it broke. But the networks were adamantly opposed to recorded programs. Their offerings were "live." Anyone could program recordings, they sniffed. So for nearly two years after America entered the war Americans heard very little that came directly from a fighting front. The BBC was meanwhile pressing ahead with recorded radio documentaries of modern warfare.

Some of these were broadcast in the United States. One BBC reporter became celebrated on both sides of the Atlantic by outrunning British lines during an offensive in North Africa. He found himself facing an oncoming enemy formation. He was heard shouting into his microphone, "I can't see. . . . I can't. . . . Good God! It's the enemy! . . . Oh. . . . It's all right. . . . They've got their hands up. . . . They're Italians!"

As was indicated before, people were reading more. Publishers had been caught unprepared for the war in the Pacific, with carloads of books on the war in Europe, and still more on the way. But people wanted books on the Pacific when they were at war with Japan.

The war also spurred the trend away from fiction, toward nonfiction. Possibly it was part of the serious temper of the Depression years, but fiction sales dropped by nearly 50 percent between 1929 and 1939. There was also a blurring of the lines between these two categories, as in works like George Stewart's 1942 novel *Storm*. Was it meteorology or fiction?

The biggest literary argument in 1942, however, centered on John Steinbeck's *The Moon Is Down*. Steinbeck portrayed German officers in occupied Norway as being men much as other men, even if serving an evil cause. He made a passionate assertion of the spiritual supremacy—and inevitable victory—of democracy over tyranny. Soon it seemed that every educated person in the country was asking: Is it art? Or propaganda? Is Steinbeck soft on Nazis? Or just realistic? Within a single month the book sold half a million copies. But the stage version was roundly panned as being preachy and unconvincing.

Upton Sinclair admitted that the book had made him feel uneasy. "I have given a great deal of thought to the question of what I would do if I fell into the hands of the Nazis." Clifton Fadiman, reviewing the book in the *New Yorker*, came out firmly against it. "It seduces the rest of us to rest on the oars of our moral supremacy." According to Fadiman, "The only way to make a German understand is to kill him. . . ."

The war had not done much for literature as such, even if people were reading more. It provided the central experience in the lives of almost everyone, but it would take years for it to be digested and provide adequate materials for American writers. Even poetry editors found themselves with almost nothing to do. Poets fell silent. No one was sure why. Letters appeared to have marched off to war and come back looking like journalism.

Hollywood could simply not make up its mind what to do with the war. Did moviegoers want escapism or realism? Nervously the studios placed their chips on escapism. At the beginning of the year some 20 percent of the films in production were musical comedies; at the end of the year the figure was 40 percent.

The studios had no qualms about smearing the Issei and Nisei. Twentieth Century-Fox quickly ground out *Little Tokyo, USA*. With the aid of Chinese actors it showed Los Angeles' Little Tokyo district as a hotbed of Japanese espionage and sabotage. Warner Brothers did the same for Hawaii's Japanese and Nisei in *Air Force*. More fanciful still was RKO's *Betrayal from the East*, in which a popular, trusted Stanford cheerleader proved to be a traitor secretly commissioned in the Imperial Japanese Navy.

The film industry was troubled at the end of the year with the very disparate cases of Lew Ayres and Errol Flynn. Each seemed determined to make his private life congruent with his screen roles. Ayres had become famous for his portrayal of a sensitive young soldier tormented by the horrors of war in *All Quiet on the Western Front*. Summoned for induction in 1942, he asked for classification as a conscientious objector. Reviled by his profession, Ayres was assigned to one of the CPS camps.

Flynn was charged with statutory rape. His trial in the winter of 1942–1943 regularly drove the war onto the inside pages. Hollywood in its collective wisdom was certain that Flynn's career was over. Instead, movie theaters offering Errol Flynn films were sold out for every performance. Any allusion to his wicked ways was loudly cheered. The preview of a forthcoming Errol Flynn film, *Desperate Journey*, had the narrator intoning, "They knew but one approach—Attack!" It brought the house down.

For weeks the question on most people's lips was not about Stalingrad or the battles in North Africa and Guadalcanal, but if what Betty said about Errol was true. The jury of nine women and three men was probably the most envied jury in history. Three women were indicted for trying to bribe their way onto it. The conclusion of the trial was a true-to-Hollywood ending: The jury declared the defendant innocent; reporters scrambled for the telephones; flashbulbs popped incandescently; the handsome defendant leaped to his feet with a dazzling smile; the spectators clapped noisily, while the women jurors stood in the box, applauding and shedding tears of purest joy. The jury offered its congratulations to the defendant. The judge offered his own and discharged the jury, saying, "Thank you . . . I have enjoyed this case and I think you have too."

Some mention should be made of fashion, for 1942 brought the toll on fashion the defense crisis had presaged. The need for parachutes put an end to nylon stockings. Slacks became enormously popular with middle-class women. Skirts rose several inches above the knee. Short coats, reaching only to the top of the thigh, became popular. Patches on elbows, knees and bottoms began to appear, hinting vaguely at patriotic sacrifice. With the advent of slacks, short coats and calculated shabbiness, the demand for bras, slips and panties fell off.

Fashion magazines and designers despaired, but swore to make the best of it. They decreed ornate ruffles and frills to soften the austerity and masculinity. And when the WPB disapproved, they found a powerful ally in South Carolina's Senator "Cotton Ed" Smith, who rose on the Senate floor to ask his colleagues, "How in the hell are you going to win a war by taking the ruffles off of ladies' lingerie?"

The fashion austerities were not limited to women. The WPB promoted the "Victory Suit" for men—no cuffs, slimmer trousers, narrower lapels. And production of zoot suits was ordered stopped. Zoot suiters were already annoyed over the trend to slow, sentimental music, but this, they complained, was the "persecution of a minority." No longer could a hepcat go to his tailor and command, in best hepcat style, "Construct for me a sadistic cape, with a murderistic shape, shoulders Gibraltar, shiny as a halter. Drape it, drop it, sock it and lock it at the pocket. Give me pants that entrance; a frantic 31 inch knee that's draped lightly, politely and slightly to a 12 inch cuff, making it *eeeemperative* for me to grease my Garbos to slip 'em on. As for the color, Jack—let the rainbow be your guide."

XXI

Turnabout, Turnabout

THE country was supposed to be as close-knit politically as it was emotionally and socially. The Democratic Party boss Ed Flynn pledged, "In the face of war politics are adjourned." Joe Martin, his Republican counterpart, responded, "Republicans will not permit politics to enter into national defense." But that was all surface. The bitter clashes of recent years had left antagonisms too sharp, too fresh to be so quickly overcome. Virtually no one opposed the war. But the Depression and the painful fight over isolationism left wounds that could not be healed in an instant, even by enemy attack. Also, liberals and conservatives hold fundamentally different views of human nature. Those views were not to be reconciled by Japanese bombs.

The façade of political solidarity cracked under the strains of defeat. Roosevelt found himself on the defensive by February, trying to still rumors about Pearl Harbor, defending the strategy in the Pacific. By April he was lashing out at "sixth columnists." By summer the notion of political accord had completely broken down. The euphoric sense of community still prevailed among most people, but in the middle of it there was a free-fire zone marked POLITICS.

Its central feature to most people was the mismanagement of the domestic side of the war. The sense of bungling and futility cast a shadow over Washington and over political life generally. In the country at large, said one observer, a profound cynicism had developed toward "the system." Roosevelt was still popular, but not the major political and economic institutions which affected people's lives. In the late months of 1942 a joke was being told of a Japanese spy sent to discover which agencies of American government could be sabotaged and thereby cripple the American war effort. He reported back: "Suggested plan hopeless. Americans brilliantly prepared. For each agency we destroy two more are already fully staffed and doing exactly the same work."

Polls charted the growth of dissatisfaction. Had the 1942 Congressional elections been held in May, they showed, the Democrats would have gained thirty-eight House seats; in June the Democrats would have gained only ten seats; in August that figure would have dropped to eight; in September the Republicans would have gained twenty-one seats. With

247

Congressional elections set for the first week of November the President and his party were clearly in trouble.

The Seventy-seventh Congress was itself vastly unpopular. Roosevelt found it difficult to deal with from the first. And before its term ended, it was probably the most despised political body in twentieth-century American history.

Yet it was also one of the most historic Congresses. It voted the country into war with Japan, Germany and Italy. It had passed lend-lease. It narrowly rescued the draft. Its response to Pearl Harbor was the $150 billion Victory Program. It freely gave Roosevelt the power to reorganize government agencies, establish censorship, seize alien-owned property and award contracts without competitive bidding.

But it fought the administration doggedly over the domestic economy. Whenever it could, it fought for conservative economic interests. To those who traced their political education to the New Deal and their social education to the Depression, this alone made the Seventy-seventh Congress unpopular. And when the run of Japanese victories went on and on, angry letters poured into the Capitol. The Congress was derided as being both cowardly and stupid. To liberals, every Congress since the first New Deal Congress of 1933 had been worse than the last, but the Seventy-seventh had outdone itself.

These antagonisms peaked when the Congress decided in its waning months—with scores of its members facing certain defeat—to put itself onto the Civil Service pension list. Senators and Representatives with only five years' service could join the pension fund for as little as $1.39. That entitled them to life pensions worth up to several thousand dollars a year. Only one member of Congress spoke out against it, Virginia's junior Senator, and millionaire apple farmer, Harry F. Byrd.

From coast to coast came the greatest outpouring of public anger in years. There was a spontaneous wave of revulsion and outrage, war or no war. Protest meetings drew large crowds. Mail poured in to Congressional offices. In Spokane, Washington, a Bundles-for-Congress drive was launched. It caught on nationwide. Within days Senators and Representatives found their desks loaded down by mailsacks full of old clothes, false teeth, eyeglasses, rotten vegetables, last week's leftovers and used books (sample titles: *Twenty Ways to Save Money* and *They Shall Inherit the Earth*).

Hurriedly, the Senate and House abandoned the pension scheme. Their constituents then found *their* mailboxes full of letters saying I-wasn't-there, or I-didn't-know-what-it-was, or It-was-all-a-terrible-misunderstanding. One Congressman after another took the floor to give his own alibi and get it into the *Congressional Record*. For once, Congress had been slapped down by an aroused citizenry. (Still, that did not deter it from voting its members unlimited quantities of gasoline for their personal use.)

To an appreciative readership Raymond Clapper penned: "People just don't give a damn what the average Senator or Congressman says [because] what you hear in Congress is 99% tripe, ignorance and demagoguery. . . ." And Drew Pearson laughed that putting soldiers on guard duty around the Capitol was "the worst use of manpower in Washington." After all, "No one wants to steal Congress."

The sole exception to this prevalent contempt in which Congress was held was the Truman Committee. In the course of a single year it had established itself as the one Congressional body promoting the general welfare. After it attacked the dollar-a-year men in January, Nelson silenced it temporarily by accusing it of hampering production by intimidating patriotic businessmen. But in June, 1942, Truman could keep quiet no longer. He issued a report that the dollar-a-year men had proved "unable to divorce themselves from their subconscious gratification to their own industries." In that way he spared their integrity, but not their incompetence.

Truman's committee continued to probe, scrupulously trying to avoid making a nuisance of itself in the prosecution of the war. Made up principally of small-town, small-business types, it was not much impressed with big business and its big-time lawyers. It was what it needed to be: conscientious, unimaginative and led by a man who compensated for his limited formal education by developing a passion for fact gathering.

For this one committee, then, there was respect. But the rest of the Congress was regarded as a sort of highly paid, highly privileged comic sideshow. And people were starting to weary of it. It was no longer funny. No one looked to it for leadership; no one regarded it as a realistic counterweight to executive power.

For its own part, the Seventy-seventh Congress felt badly maligned. Had it not given the President almost everything he had asked for, including powers never before granted an American President? Had it not voted appropriations for every dollar the administration requested? Even if some votes had been close, as on Selective Service, had it not followed faithfully where the President had led? And there was some truth to their complaint that it had been treated unfairly. Nevertheless, it knew beyond a peradventure that its ranks would be decimated in November.

Physically, government was growing at a rate and on a scale that eclipsed even the headiest New Deal days. Civil Service examinations were being given two and three times a day, every day. The U.S. Employment Service put the state employment services out of business, to consolidate the federal government's control of manpower. State governments, though they grumbled about federal incompetence in solving the problems of boom towns, were not much bigger than before, but they were much richer. They literally had more money than they could spend. It forced many of them to drop state tax rates and license fees.

Part of the federal government's growth was the spectacular inflation of old agencies, such as the military services and the IRS. But mostly it was the creation or expansion of newer ones, such as Selective Service and the OPA. Every time government cut back in one area it seemed to expand in another. When something was shut down, something else was opened up. When, for instance, Washington's most popular acronym—"Purp" (PRP = Production Requirements Plan)—was scrapped, another body was created to do almost exactly the same thing. The acronyms were also becoming longer and more unpronounceable, like PWPGSJSISIACWPB.*

As if to memorialize for decades to come how big, why and in what way American government was growing, there was an enormous construction project under way on the other side of the Potomac. Since it began in September, 1941, choking clouds of dust had risen from the site, which nettled Washingtonians bitingly called the Dust Bowl. Work continued day and night, and even before it was finished, War Department workers started to move in. Both military services were supposed to move into the building together, inspiring feeble jokes about the lion lying down with the lamb. But at the last moment the Navy refused. The Pentagon, it said, was not big enough for both of them.

With the physical growth there went an expansion of those areas which came under governmental control or influence. Much of it was welcome, and in some instances—such as price controls—government was faulted for not doing enough rather than for doing too much. Most sensitive of all, however, was the matter of domestic propaganda. With a six-month run of defeats, what had been an academic question assumed immediate, practical importance.

Pro-Fascist journals were suppressed, some by the Sedition Act, some by having their mailing privileges revoked. The Office of Facts and Figures under Archibald MacLeish was supposed to be the primary source of official factual information. It had the eminent political scientist Harold Lasswell, of Yale, work out an elaborate chart by means of which the patriotism of a publication could be scientifically measured. Guided by Lasswell's chart, government officials picked out periodicals to be suppressed. One sorry specimen, called X-Ray, was, for example, found to be "65% subversive." It was thereupon banned from the mails. Meanwhile, MacLeish urged the country's newspaper editors to purge from their payrolls anyone whose work was "defeatist." And the FBI harassed black newspapers which continued to complain about racial discrimination.

---

* Pipe, Wire Products and Galvanized Steel Jobbers Subcommittee of the Iron and Steel Industry Advisory Committee of the War Production Board.

Beyond these steps government could impose overt censorship if it wished. But that went very much against democratic traditions and practices; it would also have been too administratively difficult to make it effective. Besides the cooperation of the working press obviated the need for any such system. Far more troublesome was the question of how to keep defeats from leading to defeatism; at least, that is how Washington looked at it. The more sober information agencies, such as the OFF and the Office of Government Reports, were disbanded. The Office of War Information was created to take charge of domestic propaganda and, in effect, sell the war.

By the fall the efforts of the OWI and other federal agencies working on government public relations carried an annual cost estimated at $30,000,000. These programs were also beginning to be resented. To much of Congress, the press and the public, it appeared that they were being treated like children, that they could not bear the unvarnished truth but must be cosseted and pacified. The working press scorned the official press agents as amateurs, mediocrities and apologists for failure. Congress made at least one serious effort to ban all government publicity operations. And it is altogether possible that official propaganda efforts backfired, that they served only to aggravate the sullen mood that hung over the war effort for most of 1942.

There was one great exception to the pattern of mushrooming government growth these days: Much of what was left of the New Deal was being shredded. The spirit of the New Deal in Washington had been dead for some time. Now, one by one, many of its monuments were being destroyed —some because they were redundant, some because they were weak and their enemies were now strong, some because they had failed.

The *New Republic* had crowed at the beginning of the year that the New Deal was not a war casualty. But it was obviously moribund. The only New Dealers of Cabinet rank—Harold Ickes and Frances Perkins—were the most unpopular and least powerful members of what was itself now an expendable body. All through 1942 one New Deal agency after another disappeared. The Federal Writers Project, the WPA, the CCC, the NYA— all were told by Congress to wind up their affairs. Thurman Arnold, the head of antitrust operations, was told by Roosevelt to stop. And before the year was over, the abrasive New Dealer at the head of OPA, Milo Perkins, was forced to resign. Liberals generally were being harassed when they sought government employment. Several hundred were forced out of their jobs. And "the principal motive," noted one famous Washington correspondent, "is to use the war to smash the New Dealers."

The change was certainly fundamental. The Washington editor for *Newsweek* summarized it this way: "Three years ago the New Dealers were in the saddle. The TNEC investigation was going full blast. . . . The cleavage between Roosevelt and the conservative (southern) Democrats was wide and deep." Now the Southern Democrats were solidly behind a wartime President, the New Dealers were gone from Washington, and the chief figures around the President were military and businessmen. Thus, far more was involved here than the simple demise of the New Deal liberals. As their star had flickered out, that of conservative political and economic interests flared up incandescently. In the power struggle which had been going on under the rubric first of the defense program and now of war production those interests had gone from strength to strength.

Liberals and conservatives alike were nervous about the upcoming fall elections. The former hoped to check the conservative tides or at least not give up more ground. Conservatives feared that the sour public mood might vent itself on them. For both sides the outcome would be critical.

Roosevelt set off on a cross-country tour of war plants in the weeks before the election. What he found so upset him that he returned to Washington and berated the Congress, the press, even members of his own administration. Not since the Supreme Court fight in 1937 had he been so splenetic. He was angry with the domestic propaganda efforts that insisted "We can lose the war" and "Production is faltering." These clumsy attempts to work up public support had backfired. Over the radio he praised the spirit of public sacrifice. He was moved, he said, by the American people's "unbeatable spirit." But it was too late. People were tired of being told they didn't know there was a war on, that their complacency was responsible for defeats and failure, that they were letting the country down. And this sudden turnabout was so transparent that it was impossible to consider it sincere.

People were not so much angry any longer as they were fed up. Let the politicians do as they like, let them sort out the mess in Washington, just leave us alone—such was the commonest sentiment. Everyone had jobs and enough to eat and some excitement in their lives. The war was still going badly, but how was that going to be altered by a vote for this man or that? So while voting in party primaries is always fairly low, in 1942 it was lower than usual. All over the country, wrote one observer, "There has been a reversion of the politics of peace and prosperity. People are saying what they used to say in the pre-Roosevelt days—that there isn't any difference between the Republican and Democratic parties."

Alarmed at the rise in political indifference, the *New Republic* pleaded with its readers, "Remember that Hitler is looking over your shoulder as you vote."

On election day Americans went to the polls in modest numbers. In North Africa the British and Germans were still locked in battle at El Alamein. On Guadalcanal there was still a stalemate. At Stalingrad the

Russians and Germans were fighting tenaciously in the rubble, the outcome still in doubt.

The Gallup Poll predicted a Republican gain of one seat in the House and two in the Senate. The Republicans gained forty-four House seats and nine in the Senate. They also won the governorships of nearly every big state, including New York, Michigan and California. Liberal Democrats and Progressives were swept out of office. Conservative candidates swept in. Party representation was almost evenly divided now in Congress. But control would be effectively exercised by the conservatives there—Southern Democrats and run-of-the-mill Republicans. Together they held a working majority.

Yet though it looked like a popular swing over to conservatism in political life and, presumably, beyond that in society at large, that was not what had happened. The result was brought about almost entirely by a low voter turnout, the return to the "politics of prosperity." Most Republicans went to the polls; most Democrats stayed home. Of 80,000,000 potential voters only 28,000,000 exercised that right. It was paradoxical, but with the war raging along in its most critical stage, people were so fed up with the way both it and the country were being run that they cast the smallest vote of any national election in a generation.

It was not a protest against the war, just against the way it was being run; more accurately, against the way people thought it was being run. The shortages of meat, sugar, fuel oil and gasoline were attributed to bungling rather than genuine shortages. The efforts to explain what was happening and why were disbelieved. There was also a sour conviction that Americans were going without all kinds of scarce and desirable things so that the British and the Russians would not have to. The reason, supposedly, was to keep them in the war.

When the Seventy-seventh Congress wound up its business just before Christmas, more than 100 of its members said their farewells to the Capitol. No one lamented the end of the Seventy-seventh.

Yet few Congresses have ever had such demands placed upon them; fewer still have ever enacted so much historic legislation. But none has been more ridiculed. It had, even if selfish in some things, worked more diligently than any other Congress in history: It set a record for the number of days it was convened—700 out of a possible 730. Its only break was a two-day weekend between its first and second sessions. The conservative, pro-Republican press was behind much of the scorn heaped on it. But popular opposition to it was also genuine. The roots of contempt lay in that search for scapegoats during the terrible months before November, 1942. And like the other victims, the Senators and Representatives were bewildered by it. They were convinced—not without cause—that they had done more than any Congress in history. Yet they were being punished as if they had done the least.

More ironic yet, if they had been able to hold on for one more month, if the elections had been held in the first week of December, 1942, it is likely that the results would have been entirely different. They would have then been the heroic Seventy-seventh Congress that was sitting when the tides of war were turned. They would have been the Victory Congress.

XXII

Sonorous Metal Blowing Martial Sounds

THE United States had entered 1942 with a Victory Program most of whose goals had been established just before Pearl Harbor. Its three central targets were planes, tanks and merchant shipping. It called for 60,000 planes, 45,000 tanks and 8,000,000 tons of merchant shipping in 1942. Its goals for 1943 were 125,000 planes, 75,000 tanks and 10,000,000 tons of merchant shipping. When these were submitted to Congress in the shape of Roosevelt's first war budget, there was no sense of resignation at the effort involved or the long-term indebtedness to be borne. On the contrary, there was a sense of elation. Such heroic proportions carried a reassurance of their own. America's traditional sentimental optimism had returned at last. Hardly anyone paused to remember the fuss which the call for 50,000 planes had created less than two years before.

The British were almost as excited at these high goals as their American allies. But Radio Berlin sneered that it was just more American bluff and bluster.

Industry went onto a seven-day workweek of twenty-four-hour working days. The mood among workers changed, literally overnight. Red, white and blue signs appeared at factory gates proclaiming THIS IS ONE PART OF THE ARSENAL OF DEMOCRACY. War production was the key to victory and revenge. A worker in a bomber plant near Los Angeles noticed how before Pearl Harbor "most of the men worked no harder to turn out planes than they would have worked manufacturing ashtrays—just hard enough to satisfy the boss." But after, production soared. As one of his friends pointed out, "The guys used to hang around smoking in the toilets. Now they only go when they have to."

War production was invested with a glamor it never had before, or since. Prisoners at San Quentin staged a near riot to demand that they be allowed to bid on war contracts. Before long, they were working twelve-hour shifts, turning out everything from antisubmarine nets to nightsticks for national guardsmen patrolling West Coast beaches.

Yet while production was climbing, there was still profound dissatisfaction with the upper levels of war production management. The White House and much of the nation had little or no confidence that delivering

255

the war economy over to big business was the best course. But it now looked like the only feasible one. There appeared to be no way to reverse the trend of the past eighteen months. The alternative would have been to spend a year or more shifting to a fundamentally different system. Under the exigencies of war that was hardly a realistic proposal. Consequently, war production was made a captive of business interests, even though no one was happy about it.

But changes were unavoidable in the   highest echelons. The Supply Priorities and Allocations Board had nagged the OPM into raising its sights. But that was not enough. In January, 1942, the Truman and Tolan committees released their separate reports on the defense program. Each concluded that it had been a failure. Tolan accused manufacturers of dragging their feet when it came to producing arms and criticized federal officials for not pushing them harder. Truman, however, traced all the shortcomings to the dollar-a-year men.

There was also an angry quarrel going on between the heads of OPM and SPAB. Press and public demanded a "czar" to take overall command of war production, put an end to the quarrels, curb the dollar-a-year men, prod the manufacturers and increase output.

Roosevelt was aware of the contents of Truman's report before it was released on January 15. On the sixteenth he named Donald Nelson, the head of SPAB, his production czar and created a new entity, the War Production Board. Nelson was given "final authority," a grant of power said to be greater than that given Baruch in World War I. Formerly the chief purchasing agent for Sears, Roebuck and Company, he was the man behind the 70,000 items in the Sears catalogue. Liberal journalists gave Nelson their blessing, while businessmen counted him as one of their own. A magazine profile gurgled, "When the nation was in deadly peril it called in as a savior a businessman so much like Babbitt that he could have sued the author of that famous work for libel." Nelson's appointment was taken as "poetic justice" for an entire generation of badly wronged American businessmen.

For the moment, then, the high-level infighting over control of the war economy was stilled and public confidence somewhat restored. The angrier criticisms and the larger doubts dropped off. Yet a reputation for futility and failure still clung to the eighteen months of defense production. Even to our day it has not shaken off the mistaken notion that its accomplishments were pathetically small. But perhaps a generation familiar with the principles of missile takeoff will appreciate the importance of the parallel when I say that those eighteen months were the vital first stage of arms output. The usual charts of economic growth during the war measure it in terms of absolute quantities, looking something like this:

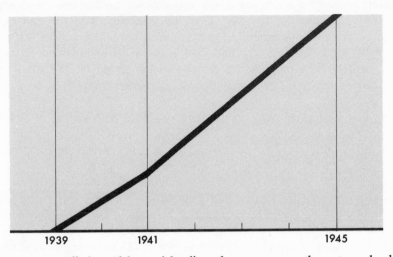

Yet a more realistic and less misleading chart measures the rate and relativity of growth. In which case it looks like this:

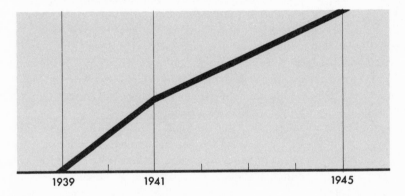

Using a dollar yardstick it becomes readily apparent how this worked. On July 1, 1940, U.S. defense spending was at a rate of $165,000,000 a month. Six months later, on January 1, 1941, that rate had tripled to $500,000,000. Six months after that it had quintupled, to $900,000,000 a month. And by December, 1941, it had increased twelve-fold, to nearly $2 billion a month. In the same period the Army had grown by 800 percent. That kind of growth was no longer possible after 1941. The rate fell off, though the absolute numbers—of dollars, of planes, of divisions, of ships—continued to rise. Without the accomplishments of those eighteen months who can doubt that the war would have lasted substantially longer than it did and taken more lives than it did?

Thus, it was an anomalous situation. Hand wringing and accusations of failure and unreadiness—while the factories were built or building, the arms were pouring forth, and not a single major agency need be created for the prosecution of the war. Even the shakeup of SPAB and OPM involved firing only a handful of people and a reshuffling of hats. Most of the WPB was made from the flesh and bones of its predecessors. It came as a surprise, therefore, when it dawned on the country in the late spring and early summer of 1942 that in war production "The U.S. need only step on the gas."

As that realization sank in, it helped moderate the sourness of defeats. "Something is happening," said *Time* (with more truth than it realized), "that Adolf Hitler does not understand . . . it is the miracle of war production." Henry Ford was the great symbol of what had happened. Just two years earlier he had been a perfervid isolationist. Now Willow Run, which almost no one outside Detroit had ever heard of before, was already one of the best-known places in the country. To some it was the quintessential symbol of the miracle of war production; to others it was the perfect example of boom-town miseries at their worst. But just being caught up in the production of arms, "Henry Ford is happier and younger than he was two years ago." So, the magazine implied, was the entire nation.

At the end of May the United States celebrated Maritime Day by launching twenty-one ships in twenty-four hours. In June, only six months after Pearl Harbor, nearly half of everything produced in the United States that month consisted of war matériel. At the end of July plane production hit a rate of 1,000 a week, and was still rising. In September a 10,500-ton Liberty ship was built in a Portland shipyard in only ten days and was delivered to the Navy four days later. In October the output of merchant ships reached three ships a week.

Most of this production was "for the shelf." Not until September did the Allies work out a strategy beyond the general principle of Germany First. That was bound to result in some waste and inefficiencies. But raw energy was more productive than efficiency. As a headline at the end of November summarized it:

WAR PRODUCTION NOW LICKED—
CURRENT PROBLEM IS BALANCE

Pearl Harbor was not yet a year past.

The most worrisome single problem dogging the ascending curve of war production was manpower. Before 1942 ended, the problem was becoming critical. It affected the entire economy, not just the war industries. The shortage of manpower was characterized by a classified advertisement that appeared in a Chattanooga paper in September:

WANTED—Registered druggist; young or old, deaf or dumb. Must have license and walk without crutches. Apply Cloverleaf Drug Store.

The prison population, federal and state, was enlisted in the battle of production. Prisoners manufactured bombs, cartridge clips, gun parts. San Quentin's prisoners tried hard to win a Navy "E" Pennant for their submarine nets. It stood for excellence.* Prisoners at a federal penitentiary in Puget Sound were building entire patrol boats for the Navy. High school students were meanwhile busy in the vocational training shops, turning out small war items. It seems strange, then, that the greatest reserve work force—America's women—were brought into war work reluctantly.

Of the male population aged fourteen and over, some 84 percent were either in uniform or at work. The figure for women in the same age group was 29 percent. The remaining 71 percent were at home. (In Russia and Britain only 30 percent of the women were at home.) American women were not so much lacking in courage and patriotism as they were victims of a foolish policy of placing women in war work only as the last resort. Those who did surmount the discouragements were often either badly trained or well trained but improperly employed. The brightest, most enthusiastic were frequently put in the dullest, most peripheral jobs because they were *too* keen: They aroused the suspicions of workers and management alike.

Besides the manpower problem, there was the shortage of critical raw materials, the chief of which was rubber. A serious lack of rubber could hobble a modern army as effectively as a shortage of steel or explosives. While all sorts of used rubber were being rounded up, most of it useless for military needs, the country's scientists worked feverishly to perfect a trinity of synthetics called Buna, Butyl and guayale. On a park bench in Washington's Lafayette Square that September the President's newly created Rubber Commission held its first emergency session, a shirt-sleeved Bernard Baruch presiding. With him on the bench were the presidents of Harvard and MIT.

All spring and summer the country worried over the rubber problem. But here too the managers of war production conveyed an ineradicable impression of fatuity. In a government short which was going the rounds of movie theaters Donald Nelson begged his countrymen to round up scrap rubber and steel. At the same time another government film was being shown to warn against loose talk, explicitly denying rumors that the country lacked vital war matériel. To prove its point, it showed warehouses bulging with rubber and steel. And in the stores there were still piles of rubber balls, sponges, erasers, rubber baby pants, paper clips, golf clubs and metal-edged rulers.

* Theodore Roosevelt had ordered an *E* to be painted on warship gun turrets for those gun crews which had performed well in the Spanish-American War. In 1942 a captain in the Navy Reserve, Lewis L. Strauss (later an admiral and head of the Atomic Energy Commission), recommended that the E be granted by the War and Navy Departments to plants which did especially well in weapons and munitions production.

Now that the country was truly back onto its long-term path of economic development it was possible to calculate at last the economic cost of the Depression in terms of lost production. The figure was $380 billion (more than it would cost the United States to fight the Second World War).

Inflation was still eating up some of the gains of economic recovery. In the first six months of 1942 the cost-of-living index rose by 7 percent. Wages were to be controlled by the War Labor Board, successor to the ill-fated National Defense Mediation Board. After months of Congressional infighting a price-control bill was sent to the White House in January. As a curb on inflation it was illusory, thanks to the generous concessions made to farm interests. In May the Office of Price Administration issued its first price-freezing order, commanding that commodities prices rise no higher than the levels reached in March, 1941. At about the same time Roosevelt came out for a $25,000 legal limit on incomes. Congress rejected the idea out of hand. All the while inflation continued to rise. Roosevelt took James Byrnes, formerly a Senator from South Carolina and a man much respected by Congress, from the Supreme Court and put him in charge of the fight on inflation. The idea seems to have been that if Byrnes could not get Congress to cooperate, no one could.

Inflation was one point at which people found economic issues impinging on their daily lives; the other was taxation. The Internal Revenue Service was promoting a publicity campaign allying taxation with patriotism: "Taxes to Beat the Axis." And most people appeared willing enough to pay higher taxes for the war.

The important thing about it as a social phenomenon was, as a Treasury expert observed, that "As America changed to a wartime economy, its citizens became intimate with it as they had never been before." In 1929 some 4,000,000 income tax returns were filed. That figure increased only slightly before 1939. But with economic recovery, entirely new groups of taxpayers were being created as incomes rose and exemptions dropped. In 1941 more than 26,000,000 returns were filed. By the spring of 1942 nearly 30,000,000 people were liable for individual income taxes. And at the end of the year another 20,000,00 who were subject to a 5 percent victory tax were added.

One result of so many millions of new taxpayers being initiated so rapidly in the mysteries of income tax was confusion—especially when the mysteries themselves were in flux. Most of the new taxpayers were unaccustomed to saving up to pay their taxes. A massive enforcement problem loomed. Thus when the chairman of the New York Federal Reserve Board, Beardsley Ruml, proposed a system of withholding it was overwhelmingly popular. Everyone favored it—except the Treasury.

Ruml's plan would have people paying their 1943 taxes in 1942; but if they paid for a year ahead, it was surely too much of a burden also to pay for the year behind—that is, 1941. Not that that would affect the Treasury's intake, for there would be no interruption of the cash flowing into its coffers. In fact, using the 1943 schedules, which were higher than those for 1941, more money would be coming in.

The Treasury's loss was really a problematical loss, "difficult to demonstrate without the use of logarithms and longevity tables." But the notion of "tax forgiveness" on an entire year's income went absolutely against the grain of the efforts to fight inflation and clashed with the idea of wartime sacrifice. And some people would, indeed, reap large windfalls from Ruml's idea if it went into effect.

So the tax wrangle went on and on. The country staggered into 1943 still wrestling with it and the chairman of the House Ways and Means Committee was groaning, "We are dealing with one of the most hateful, difficult problems that ever came along in the annals of mankind." What most people wanted was a system that was equitable and intelligible. At the moment it was neither.

The other chief means of financing the war and trying to brake inflation was the sale of bonds. After Pearl Harbor the monthly sale of bonds tripled, bringing in more than a billion dollars a month. Besides bonds there were defense stamps, in denominations from a dime to $5. Bonds were sold in banks and post offices. The stamps were sold everywhere else—drugstores, schools, newsstands, street corners.

Even after Pearl Harbor the automobile companies had continued to resist conversion. They forced one more concession from government: materials to make another 250,000 cars before the shift over to war production. Thurmond Arnold, the Assistant Attorney General, was disgusted. It was not just Detroit, he said, but business that was to blame. "There is not an organized basic industry in the U.S. which has not been restricting production by some device or other." But resistance could not be continued indefinitely. Besides, the backlog of war contracts was in the tens of billions of dollars, and corporate tax laws were generous.

Where production was held up now, it was usually due to incompetence, not resistance. There were some firms like Brewster Aeronautical which greedily stuffed themselves with war orders, then proved unable to digest them. The government was eventually forced to take over Brewster and install a new group of managers.

There were also the inevitable scandals. At Curtiss-Wright the Truman Committee "found that Army inspectors were more zealous in protecting the welfare of the company than in protecting the interests of the Air Force." High-ranking officers transferred or demoted inspectors who proved troublesome over such items as brand-new engines which leaked gasoline or engines made with substandard, dangerous materials. Curtiss-Wright responded with a national advertising campaign praising its engines and accusing its critics of prolonging the war. The company was second only to General Motors as a war contractor. Before 1939 it was a relatively small manufacturer. Its three-year growth into a corporate giant was financed almost entirely out of taxpayers' money. So, in effect, was the advertising campaign.

When American forces eventually met the Germans in combat and were routed at the Battle of Kasserine Pass, it was chastening, but understandable: Green troops were fighting veterans. The humiliating and, to many people, inexcusable part was the failure of the weapons produced by American business: American tanks were not as good as German tanks; American planes were no match for German planes; American guns were outshot by German guns. With time and experience the quality of U.S. weapons would improve. But they never really caught up.

Big business waxed rich all the same. It was recovering all that it had lost, and more. But most businessmen were not waxing rich. If anything, they were clinging by their digits to their share of the economy. For 90 percent of them were small businessmen. Between them they owned more than half of the country's total manufacturing capacity. But they were shut out from the war boom unless they were lucky enough or diligent enough to secure subcontracts from the big corporations. Those small businessmen who sold services rather than produced goods were the most hard pressed of all.

To get more small companies into arms production, Nelson ordered an end to competitive bidding. Procurement was henceforth to be by negotiation instead of bids. But even in negotiation big companies have powerful advantages over small ones. Nelson was not much interested in small business anyway. His sole concern was production. Economic costs or long-term social consequences were of no interest to him. Wittingly or not, he thereby played a large role in the delivery of control of the American economy back into the hands of big business. One businessman's Washington tip sheet, the *Kiplinger Washington Letter,* realized what was at stake. In January, 1942, it quoted "business-minded men within government" as looking on Nelson and the new WPB as being "the last stand of private enterprise."

Yet the creation of the WPB really signaled not the last round but victory. That fact became undeniable in the case of excess profits. All through the spring of 1942 government officials, from Nelson down, trooped over to the Treasury Department to tell its tax experts that corporate taxation should be trimmed to no more than 80 percent of gross profits, or war production would fall off. Called incentive, it sounded like blackmail. No matter. Congress consulted with the Treasury; it consulted with the spokesmen for big business; then it wrote an Excess Profits Tax Act which set the level of taxation at 90 percent—or so it seemed. For most companies, however, once they had claimed the exemptions to which they were entitled, the figure was really 80 percent. And there was a 10 percent postwar refund provision; this meant that the Excise Profits Tax Act was in part only a device for compulsory lending. With the postwar refund the tax level was therefore about 70 percent.

The Supreme Court was similarly sensitive to the requirements of a new day. The Justice Department had been considering legal action to recover "unconscionable" profits on government contracts. That idea was dropped when the Court wound up seventeen years of litigation stemming from a World War I steel contract. Not only did the Court stop the attempt to recover $8,000,000 in unconscionable profits from Bethlehem Steel, but it ordered the plaintiff (the government, that is) to make an additional payment of $5,000,000. Whatever the cost, said the Court, war contracts must be upheld. Regulation of excess profits was for Congress, not the courts, to decide. Business rejoiced.

There was at the same time a revival of that uniquely American phenomenon—the businessman as folk hero. There was, for instance, a young industrialist named Howard Hughes, who proposed to build a fleet of 5,000 giant cargo planes to circumvent the U-boat. There was a dynamic young New Orleans builder of landing craft called Andrew Jackson Higgins with a flair for making news. But towering over all was Henry J. Kaiser. His yards kept turning out more and more Liberty ships in less and less time. Years before, when he had built Boulder Dam, hardly anyone had heard of him. The war made him famous.

These days even the Communist Party loved big business. The *Daily Worker* even sallied forth to defend Standard Oil and scolded the liberals who criticized it for its prewar dealings with I. G. Farben and Krupp.

Young people were no longer being reared to regard business as the weak reed which had brought the country down. Instead, the National Association of Manufacturers and the National Education Association were holding get-togethers to reduce the "misunderstanding" between the marketplace and the schoolroom.

The stock market's performance that year proved especially instructive. Just after Pearl Harbor it rose sharply. Then, as the Japanese inflicted one defeat after another, it started a downward slide. By February, 1942, it was plummeting. At the end of that month a seat on the New York Stock Exchange changed hands for $18,000—the lowest figure since the 1890's and a far cry from the half million dollars which a seat cost in 1929. In March the turnover of stocks on the NYSE dropped to an average of 420,000 a day—the lowest since the Ludendorff Offensive almost won the war for Germany in the summer of 1918. In April the average price indexes hit their lowest level since the worst days of the Depression. And all this time the index of industrial production was climbing like a rocket. As the fortunes of American forces in the Western Pacific dropped, so did the stock market, reflecting a decline in middle-class confidence.

In May the market leveled out. After the Japanese were stopped at Midway in June, it started to rise slightly. American forces took the offensive in August, and it rose more sharply. By the end of the year the forces of the United Nations had wrested the initiative away from the Axis, and the stock market started to soar. Certainty and confidence were returning to the moneymen's world. Nearly all the new money coming into the market during the past year or two had been from the small investors who are usually the last to get into a rising market. Before 1942 ended, the big individual and institutional investors were starting to plunge again. America's economy was, as Harding would have said, returning to normalcy— and in the middle of a war.

When Roosevelt went before Congress to deliver his State of the Union address in January, 1943, he bowed to the changed realities. "For the first time, in a major speech," crowed *Newsweek* in delight, "Mr. Roosevelt lauded the owners of American industry without qualification." A month later he went even further. He upbraided the farmers and organized labor for the country's economic problems and breathed not a hint of criticism about business. On the contrary, he went out of his way to speak a few kind words about the blessings of free enterprise.

Organized labor was meantime fighting to hold onto its gains. Roosevelt had not signed the Draconion labor legislation passed in December, 1941, but the threat was always there. For the most part, labor leaders and the rank and file recognized that they must give up the strike. Yet wildcats broke out sporadically. And when a welders' strike erupted in the San Francisco shipyards over a union shop the AFL and the CIO, in a rare show of unity, formed a united front behind the strikers. Troops with fixed bayonets and loaded machine guns rolled into the shipyards in armored cars. The strike was crushed.

The press was chiefly antilabor, and during the defense crisis it had portrayed the forty-hour workweek as a form of labor resistance. By the spring of 1942 millions of people were convinced that the forty-hour week was crippling war production. Editorial writers lamented piteously over how France had fallen because of the forty-hour week. Not until Roosevelt explained that it was really not a disguised form of strike did the furor die down. Then it started up again, over time and a half and double time.

The administration had no wish any longer to take the side of labor or business. All it wanted was labor peace. But after Lewis torpedoed the National Defense Mediation Board, Roosevelt created a National War Labor Board. It represented business, labor and the public at large in equal proportions: four members for each. It too found that the hardest and most important problem before it was not money, but security. And the initiative in the fighting was no longer with labor but with business.

U.S. Steel, through one of its subsidiaries, Federal Shipbuilding and Drydock, was spearheading (intentionally or not) industry's counterattack on the maintenance of union membership. All through the first half of 1942, with America's shipping losses soaring, the shipbuilders toyed with national security. But still the unions would not yield, despite outraged public opinion.

It had been possible during the earlier war for labor and management to strike a rough bargain that was essentially fair to both; the companies would not discriminate against workers already in the union; the union would stop recruiting new members. But that bargain was no longer possible—the companies were already forbidden by law to discriminate against union members. The NWLB took up the compromise its luckless predecessor had tried to effect: maintenance of membership. Business was to stop trying to turn back the clock; a union with X number of members now could recruit just enough members to keep at that level for the duration. Labor readily agreed. And however grudgingly, business gradually accepted maintenance of membership. When it did, the unions went back to pressing for more money and better benefits.

The NWLB's principal answer to the problem of wages was a formula called Little Steel, because it was first worked out in a dispute involving workers from the smaller steel mills. The cost-of-living index had risen 15 percent from January 1, 1941, to May 1, 1942. The board correspondingly allowed wage rates to rise 15 percent over the levels of January, 1941. This was just the rate, of course; with overtime the amount a worker earned would be more than 15 percent above his January, 1941, paycheck. And these days there was plenty of overtime.

Once union security and wages had been settled, labor peace was generally secured. Yet there was still one person capable of undoing it all: John L. Lewis. But with the settlement securing a union shop for the "captive mines" Lewis had promised that there would be peace in the mines at least until existing contracts expired in August, 1943. And Lewis surprised everyone, including his colleagues, by proposing a truce with the AFL and eventual accouplement of the two great labor organizations. The White House and most liberals had long been eager for such a union; to them it was the fundamental solution to labor problems, and Lewis was the key to it.

Both William Green, president of the AFL, and Philip Murray, president of the CIO, were Lewis's protégés. So long as Lewis was alive, the AFL and the CIO could never be joined over his opposition. But with the country at war Roosevelt had to try to bring about some kind of accord between them and between them and business. Days after Pearl Harbor he had called for a national labor-management conference to reach an accommodation for the duration of the war.

Lewis had dominated the meeting from the start. When a spokesman for business earnestly had begged for the survival of the open shop, Lewis had mocked him. "I have heard this open shop talk before. The open shop is a harlot with a wig and artificial legs, and her bones rattle. But how much will she produce?" The labor leaders had roared with laughter. And Lewis had kept it up for every day that the conference had met. He was well on his way to becoming labor's acknowledged spokesman for the duration. Roosevelt had abruptly called the conference to a halt. The President also moved to preclude the accouplement Lewis had spoken of. A joint AFL-CIO Labor Victory Board was patched together by labor leaders friendly to the President. The merger of big labor was thus put off for another decade.

The administration had not become overtly antagonistic to labor or indifferent to its interests. All it desired was a minimum of trouble. Because it never adopted a coherent, sensible, effective manpower policy, it could bring little pressure to bear on individual workers. It tried to work through Sidney Hillman and the force of public opinion to secure labor's cooperation. But there too the absence of intelligible policy made for unnecessary, costly mistakes. The Manpower Mobilization Board, for instance, at one point ordered that any war worker who quit his job could not be hired by anyone else in war work. He would thereby lose his draft exemption. In effect, it took away the right to quit a war job. Labor leaders were incensed. Labor had already, to all intents and purposes, given up the right to strike; it had stopped pressing for a closed shop; it accepted Little Steel; it kept wildcats to a minimum. But this directive had been issued, and labor was not even consulted about it beforehand.

Recognizing their error, federal officials soon stopped enforcing this policy. The WPB always preferred to achieve its ends by persuasion and agreement. It pressed for joint labor-management committees in the factories. Both sides scoffed at the idea at first. But by the summer of 1942 more than a thousand committees were in operation. Ostensibly they were charged with exploring ways to speed up production. To workers the committees were merely window dressing. But their existence manifested a general willingness by both sides to cooperate now.

There were still serious grievances, of course. And with the strike no longer available for seeking redress there was a rise in absenteeism. Between Pearl Harbor and December, 1942, absenteeism rates increased by 300 percent. Poor transportation, the housing shortage, the lack of child-care facilities—all were partly to blame. So too was good pay. It is unlikely, though, that these accounted for all the increase. But more important was the fact that the loss of manpower owing to wildcats, sick-

ness and absenteeism still came to just 1 percent of all the time worked.
And the fruits of the remaining 99 percent had sealed the Axis' fate.

> . . . . all the while
> Sonorous mettal blowing Martial sounds:
> At which the universal Host upsent
> A shout that tore Hells Concave, and beyond
> Frighted the Reign of Chaos and old Night.
> All in a moment through the gloom were seen
> Ten thousand Banners rise into the Air
> With Orient Colours waving: with them rose
> A Forrest huge of Spears: and thronging Helms
> Appear'd, and serried Shields in thick array
> Of depth immeasurable. . . .
> —JOHN MILTON, *Paradise Lost*, Book One

XXIII

Onto the Offensive

JUST two days after the Congressional elections everything changed. On the evening of Saturday, November 8, the country learned that its troops had gone ashore in North Africa. The immediate, heartfelt response was expressed in three words: "This is it!"

At almost the same time came news that the British had smashed the Afrika Korps at El Alamein and sent it reeling along the North African coast toward the American force.

Off Guadalcanal, where the marines had been stuck futilely in the jungles for more than three months, Admiral William Halsey destroyed a Japanese fleet on the night of November 14. Their seapower in the area shattered, the Japanese on Guadalcanal were doomed.

After twenty-four days bobbing about on a tiny raft after his plane crashed into the sea, Eddie Rickenbacker was found alive.

On the other side of the world the Russians went on the offensive in and around the pulverized ruins of what had once been Stalingrad. In subsequent weeks the Red Army smashed Hitler's Sixth Army, driving around its flanks, encircling it, turning back the army sent to relieve it. By the middle of December it was plain that, as one journal said, "The Germans are losing the war in Russia, which means they are losing World War II."

By the New Year, with the Allies winning everywhere, the feeling took hold that 1943 would see the enemy set up for a knockout blow, to be delivered in 1944.

The siege of Leningrad was lifted. Stalingrad—what there was of it—was saved. And a great Russian offensive was launched across a front thousands of miles wide. Within just one year, the first year of America's entry into the war, the Axis had been defeated everywhere. How unready, then, had the United States been for war?

Almost all the tanks and many of the guns which gave Montgomery his victory at El Alamein were made in the United States. Without them Montgomery's meat-grinder tactics and "perfectionism" would have been impossible. He would doubtless have lost. Just six months after Pearl Harbor the Japanese had been turned back at Midway. Two months later, at Guadalcanal, the initiative was wrested away from them, and the

268

Japanese were put on that path which led without a break to the surrender in Tokyo Bay. Yet it still was commonly believed that the country had been unready for war at the time of Pearl Harbor.

The first six months of 1942, however, were merely modern America's introduction to an ancient fact: The outposts of power are vulnerable. The British learned that again and again in the course of winning one empire, losing it, then acquiring a second. In Africa and India they repeatedly lost the battles and won the wars. Modern America had reminded the Spaniards of the vulnerability of far-off outposts in 1898. Now, having lost a few battles, the United States and its allies were about to win the war. And it seems unlikely that it could have been done much faster than it was.

There is a tendency to think of the losses at Pearl Harbor as being devastating. But they were not much more than a pinprick attack on American military and industrial strength. On December 7, 1941, the combat strengths of the American and Japanese navies were:

	U.S.	Japan
Battleships	17	10
Carriers	7	10
Cruisers	37	35
Destroyers	171	111
Submarines	113	64

The United States also had under construction 15 battleships, 11 carriers, 54 cruisers, 193 destroyers and 73 submarines. Besides these, there were more than 500 auxiliary vessels, such as minesweepers and patrol boats, also under construction.

There was, then, the greatest disparity in the strengths of the two navies, a disparity which was growing wider each month. Even the superiority in the number of Japanese aircraft carriers is something of an illusion. For their carriers were smaller and carried fewer planes than their American counterparts.

At Pearl Harbor the brunt of the attack was borne by the battleships of the Pacific Fleet. Of eight battleships in Battleship Row seven were sunk or damaged. Every single one of them was either obsolete or obsolescent. They were all twenty years old or more. Also, only one—the *Arizona* —was a total loss. The other six were repaired and sent back into action, some as early as February, 1942. But more than that, not one naval operation in 1942 was handicapped by a shortage of battleships. The first action where those ships played any role was off Guadalcanal in the fall of 1942, by which time several brand-new battleships had joined the fleet.

Three cruisers were also hit, but none was sunk. Two of them were ready for combat again two months later. Two destroyers were sunk, and one was damaged. A tender was shot up, a target ship was sunk and a minelayer destroyed. Not one of the Pacific Fleet's four precious carriers was even scratched—they were all at sea. Some sixty-five Army planes were lost—equivalent to a single day's production.

Thus, of 345 combat vessels in the U.S. Navy, the Japanese had gone to war by doing some measure of damage to 4 percent of them—that is, 14. Permanent losses amounted to less than 1 percent. Some 2,403 servicemen were killed; another, 1,178 were wounded. That loss of life and limb could not be made up. But in the context of the war these came to less than 1 percent of American casualties.

Whatever Pearl Harbor was, it was not a military disaster. Whatever it proved, it was not that the U.S. was unready for war. Three hundred and forty-six new warships were under construction. The Army had thirty-four combat divisions in place and was building up thirty-two more in the year ahead. And the final proof was how things stood just one year later.

On a blustery December day a Washington bus driver on his day off took a streetcar from its shelter and went joyriding through the streets of the capital, picking up passengers and waving their fares away, saying, "This is on me!" Blithely he toured downtown Washington, while startled passengers at the bus stops watched a streetcar marked MOUNT PLEASANT roll up, far from its usual route. It was a spontaneous celebration by one private citizen who sensed victory in the air.

At about the same time, in the same city, other men sensed the same thing. They turned their minds to setting the terms of enemy surrender.

And with the New Year only a week old Roosevelt and Churchill journeyed to Casablanca. It was the President's first trip by air since he had flown to the Democratic Convention in Chicago in 1932 to accept his party's nomination. Most people were excited. *Time* found it irresistible: "The trip, through air in which Axis planes roamed, over waters infested with Axis submarines, was . . . a dazzling *fait accompli*."

From Casablanca the President and the Prime Minister issued their terms: "Unconditional surrender." Germany, Italy and Japan had made their bid and lost.

PART THREE

✣

The Remaking of a Nation

January, 1943–August, 1945

XXIV

New Horizons

FAR sooner than anyone expected Tunis and Bizerte fell. The war in North Africa was over by the summer of 1943. A heady idea took hold that once a landing was made in Europe, German resistance would collapse. All through May and June invasion was in the air. Then, on both sides of the globe, American forces attacked—in the Aleutians, in the Solomons, in Sicily.

Spirits soared. "The war began to look like a movie: brave Americans dashing across the blue Mediterranean and up golden Sicilian beaches to plant the Stars and Stripes among a grateful populace." To calm the sudden rush of optimism that the war would soon be over, the Vice-Chief of Naval Operations in a burst of inspired pessimism predicted the war would last at least until 1949.

On September 3, 1943, four years to the day after the war had begun, Sicily was in Allied hands and Allied soldiers were landing at Reggio Calabria in southern Italy. Soon the Fifth Army was storming ashore at Salerno. Mussolini fell from power, was locked up in a castle on a northern Italian mountain and was promptly rescued by a team of German SS parachutists.

Between Mussolini's downfall and escape Italy surrendered. The news arrived just before noon in New York. Lunchtime crowds hurriedly set up modest, spontaneous demonstrations in the streets while twenty-two tons of ticker tape, confetti and shredded telephone books cascaded down.

When the fighting in Italy bogged down in the fall into a toe-to-toe hammering, it took the edge off the high spirits and undercut optimism about a quick end to the war. But it was an exhilarating summer all the same. Bernard De Voto, looking back just three years, marveled:

> All my life I shall remember waking in an infinitesimal Idaho village to hear that the Nazis had entered Paris . . . we had to realize that there was no more France; it seemed certain that there would soon be no more England. Those of us who, in May of 1940, knew that the United States was in the war found that summer a more exhausting strain than any- thing that has come since. At least, nothing since then has required such endurance in darkness, not even Pearl Harbor. That dreadful day, in fact, had a kind of reassurance . . . for in the summer of 1940 there was no knowledge, there was hardly even an insane man's hope, that the fall of

Europe could be repaired. . . . This is a summer of discontent. . . .But, three years ago, you would not have believed a summer so tranquil, so bright with hope, would ever again be possible on earth.

American forces were meanwhile marching from victory to victory. But not without scandals, disappointments, heartbreak and soul-searching. Drew Pearson, evidently retaliating for Roosevelt's calling him a "chronic liar," reported that during the invasion of Sicily General George Patton, in a rage, had slapped the face of a hospitalized American soldier.

The story created an uproar in the press. *Time* added some details, then called it "unforgivable." Dozens of Congressmen called for an investigation. The *Nation* described it as "the beating of a soldier—a hospital patient—by an American general" and suggested that Patton was mentally ill. The *New Republic* was horrified and demanded to know how anyone so ignorant about shell shock could be trusted with a military command.* PM said Patton should be court-martialed.

Yet for all the storm in Congress and the press, most people took it in stride. They were more angry over the way the War Department had tried to hush it up than they were over the face-slapping incidents. The father of one of the slapped soldiers dismissed it philosophically.† And the week the story broke, ironically, *True Confessions* had an interview with Mrs. Patton. "The general makes a lot of noise, but he's really quite sweet," she confided.

Christmas came, laboring under a pall that buried all the bright hopes of summer. The Army panicked the entire East Coast by warning of an impending German attack on Christmas Eve. American forces meantime went on the offensive in the Central Pacific, landing on Tarawa. Within three days the country lost more men than were lost in the six-month battle for Guadalcanal. Of the 5,000 marines landed on the beach to fight for just one square mile of sand and coral, more than 3,700 were killed or wounded. The War and Navy Departments hailed Tarawa as a wonderful victory, but there was no joy in it.

The War Department, still under a cloud for its mishandling of the Patton story, was caught trying to hide more bad news. Allied forces in Italy suffered a surprise attack just before Christmas, 1943, that was costlier in terms of ships sunk than the attack on Pearl Harbor. At Bari, in southern Italy, seventeen Allied ships were sunk and thirteen were damaged when German aircraft broke through what had been proclaimed invincible air supremacy.

---

* They should, in fairness, have called for the dismissal of the entire officer corps of the Red Army. The Russians never considered a mental or nervous collapse a true war casualty.

† There were two face-slapping incidents, but the news of the first overshadowed the later revelation of the second.

The fighting in Italy had turned into a weary, painful, bloody crawl up the boot-shaped Italian peninsula, exacting no apparent strain on German resources elsewhere. Rome looked as far away as ever, and the promised benefits of making Marshal Badoglio's government a cobelligerent seemed so much wishful thinking. Worse, the superb generalship of the Germans was making their American and British opponents look like clumsy amateurs. As 1944 dawned, government officials were predicting that the new year would bring a 300 percent rise in casualties by spring. So far the cost had been light: fewer than 80,000 dead and wounded in more than two years of war.*

But 1944 would also, as everyone knew, bring the invasion of what the Germans grandiloquently called *Festung Europa*—Fortress Europe. From the first 1944 was hailed as the invasion year. General Eisenhower predicted victory before another Christmas came around.

The Germans boasted of secret wonder weapons which would turn the tide of war. *Newsweek*'s Stockholm correspondent surmised that these would be "heavy-water atomic bombs dropped from radio-directed planes."

A landing was made at Anzio. It too bogged down. And, at British request, American planes reduced the fifth-century Benedictine monastery Monte Cassino to rubble. The British imagined that hundreds of Germans were holed up in this treasure of Western civilization; real Germans turned its rubble into formidable defenses. The abbey was gone, and no advantage was gained.

At about the same time, a reporter with *Stars and Stripes* disclosed that during the invasion of Sicily the Army had shot down twenty-three of its own planes, killing 430 airmen and paratroopers. The Germans knew about it; war correspondents knew about it; many soldiers knew about it. Only the American people were supposed to remain ignorant of it. Stimson, whose enormous reputation for integrity had been badly tarnished in recent months, again tried to bluff his way through. Eventually he conceded the truth of the story.

In April, the much-praised "high-precision bombing," the subject of endless Air Corps self-love, suffered another blow. In what the Swiss angrily described as the worst violation of their historic neutrality, American bombers attacked the town of Schaffhausen, killing forty-eight, wounding hundreds more.

Yet May opened full of promise. The entire country went about its business with an eye and an ear reserved for the news of invasion. Special church services drew large crowds. The head of the OWI made a plea that this solemn enterprise not be cheapened by commerce once it began.

---

* The toll was far higher at home. Since December 7, 1941, accidents had claimed 190,000 dead and 18,500,000 injured. But these did not weigh on the conscience.

All across the land in the last days of May there was a powerful sense of occasion. In Washington, officials nervously wondered how people would bear up to the inevitable rise in dead and wounded. Though outwardly life went on much as before, there seemed to be a hush in the air.

At a special preinvasion service in San Francisco's Grace Cathedral the British consul general in that city read to a deeply moved congregation St. Paul's Letter to the Ephesians:

> Put on the whole armor of God, that ye
> may be able to stand against the wiles
> of the devil. For we wrestle not against
> flesh and blood, but against principalities,
> against powers, against the rulers of
> darkness of this world, against spiritual
> wickedness in high places. . . .

On June 4 the London office of Associated Press flashed a bulletin that the invasion had begun. A few minutes later the bulletin was canceled. But already church bells were ringing and crowds were forming in the streets.

Two days later, just after midnight on the East Coast, the urgent bell on news tickers started clanging while the machines clattered out: FLASH . . . GERMAN TRANS-OCEAN AGENCY CLAIMS INVASION HAS BEGUN. So it came in the dead of night. By the time most people heard the news the invasion was half a day old. Yet throughout that night radio stations fed a stream of news bulletins to an audience that, however small, was as captive as any in history, alert to the greatest venture in the annals of American arms.

At first, all the bulletins came from Berlin. Just before dawn in New York, Eisenhower's press aide appeared over shortwave to make the official announcement. A few minutes later Eisenhower himself came on the radio. An hour later came the first eyewitness accounts of the fighting on the Normandy coast by a reporter who had gone in with the paratroopers and already returned.

Morning newspapers were coming onto city streets, often with a one-word headline: INVASION! The largest, eight inches high, was printed by the Los Angeles *Times*. For this and the days that followed most papers threw out nearly all of the advertising to make room for news from the beachhead.

All across America that Tuesday, June 6, church bells were pealing; air-raid alarms sent up their mournful sounds; trains and factories blew their whistles; motorists zealously honked their horns and flashed their lights at one another. Through Hartford, Connecticut, there rode a man on a horse shouting the good news. But below the outward excitement there ran a solemn mood. Stores quickly closed or did not bother to open. Streets were generally deserted. Sports events were canceled. In cities, towns and villages the churches were packed with people—many of them hitherto unknown to local pastors and priests—praying and silently weeping.

At sunset, the Statue of Liberty, its lights extinguished since Pearl Harbor, blazed forth in the darkening sky for fifteen minutes. At ten o'clock in the evening Roosevelt finally spoke, and over the radio he led the country in its prayers

> Almighty God—Our sons, pride of our nation, have
> this day set forth on a mighty endeavor, a struggle
> to preserve our Republic, our religion, and our
> civilization and to set free a suffering humanity. . . .
> Lead them straight and true, give strength to their
> arms, stoutness to their hearts, steadfastness in
> their faith. They will need Thy blessing. . . .

His prayer concluded with a plea for people of the United States while they awaited the outcome: "Give us faith in Thee; faith in our sons; faith in each other."

For the rest of the week there was a somber, religious mood. There was also a strong, if muted, sense of satisfaction. America waited patiently for once in a mood neither cocksure nor apprehensive. No one strayed far from the radio. Radio, in fact, was enjoying its finest hour of the war. All commercials were canceled. With the aid of shortwave, tape recordings and daring reporters, it brought into American homes the authentic sounds of battle and vivid descriptions of the desperate fighting on the Normandy beaches.

In war industries absenteeism dropped to record levels. Factory loudspeakers broadcast a steady stream of news bulletins. Strikers went back to work. Red Cross blood donations soared. The turn in of defense bonds dropped, while bond sales turned steeply upward.

For one entire week the most boisterous, noisy, rambunctious people in the West went about with a restraint, a soberly responsible sense of purpose, that was not only striking, but without parallel in living memory. As an emotionally unifying, satisfying experience it was unique. It was the unity not of grief, but of accomplishment and hope.

In the war, the month of the invasion brought the first of the German terror/wonder weapons when V-1's began to strike London. Radio Berlin promised even more devastating marvels.

In the Far East, meanwhile, the air offensive against Japan was launched in spectacular style. From airstrips painfully carved out among the rice paddies of South China the newest of America's big bombers, the B-29, made its combat debut by demolishing Japan's largest steel mill.

In July, Saipan fell, Guam came under heavy attack, and the Tojo government was forced to resign. The fighting in France broke down into isolated actions in the Normandy hedgerows, but the Allies daily gained ground. At his Prussian headquarters on July 20 a group of Hitler's officers made a desperate effort to kill him, and won for their pains only a bloody retribution.

In the following weeks, Patton redeemed himself. His drive toward the Seine after the breakout from Normandy made him a national hero once again. Hurriedly the Senate took up his promotion to the permanent rank of major general, which had been in limbo since the face-slapping incidents, and unanimously approved it.

Late August brought a rehearsal of sorts for V-E Day. Paris was liberated—first by Charles Collingwood of CBS News, shortly thereafter by American and French forces. A hundred tons of confetti and ticker tape poured out of Manhattan windows. In the streets below, people wept openly and hugged one another. Some exuberantly broke into song and danced. A huge crowd of sobbing, singing New Yorkers and European refugees crammed into Rockefeller Plaza to be addressed by celebrities in exile intoning the glories of the day, the promise of the future. And half a dozen bands materialized, playing the "Marseillaise" over and over again. On the radio every song about France or in French was going onto the air. The number one hit song of moment, "I'll Be Seeing You," was spontaneously taken up as the anthem of liberation.

Lloyds of London posted odds of five to eight that the war in Europe would be over by October 31. Washington buzzed with a rumor that the War Department had an employee whose job consisted solely of predicting when wars would end. And he predicted V-E Day for October 10–15. Businesses and local governments began planning their V-E Day celebrations. They gave up all hope of keeping it sober; they concentrated on keeping it safe. Hotels started taking "Armistice Day" reservations, whatever date it might be; barbershops posted signs warning customers that they ran the risk of being deserted in mid-shave or mid-haircut. The flag industry started working overtime to produce tens of millions of small, hand-held flags.

Washington officials talked of how, on that happy day, there would be mountains of extra food, an end to rationing, no more price controls, no more manpower controls. Manufacturers would be able to make whatever they wished. Consumers would be allowed to buy whatever they liked.

But the Germans showed no signs of being willing to surrender, even though American, British and Russian armies were pressing up to their borders. A worrisome thought began to intrude: What if the Germans would not surrender? By fall, 1944, all kinds of stories began to circulate; of clandestine Nazi presses, secret radio stations, vast caches of arms and ammunition; of guerrilla training programs which involved hundreds of thousands of people. A new leadership corps was reported to be ready to carry on the struggle, "While Hitler will preferably have to be sacrificed— the Führer must die the death of a hero for the sake of legend." Churchill openly gave credence to such stories, and Eisenhower glumly confessed that there might never be a surrender, that V-E Day might have to be arbitrarily set by the Allied governments.

It was a disheartening prospect. And as the Christmas that was supposed to have been a Christmas of peace in half the world drew near, the fighting was becoming more fierce. Before the end of November, V-2 rockets started slamming into the southeastern part of England. Inaccurate though they were, the V-2's traveled so high and so fast there was no warning of their coming or means of defense. And rumor credited the Germans with a V-3, armed with an atomic bomb and perhaps capable of crossing the Atlantic.

Hopes that the big push—a winter offensive across the Rhine—would knock Germany out of the war by Christmas were dwindling fast. Officials talked now of perhaps stopping the tentative steps toward reconversion. American forces were using up their stockpiles of shells, planes, tanks, jeeps, guns and trucks at a rate never dreamed of. And the human cost so far exceeded earlier estimates that the Army began putting youths under the age of nineteen into combat units for the first time and draft boards starting inducting men over twenty-six.

Daylight precision bombing lost more of its standing in public esteem when a 15th Air Force bombing mission over Yugoslavia missed its target by three miles. Part of Belgrade was devastated, killing 2,000 people, injuring many thousands more.

A week before Christmas Day the Wehrmacht smashed through the forest of the Ardennes. Before the New Year began, they had struck the United States two staggering blows: one against its army, one against the hopes of its people. Overnight, everyone who had ever warned against overoptimism felt vindicated. Nettled, federal officials lashed the country for its complacency, making everyone a modest scapegoat for military defeat. Racetracks were ordered to close immediately. Where rationing had been relaxed, it was made stringent again. Production of consumer goods was ordered not to rise above specific levels. Draft quotas were raised.

So 1944 dragged to a close. Admiral Ernest King now predicted war with Germany at least until 1946. Most people gloomily agreed. A year that had opened with the highest hopes, the brightest promises came to a sour conclusion. And the expected increase in casualties had been realized in full. A chastened nation counted its war dead, wounded, missing and captured. The total was nearly 600,000. The casualty lists could only grow longer before victory came.

Once victory was certain, the terms of surrender began to appear less important than the objects for which the war was being fought. But no one seemed to know what they were. Certainly no one thought of the thirties as the good old days, to be returned to as quickly as possible. Isolationism flaunted its fading charms in the moments when the war was going badly and the Allies fell to quarreling. But most of the time the war went well, and the alliance held. American forces were on the offensive around the globe; the country must look outward. Some new consensus must be forged, and it must manage somehow to be both selfish and selfless: It must serve the airiest ideals and specific American interests.

Yet during the months of defeat the only leadership that Roosevelt had offered was to deny any passion for conquest and to gesture vaguely toward what he hoped would be a better world. Elsewhere, however, that crusading spirit which had raised its head even before Pearl Harbor was asserting its claims. In 1942 it carried a New York *Times* reporter, James Reston, and his *Prelude to Victory* into national acclaim and best sellerdom. "We cannot win this war," wrote Reston, "until it . . . becomes a national crusade for America and the American Dream." At the end of the road down which he pointed Reston could see the millennium: "We shall not only achieve victory over our enemies but we shall regain that simple, Christian, resolute way of life which always was, and despite the past two decades, still is the strength of our people." And with all the fervor of a Scots Calvinist Reston preached a militant faith: If the war ended with a single totalitarian state left anywhere in the world, the crusade would have failed, for "then it would be possible for that dictator to raise another warrior generation and challenge us on the field of battle."

Maxwell Anderson's play *The Eve of St. Mark's* was meantime assuring enthralled middlebrow audiences that all this discussion of war aims was unnecessary because We were right and They were wrong. But liberal intellectuals were clamoring, "This is a people's war for worldwide democracy." Scholars and geographers were busily redrawing the map of the world. *Life* started warning people against unwittingly fighting to save the British Empire and demanded that Britain's contribution to the war effort should be deference to American policies.

On New Year's Day, 1943, the *ad hoc* United Nations had assumed a more formal character when the respresentatives of twenty-five countries met with Roosevelt in the White House and solemnly pledged to sign no separate peace with the Axis. On this emerging structure American liberals began to fix their hopes; people of goodwill generally began to see in it the framework for a lasting peace. The road to it was well enough prepared.

Just three years before, a New York *Times* foreign correspondent named Clarence Streit had published a blueprint for a federal union of the world, called *Union Now!* It drew heavily on American experience—e.g., each nation would have two senators in the world legislature. The crux of Streit's idea was a union of the United States with Britain, its Empire and Commonwealth, plus the Scandinavians. Other nations would be permitted to join if and when they became democratic. With representation based proportionately on population the United States would dominate the union into the foreseeable future. This was Streit's vision: "When we reunite the 200,000,000 who speak English let us do it on the model of our own United States."

Streit was not laughed off as another crank. He was, after all, a former Rhodes Scholar. The *New Republic* and the *Nation* shared much of Streit's vision. The former urged, "Let the United States and Great Britain jointly assume responsibility and leadership for the whole world. . . ." The famous political scientist Hans Kohn called Union Now! "the only rational solution to the world crisis." Robert Sherwood, the playwright and Presidential speech writer, also suggested a union of English-speaking peoples with a joint government. His proposal was sufficiently like Streit's that, as *Life* noted with pleasure, "the U.S. could outvote all others." Conservatives, nevertheless, were sure that behind all such schemes they could detect the machinations of the British government.

By the time of Pearl Harbor millions of Americans wanted some kind of federal union or international organization of the world. The North Carolina legislature passed a resolution "That all peoples of the earth should be united in a Commonwealth of Nations." A *Fortune* poll in November, 1941, had shown more than a third of the country to be in favor of a permanent world federation. Even Henry Ford spoke kindly of a federal world union. Massachusetts voters on the eve of Pearl Harbor had approved a world union referendum by a margin of three to one. For all the disappointments with the League of Nations, by 1942 the United Nations was an idea whose time had come.

So when it came into existence piecemeal throughout 1942 and into 1943, it evoked, unlike its luckless predecessor, not argument but cheers. And by the time Roosevelt returned from Casablanca the whole country, it seemed, was arguing about postwar reconstruction and foreign policy.

The search for a new view of the world and America's place in it took an important turn with the return of Wendell Willkie from a round-the-world journey to Russia, China, the Middle East, North Africa and South America in the fall of 1943. Willkie called for a second front as soon as possible to relieve the pressure on the Russians. He portrayed the current struggle as "a war for men's minds." But Willkie's overriding theme, and the title of one of the war's most important books, was that he had seen "One World."

Willkie's book was an epochal point in America's education in internationalism. It marked the high tide of the moralistic, selfless component in the emerging consensus. Without a single book club sale Willkie's *One World* sold faster than any book had ever done in American history. Simon and Schuster projected a sale of 200,000 copies. Within seventy-two hours that printing was exhausted. A million copies were sold in a matter of weeks. In all, more than 2,000,000 hardbound copies were sold in a year. "*One World* was probably the most influential book published in America during the war," thought one reviewer. "Like *Uncle Tom's Cabin* it was part of the country."

After thirty years it seems bland, even banal. The world was a single political and geographical unit, said Willkie. The war must be fought with that in mind; the peace must be made with that in mind. Spheres of influence and policies of national exclusiveness could no longer prevail. The people of the world would no longer tolerate them. Wherever he went, he wrote, he had found a reservoir of goodwill toward the United States, but much confusion and worry over what it was fighting for in terms of positive goals. At home, there must be an end to racism, tyrannies of the majority and of anything else that was bigoted, small-minded or intolerant. At home and abroad he wanted a world safe for diversity and change.

Yet even as Willkie wrote, others were teaching a different lesson: the lesson of power politics in a harsh age. The most influential of these was Walter Lippmann, whose *U.S. Foreign Policy: Shield of the Republic* dominated best-seller lists throughout the summer of 1943. Lippmann argued that the United States must rectify the error of imbalanced ends and means which, he said, had characterized its foreign policy since the Spanish-American War. For nearly fifty years America's overseas reach had exceeded its grasp. In the postwar world, he saw American interests penetrating to almost every part of the globe. But the nation would not have the raw power to secure interests so scattered, so vast, so remote. It must therefore seek allies in Europe and Asia to help share its burden. Unabashedly, Lippmann embraced a new balance of power, new spheres of influence and summoned his countrymen to follow suit.

Everything could be made secure, save in one area alone: Central Europe and Germany. If the postwar settlement in that area ran into deep conflicts, then, thought Lippmann, "every nation must get ready and choose sides in the eventual but unavoidable next war." The lesson taught by Nicholas Spykman's 1942 book *America's Strategy in World Politics,* the work of an academic fascinated by doctrines of *Realpolitik*, was taught by Lippmann to an audience of millions. It was the lesson of naked self-interest advanced by power politics.

When the war went into its final year, the foreign policy debate began to turn angry. It was to develop into an angry fight between liberals and conservatives. It briefly flared around the immaculately tailored person of Sumner Welles, Undersecretary of State for six years. Welles clashed with the conservative elements in the State Department, especially with Cordell Hull. The Secretary openly laughed at literal believers in the Four Freedoms as "star gazers," as "the hosanna boys." He forced Welles out, then turned on Welles' defenders and accused them of treason.

Welles, a courtly, urbane product of a rich Eastern family, passed for a foreign policy liberal. He gave his blessings to regionalism, the UN, the world revolution and good neighbor policies. The suffering of the world's distressed touched the kindly side of his patrician nature. But on specific cases—such as Franco, the Vichy government, Argentina—the liberal gloss rapidly faded. Expediency and "military necessity" carried weight with Sumner Welles.

In a book almost as popular as Willkie's and Lippmann's, called *Time for Decision*, Welles carried the muddle of moralism and tough-mindedness to heights not theretofore scaled. In Welles' postwar international organization no country would be allowed to enter until it had first proved its moral fitness. It must demonstrate that it had a democratic government; that it was neither racist nor colonialist nor imperialist; it must give any and all overseas possessions into an international trusteeship. Yet the United States, because it was so very moral, would, of course, be exempted from this last provision.

The real champion of the liberal and progressive viewpoint was not Welles but Henry Wallace, the Vice President. He had already entered the fray with a work called *The Century of the Common Man*. The title plainly cast Wallace's work as a rejoinder to Luce's *American Century*. Suffused with goodwill, it was hopelessly ephemeral, rising to platitudes like "This is a fight between a slave world and a free world." Phrases like that could be used by anyone, and were in later years.

Conservatives pounced on a chance remark Wallace let fall. He had said that everyone should enjoy the benefits of modern technology and used the example of having milk every day to make his point. The president of the National Association of Manufacturers fumed to thunderous applause, "I am not fighting for a quart of milk every day for every Hottentot, nor a TVA on the Danube. . . ." But conservatives, agree as they might that these were not the things they wanted to see, were as confused as the liberals about what they did want.

Isolationism was shattered in so many pieces, every one of them tainted, that no one openly suggested picking them up and putting them back together. Even the *Saturday Evening Post*, recognizing that a new day was upon it, expelled its longtime isolationist editor, Wesley Winans Stout, and put its fortunes in the hands of a new editor, one who was a Republican internationalist.

When the Republican Party's leadership met on Mackinac Island at the top of Michigan in the late summer of 1943, they had publicly severed the last ties to isolationism. The *Saturday Evening Post* helpfully discovered that isolation had nothing to do with real Republicanism after all; it was merely a stopgap adopted by the GOP in 1920 to help oust the Democrats from the White House.

At about the same time that the GOP leaders were meeting in Michigan the editor of *Foreign Affairs*, Hamilton Fish Armstrong, was propounding a set of foreign policy views that the most eminently reactionary small-town Republican newspaper editor could be happy with. The most prestigious American periodical on international affairs, published by the politically moderate Council on Foreign Relations, was arguing that American interests were limitless, that there was no part of the globe which did not concern the United States, now or in the future. Like Lippmann's, Armstrong's conception was of one world, with a vengeance. Like Lippmann too, he wanted to secure "the unlimited range of our national interests" by forming alliances all over the world. And, he suggested, if the British and the Russians did not like the new dispensation, so much the worse for them.

This kind of ultranationalism was not very far removed from the traditional outlook of American conservatives, who have maintained a conservative view of human nature but have been only semiconservative in their view of the state. In their eyes an assertive state can do no good at home; abroad it can do no wrong. And here was a call for an America whose writ would run far and forcefully beyond its shores. Armstrong's article signaled a growing accord between the political right and the center. And liberals need only carry their crusading mission into the postwar world to be qualified to join them.

Even the New York *Times* was striking ultranationalist attitudes. When the Dumbarton Oaks Conference proposed to set up an International Monetary Fund to stabilize postwar currencies, the *Times* attacked it as a giveaway in which billions of good American dollars would be siphoned off to prop up the tottering British pound. The IMF, sniffed the *Times*, was nothing more than a scheme for suckering the United States into financing British imperialism.

No one was openly embracing an American imperium these days. The *Saturday Evening Post* was as aghast at the thought as was the *New Republic*. Everyone spoke warmly of the need for international cooperation. But the emerging internationalism more and more appeared—especially where isolationism had once held sway—to be a new nationalism. It was fiercely anti-British and anti-Russian. Among conservatives its catch-phrase was "national sovereignty." And Senator Gerald Nye, once an arch-champion of isolationism, was so entranced by national sovereignty that he thought Germany should be allowed to remain Nazi at the end of the war if that was what the Germans preferred.

The moralistic element remained strong, at least on the surface. For several years the Federal Council of Churches had a commission at work "to study the bases of a just and durable peace." It was chaired by an international lawyer from Wall Street, John Foster Dulles. The commission's report, issued in 1943, was yet another attempt to bring morality and goodwill to international politics. It called for a postwar international organization and a strong use of American resources to help maintain the peace.

Most people wanted to be generous. They overwhelmingly favored international cooperation. By four and five to one they favored cooperation in a postwar international organization. They approved an international police force, even one which would police the United States. They were willing to go on being rationed beyond the end of the war if that would help feed the world's hungry. And by two to one they were willing to pay higher taxes to help restore war-ravaged nations. That was how they felt in 1943 and 1944.

The administration actively encouraged the burgeoning spirit of internationalism. It set aside one day in June each year as United Nations Day, to be celebrated with parades, speeches and whatever else was appropriate. Federal officials promoted the growing interest in Latin America. Pan American Day was taken seriously, at least in the schools, during the war years. Enrollments in Spanish-language classes continued to soar.

Yet, some people recalled, there had been a comparable surge in internationalist sentiments during the earlier war. A League to Enforce Peace came into existence in 1915 and claimed the loyalties of many prominent people. In 1916 Wilson had given it his blessing. By April, 1917, most people had favored such a League in the postwar world. And by Armistice Day by a margin of three to one people were in favor of joining the League of Nations as soon as it came into existence. Still, not only had the United States never joined the League, but the twenties had brought the ascendancy of isolationism. While that history seemed unlikely to be repeated in detail, it was altogether possible that the fruits of the new internationalism could be as bitter and galling as those of the old.

For when people were asked which country should have the greatest say in the peace that was to come, four people out of five said the United States should. About half the country openly agreed that this was America's century and wanted the world to be organized accordingly. There was also a growing cynicism about what America could hope to expect from the war. As *Life* sarcastically put it, "We are fighting in Europe because we were attacked in the Pacific." And cynicism will undercut the generosity of anyone.

In response to a growing public clamor that even the administration did not know what it was fighting for, that the country was without a foreign policy, the State Department pasted up a collection of Hull's speeches and statements, distilling from them seventeen points. These, Hull grandly announced, were America's foreign policy. But Hull's points were laughed away. Hull, joked one radio commentator, was now three up on Wilson, seven on God.

America's emerging internationalist consensus was so far inchoate and unsettled, though the general lines were clear enough by the summer of 1944. But the real test of it was not yet at hand. That test would come when the war went into its last months and the Allies sought to transform what they had hammered together in wartime into a peace-keeping organization for the postwar world.

XXV

Turn to the Right

THE social experience of the United States in the war presents a grand paradox: There were novel, revolutionary, social effects, while the immediate interests of conservative elements were being advanced. Nowhere was this latter more evident than in government, especially after the 1942 elections. "Conservatives were coming to Washington," wrote one historian, "to run the government, achieving during the war what they could not previously achieve by popular vote." They were not particularly concerned with postwar organization or with the conduct of the war. They were out to secure the economic gains of specific interest groups, most particularly those of the farmers, labor unions and big business. But this revival of conservatism taught America once again the conservative way in thought, speech and deed of how to exalt the state abroad and limit it at home.

In Congress the revival centered on the lower House, suggesting how close to the grass roots it lay. Through the House's control of appropriations it was possible to choke nearly every big agency born of the New Deal. These buried, it was possible to move on to the liberal war agencies, such as the OWI and the OPA. And by driving out liberal luminaries like John Kenneth Galbraith, a conservative Congress put an end to any serious effort at price control.

Not content with substance, the conservatives sought victims. One, an economist of strong liberal views, John Bovingdon, was hounded out of Washington, ridiculed in the nation's press for being a devotee of modern dance and smeared as a potential subversive. Even the loss of his only child in combat could not deter his tormentors. Three very famous liberals, including Dr. Robert Morss Lovett, formerly an editor of the *New Republic*, were meantime persecuted under what was, in effect, a bill of attainder.

From the White House Roosevelt tried to curb the excesses of Congress, but it was beyond his control. It had been slipping away even before 1939, and by January, 1944, the Democrats no longer held a majority in the House. It seemed to at least one Washington reporter that the President by now had one policy only: "placating Congress in order to obtain its support for winning the war and the peace after it." Frustrated, Roosevelt now and again roused some of the old fire from his wasting frame. But when he slapped down the general revenue bill for 1944–1945 even the Senate and his friend Alben Barkley revolted.

This Congress, the Seventy-eighth, was hailed for having broken the shackles which had yoked the legislative to the administrative will for a decade. But they were contentious only over domestic affairs. The Fulbright Resolution, glowingly internationalist in word and spirit, passed on the scale of sixteen to one. A bipartisan outlook on foreign affairs was carrying all before it. The OWI's fate was revealing. Its domestic side was trimmed to the bone. But when government spokesmen told Congress that its other side was America's propaganda branch overseas and was serving as a counterweight to British propaganda in liberated areas, that it was boosting America to the ends of the earth, the overseas branch of the OWI saw its 1944 budget fattened by 50 percent.

Republicans expected this burgeoning conservatism and ultranationalism to redound to their profit. *Life* reported after the off-year elections in 1943: "The U.S. is now a Republican country . . . the Republicans are now the majority party." Republicans had captured the governorship of Kentucky. Negroes were falling away from the Democrats. In city elections, only Cleveland and Chicago held firm to their Democratic machines. Walter Lippmann gloomily conceded the White House to whoever secured the Republican nomination in 1944. With 10,000,000 servicemen of voting age the election might well rest with them, and the Soldier Vote bill that emerged from the House and Senate was sufficiently difficult that many servicemen (most of whom were Democrats) would not bother to vote. Roosevelt, disgusted, allowed it to become law without his signature. The Republicans had carried the fight to him and won.

Wendell Willkie tried to win a second nomination. But while he was his party's nominal head, it was really beyond his control. He scorned the party leadership and took himself to the rank and file. But they now preferred Dewey by 55 percent to 35 percent.

By the spring primaries of 1944 Dewey's lead was insurmountable. Two years before, he had pledged that if elected he would serve out a full four-year term as governor of New York. Another thought had since occurred to him, however; if drafted, he would feel it his duty to obey, for refusing a draft in wartime would be "an act of treason."

The Republicans were growing ebullient, and the Democrats, their Southern wing siding more and more with the opposition, were downcast. Their champion was ailing; his fortunes looked more problematical than ever. But though there was a powerful shift to the right in these years, America had not swung over to the Republicans. The whole country had gone to the right, including the Democratic Party. Its liberal fires were banked. Whatever social reforms it countenanced now were oblique and were wrung from it grudgingly by those interests organized to fight for social change. Those who were not organized got very little these days from the party of the New Deal.

So try as they might, the Republicans could not pit themselves convincingly as the custodians of conservative values and views in opposition to a party of reform-verging-on-radicalism. It would then have to be the GOP's standard-bearer against the Democrats'—Dewey against Roosevelt. And with the victories mounting, it was something to be Commander in Chief.

Roosevelt did not even bother to announce his intention of seeking another term. But once it sank in that he would run again, Dewey's nomination bandwagon seemed less unstoppable than irrelevant. Dewey's only chance lay in the prospect of an end to the war before election day. Only if it were over could he win.

Democrats worried less over that prospect than over the health of their champion. He was aging rapidly; perhaps, some wondered, he was literally dying before the country's eyes. There were persistent rumors that he might die at any moment. Each time he left the White House it was whispered he would never return to it alive. His doctor said he was simply fatigued from overwork, but even his wife confessed in "My Day" that she was worried. In the spring he went down to Baruch's estate at Hobcaw Barony, South Carolina, and rested for a month. His doctor pronounced on Roosevelt's return: "I am perfectly satisfied with his physical condition." But reporters, accustomed to seeing Roosevelt every few days for twelve years past, were shocked to realize when they saw him after his absence that he was now a worn-out old man. The tiredness had gone from around the eyes. But the flesh wasted on his large frame and made him look emaciated. He was nearly bald. And to all their questions he responded no longer with his old tartness or humor but with an old man's querulous irascibility at being bothered.

For only the second time in American history there would be a Presidential election with the country at war. The war would determine its outcome. But it was important even so, for in it were some deadly seeds.

Willkie, all hope of influencing the convention to adopt his brand of liberalism gone, stayed at home during the conventions.* Bricker, supported by Taft, fought doggedly to be nominated. Stassen, still on active duty with the Navy, was ostentatiously "available." But Dewey could not be overtaken before the convention opened in Chicago.

The men who organized this quadrennial gathering of the GOP labored diligently to achieve a properly dignified "tone" (something like what our

* Willkie died suddenly in October, just weeks before the election.

more visually minded age calls "image") to suit the sacrifices of the hour. And for that the stiff, grave Dewey was the ideal nominee. The convention was, at its most exciting, lethargic. Defeatism made the rank and file sullen and depressed. What spirit remained was sapped by a heat wave so intense it buckled the streetcar tracks.

California's governor, Earl Warren, made the keynote address. Clare Boothe Luce, speaking to a convention nearly one-third of whose delegates were women, presumed to speak for America's war dead. With a rare taste for political necrophilia she snatched dead men from their graves and, treating them much like ventriloquists' dummies, put into their lifeless mouths her words, her wishes, her thoughts.

Dewey won the nomination on the first ballot. One delegate from Wisconsin provided the sole note of spontaneity by shouting, "I am a man, not a jelly fish. I vote for MacArthur." Adamantly clinging to his choice, he denied Dewey the traditional show of a unanimous vote.

Bricker was tossed the Vice Presidential nomination after Warren, foreseeing certain defeat in November, turned it down.

The convention managers coached the delegates to greet Dewey's entrance to accept the nomination by singing "Mine eyes have seen the glory of the coming of the Lord. . . ." A local judge hailed the nominee as a Sir Galahad in shining armor who, gone forth to seek the Holy Grail, had performed the Augean task of smashing big-time racketeers. But defeatism still clung to whatever the delegates did. Dispirited, exhausted by the heat, they cut the convention from four days to three and hurriedly left town.

Republican newspapers and the old guard of the Republican Party announced that Republican fortunes had been graciously turned over to the younger men. Dewey and his advisers and backers were indeed the youngest group of Republican leaders since the days of Teddy Roosevelt. But the nominations of Dewey and Bricker signaled less the coming of a new day than the restored supremacy of the GOP's conservative wing.

Shortly after the Republicans fled from Chicago, Roosevelt had the White House correspondents ushered into the Oval Room and mysteriously ordered the door locked. He had, he said, an announcement to make—one of national importance. To a hushed, now solemn-looking assemblage, he assumed his best poker face and drawled: "If the convention nominates me, I shall accept. If the people elect me, I will serve."

The great issue the Democrats must face was the choice of a Vice Presidential nominee, an issue made doubly important by the President's failing health and the unpopularity among powerful Democrats of Vice President Wallace. Wallace, the Southerners and the big-city bosses said, was a drag on the ticket. Yet among Democratic voters he was, in fact, the overwhelming choice, outdistancing his closest rival, Alben Barkley, 64 percent to 13 percent. Wallace was nonetheless too liberal for Southern and boss tastes.

And never had Roosevelt so needed the big city machines as he did now. The traditional rural and Southern base of his party had been much eroded since 1932. Its base was now urban and Northern. But having let go of the one, it did not yet have a sure grasp on the other. Lest it fall between these two, Roosevelt had to choose between Wallace and the conservative political interests within the Democratic Party. He threw Wallace to the wolves: He gave the choice of Vice President to the convention.

Had the choice gone to the delegates, Wallace would have won. But like other conventions, this one was a possession of the traditional party leadership. And in they trooped, the hard-eyed, strong-willed men—Flynn of the Bronx, Hague of Jersey City, Kelly of Chicago, Crump of Memphis—while the galleries chanted plaintively "We Want Wallace." The liberal, progressive wing rallied, made a concerted bid for Wallace and fell short. The Northern machines and the Southern wing could hold firm indefinitely for anyone-but-Wallace.

But if not Wallace, who? Had Barkley not clashed with Roosevelt over the revenue bill veto, it might well have been he. Beyond Barkley were many possibilities, only one of whom said he did not want the nomination. That was Senator Truman. But in the three-way fight between the Northern bosses, the Southerners and the progressives Truman emerged as the ideal compromise nominee. No one was strongly for him; no one was strongly against him. From Missouri, he was acceptable to the South. A protégé of Kansas City's Pendergast machine, he was acceptable to the bosses. Chairman of the committee investigating the wickedness and stupidities of business and the military, he was acceptable to liberals.

Wallace graciously agreed to nominate Roosevelt for a fourth term, then used the opportunity to scold the convention. Political and economic democracy must be extended to all Americans, he said. "The poll tax must go. Equal educational opportunities must come. The future must bring equal wages for equal work, regardless of race or sex." In something like despair, he concluded: "The Democratic Party cannot long survive as the Conservative Party."

The Republican campaign began by being dull. It moved on to become scurrilous. When it coasted to a halt, it was running on pure venom.

It featured a candidate who was little loved even within his own party. Alice Roosevelt Longworth sniffed, "How can we be expected to vote for a man who looks like the bridegroom on a wedding cake?" As Lincoln had in 1864, Roosevelt campaigned now on the theme that it was unwise to change horses in midstream. And a Midwestern farmer was supposed to have protested Dewey's nomination, "We keep saying it ain't so dangerous to switch horses in the middle of a stream. Maybe so. But I sure draw the line at a Shetland pony." Even one of Dewey's aides was reputed to have said, "You can't really dislike Tom Dewey until you get to know him."

Reporters were usually cool to him. He was stiff, formal, invariably dull and banal. At his most excited, Dewey would indulge no expression stronger than "Oh, Lord!" or "Goodness gracious!" Though not incapable of kindness, he was always difficult to like. He turned punctuality into a fetish. The early stages of his campaign were organized with a passion for regularity and routine. Dewey was aloof and condescending, saying hardly a word except for periodic, tightly managed press conferences for small-town newspapers. He saw himself as Efficiency Man. "Selling Dewey," grumbled one reporter, "was organized like a campaign to sell soap." Reporters had never seen anything like it. But it looked futile, for all its novelty. Because two things became increasingly evident: No one expected Dewey to win, and almost no one cared what he said or did.

Republicans desperately attempted to infuse life into their campaign by stepping up their attacks on Roosevelt. The onslaught was at first relatively indirect. They claimed that Roosevelt had told the big-city bosses at the Democratic Convention that when it came to picking a running mate, they should "Clear it with Sidney." Such an instruction made no sense at all, for the choice of Hillman's CIO was Wallace. But "Clear it with Sidney" became the Republicans' battle cry for the 1944 election. It sprang from the nervousness and apprehension with which they viewed the CIO's newly created Political Action Committee.

Organized in 1943, the PAC was an important political factor in 1944. It had lost the fight to keep Wallace on the ticket. But its promise was huge. As late as the 1930's labor was too fragmented to have much effect at the polls. The PAC was the wartime response to the Smith-Connally Labor Act and the increasingly powerful antilabor bloc in Congress. If it could organize 5,000,000 workers and their families to vote as a counter-bloc at the polls in November, it might well become, by 1948, the predominant force within the Democratic Party, something not unlike the Trades Union Congress within Britain's Labor Party.

Conservatives viewed any such step with alarm. *Life* damned the PAC as "a foreign object," as something appropriate to totalitarian states, as an instrument of class warfare, as, in a phrase, a Communist front.

The tempo of the Red-baiting attacks was accelerated as Dewey's campaign bogged down, and the attacks on Roosevelt became more personal. Dewey never went beyond referring to Roosevelt as being "old and tired." But a whispering campaign was set in motion that the President was dying of everything from cancer to syphilis. And Republicans proudly hailed Bricker as an obviously better Vice Presidential choice than Truman in case something happened. Truman too was the object of scurrilous rumors that he belonged to the Klan.

Then Drew Pearson wrote that at great cost to the taxpayers a Navy destroyer had been dispatched to the Aleutians to bring the President's dog Fala home after he was inadvertently left behind. Congress debated it and threatened an investigation; Republicans seized upon it with glee. But Roosevelt turned the tables on them.

At a banquet given by organized labor he answered his Republican critics. He grew angry at the talk of a Roosevelt Depression. It smacked of the Nazi technique of the Big Lie—effective precisely because it was outrageous. Then, in mock solemnity, he went on: "Those Republican leaders have not been content with attacks on me, or on my wife, or on my sons— no, not content with that, they are now including my little dog Fala." He was used to being misrepresented, he said. But he would not tolerate "libelous statements about my dog." A national radio audience of millions roared with laughter.

Stung, Dewey and Bricker became intemperate. For the rest of the campaign they worked assiduously to portray Roosevelt as a dupe of international Communism. Nor were they without success. They portrayed the PAC as a Communist front, out to win control of the Democratic Party and, through it, the United States. Dewey drew a line between America's valiant Russian allies and the evil Communists who, he said, were in control of the Democratic Party. Earl Browder had been released from prison to organize Roosevelt's campaign for a fourth term, according to Dewey. Dewey also promoted the idea that Roosevelt egged the Japanese on to attacking Pearl Harbor. Bricker argued that the New Dealers had maneuvered the country into war because they could find no other solution to unemployment. And Senator Taft stumped about the country insisting that Roosevelt's reelection would put the United States into the hands of the Communists.

Roosevelt grew angry. To a cheering Boston crowd he repudiated Dewey's charges. He explicitly renounced any and all Communist support for his reelection. But Dewey doggedly called them "soft disclaimers"; in so many words, Roosevelt was "soft on Communism."

To refute the whispers and the doubts about his health, the President repeatedly exposed himself in public to cold and rain, at one point spending four hours in an open car driving through a heavy New York drizzle. It did not dispel the doubts, and it probably taxed his ebbing strength.

Dewey steadily closed the gap in the polls until, by election day, the pollsters said that it was too close a contest to call. Having suffered a stunning defeat in 1942, they were very cautious now. But professional gamblers were positing odds of two and a half to one on Roosevelt.

The President traveled up to Hyde Park Village to cast his vote and await the outcome. Through the green curtains of the voting machine that familiar voice was heard swearing, "This goddamned thing won't work," to an accompaniment of clashing gears. It was the only thing that did not work for him that day. A little after 11 P.M. his neighbors marched up his driveway to cheer Roosevelt's fourth Presidential victory.

The vote was the closest since Wilson defeated Charles Evans Hughes in 1916. Roosevelt's plurality was 3,000,000 votes. But in the Electoral College the Democrats' organizational triumph was reflected in a margin of 432 votes to 99.

Roosevelt's last victory was variously credited to the big-city machines; to Republican moderates who had deserted the GOP now it was back in conservative hands; to the 3,000,000 servicemen who cast absentee ballots; to the 3,000,000 federal employees. Negroes claimed that they had given Roosevelt his reelection. But most people were inclined to credit it to Sidney Hillman and his friends in the Political Action Committee. They had registered millions of voters and got them to the polls. Organized labor for the first time had delivered a bloc vote. At a bound, Hillman supplanted John L. Lewis as the principal figure in American labor. In all, the PAC had come up with 6,000,000 votes. Republicans examined its organization and tactics, noticed a strong resemblance in both to the Anti-Saloon League which had led the successful drive for Prohibition and shuddered to think.

As for Dewey, his political career seemed at an end. A reporter thought to stop by his headquarters in the early hours of the morning after, shook the governor's hand and wished him better luck in 1948. "I have no illusions about that," he replied. In the days that followed what little national standing Dewey had ever enjoyed appeared to evaporate. And in all probability, it seemed to those who looked ahead, the next Republican Presidential nominee would be a returned war hero, like General MacArthur.

For of all the conservative elements that had flourished in wartime none had exceeded the military. They cut a swath through American life that almost no one had ever seen before. John Dos Passos nervously pondered it: "For the first time since the Civil War, military brains were coming to the top. The farmers would go for a general at the polls. But what would the generals do with us now that they were back at the top? Would the brass hats of today show the restraint and civic decency of the brass hats of eighty years ago?"

Parallel to the renewal of conservative politics was an equally sharp turn to the right among leading intellectuals and literati. We saw how the New Nationalism began to emerge in the late 1930's. It flowered in wartime. The result was neither great ideas nor great literature; if anything, the opposite was true. Yet it had the not inconsequential effect of narrowing that yawning chasm of hostility which had run through American society for most of the twenties and thirties when most of its intellectuals and serious writers had looked on the country as being rotten and doomed.

The war—the eminently justified, long-overdue, anti-Fascist war—had forced a rethinking. To most American intellectuals and their European refugee counterparts Nazism was an evil that had to be destroyed; anti-Fascism was the touchstone of their faith long before 1939. But that was a faith with a creed *against* something. Once Fascism and Nazism were doomed to certain defeat, they needed a creed *for* something. With the Nazi-Soviet Pact still embarrassingly fresh, the flirtation with Marxism of the 1930's, with Russia as "the Noble Experiment," was not to be revived. Some of the transplanted Europeans, like Somerset Maugham in *The Razors' Edge* and Aldous Huxley in *Time Must Have a Stop*, took up the higher mysticism. They turned to Eastern religions and the possibilities of transmigrating souls.

Among American intellectuals, however, there was quarreling rather than quiescence. Long-standing tendencies to faction and sectarianism revived. Proscription lists were drawn up and were smuggled into scholarly articles. Bernard De Voto turned on Van Wyck Brooks and publicly called him a liar and a fool. Brooks in turn damned the heroes of modern literature—men he had once praised—casting into outer darkness the works of Hemingway, Pound, Eliot, John Dos Passos and Henry James and exalting Socrates, Milton and Emerson. While this turbulent struggle for new hagiographies and demonologies was boiling up from the search for a new faith, something comparable was going on among the less intellectually distinguished.

Ayn Rand's *The Fountainhead*, an interminable, badly written opus which sang the praises of individualism over collectivism, appeared in the summer of 1943, to a highly mixed reception. It popped up briefly on some best-seller lists, then sank out of sight, apparently gone the same way as scores of other novels which each year have a brief flirtation with glory. But it kept on selling so steadily, if in unspectacular numbers, that by the end of the war more than 300,000 copies were sold in hardback. Millions of copies were later sold in paperback. It was made into a popular motion picture, and *The Fountainhead* is still in print.

One of the war's best sellers, a work which was hailed, even in serious journals, as being important, was a rambling, almost incoherent book by Herbert Agar, a noted liberal editor, called *A Time for Greatness*. From the reception it received, Agar's book evidently struck a highly responsive cord. He described his thesis as being "optimistic, conservative and moral." But it was an explicitly tough-minded optimism, a high-minded conservatism and a vigilant morality. "The central task of our world is to preserve it," Agar wrote. "This is a conservative task which we must perform whether or not we like to be called conservatives. Democracy has become the one effective conservative force in the world; and we are its guardians."

Peter Drucker was still attempting to unravel the present and cast light on the future by the examination of economic forces. In *The Future of Industrial Man: A Conservative Approach* he offered a sequel to his earlier work and explicitly refuted Burnham's arguments. Drucker's latest thesis was that while the basis of modern Western societies is industrial, their social, political and international affairs are still rooted in preindustrial times, needs and values. The proper realignment, said Drucker, would be a society organized along the lines of a self-governing factory. In his work epigrams, paradoxes and aphorisms flashed by at a dizzying pace, conveying a welcome sense of intellectual movement. Drucker's work was widely considered brilliant. But there were, unhappily, too many errors of fact and too many places where rhetoric was a stand-in for knowledge, for his analyses to be of much use to serious inquiry.

The famous academic economist Joseph Schumpeter offered his analysis in *Capitalism, Socialism and Democracy.* He asked, "Can capitalism survive?" and answered that it probably could not. Schumpeter thought that there were ample proofs that it was already dying, thanks to its success. The forces which had given rise to the Western bourgeoisie and then driven it on were vitiated. Spiraling modern economic growth rates could not be sustained much longer. Investment possibilities were drying up. Hordes of intellectuals were being spun off and were chipping away at established authority. In capitalist societies the will to persevere in the face of difficulties was eroding away. Schumpeter did not prophesy the immediate end of capitalism; it might take a century or more. But in the long sweep of history a mere century is the short, not the long, run.

On the horizon he saw the emergence of Socialism. For those who associated Socialism with Marxism and thought that he was thus forecasting revolution, Schumpeter was at pains to point out that Marx was not quite the bloodthirsty revolutionary of popular fancy; on the contrary, he was a sober scholar whose mature thought was conservative and evolutionary. Schumpeter thought that it was possible for a democratic Socialism to emerge from the currently mushrooming panoply of bureaucratic organizations in the advanced capitalist countries. Indeed, there was very little in this, the best known of Schumpeter's works, to trouble those conservatives who assumed that professors of economics were wild-eyed radicals.

But the great delight of conservatives was another expatriate Austrian economist, Friedrich Hayek, and his little volume called *The Road to Serfdom.* It was the intellectual success story of the war. Hayek taught that modern liberalism was the short path to tyranny.

He saw the Renaissance giving rise to individualism as the center of Western civilization moved westward toward England. The result had been a crude laissez-faire dogmatism, but at its peak it also produced the liberal humanism of the late eighteenth and early nineteenth centuries. Then the tide had shifted back to the East, to Germany. The result was Socialism and its tyrannical offspring, Russian Communism. Western intelligentsia had embraced Socialism as the logical successor to liberalism even when their infatuation with collective life and action degenerated into totalitarianism. Their pursuit of a secular utopia had produced—even if from laudable motives—the monstrous growths of Fascism and Stalinism.

Hayek had no desire to bring back the rough-hewn days of laissez-faire. He thought that everyone was entitled to the necessities of life as a matter of right. He had no patience with privilege. But his call for a renewal of free enterprise, curbing state intervention in the economy and getting rid of the planners was a welcome tocsin to conservative ears. Hayek's credentials for an attack on the left-liberal intellectuals were impeccable. He had taught at the London School of Economics since 1933. He had once been editor of the Socialist journal *Collectivist Economic Planning*.

In England, where *The Road to Serfdom* first appeared, it was not a great success. That country was already explicitly committed to creating a postwar welfare state. It found little use for Hayek's polemic with its grotesquely inflated title. But in the United States Hayek became a national celebrity. He was deluged with invitations to speak to chambers of commerce; organizations like the Lions and Rotary hung on his every word. The ultimate accolade was a book by another academic economist, Herman Finer, explicitly aimed at refuting Hayek's arguments. (Called *The Road to Reaction*, it was even worse than its protagonist.) According to one 1944 issue of the *Saturday Evening Post*, "Businessmen do not regard professors as crackpots in their own fields of activity, unless that field happens to be economics." But for Hayek they gladly made an exception.

It was noteworthy that in just a few years three Austrian economists—Drucker, Schumpeter and Hayek—should come forward as important spokesmen on the crisis of Western civilization. All three were economic conservatives; all three were concerned with the future of capitalism. But more interesting still, the two who were academic economists did not offer economic theories of that crisis. Instead, they turned to social history and ideologies, as if agreeing with Drucker's thesis of the end of economic man.

The Depression had cast a shadow over their generation. And there had been, as many people could see, no economic imperative for it. The readjustments made necessary by speculative excess and shortsighted policies did not require a depression in order to be made. Nor was there any essentially economic reason for the Depression to linger on for years; the manpower, the skills, the plants, the social cohesion, the raw materials necessary for full employment were all at hand. There was also no economic necessity for the war. Thirty years later Germany and Japan would have larger populations occupying smaller national territories and yet would have vastly higher standards of living, as we now know.

Schumpeter and Hayek had grasped, however unwittingly, that the sociopsychological crisis of the West was not really economic in origin and that it was not amenable to economic solutions. In that perception they made common ground with yet another distinguished Austrian refugee, the psychoanalyst Erich Fromm.

For the moment, however, they had cloaked the revival of conservative attitudes and beliefs in a new mantle of respectability. Conservatism in American life need no longer go about intellectually naked, once the intellectual initiative, like the wartime shift in politics, had gone from left to right.

XXVI
Economics of War and Peace

VOLUNTEER bond salesmen were on street corners again and were called Minute Men again, but gone was the earlier brashness. No more heart-rending stories of brave soldiers dying—from shortages of food or ammunition or medicine—because of the misers back home. The latent sense of guilt in most civilian breasts was tapped now by oblique approaches. Sacrifice was the theme—the sacrifices of soldiers compared to the sacrifices of civilians. And it worked.

As in the First World War, show business celebrities were the most effective salesmen of bonds, and the successor to Elsie Janis when it came to selling bonds was Kate Smith; no sweetheart of the forces, but "just fat, plain Kate Smith." In a single sixteen-hour stint on the radio on September 21, 1943, she was able to raise nearly $40,000,000.

Every one of the seven war loans was oversubscribed. But most of the money came from banks, corporations, insurance companies and the like. Bonds were portrayed as "sacred rather than secular," but they still paid a dividend. Treasury officials kept trying to sop up individual purchasing power and put a brake on inflation, and in their efforts to reach the ordinary citizen the bond drives grew increasingly vulgar and stunt-ridden. Betty Grable's stockings, Jack Benny's violin, circus tickets, Man o' War's horseshoes—all were auctioned off for bond-buying pledges. And still the individual quotas were never met, while institutional quotas were always oversubscribed.

Federal officials were suspected of manipulating the war news to boost bond sales. News of the Bataan Death March, for instance, was kept secret for nearly two years and then, without explanation, was released in February, 1944, on the eve of the Fourth War Loan. For several days the sale of bonds doubled. More disturbing, though, was the fact that while every bond drive more than met its overall quota, the country was paying barely a third of its war costs from current income. By comparison other democracies were paying half. What it meant was that the burden of the war's cost would be borne by the lower- and middle-income groups for years to come while for the rich and the big corporations the war was little more than a profitable long-term investment.

The other pillar of war economics was taxation. As with bonds, it wore a conservative face. When Roosevelt in the winter of 1942–1943 issued an executive order limiting net incomes to $25,000 a year, it very quickly became the first executive order ever to be slapped down by act of Congress. The demand for pay-as-you-go income taxes by ordinary taxpayers had become so strong, meanwhile, and the arguments against it so elusive, that by the summer of 1943 Roosevelt agreed to a compromise bill. Since then, Americans have had most, if not all, of their income taxes withheld.

But no sooner was the tax levy approved than it seemed that the Treasury wanted still more. Having extracted as much as it thought it could or should get from the mass of Americans, it proposed to fight inflation by putting a bigger bite on incomes in the upper ranges. Congress tore the proposal to shreds, damning it as yet one more attempt to smuggle Socialism into America. Congress wrote its own tax bill for extra revenues. It lowered taxes on incomes in the $6,000 to $12,000 a year range (Congressmen earned $10,000 a year) and increased taxes on those making less than $1,200 a year. It also put a stop to renegotiating war contracts. Whatever the military had said it would pay it must pay, no matter how outrageous. And the new tax bill raised an extra $2 billion, chiefly from the poor, whereas the Treasury bill would have raised $10.5 billion, chiefly from the well-to-do. Roosevelt ruefully wished aloud that he had that much nerve.

Americans were soon struggling with new tax forms, also the creation of Congress. The forms baffled the IRS as much as the average taxpayer. People were, in some cases, filing under four different schedules at once.

1. Withholding installments for March and June, 1943, based on 1942 returns.
2. Victory tax for the first half of 1943.
3. Income tax for the second half of 1943.
4. Withholding installments for September and December, 1943, based on estimates of overall 1943 income.

Here was fertile ground, indeed; overnight, "tax experts" proliferated. Few were competent or honest. Newspapers would send a reporter out to present himself at a half dozen IRS offices as a worried taxpayer; each office invariably estimated his tax differently. With something verging on glee, newspapers reported the case of a man in Fort Myers, Florida, who was believed to have committed suicide in despair over his tax forms. He was found to have owed $7.50—more or less.

When the revenue bill written by Congress reached him in the spring of 1944, Roosevelt vetoed it. For the first and only time in American history a President struck down a general revenue bill. And he penned an acidulous message to Congress. "This," he wrote, "is not a tax bill, but a tax relief bill, providing relief not for the needy but for the greedy."

Roosevelt and Congress had been coming to this showdown for a long time. They had clashed repeatedly over every federal initiative to curb inflation and spread the burden of the war equitably. He had rammed through a program to subsidize key commodities as a brake on overall prices. Congress passed an antisubsidy bill by a two to one margin. But he used his executive powers and warily trod some shaky legal ground to bring subsidies into existence.

Most of the victories in the fight over who should control the economy went, however, to those conservative interests whose wishes Congress was serving more and more. The Senate majority leader and close friend of the President, Alben Barkley, led the Congressional revolt against Roosevelt's veto. The Senate overrode it 72–14; the House by an equally emphatic 299–95.

For the past year the stock market had been bulling along, though news such as the fall of Tunis or the Italian surrender had depressed it periodically. By 1944 the New York Stock Exchange was operating in the red for the first time in more than a decade.

War production peaked in November, 1943. In that month $6 billion in arms and munitions came pouring out of America's factories. More than two-thirds of all goods produced these days were for the war. Ships were being delivered at the rate of six a day. The *Normandie* was being refloated in the greatest salvage operation in history. Only a shortage of manpower kept the production figures from rising even higher.

But about the time the manpower problem became acute the overall task of war production was done. By 1944 the Army was handing out contract cancellations on a vast scale. Tens of billions of dollars in appropriated but unspent funds were turned back to Congress by the War and Navy Departments. With the battle of production won small-arms plants were closing down, jeeps were showing up on the civilian market, and the toll of highway accidents began to rise for the first time since Pearl Harbor. By June, 1944, the number of employed workers had dropped by more than a million from the figure six months before.

The course of the production miracle had left a rash of scandals in its wake, most of them attributable to plain and simple greed. Business heroes there were, like Henry J. Kaiser and Andrew Jackson Higgins, but the villains outnumbered the heroes, though those who were neither exceeded them both.

When a Kaiser-built tanker split into two shortly after being launched, investigation laid the fault at the door of a U.S. Steel subsidiary which was turning out low-grade steel, faking the quality control tests and selling it as high-grade, premium-price material. Anaconda Copper Company officials pleaded no contest when charged with systematically and persistently selling the military copper wire and strip that they knew to be defective. Anaconda too had faked its records and inspections.

Probably the most outrageous case involved the top management of a primary war contractor, National Bronze and Aluminum Foundry Company of Cleveland. A federal court found it guilty of repeatedly and willfully passing off parts for fighter-plane engines knowing them to be defective and dangerous. Imperfect parts were scrap metal, worth fifteen cents a pound. Disguised, renumbered and reshipped, they were worth much, much more. Several of the accused executives were sent to jail, and the company was heavily fined.

A similar fate befell eight employees of the world's largest manufacturer of small-arms ammunition, the U.S. Cartridge Company of St. Louis. They had passed off millions of rounds of faulty ammunition as being sound in their eagerness to swell profits and business.

The Truman Committee kept up its quarrel with Curtiss-Wright, charging it in 1943 with cheating on tests and forging official documents in order to sell defective planes and engines to the government. That summer the plant built to turn out the Helldiver ("world's best dive bomber," according to Curtiss-Wright advertising) was idle. Its 21,000 workers were sitting around because not one of the planes so far turned out was combat-worthy. And the company made no move to get the plant back in operation, finding it a handy stick with which to beat the Truman Committee, accusing it of obstructing the war effort.

Onerous as the scandals were, however, they were kept to what was probably the minimum, given private industry's supremacy in the task of war production. William Allen White put the blame for the failures and the scandals squarely on the shoulders of the dollar-a-year men. "It is silly to say the New Dealers run this show," he wrote in his Emporia *Gazette*. "It's run largely by absentee owners of amalgamated industrial wealth. . . . If you touch them in nine relations of life out of ten, they are kindly, courteous, Christian gentlemen. But in the tenth relation, where it touches their own organization, they are stark mad, ruthless, unchecked by God or man, paranoiacs, as evil in their design as Hitler."*

Nor was business greed confined within the narrower channels of war economics or limited to fat profits on war contracts. The traditional shape of the civilian economy had changed; it was now overwhelmingly a seller's

---

* Yet there may have been something at work beyond a mere dollar-a-year man's powers to add or subtract. For there was a tradition, of sorts, at work. In November, 1775, George Washington wrote with unmitigated bitterness at the way the Revolutionary War was being fought: "Such a dirty mercenary spirit pervades the whole that I should not be surprised at any disaster that may happen." Yet Washington himself seems to have been imaginative and ambitious when given an expense account; cf. Marvin Kitman's *George Washington's Expense Account*.

market. The result was just as traditional. Somewhere between 25 and 50 percent of all American business was estimated to be in the black market, and the higher figure is probably more accurate than the lower: In 1944 OPA investigations of several hundred thousand businesses revealed that no less than 57 percent were violating price controls. In some areas the figure soared to 70 percent.

Tax evasion and grotesquely lavish expense accounts provided further opportunities. And as one reporter noticed, the possibilities of milking the war for personal gain were not yet exhausted. A new crop of war millionaires would probably be created after the war. "It will consist in turning over to private industries the gigantic war plants built, financed, and at present owned, by the government."

Yet mere incompetence probably cost the country more than greed. For despite the undeniable and historic achievement of American production an unshakably second-rate character clung to many a big war contractor. Willow Run was simply the most notorious example.

Construction of the plant began in March, 1941, and production of the first B-24 which it turned out began a week before Pearl Harbor. At its peak, the plant produced a bomber every sixty-three minutes. When it closed down in 1945 Willow Run had turned out 8,685 bombers in forty-three months, an average of 202 a month. It was a far cry from Henry Ford's loudly reiterated boast that he would turn out 1,000 planes a week. And while the plant's management proudly called it "The biggest bomber plant in the world," among the workers who made the planes a common gibe was "Willit Run?"

To a casual observer it might easily appear that government was keeping a tight rein on business. Early in 1944 a rail strike was threatened, and Roosevelt ordered federal officials to take control of the railroads. The top railroad executives were given commissions, put into uniform and told to go about their business. Labor troubles elsewhere brought a government take-over of the coal mines. Thanks to a labor dispute, Roosevelt ordered the take-over of Montgomery Ward in May, 1944.

From Chicago to both coasts people began to argue. Was Montgomery Ward a defense industry? Did Roosevelt have the right to seize it if it was not? The Attorney General was dispatched to supervise the operation and to make a final plea to Ward's crusty seventy-year-old president, Sewell Avery. Avery, shaking with rage, fumed and spluttered in Biddle's face: "You . . . you . . . New Dealer!" When he refused to leave the building, two burly MP's cradled the aged millionaire in their arms and carried him out into the streets of Chicago. Before a court could rule on the legality of the seizure, however, a compromise was reached, and the take-over was ended.

Yet appearances to the contrary, business was not being closely regulated by federal officials. With the Army canceling contracts at the rate of more than $1 billion a month American business managed to void the entire Renegotiation Act of 1942. Between 1919 and 1942 more than 170 bills and resolutions had been introduced into Congress to prevent war profiteering. Only two—and those were two of the weakest—were passed. With contracts being let on a cost-plus basis, renegotiation was thus the sole safeguard left against major abuses. And now it was gutted.

The Office of Price Administration, within which burned not a little of the spirit of the New Deal, nursed a fond hope of introducing grade labeling to a wide range of consumer goods. The FDA had been doing it for years with medications, and the Agriculture Department did it with meat and eggs. But the OPA ran head on into a national campaign against grade labeling, which was portrayed in the press as a left-wing campaign against free enterprise. It was viewed as a plot hatched by Communists and left-wing extremists. Advertising agencies insisted that it would destroy the consumer's freedom to buy whatever he chose, that it would regiment individuals into collectivist, totalitarian consumerism, that it would lower the standard of living. Grade labeling was stopped by Congress. Congress even ruled that no one on the staff of the OPA could help set price-fixing policy unless he had at least five years' practical business experience.

Even small businessmen were growing assertive. One of the Palm Beach hotels leased by the Army had been turned into a convalescent center for wounded servicemen. With the revival of winter vacations local realtors, hoteliers and rich local citizens clamored in the winter of 1943–1944 that the charms of the area were being spoiled by the sight of cripples and invalids, and this was depressing business. Meekly, the War Department surrendered. In January, 1944, it moved its wounded men to the less salubrious winter climate of central Indiana, where no one would notice them.

Military and businessmen were, all this while, becoming increasingly well met. Rarely did their interests clash directly, and their views of society and the state tended to be similar at so many points that it was only natural that they would get on well together. And looking to the future, Lieutenant General Brehon Somervell, the Army's Chief of Supply, established a quasi-secret school for business executives at Fort Leavenworth, Kansas. There, in a four-week course run by Army officers, the managers of the great corporations learned all about the necessity of military control as a curb on civilian bureaucratic inefficiency. The students were invariably hostile to the New Deal and what it stood for and were told that they were being trained for "service in special posts." So far as one can judge, they were all flattered and impressed. Hundreds of them were graduated before several curious and irate Congressmen learned of the school and forced its extinction.

Before the war ended, the Secretary of the Navy, James Forrestal, was calling for government henceforth to be entrusted to an administrative elite trained and organized along military lines and drawn from the ranks of big business. Charles E. Wilson, president of General Electric and the number two man in the War Production Board, informed the Army Ordnance Association that businessmen should be given reserve commissions so as to help carry the wartime unity of business and military into the postwar era. It was perhaps none too surprising, therefore, that it was a World War II general, later President of the United States, who gave us the phrase "military-industrial complex."

For the moment, American business was waxing in the fullness of prestige, power and profits. Even small businessmen managed to grab enough crumbs that fell from the tables above them somehow to survive. And while in looking to the future there were prophecies of disaster ahead, rarely did they come from businessmen. Individual bank deposits had gone up by 50 percent in the five years since war began in Europe. With more than $100 billion saved up, people obviously had plenty of money to fuel a postwar boom in consumer goods. According to *Fortune*, they were lusting for automobiles, houses, refrigerators and washing machines.

Now and then, it is true, there was an executive who was dismayed by the greed of his friends and colleagues. One of them, WPB's Wilson, was so chastened by what he had seen in Washington in recent years that he bared his soul to the NAM convention in December, 1943. Never had the country faced such peril since the Civil War, he told them. Yet businessmen were using the war effort "to work for their own special purposes and private ambitions. Too many people," Wilson thundered, "are trying to position themselves for the postwar period, long before the country is out of danger. . . ." During the Depression businessmen had feared a left-wing fury that would pit labor against business. But "I am alarmed today over the possibility of a right-wing reaction." Most of the assembled delegates, sleek and well fed, yawned and politely applauded. For this was an NAM convention not the least bit introspective but one that was optimistic and ebullient. Business "confidence" had returned at last.

Strikes were marginal in wartime, but antilabor elements found that absenteeism would serve as almost as heavy a club. Congressman Rankin at one point assured the House that God had spared the life of Captain Eddie and sent him safely home to warn America of the dangers of absenteeism.

The nagging over absenteeism and the forty-hour week obscured the fact that American workers were laboring hard these days; indeed, had they not, there could have been no miracle of production. In a Midwestern shipyard, for instance, the average worker was putting in six days of nine hours each week, for a total of fifty-four hours. With time and a half unskilled men were earning $50 a week and craftsmen $80 a week. To keep men from drifting, a 5 percent Christmas bonus was given to men who stayed more than six months on the job. And there was extra pay for the graveyard shifts. Business grumbled, but it had no cause. Labor's cooperation was, like business's, being bought instead of compelled.

Workers in some instances waged their own campaigns against absenteeism. A young woman in a Portland shipyard refused to accept a date without seeing a man's time card for the previous week. Soon "No Work-No Woo" clubs came into existence. But the principal absentee fighting device was the lottery, run by management. Only workers with perfect attendance records could compete. The War Labor Board insisted that "loyalty cannot be bought." But business was willing to try. The prizes ran as high as $1,000 in cash.

The results of the lotteries as a check on absenteeism were mixed. And the nearer victory drew, the more the onus on strikes began to break down. With business clearly out to wring the last full measure of private gain from what was left of the war effort, labor felt entitled to do the same. Each blamed the other, of course. Labor also pointed angrily to the rising cost of living, which government had failed to curb and which business was helping promote by hampering the fight on inflation. The first big strike came with, naturally, a walkout of Lewis' miners when their contracts expired at the end of April, 1943.

Roosevelt and Lewis by now were waging a private war of their own. Lewis was cursed in every part of the nation, but American labor grudgingly conceded that his demands were fair. In both the AFL and CIO Roosevelt's patchwork attempts at economic stabilization were denounced as a fraud. The miners were obviously out for themselves, but they were also the spearhead of growing labor grievances.

Ickes, as fuel coordinator, assumed control of the 3,300 struck mines and ordered the Stars and Stripes to be flown at the entrance to each of them. He hinted darkly that soldiers might soon be sent in, and the miners jeered, "What will they do—dig coal with their bayonets?" Lewis proceeded to outmaneuver the President and publicly humiliated him by having his miners back at work minutes before Roosevelt went on the radio to plead with them to go back.

The miners felt their grievances strongly. They earned an average $40 a week for work that was dirty, difficult, dangerous and skilled. Workers in war industries made far more money for work that was easier and less dangerous. But the WLB, stung in its pride and doubtless remembering the fate of its predecessor, called Lewis a man who "gives aid and comfort to our enemies"—the classic definition of treason. They ordered him to negotiate with the mine operators. He flatly refused. Liberal intellectuals were furious. The *Nation* belabored Lewis, his miners and everyone who supported them: "The strike was irresponsible and unpatriotic and unjustified, *no matter what the miners' grievances* [My italics]." And *Stars and Stripes* chimed in: "Speaking for the American soldier—John L. Lewis, damn your coal-black soul."

Yet labor unrest neither began nor ended with the coal miners. In Akron, Ohio, some 50,000 rubber workers went on strike in May, 1943, until forced back to work by federal officials. Almost the entire record industry was shut down for nearly a year by a musicians' strike. And the threat of a railroad strike loomed over the whole war effort for the best part of three wartime years.

But still there was no settlement of the miners' strike, and Lewis set a deadline of October 31, 1943, for a new contract. Congress angrily and rapidly passed the Smith-Connally Labor Act. It banned strikes in defense-related industries, imposed a mandatory thirty-day cooling-off period, made organizing an illegal strike a federal offense and forbade union contributions to political parties. Roosevelt vetoed it. Congress promptly passed it again over his veto. "In doing so," reflected *Time*, "it dealt Franklin Roosevelt the most stinging rebuke of his entire career, his worst domestic defeat of World War II." Its significance lay in its being a signal that Congress and much of the nation were no longer confident that the President could effectively discharge his responsibilities at home.

Lewis' fertile brain was at work, however, seeking its ends by finesse rather than showdown. It had long been a grievance of miners the world over that they frequently had to work in mines where the coal face was miles from the pithead. They had to scurry, bent double like apes, for hours each day and were paid only for their time at the coal face. By 1943 the United States was virtually the only industrialized country where there was still no portal-to-portal pay. But Lewis managed to isolate a group of Illinois mineowners and get them to agree to such pay for his miners.

The WLB, which he had once called "a court packed against labor," slapped down the agreement, arguing that it violated Little Steel. To them, portal-to-portal pay was simply a hidden wage increase.

But Lewis still was able to negotiate a settlement of his original demand for a basic pay increase of "$2 a day—no more, no less." He got more, in fact, an extra 18 cents, and took it. Having been the man who killed off the NDMB, he was well on his way to destroying Little Steel. That formula had been loved at first by labor because it allowed raises up to 15 percent. Once the raises were granted, it became a ceiling, and business now loved it. So Lewis' victory was a victory for most of organized labor, which was, by the end of 1943, more restive than at any time since the summer of 1941.

Just before Christmas some railroad locals went on strike. Roosevelt hesitated, then seized all of the country's railroads. But 30 percent of the railwaymen stayed out on strike. Meanwhile, millions of his fellow countrymen were shaking their frozen fists at John L. Lewis. There was a huge coal shortage. Along the East Coast, where there was hardly any anthracite left for civilian consumption, millions of homes were dark and cold. People turned to Ickes for relief, and he lamented, "I'm not God." Then, he laughed. "We can fuel all of the people some of the time, and fuel some of the people all the time. But in war we can't fuel all of the people all of the time." The shortage was not entirely Lewis' fault; much of it was due to a labor shortage.

The railroad workers were meantime proving as obdurate as the miners. General Marshall cursed the rail strike as "the damnedest crime ever committed against America." But the railwaymen refused to yield. After three weeks of government control the lines were restored to their owners, and the strikers had won a settlement that skated all around the outer limits of Little Steel but technically could be held to be within it.

And by now the legitimacy of labor's grievances was grudgingly acknowledged even by the conservative press. *Life*, after berating irresponsible strikes, put the blame for labor unrest on "administration so bad that it amounts to bad faith."

Labor was constantly told that while it was nice and safe at home, men in uniform were suffering, that organized labor was a parasitic ingrate. But the dead and wounded in American industry exceeded the war dead and wounded in 1942–1943 by more than twenty to one, as inexperienced workers flocked into the factories to operate increasingly complex and dangerous machinery.

There was no little talk of the factories being full of draft dodgers. Yet factory walls were covered with posters urging workers not to enlist. Repeatedly they were told they could serve their country best by staying where they were. It was their patriotic responsibility to wait to be drafted. They were told such things by management and government. But no one bothered to tell the rest of the country. And while from Casablanca to D-Day there was a growing impression that war production was being hobbled by strikes, the time lost to strikes amounted to less than one-tenth of 1 percent of the time worked.

But even Roosevelt was by now unsympathetic to labor. He used his 1944 State of the Union address to call for a National Service Act. It was a call for work-or-fight. And under the circumstances it clearly cast labor as the villain, even though Roosevelt also wanted stiffer taxation of the rich, better food subsidies and effective price control. But it was hardly possible to argue that everyone must work, not when tens of thousands of workers were being laid off each week. At Brewster Aviation on Long Island the spring of 1944 brought the first genuine strike-to-work in the history of American labor. Four thousand workers protested being laid off and seized the factory. Embarrassed, federal officials came up with some make-work for them. But labor and business shuddered; the WPA might be resurrected yet.

Little wonder that American workers were looking toward victory with the most ambivalent emotions. Most expected the coming triumph to taste distinctly of ashes. The nearer victory drew, the more it depressed them. Women began to be forced out of the factories or simply quit, in rising numbers. With the future looking so bleak, men too started to tire of the long working hours. The level of output per worker was dropping, and the only corrective proved to be more money.

Employers, as well as workers, were becoming worried that the post-war era might indeed bring a return of massive unemployment, once the consumer-goods boom had burned up the savings. That, they believed, might be the last straw; it might really bring the end of free enterprise. So during the war they at last accepted, if not without grumbling, collective bargaining, union organizers, Social Security and almost anything else that might help to stabilize future labor relations. They even turned on the Smith-Connally Act because it was making labor militant again. Smith-Connally was quietly abandoned.

XXVII

Black Man, Brown Man

AMERICA'S abrasive racial heritage was working its way to a murderous pitch in the two years after Pearl Harbor. Ironically, the United States at the same time was doing more to redress inequalities than it had done for decades. But to a nation long grown accustomed to callousness, sensitivity was not easily or quickly acquired.

The *Saturday Evening Post* blithely started up a weekly cartoon series called "Ambitious Ambrose." Ambrose, a young Negro grocery clerk, was supposed to be funny because he was dim-witted, incompetent and unable to understand the ordinary requests of white people. The Red Cross routinely segregated blood supplies into "colored" and "white."* When the Treasury Department hired a Negro, William Pickens, who had just been graduated from Yale, the House on a secret vote approved an amendment that said "no part of any appropriation" could be used to pay Pickens' salary.

Negroes were told to put their trust in the FEPC, and when it scheduled public hearings into discrimination on the railroads, the Negro press and civil rights leaders gave it their blessing. But at the last possible moment the hearings were canceled by the War Manpower Commission, to the anger of millions of blacks. Not surprisingly a tense, uneasy feeling was in the air throughout 1942 that the entire country was heading toward some kind of showdown on race. *Time* tried to assure its white readers there was no need for alarm, that American Negroes were loyal to a "fighting democracy" even though they were themselves only "semi-citizens." But *Newsweek* was less certain and worried about the Black Muslims and other Negro cults.

As a counter to whatever incipient fifth column might have been lurking within the poisonous weeds which race hatred had fostered, government press agents mounted a noisy propaganda campaign. But as often as not their clumsy efforts backfired. A film produced by the OFF, for example, showed a battalion of Negro soldiers just a-diggin' and a-singin' away for victory and democracy. Whites loved it. Negroes hated it.

---

* This was especially galling, considering that blood plasma storage and transfusion was developed under, and the American Red Cross Blood Bank was created by, Dr. Charles Drew, a Negro.

Federal officials even flirted with censorship as they tried to head off disaster. Elmer Davis, the kindly, liberal head of the OWI, gave special commendations and favors to editors who minimized racial clashes. Those who reported them at length were told they were dabbling in treason. Negro newspapers were harassed by the FBI, and hints were dropped to their editors that they might find their paper ration had shrunk if they continued to publicize racial grievances.

But the crisis only grew. A famous Southern newspaper editor and civil rights champion was just one of many who saw what lay ahead when he wrote an article in January, 1943, called "Nearer and Nearer the Precipice." The United States was now, he said, on the brink of the worst race riots since 1919.

The combustibles for a social explosion were all about and trailing long fuses. But what would provide the spark? So far as one can tell in retrospect, the answer appears to be rumor. Some years ago in a famous work George Rudé showed how rumor turned the militant crowds of the French Revolution into murdering, rioting, bloodthirsty mobs. And race rumors were rampant in wartime.

Almost everyone had heard of the black sharecropper who, on December 8, 1941, was supposed to have said to his landlord, "Ah hear dem Japanese gone done dee-clare war on yo' white folks. That right?" All across the South there were rumors that when all the able-bodied white men had been drafted, the Negroes were planning to assuage the sexual desires of the women left behind. All kinds of rumors had Negroes working closely with the Japanese. Negroes were said to be holding the hands of white salesgirls in the five-and-dime stores on the pretext of accepting their change. And there were the ice pick rumors—e.g., "The niggers are buying up all the ice picks in town and just waiting for the first blackout."

Even the prointegration *New Republic* peddled race rumors. One of its editors angrily reported that prior to Pearl Harbor the Japanese were establishing sukiyaki cafés "wherever there are large numbers of Negroes." And A. Philip Randolph, he said, was going to undermine the war effort by mounting a massive campaign of civil disobedience in the fashion of Mahatma Gandhi.

There were also rumors of Negro cowardice in battle. One story, believed even by the Army's Chief of Staff, General Marshall, told how the 93d Division had made contact with a much smaller Japanese force at Bougainville, in the Solomons, and the entire division had utterly disintegrated once the shooting began. Thousands of Negro soldiers, the story went, had run into nearby caves and refused to fight.*

* The grain of truth here was that a company of green young soldiers were routed by a smaller force of Japanese veterans. The same thing happened, and on a much larger scale, to white soldiers at the Battle of Kasserine Pass in 1943 when they met the Afrika Korps.

There was also a rumor that Negro children were being taught to sing "America" to the following words:

> My country's tired of me
> I'm going to Germany
> Where I belong.

And pacing the rumors was a rash of bloody incidents. Just weeks after Pearl Harbor a mob in Sikeston, Missouri, dragged a Negro from the town jail while he was still suffering from three gunshot wounds inflicted by police. A rope was put around his neck and the free end tied to an automobile. The man was then dragged around town, screaming and kicking in the dust. Then, to the ecstatic cheers of an estimated 600 spectators, he was drenched with gasoline and burned to death.

When Negroes attempted to move into the Sojourner Truth housing project on the edge of an all-white Detroit neighborhood in the spring of 1942, hundreds of whites rioted, beating and stoning them. Police aided the rioters by turning their clubs on the blacks. Twenty people were injured, a hundred arrested—all of them black.

Bloody clashes at military posts were an almost daily occurrence. The dead and wounded ran into the scores. For all over the South white people were being confronted for the first time with Negroes who were not ignorant, terrified sharecroppers but men who were proud, literate and armed. Lynchings and beatings rose alarmingly. In a period of a few weeks in the fall of 1943 Mississippi alone admitted to being the site of three lynchings. But attempts to frighten Negroes back into subservience would work no longer, and the cycle of American race riots had come around once again.

The northward migration of Southerners into Detroit begun in 1914, when Henry Ford introduced the $5-a-day wage, had revived in the defense boom of 1941. And a year after Pearl Harbor Detroit was a city of transplanted Southerners of both races crammed hugger-mugger with Slavic immigrants. In all the United States nowhere were race tensions more venomous.

The Ku Klux Klan had flourished in the Motor City in recent years. The avowedly racist Southern Society boasted 16,000 paying members. After Huey Long's assassination his Fundamentalist, racist crony Gerald L. K. Smith had moved to Detroit. Father Coughlin's headquarters were in one of its suburbs. Though the leadership of the powerful UAW was antiracist, the white rank and file was emphatically not. And wartime congestion set whites and blacks at each other's throats all over the city.

The first months of 1943 brought racial clashes in different parts of the country. Fighting between white and Negro gangs in Newark, New Jersey, left one Negro dead and several wounded; four Negroes were severely beaten by a mob in Philadelphia; a race riot in Centreville, Mississippi, left one black soldier dead; a riot involving white and Negro soldiers in El Paso resulted in two deaths; in Marianna, Florida, a Negro twice tried for, and acquitted of, the murder of a white man was lynched by a mob; at Camp Stewart, Georgia, black soldiers and white MP's fought a gun battle that left one MP dead, four others wounded.

A race riot broke out in Mobile, Alabama, when a dozen black welders at the shipyard were promoted. Thousands of white shipyard workers went on a rampage, beating up the black workers, severely injuring twenty. In Beaumont, Texas, a rumor ran through the shipyard there that the wife of a white worker had been raped by a Negro. A mob descended on the city jail, discovered that no suspect had been apprehended, armed itself with guns, clubs, hammers and crowbars and then went on a rampage through the nearby black slum. Peaceful Negroes were dragged from their homes and beaten; their businesses were looted and burned. Two blacks were killed; more than fifty were badly injured. And after the riot had run its course, a doctor found no evidence to support the claim of the woman who said she had been raped.

On June 13, 1943, a riot broke out in the Detroit suburb of Inkster Park when several hundred youths of both races fought a pitched battle with fists and rocks. Two days later an amusement park in the suburb of East Detroit was the scene of a similar outbreak.

The following Sunday, June 20, was a very hot day, with temperatures over 90°. As Detroiters do even now on such a day, tens of thousands of them flocked to Belle Isle, the 1,000-acre island in the Detroit River. Perspiring blacks and whites were pressed together at a density of 100 or more to the acre.

Scuffles broke out all afternoon, and when evening descended, it was a tired, angry crowd that jostled its way over the bridge connecting the island to the city. Tempers flared; fights broke out. By 11 P.M. a number of the fights had coalesced into a free-for-all, and it was spilling from the bridge into downtown. The police moved in and started to bring the fighting under control.

At this point, however, a rumor swept along the riverside and into the Negro ghetto. Here was a dirty, overcrowded area of sixty square blocks with the preposterous name of Paradise Valley. It was a miserable slum that could be smelled from afar, for thousands of Negro homes were served by outdoor toilets perched precariously over sluices running off into the sewer mains. The rumor which now swept through the slum late on a Sunday night was that a group of white men had killed a Negro woman and her baby on Belle Isle bridge, then thrown their mutilated bodies into the river. By midnight thousands of angry blacks were pouring into the downtown area, thirsting for revenge.

For the rest of the night the riot spread. The mayor, the governor, the police and federal officials bickered while the beatings, killings and looting mounted. By Monday afternoon Negroes were being hunted down on the streets of Detroit and brutally murdered to squeals of delight from sidewalk crowds. Rarely did the police intervene to trap any Negro luckless enough to be caught. When they broke up gatherings of whites, they used tear gas; on blacks they used guns. Some seventeen Negroes were shot by the police; all were accused of "looting." Whites were looting, burning and killing. Not one was shot by police. Only when soldiers arrived was the riot brought under control. There were 35 dead, more than 700 wounded and 1,300 arrested.

In its aftermath the mayor blamed it all on Detroit's Negroes. They had, he reported, set out to destroy white-owned property and kill white people. He concluded, "The white people were slow to get started, but when they did get started they sure made up for lost time." Michigan's governor set up his own commission to look into the riot, and its report concurred with the mayor's. It placed the entire blame on the city's Negroes, especially local black leaders and the local black press.

The bloody glow cast by the Detroit riot obscured the other racial clashes that broke out in its wake, in El Paso and Port Arthur, Texas; in Springfield, Massachusetts; in Hubbard, Ohio; and in Harlem, where a rumor of police brutality triggered a riot that left six dead and scores injured. But there was one riot that it did not overshadow, and that was in Los Angeles two weeks earlier. The victims there were not so much black as brown.

For decades the city had ignored the Mexican-American ghetto sprawling along its eastern edge. And roaming the ghetto in wartime were more than three dozen gangs of pachucos.* Most of these young thugs wore zoot suits. They wore their hair long. Usually they were poor, unemployed, self-styled tough guys.

When racial tensions rose all over the country in the frantic, fearful months after Pearl Harbor, the two major Los Angeles newspapers, both of them part of the Hearst chain, whipped up a mythical Mexican crime wave on the front pages. The mayor leaped aboard the crime-wave bandwagon and called for a crackdown. The city council passed an ordinance making it a crime to wear a zoot suit. Soon heavily armed police units were sweeping into the East Los Angeles *barrio* at all hours, making mass arrests and sudden searches. Possession of anything remotely resembling a

---

* Pachuco has been defined as (1) "an underworld character, originally a marijuana runner" or (2) a slang term for Mexican toughs who came to Los Angeles by way of El Paso. In either case it referred to young Mexicans on the fringes of society, who often took to petty crime and had a penchant for violence.

dangerous weapon (*e.g.*, a beer can opener) was put down as evidence of criminal intent, and local judges agreed. The county sheriff justified the wholesale arrests and calculated terror by arguing that Mexicans had "a biological pre-disposition to criminal tendencies" because the Aztecs practiced human sacrifice. And throughout the city insulting signs quickly proliferated, reading: SE SERVE SOLAMENTE A RAZA BLANCA.

Then, on August 2, 1942, a young Mexican named José Díaz was found lying by a dirt road on the outskirts of the city. There was no proof of foul play; indeed, his injuries suggested an automobile accident. But Díaz died without regaining consciousness, and the Los Angeles Police Department used his corpse as an excuse for a new round of terror. Twenty-two Mexican gang members frequenting a scummy pond called Sleepy Lagoon near where Diaz's body was found were arrested and charged with his death. Confessions were beaten from most of them.

Two, however, had the sense to ask for a separate trial and hired a former district attorney to defend them. The case against them, which was the same as the case against the rest, was promptly dropped for lack of evidence. Their twenty less sensible friends were prosecuted. Twelve were convicted of murder and sentenced to life imprisonment in San Quentin. Five were convicted of manslaughter and received lesser sentences. Three were put on probation. Two years would pass before this travesty of justice was reversed.

Meanwhile, Los Angeles was rocked by the worst riot in a generation. In the first week of June, 1943, a rumor ran through the downtown area that a gang of pachucos had beaten up a sailor and run into a movie theater. Within minutes a mob of soldiers and sailors was forming, and egged on by cheering crowds, it plunged into the movie theaters and cafés, dragging out scores of zoot-suited Mexican youths. Their clothes were ripped off; they were beaten into bloody insensibility and were arrested for indecency and vagrancy. The following night the same pattern of attacks was repeated. And the night after that. And the night after that. By this time, however, few Mexican adolescents would leave the *barrio* at night. For want of victims the violence played itself out. But other California cities, such as Pasadena, Long Beach and San Diego, had similar "zoot suit riots" in the days that followed.

Among the spectators in Los Angeles was one serviceman at least who was disgusted. "I could find nothing to distinguish the behavior of our soldiers from the behavior of Nazi storm-troop thugs beating up outnumbered non-Aryans," he wrote. And he saw it for what it was: Disgruntled servicemen were venting their personal frustrations on social outcasts. "This is a form of class war."

The riots put the cities with large black or brown populations on edge for the rest of the war. Cleveland, Chicago, Pittsburgh, Oakland, St. Louis, each wondered when its riot would begin. They, and more than 200 other cities and towns, hastily set up interracial committees to work on social problems, thus creating a grass-roots concern with racial equality unprecedented since Reconstruction. Even the city of Los Angeles was sufficiently shaken to call off the police terror, and a score of interracial bodies were set up to diminish the tensions.

In Detroit, too, there were efforts to seek reconciliation. The police had a mandatory six hours of instruction on the social problems of Paradise Valley. Scores of religious, civic and educational groups sprang up to promote racial tolerance. An Inter-Racial Fellowship brought leading blacks and whites together each month.

At the same time the riot squad, much enlarged and more impressively armed, ostentatiously practiced on Belle Isle every week with its rifles, bayonets, machine guns and tear gas grenades. The fundamental problem in jobs, housing, education, health and the legal system had not yet been solved. But something had been gained, nevertheless—a breathing space.

Negroes had endured job discrimination from generation to generation. During the Depression, when millions of white people were out of work, it was somehow a little easier to accept. But the attempts to freeze Negroes out of the 1940–1941 defense boom had roused them as almost nothing else could, for then even industries which had formerly hired Negroes began, in their fears over growing Negro militancy, to adopt discriminatory hiring policies.

And when they sought redress, Negroes were told to appeal to the FEPC. But the canceled railroad hearings completely undercut that body before it managed to establish its credit with blacks. Its chairman had resigned in protest, and for six months no one would take the job. Washington wits joked of raffling it off on *Horace Heidt's Treasure Chest*, a radio giveaway show.

Eventually Roosevelt was forced to create a second FEPC, naming a Catholic monsignor of impeccable liberal credentials its chairman. Like its luckless predecessor, it began its career under the direct control of the White House. And this time, business was better represented, labor less so.

But most businessmen were still hostile to hiring Negroes, even with the labor shortage. Only where direct pressure was brought to bear did Negroes get into war industries. As a food contractor explained, "We were shoved into hiring Negroes. The Quartermaster said the soldiers were hungry, so we didn't dilly dally." And those plants which bowed to the FEPC or the NAACP or some other pressure group often did so along segregated lines. The Kingsbury Ordnance Plant in Indiana, for example, constructed entirely with federal money, had a production line set aside exclusively for Negro workers. Toilets were of two kinds, white and "Colored." In case of air raids Negroes had to go to a BOMB SHELTER—COLORED ONLY.

Yet Negroes continued to press to get into the factories; they still migrated from South to North in search of work, drying up the traditional Southern pool of cheap black labor. An editorial in the Ruston, Louisiana, *Leader* expressed the bitterness of the masters they were leaving behind: "Numbers of good Negro workmen have left . . . and the hardship they are putting on us who need them is going to ruin this section of the nation. . . . The bad part about this is that the very best of our Negroes are leaving. Those we have educated and trained to be useful. . . ."

Slowly and angrily Negroes continued to force a way into the war industries. By the time war production reached its peak in the late fall of 1943 a million had made the breakthrough. Almost without exception they were employed as unskilled labor, even if they were skilled. They were hardly ever promoted. Negroes hired into war production in the First World War were the first fired at war's end; everyone assumed that would happen again. But for the time being many a wall had been breached.

The military involved an identical pattern: mounting pressure, resistance, then concessions grudgingly made. Neither Knox nor Stimson had the least sympathy with Negroes' demands. The Army pressed ahead with separate-but-equal until it produced the ultimate absurdity: an all-Negro invasion. When American forces went ashore in North Africa in November, 1942, a small detachment of black soldiers was given a landing of their own, in Liberia. They were to set up an air base. With not a hostile native in sight they waded ashore from landing craft, armed to the teeth. And to underscore the point, Roosevelt proceeded to Liberia after reviewing white soldiers at Casablanca and reviewed the Negro soldiers who were building the airfield.

Disgusted, William H. Hastie meantime resigned his position as aide to Stimson, vehemently protesting the continued segregation in the armed forces and scorning the sops and pacifiers.

Not until 1944, when rising casualty lists and the general manpower shortage conjoined, did the military begin to relent. The Navy, the Air Corps, the Marines had all accepted only a minimal number of Negro volunteers. Draft boards regularly inducted whites ahead of Negroes, even those who were single and healthy. By the end of 1943, however, whites were grumbling about such policies. Even Southern Congressmen were complaining that minimizing Negro enlistments was an intolerable form of racial discrimination. From this point to the end of the war Negroes were taken into the military in numbers reflecting their population base. And the military was forced to make major concessions to the influx of black troops.

The Army put a stop to segregation in PX's, recreation facilities, troop trains and troop ships. With the European battles in their final months it experimented by putting black and white platoons side by side in combat and discovered that even this timid step toward integration worked a revolution in the combat performance of black soldiers. The Marines meantime accepted 20,000 black recruits, intending to put them into service units, but the corps was so combat-oriented that it absentmindedly started to ignore its own policy before the war ended. Yet nowhere were the changes more striking than in the Navy.

A Negro mess attendant named Dorie Miller manned an antiaircraft gun at Pearl Harbor and, exposing himself to danger, brought down a Japanese plane. Awarded the Navy Cross, Miller had made mockery of the premise on which the Navy accepted Negroes only as mess attendants. Grudgingly, the Navy started to accept more black recruits—and put most of them to work at the dirty, dangerous service jobs such as ammunition handling. But Negroes pressed hard for real changes, pointing to the example of the Royal Navy, which had commissioned a black officer from Jamaica.

When the Liberty ship *Booker T. Washington* was launched by Marian Anderson in September, 1942, her captain was another native of the British West Indies, Hugh Mulzac. The U.S. Navy commissioned a destroyer escort in 1943 and named it the *Harmon* after a Negro sailor who had perished heroically at the battle of Guadalcanal. It put more Negro sailors in combat jobs. And before 1943 ended, the Navy agreed to commission black officers. By the end of the war it had commissioned fifty-eight of them. If anything it was by then less Jim Crow than the Army.

The Coast Guard had gone even further, commissioning 700 Negro officers and accepting, 4,000 Negro recruits. And in the Merchant Marine, which in 1942 and 1943 saw more danger than any of the military services, integration had been accomplished. Negroes saw the Merchant Marine as irrefutable proof that equal treatment elicited equal performance.

The wartime militancy of American blacks annoyed many, perhaps most, white people. "Mobilization had rubbed the nation's race problem raw," grumbled *Time*:

> Pinko agitators, self-styled liberals and other citizens of goodwill had plucked at the sore. The thin-skinned and irritable Negro press, which has seldom missed a report of injustice to Negro troops and has played it for all it would stand, continued to print . . . sensational and baseless yarns. . . .

Newsweek was still able to stand criticism on its head and turn it into praise—*e.g.*, "The history of bigotry in this country can also be called the battle *against* bigotry. . . . Never has intolerance gained a hold over the majority of the American people as it has over other peoples of the earth." But by 1944 it was plain to most people, as the editors of *Life* concluded, that "America's No. 1 social problem, its great, uncured, self-inflicted wound, is aching violently, perhaps reaching a crisis."

White champions of civil rights found the current pace too brisk and some began to fall back. One, a noted newspaper editor, angrily attacked the militancy of Roy Wilkins and A. Philip Randolph; he called the Negro press "rabid" and assailed the extremists who were demanding "an overnight revolution in race relations—that is, complete social equality." Another Southern liberal cautioned that those who proposed to use federal power to break down discrimination were running the gravest risks. "Let them beware. I have no doubt that in such an event . . . the country would be swept by civil war."

It was at this juncture, in 1944, that Gunnar Myrdal's massive, historic study *An American Dilemma* appeared. Myrdal's work summarized the findings of seventy-five assistants who had studied the race problem for five years. America's great failure on race was its failure to turn its precepts into practice, they found; it was a failure of public morality. The dilemma in which the United States was caught, said Myrdal, was between what it said and what it did.

Myrdal's work offered little cause for optimism that once the country's attention was drawn to its moral shortcomings, it would produce an effective response. For he found a historic pattern of responses to moral failure —passing new laws. Inept public administration and waning public interest soon made the new laws unworkable. The result was a new layer of bureaucracy, no resolution of the original problem and a rise in contempt for the authority of law as it became unworkable. "In principle the Negro problem was solved long ago; in practice the solution is not yet effectuated." Nor did it seem likely to be, so far as Myrdal could tell.

For though a tiny black middle class was coming into existence, it was shut off from normal contact with white society just as rigorously as were poor blacks. Poor blacks in turn were themselves starting to become self-conscious. As they did so, they demanded racial separation. Myrdal glumly concluded that postwar race relations would tend to even greater social separation than in the past. He placed little faith in the legalist, integrationist program of the Urban League and the NAACP. Yet Myrdal, for reasons he could not fully explain himself, felt optimistic that America would somehow manage to resolve its racial dilemma.

The militancy of blacks these days certainly did not encourage optimism, though we can see now that it should have. The constant talk of the war being fought for democracy grated on most Negroes as so much hypocrisy. Yet the war was the culmination of the development of a global racial awareness. Negroes hotly argued the case for Indian independence. A black journalist was forcefully struck that "Whereas for years Negroes have felt that their position was isolated and unalterable, some of them are beginning to feel that dark people throughout the world will soon be on the march."

New leaders, new tactics, new organizations had come into existence. When Randolph's March on Washington Movement called off the march set for July, 1941, it did not simply fold up. It went on to launch the modern phase of the struggle for equality. Before MOWM the civil rights movement had been integrated; it was essentially an extension of the New Deal, with no mass base among poor blacks. But Garvey had stirred the Negro masses, they had been made militant, and MOWM was able to build on that foundation. It captured the imagination of American Negroes. At first it was, unlike other civil rights groups, entirely black. From Gandhi it took the techniques of passive resistance.

To continue to protest injustice after Pearl Harbor posed a dilemma: "They wanted something more pointed than a warning but less dangerous than a march." The solution was a series of massive public rallies wherever a large population of Negroes was to be found. All across the country in the summer of 1942 MOWM held its rallies. But it could not keep them up indefinitely. And the prospects for the ultimate weapon—the march on Washington—dimmed as the war ran on. MOWM disintegrated.

But it was not a failure; far from it. The struggle for equality had finally struck out along the path of independent political action with the support of ordinary black people. A proving ground had been provided for a new corps of leaders and organizers. A new generation of young Negroes, college-educated and militant, was coming along to push even harder. Since the First World War the number of Negroes in college had increased fifteen-fold, from 3,000 to 45,000. There was the vigilant Negro press, which had been but a shadow a generation before. There was even a charismatic new leader emerging to stand where Garvey had stood, Adam Clayton Powell, Jr.

Powell was the son of the pastor of Harlem's enormous Abyssinian Baptist Church. He was tall, muscular and handsome, and women swooned in his presence, calling him "Mr. Jesus." While still in his early thirties, Powell rose during the war with all the speed his advantages allowed. He was, to all appearances, virtually white, with blue eyes, an aquiline nose and straight light-brown hair. Negroes laughingly called him their own "Great White Hope." Yet, said the editor of Harlem's *Amsterdam Star-News*, there was another side to Powell's lightness: "Being *white* he constantly has to prove that he's a *Negro*." Before the war ended, Powell was in Congress, taking all American Negroes for his constituency.

The gains derived from the new techniques, leaders, organizations, race consciousness and militancy were often small, unimpressive in themselves, but the cumulative effect was devastating. No important part of American life went untouched.

The change was literally visible. Before 1941 Hollywood turned out an all-Negro film once every three or four years. Before the war ended, it was turning out that many each year. And in other films, such as *The Ox-Bow Incident*, Negroes were being portrayed intelligently in serious roles. *In This Our Life* showed a young Negro chauffeur struggling against discrimination as he tried to study law. The Negro press was even able to keep MGM from making a film version of *Uncle Tom's Cabin* because it would serve as a painful reminder of slavery.

Broadway went the way of Hollywood. The toast of the 1943 season was Paul Robeson, starring in *Othello*. The glittering first-night audience gave him a twenty-minute standing ovation and ten curtain calls, making it one of the legendary Broadway stage debuts. Meanwhile, two all-black productions, *Carmen Jones* and *Anna Lucasta*, settled in for long runs.

In 1944 a Negro journalist was admitted to Presidential press conferences for the first time, over the fierce opposition of the White House Correspondents' Association. The Supreme Court opened up party primaries to black voters, reversing a ruling of just a few years before that primary voting was a privilege, not a right. Even the most lily-white bastions of society were crumbling. The Daughters of the American Revolution had refused to let Marian Anderson sing in Constitution Hall in 1939. She sang there on behalf of war relief in January, 1943, to an integrated audience that was one-third black. The American Bar Association similarly bid adieu to Jim Crow. In 1943 it admitted its first Negro member since 1912 and explicitly dropped its longtime policy of racial discrimination.

Ordinary Negroes were feeling the benefits of the new militancy and new sensitivity long before the war ended. The skills, the wages, the work opportunities of Negroes had all been transformed. The number of black workers in manufacturing had jumped from 500,000 to 1,200,000 in only three years. The number of Negroes in labor unions was more than 500,000. The number of Negroes in government had gone from 50,000 in 1939 to 200,000 five years later.

Negroes were leaving the South in droves, moving into the big cities of the North and Far West. San Francisco saw its tiny, prewar black population increase to more than 20,000, and it was still rising as the war ended.

Public institutions began to break down racial barriers. At San Quentin, prison officials integrated the mess hall. The 1,100 white prisoners at first refused to eat with Negroes. But after being served meals in their cells, they changed their minds. Racial tensions in the prison dropped. An anthropology professor, Hortense Powdermaker, wrote a textbook, called *Probing Our Prejudices*, which taught that racism was cruel, insidious and indefensible. Thousands of schools adopted it. Some big-city school districts, such as

Chicago, revised elementary-school textbooks to include chapters on black history and culture.

Negroes remained unimpressed by the FEPC, which Senator Theodore "The Man" Bilbo insisted was encouraging "the Negro's dream of social equality and intermarriage." It was supposed to produce jobs, and most black workers thought it had failed. Yet before the war ended, it was becoming genuinely effective. For five days in the summer of 1944 Philadelphia was paralyzed by a strike of streetcar motormen protesting the promotions of eight Negroes. The city's 1,600 streetcars, 600 buses and 500 railway carriages which took 1,000,000 people into and out of the city each day were stopped.

Second only to Detroit as a center of war production, Philadelphia's paralysis was a national crisis. And racial tensions, already high, became inflammable. Outbreaks of violence produced hundreds of arrests. Despite pleas to their patriotism, the strikers stayed out, one leader complaining, "Colored people have bedbugs. I don't want any bedbugs." A young Negro Muslim went over to Independence Hall and despairingly threw a heavy paperweight at the Liberty Bell, sobbing to its mournful resonance, "Liberty Bell, oh, Liberty Bell—liberty that's a lot of bunk!" He was seized and placed under psychiatric observation.

Only when 8,000 heavily armed soldiers moved in was the strike broken. Tensions remained high for months; for the first time in nearly twenty years Philadelphia police carried nightsticks. Would-be strikers passed out cards on the street reading:

FRANKLIN TO ELEANOR
You kiss the Niggers
I'll kiss the Jews
And we'll stay in the White House
As long as we choose.

But the FEPC had nonetheless won its first great victory. Eight Philadelphia streetcars were now being driven by Negroes, and rather than have a repetition of this showdown, the city opened up more and more jobs to blacks.

Once it had shown what it could do, civil rights groups fought to turn the FEPC into a permanent government agency. Its writ ran only to industries affecting the war effort, and its mandate was for the duration only. But by 1945 Negroes were insisting that it not be allowed to expire.

Senator Bilbo led the Congressional campaign against a permanent FEPC, telling his colleagues in the Senate, "If you go through the government departments there are so many niggers it's like a black cloud all around you. . . . The niggers and the Jews of New York are working hand in hand on this damnable, Communist, poisonous piece of legislation." Mississippi's other Senator, James Eastland, seconded him. "We are dealing with an inferior race . . . They will not fight. They will not work."

The FEPC's last wartime appropriation was for less than half the amount the administration had requested, and it was hinted that it might use the money to liquidate itself. But elsewhere the pressure for a permanent FEPC was growing. New York State created one of its own. Some twenty other states were beginning to do the same before the war ended.

And with more than 1,000,000 black veterans about to return from military service it was simple prudence not to have them come back to racism as usual; to allow that was to risk a national catastrophe that would eclipse the bloody riots of 1919. This time, however, there was the GI Bill. Negroes were entitled to the same educational, medical, business, homeownership assistance as other veterans. The VA solemnly pledged itself to a "Four Freedoms" policy for returning black servicemen, swearing in four different ways not to discriminate.

No one had expected it, and no one intended it, but the war had been the watershed of the postemancipation struggle for equality. These were the years when American Negroes began for the first time to fight for their rights effectively and independently. Their relationship to white America had undergone a fundamental change. Here was where the modern civil rights movement began; here was where it scored its first important victories.

Superficially, parallels could be drawn with the earlier war. Government tried to purchase loyalties with tokens. But this time it was forced to pay a fair price. And what a difference in results! This war would leave no trail of race riots in its wake; it would give the KKK no chance to return to power in the South; it would not leave ordinary black people as poor as they were before the war—indeed, something of a health revolution had increased the life expectancy of Negroes by approximately five years. A quarter of a million black veterans were going to attend college under the GI Bill. And hope stirred people's hearts where once was black despair: No other part of American society was as confident as Negroes were that young men now had a better chance to get ahead than their fathers had had.

There are eminent scholars who argue that in war interest groups are rewarded for their participation. But in a total war no important segment is allowed not to participate. And in the earlier war American Negroes constituted more than 10 percent of the armed forces; in this war they were 8 percent—a difference really of 25 percent. Yet the gains this time were far greater. To what, then, are we to attribute the difference?

It might be put down to a more tender social conscience. But that is unlikely, given the experience of the Japanese and Nisei, the rise in anti-Semitism, the increased callousness toward the bombing of civilians. What

Negroes had won was due to militancy doubly armed with organization and justice.

The wartime gains were enhanced and consolidated by growing political and organizational strengths. There was, as we have seen, a national Negro press. Where there had been one black Congressman, there were two after 1944. All across the South whites and Negroes were joining together at the local level under the Southern Regional Council. In 1944 the American Council on Race Relations was established in Chicago and set up biracial organizations across the Midwest. Two years before, Negroes and white pacifists had created the Congress of Racial Equality. Since then it had pressed for integration by adopting the militant, nonviolent tactics of Gandhi's *satyagraha* campaign against British rule in India. Older, less militant organizations had also grown strong in the war years. The Urban League tripled in size. The NAACP did even better. It had 50,000 members and 355 branches in 1940; by the end of the war it had nearly 500,000 members and more than 1,000 branches.

This, then, was the way in which the gap between belief and practice was narrowed: by the pressure tactics of an organized interest group. And the means whereby the gains were made helped assure that they could not be taken away when the war ended. Perhaps the gap would not be fully closed; even now no one can be sure that it will be. But the war had brought a historic narrowing—the greatest since the slaves were freed.

XXVIII

Social Welfare, the American Way

WE have seen how the war had ushered in a massive revival of conservative interests, especially of big business and the military. At their feet were strewn the corpses of most New Deal programs and ambitions. Whatever surplus energies the country possessed would evidently go into defeating the Axis, instead of reducing social inequities. There was also an inclination to consider war abnormal, a form of social pathology, which lent its fruits an aura of shaky impermanence. What hope then of real social change?

No one could fail to be conscious of the widespread social dislocations of wartime. Total war is itself a social crisis which regiments society while cutting people adrift from normal emotional and ethical moorings. More than 16,000,000 people were physically set in motion as they went off in search of jobs or loved ones. Most of these wartime migrants were women. Another 16,000,000, nearly all men, left their homes and went into the Army and Navy.

There was also a vague but pervasive idea that the revival of the economy had given everyone a job and made social reform unnecessary, even though there were still at least 20,000,000 people living on poverty-level incomes in the fall of 1943. Social welfare programs, like food stamps, were meanwhile being cut back. Yet here was the other side of the grand paradox of wartime: This was a period of massive social change, including a quantum leap in social welfare. It was hidden or at least heavily disguised, but it was nonetheless real and its effects were long-lasting, as this chapter—which treats of social problems, social welfare and social change —will show.

Generally speaking, social welfare is half the world of governmental responsibility (the other half being national defense). But it conveniently breaks into four interlocking parts: education, housing, health and social insurance. This latter comes down to programs of social security and direct relief for the distressed. In all four areas (only three of which are discussed here, education being treated separately) the war had the greatest consequences. But, as with so much else, we must first take a brief look at the years before the war—specifically at the New Deal's achievements and limitations—in order to comprehend the importance and the scope of what now occurred.

The question of how much desirable social change had been effected from 1933 to 1939 is endlessly debatable. The orthodox view of its admirers was expressed by Frederick Lewis Allen two decades ago: The New Deal "had repealed the Iron Law of Wages. We had brought about a virtually automatic redistribution of incomes from the well-to-do to the less well-to-do. . . . We had discovered a new frontier to open up: the purchasing power of the poor. That, it seems to me, is the essence of the Great American Discovery." (As we shall see, Allen was not only wrong, but far more wrong than he ever realized.)

A less starry-eyed but still sympathetic view of the New Deal's major accomplishments makes, at best, a short list: welfare as a right; Social Security provisions for the old, the disabled and the unemployed; a minimum wage for millions of workers; bank and stock market regulation; smashing the near monopoly on government of the propertied elements— usually WASP's—by bringing Negroes, workers and ethnic minorities into national politics; and forging the tools to avoid future depressions. But the limitations are obvious: Minimum wages are frequently more a ceiling than a floor; in 1939 there was one Negro in Congress; only a third of the nation was covered by Social Security; and who, even now, can guarantee there will never be another depression?

Yet many good things were done, and were done in a swirling environment of social experiment and innovation. The federal government directly subsidized thousands of artists, writers, actors and musicians. With federal money about 200 cooperative living projects were set up, over conservative grumbling that they were "soviets." The Solicitor General, Robert Jackson, had affronted conservative sensibilities even further by demanding legal aid for the poor, a proposal called "socialized law" by the president of the American Bar Association, who attributed it to the workings of "Termites in the temple of justice."

The federal government had launched a modest school-lunch program in 1935 that less than ten years later was feeding 9,000,000 schoolchildren at least one hot meal each day. Federal and local authorities split the cost, and the PTA, the Junior League, the American Legion and others provided labor and equipment. There was no discrimination in the program, and in the poorest areas breakfast was often available, too.

Nor had the innovations ended when the war began. In November, 1939, the federal food stamp program had begun, to popular approval. On the first of January, 1940, the new Social Security System mailed out the first 900,000 old age pension checks. But no one believed that the Depression had been beaten; only the most fervent New Dealers thought it was about to be. When people were asked late in 1939, "Do young men have a better chance to get ahead now than they had thirty years ago?" by a margin of three to one they chose "30 years ago."

For despite the impassioned efforts of recent years, the foundations of pessimism were unshaken. In 1937 Roosevelt had seen one-third of a nation ill-clothed, ill-housed, ill-fed. Two years later the chairman of the New York city housing authority saw 40 percent. In terms of housing alone, it was possibly even higher, for half of U.S. housing was substandard, and Congress turned back a proposal for a major assault on the housing problem in 1939. Moreover, average weekly earnings in industry and agriculture were lower in 1939 than they had been in 1937.

More disheartening still was the pattern of income distribution. What redistribution occurred under the New Deal chiefly benefited the comfortable middle class and the very top income groups—that is, the top 5 percent. Middle-class families who held onto their homes and their regular incomes had, given the depressed prices of the 1930's, enjoyed a substantial increase in their standard of living. For them, the Depression was something to read about or look at from a distance. In the country as a whole income had been more fairly apportioned in 1918 than it was twenty years later:

Shares of National Income	1918	1929	1937
Lowest Fifth	6.8	5.4	3.6
Second Fifth	12.6	10.1	10.4
Third Fifth	14.6	14.4	15.7
Fourth Fifth	18.3	17.9	21.8
Highest Fifth	47.4	51.3	48.5

It may be asked, did not the system of relief to the unemployed make up in benefits what was lost in cash income? It seems a fair assumption that it did not and never could. For the answer to unemployment was not relief, but jobs.

Before the Depression, systematic succor was extended primarily to the "deserving poor"—the temporarily unemployed but responsible, hardworking family man; the physically handicapped, such as the blind; and survivors—that is, widows and orphans. This was relief rooted in private charity and local control, tracing directly back to the poor laws of Elizabethan England. Almost last among industrialized Western nations did the United States enact permanent social legislation based frankly on the principle of governmental responsibility to alleviate the sufferings regularly visited on those least able to bear them by the mysterious workings of business cycles which no one knew how to regulate.

But by 1939 a new system had been developed, holding out five kinds of relief: general relief—that is, cash allowances for food and other necessities; aid to dependent children; old age insurance; aid to the blind; and public works employment. In all, some 16,500,000 people were receiving some kind of relief in 1939, and the number was rising.

Most of these measures were simply prudent. For a Western nation, none of them was exceptional. But in the popular imagination the public works programs came, in later years, to dwarf the other relief programs. And it is true that the Works Progress Administration built thousands of useful schools, post offices, bridges and dams. The Civilian Conservation Corps planted 2 billion trees and saved millions of acres of land from destruction. But all this obscured two important facts. First, public works were not an innovation of the New Deal; in fact, more money was spent on public construction each year under Hoover than the New Deal public works projects approached except at their peak. This points to the second —that despite New Deal public works, the country was losing ground each year: America was physically running down, falling apart, decaying.

New Construction (in billions of dollars)	1929	1930	1933	1939
Public	2.39	2.75	1.00	2.44
Private	7.52	5.31	1.22	3.62

And the drop in private construction showed no prospect of being closed for many years, if ever.

The central problem, of massive unemployment, was so profound that not until mid-1943—after a year and a half of defense crisis and another year and a half of war production—was full employment achieved. If it took four years with these stimulants, it is reasonable to suppose that it would have taken much longer without them.

And no sooner had recovery seemed imminent than conservative elements were at work trying to lay the ghost of the New Deal. We have seen how throughout the war a large and powerful bloc in Congress forced the dismantling of New Deal agencies and programs with a zest born of bitterness.

The CCC was abolished at the end of 1941. Two years later Roosevelt gave the WPA what he lightly called "an honorable discharge." The National Youth Authority survived only as a vocational training program for war industries. The National Labor Relations Board was in a state of suspended animation. The Agricultural Adjustment Agency was a prize trophy of conservative interests. The Justice Department stopped its trust-busting attacks on monopolies. The SEC had merged into the Wall Street Establishment. Almost without exception New Deal agencies were dead, dying or under a cloud, including even the free lunch program. Selective Service had demonstrated that young men from homes where the diet was poor provided most of the physical rejects. But Congress slashed the subsidies for the school lunch program to the bone. It was pointless, as well as cruel, for free lunches had improved health standards, school attendance, learning and discipline. Hungry children have never made alert or orderly pupils. But conservatives argued that there was no longer a food surplus to go into these subsidized meals; that there were now plenty of jobs, and parents should be able to take care of children themselves; that free meals undermined the spirit of free enterprise.

Congressional conservatives were meantime dismantling the Home Owners Loan Corporation. When the HOLC had been established in 1933, foreclosures were running at a rate approaching 1,000 a day. Ten years later it was 58 percent liquidated, and with a loss rate of only 2 percent there was every likelihood that before much longer the HOLC would liquidate itself entirely, with no overall loss, perhaps with a small profit, to the taxpayers. As if to indicate that what was involved in the dismantling of the New Deal was more than ideology, the savings and loans associations and the banks forced the HOLC to wind up its business in short order. By putting the HOLC out of business, many thousands of weak loans were foreclosed, at a cost to the taxpayers of hundreds of millions of dollars. Then the sound loans were refinanced by the banks and others, at higher rates. With Congress' help a public agency was forced to commit suicide for private gain. Even the president of the New York Stock Exchange was willing to concede these days that "There is a conservative reaction in progress."

Conservatives were strong enough by now to easily turn aside any attempt to reintroduce overt social reform. In 1939 Roosevelt had created a National Resources Planning Board to make a long-range study of work relief and Social Security programs. Almost everyone had forgotten it, until late in 1942, when it issued its report. There was general anticipation that it would parallel Britain's Beveridge Report, which, when adopted, had committed that country's government to the creation of a postwar welfare state.

Using the NRPB report as a springboard, Roosevelt early in 1943 sent his recommendations to Congress. The second part of his proposals followed some weeks later. Together, they formed a whole that was both vast and vague. Rarely did he ask for anything specific. "The most striking characteristic of the reports," thought one political editor, "is their essential conservativism . . . specific suggestions will be controversial but none is revolutionary or even novel." As it proved, there was not even much controversy. It was simply too nebulous to encourage debate. It was, summarized *Time*, merely "480,000 words of foggy goodwill."

Even so, Congress disapproved both the NRPB reports and forced the NRPB itself out of existence. Business set up a postwar planning body of its own, the Committee for Economic Development. Jesse Jones, the ultraconservative Texas banker who was both head of the Reconstruction Finance Corporation and Secretary of Commerce, kindly provided the fledgling CED with free office space in the Department of Commerce building in overcrowded Washington.

Liberals were thrown into angry despair over developments like this.

The accomplishments of a decade were, it seemed to them, being trampled underfoot by the most predatory elements of an avowedly competitive society. The *New Republic*'s literary editor, Malcolm Cowley, vented sentiments known to millions when he publicly mourned "The End of the New Deal" in mid-1943.

Roosevelt himself acknowledged that an era had ended. In 1932 the nation had been gravely ill, so he had called in Dr. New Deal, he said. The patient had since recovered, but still needed help, so he had called in Dr. Win-the-War. A mock-serious obituary soon followed, announcing: "Death Revealed. The New Deal, aged ten, after long illness; of malnutrition and desuetude."

Thus, the New Deal and its fate. In large part it explains why even thirty years later there is a common assumption that social change and social welfare advanced little or not at all during the war. But when we turn to those specifics by which the social welfare of a nation are measured, a different picture emerges.

Conscription provided a rough yardstick for measuring the social costs of the Depression. Nearly 15 percent of the nation—and that presumably the healthiest, most vigorous part—was examined for military service. No census had examined so many so thoroughly.

By setting its minimum requirements low, the Army expected to keep the rejection rate at about 20 percent. During the defense crisis period it required only a minimum height of 5 feet, minimum weight of 105 pounds, correctable vision, half the natural teeth, no flat feet, no hernias, no venereal disease. Not a very exacting set of physical requirements for a rich, modern nation. But rejections were running as high as 70 percent in some areas in 1941, and the overall rate was 50 percent. Bad teeth and bad eyes were the two chief causes for rejection, and they could all too often be traced to malnutrition. Beyond a commonality of diets deficient in essential vitamins and minerals there was a more fundamental deficiency responsible for this stunning rejection rate—an acute shortage of basic medical care.

Providing adequate medical care was already difficult in a nation devoted to commerce, and the Depression had been a tremendous setback. For a decade the annual production of doctors had remained much the same from one year to the next. The same was true of dentists. It was also true of the number of hospital beds. Population had meanwhile increased by 9,000,000. There were thus fewer medical services per person in 1939 than there had been in 1929. And even though federal public health expenditures had doubled in that decade, they still came to only 22 cents a person each year.

The introduction in 1940 of dried, bleached, ground grass to be added to wheat, rye or barley to produce a food fit for human consumption but rich in vitamins for only six cents a pound spoke of a need that literally gnawed at the flesh of millions.

Much of this distress was hidden away in rural areas and small towns. But the cities, where half the population now lived, were usually a menace to public health. They were filthy, pestilential and, for the most part, ugly. The smoke in industrial towns was frequently so thick that daytime traffic could navigate the gloom only with headlights on and all the street-lights blazing. Smog, a word just coming into use, took an economic toll estimated at $3 billion. Industrial urban areas each year labored under a new accumulation of as much as 1,000 tons of fresh soot per square mile. Women's stockings, whether nylon or silk, were commonly pitted and holed by particles of sulfuric acid cast out by smoke-belching chimneys.

The sum of these distresses—the shortage of doctors, dentists and hospitals, the inadequate public health programs, the malnutrition and hunger, the pestilential cities—added up to a staggering health problem. And all were aggravated by the commercialized character of American medicine. Most people wanted something very much like the national health schemes of Scandinavian countries. Most doctors took the position of the American Medical Association, which was characterized by the notion of every man for himself and a fat profit to the tradesman with medicine to sell.

Against the AMA the New Deal had offered only token opposition. A few small-scale federal programs provided health care to the utterly destitute. For the rest, it relied on a modest expansion of public health facilities and looked to the food stamp program to approach the problem obliquely by reducing both farm surpluses and hunger. By combating malnutrition, food stamps would make millions of people less susceptible to the infectious diseases associated with poverty.

Not surprisingly, works like *The Modern Home Medical Adviser* enjoyed a large and profitable sale from year to year. And after Pearl Harbor sales doubled. Patent medicines and home remedies were hoarded on a scale not seen since the end of the frontier. Many a family medicine chest bulged with arnica, eyewash, ipecac and milk of magnesia. Cough drop sales doubled before sugar rationing curtailed production. When German propagandists credited the Third Reich's military prowess to the vitamin-rich diet of its soldiers, a massive demand for synthetic vitamins was created overnight. Before the war ended, an entire mythology had developed, especially around Vitamin B, which was hailed as "The morale vitamin." Besides the large home consumption, employers handed vitamins out to their workers in the hope of raising production.

Hundreds of new community service hospitals and thousands of new clinics were spun off from the economic gains of the pre-Pearl Harbor defense boom. But these badly needed facilities no sooner opened than they began to lose their doctors. By 1943 almost every American community suffered an acute doctor shortage. One news story told of an Albuquerque housewife who was jubilant when a doctor came to her house six hours after she called him: "Good heavens! Imagine calling a doctor and getting him to come over the same day!" A third of the country's doctors were in uniform. And in poor communities tales were rife of babies being delivered by the father or by friends of the family.

At first, the young doctors in whom the military services were most interested effectively resisted appeals to their patriotism. Many had lucrative practices for the first time in their lives. Only after General Hershey threatened to draft them into the Army as private soldiers—promising to keep them at that rank for the duration—did the military acquire the doctors it needed.

By 1943, where there was one doctor for every 100 servicemen, there was one doctor for 3,500 civilians. Those physicians and surgeons tending the civilian population were old or ill or both. Anonymously and courageously many of these men and women literally, if sometimes with rusty skills, worked themselves to death.

The strains on the reduced supply of medical resources at times seemed likely to swamp them. Syphilis and gonorrhea affected 3,000,000 people a year in peacetime. It was predictable that the incidence of those diseases would reach epidemic proportions in wartime, and it did. The world's first hospital devoted exclusively to venereal disease was opened in Chicago in 1942.* Aggravating the epidemics of these and other infectious diseases was the decision to assign nearly all production of penicillin to the military.

Polio also increased spectacularly in wartime. In 1943 the incidence of this disease was twice the prewar rate, reaching epidemic proportions in some states. California alone suffered more than 1,000 cases in a matter of weeks that summer. In 1944 polio was still more virulent, reaping the largest harvest of victims—principally children—since 1916. And no one knew the cause, the means of transmission or the cure. An angry controversy swirled around an Australian physiotherapist named Sister Elizabeth Kenny, who had worked out a system of baths, massages and exercises that were clearly effective. But her theories of why and how her methods worked made little or no sense to doctors engaged in polio research.

Besides physical illness, the country had a staggering incidence of mental illness the dimensions of which were only just beginning to emerge. Psychiatric screening had been almost nonexistent in the First World War. It was far more rigorous this time, yet the rate of admissions to Army hospitals for neuropsychiatric diseases was twice as high. About one-fourth of the teen-agers examined for induction into the military were turned away

* It soon became a landmark for men in search of wayward women, presumably just cured.

for psychiatric reasons. And the overall rate of psychiatric rejections was nearly 20 percent, or about seven times the First World War rate.

There was, then, a critical national health problem, exacerbated by the war. Yet, as we shall see, just as matters seemed to reach a breaking point there was a startling reversal. Rather like a person who falls ill, grows more desperately ill yet is ultimately saved by timely, drastic measures, so did the U.S. go from being unhealthy to being very unhealthy to recovering (or as much so as a reasonable distribution of available resources allowed).

An important obstacle to recovery however was the AMA, especially in its ardent opposition to prepaid medical care. It brought lawsuits charging that health insurance plans were a restraint on trade and therefore illegal. The AMA vehemently attacked Blue Shield, a surgical insurance plan comparable to the Blue Cross hospitalization insurance plan begun in 1937. And leading the counterattack to the AMA was not the federal government or a liberal social reformer, but none other than that preeminent businessman-hero of the war, Henry J. Kaiser.

Probably the place where the health crisis was most acute and most immediate was in the war industries. War plants were burdened with 4-F's, dangerous machinery, unsanitary conditions. Many were located in squalid, overcrowded boom towns where the menace of epidemics was ever-present. But the more than 125,000 war workers employed by Kaiser were enrolled in a health plan which, for a few cents each day, provided every one of them and their families with excellent medical care. Alongside every Kaiser shipyard or assembly line there was invariably a modern hospital or clinic.

Other companies launched comparable plans, and the Farm Security Agency had operated a similar plan of its own in rural areas in the 1930's. But with Kaiser they were a passion. He waged a national publicity campaign for prepaid medical care for everyone. He argued endlessly that a healthy, worry-free work force was a positive aid to production and pointed to his shipyards as proof. Kaiser, however, was not simply a pragmatically minded businessman, but a social crusader with a business background. It was also said that he had a strong personal grievance against the medical establishment, that he believed his mother had died prematurely because she could not afford simple medical care.

Kaiser had been experimenting with health programs for years before the war began. His current system was thus ambitious, proved and potentially very popular. Each of the clinics and hospitals was staffed with a balanced team of specialists, carrying group medicine to new levels of practice. Preventive medicine was practiced, with vaccinations, inoculations and periodic physical checkups being provided at nominal charges. House calls were free. Ambulance service and outside consultants were provided at reasonable prices. By 1943 Kaiser was operating the biggest prepaid medical plan in the country. The AMA bitterly assailed it, calling it "contract medicine," and opened a private war on Kaiser's clinics.

Doctors who worked in them were threatened with expulsion from the association; to show its sincerity, one was expelled. Where doctors took up group practice on the Kaiser model, they found local hospitals closed to them. There were long legal battles. Local draft boards were pressured, sometimes with apparent success, into reclassifying and drafting Kaiser's doctors. There was a national publicity campaign charging that Kaiser was bribing doctors into mollycoddling his workers, the result of which was that wounded soldiers were going without medical attention.

Kaiser stubbornly refused to give ground. And the AMA was soundly defeated in the courts. The Justice Department brought its own antitrust suit against the AMA. The harassment of doctors in group practice resulted in the conviction of the AMA leadership for illegal conspiracy. So Kaiser's plan was saved. Beyond that, the AMA gave up the fight against health insurance. In the next few years Blue Cross and Blue Shield would enroll tens of millions of subscribers. It would still be true, as one writer said in 1943, that "The cost of complete medical care is outrageous. It is bearable only by the rich." Yet, thanks in large part to Kaiser's crusade, a major advance had nevertheless been scored.

The war had also brought a more rational, more effective, more just distribution of the country's medical resources. There were still 8,000,000 people receiving food stamps a year after Pearl Harbor, but the emphasis had shifted from simply feeding people to making sure that they had properly balanced diets. In war plants, when large numbers of women were employed, sanitary and safety conditions often improved dramatically: Hot meals were provided; heavy work was simplified or mechanized; women workers were given complete physical examinations at company expense. Dentists had recently discovered the decay-resisting properties of fluoride, and some towns were putting it into their drinking water.

In the boom towns the federal government financed the construction of new clinics and hospitals and found doctors and nurses to staff them. The experience of Seneca, Illinois, was typical of hundreds of boom towns. The U.S. Public Health Service set up a community health center. The local hospital was expanded with the aid of a government grant. A PHS nurse was assigned to the town and she supervised immunization drives, school health services, first-aid classes—none of which had ever been seen before in Seneca. Both of the town's prewar physicians had been drafted. Yet never had its citizens been so healthy.

A small revolution, in fact, had been worked in the nation's health even though nearly all its youngest, best-trained doctors were in uniform. In the state of Indiana, for example, public health had improved beyond all expectation. Typhoid fever, scarlet fever, tuberculosis, diphtheria and pneumonia dropped to unprecedentedly low levels. The typical diseases of infancy, such as measles and whooping cough, dropped off sharply. In the country at large, the war saw a drop in the death rate and a rise in the birthrate. People were eating more, and eating more sensibly. And the improvement in the health of children was so marked that their elders were amazed.

One of the reasons for the improvement in health was that some 16,000,000 men and many of their dependents were the beneficiaries of what was, in effect, a short-term program of socialized medicine. About half the men examined for induction needed immediate medical care. Nearly 2,000,000 were salvaged for military service at government expense. Military authorities put nutritionists to work ensuring that menus provided a balanced diet. Army doctors fitted millions with glasses, made the fat lose weight, built up the undernourished, performed minor corrective surgery. The Army Dental Corps had many of its stations working around the clock. At government expense tens of millions of teeth were saved; hundreds of thousands of dental plates and bridges were installed.

People were also better able to provide for themselves. During the Depression medical expenditures had dropped by a third. Most people were forced to cut back heavily on what they spent on doctors, dentists, health insurance and prescriptions. But now that they had money to spare, they were spending it freely on their health. Before the war ended, the amount spent on purchasing accident and health insurance was up 100 percent over the 1939 level.

Whereas the number of doctors and dentists had changed hardly at all during the Depression, the number graduated in 1944 was twice that of any prewar year. The number of hospital beds per 1,000 people increased only marginally during the 1930's; during the war it rose 50 percent. Federal, state and local government expenditures on health meanwhile went from several hundred million in 1939 to more than $1.1 billion in 1945. With these increased resources there also went, as we have seen, a fairer and more effective utilization.

The results were as astonishing as they were welcome. Life expectancy had altered hardly at all, for either race or both sexes, between 1932 and 1939. But in the six years from 1939 to 1945 there was an overall increase of three years. For blacks it was five years. At the same time, the death rate for infants under one year of age per 1,000 live births (which is a common index of public health standards and general economic conditions) was cut by more than a third, from 48 to 31 per 1,000. The 1942 overall death rate of 10.3 per 1,000 people was the lowest in the country's history.

Even the war's cost in combat dead and wounded could not blunt the great advance in America's physical health. Some 292,000 men were killed in battle; another 671,000 were wounded. It was a painful loss. The premature death of so many young men weighs heavily; the grief of their families and friends should never be discounted. Yet the effect on the overall death rate was small. They represented less than 5 percent of all the Americans who died between Pearl Harbor and the end of the war.*

Social insurance is nearly always thought of in terms of special programs set up by government in a direct and explicit attempt to relieve individual distress; unemployment compensation is a typical example. But in a country where central government is strong, yet centralized administration is weak, that view is too narrow to deal with the realities. By European standards American social policy has long been Victorian in its petty cruelties and structural inadequacies. Recent crises have done much to justify the critics. What has gone unappreciated is the fact that the American approach has, until recently, been possible because it has been better able to preclude distress than to alleviate it, and do we not all say that prevention is better than cure? And that was what occurred in the 1940's. It was done in a uniquely American way; it is probably unrepeatable. But for a generation it worked.

Unemployment, the scourge of the thirties, was a thing of the past, the fear of the future. Jeff Davies, the president of Hoboes of America, Inc., filed his annual report with Indiana authorities in 1942 and reported that all 2,000,000 members were "off the road." Some were in uniform; more than half a million were in war industries. Those few who were still on the road or riding the rods were not hoboes, Davies sneered. "They're just bums."

In retirement towns like San Diego and Long Beach up to 40 percent of the retirees went back to work. The country was literally sweeping the streets for labor as urban police forces rounded up skid row denizens, screened them for useful skills and offered suspended sentences to those who would go to work. Midgets were employed as aircraft inspectors, being able to crawl inside wings and other cramped spaces. Deaf-mutes were employed in factory areas where machinery noise was intolerable to others. Handicapped workers generally were, for once, welcomed by employers. Ford, for instance, had a wartime work force 10 percent of which was blind, deaf or crippled.

Farmers no longer brutalized migrant workers. Instead, they welcomed them with open arms—when they could find them. Big-farm interests demanded unrestricted immigration of Mexican *braceros*, and nearly 200,000 Mexicans and West Indians were brought into the country.

Everywhere the shortage of labor made itself felt. A Manhattan restaurant chain posted signs reading, "Please be polite to our waitresses. They

* I calculate that from December, 1941, to August, 1945, inclusive, some 5,231,000 deaths were recorded in the United States. For raw data see the 1947 edition of *Statistical Abstract of the U.S.*

are harder to get than customers." A shortage of mailmen inspired the Post Office to start zoning and numbering the nation's cities. Child labor started to make a comeback, often with the explicit encouragement of conservative state governments which used the present emergency to set aside anti-child-labor laws. By the summer of 1943 nearly 3,000,000 youngsters aged twelve to seventeen were at work.

Even the pathetic Okies and Arkies chronicled by Steinbeck were no longer pariahs. Farmers sought them out and offered living wages. But they were leaving the land at last, drifting into war industries. The Okies and other poor white migrants were still stock figures of contempt and derision. They were still taunted as being stupid, shiftless, ignorant and dirty. West Coast shipyard urinals were nicknamed "Okie drinking fountains." The Okies struck back by writing on lavatory walls:

> The miners came in '49
> The whores in '51
> And when they fucked each other
> They begot the Native Son.

Yet when all was said and done, the poor white migrants (of whom there had been more than 4,000,000 in 1939) were passing into the lower-middle and skilled working classes; they acquired new skills, new attitudes, bank accounts and permanent homes. They were becoming urbanized, sending their children to school, and year by year throughout the war their old life lost its hold on them.

But a cloud hung over the humming factories and fields. It prayed on people's minds even as they worked. For with war production at its peak, when asked what would be the principal problem of the postwar period, only 13 percent said a lasting peace, while 58 percent said jobs.* The National Resources Planning Board had projected postwar unemployment would reach 8,000,000 to 9,000,000. The Department of Labor predicted 12,000,000 to 15,000,000 unemployed. And by the summer of 1944, with some factories already cutting back, federal officials were forced to devise make-work expedients to maintain full employment. This was the pall that hung over all the social gains of wartime. But for the moment everyone who wanted a job could find one, and the immediate problem was not how to make a living but how to make living more pleasant.

Boom-town life, wretched before Pearl Harbor, often became still more miserable after it. By universal agreement the worst of everything could be found in Willow Run, Michigan, where most of the plant's 42,000 workers would rather commute 60 miles each day than live in the squalid camp of trailers and temporary shelters that had sprung up about it, complete with dysentery and periodic typhoid scares. Years afterward, when

* Interestingly, most workers thought *they* would still be working; other people would be laid off.

the question was raised of how war industries should be decentralized, one authority wrote: "Willow Run supplied some answers by demonstrating with impressive finality how not to do the job." But Willow Run exemplified wartime living at its worst, not its most typical.

Federal agencies had been working since 1940 to ease the miseries of boom-town life, and after Pearl Harbor the Community Facilities Act (popularly known as the Lanham Act, after its sponsor) provided an effective instrument. The Federal Works Agency was authorized to provide money for nursery schools, child-care centers, clinics, elementary- and secondary-school expansion, the construction of recreation facilities and almost anything else for which a war-created need could be shown. In this way, thousands of U.S. towns and villages got new schools, playgrounds, clinics, community centers, all completely paid for out of federal funds. The gain to each community and to the country as a whole was enormous. Many of those wartime creations are even now in daily use. Of all the countries at war only in America was there such an awesome rebuilding of physical plant while the war was still under way.

All this was improvised. It was treated and looked upon as something temporary and unimportant. Certainly it did not come within the ambit of explicitly planned social reform, and for that reason it was invisible to most liberal reformers. For all the credit attached to it, it may as well have been nonexistent. The advocates of planning loudly despaired that the country was edging its way willy-nilly into disaster.

What planning there was for the postwar world took for its object not something avowedly aimed at social welfare but the provision of veterans' benefits for 16,000,000 servicemen and their families. It was not thought of as a program of social welfare in the traditional mold. It was seen principally as a payment for services rendered.

Soldiers' bonuses had, in the course of three wars, become overwhelmingly unpopular. Roosevelt himself had vetoed two bonus acts. When he made his first public address after a six months' silence in 1943, he made provisions for veterans the subject of his speech. His proposals looked to providing education, improved hospitalization and rehabilitation programs, more generous pensions for the disabled and other measures to help veterans get ahead instead of just paying them off. Congress took a similar approach, as did most veterans' organizations.

The biggest of these, the American Legion, drew up its own plan and submitted it to Congress as an omnibus bill. It combined every one of the measures others had proposed, except for a bonus. The object of its bill, said the Legion, was the readjustment of the veterans to civilian life, calling its proposal "a bill of rights for G.I. Joe and G.I. Jane." Eighty Senators rushed to attach their names to it before it appeared on the floor, and most of the remaining sixteen complained that they had not been given a fair chance to do likewise.

The administration was not entirely blind to the potential of veterans' benefits in advancing social welfare. Some of Roosevelt's staff tried to link these benefits to the needs of the entire nation. But Roosevelt would not fight for them. A handful of New Dealers fought against the principle of veterans' exclusiveness, without the support of the White House. The Legion was therefore under no serious pressure to compromise, and its bill passed almost intact. Liberals mourned it as a great opportunity lost. Yet, as we shall see, the GI Bill still represented an unprecedented achievement.

Veterans were returning in large numbers long before the war ended. These first returnees were usually war-wounded or combat heroes, like Pittsburgh's "Commando" Kelly, credited with killing forty Germans at Salerno. He went to the White House to receive the Medal of Honor. His hometown honored him with a parade, and one excited citizen threw him a three-foot length of salami. But most of the homecomings were not like this. Many were touched with a bitter hostility.

Nasty incidents between civilians and returning veterans kept breaking out, especially in overcrowded trains, restaurants and buses. A soldier at Camp Shelby, Mississippi, wrote a poem called "Back Home," expressing sentiments commonly found around Army bases:

> Money and liquor and girls
> They are grabbing for all they are worth.
> Why do the swine get the pearls
> And the meek inherit the Earth?

Football hero and fighter pilot Tom Harmon returned to Detroit after being shot down in China and told the crowd that turned out to cheer his safe return that they made him ashamed. On their heads he wished the descent of enemy bombs.

Civilians were nervously defensive, squirming at any mention of relative sacrifices. "The fighters of course suffer far greater perils, pains and hardships" was a typical remark. It was a half-truth at best, for only one serviceman in ten was ever exposed to combat. For the rest, they were in no more danger than they would have been at home. With an overall death rate of 5 per 1,000 the military was a safer place to be than at home, where the death rate was more than twice as high and where the death and injury rates were higher still in war industries.

The frictions were also aggravated by the high proportion of neuropsychiatric cases among the men being discharged. These men should never had been inducted, but they were. Once they had been discharged, they were not always averse to hiding the reasons for their separations from duty and to creating fictitious combat records.

Readjustment, despite the aid of a grateful nation, often proved to be rocky. The last year of the war brought the ominous phenomenon of the veterans who turned to crime, frequently violent crime. Unable to settle down, troubled by physical or mental illness, they invariably pleaded when caught that America did not appreciate what they had done for it. Police and courts could not have been more sympathetic. A Chicago judge typically sentenced a veteran convicted of armed robbery and serious bodily harm to just six months in prison. Passing sentence, he said, "We will try to forget the crime you have committed and remember what you have done for your country." People were less worried at such leniency than they were at the prospect of what was in store if millions of the returning veterans took this man's path.

By the spring of 1944 a million veterans had returned to civilian life. Veterans often felt cut off from the security of military life; they found themselves adrift in a hostile, alien environment which was without obvious regularity, discipline, authority and predictability. They missed the comradeship of service life. All too often their friends and relatives seemed remote, stupid, lackadaisical inhabitants of a world they no longer knew as their own. Their old jobs seemed pointless and boring. Congress, thinking it was doing what the veterans wanted, required employers to restore these men to their former jobs. But 70 percent did not want them. Thanks to the GI Bill, they now had a good chance to prepare for better-paying, more interesting work. Or they could go into business for themselves backed by government-guaranteed loans.

More and more men were showing up on city streets short of a limb. Most were victims of industrial accidents, but unless an amputee was very old or very young, he was tacitly assumed to be a combat veteran. There were also persistent rumors that the military was hiding away hundreds, perhaps thousands, of multiple amputees, especially quadruple amputees, callously nicknamed "basket cases." In vain did military officials deny them. One man wrote to *Time*: "There is a whole ward of the ———— hospital devoted to these pitiful [basket] cases. They are brought in at night so the squeamish public will not know they exist."*

Most amputees were annoyed; not without cause. They endured the torments of prosthetics which had not been improved on since the Civil War. Plastics, fiber glass, lightweight alloys may as well not have existed so far as prosthetics manufacturers were concerned. An artificial arm, for example, weighed 10 pounds. These false limbs, besides being clumsy and uncomfortable, were very expensive. And the demand far exceeded the supply. There were 17,000 military amputees. Industrial accidents in the war years produced over 100,000 more. Polio contributed its thousands of victims. Amputees were commonly simply given some money, then told to go and buy an artificial limb, if they could find one.

The Veterans Administration found this and a host of other sins laid at

* There were, in truth, only two such cases in all: one caused by an accident, the other resulting from combat.

its door. Returning veterans waxed wrathful over what they considered the VA's heartless, bureaucratic approach to their problems. The medical care it provided was dismissed as being third-rate. VA officials pleaded that they were simply swamped: Their work load had increased 400 percent over the levels of the First World War, but their work force was no bigger. Angry Congressmen brushed the rejoinders aside and brandished letters from their constituents in VA hospitals: "I refused to eat the food because it wasn't fit for a dog." "Personally I would much rather be on Iwo Jima." It was a cause for national rejoicing when the head of the VA since 1920 was fired in 1945 and replaced by General Omar Bradley. For the country sincerely wanted to treat its returning veterans, if not as heroes, at least as men who had fought a just war with honor and courage.

America certainly did not let the veterans down. If anything, it turned them into a privileged group. But it was, when veterans' dependents were included, a group so large that it enhanced, and was enhanced by, a powerful wartime trend to the creation of a genuine middle-class democracy. It was one of the most remarkable and successful instances of social welfare without Socialism.

This war's veterans were provided for by legislation going back to 1940. Ever since then, more and more benefits had been added. By 1945 a grateful nation would help a veteran buy a home, set himself up in business, take up farming, go to college, learn a trade, finish high school or get a government job. Those in small business had access to a billion dollars' worth of surplus government property. Veterans and their families could be buried at government expense in government cemeteries. Millions of these families carried inexpensive, government-subsidized life insurance. To federal benefits, the states, municipalities and private organizations added their own. There was also a bonus—though it was never called that—which amounted to $1,300 and was supposed to ease the return to civilian life. Twenty-one states also gave their own bonuses, totaling $2.4 billion.

Though not explicitly a program of social welfare, the results were the same as if it had been. Veterans' benefits were a variety of Socialism that, counting the 16,000,000 veterans and their families, by 1950 embraced approximately one-third of the total population. The true nature of veterans' programs was occasionally acknowledged. The purpose of the loan program was said to be primarily to help veterans readjust by buying homes or businesses. But second, "to help overcome the national housing deficit," a deficit which by 1945 ran to millions of units. Ten years later some 4,300,000 home loans had been granted, with a face value of $33 billion. Veterans' loans accounted for 20 percent of all the new homes built in the decade after the war. Nearly 8,000,000 veterans went back to school or learned a trade or went to college under the GI Bill. They represented an infusion of $14.5 billion in federal money into the nation's schools and colleges by 1955.

The total money cost of veterans' benefits cannot be computed precisely. But excluding insurance dividends, surplus property and intangibles such as Civil Service preference, $50 billion is a conservative minimum estimate. To date, the entire sum is probably twice that amount.

No status group of comparable size prospered as did veterans after the war. They did not, could not, see themselves as the recipients of welfare programs. To the largess spread before them they brought not the sullen, self-destroying agonies of welfare clients but the assertive, self-respecting attitudes of people whose claims are based on having earned, not simply deserved, what they received. It was a very middle-class program, all the more effective for the disguise that it wore. And now, in the professional and managerial ranks, the veterans of World War II are represented out of all proportion to their numbers in the total population. They have, on the average, three years more formal education than the average nonveteran of the same age. The GI Bill more than made up for the wartime deficits in training lawyers, doctors, engineers, teachers and other highly trained persons. Today war veterans make more money, are more likely to own their own homes, and their families are better fed and better educated than the nonveterans of their own age. They and their children are the bedrock of America's modern middle class.

It was with good reason that Roosevelt had included housing in his pithy summary of social distress when he saw a third of the nation ill-fed, ill-clothed, ill-housed. The administration had saved millions of homes from foreclosure through the HOLC. Rural electrification programs had brought light into millions of homes. The Farm Security Administration had striven valiantly to improve sanitation in rural homes. But throughout the New Deal years the government fought a losing battle with the housing problem.

During the twenties more than 7,000,000 new nonfarm dwellings were constructed; during the thirties construction fell by nearly two-thirds. Population grew while the existing housing stock deteriorated. Between 1932 and 1939 public agencies financed the construction of only 23,000 new homes. Just as war began in Europe, an administration request for $800,000,000 to make a serious assault on the problem of low-cost housing was rejected by Congress. It was a gloomy prospect indeed. About half the housing in the United States was in need of major repairs or was a menace to health, and there was an overall shortage of 4,000,000 to 5,000,000 units.

"The picture is one of barriers built up from every side," wrote a housing expert. "The housing industry in 1940 remained in the grip of ancient traditions. No trends visible in that year showed sufficient strength to promise any radical break from these traditions for perhaps another decade."

Then "The impact of war speeded up the rate of industrial change. [It] brought about increased efficiency in the design of dwellings, in the use of materials in building dwellings, and in the building processes themselves. At the same time government orders permitted producers to by-pass many of the obstacles existing in the private market."

The results were evident before the war ended. From 1933 to 1939 roughly 1,500,000 new houses were built, few of them, as mentioned above, with public financing. In the next six years, to 1945, despite the wartime shortages of materials and labor nearly 3,000,000 houses were built; more than 600,000 of them were publicly financed, an increase of nearly thirty-fold. Wartime prosperity also saw the number of houses owned by those who lived in them jump from 15,000,000 in 1940 to 20,000,000 in 1945.

That prosperity, carrying over into the postwar era, fueled a housing boom that, in conjunction with the veterans' programs, saw the housing problem solved within another decade. Ironically, the United States was the only Allied country which did not have a set of housing policies for the postwar world to offer as an incentive to its people to endure the rigors of wartime. There was no overall housing plan. Yet it was the United States which was the first to solve its housing problem.

Women posed a special problem in wartime. They were supposed to be cosseted as tradition required. But they were also the country's largest labor reserve. Though employers were cool to the idea, sooner or later they would have to put women into war work if the Victory Program were to meet its targets. By the fall of 1943, with war production at its peak, 17,000,000 women made up a third of the total work force, and of those about 5,000,000 were in war industries. In some plants, particularly the airplane factories, women did most of the work while men did most of the supervising. The bombers and fighters which pounded Japanese and German cities were predominantly built by American women. Yet there was a lingering notion that they were unwilling to go into the factories. Unfavorable comparisons were drawn with the women of Russia and Britain. *Life* jeered:

AMERICAN WOMEN
Draft Them? Too Bad We Can't
Draft Their Grandmothers

But they were, in truth, working harder than they had ever worked, at home and elsewhere. They did heavier and more dangerous work than they had ever done. On jobs which did not require unusual muscular strength women proved to be more productive than men, *if* they were kept happy. Often enough that was difficult to do. For too many were trying to work full time and still run a home. One woman sarcastically replied to the question of why more women did not go into war work: "Because they don't have wives."

Industry was caught unprepared for this wartime influx of women workers. The telephone and insurance companies had, in recent years, been studying menstruation as a work problem. But industry had not. Rare was the factory manager who was prepared for tears, dermatitis, jewelry and child-care worries. Hastily they scraped up countermeasures. For the dermatitis, special creams were handed out. For the tears, sympathetic women counselors were hired. For the jewelry, there was an absolute ban. And for the children, there were full-time nurseries, at nominal cost. Clean, comfortable washrooms were installed. Lessons on diet, grooming and posture were offered. There were education and recreation programs. Cafeterias, rest periods, vitamin pills, periodic physical examinations, free inoculations—all followed women into the factories. The few plants which had offered these things before the war were considered radical; suddenly they were commonplace.

Employers were forced to make adjustments and grumbled endlessly about them, especially about the rest periods which most states began to require by law. Most of the changes, however, worked to the advantage of workers generally, for they usually resulted in safer, cleaner plants. Even then, war work was dangerous. One highly educated woman working in a munitions plant finished her stint with burned hands and a badly gashed face. Of the 10,000 workers in the plant where she worked, some 200 were injured on the average working day.

Women were also susceptible to fears that war work was harmful. It was widely believed that heavy work increased the chances of breast cancer. Rosie the Riveter was supposedly prone to a mysterious ailment called "Riveter's arm." There was also a new malady called "Riveter's ovaries," supposedly caused by excessive vibration. But the greatest barrier to counteracting the tears and absenteeism was not the fearful rumors but unequal treatment.

As one woman worker pointedly said, "No working woman (in whatever line of work) labors under the delusion that any woman is actually, either socially or economically, equal to men in the U.S. in 1944." It was federal government policy that women should be paid the same as men for doing the same work. But it was an open secret that the policy was never implemented except by accident or as a token. That was true even in the eight federally owned and operated shipyards. The highest pay for women working in these yards was $6.95 a day; for men, $22 a day. Most women earned the bare minimum, $4.65 a day. Sanitary conditions were often poor and the rest periods theoretical. And no matter how long or how hard they worked, the chances of women being promoted into the better, or better-paying, jobs were virtually nonexistent.

In vain did women war workers look to organized labor to help them. Of the 15,000,000 union members at the end of 1944 about 1 in 5 was a woman. But most union organizers and much of the leadership considered women a threat to the other four-fifths of the membership. Women had gone into war work in the earlier war, and by 1918 of every 1,000 workers in war plants 139 were women; those gains had not been reversed, so that in 1939 the figure was 135 per 1,000. With women now constituting a third of the war industry work force, male workers were apprehensive indeed. The country as a whole when asked if women should surrender their jobs to returning soldiers said yes by more than four to one. "Americans may no longer believe that a woman's place is in the home. But more important, we believe even less that a man's place is on the street without a job," concluded one observer. And most women agreed.

But as the war drew to a close, many women workers surrendered their jobs with the greatest reluctance. Their families had come to rely on the money they earned. A new sense of independence had taken root once they were earning money of their own. And the war had opened up all manner of opportunities, not just in the factories but throughout the economy. Even before the end of 1942 one journal observed, "There is hardly any job that women cannot get if they want them. . . ." Many a predominantly male bastion crumbled. By 1944 *Editor and Publisher* estimated that the 8,000 editors and reporters in uniform had been replaced by 8,000 women. Dozens of the smaller papers, in fact, were almost fully staffed by women. Nine of the country's major symphony orchestras each had ten or more women musicians. The New York Stock Exchange in 1943 hired the first female clerk in its history, turning half of Wall Street apoplectic.

The Army and Navy had likewise succumbed. When the Women's Auxiliary Army Corps was established in the summer of 1942 less than 500 officer openings brought 50,000 applications in a matter of days. The Navy established the WAVES—Women Accepted for Volunteer Emergency Service. The Marines, who had accepted female recruits in the First World War for clerical work, followed suit. But to them a marine was a marine, regardless of sex, and they steadfastly refused to give female marines a separate name, such as mariness, she-marine, femarine or marina, all of which were suggested by civilians.

The WAAC's (shortened to WAC's with the dropping of "Auxiliary" in 1943) were at first the very byword for military glamor. They completely overshadowed the elite paratroop division which was being formed at the same time. But the WAC was dogged by rumors of promiscuity. It was widely believed that thousands were illegitimately pregnant. The rumors kept interest high but enlistments low. Enlistments were further discouraged by the dull, dusty-looking uniform. The WAC hoped to have 150,000 women at its peak, but it never numbered more than 60,000.

All-women ROTC units were meanwhile set up at Smith and the University of New Hampshire. These provided officers for the WAC's and the WAVES. There were also more than 1,000 WASP's—Women's Auxiliary Service Pilots. They ferried planes, towed targets, flew weather observation flights and generally released male pilots for more dangerous work.

In all, more than 100,000 American women were in military uniform during the war. But some military men never became entirely reconciled to it. One marine officer, told that women were being posted to his camp, was said to have cursed, "Goddamn it all. First they send us dogs. Now it's women."

Other women were knitting for servicemen and rolling bandages for the Red Cross. Volunteer all-women fire brigades appeared in scores of small towns. An American Women's Volunteer Service came into existence, patterned after the British WVS. Its 260,000 members drove trucks, navigated for military convoys, made maps, chauffeured Army and Navy officers, taught housewives what to do during an air raid and manned information centers for the Air Warning Service.

The American Legion's female auxiliary, with 2,500,000 members, snorted derisively at other women-come-latelies: "We see this emergency a little more clearly than the others. . . . We stand ready." And when 10,000 women doing volunteer war work showed up for a parade down Fifth Avenue in 1942, there were so many organizations represented, each with its own uniform, that no one managed to keep track of which was which.

Had the feminist movement been as strong at the beginning of this war as it had been in 1914 it could doubtless have scored great gains, as it had then. But the Depression had absorbed whatever energies people had for social protest, and feminism, though still alive, was not vibrant in 1939. Lacking its earlier leadership and organizational base, it could not capitalize on the wartime gains. There was nothing comparable to the impassioned movement of the pre-World War I suffragettes to press home the wartime opportunities and capitalize on the new importance of women, to turn a temporary advantage into permanent gain. Dorothy Thompson was demanding that the postwar world be reorganized on "feminine principles." Eleanor Roosevelt provided inspiration and example, as ever. But these were voices from the mountaintop. No one was working down below.

Thus are great opportunities lost. By 1944 there were a dozen women in the House and one in the Senate. More than 100 of the Democratic Party's county chairmen were women, compared with 12 in 1940. At both the nominating conventions that year more than 25 percent of the Republican and Democratic delegates were women. Usually they made up less than 10 percent. Both major parties incorporated into their platforms the Equal Rights Amendment that the National Woman's Party had been pressing for for years. But once the election was over and the men started to return from the war, the amendment was allowed to die a natural death.

Anyway, most women were currently less interested in equal rights than they were in the shortage of men. One mourned:

> Of all sad words of tongue or pen
> The saddest are these: there are no men.

Widows were told by the president of the Widows and Widowers Clubs that it was their duty "to keep love alert for the duration." She conceded that that was no easy task. For while "it used to be that a woman could get any man she liked, now she has to like any man she can get." The response to "Don't Sit Under the Apple Tree with Anyone Else but Me" was a song called "They're Either Too Young or Too Old," which plaintively concluded "I *can't* sit under the apple tree with anyone else but me."

Probably the most poignant sight in wartime America was the "strange, unorganized home-front battle being fought all over the U.S. by a vast, unorganized army of women. They are the wives, mothers, sweethearts or fiancees of servicemen. Their only plan of campaign is to follow their men." For many, perhaps most, the only married life they had ever known was built around suitcases, rented rooms, frequent good-byes, packed trains and buses, soaring prices and low, fixed incomes, missed connections, exorbitant rents and unscheduled changes in military orders.

These women more often than not were disheveled and careworn, dressed in mismatched odds and ends that happened to be handy when the time came to pack. On their coats they sported costume jewelry denoting which service their men were in. About one in five seemed to be pregnant at any given time. But they all refused to be deterred. These women seemed to mix easily, sharing whatever they had to make this nomadic life more bearable. Long before the war ended, they were the saddest and the most predictable feature of the crowded train stations and bus terminals in the great cities.

At one time or another almost all the women under forty were caught up in this migration. They were more self-aware, more self-reliant than their mothers had been. But above all, they were lonely. The tensions and separations of wartime had created in them one overwhelming desire: to settle down and have children. Very few by 1945 wanted anything else.

As with the Depression, a disproportionate share of war's social strains was shouldered by America's children and adolescents. Pearl Harbor was not a year past before there were hundreds of thousands of "eight-hour orphans" roaming the streets of the boom towns, latchkeys often tied to a string around their necks. Tens of thousands more children were locked inside automobiles in war-plant parking lots. Still others could be found in trailer camps chained to the family trailer by a length of chain, much like dogs. Unlicensed, unregulated nurseries sprang up. Tales of squalor, brutality and child molesting clung to many of these places, and not all the stories could be wrong.

Here was a national child welfare problem at its worst. But the chief manifestation of it was a staggering rise in juvenile delinquency. The delinquency usually involved vice or violence. Of the two, vice was the more obvious.

The bus depots of the larger cities and towns were crowded with teen-age girls, variously called Victory Girls, Patriotutes, Cuddle Bunnies and Round-Heels. Hauled in by the police, they protested that they were performing a patriotic service, maintaining military morale. Some were as young as twelve years old. There are no unimpeachable figures, but it seems clear that vice by girls was more common than violence by boys.

Nor were servicemen the only recipients of adolescent favors. Federal housing projects spawned "wolf packs"—clubs for teen-agers where girls seeking admission paid their dues by copulating with every male member. One determined young initiate joined a club with ninety boys. A New York City court in 1943 tried and convicted a seventeen-year-old girl named Josephine Tencza for running a vice ring of thirty young hookers aged twelve to fifteen catering to a clientele of middle-aged men. Older, more established practitioners fiercely resented the competition. A San Antonio social worker reported, "The girls are sore as all get-out. They say the young chippies who work for a beer and a sandwich are cramping their style." The head of Vassar's Child-Study Department was more sympathetic. To her, these young girls were really "war casualties."

Much of the problem could be traced to the fact that there was no explicit place in the war effort for youngsters below draft age. There was also the parental neglect attendant on the wartime disruptions of everyday life. And juvenile delinquency not only rose steadily during the war, but was growing uglier and more violent. There was a growing callousness that made it possible for twelve adolescents to rape a seventeen-year-old girl in a crowded movie house in the Bronx in 1943 without one of the patrons moving to interfere. In 1944 two girls aged eleven and thirteen cold-bloodedly planned and then carried out the ritual execution of a nine-year-old in a New York schoolyard during the morning recess. Again, no one interfered. These days schoolteachers in the city were terrified. They begged, then through their union demanded, that policemen be placed in the schools. La Guardia scoffed that they were exaggerating the dangers—until a teacher was tortured to death in her classroom.

It was this evident readiness to employ deadly force that was the most frightening feature of the youth gangs which sprang up during the war in most big cities. This was the first zip-gun generation. The gangs, organized on racial and ethnic lines, waged pitched battles in the streets with as many as a hundred participants to a side.

Younger children were showing an ominous propensity to vandalism. An El Paso movie house manager was confronted nightly by so many marijuana-smoking, rebellious young patrons that he literally armed himself to the teeth and patrolled his theater like a one-man army. After he had been thrown out of his own establishment several times, he dressed for work each night in a Sam Browne belt complete with a .38-caliber automatic and three clips of ammunition; a bone-breaking device called an "iron claw"; a blackjack; a pair of handcuffs; a shiny police-type badge; and, "on extra busy nights," a 24-inch police nightstick in one hand and a long, heavy flashlight in the other.

Zoot suits had meanwhile gone from being the fad of harmless jitterbuggers to being the uniform of young thugs organized in street gangs. Youth dances frequently ended up as free-for-alls. To the standard zoot suit accessories there had been added an ornate switchblade knife for boys and a whiskey flask shaped to fit inside a brassiere for girls.

Some communities tried to curb delinquency by simply imposing a curfew. Others tried more positive measures, such as "Teen Canteens." A few tried a combination of restraint and diversion. The High School Victory Corps also managed to siphon off some of the excessive youthful energies into parades, scrap drives, bond sales and physical education. But there were any number of cities with mayors like La Guardia, who cut the number of city-operated parks from 400 to 35 despite social workers' warnings that he was aggravating delinquency; opposed child-care programs ("The worst mother is better than the best nursery school"); and said, "Let the police deal with juvenile delinquency. There is no need for after-school programs to keep children off the streets."

Ironically, despite the current rise in youthful violence, the streets had become safer than ever and property was more secure. Adult crime rates dropped, and the big prisons holding the most dangerous prisoners—like San Quentin, Sing Sing and Folsom—lost up to half their inmates.

Gradually the rising tide of delinquency was turned as the initial hard-nosed attitudes proved futile. The era of physical fitness programs and scrap drives gave way to a new phase in which the rudiments of an adolescent subculture asserted themselves. Social recreation schemes meshed easily with the demand of adolescents to have something of their own. Social centers, glamorized as counterparts to servicemen's "canteens," were established in thousands of American communities in the last two years of the war. Dances, swimming parties, jam sessions, table tennis tournaments —every kind of recreation short of sexual intercourse or drinking was encouraged. Public and private money poured into these centers with names like "The Rec," "Coke Bar," "Club Victory" and "Teentown Night Club." Adults launched most of the centers; soft-drink manufacturers underwrote many of them. But everyday operation was predominantly exercised by the patrons, who were usually high school students.

The upshot was the creation of a new social phenomenon: the teen-ager. Before the war there had been children and adults. Now there was an entirely new category of social and individual identities that had sprung up between them. By the time the war ended, advertising, clothing styles, sociological surveys, scores of magazine articles and considerable parental interest revolved about this novel subculture. Where women's magazines had traditionally catered to the mature woman, the new need had spawned *Seventeen, Mademoiselle* and *Glamour*. The *Saturday Evening Post* waxed angry over the development of "Your generation" and "Our generation" and demanded to know, "Who Made Our Youngsters 'Generation' Conscious?" hinting darkly that it was another left-wing initiative.

It was, in truth, an extraordinary act of social regeneration. Yet among the nation's elders there was a profound pessimism. One sensitive woman reporter pitied the youngsters. They were too young to go into the Army, they had been generally left to fend for themselves, and the loftiest role they had been offered in the war effort was to collect junk. The famed sociologist Robert Lynd thought it was "a hell of a world for kids to be trying to grow up in." He prophesied a new Lost Generation. La Guardia grimly forecast such massive postwar unemployment that it might be the better part of wisdom not to train this violence-prone younger generation for anything but menial jobs. When the inevitable disappointment of high expectations set in, he said, they would turn on society and ravage it. And a noted psychiatrist predicted such an orgy of violence and wildness in the postwar world that it would make the Jazz Age look timid and introspective in comparison.

Yet there was also at least one authority who saw the war as being "far better for adolescents than Depression; for it does meet that one great need, the need of youth to count in the world of men, the need to belong, the need to serve."

Seneca, Illinois, had been a sleepy little town of 1,200 people on the Illinois River before the fall of France. Four years later, in 1944, it was a bustling town of 6,600 people busily turning out oceangoing LST's for the Navy. Like other boom towns, Seneca had been suspicious of the boom at first. A peacetime boom seemed natural somehow; a wartime boom seemed pathological. Yet Seneca was in no position to quibble. In 1940 it was virtually dead on its feet. Its businesses limped along from year to year. Its houses, streets, schools, stores and churches were crumbling, while new construction was rare. Old-time residents liked to look back to the years before the war as a sort of golden age, and they looked on the newcomers as a form of social blight. The incoming war workers laughed at Seneca's mythical golden age. They pointed to the 1,500 new houses and apart-ments. Where there had once been a single policeman there were now seven, plus a police car, all underwritten by the federal government. Even the churches prospered, catering to thousands of new parishioners. The wife of one of the war workers huffed, "Seneca people needn't be so snooty. There were only four bathtubs in Seneca before the shipyards came. And look at all the new things they've got: two new churches, two new schools, a lot of extra teachers and police, good sidewalks and a sewer system."

The antagonisms between old residents and new also obscured an important social fact: "For the vast majority of people, old and young, newcomers and oldtimers, life in wartime was an exhilarating experience." There was plenty of money for almost everyone; there was a satisfying sensation of helping play an important part in the greatest, most worthwhile enterprise of the century; there was the chance to meet new people; there was the exposure to novel experiences. The gambling, the drinking and the overcrowding in the boom towns often made life unpleasant. But the exhilaration was never destroyed, nor was the sense of importance.

The country as a whole was meantime achieving a close-knit texture, a degree of social cohesion, rarely, if ever, known in its history. American factories, for instance, were notorious for remaining aloof from the communities where they were located. But wartime pressures had forced them at last into a close relationship with local health, education and housing authorities. The labor shortage made them sensitive, as they had never previously been, to the welfare of their employees.

Nowhere was the new social cohesion more evident than in the South. Labor costs were lower there, and the climate was conducive to the year-round training of troops. One reporter discovered in 1943 that "There are scarcely a dozen towns with a population of 10,000 or more that do not have a military installation of some sort" and "there is now a Yankee briskness about them." Thanks to the war, millions of Northerners discovered the South and its poverty and backwardness. Their shocked surprise ruffled Southern complacency and prodded the entire region into a new restiveness about its traditional burdens. Southerners were also meeting first- and second-generation Americans for the first time. Like armies everywhere, the presence of a Northern army in the South resulted in many a Northern boy marrying a Southern girl. Liberals feared that what was occurring was the transmission of Southern prejudices to Northerners. But the more likely result was a modest liberation of the South, easing the grip of the dead hand of its past. Beyond that there was a great advance in social cohesion, a breaking down of regional and provincial ignorance and hostility.

Many another wartime social program which started out with only the most limited ambitions concluded by scoring a major advance. For example, the block-mother plan set up by the PTA as part of the civil defense program in 1942 was supposed to protect children during air raids;

it turned up tens of thousands of instances of neglected children. Before the war ended, it had become a program for protecting the welfare of young children, at a local level and on a voluntary basis.

The Office of Defense Health and Welfare, created before Pearl Harbor, became the Office of Community War Services in early 1943, with two branches—Social Protection and Recreation. The former made sure that every community had enough doctors, dentists, schoolteachers; it interceded with the OPA for extra rations when special needs arose; it cleaned up the shanty towns spawned by the boom; it regulated the worst of the trailer parks; it set up nurseries and child-care centers, it built VD clinics; and so on. The Recreation Division maintained adult education centers, supported little theaters, sponsored athletic contests, built hundreds of community centers and more than 3,000 teen-age recreation centers. The federal government provided money and often the initiative and then found hundreds of thousands of local volunteers to take over what it had created.

But none of this—the creation of wartime community health, education and recreation facilities—counted as social reform. It occurred to hardly anyone that that was what it was. Instead, it appeared to be a congeries of hastily contrived, *ad hoc* measures to cope with wartime social problems. And those people strongly concerned with social reform never stopped demanding that government come up with some overall, long-range program for the attainment of social welfare and justice.

The liberals and progressives who still looked on "planning" as the panacea of social ills focused so much on economic planning as the counter to a postwar depression that they hardly noticed the wartime gains. And the recrudescence of conservatism had brought this, like other liberal remedies, into disrepute. New York's Robert Moses, the mastermind behind the 1939 World of Tomorrow, was leading the counterattack. To him, refugee intellectual architects and planners like Walter Gropius and Eero Saarinen were snobs, ingrates and anti-American. Worse still, they were revolutionaries. They did not soil their own hands in the work of demolition, but "They make the TNT for those who throw the bombs." For what they envisioned, said Moses, was not merely the planned use of space but fundamental changes in the existing social order, and planning was the cutting edge. If their views were adopted, the result would inevitably be "land nationalization."

A noted apostle of economic planning, George Soule, had already announced that planning had won. But what planning there was stood in stark contrast with planning elsewhere. "In America," as one observer noted, "it [planning] has dealt with large, abstract speculations about world affairs." In Britain, on the other hand, the government had turned its energies to hammering out specific policies and plans for the country's domestic life in the postwar world.

Wartime America in general did not appear to be an encouraging place for social change. When *Fortune* asked if Socialism would be good or bad for America, 40 percent said bad, only 25 percent said good. People were more conservative than the British, most of whom were avid for fundamental reform in the postwar era. The counterattack on New Deal programs carried out by Congress from 1942 to 1945 occurred in an environment that was overtly hostile to social experiment.

But it would be a mistake to think this a conservatism which had sprung from ideological reaction. Ordinary people were conservative now because they had something to conserve. They viewed the postwar world apprehensively, seeing in it a possible economic collapse that would rob them of their wartime gains. And those gains were spectacular. They added up to a historic advance in social justice. We have seen some of them. And their wellspring was the same criterion on which Frederick Lewis Allen relied to prove the accomplishments of the New Deal. For to liberals, as John Kenneth Galbraith remarked, "No other question in economic policy is ever so important as the effect of a measure on the distribution of income." Who got the money in wartime? Everybody did. But some got more than others, and thereby hangs the tale of social change and welfare in modern America.

It is a commonplace to remark that the war solved the problem of unemployment. What goes unremarked is that the war also provided the principal means of achieving social justice in a capitalist society: money. The money needed to finance new housing, wider educational opportunities, more adequate programs of social insurance and better health care had been churned out in six years of wartime economics. The New Deal had good intentions, but the war had better results. It provided the money to pay for social welfare. Personal income rose from $72.6 billion in 1939 to $172 billion in 1945. Even allowing for inflation, the real growth was 68 percent in only six years. It was also more fairly distributed than anything liberals, progressives and planners had ever envisaged.

The First World War had also had the net economic effect of reducing economic inequalities. But in the twenties there had been much slippage. For the two decades before 1939, therefore, the top 5 percent of the population from year to year held onto 30 percent of the national income. And the breakdown of family incomes was perfectly pyramidal—that is, it showed a country sharply divided into economic classes. In 1935–1936 it looked like this:

Incomes of less than $1000 per annum	43.5%
Incomes of $1000–1999 per annum	34.2%
Incomes of $2000–2999 per annum	13.1%
Incomes of $3000–3999 per annum	4.4%
Incomes of $4000–4999 per annum	1.7%

and so on into the economic stratosphere.

By 1945–1946 that pyramid had been smashed. There were still rich people at one end and poor people at the other. But America had at last become what it said it was and what it had so long wanted to be—a middle-class nation: an economic and social democracy. The distribution of family incomes now looked like this:

Incomes of less than $1000 per annum	8.8%
Incomes of $1000–1999 per annum	17.6%
Incomes of $2000–2999 per annum	20.3%
Incomes of $3000–3999 per annum	19.8%
Incomes of $4000–4999 per annum	12.4%
Incomes of $5000 and more per annum	21.1%

The share of the top 5 percent of the population had meanwhile dropped sharply, to 18 percent of the total national income.

What had occurred was a fundamental reversal in the way in which economic gains were divided. Because this redistribution came from an expanding economy, it was painless; it did not require that the gains of one sector be wrested from another. Since Pearl Harbor, every economic group had gained, but the biggest advances were scored at the bottom of the social pyramid. This is how family incomes increased between 1941 and 1945:

Lowest fifth	+68%
Second fifth	+59%
Third fifth	+36%
Fourth fifth	+30%
Top fifth	+20%

This achievement, unprecedented and still unparalleled, was paced by other important changes. The portion of national income going to property in the form of profits, interest and rent had dropped by 20 percent in the fifty years preceding the war. It dropped another 20 percent during the war years. It has not dropped significantly since.

Excise and business taxes were a bigger source of revenue under the New Deal than were personal and corporate income taxes. By the end of the war these regressive tax policies were ended. Indirect taxes provided only 15 percent of federal revenues now. This shift in taxation policy was government's principal wartime attempt to redistribute income. Yet even then it was responsible for less than a tenth of what redistribution occurred. The rest was done silently, unplanned by anyone, and the more effective for being so.

The prosperous, conservative elements grumbled that "In the wartime U.S. the poor were getting richer, the rich poorer," and went on to bemoan that workers were getting high wages while the rich were being taxed without mercy; that the Junior League had been forced to drop its dues from $120 to $75 while the proletariat had more money than it knew what to do with; that sales of classical records were dropping, while sales of "Old Black Joe" were soaring. Middle-class housewives were learning to do their own housework. In 1936 virtually every middle-class home had a servant. The upper third of the population was literally waited on by the other two-thirds. Now almost no one had a servant. And the good bourgeoise, whether newly minted or to the class born, was lamenting that the postwar world held no promise of a return of the domestic servant. The feelings of the former servants can be guessed at: Their average wage in 1941 had been $7 a week, plus board, in exchange for an average workweek of seventy hours.

There was some slippage in income distribution after the war, but it was minor. The magnitude of what had been achieved may be grasped when we consider that it took twenty years for family incomes in the United States to rise another 50 percent after the war ended. With that gradual increase there has gone no further redistribution. The breakdown of family incomes is now almost exactly what it was twenty-five years ago. In the interim a new generation of poor has been born, and has come of age, and has been fed into the welfare bureaucracy.

Even a highly critical economist was able to write that despite those wartime economic policies of which he disapproved, "The more cheerful side of this tale is that the underprivileged third of America's population undoubtedly lived better during the war and for some time afterward than they had ever lived before." While other liberals were gnashing their teeth over the death of the New Deal, one at least, Stuart Chase, looked around and said, "So what?" Just look, he said, at what has happened. Practically every common man has a job; he feels that he belongs; he makes more money than he needs; he has paid most of his debts; he usually has some money put away in defense bonds or a savings account; rationing and progressive taxes have combined to reduce class differences; the government has assumed responsibility for seeing that everyone at least has the necessities of life—"In short, the facts show a better break for the common man than liberals in 1938 could have expected for a generation." As for talk of a postwar reaction, it was obvious to him that only at gunpoint would people surrender their wartime gains; they would bring down the government first. It was no ideological conservatism, then, which made America conservative in wartime. It was a conservative outlook that was a luxury of sorts; it could be afforded because no longer was the country rich, the people poor.

The nation as a whole, in fact, favored modern social welfare programs. Ninety-four percent supported old age pensions, 84 percent favored unemployment insurance, 83 percent favored national health insurance, 79 percent wanted direct governmental aid to students, and 75 percent favored the government making itself the employer of last resort. Opposition to a Cabinet level Department of Health, Education and Welfare had dropped to half its prewar level and stood at 22 percent. The seeds of such an agency were already at hand in the Office of Community Health and Welfare Services.

And a great change had come over the nation's life that would not be shaken off with the end of the war. Through half a dozen major agencies —Social Security, Internal Revenue, Selective Service, the Office of Price Administration, the Office of Community War Services—Americans were now more closely tied to their government than any other generation in history. It eclipsed anything envisaged during the New Deal. Big government had come of age. It was no jerry-built creation of wartime but a permanent shift in American life. Republican politicians tried to make a political issue of it, to no avail. For while people grumbled about the failures of this agency or that, big government had produced results which, planned or unplanned, made life sweet to almost everyone in the world's most heterogeneous, noisy democracy.

The thirties were, as Irving Kristol has said, "America's last amateur decade"—amateur in its politics, in its economic ideas, in its approach to social problems. And the war was fought largely by an amateur bureaucracy which came swarming into government or into uniform from big business, the universities and the law firms. But they did not swarm out again. They kept their hands on the levers of power; doing so, they lost their amateur standing. Meanwhile, a vast and silent social revolution had run its course, remaking American society, healing it in mind and body, drawing its people together. It would roar into the postwar world no longer ill-fed, ill-clad, ill-nourished. There was a conservative revival. But once people had the social substance, who cared about ideological dressing?

XXIX

The Civil Liberties Disaster

A S far as civil liberties were concerned, the war was a disaster. As far as civil libertarians were concerned, it was a triumph.

The legs on which this triumph rested were two: All important violations were singular—exceptions which proved the rule; and only violations of free speech were really important.

The ACLU's 1943 report *Freedom in Wartime* set the pattern: "Undoubtedly the worst single invasion of civil liberties under war pressures was the wholesale evacuation from the Pacific coast of over 70,000 Americans of Japanese ancestry."* Having reduced 70,000 instances of injustice and persecution to a single regrettable lapse, the report went on to enthuse, "We experience no hysteria, no war-inspired mob violence, no pressure for suppressing dissent . . ." and carried this rhapsody on at some length. So tens of thousands of victims became one victim, and that one was made an exception. And to our own time serious writers on the internment portray it as the sole lamentable, anomalous, quirky exception to a record that is otherwise splendid.

In the same vein one academic authority on pacifism writes: "Despite a generally good wartime civil liberties record, the nation often made life difficult for pacifists."

An authority on religions meanwhile writes: "The Jehovah's Witnesses fared badly it is true. Yet the record on civil liberties appears better this time than for the previous war."

Yet as the exceptions mount, they cease to prove the rule—they become the rule. In truth, the number of victims of persecution far exceeded those of the earlier war; the treatment of them was at least as harsh; redress was just as difficult.

In the First World War the number of victims of mob attacks, the people suppressed under the Sedition Act, all of those arrested and ordered deported, all of those sent to prison for conscience, total (so far as it can be gauged) about 8,000 to 10,000. The interned Japanese and Nisei alone numbered 120,000 in 1942. The likelihood of a CO's being jailed, which was four times greater in this war, resulted in 6,000 men being imprisoned for conscientious objection. The victims of mob violence ran into the

* They excluded the 50,000 Issei from consideration.

thousands. And small antiwar cults like Elijah Muhammad's Black Muslims were vigorously suppressed, producing still more victims. Thus, for every person falling foul of official or spontaneous persecution in the First World War, there were more than ten times as many victims in the Second.

The civil libertarians, however, defined infringements in the narrowest possible way. They hovered alertly over the First Amendment. But hardly anyone openly opposed this war. That meant there could be at most a relative handful of prosecutions for utterance. (Yet what there could be, there were.) This sort of logic chopping cut off the other nine amendments and with them the spirit that informs the Bill of Rights which secures the individual and restrains the state.

Such were the ways in which calamity was presented as an achievement for free men to be proud of. Compared with the other four English-speaking democracies fighting in this war, America unhappily had the worst civil liberties record of all.

Nevertheless, the Attorney General, Francis Biddle, was revered by American liberals. Only Justice Frank Murphy, himself a former AG, remained unimpressed. He called Biddle's vendetta against Harry Bridges "a monument to intolerance."

Biddle's actions throughout the war followed a general pattern: Scapegoats were identified and persecution begun; Biddle would resist official involvement; the pressure on him would increase; he would soon cave in. And there was a larger historic pattern of which these things were merely a part. The worst excesses against civil liberties in the Great War had come not during the first months of American involvement, in 1917, but when Allied fortunes were at the nadir, in the spring of 1918. The Sedition Act was easily defeated in 1917; it sailed through Congress in short order one year later. With the Ludendorff Offensive smashing across the western front in 1918, it was then that Germans in the United States and leftist antiwar elements were subject to the worst mob violence and official persecution of the war.

And self-congratulation that such things had not been repeated went from left to right in the Second World War. It was the work not of hypocrisy, but blindness. America's left-liberals were blind to the real nature of what had occurred because they had not suffered, as many of them had in the earlier war. More than that, this was as just a war as any could be. Opposition to it was, in their own eyes, little better than aiding Fascism.

On those rare occasions where a leftist opposed the war it was plain that very little had really changed from one war to the next. Harry Weber, for example, belonged to a tiny Marxist splinter group, the Socialist Labor Party. Married, father of three children, he was, contrary to Selective Service policy, ordered to report for induction. Weber asked to be classified as a CO, but expressed willingness to serve in the Medical Corps. His draft board classified him 1-A; the Army ordered him to drill with a rifle; he refused; he was sentenced to hang. This was reduced on appeal to life imprisonment.*

Of the 10,000,000 men ordered to report for induction some 42,973 were officially classified as conscientious objectors. But there is good reason to believe that the true number of objectors was close to 100,000.

Most of them accepted noncombatant service. Of the rest, roughly 12,000 worked in the Civilian Public Service camps. The remaining 6,000 went to prison. These jailings ran at four times the World War I rate and ten times the then-current British rate. The conditions under which jailed CO's lived in federal prisons were hard: Beatings were frequent; food was execrable; petty harassment was routine; worst of all, sentences were long. They averaged five years in the first years of the war, less than four years by 1945.†

The worst treatment was reserved for Jehovah's Witnesses, who made up the bulk of the imprisoned CO's. At one time, draft boards routinely inducted them and sent them along to the Army. Once forced into uniform, they were court-martialed for refusing to salute the flag. Sentences for this offense ran as high as life imprisonment. The hundreds of Witnesses held at Fort Leavenworth, Kansas, were kept in solitary confinement for sixteen straight months, half the time on bread and water. And all the earmarks of calculated persecution attended their miseries. "As many as forty-two of them were recently sentenced in one court in a single day," wrote one reporter, "reminding lovers of freedom somewhat painfully of similar occurrences in Fascist countries."

Civil libertarians made a great fuss over the freedom of speech that objectors enjoyed. And they could indeed speak out in prison, at home, in church and in the CPS camps. A pacifist press worked unmolested throughout the war. Yet it was illusory freedom, being mere symbolic protest. For "whenever personal expression of belief turned into organized public protest it ran head on into adamant (and effective) opposition."

The CPS camps were also pointed to as a triumph of decency over primitive passions. Yet what novelty they boasted lay in their harshness. In the First World War most objectors had been able to do alternative service on "farm furloughs." They worked long hours, their movement was somewhat restricted; but they were paid for their labor and were never kept under close guard like prisoners sentenced to serve at hard labor. In this war, men in the CPS camps worked fifty hours a week and received

* As the war drew to a close, Weber's sentence was reduced to five years.
† In Britain, on the other hand, sentences were usually for several months; rare indeed was the objector who spent more than six months in jail.

not a penny for it. On the contrary, they paid the government for their food and clothing, to the hardship of many families. They did dangerous work, such as fire fighting and smoke jumping; they participated in potentially fatal or disabling medical experiments. Yet they were denied accident or mortality insurance.*

Life in the camps, which were taken over by Selective Service in 1942, became so regimented and militarized that by the end of 1943 more objectors chose to go to prison rather than into the camps. Ordinary people by this time favored good wages and family allowances for men on alternative service. But federal authorities never relented.

Even after the war ended, the government was reluctant to disband the CPS camps and let the men in them go home. Revolts and strikes flared. To the tune of one of the war's most popular songs, "Pistol Packin' Mama," the rebellious inmates would down tools and sing:

> We labored lo! these many years
> For all those hazy goals.
> The Forest Service got our sweat,
> The Brethren got our souls.
>
> Break the system down, boys!
> Break the system down!
> Strike the lick that does the trick
> And break the system down!

But not until 1948 did the last of these men return home.

In 1942 approximately 150 people were indicted under the Espionage Act for hampering the prosecution of the war. More than 100 publications were suppressed. Most, like *Social Justice*, were publications of the right-wing lunatic fringe. A few, like *The Militant*, were ultraleftist. And two—*Police Gazette* and *Esquire*—were banned from the mails in the name of morality. The idea seems to have been that wartime morale could best be upheld by keeping it pure. The ACLU protested the suppression of these two magazines, but not of the rest.

The government meantime charged two dozen leading pro-Fascists with sedition. But, presumably for lack of evidence, they were not brought to trial. Then, early in 1944, a federal grand jury reindicted twenty of them, plus ten other persons, under the 1940 Alien Registration Act, and charged them all with conspiring to foment disloyalty and topple the government. It was clearly a free speech case. Yet again the ACLU refused to intervene.

* In Canada, by comparison, objectors in alternative service lived at home, did work assigned by the government and were paid for it.

The accused included Joe McWilliams, the former Christian Front organizer; Elizabeth Dilling, author of *The Red Network* and head of the "Mothers' Crusade"; James True, founder of America First, Inc., and inventor of a billyclub called "The Kike-killer" (U.S. Patent 2026077); and Harvard-educated Lawrence Dennis, author of *The Coming American Fascism*. Told of his indictment, Dennis complained, "My prophecy is coming true. This is Fascism."

Individually and collectively the accused did not look like much of a threat to national security. All they had in common was hatred for Roosevelt, Jews and Communism. Some were bright; others were stupid. Some were rich; others were poor. Some were successful in their work; others were failures. Between them they hired twenty-two lawyers, and they all —lawyers and defendants—bickered endlessly. Yet the thirty defendants were nonetheless charged with conspiring together to undermine the military services of the United States. Most of the country dismissed it as a farce.

But not the liberal press or Attorney General Biddle, who sought the indictments. James Wechsler, national affairs editor of the liberal daily *PM*, insisted that the country's existence was at stake. "Disastrous consequences would follow a government defeat in the prosecution. . . ."

The defendants made a shambles of judicial dignity. While government lawyers and the judge tried to adhere to established procedures, the defendants and their lawyers wailed hysterically that it was all a Jewish-Communist plot to curb their freedom of speech. They moaned, groaned, laughed aloud, cheered and clamored, abetted by friends in the spectators' seats. The judge gaveled from morning till late afternoon, demanding, "Order! Order in the court!" Bailiffs rushed to and fro trying to get the defendants to sit down. "It was as though Justice had hiked her robes to jitterbug in the aisles."

The *Nation* was outraged. The defendants were prolonging the trial indefinitely by exploiting every procedural safeguard, "thus making a farce of democratic justice." These tactics, they glowered, had been pioneered by Hitler's followers in the courts of the Weimar Republic, and "Like the Nazis these defendants are bound by no rules of civilized conduct. . . ." The *New Republic* doubted that the country's judicial system would survive "the strain of this unprecedented type of mass disorder." For these were "tactics first organized scientifically by the Nazis."

The trial wound its chaotic way through the spring and into the summer of 1944. By August the number of defendants had dropped to twenty-six; one had died during all the excitement, two others were taken ill, a fourth was severed from the trial because he outdid the rest in disruptive behavior. One lawyer was heavily fined and was barred from the case. Five others were cited for contempt of court. The defendants wore Halloween masks and carried signs reading I AM A SPY. Exhausted, judge and prosecution agreed to a two-week respite while defense lawyers sardonically asked if they could count on having a summer vacation every year.

When the trial resumed, so too did the charade. But it came abruptly to an end, with the prosecution just getting to the core of its case, when the judge died in November. Liberals blamed the defendants for his death and insisted that the case be started up again. Only the Washington *Post* among liberal newspapers was opposed to resumption. It appears to have been one of the few to carefully examine the prosecution's case. The trial, it concluded, was a farce and predicted that it would stand as a shameful reminder of wartime hysteria. The conservative *Saturday Evening Post* agreed. It was a show trial, a propaganda trial; it should never have been staged.

The contempt that liberals felt for the views of most of the defendants, especially their anti-Semitism, was understandable and immediate. For it was not the least of the war's ironies that while America fought Nazi Germany in the name of decency, democracy and civilization, American Jews were the victims of a nasty rise in bigotry.

Jews in New York complained not only that were they being attacked in the streets but that the police often looked the other way or made only halfhearted efforts to catch their attackers. Similar complaints were made in other cities. But nowhere was the situation worse than in Boston, where Coughlinite gangs roamed the streets at night, terrorizing any luckless Jew they stumbled upon, smashing Jewish-owned businesses and vandalizing synagogues. Boston newspapers refused to report the incidents. And the patrician Governor Leverett Saltonstall angrily called a New York reporter who had exposed the attacks "a liar" and had him thrown out of the State Capitol building.

The terrorism continued unabated. And by 1944 in Boston's Ward 14, a section more than 90 percent Jewish, "the residents were living in a perpetual state of alarm." Beatings and property destruction occurred almost daily. And throughout the city there circulated anti-Semitic literature, such as a pamphlet called *The First American:*

> First American killed at Pearl Harbor—John J. Hennessey
> First American to sink a Jap ship—Colin P. Kelly
> First American to sink a Jap ship by torpedo—John P. Buckley
> Greatest American air hero—"Butch" O'Hare
> First American killed at Guadalcanal—John J. O'Brien
> First American to get four new tires—Abraham Lipschitz

This sort of venom washed over into Congress where Mississippi's John Rankin attacked Jews almost as often as he attacked Negroes. At one point he called Walter Winchell "that little kike" and concluded his anti-Semitic rantings to loud, prolonged applause.

And when people were asked which groups should be allowed to immigrate to the United States after the war, the British were approved by 68 percent, the Russians by 57 percent, the Chinese by 56 percent, and Jews came last with 46 percent.

But this rising tide of intolerance was not to be turned back by persecuting anti-Semites or crypto-Fascists, although the government had not had enough of conspiracy trials. Even with the end of the war in sight it tried to revive the sedition indictments. Not until 1946 was this farce ended by the federal courts.

Distinguished refugees, like the Danish physicist Niels Bohr, still trickled into the wartime United States. Max Lerner exulted, "If Aristotle were alive today he would be a New Yorker." And the influx of refugees and governments in exile had indeed given the nation's premier city a new cosmopolitanism. In and around Rockefeller Center there had sprung up an émigré press, full of dreams, claims, plans, demands, in everything from slick, expensive magazines to smudgy mimeographed handbills.

But most of the refugees who had managed to reach America's shores were not dreaming of repatriation. They were becoming Americanized as fast as they could, and counted themselves lucky. For most people—that is, about 80 percent—were opposed to any substantial immigration in the postwar world.

Yet there would be a monumental refugee problem when the war ended. Everyone knew that. The administration spent much time and effort on the problem, thinking wistfully of colonization. Hundreds of sites were considered—all of them outside the United States. Roosevelt personally was enthusiastic about settlements along the Orinoco River, in Brazil. Congress would willingly help finance such schemes.

A newspaper columnist, Samuel Grafton, proposed in 1944 that the United States should set up "free ports" for persons. Why not, he asked, let people come into the United States freely in wartime, on the understanding that they would, in a sense, be "reexported" when the war ended? Roosevelt agreed—for no more than 1,000 people, most of them Italians. At the same time the House was slashing the proposed appropriation for the UN Relief and Rehabilitation Agency by more than two-thirds.

The Oriental exclusion acts of 1888 were repealed meantime, and a few thousand people already in the United States on visitors' visas were allowed to remain. These gestures provided a fig leaf for what was really a harsh immigration policy.

As one writer sadly concluded after studying America's treatment of refugees from 1933 to 1945, "The lamp remained lifted beside the golden door, but the flame had been extinguished and the door was padlocked."

Two significant events had coincided on August 7, 1942: The Army announced the completion of the evacuation of the West Coast Japanese and Nisei to the assembly centers, and American forces in the Pacific went on the offensive as the marines stormed onto the beaches of Guadalcanal. From that date forward the treatment of the internees steadily improved.

From the camps which the Army had hastily knocked together they were moved to more permanent, prisonlike facilities euphemistically termed "Relocation Centers."* The Army handed the internees over to the newly created War Relocation Authority, which was staffed chiefly by people drawn from the Indian Service, the moribund CCC and WPA and the Department of Agriculture. To them, the WRA camps were one more opportunity for New Deal good works, for "social engineering." Fondly they conjured up visions of the desert in bloom.

The internees were soon faced with more forms to fill in, were fingerprinted again and required to take a loyalty oath to the United States "in thought, word and deed." They were required to sign up for WRA-assigned work, "for the duration of the war and fourteen days thereafter," promising to accept "whatever pay, unspecified at this time, the War Relocation Authority determines." The top pay, as it turned out, went to doctors. They were paid $19 a month.

To the WRA administrators these camps, which were really prisons, were "wartime communities." The people in them were "residents" or "colonists." But now and again reality intruded. For in these camps all "Japanese" were subservient to all "Caucasians." And when inmates were murdered by guards, the guards went unpunished.

There was, as in most American prisons, boredom, dull food, dirt, strikes, revolts, a lack of privacy and an overriding tension. Pro- and anti-American factions clashed endlessly. And in 1943 the WRA foolishly tried to make the question of loyalty the key to its control.

Every internee was told to swear fidelity to the United States, again. This time by repudiating Japan. As Americans, the Nisei were outraged at the idea. So too were the Issei. For they were told to spurn ties to Japan, yet were barred by U.S. laws from ever becoming American citizens. They would become people without a country. What the bureaucrats of the WRA thought sensible was fundamentally misguided and unjust. Some 7,000 internees refused to take the new oath. They were then segregated in a maximum security camp at Tule Lake.

Yet this development did not indicate a tougher policy toward the Japanese and Nisei. Early in 1943 the Army began accepting recruits for the all-Nisei 442d Regimental Combat Team. Older people sneered that it

---

* Roosevelt inadvertently called them "Concentration Camps," to the dismay of the War Relocation Authority bureaucrats.

was "Jap Crow"; young men enlisted over parental objections. But when the 442d earned fame for its bravery, the spirit of *bushido*, the warrior code of an ancient culture, stirred in these dreary camps on alien soil and parents pressed their sons to enlist.*

Public hostility was still being encouraged by public officials and the conservative press, especially on the West Coast. The revelation of Japanese atrocities, such as the execution of the Doolittle raiders, brought calls for reprisals against the internees. And in December, 1943, a riot broke out at Tule Lake. The WRA suppressed it by applying main force. A thousand soldiers moved into the camp, gassing, clubbing and shooting, leaving two dead and fifty seriously injured behind them.

Governor Warren, who spent his first year in office agitating for permanent barriers to any postwar return of the Issei and Nisei, went into a frenzy of rage. For two weeks the war was forced onto the inside of West Coast newspapers which blazoned with headlines like this one:

DEADLY PERIL AS ARMED JAPS
STREAM INTO CALIFORNIA

There were long articles relating how drunken orgies, wholesale slaughter, the raping of white women were all daily occurrences at Tule Lake, thanks to spineless mollycoddling of the apelike Japanese.

But despite the furor, conditions in most of the camps continued to improve, and early in 1944 West Coast draft boards started to induct Nisei registrants. By the end of that year many of the Nisei had left the camps, either to go into the Army or to move to the East (over La Guardia's strenuous protests) and Midwest. And even before the war ended, the internees were going back to California. There were a few nasty incidents. But for all the fury of the local press and politicians, hatred for the Issei and Nisei had never gone very deep. Already, indeed, the wisdom of the evacuation was being questioned.

It is tempting to wonder what the Supreme Court's performance in wartime would have been without the fight over the Court in 1937. But no amount of speculation can provide a satisfactory answer. What is certain is that though the Court was not rearranged to Roosevelt's wishes, the shadow of the fight hung over the federal judiciary for nearly a decade. Eight years passed before the Court again ventured to declare an act of

---

* In all, some 33,000 Nisei served in the Second World War. It was ironic, but the segregated, Oriental 442d was one of the most elite of all Army units, and only the cream of the Nisei recruits served in it. Its average strength at any one time was 3,000 men. By the end of the war it counted 9,486 dead and wounded. It was the most decorated combat force in the Army, with one Medal of Honor winner, 52 DSC's, 560 Silver Stars. Men with three and four Purple Hearts were commonplace.

government unconstitutional. It is not surprising then that the Supreme Court, the penultimate bastion of individual liberties (the ultimate being, of course, the conscience of the community, however roughly expressed), was a porous defense at best against the current hysteria.

The Court allowed the convictions of the eighteen Minneapolis Trotskyites to stand. It persistently turned a deaf ear to appeals by conscientious objectors and pacifists. It ducked the constitutional questions in the internment of the Japanese and Nisei. Not until the war was nearly over would it even touch the internment and then, like Cromwell looking at the head of Charles I, mourned "harsh necessity." After the war, once the issue was moot, it was much braver and ruled that military suspensions of civil liberties should not be allowed to run on for years at a time.

Yet as victory drew near, popular and official tempers mellowed, and the Court modified or reversed some of its worst wartime rulings. In 1943 it set aside the convictions of Jehovah's Witnesses who, in their zeal to preach, had violated municipal ordinances. A few months later the Court reversed its earlier flag salute ruling. The ex post facto prosecution of George Sylvester Viereck was also turned aside and his six-year sentence struck down.

These things were, in themselves, nothing more than elementary justice. Yet almost every ruling carried a train of impassioned dissents in its wake. For the Court, like many other important institutions, was changing its character, or rather, it was not so much changing its character as its character was being split. In the early years of the war the Court was generally complaisant about civil liberties questions. But it bore within it a fundamental division into antagonistic halves. And before the war ended, the conflicting judicial philosophies of Justices Black and Frankfurter had erupted into an angry quarrel which embraced the entire high court bench. By the spring of 1944 it led one observer to write, "What the members of the Supreme Court will do with matters that are laid before them is as predictable these days as what a cage of chimps will do with a bunch of bananas." Similarly, Justice Roberts was admonishing his fellow Justices that they were throwing out so many earlier decisions that a Supreme Court ruling was beginning to look "like a restricted railroad ticket—good for this day and train only."

What was really occurring was that the Supreme Court was now becoming the liberal, activist Court that would flower in the postwar era. The Court opened the way for Negroes to vote in party primaries, and it supported the demands of Negro firemen for equal pay and equal promotion opportunities. In these things it succeeded where the FEPC had tried and failed. So while the Court had not served civil liberties well in wartime, it was to American liberals a shining hope in an uncertain future. As one of them wrote in the spring of 1944, "The Federal Judiciary, led by its

Supreme Court, may well prove to be, in the coming decade, the most liberal of the three branches of national government."

It was an accurate appraisal. Yet though the postwar Court proved to be right in the essentials, that fact does nothing to exonerate a wartime showing that was, at best, disappointing. For as everyone knows, the test of the protection of fundamental rights is not how they are served in times of calm but how vigilantly they are defended in times of danger. By that test the wartime experience may be fairly described as a disaster for tens of thousands of Americans.

XXX

Wartime School Days

AMERICA'S schools and colleges had thrown themselves into the defense crisis with so much vigor that their momentum carried them easily through the school year in the middle of which came the Pearl Harbor attack. Defense courses became war courses. The purges of radical teachers and the hunt for fifth columnists were kept going.

To absorb the excess energies of students who wanted to join in the war effort, a High School Victory Corps was created in the summer of 1942. There was a badge and a uniform of sorts: white shirt and dark trousers for boys, white blouse and dark skirt for girls. Ostensibly they were being prepared for war work or the services, but for the most part they were kept busy with parades, scrap drives, bond sales and calisthenics. For these activities the high schools gave academic credit.

Secondary school curricula tended strongly to vocational training and physical education all through 1942 and 1943. War reached down into the most exalted private schools and had the preppies learning close-order drill, motor mechanics, navigation, map reading and aeronautics. The passion for teaching democracy was over; it had proved too elusive. War became the fulcrum of American education. Spelling lessons mixed military terms with everyday words; English classes offered propaganda analysis; arithmetic problems used airplanes where once they used apples. Elementary schools tried to keep up by having one scrap drive after another and air-raid drills two and three times a week.

A model wartime curriculum was drawn up by the executive secretaries of State Teachers Associations and Chief School Officers:

A. Courses in arithmetic, algebra, geometry, general mathematics and in some cases trigonometry . . . where many of the problems will be drawn from the fields of aviation, navigation, mechanized warfare and industry.

B. Courses in industrial arts related to war needs.

C. Courses in auto mechanics in cooperation with local garages and farmers, with particular emphasis on the repair of trucks, tractors and automobiles. . . .

D. More practical courses in cooking and sewing. . . .

E. Courses in physics particularly stressing the characteristics of mechanics, heat, photography and electricity.

F. Teaching units giving increased emphasis on health. . . .
G. Revised social studies courses to give a knowledge of war aims and issues as well as actual experience in community undertakings.
H. One or more units of study dealing with an understanding of the armed forces. . . .
I. Unit pre-flight courses as outlined by the armed forces. . . .

Not every school followed the same curriculum, but this was representative of the regimen on which tens of millions of children and teen-agers were educated between 1942 and 1945.

If, besides war, secondary education had a central theme in these years, it was "air age education." More than 75 percent of the boys were enrolled in "preflight" courses; most of them were useless, however, save as a means of making youngsters "air-minded." History's great men were Leonardo da Vinci and the Wright brothers. Biology classes explained the physiology of a blackout in a tight turn. Spelling classes smuggled in such words as "nacelle," "troposphere" and "advection." The literature of flight was ransacked to provide new anthologies for English literature classes. Textbooks with flying themes rolled from the presses.

It was in this militarized atmosphere that progressive education tried to claim the prize it thought it had won. But just as *Time* was concluding from the Eight Year Study, "Many considered the report a death sentence for the traditional system of U.S. high school education," the exigencies of war placed a new premium on overt displays of regimentation. The call now was for "discipline." Private schools prospered, especially those with reputations for being spartan. Military schools, which had languished in the thirties, had their pick of applicants. Even the least known of them, like Northwestern Academy and Wentworth, were inundated. And people like Nicholas Murray Butler, who had once called progressive education "the rabbit system of education" (presumably for the timid, the mindless and the undisciplined), laid the incredible rise in juvenile delinquency squarely on the progressives' doorstep. When terror struck big-city classrooms, many a conservative school board which had been on the academic defensive for years set off in full cry after progressive education and blamed the classroom violence on "permissiveness" in the schools.* All the schools in the city and state of New York were set to become progressive in 1942–1943. Instead, that entire program sank rapidly out of sight. School districts everywhere began to retreat from progressive methods and philosophy.

Army generals were blaming progressive education for desertions, AWOL's, incompetence in the ranks and anything that smacked of "soft-

---

* It is worth noting that progressive school districts, such as Tulsa, Oklahoma, had a markedly lower wartime incidence of violence and delinquency than those school systems which had never been progressive—*e.g.*, Chicago.

ness" or ill discipline. Navy admirals grumbled about the low level of training in mathematics and blamed it on progressive education. Few of the critics appeared to grasp that only a handful of American children had ever been exposed to progressive methods and teachers. Progressivism's brief golden age was over all the same. The Progressive Education Association phased out its publication, *Frontiers of Democracy*, promised to shift its attention from the child to the community, and hastily turned itself into the American Education Fellowship. PEA was dead. Progressive education was but another victim to the conservative revival. Long regarded as a left-wing pedagogy, it went the same way as scores of left-liberal institutions. In American schools authoritarianism had come back with a rush.

The classrooms were meanwhile being placed in the hands of hordes of inexperienced teachers, many thousands of them without as much as a high school diploma. More than 350,000 experienced teachers had left the schools to take up war work or go into the services. Enrollment in teachers' colleges plummeted. Emergency teaching credentials were issued at ten times the normal rate and were renewed year after year. Teaching standards, which had never been very high in the general run of schools, dropped to rock bottom. And despite a rise in state revenues, often resulting in lower tax rates, many a school district's budget was cut.

It was thus with considerable heat that the National Education Association criticized America's educational policies and contrasted them with those of Great Britain, where tens of thousands of drafted teachers were sent back to their schools and where education budgets increased each year despite the war.

Not only were the teachers gone, but so were many of their students. Some 4,000,000 high school students went off to work in the summer of 1943, and when the schools reopened in the fall, more than 1,000,000 refused to come back.

Yet there was at least one heartening development. No one intended it, but thanks to the war, ties between the schools and the communities they served were drawn close. The school became the center of community war work. For many that meant no more than that the school became the place to organize a scrap drive or set up a ration board. But to millions more the school—its problems, its resources, its teachers and administrators, its responsibilities, its needs—became for the first time an object of serious interest. Rationing alone brought 1,000,000 teachers face to face with 20,000,000 parents as the PTA had never done and could never hope to do. Teachers found it an important experience; presumably parents did, too. Local citizens had paid for the schools, but rarely had they ventured inside them before. They knew the names of their children's teachers, but had never met them. They had felt remote from the schools and what went on in them. For the moment, at least, that was no longer true. This development gave new impetus to the fight for federal aid to education.

For though the government had borne down upon the nation's schools as never before—using them, for instance, to give vocational training to 9,000,000 people prior to sending them into war work—there was still strong resistance to tying local schools to the federal government. Large amounts of federal money were coming into the secondary schools (for vocational training and aid to impacted areas), but ideological conservatives persistently tried to turn it aside. Every year since 1937 a federal aid-to-education bill came up in Congress with a suggested appropriation in the hundreds of millions of dollars. More than 1,000 schools closed each year for want of teachers. The Army had lost the equivalent of scores of divisions because more than half the adult population had not gone beyond the eighth grade. There were 10,000,000 adults who were functionally illiterate. But by loading the aid-to-education bill with civil rights amendments, Senator Taft each year managed to provoke enough Southern Senators into voting against it to turn the tide. The conservatives, however, had been outflanked by the aid-to-impacted-areas program. And now that they were taking an interest in their schools, millions of American parents were pressing for federal aid to them.

Local control, though there were always those who grew misty-eyed over it, was not quite as wonderful as it was made out to be. La Guardia, for instance, never tired of interfering with the administration of New York's schools. The NEA admonished him for the forceful, vindictive fashion in which he continually cowed the city's school board. But La Guardia was simply far less interested in schoolchildren than he was with controlling the board; he had found it useful in the course of his political career. And what La Guardia did in New York lesser tyrants repeated on a smaller scale in communities all over the country.

On the college campuses the pre-Pearl Harbor defense courses looked altogether tame once the country was at war. Army officers made no secret of their opinion that the courses were useless. The University of Chicago, self-consciously innovative as ever, responded by setting up its own Institute for Military Studies. Undergraduates enrolled there were taught marksmanship, grenade throwing, the art of the bayonet, close-order drill and hand-to-hand combat. Other colleges soon set up obstacle courses and rifle ranges. But most could afford only to cook up more classroom studies: military law, the chemistry of explosives, camouflage techniques, military German and Japanese, map reading.

But the principal response to the shift from defense to war at the colleges and universities was to accelerate the normal tempo of things. The high schools followed suit, and before long, graduations were being

held somewhere by someone on any given day. Scores of colleges had
moved even before December, 1941, to offer three-year bachelors' degrees
to minimize the impact of the draft. Medical schools now lopped a year
off their programs and offered a three-year MD. Law degrees were cut
from three years to two. Year-round operations, increased course loads,
entering classes in June instead of September, correspondence courses for
students who were drafted, combining the high school senior year with
the college freshman year—such was acceleration. Classes were hurried
through and sent out into a warring world without caps, gowns, parades,
speeches or ceremony.

Besides falling enrollments, the colleges had to contend with the fact
that the military had a virtual monopoly on graduating high school
seniors. And some college administrators, such as Harvard's Conant, worried that something entirely undemocratic was likely to emerge: Only
those the Army and Navy wanted to train as officers would be able to go
to college. But Congress laid such fears to rest by initiating a program
hitherto unprecedented. As a war measure the federal government began
to offer scholarships and low-interest loans to students in fields of study
it thought bore on the nation's security.

The Army and Navy were eager to take over the colleges, pick the
students, prescribe their curricula and eliminate everything but technical
and military-related subjects. That would not require all 1,400 colleges
and universities. Those they did not need would probably have to shut
down. During the First World War the Army had virtually taken over
higher education. Almost every male college student had been put into
uniform, given a private's rank and pay, and kept busy drilling back and
forth across the campus. Thousands of professors and administrators
recalled the scene and despaired.

To preclude any repetition of that experience, the colleges proposed to
contract themselves out to the military. A set of rough compromises was
worked out. One program committed the Army to send several hundred
thousand selected high school graduates to college for a year or two; then
the Army would send them off to Officers' Candidate Schools. Another
program had young men with marked technical aptitude going straight
from basic training to college for a year or more. As with other war contracting, most of the contracts went to the top institutions; more than
1,000 small colleges were driven to—but not quite over—the brink of
disaster. All told, more than 400,000 young men received a college education in 1943 at government expense.

With the military all over the campus "collegiate" no longer meant, as
it had for years past, "something essentially callow, superficial and insignifi-
cant." And the military presence was all-pervasive. At Harvard's two hundred and ninety-second commencement one famous alumnus hailed his
alma mater as "one of the foremost military and naval academies in the

United States." For every academic degree awarded there that day, four military training certificates were conferred. Even Quaker colleges such as Haverford had most of their 1943 graduating class in uniform. At Berkeley, Robert Gordon Sproul pronounced, "The University of California is no longer an academic main tent with military sideshows. It is a military tent with academic sideshows."

The trainees in the specialized training programs with mystifying V numbers were both envied and resented by their peers. Soldiers in combat units sneered at the programs as "college foxholes." And when casualties began to rise steeply and draft boards fell short of their quotas, the enthusiasm of military staffs for the college programs diminished. But all through 1943 the Army carried out mass testing of young men aged seventeen to twenty-one. The tests were drawn up by the civilian College Entrance Examination Board and were given to millions. From those who scored well the Army and Navy chose their officer candidates, then sent them to college. It was all very democratic. Thanks to it, more than 1,000,000 young men in wartime received college degrees or credits toward degrees at the taxpayers' expense. Here was one more program of social welfare in disguise.

But in early 1944 the Army ordered nearly all its students in uniform onto active duty, throwing the colleges into turmoil. The only trainees left were in medicine, dentistry and engineering. A pall of gloom descended over the campuses. Yet this decision did not affect the scores of smaller programs for "retooling" or "converting" hundreds of thousands of managers and supervisors to take up new positions in the war industries.

Before Pearl Harbor most of the trainees in these programs were people whose skills were being upgraded. Now they were usually people who were acquiring skills in management, engineering and science for the first time, people such as former salesmen, stockbrokers, playground supervisors, housewives. At no cost to themselves they received up to a year of intensive technical training. Employers, finding them well trained, took to bidding for entire graduating classes.

The pervasive military presence on campus had given a new thrust to the clash between the humanists and the scientists. Many a college professor became alarmed for the future of liberal education. Mass testing for aptitudes and abilities; standardized textbooks; and audiovisual aids such as films, recordings, models, graphics—all had been around for years past. But the military relied heavily on them, and the schools and colleges were beginning to do the same.

The Army also proposed that the colleges provide only technical training to its trainees. The Navy was willing to permit a smattering of instruction in English and history. This hard-nosed approach enjoyed the blessing of some noted academics. Johns Hopkins' famous Professor of Philosophy George Boas derided the calls for liberal education in wartime. "If training men in trigonometry and physics and chemistry will win the war, then for God's sake let us forget our art, our literature, our history and get down to business learning trigonometry, physics and chemistry." After all, said Boas, civilization is not trapped within the universities like a fly caught in amber. It permeates society. And if classical scholars are to be exempted from military service, why not, say, accountants or plumbers? The alternative was the creation of "a class of privileged men and women who have been kept in college at the expense of other men's lives." Princeton's Dean Christian Gauss meanwhile firmly insisted that humane learning be suspended for the duration. Knowing Plato, he said, did not make a man a better soldier.*

Here was no obscure quarrel between academics; the entire country was drawn into the fight. The New York *Times* created an uproar with surveys in 1942 and 1943 which showed that American high school students and college freshmen were profoundly ignorant of their country's history and institutions. More than 80 percent of the colleges were said to have no American history requirement. Before the war ended, however, state after state was moving to close the history gap by requiring a mandatory year of U.S. history of high school students, and most colleges introduced a similar requirement of their own as a prerequisite to graduation.

The anti-intellectualism of the Boases and the Gausses was also reaching down into the secondary schools. Even the U.S. Office of Education took up the theme. From its perspective the High School Victory Corps became an instrument for fundamental change in the schools. It should become "A campaign of community education to break down existing prejudices in favor of the strictly academic types of high school courses."

The University of Chicago had become famous in the thirties for the fight it put up against mere utilitarianism. And now liberals like Walter Lippmann and Lewis Mumford found themselves joined by moderate conservatives like Henry Luce in the defense of humane learning. But it fell to Willkie to make the most cogent defense of liberal education in wartime. To a cheering Duke University student body Willkie, a veteran of the Great War, went on the attack:

> The liberal arts, we are told, are luxuries . . . mere decorations on the sterner patterns of life. . . . Men and women who are devoting their lives to such studies should not be made to feel inferior or apologetic in the face of a PT boat commander or the driver of a tank. . . . The preservation of our cultural heritage is not superfluous—it is what we are fighting for. . . . [And] education is the mother of leadership.

* Yet is not *The Republic* a manual on training citizens how to serve the needs of the state in peace and in war?

With liberal education pressed so hard to survive it was not surprising that the panicky intolerance of the time before Pearl Harbor held over for the duration of the war, though the excesses were somewhat diminished. Bertrand Russell stayed on in the United States as genius-in-residence to a Pennsylvania health-foods millionaire and art collector named Albert Barnes. Then he had a falling out with his patron, and try as he might, Russell could not find a teaching position anywhere in the United States. Harvard, Columbia, Chicago, Berkeley, NYU—all turned him down. Unable to find a job, Russell returned to England.

At Notre Dame, meanwhile, a philosophy professor who publicly spoke out against anti-Semitism, Franco and isolationism, called for greater aid to Russia and approved the bombing of Rome was ousted from his post. At Cornell, student demands led to the teaching of courses on Russia. The faculty members who taught the courses were shortly thereafter denounced as Communists and fellow travelers. By a series of purges and gag rules the administration scurried hastily rightward and was able to expel the erring professors.

Elsewhere, the liberal president of Hunter College in New York, Dr. George N. Shuster, assembled his faculty and intimidated it as best he could. He would bring criminal charges, he said, against anyone who spoke against the war, suggested the Vatican was lenient on Fascism, made anti-Semitic remarks, said the Soviet way in government and society was better than the American way, suggested Negroes were inferior to whites or argued that the war was not just. Shuster was a prominent member of the ACLU and had an enviable national reputation as a defender of academic freedom.

So when in the summer of 1944 Conant called for more "American Radicals"—which *Time* seconded—it was plain that the radicals whom Conant had in mind were of a tame and peculiar variety. They would be, as Max Lerner observed, not radical at all but American provincial.

The war had exposed all the deficiencies in American education: a high level of functional illiteracy; a scandalous shortage of people with a basic competence in mathematics, foreign languages and science; tremendous disparities in educational opportunities; a lack of purpose or direction from grade school through college; and awesome deficiencies in vocational training. Hundreds of thousands of physically fit recruits were turned down for service because they could not read or write. And though the average chronological age of its soldiers was twenty-eight years, the Army claimed that the average mental development was that of fourteen-year-old children.

Only one American in four had finished high school. Most had not finished grade school. Thus, the biggest education demand among ordinary people was not for vocational or professional training, but secondary education. Many a returning veteran used his GI Bill benefits to pursue a high school diploma.

Looking to the future, the country's educators were seen to despair. Yet most people did not. Incredibly, they thought that the schools were adequate, and more. They saw no great need for change. Less than 10 percent even looked with favor on better-paid or better-qualified teachers. What a testament to the new infatuation with the status quo!

The National Education Association made its obsequies to the conservative mood by redundantly resolving at its 1944 convention to suppress "radical teaching." But even the NEA conceded that things could not stay as they were. For the war had irreversibly upset American education in at least two ways: Everyone could now claim the right to a college education, for the Army and Navy had shown that it could be done democratically and on a mass scale; second, federal aid to education was an imperative, for only then could genuine equality of opportunity be provided. It was, until the war, a fact—and a reflection of the class nature of an ostensibly classless society—that most of the brightest young people did not go to college. The places that merit should have claimed were filled in countless instances by dullards from prosperous homes. That situation could no longer be tolerated.

Reports and studies poured from academic and administrative bodies as the war neared its end, all of them looking toward a new system of American education in the postwar world. The NEA produced a General Purpose for America's Schools. The American Association of Colleges issued a report which it had labored over for nearly four years, calling for sweeping revisions in the college classroom. But looming over these and all other reports was Harvard's *General Education in a Free Society*. Its roots went back to the pre-1939 search for "general education." But because that phrase was now associated with progressive education, and the title of the Harvard report notwithstanding, the current catchphrase was "liberal education."

The wartime programs had expanded the standard curricula of high schools and colleges. Foreign area studies had been developed. There was a new interest in American culture, manifested in a rash of programs combining history and literature. The New York *Times'* surveys had brought a strong emphasis on the teaching of American history. A residue remained of the brief, intense fling with teaching democracy. There was the pervasive new interest in aviation. But these things in themselves contributed only to the fragmentation and confusion in the schools. The Harvard report, however, provided what was lacking and needed. It outshone its rivals because it alone provided an overarching educational philosophy that embraced everything from the humblest one-room rural school to the most exalted college on the Charles.

For years the secondary schools had been torn between "education for college" and "education for life." Unable to make up their minds fully about either, they fell short on both. Historically, the country had been trying to cope with a Jeffersonian conception of education for the elite and a Jacksonian conception of education for all, or so the Harvard report concluded. With the buoyant, assertive optimism that was coming to characterize the entire country in the final year of the war, the Harvard professors announced that the United States could and should do what no one had ever done or even tried to do: educate both the elite and the masses in a democratic, systematic fashion. Getting the natural elite through high school and into college should pose no difficulty to a rich country once the restraints of social class had been removed or lowered. But providing a liberal education—historically the prized possession of the upper, leisured classes—to the mass of its citizens was the burden and the glory of a modern democratic state.

According to the Harvard report, all high school students, whether going to college or not, were entitled to an education in the literary, artistic, political and scientific heritage of Western civilization and their own country. Those going to work at seventeen or eighteen were just as much citizens as those who were going to college. To participate fully and usefully in the life of a democratic nation, they must therefore be full heirs to its traditions, values, beliefs, history. Dividing the curriculum into general education and vocational training must be halted, and liberal education—preparation for both work and college—should be provided to all. Everyone should be able to both earn a living and cultivate the pleasures of the mind.

Many of the specific changes which the Harvard report recommended had already been implemented piecemeal in high schools and colleges. But here was a systematic approach which was rapidly taken up, and a new ideal was held out to high school students: They should strive to be "well-rounded"—equally able to change their spark plugs or intelligently discuss the development of English literature.

Harvard, Yale and Princeton set the pace by drawing up "core curricula" and revising the entire structure of their BA programs for the first postwar class. They limited electives and set up a common core of instruction to which all students would be exposed. Everyone must have some science, some social science, some knowledge of the humanities. Atop these requirements each student could then perch his own major field of study. With the most prestigious institutions moving in this direction, and Chicago and Columbia already there, the less prestigious quickly followed suit, and a mimic effect carried over into the high schools.*

* Not since American higher education at the turn of the century had gone into raptures over the German love of research had there been quite so profound a development. Then Charles Norton Eliot had reshaped Harvard College, introducing

The war had not overthrown all that had occurred for fifty years past, but it had profoundly altered it. Instead of being centers of scholarship removed from the hurly-burly immediacy of war, the colleges and universities had plunged straight in. The top third of them held war contracts. That involvement, we know, did not end with the end of the war.

The result of the various wartime military and civilian training programs was a mixed but important heritage. The colleges had staggered into the war with sagging enrollments and depleted endowments. Many of them found in the contracts with the War and Navy Departments and the Office of Scientific Research and Development a new lease on life and a new sense of purpose. When the Army cut its programs to the bone, they trembled for a time. But just as the trainees marched off to war, the first wave of veterans, GI Bill checks clutched in their hands, came marching in. And many a college administrator was hoping that programs of this kind, with federal subsidies, democratic selection and minimal government control, would be kept up indefinitely.

Yet many academics were not so impressed, and one noted administrator, Chicago's Hutchins, thought that the wartime business of having government select the students, choose their courses and pay their tuition was but the prelude to something fundamentally important in American life: "A government which has once discovered that universities can be used to solve immediate problems is likely to intensify the practice as its problems grow more serious."

Certainly the colleges wanted the money. It was no use pointing out that GI Bill money was free from government control, that it was federal money that came indirectly. For universities, said Hutchins with the authority of a man who ran one, were easily seduced by large amounts of cash. Whatever intentions they started out with, they wanted the veterans' money badly enough to drop their standards and, in effect, bid for as many veterans as possible. And once dependent on government money, they would never, he thought, be able to let go whether the money came to them in one way or another.

The government would not find itself forcing its attention on an unwilling subject. Overnight the colleges and universities had become dependent on the federal government. The last thing they could tolerate, as their anguished pleas when the military training programs were cut had shown, was to be poor but free. Better far, it seemed, to be prosperous and dependent.

American higher education had assumed the character that would prevail for another generation.

---

free electives into the curriculum. Thousands of American scholars had gone to Germany and come back to do battle for research, objectivity and positivism. They made the nation's colleges and universities over, wrenching higher education sharply away from its place directly in the path of the English intellectual tradition.

XXXI

Life, Literature and Leisure; Art, Architecture and Aviation

THEY had the money, they had the time, and war or no war, they swamped the train stations and bus depots in the summer of 1943 to go on vacation. Neither official pleas nor physical discomfort could dissuade the determined wartime vacationer. Trains were already crowded and uncomfortable, and the amenities offered by resort hotels were spartan. Yet all along the East, West and Gulf coasts the beaches were crowded throughout the summer.

And in the winter Florida was awash with vacationers, all of them apparently well armed with bulging wallets. Without intending to, they created hardship for many servicemen and their families, who saw the price of everything zoom into the economic stratosphere. Local hoteliers who just two years before had welcomed the military with open arms were now urging servicemen to leave the state as quickly as possible. It was justice of sorts that thousands of those who drove down to Florida in the winter of 1943–1944 were unable to buy the black market gasoline they had counted on for the trip home. Millions of their countrymen relished the sight of these sun-tanned and desperate tourists shamefacedly boarding the special "relief trains" diverted to the South to get them out.

The people who did not take vacations far from home went out and discovered their own region—its cities, parks, forests, museums and historic landmarks—often for the first time. And they thronged into big-city nightclubs and restaurants. Happy club owners had almost forgotten the twenties. But as if frowning on so much frivolity in wartime, federal officials put a 30 percent tax on live entertainment (reduced after angry protests to 20 percent) and sharply raised the tax on liquor.

Liquor, in fact, seemed about to become scarce. Hundreds of bars, taverns and liquor stores closed down each month. More than 1,000 closed in San Francisco alone in the eighteen months after Pearl Harbor, not for want of demand but for lack of supply. No more liquor alcohol was being made. Yet the war had brought a 30 percent increase in consumption, draining available stocks at an alarming rate. By the fall of 1943 bootlegging and hijacking were back. Whole cities, such as Minneapolis, were out of whiskey. Where hard liquor could be found, a mediocre bourbon sold for as much as $12 a pint. And as one distillery executive mourned, "If people go into a store and can't buy butter they accept it because there's a war on. But if they can't get whiskey they raise hell."

So far as popular entertainments went, the most extraordinary wartime phenomenon was a skinny young crooner from Hoboken, New Jersey, named Frank Sinatra. Not since Valentino had an entertainer been so adored. Hardly known the year before, Sinatra was the cult figure of thousands of fan clubs in 1943, from one called Moonlight Sinatra to a Frank Sinatra Fan and Mah-Jongg Club (catering to older women). He easily displaced Bing Crosby as the country's premier crooner, and in the sentimental, mellow, nostalgic mood of wartime Sinatra was the foremost figure in the trend to "sweet" music. By the fall of 1943 it was necessary to dispatch some twenty police cars and 450 policemen to New York's Paramount Theater to contain the 30,000 bobby-soxers emoting over their idol.

Their elders were variously worried and bemused. In the world's long history of mass hysteria, wrote one man, Lindbergh and Valentino could not compare with this new phenomenon. The closest comparison he could make was with St. Vitus' dance and the Children's Crusade. For wherever Sinatra went the prospects of riot were strong. Windows were often smashed; fistfights would break out; there would be a trail of hospital cases. What other private citizen needed a squad car full of policemen to accompany him everywhere?

At Sinatra's performances young girls went to extraordinary, often dangerous lengths to be near him. When he sang, they were thrown into a frenzied, noisy agitation. To our time this may not seem extraordinary, but thirty years ago it was unexpected, and to many people bewildering. When Sinatra sang "I'll Walk Alone," a desperate, pleading voice cut above the noise and in purest Brooklynese cried out, "I'll wok wid ya, Frankie." Between songs he kept up a steady patter about his wife and children, which should have been fatal but was not. And at the end of his last song he would stride rapidly offstage without warning. At that instant spotlights would blaze onto dozens of strategically placed American flags while the band swung quickly into the national anthem to defuse a potential riot.

There had been a growing craze among the young in recent years to elevate singers and musicians into the pantheon of folk heroes. The big-name bandleader had become "one of young America's gods. More so even than the movie star, and more so even than the baseball or football hero." Young girls seemed to their mothers to be inexplicably going mad these days over anything young, male and healthy. Psychologists attributed Sinatra's appeal to frustrated love on a massive scale, induced by the pressures of wartime. And when teen-age girls went berserk over Harry James, jitterbugging until exhausted, it was put down to "mob hysteria" and "body satisfaction." It took a writer for *Variety* to point out the obvious: Dancing in the aisles, which could be dated from the famous Benny Goodman concert at Carnegie Hall in 1937, was an improvement on the boozy promiscuity of the twenties, an era dear to the hearts of the parents of this generation of "hepcats."

Their parents had also danced the lindy hop. But the lindy hop was now so respectable that *Life* glowed, "With the exception of the tap dance it is this country's only native and original dance form." But to older people anyone gyrating wildly on the dance floor now was not a lindy hopper but a jitterbugger, a far different phenomenon. A young starlet won an $8,000 award for damages from the Hollywood Canteen after she danced with a "jive-maddened" marine and injured her coccyx. The judge summed up: "To one not skilled or expert in it [jitterbugging] presents a real danger."

While "swing" and "sweet" were dividing the world of popular music between them, the trend toward older, simpler pleasures was cresting, bringing a revival of what a blunter age called "hillbilly music." The biggest song hit in years was "Pistol Packin' Mama." Though the recording industry was idled for much of 1943 by a musicians' strike, roughly 1,000,000 bootleg recordings of "Pistol Packin' Mama" were circulating before the strike ended. When the union musicians went back to work, it was the first song they recorded.

With the country apparently determined to carry on as if there were no war on, the taste for fads and crazes continued to wind its unpredictable course. There was an extraordinary boom in the popularity of checkers. Millions of people took the game up for the first time. One of 1943's best sellers was a volume called *How to Play Winning Checkers*. Sophisticated Broadway sprouted checker parlors catering to a round-the-clock clientele.

The inexplicable ran on as profitably as ever. The biggest radio celebrity was a mind reader called Dunninger. The science editor of the New York *Times*, Waldemar Kaempfert, set out to debunk Dunninger's feats. The mind reader in turn denounced Kaempfert and staged several demonstrations which were supposed to confound his critic's arguments. The country rapidly split into Kaempfert and Dunninger camps. The Better Business Bureau was meanwhile estimating that Americans were spending no less than $200,000,000 a year on astrology and fortune-telling. In all, the occult may easily have been a billion-dollar-a-year business.

Comic books had been impelled into the big time just before the war, when Superman leaped from the windows of Gotham's *Daily Planet*. Whether owing to the war or not, they had also become a billion-dollar business by 1944, despite the paper shortage. Two comic book markets had come into existence, virtually overnight: one for children, one for servicemen. A special overseas edition of *Superman*, for instance, was printed each month running into the millions of copies. About a third of the country's young adults (aged eighteen to thirty) read comic books.

There was also a revival of nonsense songs. Its wartime masterpiece was "Mairzy Doats," based on the old nursery rhyme "Mares eat oats and does eat oats, but little lambs eat ivy. . . ." Rendered by a committee of three songwriters into:

> Mairzy doats and Doazy doats and Liddle lamzy divey
> A kiddely divey too, wouldn't you?*

it was the biggest freak song hit since "Yes, We Have No Bananas."

The war years saw the development of a mass market for books for the first time in American history. Before 1939 the United States each year published about one-half book per person each year, excluding textbooks. There was neither a mass market nor the prospect of one. But in less than six years there came a virtual revolution in popular culture. The number of volumes published almost doubled and would doubtless have tripled but for paper rationing. Book sales rose more than 20 percent each year after Pearl Harbor. Pocket Books had gone from a sale of several hundred thousand to more than 10,000,000 copies in 1941, 20,000,000 in 1942 and nearly 40,000,000 in 1943. The small, cozy enclave of American publishing had become a publishing industry. It was buoyed up by a seller's market in which everything but scholarly works and avant-garde literature prospered. Technical handbooks on subjects from welding to teach-yourself-geometry sold in the millions of copies. And the demand for Bibles and dictionaries was so voracious that the supply was rationed.†

The war created little good fiction, but it was an enormous human undertaking from which there would in time come a crop of "war novelists"—that is, writers who found in the events of wartime the central experience of their own and other people's lives and around which they would shape their literary careers. Most—like James Jones, Norman Mailer, Herman Wouk, James Michener and William Styron—would emerge after the war ended but while it was still fresh in the memory. A few, however, such as Saul Bellow, Irwin Shaw, John Hersey, made their debuts in wartime. There were the "war poets," too, such as Karl Shapiro and Randall Jarrell. But distinguished though these names are now, wartime saw very little first-rate literature.

* *Mairzy doats.* Words and music: Milton Drake, Al Hoffman, Jerry Livingston. Copyright © 1943 by Drake Activities Corp., The Hallmark Music Co., Al Hoffman Songs, Inc. Used by permission.

† Not that the United States was afflicted with biblomania. Of the 20,000,000 tons of paper consumed each year, only 100,000 tons went into books, while 1,000,000 tons went into advertising. Advertising interests fought energetically, and successfully, to hang onto their share.

Partly it was because, as one critic noted, "This time the radicals are more patriotic than the conservatives." The First World War spun out of its horrors a treasury of great poetry, but it was a poetry against the war. A few of the older critics, such as Edmund Wilson, still clung stubbornly to their lifelong isolationism. But for the rest it was impossible to oppose the war against Fascism, even if it did not include Spain.

A popular war not only made for a letdown in fiction, but encouraged bad poetry, such as Russell Davenport's 1944 best seller, *My Country*. It read like a parody of high school commencement addresses and conveniently blamed the war on pacifists. Hugely popular, it was probably liked by people not used to reading poetry but troubled by the thought that they ought to read more. Still worse was William Rose Benét's *Day of Deliverance*. Benét linked a strong love of cliché and platitude to a modest talent for rhyming. Equipped with these, he sang the praises of the common man as he is known only to the upper classes. Benét was editor of the *Saturday Review of Literature*.

But in Shapiro, Jarrell and Lowell the United States had a trinity of fine poets. Shapiro's *V-letter* won a Pulitzer Prize and attracted what was, for serious poetry, a considerable readership. It was an uneven collection, but it was unmistakably the work of a gifted poet. And the older poets did not lapse into silence. Robert Frost, for instance, served the New Nationalism with "The Gift Outright." But the war generally did not serve poetry well. For, as Seldon Rodman observed, "All serious war poetry is antiwar poetry."

Other writers were also bemoaning that America was what it had always been—inhospitable. Henry Miller, reduced to begging in the pages of sympathetic journals, complained: "America is no place for an artist. A corn-fed hog enjoys a better life here than a creative writer." In truth, one of the country's great modern poets, Edgar Lee Masters, the author of *The Spoon River Anthology*, was dragged out of a New York gutter in 1944, utterly destitute, dying of pneumonia and malnutrition.

A certain timidity had meanwhile overtaken American literature. The fierce alienation which had marked the fiction of the thirties had given way to a new kind of novel, resulting in "a literature of the acceptance of the *status quo*. The values of our present novels are the established values," as one critic wrote. There was a concurrent absence of heroic figures and a minimum of action. Characters struggled with their psyches instead of with society. Where there was violence, it tended to be in the past, not the present. It was, in short, a conservative literature.

The tides of sentimentality and nostalgia were washing over the stage, films and literature. All three borrowed from one another. It seemed only right that a girl named Smith should marry a private named Jones and write an epic of nostalgia, *A Tree Grows in Brookyln*. But the greatest sentimental literary success in wartime was a book which ostensibly dealt with the war, John Hersey's *A Bell for Adano*. It flattered and encouraged every sentimental notion people cherished about how the United States would succor a war-ravaged world entrusted to its care. Diana Trilling penned a caustic but accurate summary:

> Its hero, Major Joppolo, is a kind of compendium of quickly recognizable national characteristics. Joppolo is the American occupation officer of the little town of Adano. He thinks for himself, works fourteen hours a day, is realistic about taking help where he can find it, is gentle from instinct and ruthless on principle, respects authority where it earns respect and where it is unworthy countermands it at whatever risk, knows how to play with the church, has sex but knows how to keep it down, loathes protocol and red tape, and first, last and always is a man of heart who knows that a town full of Italian peasants has more need for a bell than for American sanitation; when his M.P.s get into a drunken orgy and smash up the house in which they are billeted, instead of sending them to the guardhouse he invokes the memory of their mothers.

A Bell for Adano was nevertheless a critical and popular success of historic proportions, principally because it portrayed the forthcoming occupation exactly as most Americans wanted to see it.

But more popular still were religious novels. For three years in a row the best-selling work of fiction was a religious novel: in 1941, *The Keys of the Kingdom*; in 1942, *Song of Bernadette*; in 1943, *The Robe*. But 1944 brought Kathryn Winsor's *Forever Amber*. Miss Winsor's former writing experience consisted of writing a football column—"from the woman's point of view"—for the Oakland *Tribune*. She produced an exhausting tale of a serving wench who rises by a sweaty, seemingly endless round of seductions, orgasms, miscarriages, abortions and staggering coincidences to occupy the bed of Charles II. Salacious rubbish it undoubtedly was; it was also the best-selling book of 1944. And that was as it should be. The war was a spur to both religious sentiment and practical permissiveness. As always, both must needs be served by letters.

Nowhere was the nostalgia that we have seen earlier running at a higher tide than on the screen. Between Pearl Harbor and the end of the war it resulted in, and was nurtured by, film versions of *A Tree Grows in Brooklyn, Life with Father* (which ran on Broadway for 3,224 performances during the war), *Meet Me in St. Louis, The Magnificent Ambersons* and *State Fair*. All played to full houses.

There was, parallel to the nostalgia, a passion for light entertainment. About 20 percent of the Hollywood films in production in December, 1941, had been musical comedies. A year later that figure had doubled. When *Film Daily* polled the nation's leading film critics on whether or not films should deal with controversial issues, almost half said no. One execu-

tive at Paramount boasted happily, "My company carefully avoided inject-
ing any controversial material into this picture." The picture was the
screen version of Ernest Hemingway's novel of the Spanish Civil War,
For Whom the Bell Tolls.

It became a commonplace that what people wanted was more comedies
and more musicals. Yet war films did as well at the box office as films
of any other genre. Generally, movies were prospering as never before.
Moviegoing was achieving a popularity with the young that went beyond
any movie mogul's wildest dreams of avarice. There was also a new quality to movie audiences, of detachment and casualness. It had for a long
time been something of an event to go to the movies. Now it was taken for
granted. Behind it there seemed to be "a curious atmosphere that wartime
is to some extent vacation time, a time in which life is not quite the same
as it has been before."

As with books, films were trying to cope with both fleshly indulgence
and religious sentiment. The Hays Office banned tightly fitting sweaters
from the screen in its pursuit of morality in films. But *The Outlaw* still
managed to bring the ripeness of Jane Russell's breasts to national attention. And a B picture with a minuscule budget of $170,000 called
Hitler's Children was able to smuggle in enough sex and sadism to gross
more than $5,000,000.

Religion, on the other hand, was served by screen versions of *Song of
Bernadette* and *The Keys to the Kingdom*. And both religion and sentimentality were catered to unabashedly in a low-budget, unheralded film
released in 1943 called *Going My Way*, with Bing Crosby and Barry
Fitzgerald. It swept the 1944 Academy Awards, while at the box office it
was the biggest success since *Gone with the Wind*.

But try as it might to keep the screen clean, Hollywood retained its
place in the popular mind as the national capital of concupiscence. Errol
Flynn, though acquitted, was ne'er forgotten. Less than a year after his
trial ended the attractive salesgirl at the cigarette counter in the Los
Angeles Hall of Justice had a baby. Flynn acknowledged it as his own.

Charlie Chaplin had meanwhile, at the age of fifty-four, married the
Glamor Girl of 1942, Oona O'Neill, the eighteen-year-old daughter of
playwright Eugene O'Neill. Shortly thereafter Chaplin became the object
of a paternity suit, was charged with violating the Mann Act and was
accused of illegally attempting to influence a judge. The latter charges
were eventually dropped, but the paternity suit kept the war on the inside
pages through much of the winter of 1944.

An erstwhile Hollywood starlet named Joan Barry told an enthralled
jury how she had burst into Chaplin's bedroom two years earlier brandishing a revolver. She told too of how Chaplin had disarmed her, made love
to her, let her sleep in the "Paulette Goddard Room" of his mansion.
Chaplin talked of how he had tried to further her career and tried to

improve his mistress' mind. Miss Barry conceded that it was so, recalling how "we talked about this and that and the Second Front." But the affair was over, said Chaplin, long before Miss Barry conceived. The medical evidence was in his favor. The result was a mistrial.

But Miss Barry persisted. A second jury heard her attorney attack Chaplin's character, calling him a "Piccadilly pimp" and a "Cockney cad." And though it was medically proved that Chaplin could not have fathered the child, this second, more sympathetic jury voted that he must support it and the mother.

As for the war, the Hollywood studios were as cautious as ever. Less than one-third of the films turned out in the war's closing phase had any connection with it. But the quality of what there was had improved. By returning to the documentary techniques of the late 1930's, American filmmakers produced a number of excellent war documentaries, such as *With the Marines at Tarawa, Memphis Belle* and *The Fighting Lady.* More than one critic thought the best war thriller was *Resisting Enemy Interrogation,* produced by the U.S. Army Film Unit on Long Island.

Hollywood also made its own bow to internationalism with *Wilson.* Released in 1944, it was the most expensive film to date, more expensive even than *Gone with the Wind,* costing more than $5,000,000. It was a serious treatment, if artistically lame, of America past and present.

There was at least one ambitious attempt to deal with the home front, in David O. Selznick's putative epic of 1944 called *Since You Went Away.* Thin on plot, action and characterization, it churned along for three hours. It portrayed what Selznick presumably considered an average American family. But they appeared to be enjoying about three times the average income. It had, said James Agee,* "the authenticity of authentic self-delusion."

Stage shows were prospering as films were. Broadway had never been in better financial health. Artistically its offerings were so undistinguished that there were no Pulitzer Prizes for drama in 1942 and 1944, a judgment with which the New York Drama Critics Circle concurred. The best plays were either imports, like Noel Coward's *Blithe Spirit,* or revivals, like *Othello.* Yet people packed into the theaters as if supremely indifferent to the quality of what was being offered.

It seemed to more than one observer that popular tastes had been vulgarized and jaded by the atmosphere of wartime. Burlesque and strip-tease shows played to standing room only crowds, especially when skill and artifice were minimized and stark exposure maximized. The longest-run-

---

* The emergence of James Agee as a film critic was in itself one of the most encouraging sidelights of films in these years. Auden hailed him as a critic with great creative powers, in the tradition of Berlioz and Shaw. Auden also presciently observed: "One foresees the sad day, indeed, when Agee on Films will be the subject of a Ph.D. thesis."

ning show in the history of Chicago's theaters was *Good Night, Ladies*. Based on a twenties farce called *Ladies' Night in a Turkish Bath*, it was principally a vehicle for nudity and dirty jokes. It ran for nearly three years. In Los Angeles, where no important stage production had ever run for more than two months, a show of the same kind, called *Blackouts of 1943*, played to packed houses into 1945.

Strip shows were especially popular in the boom towns. A full-scale riot erupted in Portland, Oregon, when police banned a midnight striptease extravaganza for war workers on the 4 P.M. to midnight shift. More than 700 shipyard workers went on a rampage that destroyed the theater, produced pitched battles in the streets and resulted in dozens of injuries. Police in other war boom towns appear to have been less zealous thereafter in curbing these entertainments.

As early as December, 1941, it had been possible for New York to claim that it had supplanted Paris as the art capital of the world, at least temporarily. Virtually every important European artist—with the noteworthy exception of Picasso—had left or been driven from his home and had crossed the Atlantic. Almost the entire School of Paris was in exile. Marc Chagall, Piet Mondrian, Ives Tanguy, Salvador Dali, Max Ernst, Fernand Léger, Jacques Lipchitz, André Breton and scores of other famous painters and sculptors spent the war years in the United States. Much of European art had come with them for safekeeping.

After Pearl Harbor, American museums and art galleries shipped their own most valuable works to Colorado Springs. The war did not seem likely to promise an atmosphere favorable to, or even safe for, art. The art directly concerned with the war was indeed unfailingly mediocre. Not a single great painting or even a memorable poster was produced. The most notable attempt was Thomas Hart Benton's response to Pearl Harbor—a series of eight paintings collectively titled "Year of Peril" which succeeded in being both emotionally sharp and artistically trivial. Government officials thought they were too offensive to people's sensibilities and refused to accept them for general distribution.

The Army wanted to commission artists to record the war in drawings and paintings and launched a modest art program of its own in 1942. But the next year Congress, while voting billions for defense, would not vote a penny for pictures. *Life* magazine took up the burden and became responsible for most of the country's war art, commissioning some thirty painters, who in time produced more than 700 canvases.

In these circumstances it is all the more remarkable, then, that the war years were not an artistic desert but a period of great flowering, and not among the European refugees but among America's own artists. When the war had begun in Europe, American museums and art lovers generally had long become accustomed to thinking of contemporary art as falling into two broad streams: abstract art, which was European, and realistic art, which was American.

But the influx of European Cubists, Surrealists and other moderns had this happy result: American artists, though cut off from Europe, were not cut off from its most advanced ideas and techniques. If anything, they were closer. For they could now learn directly from its exemplars. And to modern art they brought a fund of enthusiasm and excitement. The result was America's only genuinely native school of modern art—Abstract Expressionism.

Precisely defined, it was: "A combination of Abstract art and Expressionism which amounts to little more than automatic painting—i.e. allowing the subconscious to express itself (a Surrealist idea) by the creation of involuntary shapes and dribbles of paint." It also bore a strong resemblance to the outlook and methods pioneered by Kandinsky a generation earlier. But beyond that it finally broke the provincialism of American art, something many American artists had been trying to do for years. Overnight, it seemed, American art had become important and exciting.

The pivotal event of this development was the opening in October, 1942, of Peggy Guggenheim's Art of This Century gallery in New York with a benefit showing for Red Cross War Relief. For American artists it was the most important exhibition since the Armory Show of 1913. They had been trying for years to develop a style distinctively their own. But who, outside the United States, cared a fig for regionalism or the muscular but lifeless murals of the WPA? Here, though, was a new style, which if still raw in technique, exuded spontaneity and vigor and was bold enough to reject both conventional forms and techniques, willing to take up humble scrub-brushes and house paint. Ambitiously it tried to reach, through art, the subconscious world whose contours are guessed at by modern psychology. A new school, the New York School (or Action Painting), had made its debut. Within a decade the early exhibitors at Peggy Guggenheim's gallery would be world-famous artists: Jackson Pollock, Wilhelm de Kooning, Mark Rothko, Arshile Gorki.

Objectivism had gone out of American art. Henceforth it would be subjective; frequently it was pessimistic. But it was undeniably interesting. Aided in part by the limits on traditional amusements and on the supply of everyday goods, during the war art galleries were able to draw enormous crowds. Art sales leaped upward from year to year. Not until almost 1960 would art sales reach the 1944–1945 levels again. About one in three of the people buying a painting or a sculpture in wartime was doing so for the first time. The new interest in art held up after the war. A mass audience for works of art had come into existence. Thus, in 1948 more than 50,000,000 people went to art exhibits, three times as many as in the prewar years.

Art's cousin, architecture, also found the war to be its modern watershed and built up a momentum that carried it with a rush into the postwar era. Architects had for years been trying to use the latest methods and materials, but the Depression had imposed severe limitations. The principles of "Simplicity, economy and efficiency became formal, as well as functional, criteria," but there was little money to put them into practice. There were some showcases, however, like Rockefeller Center and the GM and Ford buildings at the 1939 New York World's Fair. In part, this stylistic simplification was dictated by the need for economy. It also had the desirable side effect of clearing away the clutter, the expensive gewgaws, the opulant vulgarities which had literally clung to American architecture for decades.

The country was ready to rediscover its greatest native architect, Frank Lloyd Wright. A marginal figure for more than a decade, Wright was rediscovered by a new generation of young architects with a stunningly successful one-man show at the Museum of Modern Art in November, 1940. Wright's insistence that the box was the shape of Fascism, that democracy required less rigid architectural forms, was often taken to silly extremes. But his scorn for the knife-edged simplicity and coldness of much modern design encouraged those who sought to bring to simplicity a new warmth and attractiveness.

Before American architecture could entirely break the shackles of the past, it had to exhaust the revival of neoclassical style inspired by the Columbian Exposition of 1893. The Jefferson Memorial, opened in 1939, and the National Gallery of Art, opened in 1941, did precisely that.

While architectural Toryism was breathing its last, there was a concurrent influx of great European architects, such as Walter Gropius, Eero Saarinen and Miës van der Rohe. They brought with them something that American architecture had always lacked: formal, structured, coherent theories of architecture. American architects learned to think in a new way, and they brought energy and enthusiasm to the new opportunities it opened up.

The war brought new construction on a vast scale. As we saw, housing doubled over the Depression levels. Millions of temporary dwellings were put up. Military and industrial construction was on a scale never before seen or imagined. The architectural ideas developed in recent years were put to work in novel settings. Whole cities sprang up around war plants. Some of the most important architects, like Richard Neutra, turned to designing prefabricated housing. The same structural principles on which planes, ships and bridges were assembled went into housing and factory construction. Scarce materials like steel were eliminated, never to return. The technology had been known for a decade, but this was the first chance to put it to work.

Nowhere were the advances more striking than in industrial architecture.

Able to build new plants from scratch for the first time in years, architects filled them with innovations which set them off sharply from earlier plants. They were built away from the cities and close to land where future expansion was possible; they were made windowless and were lit with fluorescent lighting; they were air-conditioned; they had basements which housed facilities for the workers—showers, toilets, lockers, cafeterias, even classrooms; the lines were clean; dividing walls were kept to a minimum; they used space instead of height; and they were incomparably cleaner and safer than factories built less than a generation before.

The war provided a unique opportunity for American architects to consolidate the thinking of the past twenty years, to learn from the Europeans and to experiment with new methods and materials. The country at large was meanwhile stirring with a pent-up desire for new houses, new buildings, new industries in the postwar world. And it had the money to pay for these things. Like the artists, the architects would emerge from the war with a new clientele, one prosperous and avid to learn how to be modern.

Advertising was the war's most curious growth industry. Most advertisers had little or nothing to offer the consumer, and what little there was would be snapped up whether it was advertised or not. The New Dealers had been barely polite on the subject of advertising, openly regarding it as a parasite on the body of commerce and a snare for the altogether too-trusting consumer. Yet advertising was waxing rich.

At first, the war had looked like a body blow. But some companies recalled that businesses which had not kept their names before the public in the earlier war had, in some cases, not lived to see the Armistice. So they were willing to advertise if only for survival's sake. And the Internal Revenue Service was persuaded to issue a ruling that money spent on advertising would not count as profits. Thus, with the American taxpayers subsidizing it, advertising entered on its golden age.

In just two years the money spent on advertising shot up 60 percent. Because of the paper shortage, which reportedly had the New York *Times* turning down as many as thirty pages of advertising a day, most of the largess went into radio commercials. Radio advertising budgets went from $195,000,000 in 1942 to $390,000,000 in 1944.

Instead of promoting products, advertisers portrayed themselves as a critical part of the war effort. There was also an underlying theme that it was business which made victory possible. And there was a Nash-Kelvinator campaign, for instance, the slogan of which was "Don't Change Anything." It said, in effect, that for the war to be worth fighting, America must welcome its returning soldiers by being once again where it had once stood, at that pinnacle of human contentment: America *circa* 1928.

The advertising agencies and their clients also succeeded in destroying the OWI as their chief rival in the arena of domestic propaganda. From the outset OWI was divided into two warring camps—liberal journalists and academics on the one side, advertising and businessmen on the other. To the former, the OWI was an instrument for making the country aware of the larger issues posed by the war and, beyond that, for raising social and political consciousness. The latter group had a particular philosophy of their own to sell. The writers also preferred a less varnished version of the war news than the advertising men cared for. The writers produced posters which urged people to use less gasoline as an aid to the war effort; the advertising men produced posters which said "Walk—and Be Beautiful." The writers responded with a sarcastic poster showing the Statue of Liberty with a frosty bottle of Coca-Cola raised aloft in place of its torch. Three more bottles were tucked under its arm. "Try the Four Delicious Freedoms—the War that Refreshes."

This quarrel could not be contained indefinitely; it eventually broke into public view. The writers looked to Elmer Davis, and Davis looked to the President. But Roosevelt had already made his peace with advertising. He went out of his way to assure its practitioners that he considered them vital to winning the war. He would later thank the War Advertising Council—a creation of big business and the big advertising agencies—for its role in the fight against inflation. By then the domestic branch of the OWI had been pared to the bone and the writers had resigned en masse.

The most famous of the wartime advertising campaigns was based on the proposition that green ink would be rationed. Lucky Strike changed its colors and proclaimed "Lucky Strike Green has gone to war." As a wartime slogan it was probably better known than "Praise the Lord and Pass the Ammunition." But there was neither a shortage of chrome green (a derivative of bichromate) nor any prospect of one, short of an Axis victory. There were suspicions that Lucky Strike had simply found in the war a heaven-sent chance to change its dark-green pack to white and attract women smokers.

Not a little of the advertising was blatantly offensive, especially when juxtaposed with incoming war news. New Yorkers were startled one night to hear reports of heavy American casualties followed by a funeral home commercial: "You never know when to expect bad news. So be prepared. Buy a family plot."

Before the war ended, many millions of people had become so angry over the mixing of commercials with war news that dozens of smaller stations voluntarily stopped doing it. When fighting was heavy, the networks did the same. But this limitation barely affected advertising's growth. And it already had its eye on television.

As early as the winter of 1943, in fact, sponsors were developing possible shows for the postwar era. Advertising agencies set up new departments to create television commercials. Five commercial stations were operating before the war ended. New Yorkers had their choice of half a dozen commercially sponsored programs each day.

In only four years the aviation industry had gone from fortieth place on the index of industrial production to first. Yet no other industry appeared to face so bleak a future. The dollar value of all the planes produced in 1944 was $20 billion. Not even the wildest optimist could foresee a postwar market calling for more than $2 billion in new aircraft each year.

Nevertheless, this was the time when aviation came of age, and nowhere more so than here. Americans grappled as no other people did with air age geography, the prospects for making the family plane as commonplace as the family automobile and raising an air-conscious generation of young people. Americans were constantly being exhorted to learn how to think in three-dimensional terms, ignoring age-old physical barriers like mountains and deserts, to become used to a realm where time was more important than distance.

A new "global geography" sprang up, from which were drawn the most ridiculous claims.* One-dimensional maps, portraying the world solely in terms of flying time, erasing all terrain features and boundaries, poured forth. In vain did professional geographers protest that the true representation of the globe is a globe.

Far from proving a disaster for commercial aviation, the war was proving to be a gold mine. Instead of requisitioning its planes, the military made it an auxiliary of the Army Air Force. Commercial airlines then found themselves with more planes, more pilots and more extensive routes than they had ever had. A decade of peacetime growth was crammed into several years, while at a gratifying level of profits they flew men and material to the battle fronts and the Army supplied them with ground crews courtesy of the American taxpayer.

Official Washington made its obeisance to the new ascendancy of airpower by belatedly atoning an earlier wrong. Brigadier General Billy Mitchell, whose death in 1926 was touched with martyrdom, was posthumously promoted to major general and awarded the Medal of Honor. At about the same time the first Presidential aircraft made its debut, irreverently and officially named "The Sacred Cow."†

Looking to the postwar world, both Roosevelt and Henry Wallace called

---

* One theory held that Minneapolis would be attacked before San Francisco: Minneapolis is closer to Alaska than is San Francisco; the direct route for a Japanese bomber flying from Tokyo to attack the Panama Canal with a refueling stop in the Aleutians is via Alaska; the shortest route from Alaska to Panama passes over Minneapolis—*q.e.d.* Minneapolis.

† Roosevelt only flew in it once before he died. It would take a different age to come up with "Air Force One."

for "Freedom of the Air." Liberal internationalists took up the cry. To conservatives, however, such a proposition was as unacceptable as the idea of free trade had been only a generation before. If nothing else, the notion of unrestrained physical mobility through the world's airspace affronted their fierce notions of national sovereignty. Clare Boothe Luce, one of the conservative victors in the 1942 elections, created a storm by using her maiden speech in the House to pillory Wallace's call for freedom of the air as "Globaloney." Her idea of the postwar world was one where the United States made certain that it, and it alone, dominated the world's airways. If America hung back, she warned, the wily British would elbow America out of dominion of the air, and the British were rotten enough to use lend-lease planes to do it.

Before the war ended, however, Mrs. Luce's fears proved vain. If the British contested American dominion in the air, it would be thanks to their lead in the development of jet aircraft. But even then, no one could effectively challenge U.S. supremacy. Though technologically lagging behind, the United States possessed in the B-29 Superfortress the military twin of the Boeing Stratocruiser, a plane big enough, able to fly far enough and available in sufficient numbers to dominate postwar international aviation.

At home, in more than a dozen states the schools were meanwhile trying valiantly to provide an air age education to all their children. Tennessee, for instance, sent its high school teachers out to local airfields to go on commercial flights. Schoolchildren spent class time touring municipal airports. Many a high school district had revised its curriculum to base it on matters aeronautical. High school students were learning to fly, their lessons subsidized by local school boards. History and economics classes probed the social and economic implications of the air age. Some 240 colleges and universities created courses related to aviation. The Army Air Force was also encouraging them by handing over more and more stores of surplus equipment. The United States could safely say, by 1945, that it had entered the air age and had the most air-minded generation of young people in the world. In that and in its wealth lay the promise of American aviation in the years ahead.

Community involvement in the war followed the same curve as war production, paralleling its spectacular rise and subsequent decline. Each city, town and village responded in its own way to unexpected needs. When the marines on Guadalcanal found, for instance, that their bayonets were too awkward for hand-to-hand fighting the citizens of San Francisco mailed them thousands of daggers and hunting knives. Later, the city also shipped off 18,000 pieces of costume jewelry to bridge the barter gap between South Sea island natives and American marines.

When Victory gardens were at their peak of popularity, hundreds of cities and towns dug up their parks and public lawns and turned them over to amateur gardeners to replant them with vegetables. High schools, prisons, convents, college campuses, almost everyone with a plot of earth took up vegetable growing. And with Victory gardens everywhere, Macy's management wondered, Why not a Victory barnyard? Macy's thereafter began selling ducks, chickens, pullets and rabbits, plus the necessary coops and hutches, to sophisticated New Yorkers. Bookstores were reportedly doing well with *A Manual of Home Vegetable Gardening* and *The Old Dirt Dobber's Garden Book*.

There were a lot of jokes, but the results were far from trivial. More than 8,000,000 tons of food came out of 4,000,000 acres of stamp-sized plots in 1943. It was an achievement that put more glamorous civil defense operations to shame. And when OCD officials wanted to mount a parade through downtown Washington to the greater glory of civil defense in the summer of 1943, they were obliged to ask the Army and Navy to send some detachments over to help flesh it out. The Air Warning Service boasted 600,000 volunteers in 7,500 posts. It kept up a twenty-four-hour watch of the skies. But there was really nothing for it to do that was useful. Before the end of 1943 it was reduced to a token force which scanned the skies for a few hours each week just to keep the organization officially alive.

There were still occasional scrap drives. The WPB set a goal of 8,000,-000 tons of scrap paper to be rounded up in 1944. Millions of schoolchildren were enrolled as Paper Troopers. Promotions to private first class, corporal and sergeant could be earned by fulfilling a quota. There was no drop in youthful enthusiasm. One thirteen-year-old in Maywood, Illinois, collected more than 100 tons of paper between Pearl Harbor and D-Day. He somehow also found the time to round up a ton and a half of waste fats.

But among adults much of the earlier zeal was gone. In most months of 1944 the paper scrap drive fell short of its quota because children could not do it all. The interest in Victory gardens was also dropping. Inspired by the 1943 success, Agriculture Department officials had called for 22,000,000 Victory gardens in 1944, an increase of 4,000,000 gardens. Instead, with victory on the horizon, what they got was a drop of more than half a million.

Overtly, fashion was going in two directions at once. On the one hand, it was all severe uniforms and work clothes. On the other, it was all frills, fluffiness and bareness. But while these tendencies were ostensibly opposed, they were also logically conjoined.

Wherever one looked, there were bare shoulders, plunging necklines, short skirts, some of them three and four inches above the knee. The summer fashions for 1944 openly boasted a "bare skin look," with dresses that were backless and sleeveless besides being short. Bathing suits shrank to a skimpiness of remarkable proportions. These things could always be conveniently blamed on the shortage of materials, but they doubtless owed more to the social effects of wartime. In what had become an unrelenting search for ways to expose their bodies, women even took to wearing romper clothes of the kind usually worn by small children. These produced the shortest, tightest shorts with bright colors, bold patterns, no stockings and low-heeled or flat shoes.

With the exposure of so much leg, the shortage of stockings became critical. Black-market nylons cost $5 a pair. Few women could afford that even when they worked. Most turned to "bottled stockings." But two years' practice at painting their legs had not brought the art above an amateurish level characterized by streaky, uneven applications. With a little luck and no baths, it was said, leg paint would last for three days. Beauty parlors offered to do it at fifty cents a leg. But the principal objects of all this effort and expense were never reconciled to painted legs. As the words of a popular song expressed male complaints: "It decants on your pants."

Fashion-conscious people were increasingly eager as the liberation of France drew near to discover what Paris fashion houses had been up to for the past four years. They were thrown into confusion when, on the eve of invasion, pictures arrived in New York of what were said to be the latest styles. The hats were large, the dresses lavish with costly and scarce materials; the styles were redolent of extravagance and indulgence. Sixth Avenue and its clientele hotly debated whether or not it was a Nazi propaganda trick. How could Parisiennes obtain such clothes, unless they were collaborating? How could American women have clothes like these without trampling the official clothing regulation, L-85, underfoot? It was eventually agreed that it was a German attempt to undermine the morale of American women by making them lust for the unattainable. The WPB solemnly denounced it as conclusive evidence of underhanded Nazi psychological warfare.

Then, when Paris was liberated, it turned out that the pictures were true.

By that summer of 1944 a new spirit moved through everyday life. It was the happiest, the most exciting summer of the war. Almost everyone was convinced that it would be the last summer of wartime. Rationing was becoming a thing of the past. Money was plentiful. Resort hotels and coastal beaches were crowded. Racetracks were jammed. A nation that had not had a real vacation since 1940 was making up for it.

In the past few years people had learned to make do. Not infrequently they were proud to discover how adaptable they could be when they had to. Millions learned to use tools for the first time and started doing their own repairs. Middle-class housewives were doing their own housework, which can have done them no harm. 1943 had been dubbed "the maid's year off." So, it proved, was 1944. Some housewives even did their own washing for the first time during the great wartime laundry crisis. War jobs and the draft simply stripped the laundries, as well as the middle-class home, of cheap labor. Two-day service became ten-day service. New York laundries rationed the number and type of dirty linen they would accept. Chicago's laundries refused to take any new customers for the duration. In Los Angeles the laundries washed only on alternate weeks. Detroit's laundries literally threw in the towel: They begged Detroit housewives to do their own washing.

But by the time of the invasion it was obvious that such irritants would soon be over. The U.S. Mint went back to making copper pennies. On city streets discharged servicemen were beginning to appear, with an eagle lapel pin to show they were honorably discharged. On both coasts city authorities were told to turn their lights on again, catching most of them off guard. In San Francisco and elsewhere civic groups had set up "When the Lights Go on Again" committees to prepare celebrations for that historic day. And here it was already.

People no longer accepted "Don't you know there's a war on?" as the final, crushing answer to requests that could not be met. One young woman in Cambridge, Massachusetts, became a national celebrity by smashing the dishes in a restaurant when her request for squash instead of potatoes drew that reply. The *Saturday Evening Post* thought she deserved a place in the Hall of Fame.

After three years of informality people started wearing evening clothes again. Broadway first-nighters that fall began showing up in evening gowns and dinner jackets. White ties and black ties reappeared at night. Even in the factories dresses began, where possible, to replace slacks. Department store salespeople noticed an upsurge in sales of frilly negligees, perfumes and jewelry.

The sole interruption in the gaiety of that happy summer and fall was another terrible fire. At a Saturday matinee in July Ringling Brothers, Barnum and Bailey's main tent was set up in Hartford, Connecticut, and was crowded with children and animals. As the second act of the show began, the band suddenly struck up "Stars and Stripes Forever"—the traditional "disaster" theme of American circuses. At almost the same moment nineteen tons of paraffin-coated canvas went up in flames. The fire lasted just a few minutes. Most of the resulting 167 dead were women and children, as were the hundreds more who were badly burned.

And the gay mood petered out when fall turned to winter and instead of victory in Europe there was the Battle of the Bulge. Racetracks were ordered to close. The reconversion to consumer-goods production was stopped. A midnight curfew was placed on bars, nightclubs and theaters. Government officials justified it by claiming that the curfew would save manpower, coal and transportation. But the real reason was obviously that Washington had decided to crack down on what it saw as complacency, gluttony, overoptimism and selfishness, all of which comported badly with the increasingly bloody fighting. Most people thought it was a stupid way to deal with the problem. One disgruntled habitué of a Chicago bar grumbled, "Turn off the furnace and let us drink in our overcoats."

Most of the people affected by the curfew were either servicemen on leave or workers on late shifts. The bars, roller rinks, bowling alleys, dance halls and movie theaters normally open after midnight were in and around the boom towns, catering to this clientele. Union officials protested. Servicemen protested. Most of the country, in fact, protested, except for its liberal intellectuals who were always eager to make the war on Fascism ascetic if possible.

Something so unpopular was impossible to enforce. La Guardia pledged that New York would observe the curfew—at 1 A.M. He decreed "an hour of tolerance." But Roosevelt put his own prestige behind the curfew order, and most mayors, including La Guardia, soon started to try to enforce it. The midnight curfew rapidly gave rise to a new variant on an ancient figure—the "curfloozie," offering "curb service." Speakeasies started to reappear, offering spiked coffee and well-laced soft drinks. Flasks and bottles were carried openly. Drinking and copulating in doorways and hallways became more evident. There was increased public drunkenness as people bolted their liquor to beat the curfew. Instead of infusing public morality with the spirit of sacrifice, the result was increased wantonness.

After three months, federal officials lifted the curfew. Horses and dogs were allowed to run around in ovals again. Reconversion was set in motion again. Brownouts and dimouts were completely lifted. Measured solely by the appearance of everyday life and leisure, the war was already over.

XXXII

Winding Down a Miracle

ONCE Paris was liberated and Allied armies closed in on Germany the miracle of war production need no longer be sustained. There were, by most calculations, ample stocks of weapons and munitions to allow the first steps toward reconversion to be made. But the question of reconversion was not essentially a technical one, and it erupted into an angry public quarrel. For what was at stake was the country's economic—and, by implication, its social—future.

Big business and the military opposed reconversion, for different reasons. Big business opposed it because it would be to the advantage of those small businesses which could shift back to providing consumer goods and services more nimbly than could the big businesses which were slowly divesting themselves of their fat war contracts. Also, the big war contractors were making more money out of the citizen taxpayer than they could hope to make out of the citizen consumer. Military officers opposed reconversion because it grated on them that civilian life was getting easier just as battle casualties were reaching their climacteric.

The WPB, however, was pressing for reconversion at the earliest moment; at least, Donald Nelson was. But because the pivotal issue was the consolidation of the wartime gains of big business and conservative economic interests generally, much of the WPB was opposed to Nelson, and the opposition was led by Nelson's deputy, Charles E. Wilson. Liberals, to their own surprise, found themselves now supporting Nelson. More surprising still (to most liberals), Roosevelt threw his own weight behind Wilson. By the fall of 1944 the whole country was arguing about reconversion.

The military-industrial interests created an effective scare campaign, persuading the nation at large that war workers were slacking off, that this had created a critical shortage of arms and ammunition and that this in turn was responsible for the stunning increase in casualties. Truman's committee proved that every specific shortage that was cited could be traced to a transportation bottleneck in the war zones, but the truth never quite overtook the deception. In fact, the war industries were churning out far more arms than would ever be needed; the country was working overtime to produce surplus and scrap for the postwar era.

Nelson was meanwhile ordered to go out to China and inspect things for a while. Wilson decided to resign, bitterly attacking Nelson on his way out. And when Nelson returned from China, his resignation was asked for and given. A former New Dealer, Julius Krug, was named the new head of WPB. Krug told business to reconvert itself, in its own way and at its own pace.

Reconversion was thus up in the air. One Washington rumor said that the White House was now terrified that instead of waiting a year for the Americans to march into Tokyo, when Germany surrendered, Japan would, too. At a stroke the bottom would fall out of 15,000,000 jobs and the United States would be back in 1932. "It would be a Pearl Harbor of Peace," wrote one correspondent.

Worried workers, despite stern admonitions from the military, the War Manpower Commission, Selective Service, the White House and big business, started reconverting themselves. First in the thousands, then in the tens of thousands, each week they left high-paying war jobs and took lower-paying nonwar jobs to build up some seniority before the war ended. A new wave of migration was set in motion as millions of people drifted back to where they came from, with new skills and enviable savings. Unable to stop this reconversion, Krug suggested bonuses to keep workers on the job between V-E and V-J days. But they wanted jobs, not bonuses.

Then came the Battle of the Bulge. The mood of general satisfaction with the country's job of war production was jolted by this sudden reversal. The WPB blamed it on the Army and on the country as a whole. The Army blamed American labor and encouraged more shell shortage rumors. There were stories of infantry units going onto the attack without artillery support for lack of shells, while there were in fact enormous shell stockpiles in all the war zone. No matter. The War Department insisted on passage of a work-or-fight law. But the German offensive petered out. War workers found that overtime was disappearing. And soon Willow Run began to shut down, throwing thousands of workers onto the street each day.

It was an anticlimactic ending to an extraordinary achievement. Over some 4 percent of the war plants there flew colorful Army and Navy "E" Pennants. Half a million war workers wore the "E" in their lapels or on dress fronts.

The physical cost of war production exceeded the battle casualties. Nearly 300,000 workers had been killed; more than 1,000,000 more were permanently disabled; another 3,000,000 nursed lesser wounds.

Between the fall of France and the surrender of Japan the country had spent $186 billion on war production. For its money it got 86,000 tanks; 296,000 airplanes; 15,000,000 rifles, pistols and machine guns; more than 40 billion bullets; 4,000,000 tons of artillery shells; 64,000 landing craft; 5,400 merchant ships; 6,500 Navy ships.

When Roosevelt went to Yalta in February, 1945, Stalin raised his glass and toasted American industry. Without it, he barked in his Georgian-accented Russian, the Allies would never have won the war.

The economy on top of which this mountain of devastating matériel was built had nearly doubled in size in only six years. Much of the increase was swallowed up by inflation. But in the last two years of the war federal officials had been able to keep the cost-of-living index to an increase of roughly 3 percent.

Yet the OPA was fighting for its life. It was by the narrowest margin that it won Congressional approval in 1945 to run for another year and to try to contain the inevitable postwar inflation. People were grumbling these days that in the First World War they could always buy meat and eggs. And they could, at a price. What they had forgotten was that then there was strict rationing for the poor, no rationing for the rich.

The OPA had bungled rationing, created artificial shortages and aggravated normal ones. But most people (in this case, 90 percent) supported its efforts to control prices. Only a handful of people ever condoned the black markets which mushroomed in the last year of the war. Most people who bought black-market goods did so unwittingly.

There was a growing dissatisfaction with the way the war had been financed, and one economist complained that the war was too expensive already. U.S. forces had killed no more than 500,000 enemy soldiers. With a total war expenditure in the neighborhood of $400 billion, that amounted to approximately $800,000 for every enemy soldier killed. As for property destruction, "at that price the U.S. could have bought up everything it destroyed in Germany, Italy and Japan."

It was ironic, then, that with much of the nation convinced the government had bungled wartime economic management and with the comeback of big business in both the economy and national politics, professional economists had achieved a prominence that even New Dealers had hardly foreseen. Economic tools had proved their effectiveness more in wartime than anything Keynesian theories had achieved in peace. No President would henceforth feel free to do without a permanent body of economic advisers.

The country was meanwhile stumbling through the first steps of reconversion. There was a profound sense of apprehension that what lay ahead was economic collapse. Nowhere was the apprehension keener than along the Pacific coast, where war industries had changed the economy of the entire region. An industrial base had come into existence that would normally have taken decades to develop, perhaps as much as fifty years. By 1945 Seattle and Portland were more dependent on government contracts than any other cities in the United States. San Francisco, whose Mark Hopkins Hotel had become a sentimental landmark to hundreds of thousands of servicemen and their families, was the hub of a vast shipbuilding industry. Los Angeles was tied to airplane production. San Diego and Long Beach lived for the Navy. They were bound so tightly to the production of ships and planes—of which the United States currently had more than enough—that the West mourned the impending end of the war.

And yet, in the West as elsewhere, that silent social revolution we saw earlier had driven deep roots. America had become a middle-class country. Nearly 50,000,000 people in a population of 140,000,000 were paying income taxes. What is more middle class than income taxes? And with the obligation there went the means. Average income was almost $3,000 a year, more than twice what it had been in 1939. The gross national product had gone from $90 billion then to $213 billion now. Most of the increase went into wages and salaries. Given a chance to spend it, people did. Expenditures on personal consumption almost doubled and would have gone higher but for rationing.

So Americans stood at the dawn of a new day with their wallets bulging. Nearly 30 percent of their earnings since Pearl Harbor had been saved up. Personal savings in cash, bonds, bank accounts and the like had been $15 billion in 1940; in 1945 they were more than three times as much. And if anyone needed a loan, the banks had so much money to lend and so little demand for it that they asked for just 2½ percent in return.

Business was equally prosperous. Its capital reserves stood at $20 billion. There was another $46.5 billion in working capital. In the whole country there was, by 1945, more than $130 billion available for postwar consumption and investment.

The national debt had also gone from $40 to $260 billion. But no one was particularly concerned. For a new lesson in economics had been absorbed. It was not even a decade since the New York *Times* had admonished the Keynesians, "We can no more spend ourselves rich than we can drink ourselves sober." The war years had made a mockery of that. "In the Thirties, niggardly voluntary spending failed to produce prosperity. In the Forties, extravagant involuntary spending had produced prosperity. Economics had a new philosophy."

Most people considered the black market just another domain into which traditional criminal elements had moved, as they had earlier moved into the supply of illegal liquor. It was true that some items, like counterfeit gasoline stamps and black-market tires, were monopolized by ordinary crooks. But most of the black market was run by ordinary small and medium-size businesses and their owners. They controlled the supply of most of the scarce goods; they controlled the retail outlets; they controlled the black market. When they were caught—and most were not—they pleaded necessity: that they had to do it to stay in business. But though small business was never fully integrated into the war effort, most of them were making more than enough money legally to stay in operation. The real motive was greed.

Much of the middle class refused to consider black marketeering as a crime. The treatment of black marketeers by the courts indicated a similar coyness on the bench. And while most people would not willingly buy on the black market, among business and professional people international black-market buying was the rule, not the exception. As the war ended, the black market was waxing stronger than ever. It would be bigger in the postwar era, in fact, than it had been in wartime.

Big business was exuding confidence and strength in the waning phase of the war. It had reasons enough. When federal officials took over Montgomery Ward again in January, 1945, a federal judge slapped them down, ruling that the President did not have the authority for it. At the same time the Dow-Jones averages were at their highest point since the boomlet of September, 1939, and were lurching ahead. Speculation was back. Stockbrokers began recalling the happy days before the Crash.

All through 1944, in fact, the market had climbed steadily, with cheaper stocks setting the pace. A new Florida land boom was getting under way. Around Miami the value of many houses had tripled in four years. Scores of hotels between Jacksonville and Key West changed hands each month. Tracts of swampy land were being drained, subdivided and sold at fancy prices. Elsewhere there was a boom in farmland. Hungering to get back to a simple way of life, people were roaming the back roads on weekends looking for family-size farms to buy with their wartime savings. The price of small farms had doubled in just a few years. Speculation was so emphatically back that there was even a new automobile manufacturer. Henry J. Kaiser and a Detroit auto parts manufacturer named Frazer were preparing to launch the Kaiser-Frazer and the Henry J.

When American forces crossed the Rhine, the stock market turned down, indicating that business was not entirely confident about the postwar world. Roosevelt hinted that the government might retain wartime economic controls (such as they were) until reconversion was over, which might take several years. The market stayed down. But then Roosevelt died. Investors celebrated the event by sending the Dow-Jones indices roaring upward to heights not scaled since the mini-recovery of 1937. The final link to a new chain of belief had been forged.

American business had never been so awesome. Nearly 500 banks had been forced to close. This weeding out of the weaker elements, while assets doubled, left the banks in an unprecedentedly strong position. The gross profits of business had tripled since 1939, topping $20 billion in 1945. Taxation appeared to have held net profits down. But a "relief amendment" tacked onto the IRS codes by a complaisant Congress would allow most businesses to recover nearly half of the excess profits taxes they had paid since 1940. When the United States came out of the First World War, it was to a cry of "Back to Normalcy." The cry these days was "Free Enterprise." It was no wonder that business contemplated the postwar era with more relish than did labor.

Yet big business would not relent in its opposition to speedy reconversion, at least, not until it was ready. To get ready, the corporations were calling their executives back from Washington with an urgency comparable to that with which it had dispatched them a few years before. Having come to rely on the dollar-a-year men, federal agencies pleaded that they be called back gradually. But these businessmen on loan were being told to come back at once or not to come back at all.

Every day, in every way, it looked, then, as if the real victor in the Second World War were American business. Antitrust operations were suspended. Expansion had been underwritten with public money. Corporate assets had gone from $54 billion in 1939 to nearly $100 billion in 1945. Generous tax and amortization laws were coming into effect. Even more lavish concessions lay ahead in the postwar world. "[Business] got some $25 billion in new plants and equipment for a pittance and scientific discoveries [financed by the taxpayers] worth untold billions. The net result was that before 1950 big business was stronger, more firmly entrenched and more monopolistic than ever before in American history."

For three years it had been AFL and CIO policy not to condone strikes. In those three years more than 11,000 strikes broke out, almost all of them wildcats. As the war went into its final months, the tempo accelerated. The strikes usually lasted only a day or two. The issue was nearly always job security. By the spring of 1945 strikes were erupting at a rate of thirty to forty a day. The "no-strike" pledge, though not formally abandoned, had broken down and was virtually meaningless.

When offered the opportunity, most workers had been willing to give the union a chance, so organized labor had grown substantially in wartime. Under maintenance of membership the number of union members went from 9,000,000 to 15,000,000 between 1941 and 1945. Politically, as we have seen, labor had also been able to realize the strength of its numbers. Business had at last accepted that there could be no return to the days of the open shop (and all that that implied). The AFL, the CIO and the U.S. Chamber of Commerce acknowledged that the days of open warfare were over by signing a peace treaty in the spring of 1945 pledging each to cooperate in the postwar era. Organized labor gave its blessing to capitalism, while business smiled on Social Security and called for more of the same. The *Wall Street Journal* rhapsodized over the agreement. The NAM was cool to it. But most of the country rejoiced.

Lewis had meanwhile been supplanted by Hillman as the most powerful figure in organized labor. But Lewis had lost none of his capacity for winning large gains for his miners. He had also launched an ambitious scheme to organize the country's 3,000,000 dairy farmers in the catchall District 50 of the UMW. Had Lewis succeeded, he would have forged an alliance between workers and farmers that would have dwarfed his greatest creation, the CIO. But he no longer commanded a corps of dedicated, imaginative organizers. Instead, he relied upon paid hacks. District 50 foundered.

Labor contemplated the postwar world fearfully. Roosevelt had endorsed a call for 60,000,000 peacetime jobs, but no one knew how they were to be created. The WLB took up the idea of a guaranteed annual wage, which already had the support of the Secretary of Labor, Frances Perkins, and the CIO. It was really a guarantee of a set amount of work each year, instead of a set amount of income. But there, too, no one could say how it was to be done.

For three consecutive years the growing weather had been excellent. Despite a shortage of agricultural labor, food production had risen from year to year, until 1945. Farmers began to cut back on production, raising just enough to meet current needs. They wanted to keep up the high food prices of wartime and hang onto their gains. Those gains were substantial.

No one had prospered more in wartime than the farmers had. They had the country by the throat. They had made the most of that opportunity. Their income was now 250 percent above 1939 levels. War had virtually eliminated the hired hand. The number of tenant farmers and sharecroppers had dropped by a third. A farm population that was much too big in 1939 had been reduced by 15 to 20 percent. The use of farm machinery had increased impressively despite the shortage of tires and gasoline. Cultivation was much more intensive and much more intelligent than it had been before the war began. The result of the new methods, machinery and longer hours was a 28 percent rise in the productivity of farmers.

But the great economic gains had been secured by political organization, and the fulcrum was parity. The Farm Board created in 1930 and the Agricultural Adjustment Administration of 1933 had been charged with closing the disparity between farm incomes and nonfarm incomes. After all, farmers usually had smaller cash incomes than nonfarmers had. Yet farmers had to pay the same price for the necessities of life. Under a system of parity the price of farm products could be set so that farmers would be sure to have the same purchasing power they had enjoyed back when the United States was still a predominantly agricultural country. Government took the period 1910–1914 as the base for parity, and by 1939 parity payments assured the farmers of at least 72 percent of their

1914 purchasing power. That was a floor. Many farmers were able to rise above it.

During the defense crisis period it was obvious that food production would have to be increased if lend-lease obligations were to be met. A new tier of administration was set up between government and the farmers. Production goals were set in Washington; then incentives were offered for meeting or exceeding them. By September, 1941, this new system was in operation. At the same time, the multitude of agricultural agencies operating at state and county levels were merged into County Defense Boards (later, County War Boards). These brought better management of the various agricultural programs. But there was heated disagreement over what kinds of incentives should be offered for increased production.

Here was an argument of fundamental importance. There were three major possibilities. One, favored by the big farmers of the Farm Bureau Federation, was simply to raise the price of all farm products. The second, favored by the AAA, was to provide cash rewards for particular crops. The third, favored by the Farm Security Agency (which represented more than 3,000,000 small farmers), was to improve production and distribution and to increase agricultural services for small producers. It was at this juncture that parity, always a complex and controversial idea, bumped up against the price-stabilization policies of the OPA.

Ostensibly, the current dispute over parity was about how to divide up the gains of the defense and war booms. But below it there ran a long-standing social clash, between poor and slightly prosperous farmers on the one hand and rich farmers and agro-business interests on the other. The Farm Bureau and its allies were determined to decentralize the Department of Agriculture. They also intended to smash the FSA and its ally, the Farmers Union. For the Farm Bureau, like Congress, had a powerful Southern wing which detested the egalitarian, social-service programs of the New Deal. The fight over the best way to increase wartime food production thus became the focal point in the fight being waged by the Farm Bloc against the millions of small farmers sheltered under the umbrella of the FSA.

During the Depression the Farm Bureau had almost perished. It was rescued by the AAA, which Hoover's administration launched and Roosevelt's enlarged. But now that it, like big business, was strong and prosperous again, it turned its energies to rolling the clock back as far as it could. Yet most people saw nothing of this struggle. All they saw was that food prices were climbing almost vertically.

The Farm Bloc managed first, in 1941, to force through a Price Stabilization Act over White House opposition that raised parity to 85 percent on six basic commodities. Then, in 1942, parity went to 90 percent, and five more commodities were added. By 1943 parity had gone to 110 percent, and there was hardly a grain, root, fiber or fruit that was not covered. Roosevelt was able to hold the line on parity at 110 percent, but the Price Stabilization Act was amended so that it would run for the duration of the war plus two additional years. And the Farm Bloc henceforth spent most of its energies on smashing what was left of the New Deal on America's farms.

Its principal objective was the dismantling of the FSA. As one anonymous Arkansas farmer was said to have described it:

> Well, it's this way. The government spends a million dollars or so to buy a 40-acre farm for a down-and-out sharecropper. They give him a mule, a bathtub and an electric shoelacer. They lay a railroad track to his house to carry the tons of forms he has to fill in. A bunch of experts figure out his milking I.Q., and behold, they teach his wife how to hook rugs, can beef and spinach, and they show the feller how to plant soy beans and prune an orchard—and by damn, them government people can actually do it! After we poke fun at their red tape for a year or two, they ups and proves their experiment can pay itself off. . . . And I don't know who's more surprised, me or the 'cropper.

The FSA had its origins in the Resettlement Agency run by Rexford Tugwell in the mid-1930's. It was thus suspect to many as another attempt at "Sovietization." Yet it had done inestimable good. It catered to the poorest of the rural poor—the small owners, the tenants, the sharecroppers. Besides being poor, they were usually sick, dirty and ignorant. Most were white, and most were in the South. Because the areas where they lived were frequently worn out, the FSA bought up arable land elsewhere and resettled them. It had its failures, especially where it tried collective farming. But the FSA had turned most of the people it catered to into self-sufficient farmers. It also set up a health program that provided first-class medical care to more than half a million people. The 3,000,000 FSA farmers had since been responsible for a disproportionately large share of the increased agricultural production in wartime.

But the FSA was doomed. For besides the ideological challenge that conservatives saw in the FSA, there was an important economic issue. Much of the country's agriculture—cotton growing, truck farming, orchard crops—was still labor-intensive. They required a large, seasonal supply of cheap farm labor. And it was the rural poor, the wellspring of such labor, that the FSA was making independent. Agriculture was therefore becoming more competitive. Big farm interests have no more stomach for serious competition than has big business, generally. They waged a successful wartime counterattack. The FSA was phased out.

The AAA was simultaneously assaulted. The Farm Bureau even succeeded in getting a rider attached to the AAA appropriation for 1943–1944 which banned it from publicizing itself or its achievements. Reluctantly, Roosevelt signed it into law. Thereafter the Farm Bureau's

Extension Service was able to promote itself without competition from the AAA's county agents. If the AAA could not plead for its own continuation or seek public support for its programs, it did not have much of a future. In time, the Farm Bureau hoped, the Department of Agriculture itself would become nothing more than an advisory agency, leaving it, the Farm Bureau, to control American agriculture. By making parity mathematical instead of flexible, it had already removed parity from the administration's control.

So in agriculture, as elsewhere, conservative interests had scored great victories for their side. But for the moment, rural America was no longer the scene of hopelessness and degradation that it had been in the thirties. The indebtedness of the average farmer was much reduced. Many had cash reserves for the first time in their lives. Rural areas and small towns had been transformed. While life there was still hard, the pockets of deep poverty had been much reduced. In some places they had been eliminated entirely. And though the Farm Bloc had made a strong showing against the FSA, against efforts to keep parity levels down, against the Department of Agriculture, against the White House, there was a commonplace view among farmers that the Farm Bloc could not hold the country to ransom any longer. For while farm organizations had grown in wealth and power, big business and organized labor had grown even more. Especially when compared with the great corporations, farmers felt that they had lost ground. But for the moment would-be wits sarcastically sang:

> The farmer's in the dough,
> The farmer's in the dough.
> Hi-ho, the merry-o,
> The farmer's in the dough.

The country would go into the postwar world with enough money in enough people's pockets to forestall any swift return to the Depression. Objectively, it need have no fear of widespread unemployment. Yet most people believed the opposite was true. Employment in 1939 had stood at 45,000,000. There were currently 55,000,000 civilian workers and 12,000,000 men in uniform. Averaging out the guesses and predictions of leading economists and politicians resulted in an estimate that fell considerably short of the goal of 60,000,000 postwar jobs.

For many, the end of the war would indeed mean hello, peace, good-bye, job. There were projections of 5,000,000 unemployed by Christmas, 1945. A newly appointed director of Reconversion Programs, John Snyder, estimated that by the spring of 1946 millions more would be laid off.

With this prospect in store at home and the growing rift with the Soviets abroad there was cause enough for gloom. There was also the daunting memory of what had followed the last war—economic misery, race riots, labor turmoil, left-wing violence, right-wing terror and severe government repression. In short, a collapse of the country's social, political and economic order. Yet these days people were far from downcast. On the contrary, they felt themselves to be standing at the threshold of a promising new era.

Many of the promises were prosaic. Housewives, for instance, were told to expect a torrent of safe, clean, laborsaving wonders, from cordless irons to chipproof plastic dishes. Many of the promises excited only those most directly involved, like the millions of young people who could now look forward to going to college. World War I had brought a staggering rise in high school enrollments in its wake; this war would trigger a boom in college enrollments.

There were fears about some of the prospects. Government, for instance, had become big all of a sudden. A federal establishment that had grown 60 percent under the New Deal had grown another 300 percent in wartime. There would be some postwar trimming, but not enough to alter the new dimension of government. The modern Presidency had also come into existence in the war years, with the creation of the Executive Office of the President, though it stemmed from prewar proposals. But after Roosevelt's death there were some people who expected the development of a strong Cabinet, a very strong Congress and a weak executive. The important point, however, was that government had become big, powerful, active. There were strong fears that it would prove unresponsive. Books with plainly apprehensive themes began to appear, such as Merlo J. Pusey's *Big Government: Can We Control It?* and Thomas K. Finletter's *Can Representative Government Do the Job?*

Preparing for the postwar world also required that some thought be given to erecting suitable memorials in memory of those who had fought for the country. After the last war cities and towns everywhere had put up architectural horrors in stone, concrete and marble and dedicated them to the dead. Will Rogers had been taken to see the enormous cylindrical shaft put up by the people of Kansas City, Missouri, and had drawled, "What is it—a silo?" There was a strong aversion in most communities now to setting up useless, costly eyesores and calling them tributes. Instead, this postwar era would bring thousands of useful civic facilities, such as memorial parks, memorial auditoriums, memorial hospitals, memorial stadiums. They would be called the Veterans this and the Veterans that, but in their use they honored not just the veterans, but the entire nation in wartime.

This was, after all, a much more sophisticated country than the one which had gone to war in 1917. Many of this war's boom towns had turned their economic windfall into permanent gains, which few of their World War I predecessors had done. They demanded—and received—public works which would be valuable in the postwar years. Many put their own inflated wartime revenues into expanding and improving public facilities and services. They had new schools, new sewer systems, new recreation facilities. State and municipal debts had been retired at a dizzy rate, on an unprecedented scale. The small towns like Seneca, Illinois, found that after the war workers had left something valuable remained behind. "The sleepy, down-at-the-heel village of 1940 gave way to an enterprising spic-and-span town in 1950."

All across America a new spirit moved—new, at least, since 1939— and touched ordinary men and women. Asked if people now had a better chance to get ahead than their parents had had, seven out of ten said yes, less than one in ten said no.

XXXIII
America First–Everywhere

WHEN the fighting in the Ardennes raged on into 1945, it took a toll of American casualties that eclipsed the Battle of Gettysburg as the bloodiest encounter in the history of American arms: 55,000 killed or wounded, another 18,000 taken prisoner. Germany and Japan were also trying, however feebly, to strike at the United States directly. Several large balloons carrying incendiary bombs drifted into the Pacific Northwest, starting a few small forest fires and injuring several people in whom curiosity was stronger than prudence. Two more German agents were landed on the coast of Maine. As pathetically fearful and inept as their predecessors, they remained at large for five weeks, doing absolutely no damage, before they stumbled into the arms of the police.

By the end of January the Germans had lost their final gamble in the west. On the other side of the world Manila fell to American forces, setting off a wave of national thanksgiving. It redeemed the humiliations of three years earlier, and it meant that thousands of American prisoners in Japanese hands would be set free. In following weeks American forces closed in on the Japanese main islands. From the east with a landing on Iwo Jima, from the south with an assault on Okinawa. The battle for Iwo Jima seized people's imaginations as no other battle of the war had done, largely thanks to a memorable photograph of a handful of marines raising the flag on Mount Suribachi.

But the cost of the war was beginning to wear on people's nerves. February brought a quarter of a million American casualties, including more than 50,000 dead. For the first time in its history the United States was in a war that would cost it more than 1,000,000 casualties. Letters and telegrams poured into government offices. One distraught woman wrote: "Please, for God's sake, stop sending our finest youth to be murdered in places like Iwo Jima. It is too much to stand, too much for mothers and homes to take. It is driving some mothers crazy. . . . It is most inhuman and awful—stop, stop!"

Roosevelt had meanwhile begun his fourth, and it was assumed his last, term. To liberals it seemed that with the new, strongly Democratic Congress behind him and no personal ambitions left to distract him the President could "return with vigor to the unfinished tasks of the New

Deal." He could smash monopolies, fight racism, do battle for social welfare and social justice, with no thought for himself. He could be the Roosevelt of their dreams.

His fourth inaugural was the simplest, least expensive in history. Bareheaded, without an overcoat in the freezing cold, he struggled painfully to his feet on the south porch of the White House to take the oath. Several thousand invited guests watched from the lawn. His speech was short, little more than 500 words. There was a brief reception indoors, and then it was over. It was a ceremony congruent with the bloody pitch of the war. In his State of the Union speech a few days later he sounded no heroic themes, calling merely for postwar compulsory military training. Then he was off to Yalta, knowing that he left behind him a country that was torn between high hopes and the worst apprehensions.

Will Rogers used to joke that the United States had never lost a war or won a conference. "Diplomacy," said one reporter, "is widely regarded as a sort of occult art in which Americans are usually outsmarted." In months past there had been other conferences: at Bretton Woods, New Hampshire, to establish the International Monetary Fund and the World Bank, which would stabilize postwar international trade and help developing economies; at the Dumbarton Oaks estate in Georgetown, where the question of postwar relationships between the great powers and the small was grappled with at length by the members of the emerging UN. And it was becoming evident that what was developing was something not so very different from traditional balance-of-power and sphere-of-influence policies, both of which—even if realistic—were repugnant to popular sensibilities.

By the time that Roosevelt journeyed to Yalta in February, 1945, the country trod the narrow space between hope and fear. *Time* portentously hailed it as "possibly the most important conference of the century." Walter Lippmann proclaimed it "The most impressive conference of our time." There was relief that the meeting did not break up over the question of Poland. But beyond that, a conference which began with some goodwill and optimism concluded on a sour note even before the details of its work were known. There was a strong sense of disappointment when it dawned that Yalta "was not, by itself, a guarantee of peace everlasting, even of peace in our time."

Radio Berlin called it "an unlimited triumph for Stalin." The Chicago *Tribune*, the Hearst chain and the Scripps-Howard newspapers agreed. In a two-page commentary called "Ghosts on the Roof" *Time* portrayed Yalta as a diplomatic fraud perpetrated against the West. The Russians, said *Time*, were using the peace as they had long used the war—to advance social revolution. Between America and Russia there could therefore be no compromise agreements: Any compromises reached at Yalta were

merely tactical moves in an East-West struggle to the death for possession of the world. It was an apocalyptic lesson that the American press
was teaching.

Roosevelt, haunted by the memory of Wilson's humiliating clash with
Congress over the Treaty of Versailles, threw himself with his waning
strength into the breach. He made an unprecedented effort to win support
for the Yalta agreements in Congress. Disdaining the podium, disdaining
even the pretense of walking, he was wheeled into the well of the Senate
chamber. "There, for the first time in living history, a President sat literally
on the same level with Congress . . . [and] for the first time he referred
publicly to his paralyzed legs." He tried to charm the Senators and Representatives, departing time and again from his prepared text, giving a
rambling account of Yalta full of conversational asides and anecdotes. But
it was all a little too calculated, a little too obvious to be very convincing.

Yalta was not perfect, said Roosevelt. But it was tolerable. What struck
his listeners most was less his words than his appearance. He was thin and
stooped; his hands trembled visibly; his voice quavered; he sounded
hesitant; the vibrant, self-assured Roosevelt they remembered had disappeared, and a broken old man had taken his place. The rumors about his
health now grew so many and so detailed that, as one writer complained,
"It's getting so that a Washington correspondent needs a medical degree."

Several weeks later the country learned that the United States and USSR
had secretly agreed to have three seats each in the postwar UN, whose
charter would soon be drawn up in San Francisco. There was an uprush
of public anger. Roosevelt tried to calm it by saying the United States
would take only one seat. But what residuum of trust still clung to the
accords was utterly canceled. "The bargain was bad enough, but the deceit
was worse."

In April Roosevelt went down to his beloved Warm Springs, Georgia,
retreat. Sitting for a portrait painter, he suddenly clutched his head, moan-
ing softly, "I have a terrific headache." He lay down to rest and died of a
cerebral hemorrhage.

No one should have been surprised, but it came as a shock that people
remembered for the rest of their lives. Across the country there rolled a
tidal wave of grief. The emotional burden of Roosevelt's death weighed so
heavily that hardened radio and newspaper reporters wept openly as they
went about the business of reporting his end. Front pages blossomed with
the 300-point woodblock type called the "Second Coming" size which
they had been holding back for VE-Day. It fell to Eleanor Roosevelt to
show how grief should be borne. She quickly made the White House
ready for its new occupants and left Washington for New York. To a lone
reporter who asked her for an interview she graciously declined with a
brief envoi: "The story is over," she said.

There were, of course, some who were glad it was over. The stock market surged ahead. The eulogies also obscured the fact that, as Allen Drury concluded from his post in the Senate gallery, Roosevelt and Congress were bitterly hostile to each other at the time of his death. "It is not too much to say that in those final days they despised each other."

Truman quickly made himself popular with the press and the public. He was deferential and humble. He protested his unfitness for the Presidency so convincingly that he was taken at his word. Truman was looked upon as a highly paid White House caretaker. Conservatives warmed to him. "With Mr. Roosevelt's death the era of experimentation was probably ended," enthused *Newsweek*. "President Truman could conceivably begin another, but if he did the country would be surprised."

It was a shaken and still bereaved nation that turned its attention to the UN Charter conference scheduled to open in San Francisco. The Big Three had really been three men. Now one of them was dead, and another (Churchill) would soon be out of power. The UN, which they had striven to create, would take its first tentative steps without them. The conference also opened under a cloud of public suspicion in the wake of the Yalta accords. It was further discredited by the presence of the crypto-Fascist representatives from the Perón regime in Argentina which, with the help of the State Department, had scrambled aboard the Allied side now that the war was almost over. Overnight, a host of lickspittle regimes, formerly neutral, declared war on the Axis and demanded a place at the charter-writing conference. A popular cartoon had a malevolent-looking Hirohito telling a startled Hitler, "You declare war on me, I declare war on you, and we both go to San Francisco." There were more than a few suggestions that the "San Fiasco conference" should be called off. But Truman dispatched the new Secretary of State, Edward Stettinius, whom Roosevelt had named to the post shortly before he died, and pressed ahead with the conference.

San Francisco was still the city which felt closest to the war. To reach it the charter-writing delegates had to travel all across the United States. Along the way they would see how big the country was, how prosperous its cities, how energetic its people, how vast its mountain ranges, deserts and plains, how its teeming, diversified population was well fed and free, how its factories roared and hammered and blazed by day and night, what it meant to be a nation of unlimited optimism, self-confidence and riches. It was reported that this was no accident, that when discussions were under way to pick a conference site Stettinius had heard a staff assistant humming "Home on the Range." Jubilant, Stettinius burst out, "That's it! San Francisco's the place! Make them go clear across our country."

When the conference opened in the Opera House, the sun was shining brightly; then the weather turned to rain. The scores of flags around the building, still at half-mast, flapped desultorily. Truman spoke to the delegates by radio and talked of justice. But the Russians were, from first to last, the center of attention.

A Russian ship lay anchored in the bay, heavily guarded by Soviet Secret Service men. The city ground out rumors that it was crammed to the gunwales with vodka and caviar, that Saturnalian orgies of legendary, Oriental proportions took place every day, that it was filled with Soviet frogmen who were busily probing the bay's defenses each night. On San Francisco streets OGPU agents in baggy serge suits and round-domed hats could be seen conspicuously trying to look inconspicuous.

Stettinius delivered a welcoming address which sounded a theme of one world and went on to declare: "The interests of the United States extend to the whole world [and] we must maintain those interests in our relations with other great powers." Truman was equally hard-nosed. He told the delegates not to worry themselves over the matter of captured territory in the Pacific. The United States would only retain "strategic bases." Anything left over would be assigned to international trusteeship. But the United States—and the United States alone—would decide what was and what was not a "strategic base."

By serving as Argentina's champion, the United States also found itself playing godfather to a host of semi-Fascist regimes. In contrast, the Russians were able to pose as the champions of ethics in international relations. They repeatedly cited the score of Latin American client states over which the United States now held sway as proof that the forthcoming UN would be packed with American puppets. *Time* conceded that it was a politics of expediency, but justified it: "[We] could hardly have taken any other course." It was "a straight power game, as amoral as Russia's game in Eastern Europe."

It took more than two months, but by the end of June the UN had a charter. Truman traveled to San Francisco and gave the new creation his blessing. It was noticed however that a conference which had begun by talking of peace and justice ended by talking chiefly of power and security.

In the war, April—as if intent on proving itself to be indeed the cruelest month—had brought false reports of peace in Europe. There were spontaneous celebrations. Newspaper extras blared NAZIS QUIT! For nearly two hours the country rocked with celebration. It was like the false Armistice of the earlier war, and it took some of the edge from the real thing when it finally came true.

Mussolini was killed by partisans as April gave way to May. Days later Berlin radio announced Hitler's suicide. Never did so many tens of millions of people rejoice over the death of a single man. But without Hitler's corpse the suspicion lingered on in many hearts that he was not really dead.

A few days after, an Associated Press reporter scooped his colleagues by breaking his word. VE-Day was supposed to come on a Tuesday, with simultaneous announcements from London, Washington and Moscow. Because of the leak, it came on a Monday, May 8. All the same, it was VE-Day at last. A thousand tons of paper poured down into the canyons of New York. Half a million people crammed into Times Square, chanting, "It's over, it's over." Extra police appeared on the streets. Liquor stores closed down. But it was a restrained celebration. The events of the past month had left the entire nation emotionally limp, spiritually drained. Four weeks had brought the deaths of Roosevelt, Mussolini and Hitler. Ernie Pyle, the most popular of all the war correspondents, had just been killed on Okinawa. Now that VE-Day was here it seemed somehow anti-climactic, while from Tokyo came this comment on Germany's surrender: "We can imagine what the future will be."

A week later a U-boat chugged up the Piscataqua River flying a white flag and surrendered to startled New Hampshire state police. Soon the leaders of the forces in Europe were returning in triumph. General Bradley was honored with the biggest parade in Philadelphia's history. Atlanta turned out for General Luther Hodges. Feted and cheered by the peoples of Paris and London, General Eisenhower came home, with a hundred fighters and bombers roaring aloft to greet his incoming plane. More than half a million of his countrymen cheered him as he drove down Pennsylvania Avenue to stay at the White House. A million more turned out to honor him in New York. Often he was openly called "Our next President."

But it was fitting that the most spectacular return was that of the general who loved glory most, General Patton. Almost a million people turned out for Patton's triumphal entry into Boston. He glittered with stars, twenty-four of them—four on each shoulder, four on each collar, four on his helmet and four on the holster in which rested his pearl-handled revolver. Patton beamed, he roared, he blew kisses, and when he talked of his dead and wounded men, he sobbed. The crowd sobbed with him. He insisted that he was "a better poet than a general." Then he set off for more of the same in Denver and Los Angeles.

Patton concluded with an appearance at the Los Angeles Coliseum that brought 130,000 people into an arena designed for 100,000. Red, white and blue searchlights formed a star high in the night sky. B-29's roared overhead in close formation. Patton, his voice breaking, addressed the crowd: "Goddam it, it's no fun to say to the men you love, go out and die! But by God, they did it!" He choked, as tears ran down his cheeks, "I'm living up to my name, I'm being as horrible as I can be—but I don't enjoy it." The festivities ended with a mock tank battle in the end zone.

The next Sunday, Patton visited the church in San Gabriel where he had been baptized fifty-nine years before and led a group of Sunday schoolers in singing "Onward, Christian Soldiers." He told them that they would be the ones who would have to fight the next war.

Patton's words to those children were disturbing and annoying to many; they were not the words the nation wanted to hear from returning generals. But people acknowledged their melancholy truth.

For the moment, however, there was the UN Charter. It had to win the Senate's blessing, and into Congress trooped hundreds of plain citizens who wanted to testify against it. Mrs. Agnes Waters, of the National Blue Star Mothers of America, argued that it would "set up a world government for the Soviets [and] make America into a feeding trough for the have-nots." Warming to her subject, she shrilled: "The real war criminals are in this room. . . . I name Mr. Stettinius." She concluded, as guards rushed down the aisles to eject her, by calling for armed revolution. Mr. David Darrin of the United Nations of the Earth Association called the charter "Godless . . . a monstrous crime against American liberties." Mrs. Helen Virginia Somers was convinced that the UN was simply a plot to make the Duke of Windsor "King of the World." And so it went.

There were liberal internationalists who were sincerely afraid that the UN Charter might, in fact, fare as badly as had the Treaty of Versailles and the Covenant of the League. But their fears were chimerical. For there had built up in recent months, as one reporter said, "evidence of such a popular groundswell in favor of international cooperation as to sweep aside all legislative opposition." He went on, "I can't recall anything quite like it . . . the public simply made up its mind and that was that. Voters simply don't want the Wilson-Lodge fight repeated." The fight would come, then, not over ratifying the charter but over implementing its provisions.

And in that latter lay the real test of the new internationalism. Unhappily, it gave every sign of having a thoroughly parochial core. But given the conservative revival which we have seen throughout society, economy and politics in wartime, it would perhaps be surprising if it were otherwise.

Quincy Howe had sensed as early as 1942 that the war was creating a new spirit of ardent nationalism, that a tougher, more resolute country was in the making, and he expected that the American people would be more changed than they had been since the Civil War. At almost exactly the same time the famous French journalist Raoul de Russy de Sales predicted what would come of America's victory over Germany:

> America will believe it her duty to concern herself with the rest of the world, but she will not do this without being paid for it. The payment she will demand will not be material but moral. No country is more con-

vinced than this one that she is right, or is more arrogant in her moral superiority. If she intervenes in the affairs of the world it will be to impose her ideas, and she will consider her intervention a blessing for lost and suffering humanity. The prospect is cheerless. Whether (run by the American left or right) the world will in either case suffer a singular form of tyranny at once biblical and materialistic.

He prayed, "I hope I shall not live to see this epoch of humanitarian businessmen [*e.g.* Hoover] and preaching farmers [*e.g.* Wallace]."*

William Shirer similarly tried in 1943 to tell his countrymen how they appeared beyond their own shores: "The masses of Europe have become distrustful of us. Many hate or fear us. Not one American in ten thousand probably realizes it, but this youthful Republic . . . is coming to represent to the mass of peoples of the outside world a sterile and black reaction, frightened to death of the great popular forces which this war has unleashed."

Shirer was certainly right in saying that very few Americans appreciated how other peoples were beginning to regard American power. They found it inconceivable that this could be an imperialist nation. For their idea of imperialism was like Hobson's and Lenin's—almost wholly economic. Yet colonies have rarely been a good investment; the French and British empires, for instance, never covered the economic cost of creating and maintaining them. Modern imperialism was a costly game played by individuals for profit but by nations for prestige. Imperialism as moral tyranny was far more common than imperialism as economic investment. The United States had its feet on an imperialist path and did not know it, though where money was involved, it was quick to count the cost.

The New York *Herald Tribune*'s Bert Andrews was claiming that there had been four secret agreements at Yalta, of which three had been revealed. The fourth, he said, was an agreement to extract $20 billion in reparations from Germany and give most of it to Russia. Clare Boothe Luce was insisting on "cold cash on the barrelhead" (though what the United States would do with carloads of worthless Reichsmarks was not clear). The atmosphere where money was concerned was, in fact, not so very far removed these days from where it had been twenty years before when one Congressman had intoned on the subject of war debts: "We don't want their gold; we don't want their goods; we want their money."

A majority of people wanted the British to be forced to repay lend-lease aid in cash, in full, and at once. When the House approved lend-lease for an additional year, it tacked on a requirement that no lend-lease goods could be used by the recipients to aid in their postwar rehabilitation. When it became known that Russia wanted a $6 billion loan to bind up its wounds, the country opposed such a loan by more than two to one. It was

---

* De Sales's prayer was granted. He died in 1943.

not just anti-Communism. They were equally opposed to loans to help the British recover from war.

It was a cliché by now that the soldiers overseas were "seven million isolationists." A popular ditty among servicemen in Europe and the Pacific ran:

> I'm tired of these Limeys and Frogs,
> I'm fed to the teeth with these Gooks, Wops and Wogs.
> I want to get back to my chickens and hogs,
> I don't want to leave home any more.

One of the best-selling books of 1944 was Bob Hope's *I Never Left Home,* recounting his travels to entertain servicemen. Its overt theme was that wherever he went, he saw so many Americans that he was never far from home. But there was another, unintended way to read his title. More than 10,000,000 Americans had gone overseas in this war, but most had really never left home.

The *Saturday Evening Post* was meanwhile unabashedly crowing that "We Americans can boast that we are not as other men are." More than that, "We can't see why Europe shouldn't be satisfied with making a United States of itself." If Americans contemplated "the global meaning of our own history," the *Post* went on, "we may do much to help Europe reproduce a new version of the miracle of Independence Hall." *Time* similarly portrayed Senator Vandenberg as he led the American delegation off to the San Francisco Conference over a caption which read: "At San Francisco, a Bill of Rights for the world?"

It was a very brittle kind of internationalism, this; really little more than the old-fashioned boosterism on a global scale. Analyzing his surveys, Hadley Cantril sadly concluded: "Our present 'internationalism' is not rooted in knowledge or analysis of facts. . . . Our fundamental attitude would seem to be one of self-interest."

Nor were liberal internationalists immune to the allure of a strident, resurgent nationalism. J. William Fulbright, who had bounded into the Senate in 1944 by defeating Hattie Caraway ("that pore, little widder lady" in Huey Long's phrase), thought that the war had brought a new world into existence. And "America's responsibility is to furnish leadership for this world." Its wealth and the character of its people fitted it for the task, said Fulbright. More, "The civilization to which we must devote our leadership is not, as some suppose, a vague and idealistic formula . . . it is the essence of *our way of living, the only way worthy of a free man* [my italics]."

Another eager young liberal named McGeorge Bundy was berating the college presidents who opposed postwar compulsory military training. "Peaceful peoples like ourselves get into wars for *want* of a military and foreign policy, not too much of it. . . ." If the United States were to play its destined postwar role as a great power, it must have the permanent military establishment of a great power, said Bundy. The powerful, vigilant America that Bundy imagined could never provoke a war anywhere, for "Strength in the hands of the righteous is the only guarantee of peace."

Liberal internationalists generally were becoming bellicose. Walter Lippmann was prophesying a postwar world split into a Russian orbit and an Atlantic community. He put his faith in a realistic alignment of powers to preserve the peace rather than a world organization. But Lippmann argued at the same time that "The world cannot be half democratic and half totalitarian." He shrank from spelling out the conclusion that such logic led to.

There was, then, a marked sense of impending showdown hanging over the new internationalism. Liberal internationalists were at the same time cultivating a profound contempt for neutrality. Before Pearl Harbor, Reinhold Niebuhr and a group of likeminded friends had established *Christianity and Crisis*. In its pages they had argued that Christians must press home the war on Fascism, that such was the nature of the current world crisis. The war on Fascism was now almost won. Something of that spirit, however, carried over into the rift with the Soviets.

Russell Davenport's *My Country* charged that America had allowed evil to prosper by not taking a strong stand before Pearl Harbor:

> In us the evil grew—engendered
> Evil behind the pious and empty mask
> Of pacifism and hypocrisy . . .
> We could have risen; yet we did not rise.
> We were neutral!

Herbert L. Matthews, a leading foreign correspondent on the New York *Times*, a man of staunch liberal sentiments, summarized the lesson learned in twenty years of foreign reporting: "You can't be liberal without being opposed to Communism." The most fervently interventionist organization of 1941, the Fight for Freedom Committee, was by 1945 turning itself into the virulently anti-Communist Freedom House. And those "old radicals [whom] Stalin drove crazy with rage and frustration" were ready recruits for the postwar, CIA-financed Congress of Cultural Freedom.

Meantime, there was the question of what should be done about Germany. There was no strong desire to occupy Germany unless it was necessary. But something would have to be done about the Germans. A Harvard anthropology professor, Ernest Albert Hooton, was reported to have proposed that the German elite be liquidated and the rest of the population scattered. Germany would then be given to non-German refugees. Henry Morgenthau had created a storm by making a similar proposal that would have reduced Germany to a scattering of weak, pastoral states. Ralph Slater, the "radio hypnotist," was still claiming that Lindbergh had been hypnotized. According to him, Hitler had hypnotized the German people. But he, Slater, could make them all wake up if only he could have a few hours on the shortwave.

There were numerous analyses which protrayed the enemy as being mentally ill. Germany was a nation of warriors and poets, according to one theory, and had pressed toward the poles represented by these two antagonistic types. The resulting split had created a nation of schizophrenics. The modern treatment for schizophrenia was shock, induced by insulin or electricity. It was in that light that the bombing offensive should be viewed. In the postwar years something just as shocking, but less deadly, should be applied. In time, the Germans would lose their illusions of grandeur and superiority and their worship of force. A well-known neuropsychiatrist, however, diagnosed it not as schizophrenia but as paranoia. He argued that since the days of Frederick the Great the paranoid elements in the German population had prevailed over the nonparanoid. The upshot of 200 years of national paranoia was Nazism. The Germans, he said, were homicidally insane. Recognizing that must be the starting point of the Allied treatment of Germany.

Reeducating young Nazis was dealt with on the stage and screen in *Tomorrow the World,* in which a particularly vicious specimen of the superrace is taken into the home of a kindly liberal American professor. Firmness and fairness bring about a conversion so total and so swift that Paul's experience on the road to Damascus could not compare. Preposterous as it was, however, both play and film were very popular, suggesting that that was much the way people preferred to have the Nazis turned into democrats. In the postwar era, American authorities would establish "de-Nazification" procedures in the U.S. zone of occupation, presumably on the notion that Nazism was some sort of infection that could be purged or shaken off.

But when the war was in its last months and the casualty lists were running to sickening lengths, there was a hardening of hearts. The full extent of German crimes began to be made known. In the spring of 1943 the New York *Post* had run a banner headline reading, NAZI FRENZY THREATENS MURDER OF 5,000,000 JEWS BY END OF YEAR and drew virtually no response. Individual Jews went through agonies of despair, like the man in Memphis who lamented: "The Nazis are simply murdering the civilian Jewish population in gas chambers." But the overwhelming majority of people refused to believe it. Nine out of ten people thought that the stories of the death camps were "propaganda."

But now the camps were being opened up. In the areas under his command Eisenhower made certain that American reporters and photographers saw the death camps and their contents. For the first time in this war

Americans as a people hated the Germans as a people. Radio stations revived the 1918 recording of Sarah Bernhardt reciting "Prayer for Our Enemies":

> They have revived a brutal way of living—
> Of murder, pillaging and fire . . .
> Their covenants they tear to tiny shreds.
> To Thee, who knows their inmost rage and cunning
> We pray with anguished hearts and heads laid low.
> Thou who their inmost souls and thoughts can view
> Forgive them not—they know well what they do.

A War Crimes Commission was already in existence, set up by the UN powers in the fall of 1942. The Russians, denied the sixteen places on it that they demanded to offset the British Empire and the U.S.-Latin American blocs, refused to participate. And liberals were impatient with the commission's work. It refused to list anyone—even Hitler—as a war criminal without first making exhaustive inquiries and giving full consideration to the broad issues of justice involved. To ordinary people it was obvious that Hitler was a war criminal. So were his henchmen. They should be hanged. And with the concentration camps coming to light, summary treatment of German generals and Nazi party officials seemed more fitting than ever. "We would involve ourselves in legal tangles of the most inextricable sort— and end by letting war criminals go scot free—if we attempted to judge war guilt in terms of recognized codes of law," scoffed the *Nation*. Robert Hutchins was almost alone among prominent liberals in his plea that they be treated with justice and mercy.

But no one, it seemed, could do justice to the comprehensive horrors of places like Dachau and Belsen. In the long, bloodstained history of man they were something entirely novel. It was as if the crust of civilization had split open and mankind could look down into those parts of its nature against which it had struggled for thousands of years. It was a terrible knowledge. It made a lie of civilization, a mockery of optimism.

People everywhere tried to understand it as something without precedent. But *Time* summarized it thus: "The causes that produced Belsen [were] deeper than any tendency to scientific brutality on the part of the German people. They lay in the political philosophy of totalitarianism, *which is not the exclusive property of any people* [their italics]."

Russia was an embarrassment to the West in two world wars. First czarist Russia, then Communist Russia upset the seductive symmetry of casting the struggles with Germany as democratic states making war on tyranny. The prowess of the Red Army kept the Russians high in popular esteem up to the close of the Second World War. Their declaration of war on Japan in the closing days triggered a boomlet of goodwill. But admiration for Russia as a fighting ally had never diminished suspicion of Communism as a social and political creed.

In 1943 *Life* had devoted an entire issue to the Soviet Union. The tenor was favorable, but it carefully avoided saying anything that could be taken as a kind word for Communism. Praise was lavished on the heroic Russian people, on the valiant Red Army, but not on the Soviet government. Frank Capra's *Why We Fight* series of films was much the same. These films were shown to every soldier who went overseas. The best of the series, *Battle for Russia*, surveyed Russian history from Alexander Nevsky's victory over the Teutonic Knights in 1242 to the Battle of Stalingrad 700 years later without once referring to Communism or the Russian Revolution.

As if intent on eliminating the latent fears and suspicions in Western minds and hearts, the Soviets abolished the Communist International in 1943. In death, as in life, the Comintern served Russian ends. Shortly after, the CPUSA dissolved itself, becoming the Communist Political Association, whose goals, said Earl Browder, would be purely educational, not political.

But the core of American anti-Communism remained untouched. Even people not especially hostile to the Russians were made uneasy by Soviet ploys such as the Free Germany Committee. Its aim was palpably the creation of a German puppet state in the postwar world. The execution of two prominent Polish labor officials in 1944 revived anti-Communist purges in the AFL and CIO. Russian intransigence and suspiciousness also struck millions of people as being both absurd and offensive. Yet, though the Russians fought bitterly over some things (*e.g.*, the future of Poland) on others they were entirely complaisant (*e.g.*, the American claim to dispose as it wished of those places in the Pacific liberated at the cost of American lives).

Yalta was the turning point. Every week thereafter the American press became increasingly hostile to the Soviets. A typical headline ran:

SOVIET FAILURE TO OBSERVE PROMISES
STALIN MADE AT YALTA
POSES QUESTION OF GOOD FAITH

The story underneath concluded that the United States and Britain "had reached the showdown stage with the Russians. The fate of the whole world hung in the balance." At the same time, a respected Washington reporter was insisting that the only way to deal with the Russians was by taking a tough stand against them. Any sign of weakness would be fatal, he said. *Time* claimed that the San Francisco conference had been saved from collapse only when Stettinius refused to accede to Russian demands. He forced the Russians to back down several times, and this had "preserved

Big Power unity." The press had become so obviously anti-Soviet that Lester Markel of the New York *Times* readily acknowledged it. But the hostility was all the Soviets' own fault, he said, for being suspicious and uncooperative.

But it was not only Russian Communism that aroused hostility. The recall of Stilwell from China was applauded by one journal which accused him of foolishly trying to push Chiang Kai-shek into the arms of the tyrannical, brutal, bloodthirsty Communists led by Mao Tse-tung. Anything short of war to the death, they counseled, would lead to a Communist regime in Peking. And such a government would almost certainly turn to Moscow for guidance. This, the editors concluded, would be a "catastrophic loss" to the United States.

Domestic Communism was meantime being revived as a menace. We have seen how Dewey tried to exploit latent anti-Communism in the 1944 election. *Newsweek* was warning the next spring of the "imminent possibility that American Communists might revert to their 1939–1941 position of sabotaging national defense." The editors of *Life* embraced Truman for forcefully pointing out the direction of postwar U.S. foreign policy—"U.S. leadership in world affairs." But the Russians, they complained, were being uncooperative about it. If they opposed American predominance in a reasonable way, it might be tolerable. But the United States was unfairly handicapped. "The fellow-traveler is everywhere: in Hollywood, on college faculties, in government bureaus, in publishing companies, in radio offices, even on the editorial staffs of eminently capitalist journals."

It was said that the mood in Washington in the spring and summer of 1945 was one of "Maybe we can't get along with Russia, but we are going to try." Yet there was also an undeniable sentiment in the country that the United States should bring to its postwar international relations an overwhelming military superiority. The blame and the need were placed squarely on Russian shoulders. A lengthy analysis of the case for universal military training concluded, "Thus the Soviets—as in so many things—hold the key." Noted academic Sovietologists were publicly portraying the Russians as pitiless murderers no better than the Nazis: The Russians would use the excuse of war crimes to exterminate the entire German middle class, they said.

Something very important had happened. Long before the war began, the notion had taken hold that Fascism and Communism were merely reverse sides of the same evil coin. The Nazi-Soviet Pact had looked to many like proof that this was so. Now that Fascism had been toppled, Communism slipped easily into its place in the popular mind as the menace to the world.

So now, wherever one looked—among conservatives, among liberals, among those in between and those at the fringes—there was a growing consensus on one point, at least: Russia was the mortal foe of the United States. As early as 1943 one journal had reported that among military men there was already talk of "the next war"—against the Soviet Union. When Kenneth Crawford returned home in the spring of 1945 after a year overseas, he was shocked by what had happened since he left. "War with Russia is unthinkable, yet it is being thought about constantly. It is, in fact, America's great pre-occupying fear."

The liberal intellectuals who had once derided Luce's *American Century* as imperialism in a new dress were now donning the same garb. The gap between the former interventionists and isolationists was almost entirely closed. The former were internationalists, the latter supernationalists. One spoke of cooperation, the other spoke of national sovereignty. Yet America's foreign policy would be bipartisan for the next quarter of a century because these two were not so very far apart. Both imbibed deeply at the springs of national self-righteousness, and both saw in Communism a common enemy.

A full year before the war ended Stalin was being portrayed as determined to create a host of Communist or pro-Soviet governments in Eastern and Central Europe, avoiding another war for ten years or so while Russia recovered, and then, from behind a shield of pliant, puppet states, he would launch the ultimate Communist war for world conquest. *Time*, interventionist before Pearl Harbor and moderate to liberal on domestic social questions, took this thesis even further. The world was dividing into two great camps, it said. One was Russian, materialistic and collectivist; the other was Western, idealistic and individualist. The question of which would triumph was the great issue of the age. More than that, "On all other issues . . . men and nations could compromise, but on this basic issue they could not compromise." This was in 1944. Thus was there a cold war before it was called the Cold War. And as the Second World War came to a close, Americans, though they had not taken willingly to these apocalyptic teachings, were split almost exactly about whether the Russians were peace-loving or not.

So while people wanted a speedy demobilization of the millions of men overseas, they had no wish to resume that almost unarmed state to which the United States was accustomed in peacetime, though with its monopoly on the atomic bomb and the largest air force and navy in the world the country need not choose between a vast standing army and weakness. Yet even so, more than 80 percent of the nation wanted the United States to maintain the most powerful military forces—in all arms—in the postwar world.

No one doubted for a moment whom those forces would be held ready against. "The possibility of World War III," reported one journal in June, 1945, "was more and more in the horrified world's public eye. That there were those who looked upon war between the democratic, capitalist U.S. and authoritarian, Communist Russia as inevitable was no longer news." It was not surprising, therefore, that when asked if they expected the country to be at war again within twenty-five years, Americans, by a margin of two to one, answered yes.

XXXIV

Science Works Its Wonders

B Y the summer of 1945 Japan was to all outward appearances a broken nation. American warships sailed along its coasts unmolested to bombard its ports and coastal cities at will. American bombers flew through its skies and were rarely challenged. Okinawa, the southern gateway to Japan's home islands, had been taken. But the bloody twelve-week battle had cost another 50,000 American casualties. An already war-weary nation asked: If that were the price of taking an island of only 400 square miles from 100,000 defenders, what would it cost to take Japan from an army of 2,000,000 Japanese soldiers and 5,000,000 militia?

So there was no sense of exultation at the impending descent onto the enemy's homeland. At best, there was only resignation. There was every prospect that hundreds of thousands more young Americans would die or be maimed in the coming year. VJ-Day was not expected before the spring of 1946. And for the first time there was widespread dissatisfaction with the policy of unconditional surrender. Letters poured in to newspaper offices demanding the policy be changed. Newspaper columnists openly criticized it. Millions of plain citizens wanted to know if it was prolonging the war.

Truman assured the Japanese that they could surrender without fear of being either exterminated or enslaved. But there was no positive response from Tokyo. To counteract the apparent complacency at home, the Navy asked people to take their 1945 vacations on the West Coast and to visit the ports there. Hundreds of thousands accepted the invitation. What they saw was the debris of the battle for Okinawa—ship after ship gutted, burned, torn open, bloodstained—the victims of kamikaze and close-in exchanges with shore batteries. But still Red Cross chapters appealed in vain for volunteers to prepare surgical dressings. Army planes futilely leafleted boom towns with handbills begging workers to sign on at local war plants. America was not so much complacent, however, as tired.

In Washington it was obvious that the government was desperately looking for some way to end the war without a frontal assault on Japan. One reporter hinted that the ultimate in bombing had not been used against Germany and "the Japanese have something new to learn." Truman modified the policy of unconditional surrender: that would apply only to Japan's military forces, he said. Most people approved. But the sticking point had come down to the status of the emperor; dump-the-emperor and keep-the-emperor factions formed in government and out. But Truman lapsed back into silence.

Then, on August 7, the President went on the radio just hours after coming back from the Potsdam Conference. In his flat, Midwestern voice Truman announced: "Sixteen hours ago (on August 6) an American airplane dropped one bomb on Hiroshima, an important Japanese army base. That bomb had more power than 20,000 tons of TNT. . . . It is an atomic bomb, harnessing the basic power of the universe. . . . What has been done is the greatest achievement of organized science in history. . . . If they do not now accept our terms, they can expect a rain of ruin from the air, the like of which has never been seen on this earth." A thrill mixed with dread went down the spines of millions. "We have spent two billion dollars on the greatest scientific gamble in history," said Truman, "—and won."

Three days later Nagasaki lay in radioactive ruins. Then began what was dubbed the Long Wait. The Japanese asked for clarification on what the status of the emperor would be. Twice the waiting was broken by premature news flashes of Japanese surrender. Finally, on Tuesday, August 14, at one forty-nine in the morning, eastern war time, came a message which began, "In obedience to the gracious command of His Majesty the Emperor. . . ."

People were still awake on the West Coast. They poured into the streets. From west to east a nation's lights came on as people got up in the middle of the night to celebrate. Church bells pealed. Streetlights blazed. Car horns sounded. In Salt Lake City thousands of people snakedanced in a drenching summer thunderstorm. Later in the day Truman declared a two-day national holiday. Despite the celebrations since early morning, there was energy left for still more revelry. Times Square was packed with the largest crowd in its history. On the other side of the continent, two statuesque platinum blondes cavorted naked in the fountains in front of San Francisco's City Hall to the appreciative cheers of half a million onlookers.

Yet over all this festivity, over the heartfelt rejoicing that it was over and won, there hung a cloud of radioactive dust. At a stroke the problems of reconversion and of postwar relations with the Soviets were cast into the shade. "The race had been won, the weapon had been used by those on whom civilization could best hope to depend," wrote *Time*. "But the demonstration against living creatures instead of dead matter created a bottomless wound in the living conscience of the race."

Some people could only shrug that it was inevitable: "Once you invest two billion dollars in a firecracker you have to light it." For the moment, most people felt no repugnance about using the bomb to end the war. Yet there seemed to also be a deep, troubling feeling that the world would probably be better off without it. From abroad, Churchill greeted the atomic age with evident misgiving, observing almost wistfully that the secrets of the atom had been "long mercifully withheld from man." From his jail cell Hermann Göring called it "a mighty accomplishment," then shuddered. "I'm glad I had nothing to do with it."

Truman went on the radio again to talk about Hiroshima and Nagasaki. The bomb had a "tragic" significance, he conceded. But the Germans were manufacturing one, leaving the United States no choice in the matter. He said nothing about the alternatives to using the weapon on the Japanese without warning. But buds of doubt and revulsion were already beginning to sprout. One impassioned letter to the editor read:

> [We] have this day become the new master of brutality, infamy, atrocity. . . . No peacetime applications of this Frankenstein monster can ever erase the crime we have committed. . . . It is no democracy where such an outrage can be committed without our consent.

During the 1930's and early 1940's science had nestled snugly in the bosom of popular esteem. In films like *Pasteur, The Fight for Life* and *Dr. Ehrlich's Magic Bullet,* in books like *Microbe Hunters* and *Rats, Lice and History,* scientists were portrayed sympathetically, even affectionately. Never again. After the atomic bomb's debut science loomed larger than ever in the fate of man, more mysterious than ever, more powerful than ever—and disquieting to the point where it seemed almost malevolent. Once science had been regarded chiefly as a life-cherishing, life-preserving force. Pasteur and Ehrlich and Fleming were men the public could love. Fermi and Oppenheimer and Rutherford were respected, but physicists, unless they were theoretical physicists like Einstein, were not looked on with affection. Before the war science had meant medicine. Now it meant physics, for this was the physicists' war (much as the previous one had been the chemists'). Medical and biological experiments in the concentration camps had also cast the medical sciences in a new, repellent light. It was ironic, but the Germans—and others, to a lesser degree—had managed to discredit science while serving technology.

Science is concerned primarily with our knowledge of nature. Technology is concerned primarily with the control of nature. The latter builds on the former. The United States, like Germany, excelled during the war years in technology and slighted science. Science—the realm of imagination and disinterested inquiry—was from first to last a field in which the Europeans excelled. America's major contribution to atomic physics, for instance, was the cyclotron built by Ernest O. Lawrence; it was essentially a piece of engineering. So too was construction of the atomic bomb.

It was German research before the war began in Europe that prompted the United States to enter the atomic race. The Germans proved that a sustained nuclear reaction could be set up, turning a theoretical possibility into a practical idea. But if the Germans ever built up a substantial lead, the United States might never catch up. American and refugee European scientists, alert to both these considerations, prodded the federal government into action. America would build the bomb. But without Bohr, Fermi and other European atomic scientists and the British heavy-water project, the American atomic bomb would never—possibly could never—have been built.

American wartime science had other important shortcomings. They were obscured by the atomic mushrooms welling up from the remains of two Japanese cities, but they were significant. There had been a war-inspired emphasis on teaching mathematics and science in the schools and colleges. It suggested that the United States was raising the most science-minded generation in history. But serious scientific training had really come to a virtual halt. The United States, in fact, was the only major country which stopped training scientists. When the Rockefeller Foundation examined American education in 1944, it was disturbed to find that "Except for a few 4-Fs the United States now has practically no male students over eighteen studying science."

There was an even more worrisome flaw in the wartime organization of science. Contracts were let to private laboratories and university science departments on a cost-plus basis for tackling problems in fire control, military medicine, radar, transportation and thirteen other areas primarily related to the war effort. But relations between scientists and users were rudimentary. The result was that hardly any of the wartime scientific projects initiated in the United States turned out to be of any practical use whatever. University science departments, however, grew utterly dependent on federal funds.

There was also, despite the roster of scientific personnel, a confused scientific manpower policy that saw thousands of trained scientists drafted into the military—the very thing that was not supposed to happen. Even an awestruck admirer of American science in wartime thought that "the United States dealt clumsily with the problem of scientific manpower as compared with Great Britain."

It was not surprising, therefore, that compared with the weapons of the other major powers (excepting Japan and Italy), American weapons were inferior. This seems a very harsh judgment. It requires explanation, especially in light of the fact that when it came to science in wartime—particularly when the question of credit was raised—the euphoria of a successful war brought a complete collapse of critical intelligence. Because the United States had built the atomic bomb, it somehow appeared to deserve the credit for everything else. Even before the atomic bomb was exploded, *Time* was blithely praising the United States for inventing radar, rockets, jet planes, power-driven gun turrets, proximity fuses and guided torpedoes. And just after the war ended, the Pulitzer Prize for history would go to a book on wartime science that puffed along in this vein:

> The only successful development of proximity fuses was American, sponsored by the OSRD. Except for the atomic bomb this constitutes the most remarkable scientific achievement of the war. [It was a triumph] of the highest degree of cooperation between American science, American industry and the armed services. That it was done at all borders on the miraculous.

Proximity fuses were indeed an astonishing achievement.* They were given to the United States by British scientists in 1941. At about the same time the British also handed over the cavity magnetron (the solution to the problem of how to make radar work), asdic, ship-finding radar, solid-fuel rockets of advanced design, a working jet engine, a mass of data on how to build an atomic bomb and various other useful items. The problem of large-scale amphibious landings on hostile shores was overcome by the LST, also of British design. So, to a lesser degree, was the best American fighter, the P-51 Mustang, which stemmed from the work of the British Purchasing Commission in 1940.

As for the other important applications of science to war, the Germans were obviously ahead of everyone else in liquid fuel rockets; sonar, operations research and solid-fuel rockets were pioneered by the British; German and Russian tanks and artillery were the best in the world; Germany and Britain developed the first operational jet fighters. The United States' uniquely original contributions were the DUKW and the bazooka.†

It was both fitting and fortunate that the Germans, who had been the first to organize science systematically for war (in 1914), organized more poorly than the United States in the Second World War. The Germans had a tactical edge from the first in some items, but scientifically they lagged behind from the start. Not until 1942 did they even attempt to emulate the British and American organization of science for war. By then there were few first-rate scientists left in Germany, fewer still who would willingly serve the Nazi regime. Hitler also helped matters by being blind to the possibilities of wartime science, and he grossly misused his advanced weapons like V-2's and jet fighters. The Japanese did still worse than the

---

* The secret of the proximity fuse, which had baffled American and German scientists for years, was to place a radio inside its own aerial—to wit, inside a shell casing. The fuse was a radio valve which emitted a radio signal; as the signal bounced off its target, it was picked up by the shell casing and, once a preset proximity was reached, detonated the shell. The man who hit on this solution was W. A. S. Butement. From that point it was simply a question of perfecting the fuse and the shell, then turning them out in quantity, a task for which American industry was better equipped than the hard-pressed British.

† When America's own courageous rocket pioneer, Robert Goddard, died in 1945, hardly anyone noticed.

Germans; they had no scientific organization worth mentioning. Their total neglect of military medicine resulted in great suffering among Japanese soldiers and those civilians in towns subject to American air attacks.

Surveying the course of American science in wartime, Vannevar Bush was openly worried. Almost no basic scientific research had been done in the United States for nearly four years; even before the war the United States had slighted basic science, putting six times as much money into technology. The scientific discoveries on which that technology rested had been almost without exception the result of European research. But Europe was now so ravaged and worn-out that it would be years before it had the will or the means to do much basic research. In a historic report to the President, Bush argued for "a national policy for science." He called for vast amounts of federal money, for the selection and encouragement of tens of thousands of bright students to go into science each year and for scientific advisers at the highest levels of government. Publicly Bush argued that unless it did these things, the country could expect to fall behind in military power, its international trade would suffer, and the domestic economy would stagnate. Commissioned by Roosevelt, Bush's *Science: The Endless Frontier* was taken to heart by the Truman administration. In the postwar years a National Science Foundation would be created, there would be Presidential science advisers, billions of dollars would be poured into scientific research, and for a generation the United States would become the foremost producer of scientific knowledge.

Meanwhile, the nation learned that there had secretly grown up a $2-billion-a-year radar industry within the economy; that was six times the size of the pre-1940 radio manufacturing industry. Plastics had been developed in the 1930's and seemed ready to be put to a thousand-and-one uses in the streamlined, aseptic world of the future. For in 1945 a new world was said to be in the making, a world which would revolve around electronics and synthetics. The newest magic material was silicone, made from coal, sand, oil and salt water. DDT was another wartime scientific wonder; strange as it may seem now, it was hedged about with glamor. By killing the pests which destroyed crops and the parasites which spread disease, it was seized upon as a boon second only to penicillin. Synthesized in Germany in 1874, it was made useful on a large scale by the Swiss in 1940. "Our picture of the postwar world," enthused *Newsweek* as the war drew to its close, "is already one in which aviation, plastics, electronics and a host of industrial wonders are going to transform our habits, our ways of living, our place in the world."

But what did it finally amount to in the growth of science, this war which saw mule carts drag German ammunition across the Polish frontier in 1939 and ended with atomic bombs six years later? The answer is, almost nothing. Since the middle of the seventeenth century science has grown so fast—about eight times faster than the rate of Western population growth—that wars, even the most awesome of them, have hardly nudged it from its pattern of long-term growth. They have neither speeded it up nor slowed it down. Since about 1700 science has grown about 1,000 percent every fifty years: for every 100 scientists in 1700 there were 1,000,000 in 1950.

Yet thanks to wartime technology, there now hung over the entire human race a question mark that looked like an accusing finger.

XXXV

Past and Present

EVEN before the war ended, hundreds of thousands of men who had gone abroad to fight were coming home. The average civilian felt that what he had seen and done during the past six years did not, could not, compare with the experiences of the fighting men. Yet at home, just as much as overseas, the country had been faced with and overcome a great historic challenge. And in that fact was the significance of the experience of the war years to American society and politics. For what the country really overcame in those years was less a combination of foreign enemies than itself. America triumphed over itself and its history.

However little it was appreciated at the time, the war generation had overcome the potential crisis of authority that is never far from the surface in American life. Not until another generation had come to maturity to grapple in its turn with that crisis would it be possible for the true nature of the wartime experience to be generally understood.

Without knowing it or intending it, the American people in the six years from 1939 to 1945 refreshed the springs of authority in society and politics, from the lowliest local school to the most imposing seats of power. It was a renaissance of the spirit and carried home to ordinary people the legitimacy of American ways, beliefs, aspirations and institutions. It was the supreme collective social experience in modern American history. Nothing like it has happened since, for in the unity of wartime a disparate people was fused into a community, and that community was cemented in victory, in social justice, in economic recovery, in a more democratic polity and society. It was a very creative time.

The key to its importance was the renewal of authority, for the great danger that all democracies run is a crisis of authority. It springs from the dilemma fundamental to all secular authority: that though the premise of individual freedom and responsibility has driven Western civilization forward since the breakup of medieval Christendom, the institutions created by men are unavoidably second-best as sources of authority. It is unlikely that we can ever be happy for long with the ties and objectives we fashion for ourselves. For one thing, we know our own failings too well. So all of the mystery and most of the magic is lost when authority comes from ourselves instead of from something outside ourselves. Certainly it leaves important needs unsatisfied: As divine authority has fallen,

433

absolutist politics has risen. The nation-state was barely in its infancy before the theorists of the absolute state, such as Bodin, Machiavelli, Hobbes, rushed forth to instruct it. Behind us there now stands more than five centuries of absolute politics, cosmic ideologies, millennarian parties, quasi-divine political leaders and semisacred political texts. The result has been a tidal wave of blood and tears.

The other great defect of secular authority as compared with the divine is that once the fundamental needs of food and shelter have been met, there is no distinct purpose to life. When the central aim of existence was the salvation of souls, life had a purpose that was eternal and universal, fixed from century to century and across the boundaries of language and geography. No such bond links modern men to one another or to time. In the modern world purpose must be constantly created anew; in the Biblical phrase, "from generation unto generation."

To some it seems unreal, of course, to talk of generations; the idea is hazy rather than precise. Infants are obviously born along the path of time; they do not swamp it at intervals of twenty or thirty years. Yet the idea of generations will not down in discussions of society. Polybius relied heavily on the importance of generations when, 2,200 years ago, he tried to explain the course of Roman history. Auguste Comte, the nominal father of modern sociology, posited a new generation about every thirty years and saw in generations a primary element in the life of societies. John Stuart Mill was, at about the same time, similarly trying to explain history in terms of generations. Giuseppe Ferrari saw political history changing every thirty years thanks to generational forces and thought that each generation passed through four stages: the preparatory, the revolutionary, the reactionary and the conciliatory. An entire school of German historians (the most notable of whom was Leopold von Ranke) attempted to develop a scientific theory of history around generations. In the 1920's the eminent sociologist Karl Mannheim made an ambitious attempt to formulate a generation theory of society. And in the 1930's José Ortega y Gasset tried to break modern history up into generations of fifteen years.

However crude, then, the idea persists. Prodigies of effort have gone into futile attempts to make the idea precise by determining how long a generation is. But what creates a generation is only partly chronological. For it is really a three-legged creature (no doubt that is why it is so clumsy in action and inelegant in conception). The other legs besides a roughly similar age grouping are commonality of experience and commonality of outlook on that experience.* As each generation comes of age to claim its

* It is also important to keep in mind the things *not* experienced by a particular generation, for several generations exist side by side. Young and old alike, for instance, lived through the traumatic decade of the 1960's. Those experiences were shared across generations. But instead of pulling them together, those experiences set them at odds. Why? Because the outlook on what was happening was so very different. The old had experiential resources to fall back on which the young lacked.

inheritance, authority must be legitimized within it. At the same time, it must be legitimized across the generations. It is not difficult to see that legitimizing authority within a generation is infinitely easier than across generations or that in the latter the potential for crisis is strong.

These are crucial matters in the history of any society. If at times it is hard to perceive them clearly, we can lay much of the blame on relying for too long on rusty intellectual tools. Authority has been conceived chiefly as a matter of politics. But politics and society are not the same, for all their interpenetration. This, however, is not the place to offer a primer on the subject. It is enough to keep in mind that authority in politics is concerned with the question: How shall we be ruled? In society it is concerned with the question: How shall we live? One helps set the terms of the other, but they are still two very different questions, requiring different, if related, answers.

Besides the general confusion of the things which belong to politics with the things which belong to society, we have also suffered a paucity of fresh thought on the general subject of authority. For two centuries two remarkable thinkers have preempted the field. Hobbes said that men obey because of fear. Rousseau said they consent to obey rules which they themselves have framed. These two ideas of obligation based on fear or consent eclipsed what remained of the earlier theories of the divine right of kings or "prescriptive possession" (rule by customary right) and set the terms for all subsequent discussions of authority. We have had interminable considerations of the rule of force or of social contracts and covenants. But hardly a word has been uttered on what we all can readily see has become the modern basis of authority: practical success. That has always been the American test; there is not a state or society in the world which means to be modern that is not moving toward it.

It is all well and good to insist that states and societies rest on contracts and to fume, as Burke did, that it is absurd to expect that each individual can have his obligations under that contract proved to his satisfaction. But that is an argument effective only in debate, not in life. The rise of mass education, popular journalism, political parties, and militant ideologies have mobilized what were once no more than vague stirrings of disquiet in ignorant breasts. Whether or not each person ought to have legitimacy and authority proved to his or her satisfaction, any institution —from the family to the state—courts possible disaster when it fails or refuses to do so. It is, after all, an old and critical question: If I was not there to sign the contract or enter into the covenant, why is it binding on me? In the modern world that question is asked with a force it never had before.

This does not mean that the old were smarter for their experience, only that what joins one generation together—whether it is ignorance or knowledge—helps set it off from other generations.

In responding to it, no society is entirely helpless, and habit and convenience will, if given the chance to come into play, incline the questioner to moderation. Every nation, no matter how new, has developed ways to routinize the legitimization of its authority. Usually it involves some combination of tradition, ritual, sacred relics and objects (such as flags and medals) calculated to awake powerful emotions. But whether it is done routinely or extraordinarily, the emphasis on how authority is legitimized differs markedly from one nation to the next.

The reason is simple enough. Flags, relics, rituals and the like are able to inspire powerful emotions because of the associations that surround them. They stand as the embodiment of those things which a group of people consider important, for these are things which help to define who and what these people are, have been and might hope to be. These associations are a powerful force in turning isolated individuals into a genuine community. The objects which conjure up the associations are the common possessions of all.

Now, authority is rooted in that very soil of commonality. It is the distillation of a community's fundamental agreement on ends and means. That agreement is what underlies the operative set of binding obligations which we call authority. The commonality of purpose, outlook and needs which underlies common emotional associations is, then, the mainspring of authority.

As between groups of people, particularly as between nations, the ends, the means and the associations differ, because of geography, or history, or ethnicity or religion or some other reason or combination of reasons. The important thing is that they differ. Consequently the ways of legitimizing authority also differ. And the principal differences are the ways in which common agreement is reached and the ways in which it is known that it has been reached. It is largely a matter of promises. All nations, of course, make similar professions: All declare their love of peace, their desire to be just, their concern with the welfare of their people. But though all make promises, some promises are more important than others (as we shall see).

Besides their importance in establishing agreement on ends and means, the promises play a central role in defining success. Modern Russians, for example, grow restive at the sight of a new class, a rigid bureaucracy and the suppression of basic liberties, and the more courageous among them demand, "Where is the real Communism?"—that is, the Communism of humanitarian idealism. Conversely, no one in the Third Reich contemplated the Nazi regime and asked, "Where is the real Nazism?"

In America for reasons of history and geography the essential promise has been the promise of practical success. America has ritual, tradition, sacred relics. But more than any other people Americans have historically found the legitimacy of their society and politics in practical success. The nature of the country's history made such a heritage virtually inevitable, for it began with the Puritans.

To the Puritans the divine will was everywhere. They believed that God literally made order out of chaos, not just when the world began but every day in every way. And it follows that if the world is arranged so that something means anything, then everything means something. In the falling of a sparrow was a clue to the divine will.

By the time they reached American shores the Puritans were accustomed to looking for "witness" all around them: In their daily lives they sought witness of God's will at work; particularly they sought witness of his blessings on their posterity, of his approval of their actions, of assurance of their own salvation. Believing that none but the elect of God was saved, they looked to secular success for a clue to how they stood. For if God approved of them, was it not obvious that He would make their exertions prosper and, conversely, if He disapproved, would visit poverty and futile struggle on them? Thus did the search for witness of salvation give an entirely new impetus to the pursuit of the things of this world, creating a rapid growth of the pragmatic outlook and assigning an unprecedented weight to secular success. Yet though its early growth was nurtured in the soil of Western Europe, especially in Britain, nowhere did the pragmatic, capitalist outlook triumph as it did here.

By the time of the Revolutionary War the drive of the Yankees for success here and now, measured in terms of raw economic power, was the central pillar in the edifice of American life. It was a life that was rough and competitive, but the prospects it held out never lost their allure. In the next century and a half tens of millions of immigrants poured into the country in pursuit of better wages or a chance to own some land. It is a cliché by now to portray these immigrants as people in search of opportunities to get ahead or see their children get ahead. It is also something of a cliché to portray them as people fleeing persecution. But as often as not the persecution was principally the denial of equal opportunity. To the immigrants America was promises indeed—promises of jobs, land, money, opportunity.

There was no more difficult way for a country to prove itself and create a nation. Old countries, without a profusion of untapped wealth, could never have attempted it. Instead of Success, they held out Culture or Glory or Justice or Peace. Here the practical test worked its spell. An undeveloped continent dared these white men, creeping in from the coasts, to put their creed to the test. And Daniel Boorstin has written how throughout the nineteenth century America seemed to be remade again and again, before men's wondering eyes, under their eager hands. Even in the realm of ideas the practical test exerted its hold; it was no accident that the only native school of philosophical inquiry America boasts is the pragmatism of William James.

When they went abroad or when others came to them, Americans might feel a little defensive about being less polished, less devoted to the arts, poorer in monuments and history. But they were nevertheless imbued with a fierce, bristling kind of self-esteem. For crass though they might be, they were undeniably citizens of a rich and powerful country. Europeans could taunt them, but they could not outbid them.

Equally convincing proofs were the victorious wars of each generation. The Revolutionary War was confirmed by the War of 1812. The various struggles to take territory away from Mexico culminated in the Mexican War of 1846. The questions of both slavery and Union were settled in the War Between the States. The country's entry onto the stage of world history as a major international power came with "the splendid little war" against Spain in 1898. America's full membership in Western civilization was resoundingly confirmed in the decision to go to war with Germany in 1917 rather than see Europe conquered and united under German rule. And America's supremacy within that civilization was sealed with the Second World War. What could be a more convincing proof of a nation's practical success—what is more a triumph of secular authority— than a successful war? Failure in war invariably produces a social crisis in the defeated. Success has very much the opposite result.

But America did not rely solely on wars to prove itself. It spent most of the first 200 years of its existence, first as a colony, then as a nationstate, opening up and developing the riches of a continent. There were secular challenges enough for both individuals and nation. Frederick Jackson Turner's thesis on the end of the frontier in 1893 as a turning point in American history was seized upon as a great insight, not because it offered much empirical evidence; indeed, it is a short, general essay. But it seemed right; it was felt to be right. It was not a spur to exhaustive historical inquiries to see if it was sound. It was simply accepted. For what Turner had hit upon, without realizing it, was that a vast range of opportunities for practical success had gone forever; given the nature of the American way of proving itself to itself, it was a new page of sorts in American history.*

With two successful world wars behind it, however, the country was able to avoid having a crisis of authority erupt into the open for three

---

* Turner wrote glowingly of how the frontier had taken a European and turned him into an American. His emphasis was on how the frontier shaped American character and said little directly about how the frontier encouraged a practical spirit. It is nevertheless obvious that an impractical, otherworldly character would have either perished on the frontier or never gone beyond an aboriginal existence. Turner's thesis implies much of what is stated here.

more generations, roughly seventy-five years. For what the country now faces is an old-fashioned crisis of authority in its national life. What is unique about it is that, thanks to its success for generations past, such crises have been a comparative rarity in American history. The other unique and especially worrying feature is that it has erupted in society and politics concurrently.

It is important to keep in mind that a problem is not the same as a crisis. A problem in society or politics is something that has a solution. It is an instrumental matter arising from some sort of maladjustment. It might be a matter of ignorance or badly aligned priorities or simple incompetence. The remedies are equally instrumental: Knowledge should be sought, realignments should be made, or skills should be applied. A crisis, on the other hand, is fundamental. It threatens to destroy a social or political entity or at least to alter it in a systematic way. Sometimes problems become so complex and numerous that the failure to solve them induces a crisis. But usually a problem, or a set of related problems, will work enough mischief that it will be resolved before it triggers a crisis. When Prohibition failed, for example, it was possible to deal with it by passing another law to nullify it. But no such remedy is at hand for a crisis. What has happened is that the agreement on what ends should be pursued and what means should be employed has broken down. It is a blow straight at the heart of community.

All genuine social and political crises are crises of authority, and what a subjective matter authority is! Whether or not people are turbulent depends primarily on what they believe and what they feel; only secondarily on the objective facts of their existence. The ultimate object of politics and society is not matter, but mind; the end they are supposed to serve is human happiness. And people have endured the worst imaginable evils of poverty, plague, ignorance, war, famine, injustice and tyranny without being thrown into chaos. Because despite their woes, people overwhelmingly believed that existing social and political arrangements were legitimate. To some the legitimacy of authority derived directly from a god, to others from the "cake of custom"; to still others it was part of the harmony of the universe. But once the legitimacy of authority—the authority of learning, the authority of the home, the authority of government—is thrown into doubt, then even those who are well fed, educated, healthy, even privileged become turbulent. And being educated for leadership, they become the cutting edge of protest.

The most effective counter to a crisis is a regenerative experience, something that touches everyone and calls forth a common response. Some massive, unifying, collective social experience can shape a dispirited, despairing people into a close-knit community. An experience that is broadly shared will drive the general sense of achievement home so effectively that it will counter individual failure.* The Second World War was the last experience of that sort in American history. And then, not only did people feel that the country was a success in its own terms, but it was a success in its own terms. Not only did they conclude the war thinking that life had never been so good for ordinary people, but it never had been so good for ordinary people. Not only did America seem to work, but it worked.

During the 1960's, when the next generation came of age, young people tried to create such an experience for themselves. They needed, like the generations before them, to fashion their own myths, their own legends, their own villains and heroes and martyrs; to create, in a word, their own history. In considerable measure they succeeded, though they did not set out to create a counterculture, or to green America, or to drop off the edge of history, or to be torn between drugs and mystical religions. Like their parents and grandparents, they set out to make the country work: They went on Freedom Rides, sat in at lunch counters, joined the Peace Corps, pressed for greater educational opportunities. They tried to make the country live up to the ideals it proclaimed, be what it said it was. Children of the war generation, they, like their parents, wanted the country to work. Not so incidentally, in making it work, they would make it their own. Those hopes died with a martyred President and an odious, indefensible war.

Vietnam is not simply a war the country did not win. It is a war that should not have been fought and is, consequently, a social and political disaster. Whether the war is symptom or cause of the country's faults, it is inextricably bound up with the current crisis of authority, a crisis whose cutting edge is generational.

The result has been profound unhappiness in tens of millions of homes. Yet it could not have been avoided. For the central experiences of the war generation and its children have been very different. The war generation —the people who did most of the fighting and most of the war work— now occupies most of the places of power and responsibility in society and politics. That generation carries the war experience in its bones. And to its

* In this regard it is worth noting that most of the people who came here poor lived here poor and died here poor. How the immigrants lived is caught unforgettably in *How the Other Half Lives*. It comes across starkly in the few fictional descriptions such as *Maggie: A Girl of the Streets*. The anger and rage of the younger men fueled organizations like the Molly Maguires and the IWW. But appearance triumphed over reality in the minds of most. When they failed, they took the blame on themselves, because America seemed to work; it seemed to pass its own test; it was rich and powerful even if they were still poor. Similarly, there is the myth of American social mobility and European social stagnation. To this day, most Americans can be counted on to respond with sheer disbelief when told that social mobility in the United States is almost exactly the same as in all other industrialized countries. Even educated people usually find it hard to believe, though the evidence is very convincing. Cf. the relevant studies in Seymour Martin Lipset and Reinhard Bendix, *Social Mobility in Industrial Society* (Berkeley and Los Angeles, 1959).

marrow it believes this to be a decent, democratic country. It has few illusions that America is perfect or ideal or a paradise on earth. But what it does believe, and now feels hard pressed to defend, is that American institutions, the values they are built upon and the interests they serve are legitimate. Vietnam may be admitted to be a mistake; political assassinations may be deplorable; big business may be greedy; political institutions may be slow to respond to vital needs. But these things can never be accepted as proof of some inherent proclivity for evil. For that generation has, in its time, the time with which this book is concerned, seen the springs of authority refreshed, seen the proofs of legitimacy. In a sense, it is the last generation to have lived the dream its children and grandchildren have only heard about.

It is now, nearly thirty years later, that we can appreciate what the war experience meant. The war, as a conflict between great states, has a meaning—or a multiplicity of meanings—of its own. That has not been my concern here. Instead, I have tried to understand what the experience of America in wartime meant to those who lived through it and, secondarily, to see how it fitted into the rest of the country's experience.

Had the war been a different kind of war, fought in a different way or for different objectives, its meaning would not have been the same. It was the "perfect" war. Most wars begin by seeming just and conclude under angry suspicions that they should not have been fought at all. Despite the efforts of a fringe of anti-Roosevelt cranks, the country's participation in the war was accepted by almost everyone as a just and necessary act. If anything, it looked increasingly justified as it went on and the Nazi concentration camps fell into Allied hands.

It was the "perfect" war also because the civilian population was kept from harm throughout the war. Alone of the major belligerents, the United States had almost complete immunity from domestic devastation and suffering. Half a million civilian dead and wounded would doubtless have put a different edge on the nature of the wartime experience.

More important still, however, in creating a binding, legitimizing experience was the impact of wartime on ordinary people in their everyday lives and aspirations. As we have seen, the consequences of how the country geared itself for war and how it responded to unmet social needs exacerbated by war's alarms were revolutionary. It was not a war where the nation was fed victories and glory in place of bread and butter. People ate more and better food; they were kept healthier than ever; they lived longer than ever.

Not their bodies alone, but their personalities had greater room for fulfillment. Servicemen traveled overseas; civilians moved around at home in a great migration of their own. Millions of women earned their own money for the first time and savored the mixed joys of independence. Millions of young men and women who learned valuable skills or went to college would never have done either just a few years before. Personality cannot develop much in an environment marked by hopelessness, lack of opportunities and a sense of failure. The war lifted a heavy burden from the country's soul.

We saw how in the local schools up through the colleges decades of drifting about aimlessly gave way to an invigorating new sense of direction and purpose. And behind the new sense of purpose and the opening up of educational opportunities there were billions of dollars of federal money.

In the area of social justice the contrasts with the previous decade could not have been more striking. Poor people, Negroes, old people, Mexican-Americans, all the dispossessed, the failures, the detritus of society, had a second chance; in some cases, a first chance. (The sole important exception were the Issei and Nisei, and they were barely one ten-thousandth of the total population). Those who made the most of the opportunity, such as the Okies and the Arkies in the California shipyards, climbed out of the rut of poverty for good. Not all the poor became middle-class by any means. But in no other six-year period in the country's history has so much social injustice been so quickly erased.

My own conviction is that the war experience was as close as this country has ever come to living the American Dream. Vague though that phrase is, if it means anything at all, it is that America has something for everybody. A wildly heterogeneous nation was more completely united in purpose and spirit than at any time in its history. That in itself was a rich emotional experience. It gave everyone a vital sense of community. And, as I said before, it was also as just as a war could be. On the one side, it was a response to a surprise attack. On the other, it was a war against palpable evil. It was a boon to people's hearts and ideals.

It was also good to their pocketbooks. There was something for the rich, and plenty for the rest. For the rich, there was a revival of conservative politics and economics, plus lots of money. For the rest, there were well-paying jobs and a redistribution of income. With good case do liberals gnash their teeth at trickle-down theories of social and economic justice. But in wartime it was nonetheless true that the lower levels of society scored the greatest relative gains.

The war was very much a total, modern war—a test of organizational and bureaucratic resources, a clash of metal. Whatever challenge it posed to American ideas about society or politics was indirect and inexplicit. For a nation whose strength is its pragmatism, the war was ideally suited to its history and temperament. It was also a struggle that ended in victory. There are few more powerful stimulants to a strong sense of community than a victorious, just war.

Yet the triumph over foreign enemies was a lesser victory than the war generation's victory over its own history. They—the living embodiment of the country's history—faced the test of mastering a historic challenge—and succeeded. Old myths and institutions were tested, new ones were created. Many deep wounds in society and politics were healed. And in so doing, the country both worked and seemed to work. America has lived on the accumulated social and political capital for more than twenty-five years. That account is now almost exhausted.

NOTES

Notes

PART I

Page	
	CHAPTER I *It Is War*
15	Public opinion on the eve of war: Hadley Cantril, *Public Opinion 1935–46*, p. 678.
15	Diary entry: Raoul de Russy de Sales, *The Making of Yesterday*, entry for August 21, 1939.
16	Opinions on World War I: Cantril, p. 781.
16	"War is a crusade. . . .": Jerome Bruner, *Mandate from the People*, p. 16.
16	Opinion in East and West: Richard L. Neuberger, "What the Home Folks Say," *Harper's*, September, 1939; cf. Francis L. Wickwire, "What the Polls Say," *ibid.*
16	Fears of inevitable entry into war: *Newsweek*, August 28, 1939.
17	The book was Nora Waln's *Reaching for the Stars*.
17	Polish pavilion: New York *Times*, September 9, 1939.
17	Newspapers and maps: "Personal and Otherwise," *Harper's*, November, 1939.
17	Relevant polls in *NYT*, September 3, 1939; *Newsweek*, September 4, 1939; *Time*, September 18, 1939.
18	What people thought about the Germans: *Fortune*, December, 1939.
18	Psychologists' convention: *NYT*, September 7, 1939.
19	"Armed robbery. . . .": *Life*, February 5, 1940.
19	Diminishing fears: R. E. Turpin, "Democracy at Work," *NYT Magazine*, November 26, 1939.
20–21	André Maurois, *A History of the U.S.A. from Wilson to Kennedy*, pp. 174–75.
22	Ohio relief crisis: Robert Jordan, "G.O.P. Budgets for the Hungry," *Nation*, December 23, 1939.
23	Population changes: *Historical Statistics of the U.S. 1789–1945*; Census Bureau projection in *Journal of Heredity*, December, 1941.
23	Hoarding and price rise: *NYT*, September 8, 1939.
23	"BUY NOW": *Ibid.*, September 10, 1939.
23	Economic growth: U.S. Department of Commerce, "National Income Supplement," *Survey of Current Business*, July, 1947.
24	"Glory Hallelujah!": Harold J. and Stanley Ruttenberg, "War and the Steel Ghost Towns," *Harper's*, January, 1940.

41   "The bottom would drop out": Kenneth Crawford, "War and the Election," *Nation*, February 10, 1940.
      NYT, May 17, 1940.
43   "Over-zealous prosecutions": *Newsweek*, August 6, 1945; "railroading": *Time*, August 6, 1945.
43ff. Dewey's campaign is described in Douglas Johnson, *The Republican Party and Wendell Willkie.*
43ff. Willkie's campaign is described in Warren Moscow, *Roosevelt and Willkie*, and Johnson.
45   "Street corner positions": Moscow, p. 69.
46   "The whole convention machinery was Willkie's": *Ibid.*, p. 66.
47   The reluctant McNary: *Newsweek*, July 8, 1940.
47   Willkie's theme song: *Ibid.*
48   "Grass roots": *Time*, July 8, 1940.
48   "Safe, sinless and sexless": *Newsweek*, July 8, 1940.
48   "It was just too colossal!": *NYT*, July 12, 1940.
48ff. Democratic Convention: *Time* and *Newsweek*, July 29, 1940; Moscow's account is particularly good. He was a *NYT* reporter at the convention, and it was he who tracked down "The Voice from the Sewers."
50   Willkie's lead in the polls: *Time*, August 5, 1940.
51   Roosevelt vs. Hitler: cf. *New Republic*, October 21, 1940.
52   The most angry campaign: *Life*, November 4, 1940.
52   "The fabulous Willkie train": *Time*, October 16, 1944.
52   Dunn Survey: *Newsweek*, October 21, 1940.
53   Willkie would have won but for the war: Polls cited in *Current History*, January 23, 1941.

CHAPTER IV   *Quarrel at a Crossroads*

55   "Main Street no longer exists": *Harper's*, November, 1940.
58ff. The story of the Committee to Defend America by Aiding the Allies is told in Walter Johnson, *The Battle Against Isolation.*
59   The ultrainterventionists have been chronicled by Mark Lincoln Chadwin in *The Hawks of World War II.*
59   Polls from July, 1940, to June, 1941, consistently showed sentiment in favor of aid to Britain running between 55 percent and 70 percent, but outright interventionist sentiments peaked at 20 percent in June, 1940. See Gallup's summary of his polls in *Current History*, January 23, 1941.
59   White's letter quoted in Johnson.
60   "A succulent prize": Max Lerner, *Ideas for the Ice Age*, pp. 178–79.
60   "The U.S. had taken sides": *Time*, June 17, 1940.
60   "Partisan non-belligerency": *New Republic*, June 17, 1940.
61ff. The story of the America First Committee is told by Wayne S. Cole, *America First: The Battle Against Intervention, 1940–1941.*
62   "The anti-Christ": *NYT*, May 17, 1940.
63   "America—Love It or Leave It": *Time*, October 7, 1940.
63   Bruce Barton: *NYT*, May 21, 1940.

Page

63   "In homes, clubs, churches": *Time*, July 1, 1940.

64   SWAP OF DESTROYERS FOR BASES: *Newsweek*, September 16, 1940.

65   "The mistake was made": *Time*, September 30, 1940.

65   Opinion on aid to Britain: Gallup Polls in *Time*, December 23, 1940, and *Newsweek*, December 30, 1940.

CHAPTER V   *Creating a Defense Economy*

67   The best nontechnical description, if a bit starry-eyed, of America's economic management in the First World War is in Margaret Coit's *Mr. Baruch* (Boston, 1957); cf. Frederic L. Paxson, *American Democracy and the World War* (Boston, 1936, 2 vols).

67   "No one now believes": A. J. P. Taylor, *English History, 1914–1945* (London and New York, 1970), p. 507.

68   The Industrial Mobilization Plan and the Army's unrelenting efforts to take control of the economy are described in U.S. Bureau of the Budget, *The United States at War*, Washington, D.C., 1946.

68   *Printer's Ink* quoted in *New Republic*, October 11, 1939.

70   "Mr. Forrestal's appointment": *New Republic*, July 8, 1940.

70   "The war has been a dud": John T. Flynn, *ibid.*, June 3, 1940.

71   "Edified at the splendid activity": *Ibid.*, October 14, 1940.

71   Distribution of defense contracts: *Newsweek*, June 17, 1940.

71   "Disappearance of production": There was no shortage of economists and businessmen who agreed, but this quote comes from *Nation*, July 6, 1940.

71   "Nobody invests money any more": John T. Flynn, *New Republic*, August 12, 1940.

72   "Industry will demand": *Wall Street Journal*, May 20, 1940.

72   For an insider's view of the taxation problem see Randolph Paul, *Taxation for Prosperity*, pp. 71–74.

72–73   "Governmental cliques": *Newsweek*, May 27, 1940.

73   Public opinion polls summarized in *Time*, January 13, 1941.

CHAPTER VI   *Year of Meteors! Brooding Year!*

75–77   Polls on aid to Britain summarized by George Gallup in *Current History*, January 23, 1941; cf. *Newsweek*, December 2, 1940, and February 10, 1941.

78   "From the Florida Everglades": *Newsweek*, May 19, 1941.

79   Letter from Thomas H. Joyce in *Time*, May 19, 1941.

80   "Soviet ideology was hated": Dawson, *The Decision to Aid Russia*, p. 101.

80–81   The early tribulations are described in George R. Clark, "I'm on a Draft Board," *Harper's*, April, 1941.

81   "We ask ourselves": Dorothy Dunbar Bromley in *New Republic*, January 6, 1941.

82   "Father, mother, and big brother": *Time*, March 3, 1941.

82   "Hadn't undressed for a week": *Ibid.*, March 10, 1941.

83–84 Typical of the liberal critics of the defense buildup was I. F. Stone, *Business as Usual: The First Year of Defense.*

83–84 The best work on the Truman Committee is Donald H. Riddle's *The Truman Committee*; cf. Harry A. Toulmin, Jr., *Diary of Democracy.*

84 "I want no smears": *Harper's*, January, 1945.

85–86 The boom towns are described in Blair Bolles, "The Great Defense Migration," *Harper's*, October, 1941; Lowell Clucas, "Defense Comes to Our Town," *Saturday Evening Post*, March 15, 1941; and Clark Craig, "Cape Cod Gets a War Boom," *Harper's*, March, 1941.

86 "With a wife, a dog and a car": Max Parvin Cavnes, *The Hoosier Community at War*, p. 27.

CHAPTER VII *Who's Hysterical?*

87 Justice Department tips: *Time*, June 24, 1940.

88 "Ideologies of foreign governments": *Newsweek*, November 6, 1939.

88 The inglorious history of the Dies Committee is superbly told in Walter Goodman's *The Committee*; a dull but thorough account is August R. Ogden's *The Dies Committee, 1938–1943.*

89 "Blow up the goddam Police Department" etc.: *Life*, January 29, 1940.

91 "On the edge of a Red hunt": TRB, in *New Republic*, December 6, 1939.

91 On the attacks on Jehovah's Witnesses see the ACLU's pamphlet "The Persecution of Jehovah's Witnesses" and its more comprehensive report, *Liberty's National Emergency: The Crisis Year 1940–1941*; cf. *Nation*, August 10, 1940.

92 JEHOVAH'S WITNESSES MAKE HATE A RELIGION: *Satevepost*, September 14, 1940.

92 Ku Klux Klan: *Nation*, January 11, 1941.

92 Rising intolerance: *Fortune* Poll, July, 1940.

92 "Rumors of business appeasement": *Nation*, September 16, 1939.

93 "It takes a crook": *Nation*, February 3, 1940; the *Nation* tried to tie Coughlin to Hoover's farcical "plot" in its issue of January 20, 1940.

93 The ACLU's heresy trial, including a transcript of the proceedings, is in Corliss Lamont, *The Trial of Elizabeth Gurley Flynn by the American Civil Liberties Union.*

94 "Democracy . . . cannot countenance such an extreme challenge": *New Republic*, October 28, 1940.

95 Opinion on refugees in 1938: *Fortune* Poll, July, 1938.

96 Opinion after *Kristallnacht*: Cantril, p. 1081.

96 The odyssey of the *St. Louis* is poignantly told in A. D. Morse, *While Six Million Died.*

97 Immigration figures are taken from *Historical Statistics of the United States 1789–1945.*

98 "A blonde English girl": *NYT*, July 6, 1940.

98 "Bombed to death": *New Republic*, July 1, 1940.

98 "Austrian agriculturalist": Advertisement in the *Nation*, October 21, 1939.

Page

99 Immigration policies: David Wyman, *Paper Walls: Refugee Policy, 1938–1941*; cf. Maurice R. Davie, *Refugees in America*; for the work of the refugee organizations see Lyman C. White's *300,000 New Americans*.

99 "The literary atmosphere of Paris": *New Republic*, March 31, 1941.

99–
100 Friedrich, "The Poison in Our System," *Atlantic Monthly*, June, 1941.

100 "Disguised as tourists": Edward Meade Earle, *Against This Torrent*, p. 20.

100 Dorothy Thompson: *Time*, November 3, 1941.

100 "Waging war against the whole American democratic heritage" etc.: *New Republic*, October 6, 1941.

100 Street violence against isolationists: *Life*, September 29, 1941.

100 "A powerful Fascist movement": *New Republic*, November 3, 1941.

100–
101 "It is better to be safe than sorry": *Ibid.*, February 3, 1941.

101 Edmund Wilson: Alfred Kazin, "Midtown and the Village," *Harper's*, January, 1971.

101 "I shall cancel my subscription": *Nation*, July 19, 1941.

101 "Throwing overboard in hysterical panic": *Ibid.*, November 29, 1941.

101 Hoover's opposition to wiretapping is expressed in a letter to the *Harvard Law Review*, Vol. 53, p. 870.

103 "Stalinists and fellow travellers": *Nation*, October 25, 1941.

CHAPTER VIII *Knowledge Is Power*

104 Educational economics: *Statistical Abstract of the United States, 1940.*

104 Conference on Children: *Newsweek*, January 29, 1940.

104ff. For the story of progressive education I have relied heavily on Lawrence R. Cremin, *The Transformation of the Schools: Progressivism in American Education.*

105–
106 The authoritative summary of the great progressive experiment is Wilford M. Aiken, *The Story of the Eight Year Study.*

107 "Lollipops vs. Learning": *Satevepost*, March 16, 1940; "Treason in the Textbooks": *American Legion Magazine*, September, 1940.

108 NEA convention: *Time*, July 14, 1941.

108 "Concerned with preserving Democracy": *Life*, January 13, 1941.

108 The school which tried clubs was described *ibid.*

108 "The finest land in the world": *Time*, March 3, 1941.

108 Rochester, New York, high schools: *Ibid.*, December 23, 1940.

109 The three milieux: *NYT Magazine*, December 15, 1940.

109 Democracy Readers: *Time*, January 15, 1940.

109 "Undergraduates turned in unparalleled numbers": Archibald MacLeish, "The Next Harvard," *Atlantic Monthly*, May, 1941.

110 Congress on Education and Democracy: *Nation*, August 26, 1939.

111 "Am completely without communications": *Newsweek*, March 10, 1941.

111 The best account of America's organization of science for and during the war is James Phinney Baxter, *Scientists Against Time.*

112 "l hope they never succeed": *Time*, May 26, 1941.
112– On the clash between the young and their elders cf. the exchange
113 between Arnold Whitridge, "Where Do You Stand?" *Atlantic Monthly*, August, 1940, and Kingman Brewster, Jr., and Spencer Klaw, "We Stand Here," *ibid*., September, 1940.
113 "They distrust even words in general": Archibald MacLeish in *New Republic*, July 1, 1940.
113 "I have educated myself out of a job": Paul P. Cram, "Undergraduates and the War," *Atlantic Monthly*, October, 1940.
114 "A war between beasts and human beings": *Time*, October 14, 1940.
114 "Detrimental . . . to the public interest": *Nation*, September 14, 1940.
114– Brooklyn College: *Time* and *Newsweek*, December 16, 1940.
115
115 "This case is somewhere in between": *Time*, April 15, 1940.
116 "Let us avoid being sent overseas": *Satevepost*, July 26, 1941.

CHAPTER IX *The Meaning of It All*

119 "A crisis-begotten nationalism": Alfred Kazin, *On Native Ground*, p. 504.
120 "I could not go on being a pacifist": *Time*, June 17, 1940.
120 "Sanity, not cowardice": Charles Beard, "Giddy Minds and Foreign Quarrels," *Harper's*, September, 1939.
122– National Conference on Science, Philosophy, etc.: *New Republic*, Octo-
123 ber 28, and December 23, 1940; cf. Mortimer Adler, "The Chicago School," *Harper's*, September, 1941.
123 *New Republic*'s essay contest: Results summarized in *New Republic*, April 22, 1940.
125 "Give the soldiers of America a dream": Stewart Alsop, "Wanted: A Faith to Fight For," *Atlantic Monthly*, May, 1941.
125 "To sell democracy abroad": Carl Joachim Friedrich, "The Poison in Our System," *Ibid*., June, 1941.
125 "Unless there is a free world": *What Is Democracy?*, p. 107.

CHAPTER X *Life Goes On*

127 "The specter of propaganda": *Time*, July 8, 1940.
127– "Plans complete": *Ibid*., May 13, 1940.
128
128 "By way of the Harvard Classics": Douglas Bush in *Atlantic Monthly*, October, 1940.
130 "In a mood of bitter self-examination": *Time*, December 16, 1940.
130 "A useful home education": *Life*, December 9, 1940.
131 "To dig in the earth": Malcolm Cowley in *New Republic*, July 7, 1941.
132 "A disease": *Newsweek*, September 7, 1942.
133 "Little Jack Horner sat in a corner": *Time*, January 27, 1941.
134– On fashion: cf. Winifred Raushenbush, "Fashion Goes American,"
135 *Harper's*, December, 1941.

Page

137 The story of how Washington tried to help the boom towns is told, from Washington's point of view, in Office of Community War Services, *Teamwork in Community Services 1941–1946*.

137 Rising birthrates: Genevieve Pankhurst, "Does America Need More Children?" *Harper's*, January, 1941.

140 "A Beau Brummel of the skies": *Newsweek*, December 11, 1939.

141 On aviation and the schools cf. Sarah Clayton Burrow and Corinne A. Seeds, "Community Living Through an Ongoing Interest in Airplanes," in William E. Young, ed., *Social Studies and the Elementary School*. Shooting gallery receipts: *Newsweek*, June 30, 1941.

CHAPTER XI *Negroes, Blacks and "Persons of Color"*

144 The tendency of former Garveyites to follow Father Divine was noted by Ottley, *New World A'Coming*, p. 99.

145 One young "Afro-American" was writing in "Under Thirty," *Atlantic Monthly*, September, 1939.

146 "Murderous potentialities": *Time*, March 4, 1940.

146 Relevant data on the problem of counting Negroes are discussed in R. J. Myers, "Underenumeration in the Census as Indicated by Selective Service Data," *American Sociological Review*, February, 1948.

146 On the health of black people: *Time*, April 8, 1940.

147 "Negro World's Fair": *Newsweek*, July 15, 1940.

148 "The greatest advance in civil rights": *Nation*, May 10, 1941.

148 "If one lifts his eyes": *Newsweek*, August 26, 1940.

148 "The noisy nigger in the woodpile": *Time*, June 16, 1941.

148 "It makes uneasy reading": *Newsweek*, March 4, 1940.

148 Blow-torch murders of Negroes: *Time*, January 22, 1940.

149 "The horrible fact": *New Republic*, September 23, 1940.

149 Austin Calaway: *Newsweek*, September 16, 1940.

149 Growth of the KKK: *Nation*, January 11, 1941.

150 "This is too much": in Shalloo and Young.

151 The various biracial committees in Indiana are described in Cavnes, *Hoosier Community*, pp. 112–20.

152 The employment runaround is described by Lester B. Granger, "Barriers to Negro Employment," in Shalloo and Young.

153 First M-1 fatality: *Newsweek*, January 24, 1941.

153–
154 "Is as strong as ever": *Ibid.*, December 9, 1940.

CHAPTER XII *Isolation and the Rediscovery of Latin America*

155 For a typical isolationist attack on the CDA cf. *Satevepost*, January 4, 1941.

155 "Being used to ghost dance for war": *Time*, January 13, 1941.

156 Fight for Freedom's leading personae are described in Chadwin, *Hawks of World War II*.

157 "It is as if": *Satevepost*, February 1, 1941.

157 "A violent propaganda campaign": *Time*, February 10, 1941.

158 Verne Marshall's disastrous radio appearance: *New Republic*, January 20, 1941; cf. *Newsweek*, January 13, 1941.

159 "Who Is Behind Lindbergh?": *New Republic*, May 5, 1941.
Dorothy Thompson: *Ibid.*

159 Increasing violence in isolationist/interventionist debates: *Life*, September 29, 1941.

161 "Building a Fascist movement": *New Republic*, October 13, 1941.

162 "17,000 nightly mass meetings for war": *Newsweek*, September 22, 1941.

162 "Where are our friends": David L. Cohn, "America to England," *Atlantic Monthly*, August, 1940.

162– "Burrowing tunnels underneath the surface": advertisement for *Time*
163 in *Time*, September 16, 1940.

163 "It is current vox populi": *Ibid.*, November 25, 1940.

163 "It is a New Frontier": *Newsweek*, October 30, 1939.

163 South America as compensation for lost European markets: America First advertisement in *NYT*, November 1, 1940.

163– General Wood's proposal to divide South America with Hitler: Inter-
164 view with Kenneth Crawford in *PM*, May 26, 1941.

164 Army Air Corps officers: *Time*, May 19, 1941.

164 "There are more and better rumba bands": *NYT*, February 14, 1940.

165 "Such fire and rhythm": *Time*, February 17, 1941.

165 "Rumba hips": *Ibid.*, October 21, 1940.

CHAPTER XIII   *Action in the North Atlantic*

166 "Effective guarantees by deeds": Winston Churchill, *The Second World War*, Vol. II, p. 262.

167 The *Nation*'s lecture on war aims was in its February 22, 1941, edition.

167 "Only for affirmative ends of forward movement": Randolph Bourne quoted in Max Lerner, *Ideas for the Ice Age*, p. 139.

167 "Eventually beat Hitlerism": Max Lerner, "American Leadership in a Harsh Age," in Ernest M. Patterson, ed., *Defending America's Future.*

167 "An uninspired plagiarism": TRB, *New Republic*, August 25, 1941.

169 "A Gargantuan jest": *Time*, July 7, 1941.

169 The extension of lend-lease to the Soviets is dealt with definitively in Dawson, *The Decision to Aid Russia.*

169 1,500 applications: *Newsweek*, June 30, 1941.

170 "It was a great question": *Time*, July 21, 1941.

170 Public opinion on occupation of Iceland: *Newsweek*, July 28, 1941.

171 "The foot of a frog": *Nation*, October 25, 1941.

171 "The U.S. is at war with Germany": *Time*, November 3, 1941.

171 "Whether the U.S. was winning": *Ibid.*, November 10, 1941.

171 "The incomparable U.S. Navy": *Life*, November 10, 1941.

Page   CHAPTER XIV *"Arsenal of Democracy"*

174   Typical of the liberal critics was *New Republic*, August 11, 1941, which pronounced the defense program a failure and put most of the blame on the dollar-a-year men; cf. Stone, *Business as Usual: The First Year of Defense.*

176   "It's a great war": *Harper's*, November, 1941.

177   On the evolution of the modern alliance of labor and government, especially in World War II, see Ronald Radosh, *American Labor and U.S. Foreign Policy.*

177   On Hillman see Matthew Josephson, *Sidney Hillman: Statesman of American Labor.*

177–   Rising antilabor sentiments: *Time*, April 7, 1941, and *Newsweek*, June
178   23, 1941.

178   A typical example in which grievances against NAA are acknowledged but the strike is portrayed as Communist sabotage can be found in *New Republic*, June 23, 1941.

178ff.   Government's disappointments with business during the defense crisis are retold at length in Janeway, *The Struggle for Survival*, and Bruce Catton, *The War Lords of Washington.*

179   Rising public prestige of business: Gallup Poll quoted in *New Republic*, March 31, 1941.

180   The profits of defense contractors: *Time*, December 15, 1941.

180   "As a pretext for pushing": *Fortune*, November, 1941.

181   "Tired of livin' and scared of dyin' ": E. D. Kennedy in *New Republic*, November 24, 1941.

181   "Least subject to seismic disturbances": *Wall Street Journal*, November 8, 1941.

181–   TNEC hearings and proposals in U.S. Temporary National Economic
182   Committee, *Hearings before the TNEC 1939–1941*, and *Investigation of Concentration of Economic Power: Final Report of Recommendations*; cf. Donald C. Blaisdell, *Economic Power and Political Pressure*, on lobbies and monopolies *circa* 1940.

182   Public opinion on regulation of business: *Fortune*, December, 1941; cf. Elliot V. Bell, "Planned Economy and/or Democracy," *NYT Magazine*, November 23, 1941.

183   Rise in defense strikes: *Time*, September 15, 1941.

183ff.   Labor problems in this period are covered in Irving Bernstein, *Turbulent Years: U.S. Labor 1933–1941*, and Joel Seidman, *American Labor: From Defense to Reconversion.*

183–   Lewis is portrayed, warts and all, in Saul Alinsky, *John L. Lewis*; cf.
185   Michael Klein, "Lewis Loses the CIO," *New Republic*, December 1, 1941.

184   Dangers of American mining: *New Republic*, January 6, 1941.

184   "The Administration has failed": *Ibid.*, July 14, 1941.

184   Workers should take whatever they were offered: *Ibid.*, November 24, 1941.

CHAPTER XV   *And So to War*

186   The Japanese goodwill flight: *NYT*, September 1, 1939.

186   "Did YOU Help Pay for This Bomb?": *Nation*, November 25, 1939.

186–   "This business of sending bombs": *NYT*, May 19, 1940.
187

187   "We'll be able to swing a big stick": *Newsweek*, February 5, 1940.

187   No one was afraid of Japan: cf. *Harper's*, April, 1940, and *Nation*, October 19, 1940.

187   A typical response to the tripartite alliance was Earle, *Against the Torrent*, p. 6; cf. *Fortune*, November, 1940.

188   Admiral Yarnell: *Newsweek*, October 21, 1940.

188   Washington correspondents: *Ibid.*

188   "Japan has invariably": Major George Fielding Eliot in *Life*, December 4, 1939.

188   Liberal sentiments: cf. *New Republic*, May 20, 1940.
       Satevepost: December 2, 1939.

188–   Isolationist appeasement: *New Republic*, June 17, 1940; *Nation*, June
189   22, 1940; cf. *Fortune* Poll of business executives, *Fortune*, September, 1940.

189–   Mark Gayn, *Fight for the Pacific* (New York, 1941).
190

190   "Sex-hungry": *Time*, April 28, 1941.

190   "Call Japan's Bluff!": *New Republic*, November 3, 1941; cf. *Nation*, October 25, 1941.

190   "The Hawaiian Islands are over-protected": Captain William D. Puleston, "What Are the Chances?" *Atlantic Monthly*, August, 1941.

190   Republican rank and file: *Newsweek*, October 6, 1941.

190   "The American industrial front": *Time*, December 15, 1941.

190   The editor of *The Republican*: *Newsweek*, October 13, 1941.

192   JAPANESE BOW AND GRIN FOR THE CAMERA: *Life*, December 1, 1941.

192   Betting on war: *Time*, November 24, 1941.

192   Public opinion: Cantril, p. 975.

192   "Like a civilized nation": *New Republic*, November 24, 1941.

192   The *Nation's* demand for an ultimatum: December 6, 1941.

192   Ten to one odds: *Newsweek*, December 1, 1941.

192   "Probably the last foreign policy test": *Newsweek*, November 24, 1941.

193   "Not going to be caught napping": Catton, p. 9.

193   Miseries in the Army: Harold Lavine, "Why the Army Gripes," *Nation*, August 20, 1941.

194   The physical achievements of the defense period are spelled out in U.S. Office of Facts and Figures, *Report to the Nation: American Preparation for War*.

195   "Many a U.S. youngster will die": *Time*, July 28, 1941.

195   "With a higher heart": *Ibid.*, December 1, 1941.

196   "What Rome was to the ancient world": *Life*, June 5, 1939.

196–   Luce's call for an "American Century" was expressed first in *Life*,

Page

197   February 17, 1941, and appeared several months later as a book.

197   "Europe as Nirvana is over": Irving Edman, "Look Homeward America!" *Harper's*, December, 1940.

197   Margaret Mead, *And Keep Your Powder Dry* (it was published in 1942, but written in 1941).

198   Wylie's book was *A Generation of Vipers.*

198   "The feminization of Western culture": Roy Helton, "The Inner Threat: Our Own Softness," *Harper's*, September, 1940.

198   "The Failures of Propaganda": D. C. Saunders, *Harper's*, November, 1941.

198   "Our morale today": Hadley Cantril, "How Good Is Our Morale?" *NYT Magazine*, November 16, 1941.

198   "Everything was ready" etc.: *Time*, December 8, 1941 (this issue went to press December 4, 1941).

199   "The stage was set for war": *Life*, December 8, 1941.

PART II

CHAPTER XVI   *Pearl Harbor Christmas*

203   "We lost 11 battleships": Frederick Lewis Allen, "Three Years of It," *Harper's*, December, 1944.

203   Madison Square Garden rally: Advertisement in *New Republic*, December 15, 1941.

203   "America's greatest danger": *Life*, December 15, 1941.

204   "No one seems sorry to see the war come": Correspondents of *Time*, *Life*, and *Fortune*, *December 7: The First 30 Hours*, p. 48.

204–   Incident on Main Street: Woody Guthrie, *Bound for Glory*, pp. 353–57.
205

205   Expectations of how long the war would last: Cantril, p. 1095.

205   AMERICANS ALL: *Newsweek*, December 15, 1941.

205   "We're all together now": Richard L. Neuberger, "Reveille in the Northwest," *Nation*, December 20, 1941.

205   "First invasion scare": *Ibid.*

206   "The U.S. need only step on the gas": *Time*, December 22, 1941.

CHAPTER XVII   *What News from the Front?*

207   "Everywhere there was a quiet relief": Representative Thomas Eliot in *New Republic*, December 15, 1941.

207   "This year may be one of the hardest": *New Republic*, December 29, 1941.

208   "The worst news": *Newsweek*, January 12, 1942.

208   Goldfeather and Youkovich: *Ibid.*, February 16 and 23, 1942.

208   "As thick as catfish": *Time*, January 24, 1942.

208   "A situation they never expected": *Newsweek*, February 23, 1942.

208 "This was the worst week": *Time*, February 23, 1942.

209 ATTACK! etc.: *Newsweek*, March 9, 1942.

209 *Life*'s imaginary invasion took place in its issue of March 2, 1942.

209 "Looked forward to the fight": *Time*, March 9, 1942.

209 "It sickens me": *Ibid.*

210 HERO-HUNGRY NATION: *Life*, March 30, 1942.

210 "An important victory": *New Republic*, March 30, 1942.

210 "The news was so good": *Newsweek*, April 27, 1942.

211 "Ships were sunk and seamen drowned": Samuel E. Morison, *History of U.S. Naval Operations in World War II*, Vol. 1, *The Battle of the Atlantic* (Boston, 1954), p. 130.

211– Nazi would-be saboteurs: Eugene Rachlis, *They Came to Kill*; W. A.
212 Swanberg, "The Spies Who Came In from the Sea," *American Heritage*, April, 1970.

213 "Russia was in mortal peril": *Time*, July 27, 1942.

213 "If the war ended today": *Ibid.*, July 20, 1942.

215 "We are a more united nation now": TRB, in *New Republic*, June 29, 1942.

CHAPTER XVIII *We Lose, They Pay*

217 "Wake up the fools": *NYT*, December 10, 1941; cf. Audrie Girdner and Anne Loftis, *The Great Betrayal*, p. 6.

217 Public opinion on enemy aliens: Cantril, p. 947.

217 Prewar doubts about loyalty of Issei and Nisei: cf. Magner White, "Between Two Flags," *Satevepost*, September 30, 1939; and *Life*, October 14, 1940.

217 "American Democracy will go with them": Jerome Frank, "Red-White-and-Blue Herring," *Satevepost*, December 6, 1941.

219 Popular fears of Germans and Japanese: Office of War Information, *Pacific Coast Attitudes Towards the Japanese Problem*, February, 1942, and *The Japanese Problem*, April, 1942.

219 Federal officials' view: Justice Tom Clark, interview with Edward Newman, shown on PBS, April 2, 1972; cf. Allen R. Bosworth, *America's Concentration Camps*.

219 "Throw them all into concentration camps": In the *Nation*, February 14, 1942.

219 "The West coast is more conscious of the war": Louis Fischer, "West Coast Perspective," *Nation*, March 9, 1942.

219– Lippmann: New York *Herald Tribune*, February 5, 12 and 14, 1942.
220

220 Other journalists: U.S. Department of Interior, *Wartime Exile*, p. 127; cf. John Bruce, "California Gets Tough," *NYT Magazine*, March 15, 1942, for a representative example of the odious and racist polemics which were soon being published in normally responsible periodicals.

220 "The Japanese race is an enemy race": U.S. Army, *Japanese Evacuation of the West Coast*, p. 34.

220 "A Jap's a Jap": In Morton Grodzins, *Americans Betrayed*, p. 362.

Page

220   "The very fact": U.S. Army, *op. cit.*

221   Public opinion on Germany and Japan: *Fortune*, March, 1942.

221   "It is impossible to distinguish": Carey McWilliams, "Japanese Out of California," *New Republic*, April 6, 1942.

223   "California is Japan's Sudetenland": *Time*, February 23, 1942.

223   *Tanaka Memorial* and Dies Committee: *Newsweek*, March 9, 1942.

223   Growing thirst for vengeance: Cantril, p. 1067.

223   Fate of Japanese on the East Coast: *Newsweek*, March 8, 1943.

224   "Spontaneous and cheerful": *Life*, April 6, 1942.

224   "All they forfeit": *Time*, April 6, 1942.

224   "Living in very decent conditions": Charles Inglehart, "Citizens Behind Barbed Wire," *Nation*, June 6, 1942.

224   "Will probably profit": Carey McWilliams, "Moving the West Coast Japanese," *Harper's*, September, 1942.

224   "Fear, frustration and anger": Alexander Layton, *The Governing of Men*, p. 45.

224   "It is actually a penitentiary": Ted Nakashima, "Concentration Camps: U.S. Style," *New Republic*, June 15, 1942.

225   Worsening conditions in the camps: Girdner and Loftis, pp. 187–88.

225   "Having wicked and revolutionary ideas": *Time*, December 15, 1941.

226   "Subversive doctrines are widespread": *Life*, April 13, 1942.

226   Conscientious objectors: Robert van Gelder, "The Men Who Refuse to Fight," *NYT Magazine*, May 10, 1942.

226   Selective Service policy: Mulford Q. Sibley and Philip E. Jacob, *Conscription of Conscience*, pp. 70–71.

226–   Taxing religious literature: *Roscoe Jones v. City of Opelika*, 316 U.S.
227   584; the majority opinion written by Justice Stanley Reed exudes an unmistakable contempt for "all members of the organization known as Jehovah's Witnesses."

227   "Beautifully reasoned argument": *NYT*, June 11, 1942.

227   "Damned Fascists": *Walter Chaplinsky v. State of New Hampshire*, 315 U.S. 568; Chaplinsky was preaching, an angry crowd gathered, and instead of curbing the crowd, the police seized Chaplinsky.

227   Three attacks in a single day: *NYT*, September 21, 1942.

227   "An almost fanatical believer": *Newsweek*, June 8, 1942.

227   "Stupid, ill-advised and undemocratic": Freda Kirchway in *Nation*, June 6, 1942.

227   "Curb the Fascist Press!": *Ibid.*, March 28, 1942.

227   "Make us lose the war, accept defeat": William L. Shirer, "The Poison Pen," *Atlantic Monthly*, May, 1942.

227   "It is fatal to adopt the defensive": *New Republic*, April 6, 1942.

228   New laws to prosecute Lindbergh and Coughlin: *Ibid.*, August 3, 1942.

228   "Compulsory buying of war bonds": *Ibid.*, August 10, 1942.

229–   Hawaii: Cecil H. Coggins, "The Japanese-Americans in Hawaii,"
230   *Harper's*, June, 1943; Gwenfread Allen, *Hawaii's War Years, 1941–1945*.

CHAPTER XIX *What Can I Do?*

231 "Magnificently organized": *Time*, January 12, 1942.

232 "People slept": Mercedes Rosebery, *This Day's Madness*, p. 30.

232 The overall organization of civil defense is described in Stetson Conn et al., *Guarding the U.S. and Its Outposts*; an excellent brief account is Wladislawa A. Frost, "Cities and Towns Mobilize for War," *American Sociological Review*, February, 1944.

232 "It was an exciting experience": Rosebery, p. 12.

232– On the number of people doing volunteer war work: *Fortune*, April,
233 1942; cf. *Life*, April 20, 1942, for its portrait of what the typical American family was doing.

233 "The Nakajima 96": *Life*, December 22, 1941.

233– Scrap drives: Rosebery, p. 63.
234

234 "Waste paper piled up": Fred Albert Shannon, *America's Economic Growth*, p. 821.

CHAPTER XX *Life and Leisure in Wartime*

237 "Wherever the pattern of life": Frederick Lewis Allen, "Up to Now: The First Year and a Half," *Harper's*, July, 1943.

237 "Prosperous families": *Ibid.*

237 "A complete blackout": Enid Griffis, "He Runs a Hotel," *Harper's*, November, 1943.

240 "Confusion, congestion and consecration": Richard Lee Strout (for once stepping out from behind the initials TRB), in *New Republic*, January 26, 1942.

240 "Washington in wartime": Malcolm Cowley, *ibid.*, June 1, 1942.

241 "The unwanted and long-ailing stepchild": *Time*, March 16, 1942.

242 "A good five-cent war song": *Ibid.*, February 9, 1942; cf. John Desmond, "Tin Pan Alley Seeks *the* Song," *NYT Magazine*, June 6, 1943.

243 "This is WAR!": A sample script of an entire show in all its inanity can be found in Sherman Dryer, *Radio in Wartime*; Stephen Vincent Benét's wartime radio scripts are collected in *We Stand United*.

244 "I can't see": *Time*, March 29, 1943.

244 "If I fell into the hands of the Nazis": Letter to *New Republic*, April 6, 1942.

244 "The only way to make a German understand": *Time*, December 21, 1942.

245 "I have enjoyed this case": *Ibid.*, February 15, 1943.

246 "Taking the ruffles off of ladies' lingerie": *Newsweek*, June 15, 1942.

CHAPTER XXI *Turnabout, Turnabout*

247 Martin and Flynn: Frederick Lewis Allen, "Up to Now," *Harper's*, July, 1943.

247 Polls: *New Republic*, September 21, 1942.

249 "Tripe, ignorance and demagoguery": *Time*, June 8, 1942.

Page

249   "No one wants to steal Congress": Rosebery, p. 117.

249   "Unable to divorce themselves": *Time*, June 29, 1942.

250   Lasswell's chart: *Time*, June 1, 1942.

251   Wartime information policies: Bruce Catton, *War Lords of Washington*; Sydney Weinberg, "What to Tell America: The Writers' Quarrel with the OWI," *Journal of American History*, June, 1968.

251   "The principal motive": TRB, in *New Republic*, March 30, 1942.

251–   "Three years ago": Ernest K. Lindley, in *Newsweek*, September 7, 1942.
252

252   "There has been a reversion": TRB, in *New Republic*, October 5, 1942.

252   "Hitler is looking over your shoulder": *New Republic*, November 2, 1942.

253   Gallup Poll: *Time*, November 16, 1942.

253   Congress and Congressional elections after Pearl Harbor: R. A. Young, *Congressional Politics in the Second World War.*

          CHAPTER XXII   *Sonorous Metal Blowing Martial Sounds*

255   "Manufacturing ashtrays" and "smoking in the toilets": Lewis Thompson, "Men Making Bombers," *Harpers*, May, 1942.

256   "It called in as a savior a businessman": *Life*, July 6, 1942.

257   The dollar yardstick: U.S. Office of Facts and Figures, *Report to the Nation.*

258   "Need only step on the gas": *Time*, May 25, 1942.

258   "Something is happening": *Ibid.*, March 23, 1942.

258   "Henry Ford is happier and younger": *Ibid.*

258   WAR PRODUCTION IS LICKED: *Newsweek*, November 30, 1942.

260   Economic cost of the Depression: Sumner H. Slichter, *The American Economy*, p. 67.

260   "As America changed to a wartime economy": Randolph Paul, *Taxation in the United States*, p. 319.

261   "Difficult to demonstrate": Young, p. 132.

261   "Hateful, difficult problems": *Time*, March 22, 1943.

261   "Restricting production by some device or other": *Ibid.*, January 10, 1942.

261   "Protecting the welfare of the company": Riddle, p. 921.

262–   On excess profits taxes: Paul, *Taxation for Prosperity*, pp. 108–9.
263

264   "Mr. Roosevelt lauded the owners of American industry": *Newsweek*, January 18, 1942.

265ff. Lewis, labor and Roosevelt: Saul Alinsky, *John L. Lewis*; Thomas R. Brooks, *Toil and Trouble*; cf. Seidman.

266   "A harlot with a wig and artificial legs": *Time*, January 12, 1942.

          CHAPTER XXIII   *Onto the Offensive*

268   "The Germans are losing the war in Russia": *Time*, December 14, 1942.

269   Combat strengths of U.S. and Japanese navies: U.S. Office of Facts and
        Figures, pp. 5–6; Samuel E. Morison, *History of U.S. Naval Operations*,
        Vol. 3, *The Rising Sun in the Pacific*, p. 58.
269–   All figures on U.S. losses are taken from *ibid.*, Chapter 5: "The Attack
270   on Pearl Harbor."
270   Washington bus driver: Rosebery, p. 151.
270   "Through air in which Axis planes roamed": *Time*, February 1, 1943.

PART III

CHAPTER XXIV   *New Horizons*
273   "Began to look like a movie": *Time*, June 26, 1943.
273–   Bernard De Voto: "The Easy Chair," *Harper's*, August, 1943.
274
274   "Unforgivable": *Time*, November 29, 1943.
274   "The beating of a soldier": *Nation*, December 4, 1943.
274   The *New Republic*'s reaction: In its issue of December 6, 1943.
274   Soldier's father and Mrs. Patton: Both quoted in *Time*, December 6,
        1943.
274   The disaster at Bari was reported *Ibid.*, December 27, 1943.
275   Footnote on industrial accidents: *Newsweek*, January 31, 1944.
275   "Heavy water atomic bombs": *Ibid.*, December 27, 1943.
275   The decision to destroy Monte Cassino: An excellent brief account is
        Charles B. MacDonald, *The Mighty Endeavor* (New York, 1969), pp.
        203–5.
275   Stimson's bluff and bluster: *Time*, March 27, 1944.
276   British consul general: *Ibid.*, May 29, 1944.
278   Seer in the War Department: *New Republic*, October 30, 1944.
278   VE-Day planning: *Newsweek* and *Time*, September 18, 1944.
278   "Hitler will preferably have to be sacrificed": Curt Riess, "The Nazis
        Dig In for World War III," *NYT Magazine*, August 6, 1944; cf.
        Newsweek, October 9, 1944.
279   V-3 rumors: *Time*, November 27, 1944.
280   "A national crusade for America": *Prelude to Victory*, p. x.
280   "Challenge us on the field of battle": *Ibid.*, p. 37.
280   "This is a people's war": Bruce Bliven in *New Republic*, December 21,
        1942.
281   "When we reunite": Clarence Streit, *Union Now!* (New York, 1939),
        p. 181.
281   "Let the United States and Great Britain": *New Republic*, December
        23, 1940.
281   Hans Kohn: quoted in *Nation*, March 29, 1941.
281   "Could outvote all others": *Life*, October 7, 1940.
281   Conservative suspicions: cf. *Satevepost*, March 17, 1940.

Page

281   Henry Ford: *Time*, December 15, 1941.

281   "The most influential book": Lewis Gannett, book editor of the New York *Herald Tribune*, in Goodman, p. 453.

282   "Every nation must get ready and choose sides": Walter Lippmann, *U.S. Foreign Policy: Shield of the Republic*, p. 148.

282   Cordell Hull: *Time*, September 6, 1943.

283   Welles' views on postwar international organization, morality and international politics: *The Time for Decision*, pp. 300–4.

283   "This is a fight": *The Century of the Common Man*, p. 14.

283   "I am not fighting": *Time*, December 14, 1942.

283   The *Satevepost's* fortuitous discovery about isolationism was revealed in its issue of August 21, 1943.

284   Hamilton Fish Armstrong: "Datum Point," *Foreign Affairs*, October, 1943.

284   New York *Times*, May 28, 1944.

284   Senator Nye: *Newsweek*, November 29, 1943.

285   Public opinion: Bruner, pp. 34–43.

285   Spanish language classes: cf. Cavnes, pp. 321, 356.

285   For an early expression of doubts about what the new internationalism might lead to, cf. *New Republic*, November 29, 1943.

285   Tough-minded public opinion: *Fortune*, April, 1942; cf. Gallup Poll quoted in *Time*, May 22, 1944.

285   "We are fighting in Europe": *Life*, May 7, 1944.

CHAPTER XXV   *Turn to the Right*

287   "Conservatives were coming to Washington": Young, p. 9.

287   Persecution of liberals in wartime Washington: cf. Henry F. Pringle,

287   "Snooping on the Potomac," *Satevepost*, January 15, 1944.

287   "Placating Congress": TRB, in *New Republic*, December 20, 1943.

288   "The U.S. is now a Republican country": *Life*, November 15, 1943.

288   Walter Lippmann: *Time*, November 15, 1943.

288   GOP rank-and-file preference for Dewey: *Newsweek*, November 22, 1943.

288   "An act of treason": *Life*, February 28, 1944.

288–   Wartime conservatism of the Democratic Party and Roosevelt: cf.
289   George Soule in the *New Republic*, September 6, 1943, and TRB, in the same journal two weeks later, for typical examples of the kinds of torments liberals were going through these days.

289   Poll on Dewey's chances: *Time*, May 31, 1944.

290   "If the convention nominates me": *Newsweek*, July 24, 1944.

290   Wallace's popularity with Democrats: poll cited by *Nation*, July 22, 1944.

291   Truman's disclaimer: *Newsweek*, July 24, 1944, but cf. Allen Shannon, *The Truman Merry-go-round* (New York, 1950), p. 13.

291   "The Democratic Party cannot long survive": *Time*, July 31, 1944.

292   "Like a campaign to sell soap": TRB, in *New Republic*, November 20, 1944.

292   "A foreign object": *Life*, August 21, 1944.

293   "Soft disclaimers": *Newsweek*, October 16, 1944.

293   Odds of two and a half to one: *Ibid.*, October 23, 1944.

293   "This Goddamned thing won't work": *Time*, November 13, 1944.

294   John Dos Passos: *The Ground We Stand On*, p. 260.

295   "This is a conservative task": Agar, *A Time for Greatness* (Boston, 1942), p. 58.

297   "Businessmen do not regard professors as crackpots": *Satevepost*, September 2, 1944.

CHAPTER XXVI   *Economics of War and Peace*

299   Kate Smith's bond-raising marathon: Robert K. Merton, *Mass Persuasion: The Social Psychology of a War Bond Drive.*

299– Conservative tax policies: It is true that the level of corporate taxes
300   doubled, going from 19 percent in 1939 to 40 percent in 1944; but net profits nonetheless tripled, thanks to a generous excess profits tax and a variety of ingenious loopholes written into the wartime tax codes. For a good short analysis see Chandler, *Inflation in the U.S., 1940–1948*, especially pp. 97–103.

300   The man in Fort Myers, Florida: *Newsweek*, February 28, 1944.

302   "It is silly": quoted in *Nation*, May 22, 1943.

302– OPA investigations of price violations are dealt with at length in Marshall
303   B. Clinard, *The Black Market*; cf. Harvey Mansfield, *A Short History of the OPA.*

303   "It will consist in turning over to private industries": TRB in *New Republic*, April 12, 1943. He predicated a vast giveaway on the election of a Republican President. That proved unnecessary.

303   "Will it Run?": *Time*, April 19, 1943.

304   For an example of the campaign against grade labeling, cf. Millard Faught, "Customer's Nightmare," *Satevepost*, February 5, 1944.

304   Removal of injured soldiers from Miami Beach: *New Republic*, January 31, 1944.

304   School at Fort Leavenworth for business executives: *PM*, March 9 and 10, 1943.

305   "The possibility of a right-wing reaction": *Time*, December 20, 1943.

305   God, Captain Eddie and absenteeism: *Nation*, March 13, 1943.

306   AFL and CIO attacks on administration's economic policy: *Newsweek*, May 10, 1943.

306   "What will they do?": *Ibid.*

307   "The strike was irresponsible": *Nation*, June 12, 1943.

307   "Speaking for the American soldier": quoted in *Time*, June 28, 1943.

307   "The most stinging rebuke of his entire career": *Time*, July 5, 1943.

308   "It amounts to bad faith": *Life*, January 17, 1944.

308– Falling production and efforts to reverse it: *Newsweek*, November 29,
309   1944.

Page   CHAPTER XXVII   *Black Man, Brown Man*
310   "Fighting democracy" and "semi-citizens": *Time*, March 2, 1942.
310   *Newsweek*'s doubts: Its issue of June 1, 1942.
311   OWI policy: *New Republic*, September 7, 1942.
311   Harassment of Negro newspapers: Ottley, pp. 269–70.
311   "Nearer and Nearer the Precipice": *Atlantic Monthly*, January, 1943.
311   George Rudé, *The Crowd in the French Revolution* (London and New York, 1959).
311   "The niggers are buying up all the ice picks": Howard W. Odum, *Race and Rumors of Race.*
311   Sukiyaki cafés and A. Philip Randolph rumors: *New Republic*, February 8, 1943.
311   93d Division: Lee, pp. 509–12.
312   "My country's tired of me": *Nation*, April 15, 1944.
312   Sikeston, Missouri: *Newsweek*, February 2, 1942.
312   Bloody clashes in and around military bases: Lee, p. 306.
312–   Racial tension in Detroit before the riot: Earl Brown, "The Truth
313   About the Detroit Riots," *Harper's*, November, 1943.
313   Beaumont riot: *Newsweek*, June 28, 1943.
313–   The Detroit riot: Alfred McC. Lee and Norman D. Humphrey, *Race
314   Riot* (New York, 1943); Robert Shogan and Tom Craig, *The Detroit Race Riot*; Thurgood Marshall, "The Gestapo in Detroit," *The Crisis*, August, 1943; cf. the photographic coverage in *Life*, July 5, 1943.
314   "The white people were slow to get started": Thomas Sancton, "The Race Riots," *New Republic*, July 5, 1943.
315   The Díaz case: S. Guy Endore, *The Sleepy Lagoon Mystery.*
315   The Los Angeles riot: Ruth D. Tuck, "Behind the Zoot Suit Riots," *Survey Graphic*, August, 1943; Carey McWilliams, "The Zoot Suit Riot," *New Republic*, June 21, 1943.
315   "The behavior of Nazi storm-troop thugs": Letter from Staff Sergeant William D. Eastlake to *Time*, July 5, 1943.
316   Aftermath of Detroit riot: *Newsweek*, June 26, 1944.
316   Discrimination in industries formerly not discriminating: P. L. Prattis in *New Republic*, October 10, 1943.
316   General hostility of businessmen to hiring Negroes: *Fortune*, February, 1943.
316   "We were shoved into hiring Negroes": Cavnes, p. 120.
316   BOMB SHELTER—COLORED ONLY: *Ibid.*, p. 134.
317   "Numbers of good Negro workmen have left": quoted in *New Republic*, July 5, 1943.
317   Southern Congressmen complaining about discrimination: *New Republic*, December 27, 1944.
318   Integration of the Merchant Marine: John Hope Franklin, *From Slavery to Freedom*, pp. 588–89.
318   "Mobilization had rubbed the nation's race problem raw": *Time*, July 10, 1944.

318– "The history of bigotry in this country": *Newsweek*, June 28, 1943.
319

319 "America's No. 1 social problem": *Life*, April 24, 1944.

319 "An overnight revolution in race relations": Dabney, "Nearer and Nearer the Precipice," *Atlantic Monthly*, January, 1943.

319 "Let them beware": David L. Cohn, "How the South Feels," *Atlantic Monthly*, January, 1944.

319 "In principle the Negro problem was solved long ago": Gunnar Myrdal, *An American Dilemma*, p. 24.

319 Prediction of greater social separation: *Ibid.*, pp. 644–50.

319– "Negroes had felt that their position was isolated": Horace R. Cayton,
320 "Fighting for White Folks," *Nation*, September 26, 1942.

320 "They wanted something more pointed than a warning": Herbert Garfinkel, *When Negroes March: The March on Washington Movement in the Organizational Politics of the FEPC*, p. 82.

320 Black education in the interwar years: Virginius Dabney, "The Negro and His Schooling," *Atlantic Monthly*, April, 1942.

320 "Has to prove that he's a Negro": Ottley, pp. 231–32.

321 On Hollywood's sudden interest in Negroes: cf. Manny Farber in *New Republic*, March 1, 1943.

321 White House Correspondents' Association: *Time*, February 21, 1944.

322 "The Negro's dream": quoted in the *Nation*, July 1, 1944.

322 "Colored people have bedbugs": *Newsweek*, August 14, 1944.

322 Liberty Bell incident: *Ibid.*, September 11, 1944; *Time*, August 14, 1944.

322 FRANKLIN to ELEANOR: Ruchames, p. 117.

322 Bilbo and Eastland: quoted in *Time*, July 9, 1945.

323 Negro opinion on chance to get ahead: Cantril, p. 830.

323 On the callousness toward bombing victims: see George F. Hopkins, "Bombing and the American Conscience in World War II," *Historian*, Vol. 28, May, 1966.

CHAPTER XXVIII   *Social Welfare, the American Way*

325 Wartime migrants: Henry S. Shryock, Jr., and Hope T. Eldridge, "Internal Migration in Peace and War," *American Sociological Review*, February, 1947.

325 Hard-core poverty in wartime: *New Republic*, November 1, 1943.

326 "Repeal the Iron Law of Wages": Frederick Lewis Allen, *The Big Change* (New York, 1952), p. 286. See p. 154, where he makes it quite clear that he believed this redistribution occurred during the Depression, not during the war years.

326 The New Deal's major accomplishments: William E. Leuchtenberg, *Franklin D. Roosevelt and the New Deal*, pp. 331–32.

326 Chances to get ahead: Cantril, p. 829.

327 Redistribution of income: Simon Kuznets, *Shares of Upper Income Groups in Income and Savings*, deals particularly with the top 5 percent.

Page

Table on income distribution in the interwar years: *Historical Statistics of the U.S., 1789–1945.*

328   Table on new construction: "National Income Supplement," *Survey of Current Business*, July, 1947.

328–   Free meals and free enterprise: *Newsweek*, April 17, 1944.
329

329   "There is a conservative reaction in progress": *Satevepost*, May 29, 1943.

329   "The most striking characteristic": Ernest K. Lindley, *Newsweek*, March 22, 1943.

329   "Foggy goodwill": *Time*, March 22, 1943.

330   Malcolm Cowley: "The End of the New Deal," *New Republic*, May 31, 1943.

330   "Death Revealed": *Time*, January 3, 1944.

330   Draft rejection rates: *Ibid.*, October 23, 1941.

332   "Good heavens!": quoted in *New Republic*, May 10, 1943.

332–   Army's neuropsychiatric problem: *Time*, December 6, 1943; *ibid.*,
333   February 28, 1944.

333   Kaiser's mother: *Ibid.*, November 23, 1942.

333–   Kaiser's medical plan: Paul de Kruif, *Kaiser Wakes the Doctors.*
334

334   "The cost of complete medical care": *Ibid.*, p. 36.

334   Seneca's health: Robert Havighurst and H. Gerthon Morgan, *The Social History of a War Boom Community*, pp. 282–88.

334–   Indiana's health: Cavnes, p. 197.
335

335   Obvious good health of children: *Harper's*, February, 1944.

335   Spending on health insurance: "National Income Supplement," p. 42.

335   Hospital beds: *Historical Statistics of the U.S. 1789–1957*, pp. 34–35.

335   Public health expenditures: *Statistical Abstract of the U.S.*, 1947 edition, p. 236.

335   Longevity increases: *Historical Statistics*, p. 25.

335–   Death rates: *Statistical Abstract*, 1948 edition, pp. 66, 79.
336

336   "They're just bums": quoted in Rosebery, p. 212.

336   Handicapped workers: *Time*, June 21, 1943.

336–   "Please be polite to our waitresses": *Nation*, June 19, 1943.
337

337   "The miners came in '49": Katherine Archibald, *Wartime Shipyard: A Study in Social Disunity*. Miss Archibald euphemistically writes it "bunked together."

337   Opinion on the postwar period: Polls quoted in *Time*, October 11, 1943.

337   NRPB estimates: *Newsweek*, August 9, 1943.

337   Department of Labor estimates: *Nation*, November 23, 1943.

337   "Willow Run supplied some answers": Lowell J. Carr and James E. Stermer, *Willow Run*, p. 7; cf. William H. Jordy, "Fiasco at Willow Run," *Nation*, May 8, 1943.

338 "GI Joe and GI Jane": *NYT*, January 9, 1944.

338– The story of the GI Bill is told in David R. B. Ross, *Preparing for*
339 *Ulysses*, pp. 118–24.

339 "Back Home": Quoted in *Life*, April 17, 1944.

339 Tom Harmon: *Ibid.*

339 "The fighters of course suffer more": Allan Nevins, in Goodman.

339 Military and civilian death rates: Shannon, p. 814.

340 "We will try to forget": *Newsweek*, May 7, 1945.

340 Veterans' grievances: cf. Arch Soutar, "Homecoming Isn't Easy,"
Satevepost, December 9, 1944; Charles G. Bolte, "The Veterans' Runaround," *Harper's*, April, 1945.

340 "There is a whole ward": Letter to *Time*, April 2, 1945.

340 Treatment of amputees: *Nation*, March 10, 1945, and *Time*, August
27, 1945.

341 "I refused to eat the food" and "Personally": *Newsweek*, April 16,
1945.

341 Veterans and their families: President's Commission on Veterans' Pensions, *Veterans Benefits in the United States*, pp. 63–77.

341 Veterans and the housing problem: *Ibid.*, p. 301.

342 Federal appropriations for veterans' benefits totaled $49 billion by 1957:
Historical Statistics of the U.S., 1789–1956.

342 Representation of veterans and their dependents in the upper strata of
society: Ross, p. 289.

342 GI Bill making up wartime educational deficits: *President's Commission*, p. 299.

342 Figures on housing construction and financing in the 1930's: U.S. Housing and Home Finance Agency, *Housing Statistics Handbook*, p. 2.

342 "The picture is one of barriers": Miles Colean, *American Housing*, p. 9.

343 Housing construction and homeownership from 1939 to 1945: *Housing
Statistics Handbook*, p. 43.

343 AMERICAN WOMEN: *Life*, January 29, 1945.

344 The side effects of getting women into the factories: Elinor M. Herrick,
"With Women at Work the Factory Changes," *NYT Magazine*,
January 24, 1943; cf. A. G. Mezerik, "The Factory Manager Learns
the Facts of Life," *Harper's*, September, 1943.

344 Dangers of factory work: Josephine von Miklos, *I Took a War Job*,
p. 126.

344 "No working woman labors under the delusion": Elizabeth Hawes,
"Do Women Workers Get an Even Break?": *NYT Magazine*, November 19, 1945.

344 The federal shipyards: Susan B. Anthony II, "Working at the Navy
Yard," *New Republic*, May 1, 1944.

345 "America may no longer believe": Bruner, p. 215.

345 "There is hardly any job": *Time*, October 19, 1942.

345 Women in journalism: *Satevepost*, May 13, 1944.

345 New York Stock Exchange: *Time*, May 10, 1943.

346 "Goddam it all": Quoted in *Life*, March 15, 1943.

Page

346 "We see this emergency a little more clearly": *Time*, January 26, 1942.

346 Dorothy Thompson: *Newsweek*, January 26, 1942.

346 Women at the conventions: *Ibid.*, June 19, 1944.

347 Widows and Widowers Clubs: Rosebery, pp. 102–3.

347 "Strange unorganized home-front battle": *Time*, August 30, 1943; cf. Elizabeth R. Valentine, "Odyssey of the Army Wife," *NYT Magazine*, March 5, 1944.

347 What women wanted: *Time*, February 26, 1945.

347– Children in the trailer camps and boom towns: Warner Olivier,
348 "Eight Hour Orphans," *Satevepost*, October 10, 1942.

348 Vice more common than violence: *Newsweek*, March 6, 1944.

348 Wolf packs: *Ibid.*, May 8, 1944.

348 "The girls are sore as all get-out": *Time*, March 29, 1943.

348 "War casualties": *Ibid.*, October 5, 1942.

348 Rape in a movie house: *Ibid.*, April 12, 1943.

348 Murder of a nine-year-old: *Ibid.*, May 22, 1944.

348 Teen-age gangs: Eleanor Lake, "Trouble on the Street Corner," *Common Sense*, May, 1943; Bradford Chambers, "Boy Gangs of New York," *NYT Magazine*, December 10, 1944.

349 El Paso movie house manager: *Time*, November 22, 1943.

349 La Guardia: *New Republic*, February 22, 1943.

349 "The worst mother" and "Let the police deal with juvenile delinquency": Quoted in Elizabeth Hawes, *Why Women Cry*, p. 187.

349 Drop in prison population: *Newsweek*, September 13, 1943; cf. *Historical Statistics of the U.S., 1789–1945*.

350 "Who made our youngsters 'generation' conscious?": *Satevepost*, December 2, 1944.

350 The sympathetic woman reporter was Agnes Meyer of the Washington *Post*, whose *Journey Through Chaos* was one of the best narratives of social life in wartime.

350 "A hell of a world for kids": Quoted in *Time*, January 29, 1945.

350 La Guardia and the psychiatrist: *Ibid.*

350 "Far better for adolescents than Depression": Caroline B. Zachry, in *Adolescents in Wartime*, AAPSS, Vol. 236, November, 1944, p. 141.

351 "Seneca people needn't be so snooty": Havighurst and Morgan, p. 103.

351 "For the vast majority of people": *Ibid.*, p. 110.

351 "A Yankee briskness": Frank Smith, "Yankee Army in the South," *New Republic*, March 29, 1943.

351 For a good summary of the South in wartime see George R. Tindall, *Emergence of the New South*, pp. 687–731.

352 "They make the TNT": Robert Moses, "Mr. Moses Dissects the Long-Haired Planners," *NYT Magazine*, June 25, 1944.

352 George Soule's premature announcement was in "Planning Wins," *New Republic*, March 8, 1943.

352 "Abstract speculations about world affairs": Richard Lee Strout, in *New Republic*, November 2, 1942.

353 Opinions on Socialism: *Fortune*, July, 1942.

353 American and British opinion on postwar reform: *Time*, August 30, 1943.

353 "No other question in economic policy is ever so important": John Kenneth Galbraith, *The Affluent Society* (Boston, 1958), p. 72.

353 Real economic growth in wartime: Council of Economic Advisers, *Economic Report of the President* (Washington, 1951), p. 152.

353 Economic effects of World War I: National Bureau of Economic Research, *Income in the U.S.: Its Amount and Distribution, 1909–1919*, Vol. 1 (New York, 1922). Chapter 3 contains the relevant charts, tables and analysis.

353– Simon Kuznets, *op. cit.*, deals with the subject of top income groups at
354   great length. Kuznets' work on the top 1 percent and top 5 percent is controversial, but it is still the best authority on the subject.

354 Breakdown of incomes in 1935–1936: Goldsmith, Jaszi, Kaitz and Liebenberg, "Size Distribution of Incomes Since the Mid-Thirties," *Review of Economics and Statistics*, February, 1954. These figures may not be exactly precise but they are sound enough to support the conclusion I have drawn from them—*i.e.*, that they reveal a sharply narrowing social pyramid.

354 Breakdown of incomes in 1945–1946: *Ibid*.

354 Breakdown of increases in family income: Council of Economic Advisers, *Economic Report of the President*, January, 1948.

354 Drop in national income going to property: Slichter, p. 11.

354 Indirect taxes: Alfred H. Conrad, "Redistribution Through Government Budgets in the U.S., 1950," in *Income Redistribution and Social Policy*, Alan Peacock, ed. (London, 1954).

354 Taxation policy and redistribution: Goldsmith et al., *op cit.*

354 "In the wartime U.S. the poor were getting richer": *Time*, May 2, 1942.

355 Domestic servants: Priscilla Robertson and Hawley Jones, "Housekeeping After the War," *Harper's*, April, 1944.

355 Income distribution since World War II: S. M. Miller and Pamel Roby, *The Future of Inequality* (New York, 1970), pp. 35–41.

355 "The more cheerful side of this tale": Shannon, p. 851.

355 Stuart Chase: "So What?" *Common Sense*, September, 1943.

355 Public opinion on social welfare programs: Bruner, pp. 155, 177.

355– Department of Health, Education and Welfare: Cantril, p. 440. Sup-
356   port for it had also dropped; I think that was because such an agency seemed less necessary than ever.

CHAPTER **XXIX**   *The Civil Liberties Disaster*

357 "We experience no hysteria": ACLU, *Freedom in Wartime.*

357 Typical of the interpretation of the internment as being an anomalous, regrettable lapse is Girdner and Loftis, p. 482. They call it "an aberration."

357 "Despite a generally good wartime civil liberties record": Lawrence S. Wittner, *Rebels Against War*, p. 38.

Page

357 "The Jehovah's Witnesses fared badly it is true": Ray H. Abrams, "The Churches and the Clergy" in *Organized Religion in the U.S.*, AAPSS, Vol. 256, March, 1948.

357 Increased incidence of CO imprisonment: Wittner, pp. 41–42.

358 "A monument to intolerance": *Time*, July 2, 1945.

358 On persecution in the First World War: cf. Paxson, *America at War*; Zachariah Chafee, *Free Speech in the U.S.* (Cambridge, Mass., 1941); William Preston, *Aliens and Dissenters* (Cambridge, Mass., 1963).

358– Harry Weber: *Time*, February 19, 1945, and *Nation*, February 17,
359 1945.

359 The problem of estimating the number of objectors is dealt with at length in Sibley and Jacobs.

359 Conditions of imprisonment: Denny Wilcher, "Conscientious Objectors in Prison," *Christian Century*, March 8, 1944; the only full-length account by a prisoner is Jim Peck's *We Who Would Not Kill*. Peck was a "troublemaker" from the point of view of prison authorities for the full length of his three-year imprisonment. It is nonetheless an honest, even if impassioned, account of the treatment of CO's in prison.

359 Court-martialing Jehovah's Witnesses and sentences of life imprisonment: *Time*, April 12, 1943.

359 "As many as forty-two of them": Wilcher, *op. cit.*

359 "Whenever personal expression of belief": Sibley and Jacob, pp. 460–61.

359– "Working conditions in the CPS camps": *Harper's*, January, 1945.
360

360 Public opinion: *Time*, February 5, 1945.

360 "We labored lo!": Quoted in Wittner, p. 81.

360 1942 indictments under espionage act: *New Republic*, January 4, 1943.

361 "My prophecy is coming true": *Life*, January 17, 1944.

361 "Disastrous consequences": James Wexler, "Sedition and Circuses," *Nation*, May 4, 1944.

361 "It was as though justice": *Newsweek*, May 29, 1944.

361 "Like the Nazis": *Nation*, June 3, 1944.

361 "The strain of this unprecedented type of mass disorder": Edwin A. Lahey, "Fascism's Day in Court," *New Republic*, June 5, 1944.

362 *Satevepost's* opinion in its issue of January 6, 1945.

362 Rising anti-Semitism in wartime: cf. polls in Cantril, pp. 381–83.

362 "A perpetual state of alarm": Wallace Stegner, "Who Persecutes Boston?" *Atlantic Monthly*, July, 1944.

362 "The First American": Quoted *ibid.*

362 "That little kike": *Time*, February 14, 1944.

363 Public opinion on postwar immigration: Cantril, p. 306.

363 "If Aristotle were alive today": Lerner, p. 38.

363 Postwar immigration: Cantril, *op. cit.*, p. 306.

363 Interest in refugee settlements in other parts of the world: David Wyman, *Paper Walls*, pp. 59–60.

363 "The lamp remained lifted": Morse, p. 149.

364 The War Relocation Authority's point of view on the challenge before it can be found in *The War Relocation Work Camps* (Washington, D.C., 1942).

364 "Whatever pay, unspecified at this time": *Ibid.*

364 Work and pay: cf. S. Burton Heath, "What About Hugh Kiino?" *Harper's*, October, 1943.

364 Relationship between "Japanese" and "Caucasians": cf. Leonard Bloom, "Adjustments of Japanese-American Families to Relocation," *American Sociological Review*, February, 1947.

364 Unpunished murders: Girdner and Loftis, p. 243.

364– Recruiting for the 442d: cf. Bloom, *op. cit.*
365

365 "DEADLY PERIL": Los Angeles *Herald Express* headline quoted in Carey McWilliams, *Prejudice—Japanese-Americans.*

366 "What the members of the Supreme Court will do": George W. Martin, in *New Republic*, April 17, 1944.

366 "Like a restricted railroad ticket": *Time*, April 10, 1944.

366– A good short summary of the Court in wartime is in Alpheus Thomas
367 Mason, *The Supreme Court from Taft to Warren* (New York, 1964), pp. 119–95.

366– "The Federal Judiciary": Alexander H. Pekelis, "The Supreme Court
367 Today," *New Republic*, April 17, 1944.

CHAPTER XXX *Wartime School Days*

368 High School Victory Corps: Irving Kandel, *The Impact of the War on Education*, pp. 91–93.

368– Model wartime curriculum: Cavnes, p. 316.
369

369 "Many considered the report": *Time*, February 16, 1942.

370 Drop in number of teachers and rise in emergency teaching certificates: Kandel, p. 63.

370– Teachers and the ration boards: George Henry, "The People and
371 Their Schools," *Common Sense*, April, 1943.

372 "Something essentially callow": Felix Morley, president of Haverford, in *Satevepost*, October 16, 1943.

373 "The University of California": Quoted in the *Nation*, June 12, 1943.

374 "A class of privileged men and women": George Boas, "Priorities in Education," *Atlantic Monthly*, January, 1943.

374 Dean Gauss' remarks: Quoted in Porter Sargent, *The Continuing Battle for the Mind of Youth*, pp. 82–83.

374 "A campaign of community education": U.S. Office of Education pamphlet, "High School Victory Corps" (Washington, D.C., 1942). pp. 22–23.

374 "The liberal arts . . . are luxuries": *Time*, January 25, 1943.

375 George N. Schuster: Lerner, p. 142; *Time*, February 28, 1944.

375 Lerner on Conant's radicals: Lerner, pp. 8–10.

375 Mental development of fourteen-year-olds: *Time*, January 29, 1945.

474   DAYS OF SADNESS, YEARS OF TRIUMPH

384   "Its hero, Major Joppolo, is a kind of compendium": *Nation*, February 12, 1944.

385   "My company carefully avoided": *Newsweek*, May 29, 1944.

385   "A curious atmosphere": Manny Farber, "Movies in Wartime," *New Republic*, January 3, 1944.

386   "We talked about this and that": *Time*, January 1, 1945.

386   "The authenticity of authentic self-delusion": Agee, in *Nation*, July 29, 1944.

388   "A combination of Abstract art and Expressionism": Peter and Linda Murray, *Dictionary of Art and Artists* (London, 1965).

388   The best recent works on the development of Abstract Expressionism are: Irving Sandler, *Abstract Expressionism: The Triumph of American Painting* (London, 1970), and Alexis Gregory, ed., *American Painting* (Lausanne, Switzerland, 1969).

388   Wartime and postwar interest in art: Forbes Watson, "American Art," in *Twentieth Century Unlimited*, Bruce Bliven, ed. (New York, 1950).

389   "Simplicity, economy and efficiency": James Marston Fitch, Jr., *American Building*, Vol. 1, rev. ed. (Boston, 1966), p. 259.

389   New architectural opportunities: Douglas Haskell, "The Revolution in House-Building," *Harper's*, June, 1942.

389–   The new factories: Albert Kahn, "Architects of Defense," *Atlantic*
390   *Monthly*, March, 1942; for a more critical view, cf. Percival and Paul Goodman, "Architecture in Wartime," *New Republic*, December 13, 1943.

390   Advertising expenditures: Madison Avenue (pseud.), "Advertising in Wartime," *New Republic*, February 21, 1944.

390   Radio advertising: *Harper's*, March, 1945.

391   OWI's civil war: Sidney Weinberg, "What to Tell America: The Writers' Quarrel with OWI," *Journal of American History*, June, 1968.

391   Roosevelt's obeisance to advertising: *Newsweek*, May 8, 1944, and *Time*, August 14, 1944.

391   "You never know": Quoted in Goodman, p. 385.

396   The laundry crisis: *Life*, July 12, 1943.

396   *Satevepost's* acclaim of the dish smasher was in its issue of November 11, 1944.

397   "Turn off the furnace": *Time*, March 5, 1945.

397   Liberal intellectuals and asceticism: Cf. *New Republic*, March 26, 1945.

CHAPTER XXXII *Winding Down a Miracle*

399   "It would be a Pearl Harbor of Peace": TRB, in *New Republic*, September 4, 1944.

399   Industrial accidents in war production: Compiled from *Statistical Abstract of the U.S.*, 1942–1946 editions.

400   Public opinion on OPA: A summary of relevant surveys is in NORC Report No. 26, "Public Opinion on Controls of Prices, Wages, Salaries During the War and Reconversion" (Denver, Colorado, 1948).

400   "At that price": Shannon, p. 843.

Page

401   "In the Thirties": Randolph Paul, *Taxation for Prosperity*, p. 84.

401–   Black markets and business: Clinard, pp. 293–96; cf. Edward H.
402   Sutherland, *White Collar Crime* (New York, 1949).

402   Black markets and the middle class: Clinard, p. 94.

403   On businessmen's views on the postwar era: See Gunnar Myrdal, "Is American Business Deluding Itself?" *Atlantic Monthly*, November, 1944.

403   Dollar-a-year men told to come back at once: *Time*, July 3, 1944.

403   "Big business was stronger": Shannon, p. 854.

404ff.   The standard work on wartime agriculture is still Walter M. Wilcox, *The Farmer in the Second World War*.

406   "Well, it's this way": Oren Stephens, "FSA Fights for Its Life," *Harper's*, April, 1943.

406   FSA farmers' disproportionate share of increased production: *New Republic*, April 26, 1943.

407   What farmers thought about the farm bloc: Wilcox, pp. 250–60.

407   Fears of postwar unemployment: *Time*, January 8, 1945.

407   Predictions on postwar unemployment: *Ibid.*, March 12, 1945.

409   "The sleepy down-at-the-heel village": Havighurst and Morgan, p. 330.

409   Opinion on chance to get ahead: Cantril, p. 831.

CHAPTER XXXIII   *America First—Everywhere*

410   "Please, for God's sake, stop": *Time*, March 26, 1945.

410–   "Return with vigor": *New Republic*, November 3, 1944.
411

411   "Diplomacy is widely regarded": Ernest K. Lindley, in *Newsweek*, March 12, 1945.

411   "Possibly the most important conference": *Time*, February 19, 1945.

411   "The most impressive conference": Quoted in *Life*, February 26, 1945.

411   "Was not, by itself, a guarantee of peace everlasting": *Time*, February 26, 1945.

411–   *Time*'s indignation at the Yalta compromises was expressed in its issue
412   of March 5, 1945.

412   "There, for the first time": TRB, in *New Republic*, March 12, 1945.

412   "It's getting so": *Ibid.*, March 19, 1945.

412   "The bargain was bad enough": *Time*, April 9, 1945.

412   "The story is over": *Newsweek*, April 30, 1945.

413   "It is not too much to say": Allen Drury, *A Senate Journal*, p. 4.

413   "With Mr. Roosevelt's death": *Newsweek*, April 23, 1945.

413   "That's it! San Francisco's the place": Frederick Lewis Allen, "San Francisco Retrospect," *Harper's*, July, 1945.

414   "We could hardly have taken any other course": *Time*, May 14, 1945.

415   "Goddam it, it's no fun": *Newsweek*, June 18, 1945.

416   Mrs. Agnes Waters et al.: *Time*, July 23, 1945.

416   "I can't recall anything quite like it": TRB, in *New Republic*, July 23, 1945.

416   Quincy Howe: "Twelve Things the War Will Do to America," *Harper's*, November, 1942.

416–
417   De Sales, *The Making of Yesterday*, entry for July 7, 1942.

417   "The masses of Europe have become distrustful": Quoted in *Time*, September 13, 1943.

417   The classic work on imperialism and economics is J. A. Hobson, *Imperialism: A Study* (London, 1902). Lenin borrowed heavily from it for his own *Imperialism: The Highest Stage of Capitalism*. But cf. D. K. Fieldhouse, " 'Imperialism': An Historiographical Revision," *Economic History Review*, No. 2, 1961, for an excellent introduction to the extensive literature on the economics of imperialism, especially the major studies dealing with Hobson's nonexistent facts and imaginary correlations. Hobson's book was historically important, not historically sound.

417   "Cold cash on the barrelhead": Quoted in *Nation*, March 10, 1945.

417–
418   Public opinion on lend-lease and postwar loans: Cantril, p. 210.

418   "We Americans can boast": *Satevepost*, April 7, 1945.

418   "A Bill of Rights for the world?": *Time*, April 30, 1945.

418   "Our present 'internationalism' is not rooted in knowledge": Hadley Cantril, "How Real Is America's Internationalism?" *NYT Magazine*, April 29, 1945.

418   "America's responsibility is to furnish leadership": J. William Fulbright,

418   "The Peace We Want," *ibid.*, July 22, 1945.

418–
419   "Peaceful peoples like ourselves" Captain McGeorge Bundy, "A Letter to Twelve College Presidents," *Atlantic Monthly*, May, 1945.

419   "The world cannot be half democratic and half totalitarian": Walter Lippmann, *U.S. War Aims*, p. 149.

419   "You can't be liberal without being opposed to Communism": *Newsweek*, July 9, 1945.

419   "Old radicals whom Stalin drove crazy": Alfred Kazin, "Midtown and the Village," *Harper's*, January, 1971.

419   Hooton: Quoted in *New Republic*, May 11, 1942.

420   Germany as schizophrenic: T. E. Murphy, "Will Shock Treatment Cure Germany's Ills?" *Satevepost*, January 1, 1944.

420   Germany as paranoiac: Richard M. Brickner, *Is Germany Curable?*

420   "The Nazis are simply murdering the civilian Jewish population": Quoted in *New Republic*, May 22, 1944.

420   State of public opinion: Arthur Koestler, in *NYT Magazine*, January 2, 1944.

421   Impatience with the War Crimes Commission: cf. *New Republic*, February 19, 1945.

421   "We would involve ourselves in legal tangles": *Nation*, June 9, 1945.

421   "The causes that produced Belsen": *Time*, June 11, 1945.

422   SOVIET FAILURE TO OBSERVE PROMISES: *Newsweek*, April 30, 1945.

422   The Washington reporter was Ernest K. Lindley, *ibid.*

Page
422– "Preserve big power unity": *Time*, July 9, 1945.
423

423 Lester Markel, in Goodman, pp. 351–52.

423 "Catastrophic loss": *Time*, November 13, 1944.

423 "Imminent possibility that American Communists might revert": *Newsweek*, June 18, 1945.

423 "The fellow-traveler is everywhere": *Life*, July 30, 1945.

423 "Maybe we can't get along with Russia": TRB, in *New Republic*, July 2, 1945.

423 "Thus the Soviets": *Newsweek*, June 11, 1945.

423 Predictions of academic Sovietologists: *Satevepost*, December 2, 1944.

424 1943 predictions of "the next war": *New Republic*, March 15, 1943; cf. *Time*, June 14, 1943.

424 "War with Russia is unthinkable": *Common Sense*, May, 1945.

424 "On all other issues men and nations could compromise": *Time*, September 11, 1944.

424 Public opinion on the Russians: Cantril, p. 502.

424 Public opinion on postwar armaments: *Ibid.*, p. 19.

424– "The possibility of World War III": *Time*, June 11, 1945.
425

425 Public opinion on war within twenty-five years: *Ibid.*, May 14, 1945.

CHAPTER XXXIV *Science Works Its Wonders*

426 "The Japanese have something new to learn": TRB, in *New Republic*, July 2, 1945.

427 "The race had been won": *Time*, August 20, 1945.

427 "Once you invest $2 billion in a firecracker": TRB, in *New Republic*, July 2, 1945.

428 "We have this day become the new masters": Letter to *Time*, August 27, 1945.

429 "Except for a few 4-Fs": *Newsweek*, May 7, 1945.

429 "The U.S. dealt clumsily": James Phinney Baxter III, *Scientists Against Time*, p. 135.

429– *Time*'s assignment of credit for war inventions was in its issue of April
430 3, 1944.

430 "The only successful development of proximity fuses": Baxter, pp. 222, 242.

430 British science in wartime: Guy Hartcup, *The Challenge of War*; J. G. Crowther and R. Whiddington, *Science at War*.

431 Bush's report was *Science: The Endless Frontier*.

431 "Our picture of the postwar world": *Newsweek*, August 23, 1945.

431– On the growth of science: Derek J. de Solla Price, *Big Science, Little
432 Science*.

SELECTED BIBLIOGRAPHY

BORTH, CHRISTY, *Masters of Mass Production*. Indianapolis, Indiana, 1945.

BOSSARD, J. H. S., and BOLL, E. S., eds., *Adolescents in Wartime*. Annals of the AAPSS, Vol. 236. Philadelphia, Pa., 1944.

BOSWORTH, ALLEN R., *America's Concentration Camps*. New York, 1967.

BRICKNER, RICHARD M., M.D., *Is Germany Incurable?* Philadelphia and New York, 1943.

BROOKS, THOMAS R., *Toil and Trouble: A History of American Labor*. New York, 1964.

BROOM, LEONARD, and KITSUSE, JOHN I., *The Managed Casualty: The Japanese American Family in World War II*. Berkeley and Los Angeles, 1956.

BROOM, LEONARD, and RIEMER, RUTH, *Removal and Return: The Socio-Economic Effects of the War on Japanese Americans*. Berkeley and Los Angeles, 1949.

BROWDER, EARL R., *The Second Imperialist War*. New York, 1940.

BRUMBACK, OSCAR, *Manual of the Citizens No Foreign War Coalition, Inc.* Washington, D.C., 1941.

BRUNER, JEROME, *Mandate from the People*. New York, 1944.

BURNHAM, JAMES, *The Managerial Revolution*. New York, 1941.

BUSH, VANNEVAR, *Science—The Endless Frontier: A Report to the President*. Washington, D.C., 1945.

BUTLER, PIERCE, ed., *Books and Libraries in Wartime*. Chicago, 1945.

CANTRIL, HADLEY, *Public Opinion 1935–1946*. Princeton, N.J., 1951.

CARSKADON, T. R., *Labor in the Defense Crisis*. New York, 1941.

CARR, LOWELL J., and STERMER, JAMES E., *Willow Run*. New York, 1952.

CATTON, BRUCE, *The Warlords of Washington*. New York, 1948.

CAVNES, MAX PARVIN, *The Hoosier Community at War*. Bloomington, Indiana, 1961.

CHADWIN, MARK LINCOLN, *The Hawks of World War Two*. Chapel Hill, N.C., 1968.

CHAMBERLIN, WILLIAM HENRY, *The World's Iron Age*. New York, 1941.

CHANDLER, LESTER V., *Inflation in the United States, 1940–1948*. New York, 1951.

CHASE, WILLARD L., *Wartime Social Studies in the Elementary School*. Washington, D.C., 1943.

CHERNE, LEO, *The Rest of Your Life*. New York, 1944.

CHILDS, MARQUIS, and STONE, W. T., *Toward a Dynamic America: The Challenge of a Changing World*. New York, 1941.

CLINARD, MARSHALL B., *The Black Market: A Study in White Collar Crime*. New York, 1952.

COLE, WAYNE S., *America First: The Battle Against Intervention, 1940–1941*. Madison, Wis., 1953.

COLEAN, MILES L., *American Housing: Problems and Prospects*. New York, 1944.

COLLINS, HENRY HILL, Jr., *America's Own Refugees*. Princeton, N.J., 1941.

Committee to Defend America by Aiding the Allies, Berkeley-Oakland Chapter, *Information Letter 1940–1941*. (Collection held at University of California, Berkeley.)

CONANT, JAMES B., *My Several Lives*. New York, 1970.

———, *Our Fighting Faith: Addresses to College Students*. Cambridge, Mass., 1942.

CONN, STETSON, and FAIRCHILD, BYRON, *The Framework of Hemispheric Defense*. Washington, D.C., 1964.

CREF, JOHN R., *A Survey of the American Economy, 1940–1946*. New York, 1947.

CREMIN, LAWRENCE R., *The Transformation of the Schools: Progressivism in American Education*. New York, 1961.

CROWTHER, J. G., and WHIDDINGTON, R., *Science at War*. London, 1948.

CURTI, MERLE, *The Growth of American Thought*, 2d rev. ed. New York, 1951.

DALFIUME, RICHARD M., *Desegregation in the U.S. Armed Forces*. Columbia, Mo., 1969.

DAVIE, MAURICE R., *Refugees in America*. New York, 1947.

DAVIS, KENNETH S., *Experience of War: The U.S. in World War Two*. New York, 1965.

DAWSON, RAYMOND H., *The Decision to Aid Russia, 1941: Foreign Policy and Domestic Politics*. Chapel Hill, N.C., 1959.

DE KRUIF, PAUL, *Kaiser Wakes the Doctors*. New York, 1943.

DE SALES, RAOUL DE RUSSY, *The Making of Yesterday*. New York, 1947.

DE SOLLA PRICE, DEREK J., *Little Science, Big Science*. New York, 1963.

DOS PASSOS, JOHN, *State of the Nation*. Boston, 1944.

DRUCKER, PETER, *The End of Economic Man*. New York, 1939.

———, *The Future of Industrial Man*. New York, 1942.

DRURY, ALLEN, *A Senate Journal 1943–1945*. New York, 1963.

DRYER, SHERMAN S., *Radio in Wartime*. New York, 1942.

EARLE, EDWARD MEAD, *Against This Torrent*. Princeton, N.J., 1941.

Educational Policies Commission, *What the Schools Should Teach in Wartime*. Washington, D.C., 1943.

ENDORE, S. GUY, *The Sleepy Lagoon Mystery*. Los Angeles, 1944.

FAIRCHILD, BYRON, and GROSSMAN, JONATHAN, *The Army and Industrial Manpower*. Washington, D.C., 1959.

FEHRENBACH, T. R., *F.D.R.'s Undeclared War*. New York, 1957.

FINLETTER, THOMAS K., *Can Representative Government Do the Job?* New York, 1945.

FINER, HERMAN, *Road to Reaction*. Boston, 1945.

FITCH, JAMES MARSTON, Jr., *American Building*, Vol. 1, 2d rev. ed. Boston, 1966.

FRANKLIN, JOHN HOPE, *From Slavery to Freedom*, 3d rev. ed. New York, 1968.

FRIEDLANDER, SAUL, *Prelude to Downfall: Hitler and the U.S. 1939–1941*, tr. from the French by Aline B. and Alexander Werth. New York, 1967.

FROMM, ERICH, *Escape from Freedom*. New York, 1941.

FURNAS, J. C., *How America Lives*. New York, 1941.

GARFINKEL, HERMAN, *When Negroes March*. Glencoe, Ill., 1959.

GENUNG, ALBERT B., *Food Policies During World War Two*. Ithaca, N.Y., 1951.

GINZBERG, ELI, et al., *The Ineffective Soldier*. New York, 1959. 3 vols.

GIRDNER, AUDRIE, and LOFTIS, ANNE, *The Great Betrayal.* New York, 1970.

GOODMAN, JACK, ed., *While You Were Gone.* New York, 1946.

GOODMAN, WALTER, *The Committee.* New York, 1968.

GORHAM, ELIZABETH, *So Your Husband's Gone to War.* New York, 1942.

GRAFTON, SAMUEL, *An American Diary: Columns from the New York Post.* Garden City, N.Y., 1949.

GRODZINS, MORTON, *Americans Betrayed: Politics and the Japanese Evacuation.* Chicago, 1949.

GROVES, LESLIE R., *Now It Can Be Told.* New York, 1962.

GRUENBERG, SIDONIE M., *The Family in a World at War.* New York, 1942.

GULICK, L. H., *Administrative Reflections from World War Two.* University, Ala., 1948.

GUTHRIE, WOODY, *Bound for Glory.* New York, 1943.

HARTCUP, GUY, *The Challenge of War.* London, 1969.

Harvard University, *General Education in a Free Society.* Cambridge, Mass., 1945.

HAVIGHURST, ROBERT J., and MORGAN, H. GERTHON, *The Social History of a War Boom Community.* New York, 1951.

HAWES, ELIZABETH, *Why Women Cry: or, Wenches with Wrenches.* New York, 1943.

HAYEK, FRIEDRICH A., *The Road to Serfdom.* Chicago, 1944.

HETTINGER, HERMAN, ed., *New Horizons in Radio,* Annals of the AAPSS, Vol. 231. Philadelphia, Pa., 1941.

HOEHLING, A. A., *The Week Before Pearl Harbor.* New York, 1963.

———, *Home Front, USA.* New York, 1966.

HURD, CHARLES, *Washington Cavalcade.* New York, 1948.

IRWIN, WILL, and JOHNSON, THOMAS M., *What You Should Know About Spies and Saboteurs.* New York, 1943.

JANEWAY, ELIOT, *The Struggle for Survival.* New Haven, Conn., 1951.

JOHNSON, DOUGLAS B., *The Republican Party and Wendell Willkie.* Champaign-Urbana, Ill., 1956.

JOHNSON, HUGH S., *Hell-Bent for War.* Indianapolis, Ind., 1941.

JOHNSON, WALTER, *The Battle Against Isolation.* Chicago, 1944.

JONAS, MANFRED, *Isolationism in America 1939–1945.* Ithaca, N.Y., 1966.

JONES, ROBERT C., *Mexican War Workers in the U.S.* Washington, D.C., 1945.

JOSEPHSON, MATTHEW, *Sidney Hillman: Statesman of American Labor.* Garden City, N.Y., 1952.

JUNGK, ROBERT, *Brighter Than a Thousand Suns.* New York, 1958.

KANDEL, ISAAC L., *The Impact of the War on American Education.* Chapel Hill, N.C., 1948.

KAZIN, ALFRED, *On Native Grounds.* New York, 1942.

KERNAN, W. F., *Defense Will Not Win the War.* Boston, 1942.

———, *We Can Win This War.* Boston, 1943.

KITAGAWA, DAISAKU, *Issei and Nisei: The Internment Years.* New York, 1967.

KUZNETS, SIMON, *Shares of Upper Income Groups in Income and Saving.* New York, 1953.

LAMONT, CORLISS, *The Trial of Elizabeth Gurley Flynn by the American Civil Liberties Union*. New York, 1968.

LAMONT, LANSING, *Day of Trinity*. New York, 1965.

LANGER, WILLIAM S., and GLEASON, E. S., *The Undeclared War*. New York, 1953.

LASKI, H. J., *The Strategy of Freedom: An Open Letter to American Youth*. New York, 1941.

LEE, ALFRED MCCLUNG, and HUMPHREY, NORMAN D., *Race Riot*. New York, 1943.

LEE, ULYSSES, *U.S. Army in World War Two: Employment of Negro Troops*. Washington, D.C., 1966.

LEIGHTON, ALEXANDER H., *The Governing of Men*. Princeton, N.J., 1954.

LERNER, MAX, *Ideas for the Ice Age*. New York, 1941.

————, *Public Journal: Marginal Notes in Wartime America*. New York, 1945.

LILIENTHAL, DAVID E., *The Journals of David E. Lilienthal: The TVA Years, 1939–1945*. New York, 1964.

LEUCHTENBERG, WILLIAM E., *Franklin Roosevelt and the New Deal*. New York, 1963.

LEVER, HARRY, and YOUNG, JOSEPH, *Wartime Racketeers*. New York, 1945.

LEWIS, FULTON, Jr., *Broadcasts over the Mutual Network, 1943–1945*. Washington, D.C., 1945. 2 vols.

Life Magazine, *War Art*. New York, 1943.

LIND, ANDREW W., *Hawaii's Japanese—An Experiment in Democracy*. Princeton, N.J., 1946.

LINDBERGH, ANNE MORROW, *The Wave of the Future*. New York, 1940.

LINDBERGH, CHARLES A., *The Wartime Journals of Charles A. Lindbergh*. New York, 1971.

LINGEMAN, RICHARD R., *Don't You Know There's a War On?* New York, 1970.

LIPPMANN, WALTER, *U.S. Foreign Policy: Shield of the Republic*. Boston, 1943.

————, *U.S. War Aims*. Boston, 1944.

LOGAN, RAYFORD W., ed., *What the Negro Wants*. Chapel Hill, N.C., 1944.

LUBELL, SAMUEL, *The Future of American Politics*. New York, 1952.

LUCE, HENRY, *The American Century*. New York, 1941.

LYONS, EUGENE, *The Red Decade*. Indianapolis, Ind., 1941.

MACLEISH, ARCHIBALD, *American Opinion and the War*. New York, 1942.

————, *The American Cause*. New York, 1942.

McWILLIAMS, CAREY, *Brothers Under the Skin*. Boston, 1943.

————, *Ill Fares the Land*. Boston, 1942.

————, *Prejudice: Japanese Americans*. Boston, 1944.

MANSFIELD, HARVEY, et al., *A Short History of the OPA*. Washington, D.C., 1948.

MAUROIS, ANDRÉ, *A Short History of the U.S. from Wilson to Kennedy*. London, 1964.

MAYER, GEORGE H., *The Republican Party, 1854–1956*, 2d ed. New York, 1967.

MEAD, MARGARET, *And Keep Your Powder Dry*. New York, 1942.

MERRIAM, CHARLES E., *What Is Democracy?* Chicago, 1941.

MERRILL, FRANCIS E., *Social Problems on the Home Front*. New York, 1948.

MERTON, ROBERT K., *Mass Persuasion: The Social Psychology of a War Bond Drive*. New York, 1946.

MERZ, CHARLES, *Days of Decision: Wartime Editorials from the New York Times*. Garden City, N.Y., 1941.

MEYER, AGNES E., *Journey Through Chaos*. New York, 1944.

MILLER, S. M., and ROBY, PAMELA, *The Future of Inequality*. New York, 1970.

MILLETT, FRED B., *The Rebirth of Liberal Education*. New York, 1945.

MITCHELL, BROADUS, *Depression Decade*. New York, 1947.

MIMS, EDWIN, Jr., *The Majority of the People*. New York, 1941.

MOCK, ELIZABETH, ed., *Built in the USA, Since 1932*, 3d ed. New York, 1945.

MORISON, SAMUEL ELIOT, *History of U.S. Naval Operations in World War II*, Vol. 1, *The Battle of the Atlantic*, Boston, 1954, and Vol. 3, *The Rising Sun in the Pacific*, Boston, 1948.

MORSE, A. D., *While Six Million Died*. New York, 1968.

MOSCOW, WARREN, *Roosevelt and Willkie*. Englewood Cliffs, N.J., 1968.

MUMFORD, LEWIS, *Faith for Living*. New York, 1940.

————, *Men Must Act*. New York, 1939.

MURROW, EDWARD R., *This Is London*. New York, 1941.

MYRDAL, GUNNAR, *An American Dilemma*. New York, 1944.

NELSON, DENNIS L., *The Integration of the Negro into the U.S. Navy*. New York, 1951.

NELSON, DONALD M., *Arsenal of Democracy*. New York, 1946.

NIELANDER, WILLIAM A., *Wartime Food Rationing*. Baltimore, 1947.

NOVICK, DAVID, and STEINER, GEORGE, *Wartime Industrial Statistics*. Champaign-Urbana, Ill., 1949.

ODUM, HOWARD E., *Race and Rumors of Race*. Chapel Hill, N.C., 1944.

OGDEN, AUGUST R., *The Dies Committee, 1938–1943*. Washington, D.C., 1944.

OKUBO, MINE, *Citizen 13660*. New York, 1966.

OTTLEY, ROI, *New World A'Coming*. New York, 1943.

PARMET, HERBERT S., and HECHT, MARIE B., *Never Again: The Third Term Campaign*. New York, 1968.

PATTERSON, E. M., ed., *Defending America's Future, Annals of the AAPSS*, Vol. 234. Philadelphia, Pa., 1941.

PAUL, RANDOLPH E., *Taxation for Prosperity*. Indianapolis, Ind., 1947.

————, *Taxation in the United States*. Boston, 1954.

PECK, JIM, *We Who Would Not Kill*. New York, 1958.

RACHLIS, EUGENE, *They Came to Kill*. New York, 1961.

RADOSH, RONALD, *American Labor and U.S. Foreign Policy*. New York, 1969.

REDDING, J. SAUNDERS, *No Day of Triumph*. New York, 1942.

RESTON, JAMES, *Prelude to Victory*. New York, 1943.

RIDDLE, DONALD H., *The Truman Committee*. New Brunswick, N.J., 1964.

RIESELBACH, LEROY N., *The Roots of Isolationism*. Indianapolis, Ind., 1966.

ROSEBERY, MERCEDES, *This Day's Madness*. New York, 1944.

ROSS, DAVID R. B., *Preparing for Ulysses*. New York, 1969.

RUCHAMES, LOUIS, *Race, Jobs and Politics: The FEPC*. New York, 1953.

SADLER, IRVING, *Abstract Expressionism: The Triumph of American Painting*. London, 1970.

SANDBURG, CARL, *Home Front Memo*. New York, 1943.

SARGENT, PORTER, *Education in Wartime*. Boston, 1942.

————, *The Continuing Battle for the Control of the Mind of Youth*. Boston, 1945.

SCHLESINGER, ARTHUR M., *Political and Social Growth of the U.S., 1865–1940*. New York, 1942.

SCHLESINGER, ARTHUR M., Jr., and ISRAEL, FRED, *History of American Presidential Elections*, Vol. 4, New York, 1971.

SEIDMAN, JOEL, *American Labor: From Defense to Reconversion*. Chicago, 1953.

Select Committee Investigating National Defense Migration, *Preliminary Report and Recommendations on Problems of Evacuation of Citizens and Aliens from Military Areas*, House Report 1911. Washington, D.C., 1942.

SHALLOO, J. P., and YOUNG, D., eds., *Minority Peoples in a Nation at War*, Annals of the AAPSS, Vol. 223. Philadelphia, Pa., 1942.

SHANNON, FRED ALBERT, *America's Economic Growth*, 3d ed. New York, 1950.

SHOGAN, ROBERT, and CRAIG, TOM, *The Detroit Race Riot*. Philadelphia, 1954.

SIBLEY, MULFORD Q., and JACOB, PHILIP E., *Conscription of Conscience: The American State and the Conscientious Objector 1940–1947*. Ithaca, N.Y., 1952.

SLICHTER, SUMNER H., *The American Economy*. New York, 1948.

SOROKIN, PITIRIM, *The Crisis of Our Age*. New York, 1942.

SPYKMAN, NICHOLAS, *America's Strategy in World Politics*. New York, 1942.

STEVENS, ALDEN, *Arms and the People*. New York, 1942.

STONE, I. F., *Business as Usual: The First Year of Defense*. New York, 1941.

STOUFFER, SAMUEL A., et al., *The American Soldier*. Princeton, N.J., 1949. 2 vols.

SUTHERLAND, EDWIN H., *White Collar Crime*. New York, 1949.

SWEENY, CHARLES, *Moment of Truth: Our War Situation*. New York, 1943.

SWEET, WILLIAM WARREN, *The Story of Religion in America*, 2d rev. ed. New York, 1950.

TALMADGE, I. D., ed., *Whose Revolution? A Study of the Future Course of Liberalism in the U.S.* New York, 1941.

TEN BROCK, JACOBUS, et al., *Prejudice, War and the Constitution*. Berkeley and Los Angeles, 1954.

Time-Life, December 7: The First 30 Hours. New York, 1942.

TIMMONS, BASCOM M., *Jesse Jones*. New York, 1956.

TINDALL, GEORGE, *Emergence of the New South, 1913–1945*. Baton Rouge, La., 1961.

TOLLEY, H. R., *The Farmer Citizen at War*. New York, 1943.

TOULMIN, HARRY A., Jr., *Diary of Democracy*. New York, 1947.

TREFOUSSE, H. L., *Germany and American Neutrality*. New York, 1951.

U.S. Bureau of the Budget, *The U.S. at War*. Washington, D.C., 1946.

U.S. Bureau of the Census, *Historical Statistics of the U.S., 1789–1945*. Washington, D.C., 1952.

U.S. Bureau of the Census, *Statistical Abstract of the U.S.* Washington, D.C., 1939–1946.

U.S. Civilian Production Administration, *Industrial Mobilization for War*. Washington, D.C., 1947.

U.S. Department of Commerce, *Income Distribution in the U.S. by Size*. Washington, D.C., 1950.
U.S. Department of Interior, *Wartime Exile*. Washington, D.C., 1946.
U.S. Housing and Home Finance Agency, *Housing Statistics Handbook*. Washington, D.C., 1947.
U.S. Office of Community War Services, *Recreation Bulletin*, Nos. 1–96. Washington, D.C., 1941–1945.
———, *Teamwork in Community Services, 1941–1945*. Washington, D.C., 1946.
U.S. Office of Facts and Figures, *Report to the Nation: American Preparation for War*. Washington, D.C., 1942.
U.S. Office of War Information, *Pacific Coast Attitudes Toward the Japanese Problem*. Washington, D.C., 1942.
U.S. Selective Service System, *Selective Service and Victory*. Washington, D.C., 1947.
———, *Selective Service as the Tide of War Turns*. Washington, D.C., 1944.
———, *Selective Service in Peacetime*. Washington, D.C., 1941.
———, *Selective Service in Wartime*. Washington, D.C., 1942.
U.S. Temporary National Economic Committee, *Hearings Before the TNEC 1939–1941*. Washington, D.C., 1941. 14 vols.
———, *Investigation of Concentration of Economic Power: Final Report and Recommendation*. Washington, D.C., 1941.
U.S. War Department, *Japanese Evacuation from the West Coast*. Washington, D.C., 1946.
VON MIKLOS, JOSEPHINE, *I Took a War Job*. New York, 1943.
WALLACE, H. A., *The Century of the Common Man*. New York, 1942.
War Production Board, *Wartime Production Achievements*. Washington, D.C., 1945.
WELLES, SUMNER, *The Time for Decision*. New York, 1944.
WERNER, MAX, *Attack Can Win in '43*. Boston, 1943.
WHEELER-NICHOLSON, M., *Are We Winning the Hard Way?* New York, 1943.
WHITE, LYMAN C., *300,000 New Americans*. New York, 1957.
WILCOX, WALTER M., *The Farmer in the Second World War*. Ames, Iowa, 1947.
WILLKIE, WENDELL, *One World*. New York, 1943.
WITTNER, LAWRENCE S., *Rebels Against War: The American Peace Movement 1941–1960*. New York, 1969.
WYMAN, DAVID, *Paper Walls: Refugee Policy 1938–1941*. Amherst, Mass., 1968.
YOUNG, R. A., *Congressional Politics in the Second World War*. New York, 1956.

ARTICLES

ABRAMS, RAY H., "The Churches and Clergy in World War II," in *Proceedings of the AAPSS*, Vol. 256, March, 1948.
ADAMS, MILDRED, "A Bigger Role for Food Stamps," *New York Times Magazine*, May 18, 1941.
ADLER, MORTIMER J., "The Chicago School," *Harper's*, September, 1941.

————, "The Pre-War Generation," *Harper's*, October, 1940.

ALEXANDER, JACK, "Pugnacious Pearson," *Saturday Evening Post*, January 6, 1945.

ALEXANDER, WILL W., "Our Conflicting Racial Policies," *Harper's*, January, 1945.

ALLEN, FREDERICK LEWIS, "San Francisco Retrospect," *Harper's*, July, 1945.

————, "Three Years of It," *Harper's*, December, 1944.

————, "Who's Getting the Money?" *Harper's*, June, 1944.

ALSOP, STEWART, "Wanted: a Faith to Fight For," *Atlantic Monthly*, May, 1941.

Advertising Federation of America, "War Message Copy." New York, 1943.

American Civil Liberties Union Pamphlet, "Freedom in Wartime, June, 1943.

————, "The Persecution of Jehovah's Witnesses," January, 1941.

Anonymous, "Books and the War," *New Republic*, October 27, 1941.

ANTHONY, SUSAN B., II, "Working at the Navy Yard," *New Republic*, May 1, 1944.

BARCK, O. T., Jr., "Labor Quietens Down," *Current History*, September, 1941.

BARR, STRINGFELLOW, "A College in Secession," *Atlantic Monthly*, July, 1941.

BEARD, CHARLES, "Giddy Minds and Foreign Quarrels," *Harper's*, September, 1939.

BELL, ELLIOTT V., "Planned Economy and/or Democracy," *New York Times Magazine*, November 23, 1941.

BENEDICT, AGNES E., "Violence in the Classroom," *Nation*, January 9, 1943.

BENEDICT, RUTH, "Our Last Minority: Youth," *New Republic*, February 24, 1941.

BINCKLEY, WILLIAM C., "Two World Wars and American Historical Scholarship," *Mississippi Valley Historical Review*, June, 1946.

BINGHAM, ALFRED M., "Evolution of the New Deal," *Common Sense*, September, 1939.

————, "The New Deal Has a Future," *Common Sense*, August, 1939.

BLIVEN, BRUCE, "The Voice and the Kids," *New Republic*, November 6, 1944.

BLOOM, LEONARD, "Adjustments of Japanese-American Families to Relocation," *American Sociological Review*, February, 1947.

BOAS, GEORGE, "Priorities in Education," *Atlantic Monthly*, January, 1943.

BOLLES, BLAIR, "The Great Defense Migration," *Harper's*, October, 1941.

BOLTE, CHARLES G., "The Veterans' Runaround," *Harper's*, April, 1945.

BOYD, JAMES, "Strategy for Negroes," *Nation*, June 26, 1943.

BRANDT, RAYMOND P., "The Dies Committee: An Appraisal," *Atlantic Monthly*, February, 1940.

BRENNER, ANITA, "High School Youth: Not Flaming but Realistic," *New York Times Magazine*, October 26, 1941.

BREWSTER, KINGMAN, Jr., and KLAW, SPENCER, "We Stand Here," *Atlantic*, September, 1940.

BROMLEY, DOROTHY DUNBAR, "They're in the Army Now," *New Republic*, January 6, 1941.

————, "Women on the Home Front," *Harper's*, July, 1941.

BROWN, EARL, "American Negroes and the War," *Harper's*, April, 1942.

————, "The Negro Vote, 1944: A Forecast," *Harper's*, July, 1944.

————, "The Truth About the Detroit Race Riot," *Harper's*, November, 1944.

BROWN, J. F., "Morale for the American Dream," *New Republic*, May 4, 1942.

BRUCE, JOHN, "California Gets Tough," *New York Times Magazine*, March 15, 1942.

BUNDY, MCGEORGE, "A Letter to Twelve College Presidents," *Atlantic*, May, 1945.

BURROW, SARAH CLAYTON, and SEEDS, CORINNE A., "Community Living Through an Ongoing Interest in Airplanes," in William E. Young, ed., *Social Studies and the Elementary School*. Washington, D.C., 1941.

BUTTERFIELD, ROGER, "Our Kids Are in Trouble," *Life*, December 20, 1943.

CALAS, ELENA, "The Peggy Guggenheim Collection," *Arts*, December, 1969.

CANTRIL, HADLEY, "How Good Is Our Morale?" *New York Times Magazine*, November 16, 1941.

————, "How Real Is America's Internationalism?" *New York Times Magazine*, April 29, 1945.

————, "Opinion Trends in World War II: Some Guides to Interpretation," *Public Opinion Quarterly*, Spring, 1948.

————, "Why We Vote the Way We Do," *New York Times Magazine*, September 24, 1944.

CAYTON, HORACE R., "Fighting for White Folks?" *Nation*, September 26, 1942.

CHAMBERS, BRADFORD, "Boy Gangs of New York," *New York Times Magazine*, December 10, 1944.

CHASE, STUART, "So What?" *Common Sense*, September, 1943.

CLARK, GEORGE R., "I'm on a Draft Board," *Harper's*, April, 1941.

CLARK, KENNETH B., "Morale of the Negroes on the Home Front," *Journal of Negro Education*, Vol. 12, Summer, 1943.

CLINARD, MARSHALL B., "Criminological Theories of Violations of Wartime Regulations," *American Sociological Review*, June, 1946.

CLUCAS, LOWELL, "Defense Comes to Our Town," *Saturday Evening Post*, March 15, 1941.

COGGINS, CECIL H., "The Japanese-Americans in Hawaii," *Harper's*, June, 1943.

COHEN, JEROME B., "The Forgotten TNEC," *Current History*, September, 1941.

COHN, DAVID L., "America to England," *Atlantic Monthly*, August, 1940.

————, "How the South Feels," *Atlantic Monthly*, January, 1944.

————, "The Road Not Taken," *Atlantic Monthly*, March, 1940.

COLLIER, JOHN, "Indians Come Alive," *Atlantic Monthly*, September, 1942.

CONRAD, ALFRED H., "Redistribution Through Government Budgets in the U.S.," in Alan Peacock, ed., *Income Redistribution and Social Policy*. London, 1954.

COWLEY, MALCOLM, "American Literature in Wartime," *New Republic*, December 6, 1943.

————, "The End of the New Deal," *New Republic*, May 31, 1943.

————, "This Man's Army," *New Republic*, September 23, 1940.

————, "Writing in Wartime," *New Republic*, November 17, 1941.

CRAIG, CLARK, "Cape Cod Gets a War Boom," *Harper's*, March, 1941.

CRAM, PAUL P., "Undergraduates and the War," *Atlantic Monthly*, October, 1940.

DABNEY, VIRGINIUS, "Nearer and Nearer the Precipice," *Atlantic Monthly*, January, 1943.

————, "The Negro and His Schooling," *Atlantic Monthly*, April, 1942.

DALFIUME, RICHARD M., "The 'Forgotten Years' of the Negro Revolution," *Journal of American History*, June, 1968.

DARNTON, BYRON, "California Pulls in Her Adjectives," *New York Times Magazine*, May 12, 1940.

DE SALES, RAOUL DE RUSSY, "America Looks at the War," *Atlantic Monthly*, February, 1940.

————, "Socialism and the Future," *Atlantic Monthly*, December, 1941.

DESMOND, JOHN, "Tin Pan Alley Seeks *the* Song," *New York Times Magazine*, June 6, 1943.

DOS PASSOS, JOHN, "The People at War," *Harper's*, March–April, 1943.

DRAKE, FRANCIS VIVIAN, "Hitting Power: Does Our Air Force Lack It?" *Atlantic Monthly*, October, 1940.

EDMAN, IRVIN, "Look Homeward, America," *Harper's*, December, 1940.

FARBER, MANNY, "Movies in Wartime," *New Republic*, January 3, 1944.

FAUGHT, MILLARD C., "The Kids Aren't Hungry Any More," *Saturday Evening Post*, July 4, 1942.

FISCHER, LOUIS, "West Coast Perspective," *Nation*, March 7, 1942.

FISHER, JOHN, "Odds Against Another War," *Harper's*, August, 1945.

FISKE, IRVING, "Where Does Television Belong?" *Harper's*, February, 1940.

FOWLER, BURTON P., "What Kind of School?" *New York Times Magazine*, June 27, 1943.

FRIEDRICH, CARL J., "The Poison in Our System," *Atlantic Monthly*, June, 1941.

FROST, WLADISLAWA A., "Cities and Towns Mobilize for War," *American Sociological Review*, February, 1944.

FULBRIGHT, J. WILLIAM, "The Peace We Want," *New York Times Magazine*, July 22, 1945.

GOLDSMITH, SELMA; JASZI, GEORGE; KAITZ, HERMAN; and LIEBENBERG, MAURICE, "Size Distribution of Income Since the Mid-Thirties," *Review of Economics and Statistics*, February, 1954.

GOODMAN, PERCIVAL and PAUL, "Architecture in Wartime," *New Republic*, December 13, 1943.

GRAFTON, SAMUEL, "A New Learned Society," *New Republic*, July 21, 1941.

GRATTAN, C. HARTLEY, "Salute to the Litterateurs," *Harper's*, November, 1944.

————, "What Business Thinks About Postwar America," *Harper's*, February, 1944.

GRIFFIS, ENID, "He Runs a Hotel," *Harper's*, November, 1943.

GWARTNEY, J., "Changes in the White/Non-White Income Ratio 1939–1967," *American Economic Review*, December, 1970.

HAMLIN, TALBOT, "Architecture in America Today," *New Republic*, August 4, 1941.

HANIGHEN, FRED C., "The U.S. Army," *Harper's*, December, 1940.

HASKELL, DOUGLAS, "The Revolution in House-Building," *Harper's*, June, 1942.

HAWES, ELIZABETH, "Do Women Workers Get an Even Break?" *New York Times Magazine*, November 19, 1944.

HELTON, ROY, "The Inner Threat: Our Own Softness," *Harper's*, September, 1940.

HENRY, GEORGE, "The People and Their Schools," *Common Sense*, April, 1943.

HERRICK, ELINOR M., "With Women at Work the Factory Changes," *New York Times Magazine*, January 24, 1943.

HIGH, STANLEY, "The Liberals' War," *Nation*, June 14, 1941.

HOPKINS, GEORGE E., "Bombing and the American Conscience in World War II, *Historian*, Vol. 28, May, 1966.

HOWARD, DONALD S., "But People Must Eat," *Atlantic Monthly*, February, 1940.

HOWE, QUINCY, "Twelve Things the War Will Do to America," *Harper's*, November, 1942.

HURD, CHARLES, "E for Effort on the Home Front," *New York Times Magazine*, October 15, 1944.

JOHNSON, CHARLES S., "The Negro War Worker in San Francisco," 1944 pamphlet, Bancroft Library.

JOHNSON, F. E., "The Impact of the War on Religion in America," *American Journal of Sociology*, November, 1942.

JONES, DOROTHY B., "Hollywood Goes to War," *Nation*, January 27, 1945.

JORDY, WILLIAM H., "Fiasco at Willow Run," *Nation*, May 8, 1943.

———, "The Slicks Are Scared," *Common Sense*, December, 1942.

KAHN, ALBERT, "Architects of Defense," *Atlantic Monthly*, March, 1942.

KAZIN, ALFRED, "Midtown and the Village," *Harper's*, January, 1971.

KLEIN, MICHAEL, "Lewis Loses the CIO," *New Republic*, December 1, 1941.

KRAMER, DALE, "What Soldiers Are Thinking About," *Harper's*, December, 1943.

LAHEY, EDWIN A., "Fascism's Day in Court," *New Republic*, June 5, 1944.

LAKE, ELEANOR, "Trouble on the Street Corner," *Common Sense*, May, 1943.

LAVINE, HAROLD, "Why the Army Gripes," *Nation*, August 20, 1941.

MacLEISH, ARCHIBALD, "The Next Harvard," *Atlantic Monthly*, May, 1941.

McWILLIAMS, CAREY, "Los Angeles' Pachuco Gangs," *New Republic*, January 18, 1943.

———, "Moving the West Coast Japanese," *Harper's*, September, 1942.

———, "The Zoot Suit Riots," *New Republic*, June 21, 1943.

Madison Avenue (pseud.), "Advertising in Wartime," *New Republic*, February 21, 1944.

MAHER, EDMOND F., "Customers' Nightmare," *Saturday Evening Post*, February 5, 1944.

MANCHESTER, HARLAND, "The Diesel Boom," *Harper's*, July, 1940.

MARSHALL, THURGOOD, "The Gestapo in Detroit," *The Crisis*, August, 1943.

MARTIN, JOHN BARTLOW, "Colonel McCormick of the Tribune," *Harper's*, October, 1944.

MEAD, MARGARET, "Democracy's Scapegoat: Youth," *Harper's*, January, 1941.

MEZERIK, A. G., "Getting Rid of the Women," *Atlantic Monthly*, June, 1945.

MILNER, LUCILLE, "On the Civil Liberty Front," *New Republic*, June 26, 1944.

MOSES, ROBERT, "Mr. Moses Dissects the Long-Haired Planners," *New York Times Magazine*, June 25, 1944.

MUMFORD, LEWIS, "The Corruption of Liberalism," *New Republic*, April 29, 1940.

MURPHY, T. E., "Will Shock Treatment Cure Germany's Ills?" *Saturday Evening Post*, January 1, 1944.

MURRAY, PHILIP, "The Worker and Defense," *Nation*, June 28, 1941.

MYERS, R. J., "Underenumeration in the Census as Indicated by Selective Service Data," *American Sociological Review*, February, 1948.

NAKASHIMA, TED, "Concentration Camp: U.S. Style," *New Republic*, June 15, 1942.

NEUBERGER, RICHARD L., "Reveille in the Northwest," *Nation*, December 20, 1941.

————, "What the Home Folks Say," *Harper's*, September, 1939.

OGBURN, WILLIAM FIELDING, "The Changing Pattern of America," *New York Times Magazine*, October 13, 1940.

OLIVIER, WARNER, "Eight-Hour Orphans," *Saturday Evening Post*, October 10, 1942.

OTTLEY, ROI, "Negro Morale," *New Republic*, November 10, 1941.

PANKHURST, GENEVIEVE, "Does America Need More Children?" *Harper's*, January, 1941.

PEKELIS, ALEXANDER H., "The Supreme Court Today," *New Republic*, April 17, 1944.

PERLMAN, DAVID, "Four for the Ages," *New York Times Magazine*, August 25, 1940.

PIEL, GERALD, "Narcotics," *Life*, July 19, 1943.

POWERS, JAMES H., "What to Do with German Prisoners," *Atlantic Monthly*, November, 1944.

PRATTIS, P. L., "The Morale of Negroes in the Armed Forces of the U.S.," *Journal of Negro Education*, Vol. 12, Summer, 1943.

Presidential Commission, "The Wartime Cost of Living," Washington, D.C., 1944.

PRINGLE, HENRY F., "College with an Idea," *Saturday Evening Post*, October 14, 1944.

————, "Snooping on the Potomac," *Saturday Evening Post*, January 15, 1944.

RATCLIFF, J. D., "Health for the Backwoods," *New Republic*, June 8, 1942.

RAUSHENBUSH, WINIFRED, "Fashion Goes American," *Harper's*, December, 1941.

RIESELBACH, LEROY N., "The Basis of Isolationist Behavior," *Public Opinion Quarterly*, Winter, 1960.

RIESS, CURT, "The Nazis Dig in for World War III," *New York Times Magazine*, August 6, 1944.

ROBERTSON, PRISCILLA, and JONES, HAWLEY, "Housekeeping After the War," *Harper's*, April, 1944.

RODMAN, SELDEN, "What's Wrong with the 'World of Tomorrow'?" *Common Sense*, September, 1939.

ROLO, CHARLES J., "Germany Calling!" *Current History*, October, 1940.

ROSTOW, EUGENE V., "Our Worst Wartime Mistake," *Harper's*, September, 1945.

ROVERE, RICHARD H., "The American Left: Part 1. The Decline of the Communist Party," *Common Sense*, November, 1940.

————, "The American Left: Part 2. Non-Communist Leftists," *Common Sense*, January, 1941.

————, "American Magazines in Wartime," *New Republic*, March 6, 1944.

RUSSELL, WILLIAM F., "Illiteracy and the Manpower Crisis," *New Republic*, October 19, 1942.

RUTTENBERG, HAROLD J. and STANLEY, "War and the Steel Ghost Towns," *Harper's*, January, 1940.

SANCTON, THOMAS, "The Negro Press," *New Republic*, April 26, 1943.

————, "Trouble in Dixie," *New Republic*, January 4, 1943.

SHIRER, WILLIAM L., "The Poison Pen," *Atlantic Monthly*, May, 1942.

SHRYOCK, HENRY S., Jr., and ELDRIDGE, HOPE T., "Internal Migration in Peace and War," *American Sociological Review*, February, 1947.

SLICHTER, SUMNER H., "How Much Trade Unionism as Usual?" *Atlantic Monthly*, January, 1943.

SMITH, FRANK, "Yankee Army in the South," *New Republic*, March 29, 1943.

SMUCKLER, RALPH H., "The Region of Isolationism," *American Political Science Review*, June, 1953.

SOULE, GEORGE, "Can We Have Freedom from Hunger?" *New Republic*, June 14, 1943.

————, "Planning Wins," *New Republic*, March 8, 1943.

SOUTAR, ARCH, "Home-coming Isn't Easy," *Saturday Evening Post*, December 9, 1944.

SOUTHWORTH, H. R., "Jehovah's 50,000 Witnesses," *Nation*, August 10, 1940.

SPALDING, ALLAN, "The Poor Are Still Poor," *New Republic*, November 1, 1943.

STEGNER, WALLACE, "Who Persecutes Boston?" *Atlantic Monthly*, July, 1944.

STEIN, ROSE M., "Big Steel and the Union Shop," *Nation*, October 4, 1941.

STEPHENS, OREN, "FSA Fights for Its Life," *Harper's*, April, 1943.

STEVENSON, CHARLES, "Labor Takes in the Fair," *Atlantic Monthly*, January, 1940.

STONE, I. F., "Relaxing Too Soon," *Nation*, April 24, 1943.

STROUP, RUSSELL C., "A Soldier Looks at the Church," *Harper's*, October, 1944.

SWANBERG, W. A., "The Spies Who Came In from the Sea," *American Heritage*, April, 1970.

THOMPSON, LEWIS, "Men Making Bombers," *Harper's*, April, 1942.

TISDALE, FREDERICK, "Manhattan Headache," *Saturday Evening Post*, April 10, 1943.

TRILLING, DIANA, "What Happened to Our Navels?" *Harper's*, May, 1944.

TUCK, RUTH D., "Behind the Zoot Suit Riots," *Survey Graphic*, August, 1943.

TURPIN, R. E., "Democracy Is at Work," *New York Times Magazine*, November 26, 1939.

U.S. Department of Commerce, "National Income Supplement," *Survey of Current Business*, July, 1947.

VALENTINE, ELIZABETH R., "Odyssey of the Army Wife," *New York Times Magazine*, March 5, 1944.

VAN GELDER, ROBERT, "The Men Who Refuse to Fight," *New York Times Magazine*, May 10, 1942.

WAGG, ALFRED, III, "Washington's Stepchild: The Refugee," *New Republic*, April 28, 1941.

WECHSLER, JAMES, "Bricker's Running Mate," *Nation*, October 7, 1944.

————, "Sedition and Circuses," *Nation*, May 6, 1944.

WEINBERG, SYDNEY, "What to Tell America: the Writers' Quarrel with the OWI," *Journal of American History*, June, 1968.

WHITE, MAGNER, "Between Two Flags," *Saturday Evening Post*, September 30, 1939.

WHITRIDGE, ARNOLD, "Where Do You Stand?" *Atlantic Monthly*, August, 1940.

WICKWIRE, FRANCIS L., "What the Polls Say," *Harper's*, September, 1939.

WIERS, PAUL, "Wartime Increases in Michigan Delinquency," *American Sociological Review*, August, 1945.

WILCHER, DENNY, "Conscientious Objectors in Prison," *Christian Century*, March 2, 1944.

WILLKIE, WENDELL, "Don't Stir Distrust of Russia," *New York Times Magazine*, January 2, 1944.

WYNN, NEIL A., "The Impact of the Second World War on the American Negro," *Journal of Contemporary European History*, Vol. 6, No. 2, 1971.

FICTION and POETRY

BELLOW, SAUL, *Dangling Man*. New York, 1944.

BENÉT, WILLIAM ROSE, *Day of Deliverance: A Book of Poems in Wartime*. New York, 1945.

DAVENPORT, RUSSELL, *My Country*. New York, 1944.

HARGROVE, MARION, *See Here, Private Hargrove*. New York, 1942.

HERSEY, JOHN, *A Bell for Adano*. New York, 1945.

MARQUAND, JOHN P., *So Little Time*. Boston, 1943.

SHAPIRO, KARL, *V-Letter and Other Poems*. New York, 1944.

WRIGHT, RICHARD, *Native Son*. New York, 1940.

Glossary

AAA:	Agricultural Adjustment Administration
ACLU:	American Civil Liberties Union
AFC:	America First Committee
AFL:	American Federation of Labor
CAP:	Civil Air Patrol
CCC:	Civilian Conservation Corps
CDA:	Committee to Defend America by Aiding the Allies
CIO:	Congress of Industrial Organizations
FEPC:	Fair Employment Practices Committee
FSA:	Farm Security Agency
HOLC:	Home Owners Loan Corporation
NDAC:	National Defense Advisory Committee
NDMB:	National Defense Mediation Board
NDRC:	National Defense Research Committee
NEA:	National Education Association
NRPB:	National Resources Planning Board
NYA:	National Youth Authority
OCD:	Office of Civil Defense
OCWS:	Office of Community War Services
ODM:	Office of Defense Management
OFF:	Office of Facts and Figures
OPA:	Office of Price Administration
OPM:	Office of Production Management for National Defense
OSRD:	Office of Scientific Research and Development
OWI:	Office of War Information
PEA:	Progressive Education Association
SEC:	Securities and Exchange Commission
SPAB:	Supply Priorities and Allocations Board
TNEC:	Temporary National Economic Commission
UAW:	United Automobile Workers
UMW:	United Mineworkers
WLB:	War Labor Board
WPA:	Works Progress Administration
WPB:	War Production Board
WRB:	War Resources Board

Index

502

503

Graf Spee (ship), 19
Grafton, Samuel, 363
Grapes of Wrath (Steinbeck), 20
Great Britain: public opinion about, 16, 19, 28, 65, 127, 138, 169, 363, 418; private efforts to aid, 18, 28, 58, 59, 63–66, 76–77, 97–98, 169; and lend-lease, 66, 76, 77–78, 169–70, 171, 189, 253, 393, 417; organization of, for war, 67–68, 72, 111, 142, 259; contribution to wartime science, 111, 429, 430; war aims, 167; as potential postwar rival to U.S., 280, 284, 393
Great Dictator (film), 162
Great War. See World War I
Greece, 79, 142
Green, William, 265
Green Guards, 38
Greenland, 25, 78
Greer, USS, 170
Gropius, Walter, 352, 389
Guadalcanal, 214, 243, 245, 252, 268, 269, 274, 383
Guam, 206, 207, 277
Guggenheim, Peggy, 388
Gulf Coast, 210, 211, 379
Gunther, John, 164, 186
Guthrie, Woody, 204

Hague, Frank, 48, 291
Hall, Felix, 82
Halsey, William "Bull," 268
"Ham and Eggs," 22
Hamilton, John D. M., 46
Hamilton, Ohio, 38
Harlem, 145, 148, 154, 164, 238, 314, 320
Harmon, Tom, 165, 339
Harmon, USS, 318
Hartford, Conn., 276, 396
Haruna (ship), 207
Harvard University, 64, 90, 99, 111, 112, 113, 115, 116, 117, 121, 191, 372, 375, 376, 377, 419
Harvey, George S., 52
Hastie, William H., 150, 317
Haverford College, 373
Hawaii, 190, 223, 229, 230, 245
Hayek, Friedrich, 296–97
Health: as national problem, 136, 328, 330–31, 332; and government, 137, 331, 335, 338, 352; of Negroes, 146, 323; improvements in, 323, 334–35, 351, 352, 353; insurance, 333–34
Health, Education, and Welfare Department. See U.S. Department of Health, Education, and Welfare
Hearst newspaper chain, 219, 226, 314, 411
Hellman, Lillian, 125
Helton, Roy, 198
Hemingway, Ernest, 94, 295, 385
Hersey, John, 382, 384
Hershey, Lewis B., 40, 81, 117, 136, 178, 332
Heydrich, Reinhard, 212
Higgins, Andrew Jackson, 263, 301
High School Victory Corps, 235, 349, 368, 374
Hillman, Sidney, 70, 74, 150, 177, 266, 292, 294, 404

Hirohito, 413, 427
Hiroshima, Japan, 427, 428
Hitler, Adolf, 18, 20, 25, 26, 28, 29, 51, 60, 62, 80, 92, 127, 131, 156, 163, 167, 168, 169, 170, 172, 178, 187, 191, 211, 212, 213, 277, 278, 413, 414, 415, 420, 421, 430
Hitler's Children (film), 385
Hobbes, Thomas, 434, 435
Hobcaw Barony, S.C., 289
Hoboes of America, Inc., 336
Hoboken, N.J., 380
Hodges, Luther D., 415
Holiday Inn (film), 242–43
Hollywood, 87, 123, 157, 162, 245, 321, 385, 423
Hollywood Canteen, 381
Holmes, John Haynes, 93
Home defense, 27, 38, 39, 233
Home Owners Loan Corporation, 329, 342
Hooton, Ernest Albert, 419
Hoover, Herbert, 19, 46, 60, 168, 191, 328, 405
Hoover, J. Edgar, 88, 101, 103
Hope, Bob, 418
Hopkins, Harry, 48, 49
House of Representatives, U.S., 36, 90, 101, 193, 206, 247, 248, 287, 301, 310, 346, 393, 417; Foreign Relations Committee, 28; Select Committee on Interstate Migration, 223, 256; Select Committee on Un-American Activities, 87, 88, 90, 93, 94, 101, 104, 114, 223; Ways and Means Committee, 261
House Un-American Activities Committee. See House of Representatives, Select Committee on Un-American Activities
Housing, 86, 104, 137, 241, 266, 305, 325, 327, 341, 342, 343, 351, 353, 389
Houston, Texas, 235
Houston, USS, 209, 235
Howe, Quincy, 197, 416
Hubbard, Ohio, 314
Hughes, Howard, 263
Hughes, Langston, 148
Hull, Cordell, 57, 187, 282, 285
Hunter College, 102, 375
Hutchins, Robert M., 115, 120, 378, 421
Huxley, Aldous, 295
Hyde Park, N.Y., 87, 293

I Married a Nazi (film), 162
I Never Left Home (Hope), 418
Iceland, 170
Ickes, Harold, 51, 97, 133, 134, 189, 251, 306, 308
Illinois, 91, 98
Immigration, 95, 96, 97, 336
Imperial Japanese Navy, 209, 269
In This Our Life (film), 321
India, 319
Indiana, 151, 304, 334
Industrial Mobilization Plan, 68
Inflation, 132, 175, 181, 260–61, 299, 306, 353, 400
Information Please (radio program), 20, 45
Ingalls, Laura (later Wilder), 218

504

Inglewood, Calif., 178
Inkster Park, Mich., 313
Inside Asia (Gunther), 186
Inside South America (Gunther), 164
Internal Revenue Service (IRS), 250, 260, 300, 356, 390, 402
International Monetary Fund, 284, 411
Internationalism: among liberals, 280, 282–83, 393, 418–20, 423–24; and UN, 280–81, 285, 413–14, 416; and *One World*, 281–82; among conservatives, 283–84, 423–24; and Fulbright Resolution, 288; character of, 417–18, 424
Intervention and interventionists: popular support for, 17–18, 168, 171, 191; Non-Partisan Committee for Peace through Revision of the Neutrality Act, 58; Committee to Defend America by Aiding the Allies, 58–60, 155–57; Century Group, 59, 156; among college students, 116; among intellectuals, 120, 125, 196; Fight for Freedom, 156–57; and postwar internationalism, 419, 424
Isolation and isolationists: between the wars, 16, 55–56; popular support for, 17–18, 169, 190, 279–80; struggle over Neutrality Act, 17, 18, 23, 24, 170, 192; in Congress, 28, 32, 75, 157, 161–62, 191; opposing aid to Britain, 28, 62, 75; in GOP, 42, 58, 62, 190, 283; in American history, 54–58, 62, 155; America First Committee, 61–63, 100, 112, 120, 155, 157, 158–61, 163; among college students, 61, 112–13, 116; physical attacks on, 100; No Foreign Wars Committee, 112, 158; opposing aid to Soviet Union, 168–69; and postwar internationalism, 424
Issei and Nisei, first days after Pearl Harbor, 204, 216; attitudes toward, 217, 221, 223; mounting pressure for internment, 217–18, 220; portrayed as fifth column, 219–20, 223, 245; Executive Order 9066, 220; voluntary evacuation, 222; ACLU contests internment, 223 n., 357; internment, 224–25, 364–65; in Hawaii, 229–30; Supreme Court rules on, 366
Italy, 58, 60, 76, 145, 169, 187, 195, 270, 273, 274, 275, 429
Iwo Jima, 410

Jackson, Robert, 73, 89, 101, 326
James, Harry, 380
James, Henry, 295
James, William, 438
Janis, Elsie, 299
Japan: public opinion about, 78, 186–87, 188, 190, 192, 199, 221; signs Axis Pact, 187; U.S. takes steps against, 187, 188, 189–90; suggested appeasement of, 188–89; and Pearl Harbor attack, 190, 199, 203, 269–70; wins Pacific victories, 207–8; strikes mainland U.S., 222, 410; on the defensive, 268, 277; atomic bombing, 426; surrenders, 427
Japanese-Americans. *See* Issei and Nisei; War Relocation Authority
Jarrell, Randall, 382, 383
Java Sea, 210, 222, 235

Jefferson Memorial, 389
Jehovah's Witnesses, 91, 92, 226, 227, 230, 357, 359, 366
Jews, 96, 157, 159, 160, 161, 213, 322, 362, 363, 420
Johns Hopkins University, 374
Johnson, Hiram, 83, 160
Johnson, Hugh S., 52, 61
Johnson Act, 64, 155
Jones, James, 382
Jones, Jesse, 65, 329
Julian, Hubert Fauntleroy, 140
Junior League, 236, 326, 354
Justice Department. *See* U.S. Department of Justice
Juvenile delinquency, 348–49

Kaempfert, Waldemar, 381
Kaiser, Henry J., 263, 301, 333–34, 402
Kaltenborn, H. V., 138
Kandinsky, Serge, 389
Kansas City, Mo., 408
Kasserine Pass, Tunisia, 262, 311 n.
Kaye, Sammy, 241
Kazin, Alfred, 119
Kearny, USS, 170, 171
Kelly, Colin P., Jr., 207
Kelly, Edward J. "Boss," 48, 49, 147, 291
Kelly, Joseph "Commando," 339
Kenny, Elizabeth, 332
Kentucky, 24, 288
Keys of the Kingdom, The (Cronin), 384
Keys of the Kingdom, The (film), 385
King, Ernest J., 279
Kingsbury Ordnance Plant, 316
Kiplinger Washington Letter, 262
Kirby, Rollin, 155
Klamath Falls, Ore., 227
Knox, Frank, 42, 59, 62, 192, 217, 317
Knudsen, William S., 70, 74, 179, 180, 192
Kohn, Hans, 281
Kristol, Irving, 356
Krock, Arthur, 227
Krug, Julius, 399
Ku Klux Klan, 92, 99, 101, 144, 149, 312, 323
Kurusu, Saboru, 192

Labor: and government, 24, 177, 183, 195, 264–66, 306, 307, 308, 399, 404; union membership, 24, 265, 403, 404; strikes, 73, 133, 176, 177, 183–85, 264, 303, 306–8, 322, 403; as a political factor, 74, 292–94; and Negroes, 150, 152, 316–17, 322; -management relations, 177, 178, 265, 309, 403; and absenteeism issue, 266–67, 305
Labor Department. *See* U.S. Department of Labor
La Grange, Ga., 149
La Guardia Field, 140
La Guardia, Fiorello, 53, 136, 155, 223, 231, 348, 350, 365, 371, 397
Landis, James H., 90
Landon, Alf, 50, 52
Lanham Act. *See* Community Facilities Act
Laski, Harold, 115
Lasswell, Harold, 250

505

Latin America, 162–65, 239, 242, 285, 414, 421
Latouche, John, 35
Lawrence, Ernest O., 428
League for Peace and Democracy, 88
League of Nations, 285, 416
Lee, Gypsy Rose, 76
Léger, Fernand, 387
Lehman, Herbert, 59
Lend-lease: Roosevelt announces, 66; Congressional debate, 75–76; delivery problem, 77–78, 170, 171; sparks war aims debate, 166; extended to Soviet Union, 169; as part of British war effort, 170; effect on Neutrality Act, 155; Clare Boothe Luce attacks British use of, 393; effect on agriculture, 405; repayment issue, 417
Leningrad, 268
Lerner, Max, 59, 119, 167, 363, 375
Let Us Now Praise Famous Men (Agee and Evans), 176
Lewis, John L.: resigns as CIO president, 52; "captive mines" strike, 184–85; proposed accoupling AFL and CIO, 265–66; supplanted by Hillman, 294; attacks WLB, 306–7; 1943 winter strike, 307–8; fails to organize dairy farmers, 404
Lewis, Sinclair, 155
Liberals, 31, 32, 68, 70, 73, 92, 93, 94, 95, 97, 100, 101, 103, 145, 158, 166, 180, 184, 188, 197, 223, 228, 247, 251, 252, 265, 280, 283, 287, 306, 339, 351, 352, 355, 358, 362, 391, 397, 398, 419, 421, 423, 424
Liberia, 317
Liberty ships, 195, 258, 263, 318
Library of Congress, 123
Lidice, Czechoslovakia, 235
Life (magazine), 19, 148, 171, 209, 224, 226, 280, 281, 285, 288, 292, 308, 319, 343, 381, 387, 422, 423
Life with Father (film), 384
Lindbergh, Charles A.: becomes leading isolationist spokesman, 60; testifies against lend-lease, 75; attacked by New Republic, 100, 228; supposedly hypnotized by Hitler, 131; attacked by Dorothy Thompson, 159; creates furor by cautioning Jews, 160; relations with other isolationists, 160, 161; suggests 1942 elections may be canceled, 161
Lipchitz, Jacques, 387
Lippmann, Walter, 27, 93, 187, 189, 196, 219, 220, 223, 282, 284, 374, 411, 419
Literature, 20, 129
Little Rock, Ark., 227
Little Steel, 265, 266, 307, 308
Little Tokyo, USA (film), 245
Local Defense Councils, 232
Lodge, Henry Cabot, Jr., 17
Lombardo, Guy, 242
London, 277, 415
London After Dark (radio program), 138
Long Beach, Calif., 315, 336, 401
Long Island, 108
Longworth, Alice Roosevelt, 48, 61, 291
Look (magazine), 44
Los Angeles, 33, 99, 204, 222, 231, 314, 315, 316, 387, 401, 415
Los Angeles Coliseum, 415

Los Angeles Hall of Justice, 385
Los Angeles Police Department, 315
Los Angeles *Times*, 276
Lothian, Lord, 63, 65, 66
Louis, Joe, 145
Louisiana, 138, 146, 195
Louisville *Courier-Journal*, 65
Lovett, Robert Morss, 287
Lowell, Robert, 383
Luce, Clare Boothe, 290, 393, 417
Luce, Henry, 44, 60, 148, 156, 196, 197, 283, 374, 424
Lucky Strike cigarettes, 391
Lusitania (ship), 18
Lynd, Robert, 350

Maas, Melvin J., 214
MacArthur, Douglas, 209–10, 294
Machiavelli, Niccolò, 434
Mackinac Island, Mich., 283
MacLeish, Archibald, 94, 119, 123, 227, 243, 250
Mademoiselle (magazine), 350
Magnificent Ambersons, The (film), 384
Maier, Norman, R. F., 213
Mailer, Norman, 382
Maine, 410
Maine, USS, 234
"Mairzy Doats" (song), 382
Mangerial Revolution, The (Burnham), 120
Manila, 206, 207, 410
Mann, Klaus, 99
Mannheim, Karl, 434
Manpower Mobilization Board, 266
Mao Tse-tung, 423
March on Washington Movement, 320
Marianna, Fla., 313
Marine Corps. *See* U.S. Marine Corps
Markel, Lester, 423
Marshall, George C., 40, 73, 193, 308, 311
Marshall, Verne, 158
Martin, Joe, 46, 247
Massachusetts, 281
Masters, Edgar Lee, 383
Matthews, Herbert, 419
Maugham, Somerset, 295
Maywood, Ill., 394
McCallister Volunteers, 38
McCormick, Robert, 158, 188
McNary, Charles, 31, 47
McWilliams, Carey, 224
McWilliams, Joe, 361
Mead, Margaret, 197
Meet John Doe (film), 123
Meet Me in St. Louis (film), 384
Memphis, 420
Men Must Act (Mumford), 94
Merchant Marine, 318
Merchant shipping, 195, 206, 208, 210, 211, 237, 255, 258, 265, 399
Merman, Ethel, 165
Merriam, Charles, 124, 125
Mexican-Americans, 314–16
Mexico, 336
Miami, 38, 402
Miami Beach, 238
Michener, James, 382
Michigan, 253, 283
Microbe Hunters (De Kruif), 428

506

508

Press, 164, 211, 214, 224, 248, 250, 251, 256, 264, 300, 311, 390, 412, 413, 422, 423, 426
Price Stabilization Act of 1941, 405-6
Prince of Wales, 206
Princeton University, 78, 100, 115, 374, 377
Printer's Ink (magazine), 68
Probing Our Prejudices (Powdermaker), 321
Progressive Education Association, 104, 105
Prohibition, 55, 239
Proximity fuses, 430
Pryor, Sam, 46
Public Health Service. *See* U.S. Public Health Service
Publishing, 129, 244, 382
Pulitzer Prizes, 158, 383, 386, 430
Puritans, 437
Pursuit of Happiness, The (radio program), 35
Pusey, Merlo J., 408
Pyle, Ernie, 415

Queen Elizabeth (ship), 19

Race riots: after World War I, 143-44, 407; Harlem, 145, 314; Dallas, 149; Detroit, 219, 312, 313-14; triggered by rumors, 311; Newark, 312-13; Beaumont, 313; Mobile, 313; Inkster Park, 313; Camp Stewart, 313; Centreville, 313; El Paso, 314; Port Arthur, 314; Springfield, 314; Los Angeles, 314-16; Pasadena, 315; Long Beach, 315; San Diego, 315; Philadelphia, 322; fears for postwar, 323
Radar, 139, 169, 429, 430, 431
Radio, 20, 35, 45, 127, 128, 131, 133, 137, 138, 154, 241, 242, 243, 276, 277, 278, 390, 423, 431
Radio Berlin, 255, 277
Radio Corporation of America, 138, 139
Railroads, 307, 308, 310
Rand, Ayn, 295
Rand, Sally, 129, 234
Randolph, A. Philip, 150, 151, 311, 319, 320
Ranke, Leopold von, 434
Rankin, Jeanette, 207
Rankin, John, 305, 362
Rationing, 133-34, 253, 259, 279, 370, 395, 400
Rats, Lice and History (Zinsser), 428
Rauschning, Hermann, 119
Razor's Edge, The (Maugham), 295
Reader's Digest, 164
Reconstruction Finance Corporation (RFC), 65, 329
Recording industry, 128, 131, 307
Red Army, 213, 268, 421, 422
Red Cross. *See* American Red Cross
Refugees, 95, 96, 97, 98, 99, 363, 387, 429. *See also* Aliens
Relief, 21, 22, 137, 327
Renegotiation Act of 1942, 304
Republican Party, 22, 30, 41-43, 45-46, 51-52, 58, 61, 62, 75, 139, 190, 247, 252, 253, 283, 288, 289, 290, 292, 293, 294, 346, 356

Repulse (ship), 206
Reserve Officer Training Corps (ROTC), 113, 114, 116
Resettlement Agency, 406
Resisting Enemy Interrogation (film), 387
Reuben James, USS, 171
Reuther, Walter, 73, 150
Reynolds Metals, 179
Rickenbacker, Eddie, 61, 214, 268, 305
Ringling Brothers, Barnum and Bailey, 396
Rivera, Diego, 129
Road to Reaction, The (Finer), 297
Road to Serfdom, The (Hayek), 296-97
Road to War, The (Millis), 27
Robe, The (Douglas), 384
Roberts, Owen J., 218, 366
Robeson, Paul, 321
Robin Moor (ship), 79
Robinson, Earl, 35
Robinson, Walter, 153
Rochester, N.Y., 108
Rockefeller, Nelson, 164
Rockefeller Foundation, 429
Rodman, Seldon, 383
Rogers, Will, 408, 411
Roller skating, 128
Roosevelt, Eleanor, 140, 151, 164, 289, 412
Roosevelt, Elliott, 39
Roosevelt, Franklin D.: asserts U.S. neutrality, 17; launches defense program, 26; ponders third term, 41-42; 1940 nomination, 48-50; and 1940 election, 50, 51, 52-53, 62; speaks at University of Virginia, 60; and aid to Britain, 64, 66, 76, 77; and management of war production, 67, 68, 70, 74, 173, 179, 256, 392, 398; and labor, 70, 74, 177, 178, 184, 185, 264, 265-66, 303, 306, 307, 308; "Four Freedoms" speech, 76; and Battle of Atlantic, 78, 79, 171; and refugees, 95, 96, 363; "Arsenal of Democracy" speech, 130; and Negroes, 151, 316, 317; and Churchill, 167-68, 206, 270; and Soviets, 169, 411-12; and Congress, 252, 287, 300-1, 307, 329, 408, 410, 412, 413; and 1942 election, 252; on D-Day, 277; and 1944 election, 289, 290-94; and veterans' benefits, 338, 339; death, 402, 412
Roosevelt, Theodore, 39, 42, 58
Root, Oren, 44, 47
Rothko, Mark, 388
Rousseau, Jean Jacques, 435
Royal Air Force, 64, 169, 195, 208
Royal Canadian Air Force, 64, 77, 153
Royal Navy, 28, 77, 170, 206, 208, 318
Royal Oak (ship), 19
Rugg, Harold Ordway, 107
Ruml, Beardsley, 260
Russell, Bertrand, 114, 120, 375
Russell, Jane, 385
Russell Sage College, 116
Ruston (La.) *Leader*, 317
Rutherford, Ernest, 428
Ruthven, Alexander G., 114

Saarinen, Eero, 352, 389
St. Louis (ship), 96
St. Louis, Mo., 315

University of Oregon, 205
University of Virginia, 60
Urban League, 319, 324

V-E Day, 278, 412, 415
V-J Day, 426
V for Victory, 130, 206
V-Letter (Shapiro), 383
Vandenberg, Arthur, 42, 43, 45, 62, 188, 418
Variety, 381
Vermont, 146
Veterans, 338–42, 376, 378, 408
Veterans Administration, 323, 340–41
Victory Corps. *See* High School Victory Corps
Victory gardens, 233, 234, 235, 394
Victory Program, 180, 211, 248, 255, 343
Viereck, George Sylvester, 218, 366
Villard, Oswald Garrison, 93

Wainwright, Jonathan, 210
Wake Island, 207
Wall Street, 23
Wall Street Journal, 72, 403
Wallace, Henry, 31, 49, 51, 192, 283, 290, 291, 392
War Advertising Council, 391
War Crimes Commission, 421
War Department. *See* U.S. Army
War Labor Board (WLB), 260, 306, 307, 404
War loans, 299
War Manpower Commission, 310, 399
War production: organizing, 67–68, 70, 173–74, 180, 194, 255–56, 259; and economic recovery, 175, 350–51, 389, 401; described, 182; achievements before Pearl Harbor, 194, 195, 257–58, 269; achievements of Victory Program, 211, 255, 256, 258; and quality of U.S. arms, 214, 262, 430; peaks, 301, 343; winds down, 309, 398, 399; results, 399; cost, 400
War Production Board (WPB), 234, 246, 256, 258, 262, 266, 305, 394, 395, 398, 399
War Relocation Authority, 225, 364
War Resources Board (WRB), 68
Ward, Harry F., 93
Warm Springs, Ga., 84, 195, 412
Warren, Earl, 220, 290, 365
Washington, D.C., 76, 84, 88, 92, 103, 155, 169, 173, 207, 217, 218, 220, 228, 229, 240, 247, 250, 251, 252, 270, 278, 287, 320, 329, 389, 394, 399, 403, 415, 426
Washington *Post*, 362
Wasp, USS, 214
Waters, Agnes, 416
Weaver, Robert C., 150
Weber, Harry, 358
Wechsler, James, 361
Welles, Sumner, 282–83
Wellesley College, 116
West Coast, 16, 206, 213, 216, 218, 219, 221, 224, 229, 231, 232, 240, 241, 365, 379, 400, 426, 427
West Coast Japanese. *See* Issei and Nisei
West Virginia, 24, 91

Wheeler, Burton K., 32, 75, 157, 160
Wheeler, Oscar, 91
White, William Allen, 58, 155, 302
"White Christmas" (song), 243
"White Cliffs of Dover" (song), 242
White House, 203, 234, 280, 411, 413, 415
Why We Fight (film), 422
Wickard, Claude, 235
Wilkins, Roy, 319
Willkie, Wendell: character and background, 43, 45, 52; seeks 1940 GOP nomination, 43–45; standing in polls, 42, 52, 288; press support for, 44, 47; at Philadelphia convention, 45–46; wins nomination, 47; election campaign, 50–52; loses to Roosevelt, 53; supports lend-lease, 75; defends film industry, 161; writes *One World*, 281–82; rejected by GOP rank and file in 1944 primaries, 288; dies suddenly, 289 n.; defends liberal education, 374
Willow Run, 175, 258, 303, 337, 338, 399
Wilson, Charles E., 305, 398, 399
Wilson, Edmund, 101, 383
Wilson, Hugh R., 17
Wilson, Woodrow, 70, 143, 166, 177, 236, 294, 412
Wilson (film), 386
Winsor, Kathryn, 384
With the Marines at Tarawa (film), 386
Wolfe, Bertram, 120
Women, 134, 135, 259, 325, 343–47, 395
Women Accepted for Voluntary Service (WAVES), 345
Women's Army Corps (WAC), 345–46
Women's Auxiliary Service Pilots (WASP's), 346
Wood, Robert, 61, 155, 163, 188
Works Progress Administration (WPA), 52, 87, 115, 137, 176, 251, 328, 364, 388
World Bank, 411
World War I, 31, 32, 37, 38, 39, 56, 65, 67, 72, 73, 85, 87, 91, 92, 94, 95, 104, 111, 113, 127, 131, 134, 139, 141, 143, 149, 150, 152, 166, 170, 177, 207, 215, 228, 234, 256, 263, 285, 294, 299, 320, 332, 353, 357, 358, 359, 372, 383, 400, 408, 430, 438
World's Fair, 17, 21, 25, 128, 129, 352, 389
Wouk, Herman, 382
Wright, Frank Lloyd, 389
Wright, Richard, 146
Wylie, Philip, 198

Yale University, 60, 250, 377
Yalta, 399, 411, 412, 413, 417, 422
Yarnell, Harry, 188
Youkovich, Vladimir I., 208
Young Men's Christian Association (YMCA), 123
Young Women's Christian Association (YWCA), 235

Zoot suits, 132, 246, 314, 349
Zoot suit riots. *See* Mexican-Americans; Race riots